CASE  S IN

NU~~~ING

ETHICS

FOURTH EDITION

SARA T. FRY, PhD, RN
Brewster, Massachusetts

ROBERT M. VEATCH, PhD
Georgetown University
Kennedy Institute of Ethics
Washington, DC

CAROL TAYLOR, PhD, RN
Georgetown University
Center for Clinical Bioethics
Washington, DC

JONES & BARTLETT
L E A R N I N G

World Headquarters

Jones & Bartlett Learning
40 Tall Pine Drive
Sudbury, MA 01776
978-443-5000
info@jblearning.com
www.jblearning.com

Jones & Bartlett Learning
Canada
6339 Ormindale Way
Mississauga, Ontario L5V 1J2
Canada

Jones & Bartlett Learning
International
Barb House, Barb Mews
London W6 7PA
United Kingdom

Jones & Bartlett Learning books and products are available through most bookstores and online booksellers. To contact Jones & Bartlett Learning directly, call 800-832-0034, fax 978-443-8000, or visit our website, www.jblearning.com.

The authors, editor, and publisher have made every effort to provide accurate information. However, they are not responsible for errors, omissions, or for any outcomes related to the use of the contents of this book and take no responsibility for the use of the products and procedures described. Treatments and side effects described in this book may not be applicable to all people; likewise, some people may require a dose or experience a side effect that is not described herein. Drugs and medical devices are discussed that may have limited availability controlled by the Food and Drug Administration (FDA) for use only in a research study or clinical trial. Research, clinical practice, and government regulations often change the accepted standard in this field. When consideration is being given to use of any drug in the clinical setting, the health care provider or reader is responsible for determining FDA status of the drug, reading the package insert, and reviewing prescribing information for the most up-to-date recommendations on dose, precautions, and contraindications, and determining the appropriate usage for the product. This is especially important in the case of drugs that are new or seldom used.

Production Credits

Publisher: Kevin Sullivan
Acquisitions Editor: Amy Sibley
Associate Editor: Patricia Donnelly
Editorial Assistant: Rachel Shuster
Associate Production Editor: Katie Spiegel
Associate Marketing Manager: Katie Hennessy

V.P., Manufacturing and Inventory Control:
  Therese Connell
Composition: DataStream Content Solutions,
  LLC, Absolute Service Inc.
Cover Design: Scott Moden
Printing and Binding: Malloy, Inc.
Cover Printing: Malloy, Inc.

Library of Congress Cataloging-in-Publication Data

Fry, Sara T.
  Case studies in nursing ethics / Sara T. Fry, Robert M. Veatch, Carol R. Taylor. — 4th ed.
    p. ; cm.
  Includes bibliographical references and index.
  ISBN 978-0-7637-8031-9 (pbk.)
1. Nursing ethics—Case studies. I. Veatch, Robert M. II. Taylor, Carol, CSFN. III. Title.
  [DNLM: 1. Ethics, Nursing—Case Reports. 2. Bioethical Issues—Case Reports. WY 85 F947c 2011]
  RT85.V4 2011
  174.2—dc22

                                                                          2010017881

6048

Printed in the United States of America
15 14 13 12 11   10 9 8 7 6 5 4 3 2

Contents

Part I   Ethics and Values in Nursing

Chapter 1

Values in Health and Illness   3

Chapter 2

The Nurse and Moral Authority   35

Chapter 10

The Sanctity of Human Life   223

Part III   Special Problem Areas in Nursing Practice

Chapter 11

Abortion, Contraception, and Sterilization   259

Chapter 12

Genetics, Birth, and the Biologic Revolution   278

Chapter 13

Psychiatry and the Control of Human Behavior   313

Chapter 14

HIV/AIDS Care   333

Chapter 15

Experimentation on Human Beings   364

Chapter 16

Consent and the Right to Refuse Treatment   396

Chapter 17

Death and Dying   426

List of Cases

▍Preface

The biologic revolution has brought about radical changes in health care. It has produced corresponding biomedical ethics problems that face healthcare professionals as well as lay people making healthcare decisions. These developments have affected nursing practice dramatically. The nurse has long been the healthcare professional in closest contact with the patient, often perceiving ethical and other value differences among the patient, the physician, and other parties. Increasingly, nurses recognize that they have the responsibility to be active, participating members of the healthcare team, initiating actions when ethical questions emerge.

In the 1970s, the use of case studies in medical ethics became an important method for helping healthcare professionals prepare for their increasing involvement in ethical choices related to health care. In 1977, Robert M. Veatch prepared a collection published as *Case Studies in Medical Ethics*. That collection covered medical ethics very broadly, emphasizing medical ethical decisions made by the entire range of healthcare professionals and lay people. Although only some of those cases involved nurses, it was clear that nurses face unique biomedical ethical problems. They stand in special role relations with patients, families, physicians, and other members of the healthcare team.

The two authors of the earlier editions of this volume, having worked together for many years, realized that a special collection of cases focusing specifically on the ethical problems facing nurses was needed. The first edition of *Case Studies in Nursing Ethics*, published in 1987, was the result. Second and third editions followed in 2000 and 2006, respectively.

A major change for this fourth edition is the addition of a third editor—Carol Taylor, a PhD with a concentration in bioethics, she is also a scholar with much experience on the faculty of a school of nursing. At the same time, Sara T. Fry, who was the senior editor of the previous editions, has taken a less active role in this edition. She had originally supplied most of the cases for the earlier editions (including many that remain in this volume), and worked collaboratively in the development of the general structure of the book and the presentation of the bioethical theory. She has reviewed the manuscript of this fourth edition, but was not directly responsible for its preparation.

Several elements were important to take into consideration when we updated the book for this new edition. As the study of ethics in health care has matured, much more sophisticated literature has become available. Likewise, the study of ethics in the nursing profession has matured. New courses, new professional codes, and new awareness of the professional responsibility of the nurse combined to make a significant updating of this book essential. In this fourth edition, we have added more emphasis on methods for analyzing cases. We have also added an entire chapter on moral integrity and moral distress, issues of particular concern to nurses, who sometimes feel pressure to act on healthcare decisions of physicians or patients in ways that do not fit with their own ethics. In light of the new roles for nurses and other health professionals, such as caring for prisoners of military conflicts in places like Abu Ghraib and Guantanamo, we have added a new chapter presenting cases on the general concept of respect for patients and others. We have also added an appendix that discusses Web-based resources.

Although this collection can be used as a source of ad hoc cases covering a wide range of topics, it can also be treated much more systematically. The authors were committed to organizing the cases in a format appropriate for the systematic study of applied ethics. Part I of the book deals with cases that pose basic questions regarding the meaning and justification of ethical claims. It focuses on identifying ethical and other value problems and examining the role of codes and other sources of ethical reflection. Part II provides an opportunity to explore the basic principles of ethics as they affect nursing. These principles are general and broad. As such, they impact the ethical thinking of nurses in many different contexts. Part III provides an opportunity to apply these principles to more specific contexts in nursing practice and to examine some of the special frameworks for approaching such topics as abortion, informed consent, the care of the terminally ill, and the new context of HIV.

Taken together, the three parts of the book constitute a text in basic ethics, and at the same time show how ethical theory is applied to the field of nursing. We hope that many readers will use this volume as an opportunity to confront systematically the full range of basic problems in ethics.

Almost all of the cases in this text are based on real situations experienced by one of the authors or shared with us by one of the many nurses who helped develop this collection. Except for cases in the public domain (indicated with references to sources), the names and details have been changed to protect confidentiality and to present the ethical issues with maximum clarity. Nevertheless, they grow out of real experiences faced by nurses who provide patient care. A small number of cases, especially those involving future problems anticipated in nursing, have been constructed based on discussions with persons actively involved in clinical and policy settings.

A great number of people have helped prepare this collection. Some have preferred to remain anonymous. Others have shared cases with us without wanting their names attached to specific cases. We are grateful to Moheba Hanif for her help in preparing the fourth edition manuscript. To the many nurses who have discussed preliminary versions of cases and commentaries, we are also grateful. We especially thank our students and colleagues who have provided thoughtful comments or raised questions about specific cases, prompting us to revise and strengthen the case commentaries.

Nurses face a tremendous challenge in formulating their own ethical positions and in dealing with those of patients and members of the healthcare team. We hope *Case Studies in Nursing Ethics*, Fourth Edition, will help in meeting that challenge.

Sara T. Fry
Brewster, Massachusetts

Robert M. Veatch
Washington, DC

Carol Taylor
Washington, DC

Introduction

Four Questions of Ethics[1]

The term *nursing ethics* is controversial. Some insist that nursing ethics is a unique field posing issues that cannot be understood fully by adapting the professional ethics of physicians. They insist on the term *nursing ethics* because it connotes the uniqueness of the moral problems that nurses face in the healthcare setting. On the other hand, others argue against the term. They suggest that there is really very little that is morally unique to nursing. The same ethical principles and the same moral issues emerge in the healthcare setting, whether one is a physician, nurse, or patient.

This book puts forth the view that nursing ethics is a legitimate term referring to a field that is a subcategory of biomedical ethics. Biomedical ethics is simply the ethics of judgments made within the biomedical sciences. The analysis of the ethical judgments made by physicians can be called *physician ethics*. Similarly, the analysis of ethical judgments made by nurses can be called *nursing ethics*. Like physician ethics, nursing ethics is a subsystem derived from a larger general system of biomedical ethics.

Biomedical ethics as a field presents a fundamental problem. As a branch of applied ethics, biomedical ethics becomes interesting and relevant only when it abandons the ephemeral realm of theory and abstract speculation and concerns itself with practical questions raised by real, everyday problems of health and illness. Much of biomedical ethics, especially as practiced within the health professions, is indeed oriented around the practical questions of what should be done in particular cases. Nursing, like other health professions, is case oriented. Yet, if those who must resolve the ever-increasing ethical dilemmas in health care—patients, family members, physicians, nurses, hospital administrators, and public policy makers—treat every case as entirely fresh, entirely novel, they will have lost perhaps the best way of reaching solutions: understanding the general principles of ethics and facing each new situation from a systematic ethical stance.

This is a volume of case studies in nursing ethics. It begins by recognizing the fact that one cannot approach ethics, especially nursing ethics, in the abstract. The volume comprises real-life, flesh-and-blood cases that raise fundamental ethical questions. It also recognizes that a general framework is needed from which to resolve the dilemmas of nursing practice. Therefore, the cases are organized in a systematic way. The chapters and issues within the chapters are arranged so as to work systematically through the questions of ethics. Because the main purpose of the book is to provide a collection of case studies from which may be built a comprehensive scheme for nursing ethics, this introduction is devoted to more theoretical issues. The object is to construct a framework outlining the basic ethical questions that must be answered in any complete and systematic bioethical system.

Four fundamental questions must be answered in order to take a complete and systematic ethical position. Each question has several plausible answers, answers that have been developed over 2000 years of Western thought. For normal day-to-day decisions made by the nurse, it is not necessary to deal with each question. In fact, to do so would paralyze the nurse decision maker. Most nursing decisions—such as when to ambulate a patient, when to flush an IV, or how often to check on a chronically ill patient—are quite ordinary and do not demand full ethical analysis. Other decisions, such as those called for in the case of emergency intervention, are not ordinary at all. Still, in both ordinary and emergency situations, it is possible to act without being immobilized by the ethical and other value problems only because some general rules or guidelines have emerged from previous experience and reflection. If ethical conflict is serious enough, it will be necessary to deal, at least implicitly, with all four of the fundamental questions of ethics.

What Makes Right Acts Right?

At the most general level, which ethicists call the level of metaethics, the first question is: What makes right acts right? What are the meanings and justifications of ethical statements?

It may not at first be obvious what counts as an ethical problem in nursing. Nurses easily recognize the existence of a moral crisis in deciding to let an abnormal newborn die, in choosing which of two needy patients will get a heart transplant, in participating in a late-term abortion for what to the nurse seems like trivial reasons, or helping a terminally ill patient in pain end his or her life. These situations clearly seem to involve ethical problems. Yet it is not immediately evident why we call these problems ethical whereas we consider others faced more commonly in the routine practice of nursing not to be.

To make the distinction between ethical and nonethical problems obvious, several steps should be followed.

1. Distinguishing Between Evaluative Statements and Statements Presenting Nonevaluative Facts

Ethics involves making evaluations; therefore, it is a normative enterprise. Moving from the idea that one can do something to the position that one ought to do something involves incorporating a set of norms—judgments of value, rights, duties, responsibilities, and the like. Thus, to be ethically responsible in the practice of nursing, it is important to develop the ability to recognize evaluations as they arise in nursing practice.

To develop this ability, select an experience that, at first, seems to involve no particular value judgments. Begin describing what occurred and watch for evaluative words. Every time a word expressing value is encountered, note it. Among the words to watch for are verbs such as *want, desire, prefer, should,* or *ought.* Evaluations also may be expressed in nouns such as *benefit, harm, duty, responsibility, right,* or *obligation*; or in related adjectives such as *good* and *bad*, *right* and *wrong*, *responsible*, *fitting*, and the like.

Sometimes evaluations are not necessarily expressed in literal, direct evaluative words but clearly function as value judgments. The American Nurses Association (ANA) *Code of Ethics for Nurses*, for example, states that "the nurse . . . practices . . . unrestricted by considerations of social or economic status, personal attributes, or the nature of health problems."[2] The ANA could be describing the facts about the way all nurses behave. Obviously it is not, however. Rather, it is saying that the nurse ought to practice without discrimination and that the good nurse does so.

2. Distinguishing Between Moral and Nonmoral Evaluations

Once one has identified a normative statement, one must determine whether the evaluation is moral or nonmoral. This process can be much harder, because the difference often cannot be discerned from the language itself. The statement that the nurse did a good job of informing the patient about the reasons for instituting intravenous fluid therapy could express many kinds of evaluations. It could mean the nurse did a good job legally; that is, the nurse fulfilled the law. It could mean the nurse did a good job psychologically; that is, the job was done in a way that produced a good psychologic impact on the patient. It could mean that the nurse did a good job technically; that is, every relevant piece of information was conveyed accurately. Or it could mean that the nurse did a good job ethically; that is, the nurse did what was morally required. Conceivably, a positive evaluation in one of these senses could simultaneously be a negative evaluation in some other sense.

Sometimes value judgments in nursing practice only express nonmoral evaluations. Saying that the patient ate well does not express a moral evaluation of the way the patient consumed the food. Saying that another day's hospitalization for the patient will be good means only that the patient will be helped physically or psychologically. It says nothing about whether the patient will be helped morally. Even these apparently nonmoral judgments about benefits and harms, however, can quickly lead one into the sphere of ethics. For example, when the patient's judgment of what will be beneficial differs from the nurse's judgment, specific ethical dilemmas may emerge. A nurse who is committed morally to doing what will benefit the patient will choose one course, whereas the nurse who is committed to preserving patient autonomy may reluctantly choose another.

Ethical or moral evaluations are judgments of what is good or bad, right or wrong, having certain characteristics that separate them from other types of evaluations, such as aesthetic judgments, personal preferences, beliefs, or matters of taste. The difference between the evaluations lies in the grounds on or the reasons for which the evaluations are made.[3]

Moral evaluations possess certain characteristics. They are evaluations of human actions, practices, or character traits, rather than inanimate objects such as paintings or architectural structures. Not all evaluations of human actions, practices, or character traits are moral evaluations, however. We may say that the nurse is a good administrator or a good teacher without making a moral evaluation. To be considered moral, an evaluation must have additional characteristics. Three characteristics are often mentioned as distinctive in this regard. First, the evaluations must be ultimate. They must have a certain preemptive quality, meaning that other values or human ends cannot, as a rule, override them.[4] Second, they must possess universality. Moral evaluations are thought of as reflecting a standpoint that applies to everyone. They are evaluations that everyone in principle ought to be able to make and understand (even if some in fact do not do so).[5] Finally, many add a third, more material, condition: moral evaluations must treat the good of everyone alike. They must be general in the sense that they avoid giving a special place to one's own welfare. They must have an other-regarding focus or, at least, consider one's own welfare on a par with that of others.[6]

Moral judgments possessing these characteristics can sometimes conflict with one another. Decisions about whether the nurse ought to care for a patient in the way thought to be most beneficial or in the way that would preserve the patient's autonomy (even though harm may result) can involve conflicts among moral characteristics. That being the case, any clinical decision in nursing practice that involves a conflict over values potentially involves a moral conflict. The nurse may be faced with the choice between preserving the patient's welfare or ensuring someone else's welfare. The nurse may have to choose whether to keep a promise of confidentiality or to provide needed assistance for a patient even though a confidence would have to be broken. The nurse may have to decide whether to protect the interests of colleagues or of the institution, or whether to serve future patients by striking for better conditions or serve present patients by refusing to strike. These are moral conflicts in nursing. Chapter 1 presents a series of cases in which both moral and nonmoral evaluations are made in what appear to be quite ordinary nursing situations. The main tasks are to discern the value dimensions and to separate them from physiologic, psychologic, and other facts.

3. Determining Who Ought to Decide

The question of who ought to decide is the focus of Chapter 2. Having learned to recognize the difference between the factual and evaluative dimensions of a case in nursing ethics, one will constantly encounter the problem of who ought to decide, or where the locus of decision making ought to rest. Chapter 2 presents cases involving a wide range of sources of moral authority, from institutions, patients, families, physicians, and administrators to professional committees and the general public.

The choice among these decision makers depends, at least in part, on what it is that ethical terms mean, or more generally, what it is that makes right acts right. Several answers to the latter question have been offered. One recognizes that different societies seem to reach different conclusions about whether a given act is right or wrong. From this perspective, to say that an act is morally right means nothing more than to say that it is in accord with the values of the speaker's society or simply that it is approved by the speaker's society. This position, called *social relativism*, explains rightness or wrongness on the basis of whether the act fits with social customs, mores, and folkways. One problem with this view is that it seems to make sense to say that an act is morally wrong even though it is approved by the society of the speaker. That would be impossible if moral judgments were based only on the values of the speaker's society.

A second answer to the question of what makes right acts right attempts to correct this problem. According to this position, to say that an act is right means that it is approved by the speaker. This position, called *personal relativism*, reduces ethical meaning to personal preference. This means that behavior thought to be immoral by some could be approved by others. Some say that the reason this can happen is that moral judgments are merely expressions of each speaker's preference.

Such differences in judgment, however, may have explanation other than that ethical terms merely refer to the speaker's own preferences. Those disagreeing might simply not be working with the same facts. To claim that two people are in moral disagreement simply because the same act is seen as right by one person or society and wrong by another requires proof that both parties see the facts in the same way. Differences of circumstances or belief about the facts could easily account for many moral differences.

In contrast with social and personal relativism, there is a third, more universal group of answers to the question of what makes right acts right. These positions, collectively called *universalism* or sometimes *absolutism*, hold that, in principle, acts that are called morally right or wrong are right or wrong independent of social or personal biases. Certainly some choices merely involve personal taste: flavors of ice cream or hair lengths vary from time to time, place to place, and person to person. But these are matters of preference, not morality. No one considers the choice of vanilla morally right and chocolate morally wrong. But other evaluations appeal beyond the standards of social and personal taste to a more universal frame of reference. When these are concerned with acts, practices, or character traits—as opposed to, say, paintings or music—they are thought of as moral evaluations.

However, the nature of the universal standard is often disputed. For the theologically oriented, it may be a divine standard. According to this view, calling it right to disconnect a ventilator keeping alive a terminally ill, comatose patient is to say that God would approve of the act. This position is sometimes called *theological absolutism* or *theological universalism*.

Still another view among universalists takes empirical observation as the model. The standard in this case is nature or external reality. The problem of knowing whether an act is right or wrong is then the problem of knowing what is in nature. *Empirical absolutism*, as the view is sometimes called, sees the problem of knowing right and wrong as analogous to knowing scientific facts.[7] Where astronomers try to discern the real nature of the universe of stars and chemists the real nature of atoms as ordered in nature, ethicists, according to this view, strive to discern rightness and wrongness as ordered in nature. The position sometimes takes the form of a natural law position. As with the physicist's law of gravity, moral laws are thought to be inexplicably rooted in nature. Natural law positions may be secular, as was seen with the ancient Stoics, or they may have a theological foundation, such as with the ethics of Thomas Aquinas and traditional Catholic moral theology.

Still another form of universalism or absolutism rejects both the theological and the empirical models. It supposes that right and wrong are not empirically knowable but are nonnatural properties known only by intuition. Thus, the position is sometimes called *intuitionism* or *nonnaturalism*.[8] For the intuitionist or nonnaturalist, right and wrong are not empirically knowable, they are still universal. All persons should in principle have the same intuitions about a particular act, provided they are intuiting properly. Still others, sometimes called *rationalists*, hold that reason can determine what is ethically required.[9]

There are yet other answers to the question of what makes right acts right. One group of views—in various forms called *noncognitivism, emotivism,* or *prescriptivism*—which ascended to popularity during the mid-20th century, saw ethical utterances as evincing feelings about a particular act.[10]

A full exploration of the answers to this most abstract of ethical questions is not possible here.[11] Ultimately, however, if an ethical dispute growing out of a case is serious enough and cannot be resolved at any other level, this question must be faced. If one says that it is wrong to tell the truth to a dying patient because it will produce anxiety, and another says that it is right to do so because consent to treatment is a moral imperative, some way must be found of adjudicating the dispute between the two principles. Then, one must ask what it is that makes right acts right, how conflicts can be resolved, and what the final authority is for morality.

What Kinds of Acts Are Right?

A second fundamental question of ethics moves beyond determining what makes right acts right by asking: What are the general norms for ethics? This takes us to the realm of what can be called *normative ethics*. Normative ethics involves several questions. The one that has dominated biomedical ethics for the past generation is: What kinds of acts are right? It questions whether there are any general principles or norms describing the characteristics that make actions right or wrong. At the end of this introduction we will add for this fourth edition two more questions that have been getting attention lately. The question of what kinds of acts are right gives rise to "action guides" or norms that tell us what it is that makes an action morally right. Two major schools of though dominate Western theories about action guides.

Consequentialism

One position looks at the consequences of acts; the other at what is taken to be inherently right or wrong. The first position claims that acts are right to the extent that they produce good consequences and wrong to the extent that they produce bad ones. The key evaluative terms for this position, known as *utilitarianism* or *consequentialism*, are *good* and *bad*. This is the position of John Stuart Mill and Jeremy Bentham, as well as of Epicurus, St. Thomas Aquinas, and capitalist economics. St. Thomas, for example, argued that the first principle of natural law is that "good is to be done and promoted and evil is to be avoided."[12]

Because St. Thomas stands at the center of the Roman Catholic natural law tradition, he illustrates that natural law thinking (which is one answer to the first question of what makes right acts right) is not incompatible with consequentialism. The two positions are answers to two different questions. Although natural law thinkers are not always consequentialists, they can be.

Classical utilitarianism determines what kinds of acts are right by figuring the net of good consequences minus bad ones for each person affected and then adding up the individual amounts of net good to find the total.[13] The certainty and duration of the benefits and harms are taken into account. This form of consequentialism is indifferent to who obtains the benefits and harms. Thus, if the total net benefits of providing nursing care to a relatively healthy but powerful person are thought to be greater than those of providing it to a sicker Medicare recipient, the healthy and powerful ought to be given the care without further ethical debate.

Traditional nursing ethics, like physician ethics, is oriented toward benefiting patients. This tradition combines the utilitarian answer to the question of what kinds of acts are right with a particular answer to the question of to whom is moral duty owed. Loyalty is to the patient, and the goal is to do what will produce the most benefit for and avoid the most harm to the patient.

Nursing ethics traditionally holds that the nurse's primary commitment is to the health, well-being, and safety of the patient. Some interpret this as emphasizing protecting the patient from harm over benefiting the patient. Like the principle of physician ethics, *primum non nocere* or "first of all do no harm," it gives special weight to avoiding harm over and above the weight given to goods that can be produced.

Among physicians, the principle of doing no harm is often interpreted conservatively, so that harm is avoided by nonaction. Nurses may be more active in avoiding harm, especially when they take an advocacy role to attempt to prevent harm to the patient. In either case, however, when nursing ethics gives special weight to certain kinds of consequences (e.g., avoiding harm), its ethics is still further distinguished from classical utilitarianism.

These problems of the relationship between classical utilitarianism (which counts benefits to all in society equally) and traditional nursing ethics (which focuses on the individual patient and sometimes gives special weight to avoiding harm through the prescriptive duty of advocacy) are raised in the cases in Chapter 4.

Nonconsequentialism

Against positions that are oriented to consequences, the other major group of answers to the question of what kinds of acts are right asserts that rightness and wrongness are inherent in the act itself, independent of the consequences. These positions, collectively known as *formalism* or *deontologism* (or simply *nonconsequentialism*), hold that right- and wrong-making characteristics may be independent of consequences. Kant stated the position most starkly.[14]

Chapter 5 takes up problems of healthcare delivery and in doing so poses probably the most significant challenge to the consequentialist ethic. The dominant ethical principle of healthcare delivery is that of *justice*. Taken in the sense of fairness in distributing goods and harms, justice is held by many to be an ethical right-making characteristic, even if the consequences are not the best. The problem is whether it is morally preferable to have a higher net total of benefits in society, even if they are unfairly distributed, or to have a somewhat lower total good but to have that good more *fairly* distributed. (Among those committed to the principle of justice, there may be differences over what counts as "fair" or "unfair.") Utilitarians would argue that net benefits tend to be greater when benefits are distributed more evenly (because of decreasing marginal utility). They claim that the only reason to distribute goods such as health care evenly is to maximize the total good. On the other hand, the formalist, who holds that justice is a right-making characteristic independent of utility, does not require an item-by-item calculation of benefits and harms before concluding that a particular distribution of goods is prima facie wrong—that is, wrong with regard to fairness.

In addition to the principle of justice, many ethics hold that human beings (and perhaps some nonhuman animals) are intrinsically worthy of respect regardless of the consequences. In this fourth edition of this book, we gather several ethical principles related to respect under the general heading of respect for persons. Chapter 6 introduces the concept of respect and takes up some cases in which nurses are challenged to show respect for patients. This chapter is followed by a series of more specific principles that are related to this notion of respect.

The first of these is the principle of *autonomy*. Whereas classical utilitarianism leads to a moral principle demanding noninterference with the autonomy of others in society because this produces greater net benefits, Kantian formalism leads to the moral demand that persons and their beliefs be respected per se. The problems of conflict between the nurse's nonconsequentialist duties to respect autonomy or self-determination of individual clients and consequentialist duties to produce benefit are discussed in Chapter 7.

Another ethical principle related to respect that many formalists hold to be independent of consequences is that of truth-telling or *veracity*. As with the other principles, utilitarians argue that truth telling is an operational principle designed to guarantee maximum benefit. When truth-telling does more harm than good, according to the utilitarians, there is no obligation to tell the truth. To them, telling the dying patient of his or her condition can be cruel and therefore wrong. In contrast, to one who holds that truth telling is a right-making ethical principle in itself, the problem of what the dying patient should be told is much more complex. This problem of what the patient should be told is the subject of Chapter 8.

Another characteristic that formalists may believe to be right-making independent of consequences is the duty of *fidelity*, especially the keeping of promises. Kant and others have held that breaking a promise will at least tend to be wrong independent of the consequences. The utilitarian points out that breaking a promise often has bad consequences. If it were to become a usual practice, the act of promising itself would become useless. The formalist, although granting this danger, argues that there is something basically wrong in breaking a promise and that to know this one need not even go on to look at the consequences. The formalist might, with the utilitarian, grant that to look at consequences may reveal even more reasons to oppose promise-breaking, but this is not necessary to know that promise-breaking is prima facie wrong.

The nurse–patient relationship can be viewed essentially as one involving promises or contracts or, to use a term with fewer legalistic implications, covenants. The relationship is founded on implied and sometimes explicit promises. One of these promises is that information disclosed in the nurse–patient relationship is confidential and that it will not be disclosed by the nurse without the patient's permission. The principle of confidentiality in ethics is really a specification of the principle of promise-keeping in general. The cases in Chapter 9 present the various problems growing out of the ethical principle of fidelity.

The cases in Chapter 10 introduce a final principle related to respect that can be included in a general ethical system: the principle of the *sanctity of human life*. All societies have some kind of prohibition on killing. The Buddhists make it one of their five basic precepts. Those in the Judeo-Christian tradition recognize it as one of the Ten Commandments. The moral foundation of the prohibition on killing is not always clear, however. For people who base their ethic on doing good and avoiding evil, prohibiting killing is simply a rule summarizing the obvious conclusion that it usually does people harm to kill them. If that is the full foundation of the prohibition on killing, then killing is just an example of a way that one can do harm.

This presents a problem, however. Many people believe there are special cases where killing someone may actually do good, on balance. It will stop a greater evil that the one killed would otherwise have committed, or it will, in health care, possibly relieve a terminally ill patient of otherwise intractable pain. Is killing a human being always morally a characteristic of actions that tends to make them wrong, or is it wrong only when more harm than good results from the killing? For those who hold that killing is always a wrong-making characteristic, the sanctity of human life becomes an independent principle much like veracity or autonomy or fidelity. The cases of Chapter 10 explore these questions.

How Do Rules Apply to Specific Situations?

There is a third question in a general ethical stance. It stems from the fact that each case raising an ethical problem is, in at least some ways, situationally unique. The ethical principles of benefiting, justice, autonomy, truth-telling, fidelity, and avoiding killing are extremely general. They are a small set of the most general right-making characteristics. Application to specific cases requires a great leap. The question is: How do the general principles apply to specific situations? As a bridge to the specific case, an intermediate, more specific set of rules is often used. These intermediate rules probably cause more problems in ethics than any other component of ethical theory does. At the same time, they are probably more helpful as guides to day-to-day behavior than anything else is.

The problems arise in part because of a misunderstanding of the nature and function of these rules. Rules have two possible functions. They may serve simply as guidelines summarizing the conclusions we tend to reach in moral problems of a certain class. When rules have this function of summarizing the experience from similar situations of the past, they are called *rules of thumb, guiding rules,* or *summary rules.*

In contrast, rules may function to specify behavior that is required independent of individual judgment about a specific situation. The rules against abortion of a viable fetus or against killing a dying patient are examples of rules that are often linked directly to right-making characteristics. This kind of rule sometimes is called a *rule of practice.* The rule specifies a practice which, in turn, is justified by the general principle. According to this rules-of-practice view, it is unacceptable to overturn a general practice simply because in a particular case the outcome would be better.

The conflict between those who take the rules more seriously and those who consider the situation to be the more critical determinant of moral rightness became one of the major ethical controversies of the mid-20th century. It is sometimes called the *rules-situation debate.*[15] At one extreme is the rigorist, who insists that rules should never be violated. At the other is the situationalist, who claims that rules never apply because every situation is unique. Both positions in the extreme probably lead to absurdity. The rigorist is immobilized when two rules conflict. The situationalist is immobilized when he or she treats situations as literally new with no help from past experience in similar, if not identical, situations.

The rules-situation debate does not lend itself to special cases grouped together. The problem arises continually throughout the cases in the volume. The final question, however, requires special chapters with cases that examine the problems raised.

What Ought to Be Done in Specific Cases?

After the determination of what makes right acts right, what kinds of actions are right, and how rules apply to specific situations, a large number of specific situations that make up the bulk of problems in nursing ethics still remain. These raise a fourth question: What ought to be done in a specific case or kind of case? Nursing, being particularly oriented to case problems, is given to organizing ethical problems around specific kinds of cases. Ethics, too, is sometimes divided into the problems of birth, life, and death.

Parts I and II of this volume emphasize the overarching problems of how to relate facts to values; who ought to decide, benefiting the patient; and the principles of justice, respecting autonomy, truth-telling, fidelity, and the sanctity of human life in healthcare delivery. These are among the larger questions of biomedical ethics. Part III shifts to cases that focus on specific problem areas. The cases in Chapter 11 raise the problems of abortion, conception control, and sterilization. Chapter 12 moves to problems of genetic counseling and engineering, and intervention in the prenatal period. The next chapters take up in turn the problems of psychiatry and the control of human behavior, HIV/AIDS, human experimentation, consent and the right to refuse medical treatment, and death and dying.

The answer to the question of what ought to be done in a specific case requires the integration of the answers to all of the other questions if a thorough analysis and justification is to be given. The first line of moral defense will probably be a set of moral rules and rights that are thought to apply to the case. In abortion, the right to control one's body and the right to practice nursing as one sees fit are pitted against the right to life. In human experimentation, the rules of informed consent pertain. Among the dying, rules about euthanasia conflict with the right to pursue happiness and the right to refuse medical treatment conflicts with the rule that the nurse ought to do everything possible to preserve life.

In many cases, the conflict escalates from an issue of moral rules and rights to the higher, more abstract level of ethical principle. It must be determined, for example, whether informed consent is designed to maximize benefits to the experimental subject or to facilitate the subject's freedom of self-determination required by the principle of autonomy. It must also be explored whether concern for harm to the patient justifies withholding information from the patient or whether the formalist truth-telling principle justifies disclosure.

The problem of what ought to be done in specific cases also requires a great deal of empirical data. Value-relevant biologic and psychologic facts are gathered to assess many case problems in biomedical ethics. The predictive capacity of a flat electroencephalogram may be important for the definition of death. The legal facts are relevant for the refusal of treatment. Basic religious and philosophic beliefs of the patient may be critical to the resolution of some cases in nursing ethics. It is impossible to present all of the relevant medical, genetic, legal, and psychologic facts necessary for a complete analysis of any case, but it is possible to present the major facts required for understanding. Readers will have to supplement these facts for a fuller understanding of the cases, just as they will have to supplement their reading in ethical theory for a fuller understanding of the basic questions of ethics.

These four basic questions can be thought of as four different stages of ethical analysis. If the answer to a specific case is not apparent, one might see if some rules or rights claims are relevant. At that point, one would have to know how rules apply to specific situations. If the rules do not give a clear answer, then one would have to move to the next stage, the stage of deciding which ethical principles are morally relevant. Finally, if one questions the basic principles, he or she is forced to consider the more fundamental questions of metaethics. An ethical analysis can start at the most specific stage, that of the case, and move to other stages, or one might try to be more systematic by starting with the most fundamental questions and moving to more and more specific stages. The stages of ethical analysis are illustrated in Figure I-1.

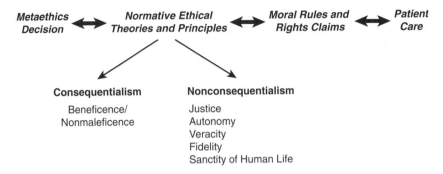

Figure I-1   Stages of ethical analysis.

Two Additional Questions of Ethics

A pertinent and pervasive critique of bioethics in the United States over the last generation has been its failure to pay sufficient attention to the character of the moral agent. One can have expert knowledge of what makes particular actions ethically right or wrong and fail to behave ethically in a reliable fashion because of deficiency in character. Similarly, individuals seemingly equally committed to respecting autonomy and benefiting others may, in practice, do this differently depending on their characters. An ethic that focuses on praiseworthy traits of character is called a *virtue theory* and such praiseworthy traits are called *virtues*. Thus, there is a renewed appreciation of the role virtue ethics plays in bioethics generally and in nursing and ethics and the ethics of the other health professions specifically. Similarly, within the health professions and nursing in particular, Carol Gilligan's groundbreaking work on *care* as a distinct moral orientation has refocused attention on the importance of the ethical norms derived from the nature of particular relationships.[16] Two questions of ethics that have commanded attention in the past several years are: "What kind of person ought I to be?" and "What does *this* relationship demand of me?"

What Kind of Person Ought I to Be?

Virtues are human excellencies, cultivated dispositions of character and conduct that motivate us to be good human beings, to flourish. A *virtue* is a trait of character that is praiseworthy. (Blameworthy character traits are called *vices*.) *Clinical* virtues are character traits that dispose nurses to provide good care to patients, families, and communities. Different schools of thought about virtues will identify different character traits as praiseworthy. Thus, while there is no official list of essential virtues of nurses, the following are frequently listed:

- Competence
- Compassionate caring

- Subordination of self-interest to patient care
- Trustworthiness
- Conscientiousness
- Intelligence
- Practical wisdom
- Justice
- Humility
- Courage
- Integrity[17]

Those familiar with the history of nursing will remember that early lists of nursing virtues included obedience, cleanliness, and order. An important responsibility of a nurse nursing as a profession is to identify the virtues that comport with professional practice and its contemporary responsibilities.

What Does *This* Relationship Demand of Me?

Carol Gilligan's research in moral development culminated in her conviction that females tend to develop *a morality of response and care* whereas males develop *a morality of obligations*. In Gilligan's theory, males and females have different ways of looking at the world. Males are more likely to associate morality with *obligations* and *rights*. Females are more likely to see *moral requirements emerging from the needs of others within the context of a relationship*. Gilligan does not claim that these two modes strictly correlate with gender or that all women or all men speak in the same moral voice.[18]

Building on these insights, philosopher Annette Baier argues not that traditional ethical theories are false or outdated, but that they capture only a piece of the larger moral world. She does not recommend that we discard categories of obligation, but that we make room for an ethic of love and trust, including an account of human bonding and friendship—elements of virtue ethics and the ethics of relations.[19] Nurse ethicists eagerly embraced the concept of care ethics to address nursing's ethical concerns, but there were many questions about the place of care in normative ethics. Most commentators that speak about *care ethics* are thinking about care in relation to virtues and relationships.

In this text, we have chosen to categorize care ethics as recognizing an underdeveloped element of morality (i.e., who we ought to be in the context of particular relationships). The ethics of care challenges impartiality and universal principles. Themes central to the ethics of care include mutual interdependence in relationships (recognizes vulnerability) and highlights a role for emotions. The nurse–patient relationship is central to *care ethics* which directs attention to the specific situations of individual patients viewed within the context of their life narrative. The care perspective directs that how we choose to be and act each time we encounter a patient or colleague is a matter of ethical significance. Ethics is not reduced to a decision to withhold or withdraw life-sustaining treatment. Characteristics of care ethics include the following:

- Centrality of the caring relationship;
- Promotion of the dignity and respect of patients and colleagues as people;
- Attention to the particulars of individual patients and colleagues and the context in which we find ourselves;
- Cultivation of responsiveness to others and professional responsibility; and
- A redefinition of fundamental moral skills to include virtues like kindness, attentiveness, empathy, compassion, reliability.[20]

ENDNOTES

1. Adapted from Veatch, R. M. (1977). *Case studies in medical ethics* (pp. 1–14). Cambridge, MA: Harvard University Press.
2. American Nurses Association. (2001). *Code of ethics for nurses with interpretive statements* (p. 7). Washington, DC: Author.
3. Frankena, W. (1973). *Ethics* (2nd ed., p. 62). Englewood Cliffs, NJ: Prentice Hall.
4. Beauchamp, T. L., & Childress, J. F. (Eds.). (1983). *Principles of biomedical ethics* (2nd ed., p. 15). New York: Oxford University Press.
5. Fried, C. (1978). *Right and wrong* (p. 12). Cambridge, MA: Harvard University Press.
6. Baier, K. (1965). *The moral view* (pp. 106–109). New York: Random House; Beauchamp, T. L., & Childress, J. F. (Eds.). (1983). *Principles of biomedical ethics* (2nd ed., pp. 16–17). New York: Oxford University Press; Rawls, J. A. (1971). *A theory of justice* (pp. 131–136). Cambridge, MA: Harvard University Press.
7. Broad, C. D. (1944–1945). Some reflections on moral-sense theories in ethics. *The Aristotelian Society, 45,* 131–166; Firth, R. (1952). Ethical absolutism and the ideal observer theory. *Philosophy and Phenomenological Research, 12,* 317–345.
8. Ross, W. D. (1939). *The right and the good.* Oxford, UK: Oxford University Press.
9. Kant, I. (1785/1964). In H. J. Paton (Trans.), *Groundwork of the metaphysics of morals.* New York: Harper and Row.
10. Ayer, A. J. (1948). *Language, truth, and logic.* London: Victor Gollancz; Hare, R. M. (1952). *The language of morals.* Oxford, UK: Clarendon Press; Stevenson, C. L. (1944). *Ethics and language.* New Haven, CT: Yale University Press.
11. For basic surveys of ethical theory, see: Boylan, M. (2000). *Basic ethics.* Upper Saddle River, NJ: Prentice Hall; Frankena, W. (1973). *Ethics* (2nd ed.). Englewood Cliffs, NJ: Prentice Hall; Warnock, G. J. (1967). *Contemporary moral philosophy.* New York: St. Martin's Press.
   For more detailed introductions, see Beauchamp, T. L. (2001). *Philosophical ethics: An introduction to moral philosophy* (3rd ed.). Boston: McGraw-Hill; Brandt, R. B. (1959). *Ethical theory: The problems of normative and critical ethics.* Englewood Cliffs, NJ: Prentice Hall; Feldman, F. (1978). *Introductory ethics.* Englewood Cliffs, NJ: Prentice Hall; Gert, B. (1998). *Morality: Its nature and justification.* New York: Oxford University Press; Taylor, P. W. (1975). *Principles of ethics: An introduction.* Encino, CA: Dickenson Publishing Co.

For readers containing classical sources, see: Brandt, R. B. (1961). *Value and obligation: Systematic readings in ethics*. New York: Harcourt, Brace & World; Melden, A. I. (Ed.). (1967). *Ethical theories: A book of readings* (2nd ed.). Englewood Cliffs, NJ: Prentice Hall.

12. Aquinas, T. (1274/1915). Fathers of the English Dominican Province (Eds.). *Summa theologica* I–II (A. 94, Art. 2). London: R&T Washbourne.

13. Bentham, J. (1823/1996). In J. H. Burns & H. L. A. Hart (Eds.), *An introduction to the principles of morals and legislation*. New York: Oxford University Press.

14. Kant, I. (1785/1964). In H. J. Paton (Trans.), *Groundwork of the metaphysics of morals*. New York: Harper Torchbooks.

15. Bales, M. D. (Ed.). (1968). *Contemporary utilitarianism*. Garden City, NY: Doubleday; Fletcher, J. (1966). *Situation ethics: The new morality*. Philadelphia: Westminster Press; Ramsey, P. (1967). *Deeds and rules in Christian ethics*. New York: Charles Scribner's Sons; Rawls, J. (1955). Two concepts of rules. *The Philosophical Review, 44*, 3–32.

16. Gilligan, C. (1982). *In a different voice* (p. 21). Cambridge, MA: Harvard University Press; Gilligan, C. (1989, Spring). Mapping the moral domain: New images of self in relationship. *Cross Currents, 39*, 50–63.

17. Taylor, C. (2012). Values, ethics and advocacy. In C. Taylor, C. Lillis, P. LeMone, & P. Lynn (Eds.), *Fundamentals of nursing: The art and science of nursing care* (7th ed.). Philadelphia: Lippincott, Williams & Wilkins.

18. Gilligan, C. (1982). *In a different voice* (p. 21). Cambridge, MA: Harvard University Press; Gilligan, C. (1989, Spring). Mapping the moral domain: New images of self in relationship. *Cross Currents, 39*, 50–63.

19. Baier, A. (1985, March). What do women want in a moral theory? *Nous, 19*, 53; Baier, A. (1985*). Postures of the mind* (pp. 210–219). Minneapolis, MN: University of Minnesota Press.

20. Taylor, C. (1993). Nursing ethics: The role of caring. *Association of Women's Health, Obstetrics, and Neonatal Nurses' Clinical Issues in Perinatal and Women's Health Nursing, 4*(4), 552–560.

PART I
Ethics and Values in Nursing

Chapter 1

Values in Health and Illness

Key Terms
Ethical conflict
Ethical values
Moral duty
Moral evaluation
Moral right
Nonmoral evaluation
Value orientations

Objectives
1. Identify moral and nonmoral evaluations in nursing practice.
2. Identify ethical conflicts in patient care situations.
3. Explain the roles that personal values and beliefs play in ethical conflicts.
4. Explain the limits of moral rights and rules as guides for ethical behaviors.

Nursing is a clinical practice that includes systematic problem solving (the nursing process) and nursing management of identified patient needs. In planning patient care, the nurse makes countless decisions concerning nursing diagnoses, construction and implementation of nursing care plans, and evaluation of patients' progress toward health. Each decision requires that the nurse combine a wide range of facts (or data) with a set of values to determine what ought to be done to help the patient fulfill his or her health needs. The facts are drawn from many different types of information about the patient: his or her medical and psychosocial histories, physiological status, economic status, and aesthetic and religious orientations. However, collection and analysis of the facts alone can never lead to a conclusion that a particular nursing intervention is morally justified. To reach a conclusion about what is morally justified in nursing practice, the nurse must combine relevant facts with a set of values. Thus, the first task in nursing ethics is to identify the many evaluations that take place in nursing practice and to separate the moral from the nonmoral components in these evaluations.

Identifying Evaluations in Nursing

Cases 1-1 and 1-2 demonstrate the various kinds of values involved in clinical decisions made by nurses in quite ordinary, routine nursing practice. Neither case raises traditional, dramatic ethical issues, but both clearly force the nurse to make ethical decisions. Moreover, they both involve many other kinds of evaluations that are not ethical at all. The evaluations include matters of taste (whether physical or psychologic risks are more weighty), matters of aesthetics (which of two environments is more pleasant), matters of law (whether it is legally acceptable to risk a baby's life to conform to the wishes of its parents), and matters of what are sometimes called **value orientations** (fundamental stances about such basic issues as whether a nurse ought to try to dominate nature or let nature take its course). However, questions of **moral evaluation** become central to the cases as they develop, and basic questions are raised about what the nurse ought to do in the moral sense. In analyzing these cases, notice the evaluations that occur and determine which of the evaluations are moral.

Case 1-1
The Patient Who Needed Help Getting Out of Bed

Isaac Livingston had led a good life. He had worked as a pharmaceutical salesman for 45 years before retiring 6 years before his most critical medical problems began. Now, at 72, he was hospitalized for what the nursing staff suspected might be his last time. He was suffering from carcinoma of the prostate that had metastasized to the bone and sapped his strength. His current hospital admission was triggered by several episodes of fainting, undoubtedly related to a serious drop in blood pressure. The pain of the tumor, the side effects of the medication (Dilaudid, 4 mg q 3–4 hours as necessary and chlorpromazine 10 mg qid as needed for nausea from the chemotherapy), and his lethargy combined to make him somewhat groggy. Moreover, Mr. Livingston often desired to get up and leave his room "to get some air" as he put it.

To make matters worse, Mr. Livingston suffered from a partial paralysis of the left leg of some 15 years' duration, apparently caused by spinal cord damage related to pressure from a spinal disc. All of these facts led the nursing team to be concerned about potential injury should Mr. Livingston fall getting out of bed.

To protect him from such injury, Mr. Livingston was placed in a room across from the nurses' station. His bed was lowered as close to the floor as possible, he was observed closely, his bed rails were raised at night, and he was instructed to press his call button to summon the nurse or nurse's aide whenever he wanted to get out of bed. Despite these precautions, however, the nurses frequently found Mr. Livingston trying to get out of bed by himself without help. His safety became a serious issue the night Ms. Howard found Mr. Livingston on the floor at 1:00 A.M. Apparently, he had slipped to the floor while trying to get out of his bed. He was not injured, but he could easily have suffered some injury. To prevent this from happening again, Ms. Howard told Mr. Livingston that he absolutely could not leave his bed without someone else being present, left a light on in his room at all times, and moved his bed so that he could not get out of it without observation by the nurses.

During the next day, Mr. Livingston vociferously objected to having to wait for a nurse or aide in order to get out of bed, use the toilet, or walk in the hallway—something he wanted to do quite frequently. Although he understood that these precautions were intended for his own good and that the nurses thought it was dangerous for him not to have someone accompany him when he was out of bed, Mr. Livingston intensely disliked all the constraints to his freedom.

That evening, Ms. Howard was approached at the nurses' station by Mr. Livingston's son during visiting hours. The son explained that Mr. Livingston had been trapped in a burning building when he was a child and since then had been severely afraid of suffocating or being enclosed or otherwise confined in small rooms. He needed to be able to get out of bed and leave his room whenever he felt confined. Were the nurses' constraints on his freedom absolutely necessary?

This explained some of Mr. Livingston's behavior, but Ms. Howard was still seriously concerned about the danger to a 72-year-old man, groggy with medication and partially paralyzed, falling as he attempted to get out of bed. It was her judgment that continued use of the protective measures were indicated for good nursing practice and Mr. Livingston's safety.

Ms. Howard explored her options. She could follow Mr. Livingston's urgent request that he be allowed to get out of bed without assistance whenever he felt like it. Or she could insist that, in her clinical judgment, good and safe nursing care required nursing assistance and close observation. Then again, she could ask for guidance from the resident on call or ask that Mr. Livingston's physician be consulted in the morning for an increase in the patient's sedation, which would make it unlikely that Mr. Livingston would try to get out of bed for any reason.

Commentary

The problem faced by Ms. Howard and her colleagues, at first, seems rather mundane. Placing Mr. Livingston's bed across from the nurses' station and requiring him to call for nursing assistance when getting out of bed hardly falls in the same class of moral controversy as the more exotic ethical issues of genetic manipulation, defining death, or even discussing a terminal diagnosis with a patient. Yet, upon reflection, it is clear that evaluations took place throughout Ms. Howard's interaction with Mr. Livingston. The brief case report presented here is full of value judgments. Mr. Livingston's life was a good life. He was suffering from carcinoma of the prostate and from partial paralysis. Suffering must necessarily be considered an evaluation. One cannot suffer and judge the sensation to be good in this respect.

The evaluations continue in the account of the immediate problem facing Ms. Howard. Mr. Livingston found it desirable to get out of his room, whereas the nursing team was worried about injury, something that necessarily has a bad connotation. Moreover, Mr. Livingston protested vociferously and objected to constraints on his freedom, many times. On the other hand, Ms. Howard was concerned about the danger to Mr. Livingston's health if he did not have nursing assistance when out of bed.

Three different levels of evaluations are taking place: choices about mental and physical health, choices about more fundamental value orientations, and choices about what is ethically acceptable behavior. At the first level, evaluations related to physical and mental outcomes seem to be in conflict. The nurse was naturally concerned about the real and significant physical risk to Mr. Livingston if he were free to get out of bed at will in his mildly sedated and disoriented state. Mr. Livingston, on the other hand, seemed to have a rather different agenda. He was relatively unconcerned about the risk of physical injury from a fall, but he was extraordinarily concerned about the psychologic sense of well-being that came from being free to move about and "get some air." That concern was, in part, derived from a unique experience in Mr. Livingston's past.

When Ms. Howard learned from Mr. Livingston's son of Mr. Livingston's history and preferences, she was able to include in her considerations the unique psychologic trauma brought about by constraints on his freedom to get out of bed at will. Still, however, she did not reach what was apparently Mr. Livingston's conclusion—that on balance, greater benefit would come from avoiding all constraints on his freedom. It could well be that the two simply compared the importance of avoiding physical injury and psychologic distress differently. If avoiding a broken hip is a good worthy of substantial psychologic trauma, then Ms. Howard's evaluation regarding the two kinds of benefits makes sense. If, on the other hand, one places more emphasis on the potential psychologic harm involved, then Mr. Livingston's behavior is understandable.

So far, this suggests only that differences are possible in essentially **nonmoral evaluations**. It does not yet get us to the level of ethics. However, other levels of evaluation may be going on in this case. Underlying the specific evaluations of physical and mental outcomes may be a second level of evaluation involving deeper, more fundamental beliefs and values. These more basic evaluations are sometimes called value orientations or, taken together, a "worldview."[1] They deal with the human's relationship with nature, whether one ought to be active and aggressive or more passive in letting nature take its course, whether it is better to be oriented to goals in the future or to focus more on the present or past, whether people are to be regarded as tending toward good or evil, and how individuals relate to other individuals and groups. Individuals as well as cultures tend to take stands on these basic value orientations. Moreover, they sometimes regard them as moral obligations rather than simply matters of preference. People sometimes believe they have a **moral duty** to plan for the future or to avoid intervening aggressively with the natural processes.

It is possible that differences in basic value orientations will, in part, account for disagreements over what counts as good nursing care of patients. In Mr. Livingston's case, physicians and nurses have made judgments about proper medication levels, but these are not the only possible levels of medication.

For example, if Mr. Livingston were to remain in pain, the nurse could increase the administration of Dilaudid up to the prescribed amount. Because the narcotic has been authorized for use "as necessary," certain judgments must be made balancing pain relief and side effects of the medication. In this case, because the sedating effect of the medication is creating a significant part of Mr. Livingston's risk, the nurse has several options. If the nurse takes the view that the role of the health professional is to make full use of pharmacologic and other medical means to control natural processes, the nurse could take steps to increase the narcotic to the limits of the prescribed amount. The nurse could even go beyond that, asking the physician to increase the dosage. More frequent administration, higher dosage levels, or adding a drug with tranquilizing effects are all available options. They would reveal a take-charge value orientation leading to increased pain relief, mood alterations, and even more sedation, perhaps decreasing the tendency for Mr. Livingston to want to get out of bed. These actions would constitute the use of chemical restraints on Mr. Livingston's autonomy.

On the other hand, if the nurse took the attitude that the health professional should use great caution in tampering with natural processes, the toxic and addictive potential of the drugs might be feared to the point that blood levels would be lightened as much as possible. The nurse could, for example, extend the time between administrations of the doses of both the narcotic and the antinausea medications. This attitude of respect for natural processes in its extreme form could lead to abandoning narcotics altogether in favor of Tylenol or other analgesics presumed by many to be nonaddictive. One of the effects of working from this value orientation might be the reduction of sedation to the point where Mr. Livingston's risk of falling due to dizziness or a feeling of disorientation would be lessened. At the same time, however, he would be able to be more active in getting out of bed, thereby increasing his chances for injury.

These basic differences in value orientation begin to sound like differences in what may be called ***ethical values***. They are often perceived as differences in obligation rather than mere personal preferences. A nurse might argue that it is wrong, even morally wrong, to sedate a patient in order to avoid having to watch a patient closely or to put in a Foley catheter in order to avoid having to help a patient out of bed to the bathroom. The nurse might also argue that it is morally wrong to eliminate the problem by lightening a patient's medication to the point that he or she is in excruciating pain or nauseated from chemotherapy or by adding medication that makes a patient more compliant with the nurse's instructions.

Beyond these value orientations, there is a third level of evaluation going on in Mr. Livingston's case. It is at this level that true moral judgments are involved. True moral problems are likely to arise if Ms. Howard remains convinced of her conclusion that preventing Mr. Livingston's getting out of bed without assistance is in his interest, on balance, even after she learns of the uniquely discomforting psychologic impact on him. If, under those circumstances, Mr. Livingston continues to insist that his freedom to move about at will should not be constrained, we have before us one of the classical ethical problems in healthcare ethics. If the nurse acts on the traditional, rather paternalistic principle that she should do what she thinks is in Mr. Livingston's interest, he will not be allowed out of bed without assistance, morally violating his autonomy (and possibly raising legal questions). If, on the other hand, she acts out of the principle of respect for the autonomy of persons and allows Mr. Livingston to move about at will, she temporarily abandons her commitment to the health, well-being, and safety of the patient. Good nursing care will be directly dependent upon whether the nurse should act to promote autonomy or should act to do what she thinks is in the interest of the patient's health, well-being, and safety. Which ought to be done is a matter of ethical principle.

Even if Ms. Howard decides to abandon her conception of patient welfare in order to promote Mr. Livingston's autonomy, she may consider the impact of the decision on other patients, coworkers, or herself. In not requiring Mr. Livingston to have nursing assistance in getting out of bed, Ms. Howard may feel compelled morally to spend more time checking on Mr. Livingston, thus providing less adequate care for other patients. If the patient falls again, as anticipated, she and the other hospital staff will have additional burdens. Even if the hospital is so well staffed that other patients are not put at additional risk, Ms. Howard and her coworkers will still suffer the inconvenience of extra work and worry in the form of an incident report. On the one hand, it is ethically questionable that a nurse should sedate a patient simply to lighten her workload and avoid a potentially troublesome situation; on the other hand, nursing ethics has to include the question of the limits of the burden a patient should be able to put on a nurse or coworkers. It seems that there should be some moral limit on how much extra work a nurse should have to do to cater to the idiosyncratic preferences of a single patient.

In dealing with these concerns about the interests of other parties—the other patients and the nurses—a full analysis of the ethics of nursing practice has to consider the legitimate moral role of various social interests. Is the welfare of others totally irrelevant morally, as some traditional ethics would have us believe? If not, is it the aggregate total of benefits and harms of an action that count? Or do certain kinds of benefits and harms take precedence—benefits to the neediest, for example?

Finally, when Ms. Howard explores her options, she has to take some stand on the ethics of her relationships with other professionals and with the patient. In deciding among her options, she will have to decide whether she stands in a relationship of obligation with the patient, her nursing colleagues, the hospital administration, the resident on call, Mr. Livingston's attending physician, and others in her personal life. Morality is, in part, a matter of loyalty and fulfillment of commitments. If Ms. Howard feels bound morally to the profession of nursing as a source of moral insight, she may well turn to sources within the profession for help in resolving her problem. She may consult a code of ethics, standards of nursing practice, or the advice of her nurse colleagues. If she feels bound in loyalty to the hospital as an institution, she may consider the legal liability of the institution as well as the standards for appropriate care established by the hospital administration. If she feels obligated to the physician involved in the case as her source of authority, she will turn to him or her for advice or even for "orders." If she sees the patient as the center of moral authority regarding his own care, she may yield to the patient—not only on the question of restraints on his freedom but also on what moral norms ought to be used for resolving the problem. Finally, because she has other centers of moral loyalty in her personal life—her church, her family, her personal system of beliefs and values—she will have to decide how these are appropriately integrated into the decision.

What starts as a simple problem of patient management ends by introducing us to virtually the entire range of ethical problems in nursing. In the case that follows, we shall see in another context how ethical and other types of evaluations raise issues, sometimes in places that are unexpected.

Case 1-2
The Nurse–Midwife and Crisis in a Home Delivery

Twenty-seven-year-old Melissa Owens was eagerly awaiting the birth of her first child. Married for 3 years, she and her husband Roger had recently opened a small business in a growing suburban community. When it became apparent Mrs. Owens was pregnant, she and her husband visited Nurse Midwives, Inc., a home birthing service available in their community. The emphasis on prenatal nutrition and childbirth preparation classes as well as the opportunity to give birth to their firstborn in their own home appealed to the Owenses' belief in birth as a natural body process. They were also strongly attracted to the relaxed approach of the four certified nurse–midwife (CNM) partners and their agreement that Mr. Owens could participate in the birth as much as he and his wife desired.

During the months of pregnancy, Mr. and Mrs. Owens attended the biweekly childbirth preparation classes given by their nurse–midwife, Ms. Lisa Bennington, and her partner, Mrs. Betty Thornton. A friendly and supportive relationship developed between the couple and the nurses based on their mutual beliefs about the birth process and the value of early infant–maternal bonding in the family setting. Because Mrs. Owens had enjoyed a healthy, uneventful pregnancy, Ms. Bennington anticipated no problems during labor and delivery.

Now, in her 41st week of pregnancy, Mrs. Owens began to feel the long-awaited contractions signaling labor. Called to the Owenses' home, Ms. Bennington found her patient in the early phase of labor, 4 cm dilated and 70% effaced. Her amniotic membranes were intact and Mrs. Owens seemed in good health and spirits. The baby's presentation (head or vertex) and position (left occipitoanterior) were considered favorable for both mother and baby. In minimal pain, Mrs. Owens was encouraged to walk around the house to stimulate labor.

Mrs. Thornton soon joined her partner at the home. She confirmed Ms. Bennington's findings, which were discussed by phone with the nurse midwives' obstetric backup, Dr. Lester Holmes. A strong believer in the overall safety of hospital delivery but supportive of the midwives' practice, he encouraged them to call him if any unexpected problems developed during Mrs. Owens's labor.

Within an hour, Mrs. Owens's amniotic membranes ruptured and the labor contractions became stronger. As time passed, everything seemed to be progressing normally until Ms. Bennington noted a marked decrease in the fetal heart rate during contractions. After a contraction, however, the fetus seemed to regain its normal heart rate. Both nurse midwives noted this pattern over several strong contractions. Changing Mrs. Owens's position did not seem to alter the pattern. They realized that an unexpected problem (i.e., umbilical cord compression) could be developing. Because Mrs. Owens was now almost fully dilated, birth of the baby could occur within a short time. Their concern about the fetal heart rate thus needed prompt attention. According to their contractual agreement with Mr. and Mrs. Owens, the nurse midwives explained the decelerations of the fetal heart rate during contractions, its possible meanings, and the various choices that might have to be made.

Mrs. Thornton thought Dr. Holmes should be contacted to arrange immediate transport to the hospital. She considered any change in the status of the fetus during labor at home a good reason to change to a hospital delivery. Ms. Bennington, however, did not think that the situation warranted hospital delivery. She thought home delivery was of such value to the parents and the child that some minimal risk to the fetus was tolerable. She also knew that her patient felt very strongly about bearing her child at home with her husband's participation. Ms. Bennington strongly supported these wishes. Her own belief in home rather than hospital delivery encouraged her to avoid transporting any patient to the hospital unless a dramatic change occurred in the fetal heart rate or other problems became evident. At this point, Mr. and Mrs. Owens voiced their own insistence on home delivery unless some definite danger to the life of their child was evident.

Ms. Bennington considered the possible choices she could make. She could yield to the Owenses' wishes to stay at home unless more than minimal risk to the fetus was evident. She could observe the fetal heart for another 30 minutes, which was as much risk as she personally thought acceptable. She could defer to her partner's judgment that the technological advantages of a hospital delivery room were immediately warranted by the situation. She could even choose not to make a decision by calling Dr. Holmes to ask for his guidance. She felt sure, however, that he would recommend immediate hospitalization.

Commentary

The safety of home versus hospital delivery is an important issue in contemporary approaches to childbirth. Believing that hospital services have been the most important factor in the improved outcomes of pregnancy over those in the past, some health professionals, especially physicians, emphasize the unpredictability of events during childbirth and the fact that they can increase risk to the life of the fetus or mother during a home delivery.[2] Advocates of home delivery, on the other hand, cite statistics demonstrating decreases in infant mortality and premature and caesarean births as well as increased psychologic benefits from home childbirth.[3] Wedged between the two extremes of high-technology, physician-managed, in-hospital births, and the lay midwife approach of the home birth movement, the certified nurse–midwife (CNM) is faced with an array of competing values.

In choosing to become a CNM, Ms. Bennington has made a significant value judgment. She has demonstrated her preference to apply her nursing knowledge to the bearing and birth of children rather than to the care of adults or even to nursing specialties such as oncology nursing. In choosing to join with Mrs. Betty Thornton and her other partners at Nurse Midwives, Inc., she has also demonstrated a value preference for independent practice over that of institutional-based practice. In 1976, nearly 90% of all nurse–midwives were employed by hospitals, public health agencies, physicians in private practice, or the military services.[4] Fifteen years later, 11% of CNMs listed their primary employer as a private CNM practice, either in a maternity service operated pre-dominantly by nurse–midwives or in a private nurse midwifery practice like Nurse Midwives, Inc.[5] Ms. Bennington and her partners have decided to choose a style of practice based on values emphasizing independent practice within nurse midwifery itself.

Ms. Bennington has also chosen to attend births in the home rather than in the hospital. This choice is based on a set of values that are important for nurse–midwives. In 1997, the percentage of births attended by CNMs increased to account for 7% of all births. Whereas births in hospitals (99%) remained the same as in 1989, births in homes increased.[6] Assuming that she and her part-ner, Mrs. Betty Thornton, have hospital privileges that allow them to admit patients for in-hospital care, choosing to deliver Mrs. Owens's baby at home indicates that they consider home birth to be of considerable physical or psy-chologic benefit to the parents and the expected child. Indeed, several studies have concluded that nurse–midwives attending home births have good out-comes when practicing within a system that facilitates safe transfer to hospital care when necessary.[7]

In several studies that compared nurse–midwife–managed prenatal care and delivery with physician-managed care and delivery, improved birth statistics in nurse–midwife–managed deliveries were demonstrated for both low-risk and high-risk obstetrical patients.[8] Another study found that urban CNMs follow a standard of care that is closer to the guidelines established by the American College of Obstetricians and Gynecologists (ACOG) than the standards of care fol-lowed by urban and rural obstetricians as well as family physicians.[9] These sta-tistics are, of course, open to debate. Some have argued that the samples are not really comparable, that fetal monitoring in modern obstetrics affects the data, or that certain critical effects (such as those stemming from anoxia) are not mea-surable for many years. Ms. Bennington has chosen to interpret the data avail-able to her in such a way that they support her conclusion that home delivery is, physically, a safe childbirth alternative. Healthcare professionals with other values might be more skeptical when interpreting the same data. Ms. Bennington has made her judgment despite other studies that indicate increased complications of delivery or increased risk of neonatal death in planned home deliveries.[10] Thus, for women who choose home delivery over hospital delivery, Ms. Bennington is ready to provide a service based on judgments of benefits, both psychologic and physical—judgments that will not necessarily be shared by other nurses, physicians, or lay people.

Even Melissa and Roger Owens have made a value judgment in deciding to consult Nurse Midwives, Inc., for the birth of their child. To them, a home delivery signifies the naturalness of birth.[11] Rather than the technological or unnatural setting of a hospital, they prefer childbirth in their own home where they and close friends can share in the event. But even the preference of home delivery for these reasons may not be the most significant value judgment for Mr. and Mrs. Owens. It may be the choice itself, the freedom to choose how one wants to give birth, that is most important.

In the past, the bearing and birth of a child was an illness-related event under little control of the consumer. Although midwife services have always been available to the rural poor or to those residing in economically depressed areas, most American women, particularly those in the middle class, have had little choice except to visit an obstetrician for prenatal care and hospital delivery. Advocates of home birth are now urging women to reclaim responsibility for childbirth by requesting birth alternatives from which to choose.[12] Influenced by the women's health movement, many women like Mrs. Owens feel that decisions concerning birth are too important to be left solely to the obstetrician. What emerges as an important value judgment in maternity services is being able to choose the mode of birth for one's child.

Up to this point, the many value judgments in this case are nonmoral and demonstrate nonmoral conflict. Mrs. Bennington's judgments in selecting nurse midwifery, independent practice, and home birth over hospital delivery all indicate nonmoral evaluations made on the basis of personal preference or tastes. The judgments of Mr. and Mrs. Owens are based on similar nonmoral evaluations. Even the conflict between physical and psychologic benefits and harms posed by home delivery versus hospital delivery is nonmoral. Neither set of judgments possesses any of the characteristics of moral evaluations. But as we have already demonstrated, nonmoral conflict can easily lead one into the realm of ethics and **ethical conflict**.

Influenced by the many nonmoral value judgments that have led her to practice certified nurse midwifery, Ms. Bennington must make additional judgments, particularly the rightness or wrongness of allowing Mrs. Owens to continue in labor at home with marked decelerations of the fetal heart rate during contractions. She must decide whether she has a duty to the fetus that would lead to hospitalization—perhaps a duty to preserve the life or protect the health and welfare of the fetus—and, if so, whether that would lead to more immediate hospitalization than the Owens would desire. She must relate her obligation to respect the values of the parents to her own values, those of her colleagues, and others involved in the case. If she decides that the situation does not pose a serious threat to the fetus's health and that Mrs. Owens's choice of home birth is to be respected, Ms. Bennington may decide to wait and see if birth occurs within a short period of time. In deciding to wait, she would be acting on the basis of the ethical principle of autonomy or respect for self-determination of persons. If more severe decelerations of the fetal heart rate during contractions should occur, Ms. Bennington might then decide to act on the basis of her duty to the health and life of the fetus. Although the autonomy of the parents would be overridden by this decision, Ms. Bennington would still be acting on the basis of some moral principle: to preserve life, promote health, or perhaps serve the well-being of the fetus.

Mrs. Thornton has already made a moral evaluation by insisting that the change in fetal status warrants delivery in a hospital with its available technology. This evaluation is based on the moral wrongness of allowing labor to continue without medical assistance once fetal distress, no matter how slight, is demonstrated. Whereas Ms. Bennington has a value preference for respecting parental choice for home delivery, Mrs. Thornton is claiming that she has a moral obligation to act in the fetus' best interest when any change in fetal status occurs in home-managed labor. Her evaluation automatically places her in the position of acting on paternalistic grounds: the Owenses' autonomous choice to deliver at home will be set aside in favor of what Mrs. Thornton judges to be the fetus's best interests and perhaps the best interests of the parents as well.

At this point, it is very hard to determine where the conflict exists. It may be that the nurse–midwives simply disagree on the empirical facts of the physical risk to the infant from the change in heart rate. They may also disagree over the relative importance of the physical risk and the psychosocial advantages of the home birth. However, there may be a moral conflict between their obligation to the fetus—to preserve life, promote health, or serve the interests of the fetus—and their obligation of loyalty to the parents, the profession of nursing, or to the backup physician. There may be, finally, a conflict over whether the autonomy of the parents should be morally prior to the duty of the nurse to serve the fetus's welfare. Thus, both moral and nonmoral evaluations permeate the practice of nursing, even in apparently routine decisions such as protecting a patient from falling or arranging in-hospital care when a patient's labor at home takes an unexpected turn.

Critical Thinking Questions

1. What are the values that are important to you as a person? To you as a nurse?
2. Are these values moral or nonmoral in nature?

Research Brief 1.1

Source: Thompson, F. E. (2003). The practice setting: Site of ethical conflict for some mothers and midwives. *Nursing Ethics, 10*(6), 588–601.

Purpose: To provide insight into the ethics of midwifery practice as well as the ethics actually being practiced by midwives. Studied were the underlying assumptions and values of midwifery practice, how mothers and midwives respond to a specific action, and how relationships emerge according to the midwife's approach.

Method: Using a snowball method, eight childbearing women and eight midwives with birthing experiences within the previous 5 years were recruited from a variety of birthing and midwifery practices, both public and private. An open-ended, in-depth interview of 1 to 2 hours' duration was conducted with each participant, at a time and place of her choosing. Participants were asked to talk about an incident in which they were involved that they felt concerned ethics and midwifery. The experience could have been good or bad, and "ethics" included anything they considered to be ethics. The interview data were analyzed and coded for personal meanings and themes, and data interpretations were validated by participants. The constructed meanings from the personal narratives were then compared and contrasted with the ethical orientations expressed in: (1) official documents, (2) the literature, and (3) commonly adopted research methods.

Findings: The central theme emerging from the narratives was the use and abuse of power in relationships. A related theme experienced by both midwives and mothers was "values conflicts"—specifically "workplace/service provider versus personal/professional midwifery ethics" and "not valuing individuals." A conflict of values between workplace/service provider and personal ethics usually accompanied descriptions of power held by another, paternalism, lack of support for the birthing woman, and restriction on or prevention of the exercise of the midwife's professional judgment. The midwives usually dealt with this conflict by becoming "silenced" or subservient to medical authority. A conflict of values over not valuing individuals often concerned procedure-oriented practices and judgments by practitioners that were viewed as impractical or not based on individual needs. This conflict was often experienced when the woman's wishes were not respected or when the woman was treated like a mere body.

Implications: This study demonstrates that an ethic of strangers with a normative and logical view of the world provides an inadequate ethical approach for midwifery practice. A care ethic alone is insufficient for midwifery practice, however. An adequate ethical approach is one that redresses the imbalance of power within relationships. An ethic of engagement reflects the values of midwives and birthing mothers and helps transform practices through its focus on the character and virtues of moral agents, human engagement within relationships, redressing the imbalance of power, and listening to the voice of women and vulnerable people.

For educators, the challenge is to inspire ethical practice from within the individual rather than mere compliance with professional codes and employer policies. This involves a change of focus from compliance with professional codes to ethical relationships, from disparate relationships to "prime relationships," from the ethic of strangers to that of intimates, and from abstract principles to human engagement. This ethic of engagement requires for midwifery that the midwife's prime relationship is with the mother and the mother's prime relationship is with her baby. The ethic of engagement fosters ethical midwifery practice by encouraging practitioners to develop virtuous character as moral agents and to focus on being with the woman during childbirth through human engagement within the mother–midwife partnership. Such an approach resembles the relational ethic of intimates with its attention to particularity and the absence of domination and subordination.

Identifying Ethical Conflicts

Once it is apparent that value choices are made constantly in nursing and the practice of other health professionals, it will not be surprising that many of the choices involve an ethical component. They may involve conflict between duty to the patient and duty to society. Ethical conflicts may involve the clash between two ethical duties (such as the duty to respect and promote autonomy and the duty to benefit the patient). They may involve tension between the ethical positions of professional and religious groups to which the nurse feels loyalty. They may involve tension between the rights of patients and the nurse's self-interest and welfare. The following cases illustrate, in turn, each of these problems.

Benefit to the Patient vs Benefit to Others

One of the most common and straightforward ethical conflicts a nurse faces is conflict between an obligation to benefit the client and an obligation to benefit others. This dilemma is signaled in the first and eighth provisions of the *Code of Ethics for Nurses* of the American Nurses Association (ANA). If a nurse were to take the ANA code as definitive moral guidance, the nurse's "primary commitment is to the patient" but the nurse also has a responsibility "to be aware not only of specific health needs of individual patients but also of broader health concerns such as world hunger, environmental pollution, lack of access to health care, violation of human rights, and inequitable distribution of nursing and healthcare resources."[13] Both the patient and public health concerns are on the nurse's agenda. The first type of moral dilemma faced by a nurse is what should be done when the two come into conflict.

Traditionally, the obligation to serve the interests of the patient takes precedence, but the realities of modern, complicated healthcare delivery systems generate pressures on the nurse to compromise the patient's welfare, especially when substantial benefits will accrue to others and very little is lost by the patient. The current movement to involve nurses in responsible cost containment in order to reduce rapidly growing healthcare costs illustrates the problem of the conflict between the welfare of the individual and that of society.

Case 1-3
The Nurse and Cost Containment: The Duty to Society

Ramón Ortega, a 42-year-old farm laborer with a history of hypertension, had been experiencing headaches on an almost daily basis for 2 to 3 weeks. Disturbed by the persistent and severe nature of the headaches, he visited the state-supported health clinic serving his rural community. Ms. Tracey Anderson, the family nurse practitioner and sole staff member of the clinic, listened as Mr. Ortega described his headaches. She then performed an initial examination, which revealed good general health with the exception of an elevated blood pressure of 190/108. Since Mr. Ortega had described some dizziness and visual disturbances during his headaches, Ms. Anderson also completed a neurologic assessment. Everything seemed within normal limits except for Mr. Ortega's peripheral vision. Ms. Anderson's assessment demonstrated that he had some difficulty seeing objects in the visual field on his left side. Ms. Anderson realized that this disturbance was probably a manifestation of his present headache in combination with his known visual deficit. Since no other abnormalities were demonstrated, the possibility of a more serious problem seemed remote, according to Ms. Anderson's judgment. Yet Mr. Ortega was very distressed by his headaches. He asked the nurse what he could do to prevent the headaches or, at least, what could be done to lessen the pain he was experiencing. Could she be sure no other problem was causing the headaches?

A few months ago, Ms. Anderson would not have hesitated to refer Mr. Ortega to University Medical Center, 110 miles away, for an examination by a physician and a neurologic evaluation of his headaches. She would have done this for no other reason than to relieve the patient of his worry and to confirm the absence of a more serious problem. She still believed that, on balance, the referral would be of some help. In recent weeks, however, the state agency that funds the rural health clinics had urged all health clinic personnel to be careful in referring patients for costly laboratory or evaluative testing and in incurring the added expense of clinic-sponsored transportation. There were decreased monies to support the personnel and services in rural health clinics because the agency had adopted a strict cost-containment program. In fact, the continued operation of the rural health clinics depended on how well individual clinics contained costs, even though they provided greatly needed services to populations like the low-income farm community in which Mr. Ortega lives.

Ms. Anderson had been cutting the operating costs of her clinic in every way she could, particularly in her judicious referral of patients to University Medical Center. But she could not overlook the fact that Mr. Ortega was distressed by his headaches, and there was always the possibility, albeit remote, that he was presenting with early signs of impending cerebrovascular disease, the effects of which could seriously affect him and his family. She was uncertain about what choice to make.

Commentary

The healthcare reform movement has generated pressures on health professionals such as Tracey Anderson to be conscious of the socioeconomic impact of their decisions. Some cost-containment decisions by nurses can be made without moral dilemma. Some procedures may turn out to be useless or even detrimental, on balance, to the patient. If the procedure under consideration is going to hurt the patient more than it helps, it is simply good nursing practice to eliminate it. If money is saved in the process, that is a fortuitous side effect.

If the procedure is one where the benefits and harms for the patient are just about equally balanced and if the patient has no strong preferences for the procedure, then the fact that it would be costly for the health clinic might plausibly be good reason to avoid doing it. In such a case, there is no good reason to go ahead.

But Ms. Anderson's dilemma is more complicated. She has concluded that, on balance, Mr. Ortega would be helped by a referral for a neurological workup. It would at least provide psychologic comfort, and there is a chance that therapeutically beneficial information would be revealed.

Moral traditions have almost all included within their lists of ethical principles some sense of moral obligation to do good for other people or "to promote beneficence," as contemporary philosophy would state it. Ms. Anderson senses that beneficence is what is at stake here. She has a responsibility, in the words of the ANA *Code of Ethics for Nurses*, to promote "the health, welfare, and safety of all people."[14] She has correctly perceived, however, that in this particular situation benefit for the patient and benefit for other people may well be in direct conflict. To make matters worse, the members of the public most likely to benefit directly from Ms. Anderson's cost consciousness are other patients in her rural health clinic area. The funds conserved by judicious compromise of Mr. Ortega's interests will be of benefit to other patients whose welfare she is also obliged to serve.

Two major options seem to be open to her. First, she could take the ANA *Code of Ethics for Nurses,* conclusion that "the nurse's primary commitment is to the health, well-being, and safety of the patient"[15] and apply it rigorously to the patient standing before her. If the patient's well-being is primary and she has concluded that, on balance, he would benefit from a referral, then her moral dilemma is solved. Concern for the welfare of others is morally subordinate to concern for the welfare of the individual. If that moral priority is chosen, following the state agency's directive to be cost conscious in such situations would be morally unacceptable. Of course, from the standpoint of the state agency, someone has to be concerned about the welfare of society. Therefore, they could impose constraints on Ms. Anderson for the kind and amount of referrals she could make. In certain special, marginal cases, she might not even be permitted to make a referral even if she thought it was in her patient's (marginal) interest.

Ms. Anderson's other option is to abandon the notion that the well-being of the patient always takes priority over the public welfare. That would permit her to take into account the impact of her decision on the welfare of others—the state agency, taxpayers, and her other clients. She might, from this perspective, try to produce the greatest good by taking the welfare of all into account. She could strive for the greatest good for the greatest number, to use the classical utilitarian phrase.

There may be other options open to Ms. Anderson, options that would permit her to take into account certain benefits to society, but not others, when she decides whether morally she should put the care of her patient above all other considerations. The balancing of the two kinds of interests might depend, for instance, on whether promises have been made either to her patient or to the state agency. It might depend upon how she, her profession, and society see the role of the nurse. It might depend upon the relative urgency of her patient's needs and the needs of others who might be helped with the funds. Any of these factors might be seen by the nurse, the profession, patients, or others in society as morally relevant, in addition to the amount of benefit and harm involved. The problem of how benefits to the patient relate to benefits to others is the first major moral issue confronted in many ethical situations in nursing. These alternatives will be explored further in the cases in Chapter 4.

Critical Thinking Questions

1. If Mr. Ortega was your patient, which action(s) would you take?
2. What factors would be important to you in making decisions about Mr. Ortega's care?

emotional problems, beginning at age 6. The unit's treatment plan centers on a reward and punishment system for eating behaviors that result in weight gain. Patients are closely watched at all times (even when in the bathrooms), and their eating and physical activities are closely monitored. Privileges, such as watching TV, phoning friends, wearing favorite clothes, listening to CD players, and the like, are withdrawn from a patient if the patient does not gain weight. Cassandra has been in the unit for 3 weeks. She is not responding well to the treatment plan and has continued to lose weight. She has lost all privileges on the unit, is withdrawing more and more into herself each day, and does not seem to care about the continued weight loss. If she does not try to eat more, gain weight, and participate in her treatment plan, her parents will be asked for permission to restrain Cassandra so she might be fed intravenously.

Miss Kaplan believes that, under most situations, people have a right to determine their own weight. Cassandra's weight loss, however, is threatening her health and may, if not stopped, lead to her death. Nonetheless, Miss Kaplan hates to see patients forced into accepting the unit's treatment plan or into gaining weight. Although she agrees that Cassandra has serious emotional and, perhaps, psychologic problems that complicate her treatment for anorexia nervosa, she dislikes treating patients harshly in order to make them "well."

Commentary

This case, like Case 1-1, which involved the need for nursing assistance in helping an elderly patient get out of bed, poses in stark form the conflict between benefit to a patient and rights of a patient. However, unlike in Case 1-1, there seems to be good reason to believe that the patient really would benefit from eating more and gaining weight. In the getting out of bed case, the course of action that would benefit the patient seems open to substantial controversy, especially when the psychologic dimensions and the patient's fear of enclosures are taken into account. In Cassandra Miller's case, it is harder to claim that, on balance, she really is better off following her own eating plan rather than the nurse's. It might be argued that Miss Kaplan's care plan is so upsetting to her that on grounds of benefit to the patient, the nurse should concede. Yet, if there were ever a case where the nurse knew best, this would certainly appear to be it.

This case is ethically interesting because Miss Kaplan recognizes and supports the patient's right to determine his or her own weight. Ethical standards for the nursing profession indicate that patients have moral rights "to determine what will be done with their own person; . . .; to accept, refuse, or terminate treatment without deceit, undue influence, duress, coercion, or penalty."[17] The nurse is to respect these rights. That makes this a case where, from Miss Kaplan's perspective, the rights of the patient and the professional mandate to protect these rights conflict with the nurse's felt duty to benefit the patient.

The first line of debate mig made. Does anyone really have a her own body? In short, is the ri the right include taking risks tha rights theorists and holders of n questions. Libertarians give primar those who are more paternalistic tects individuals from their own ch a right, does that right extend to ac disease patterns contribute to their

A rights claim, if it exists at al a substantially autonomous, indep nized that age is a relevant factor in As a general rule, minors are presum many critical decisions. However, the has a psychologic illness cannot, in incompetency for the purpose of mak sion, found capable of making autono death issues. The minor's right to ma treatment for sexually transmitted dise tion for one who accepts a general rig general principle of autonomy will be w anorexic, is capable of autonomous acti

For others who reject the principl determination on such matters that n moral problem is rather different. The c remain the principle of beneficence, a patient's interest. Several critical feature nalistic intervention such as the one M must be good reason to believe that the i There must be good reason to believe that Miss Kaplan, is qualified to know the acti lysts of paternalism and its justifications a due process to make sure that Cassandra M might, for example, include a court review petent to decide for herself—that is, whe consequences—and to determine whether th the most beneficial course.

The case poses the conflict between the about her weight and what she eats, based and the duty of the nurse to benefit the general problem of autonomy will be expl Chapter 7.

Source: Redman,
known about them

Purpose: To id
through system
questions were
nurses resolve
cal conflicts e
ethical conflic
ric nurse prac

Method: Five
1997, were id
(n = 470) wh
[n = 164], p
[n = 91], anc
mid-Atlantic
mation form
describe an
ethical princ
resolve the
by two resea
researchers
to Jameton
moral dilen

Findings: D

1. The n
disagr
given
physi
her t

2. The
cond
over
the

3. Cer
cer
the
coi
fro

The Rights of the Patient vs the Welfare of the Patient

Not all ethical problems faced by the nurse involve conflict between the welfare of the patient and the welfare of others. Often the consequences to other parties are not really an issue; the problem is rather that the nurse sees several courses of action open in which different interests, claims, or rights of the patient seem to be in conflict. Sometimes these are merely matters of different kinds of benefit to the patient. As with the cases of assistance to a patient in getting out of bed and home childbirth, the physical welfare of a patient may conflict with his or her psychologic welfare. Long-term health concerns may conflict with short-term concerns.

In other cases, however, it does not seem to be a simple matter of different kinds of benefits. Rather, other moral dimensions are added. One course of action may produce the most benefit for the patient, whereas another course protects some right or corresponds to some moral obligation. Nurses, as well as anyone, may feel that certain kinds of actions—telling the truth, keeping promises, avoiding killing, and so forth—are simply morally required even if they do not necessarily produce good consequences. Sometimes an action can be seen as having several morally relevant components: the production of good and bad consequences, the breaking of a promise, and the violation of the autonomy of another might all be parts of the same action contemplated by the nurse. If so, it is sometimes said that the action is prima facie wrong insofar as it is an act, for example, of lying but simultaneously that it is prima facie right insofar as it produces good consequences. Prima facie rightness or wrongness is thus a characterization of a component of an action, not necessarily of the action as a whole. The morality of the action as a whole—one's "duty proper," as it is sometimes called—will depend upon how the various elements are taken into account.

Often the prima facie moral dimensions of an action are expressed not as duties but as rights; that is, they are expressed not in terms of the one bearing the obligation to act but from the perspective of the one who might make a moral claim. A right is a justified claim that one may make upon another. A *moral right* is a morally justified claim, a claim justified on the basis of moral principles or moral rules.[16] As a justified moral claim, a moral right, at least as the term is normally used, cannot be defeated or overridden by pointing out that an action required by the moral right will have bad consequences.

Many situations faced by the nurse pose the problem of a right of the patient conflicting with benefit to the patient; that is, one course of action seems to protect the patient's right, whereas another course would seem to produce more good for the patient. The tension between rights and benefits is illustrated in the next case.

Case 1-4

When Promoting the Patient's Well-Being Infringes on Basic Human Rights

Sandra Kaplan is a nurse working part time on a psychiatric care unit specializing in treating teenage patients with anorexia nervosa. She is particularly concerned about the treatment program for Cassandra Miller, a 16-year-old female with a long history of emotional problems, beginning at age 6. The unit's treatment plan centers on a reward and punishment system for eating behaviors that result in weight gain. Patients are closely watched at all times (even when in the bathrooms), and their eating and physical activities are closely monitored. Privileges, such as watching TV, phoning friends, wearing favorite clothes, listening to CD players, and the like, are withdrawn from a patient if the patient does not gain weight. Cassandra has been in the unit for 3 weeks. She is not responding well to the treatment plan and has continued to lose weight. She has lost all privileges on the unit, is withdrawing more and more into herself each day, and does not seem to care about the continued weight loss. If she does not try to eat more, gain weight, and partici- pate in her treatment plan, her parents will be asked for permission to restrain Cassandra so she might be fed intravenously.

Miss Kaplan believes that, under most situations, people have a right to determine their own weight. Cassandra's weight loss, however, is threatening her health and may, if not stopped, lead to her death. Nonetheless, Miss Kaplan hates to see patients forced into accepting the unit's treatment plan or into gaining weight. Although she agrees that Cassandra has serious emotional and, perhaps, psychologic problems that complicate her treatment for anorexia nervosa, she dislikes treating patients harshly in order to make them "well."

Commentary

This case, like Case 1-1, which involved the need for nursing assistance in helping an elderly patient get out of bed, poses in stark form the conflict between benefit to a patient and rights of a patient. However, unlike in Case 1-1, there seems to be good reason to believe that the patient really would benefit from eating more and gaining weight. In the getting out of bed case, the course of action that would benefit the patient seems open to substantial controversy, especially when the psychologic dimensions and the patient's fear of enclosures are taken into account. In Cassandra Miller's case, it is harder to claim that, on balance, she really is better off following her own eating plan rather than the nurse's. It might be argued that Miss Kaplan's care plan is so upsetting to her that on grounds of benefit to the patient, the nurse should concede. Yet, if there were ever a case where the nurse knew best, this would certainly appear to be it.

This case is ethically interesting because Miss Kaplan recognizes and sup- ports the patient's right to determine his or her own weight. Ethical standards for the nursing profession indicate that patients have moral rights "to deter- mine what will be done with their own person; . . .; to accept, refuse, or ter- minate treatment without deceit, undue influence, duress, coercion, or penalty."[17] The nurse is to respect these rights. That makes this a case where, from Miss Kaplan's perspective, the rights of the patient and the professional mandate to protect these rights conflict with the nurse's felt duty to benefit the patient.

The first line of debate might focus on the nature of the rights claim being made. Does anyone really have a right to determine to take such risks with his or her own body? In short, is the rights claim being considered a justified one? Does the right include taking risks that place one's health at serious risk? Libertarian rights theorists and holders of more paternalistic perspectives differ on these questions. Libertarians give primary place to protecting individual liberty, whereas those who are more paternalistic are willing to suppress liberty if doing so protects individuals from their own choices. But even if competent adults have such a right, does that right extend to adolescents? Does it apply to adolescents whose disease patterns contribute to their apparently inappropriate preferences?

A rights claim, if it exists at all, must be exercised by an individual who is a substantially autonomous, independent decision maker. It is widely recognized that age is a relevant factor in deciding whether someone is autonomous. As a general rule, minors are presumed nonautonomous for purposes of making many critical decisions. However, the mere fact that one is a minor or that one has a psychologic illness cannot, in itself, be taken as definitive evidence of incompetency for the purpose of making such choices. Minors are, upon occasion, found capable of making autonomous judgments, even on serious life and death issues. The minor's right to make decisions in the case of abortion and treatment for sexually transmitted diseases is also recognized. The critical question for one who accepts a general right to determine self-care based on the general principle of autonomy will be whether this young woman, a 16-year-old anorexic, is capable of autonomous actions.

For others who reject the principle of autonomy and the right of self-determination on such matters that might derive from that principle, the moral problem is rather different. The overriding moral principle is likely to remain the principle of beneficence, a commitment to do what is in the patient's interest. Several critical features must be present to justify a paternalistic intervention such as the one Miss Kaplan is contemplating. There must be good reason to believe that the intervention really will be beneficial. There must be good reason to believe that the person intervening, in this case Miss Kaplan, is qualified to know the action will be beneficial.[18] Some analysts of paternalism and its justifications also insist that there must be some due process to make sure that Cassandra Miller's rights are not violated. This might, for example, include a court review to determine whether she is competent to decide for herself—that is, whether she really comprehends the consequences—and to determine whether the proposed intervention really is the most beneficial course.

The case poses the conflict between the right of the patient to decide about her weight and what she eats, based on the principle of autonomy, and the duty of the nurse to benefit the patient. This tension and the general problem of autonomy will be explored further in the cases in Chapter 7.

Research Brief 1.2

Source: Redman, B. K., & Fry, S. T. (2000). Nurses' ethical conflicts: What is really known about them? *Nursing Ethics, 7*(4), 360–366.

Purpose: To identify what can be learned about nurses' ethical conflicts through systematic analysis of methodologically similar studies. The research questions were: (1) How are nurses' ethical conflicts experienced? (2) How do nurses resolve ethical conflicts in patient care? (3) Why are some nurses' ethical conflicts experienced as unresolvable? and (4) What are the themes of ethical conflict in four specialty areas of practice (diabetes education, pediatric nurse practitioner, rehabilitation nursing, and nephrology nursing)?

Method: Five methodologically similar studies, completed between 1994 and 1997, were identified. The participants for the studies were registered nurses ($n = 470$) who were certified in one of four specialties (diabetes education [$n = 164$], pediatric nurse practitioner [$n = 118$], rehabilitation nursing [$n = 91$], and nephrology nursing [$n = 97$]) and who practiced in the five mid-Atlantic states. All participants completed the same demographic information form and the same questionnaire. The questionnaire asked them to describe an ethical conflict they had experienced in practice, identify the ethical principles that seemed to be involved, and describe what they did to resolve the conflict. The conflict "stories" were independently read and coded by two researchers. Discussion and recoding of the stories continued until the researchers reached agreement. The stories were further classified according to Jameton's typology of nurses' moral/ethical conflicts (moral uncertainty, moral dilemma, or moral distress).

Findings: Different dominant ethical conflicts emerged for each specialty.

1. The majority of diabetes nurse educators' (CDEs) conflicts concerned disagreements over the quality of medical care prescribed for or being given to patients. The CDEs were conflicted over whether to protect the physician–patient relationship or to make the patient aware that his or her treatment might be mismanaged.

2. The majority of certified pediatric nurse practitioners' (CPNPs) conflicts concerned protection of children's rights. The CPNPs were conflicted over their professional responsibility to protect the child's rights/protect the child from harm and responsibility to develop and support families.

3. Certified rehabilitation nurses (CRNs) primarily described conflicts concerning the overtreatment or undertreatment of patients, or treatment they believed did not meet the required standard of care. The CRNs were conflicted over whether to benefit the patient and protect him or her from harm or to maintain the physician– nurse relationship.

4. Certified nephrology nurses (CNNs) primarily described conflicts involving decisions about the discontinuation or initiation of dialysis, especially of terminally ill patients. The CNNs were conflicted over whether to benefit the patient/protect the patient from harm and support the patient's wishes or to openly disagree with the physician and/ or the patient's family.

Few participants experienced the conflicts as moral uncertainty. The majority of the conflicts were experienced as a moral dilemma or as moral distress. Indeed, an average of 33% of the nurses experienced their conflicts as moral distress, in which they knew the right action to take but were unable to take it—either because they lacked the power to do so or because institutional constraints made it nearly impossible for them to pursue the right course of action.

Conflicts were left unresolved by two thirds of CNNs but resolved by 70% of CNPNs. Few participants tried to resolve their conflicts by referring the patient care situation to an ethics committee. Many participants simply coped with the conflicts or removed themselves from the work setting.

Implications: There was a significant variation in the nature of the ethical conflicts experienced across the four nursing specialties studied. This means that ethics education for these specialties should be individualized to address the types of ethical conflicts most commonly experienced in the particular specialty practice. Because many of the nurses in the study reported that their ethical conflicts were unresolved, educational efforts should focus on how to resolve ethical conflicts and how to use institutional and community resources for conflict resolution. Nurses working outside institutional settings especially need to know how to use community and/or organizational ethics committees to address commonly experienced ethical conflicts. Further research is needed to study the long-term moral distress experienced by nurses in these specialties and its effects on the nurses' practices, the quality of patient care, and the nurses' length of employment in particular settings.

Moral Rules and the Nurse's Conscience

Cases 1-3 and 1-4 presented classical problems of ethics: first, where benefits to the patient conflict with benefits to others, and second, where benefits to the patient conflict with the rights of the patient. Sometimes, however, the nurse may experience ethical conflict even though there is little apparent disagreement or doubt over these basic questions of principle. People may agree on the ethical principle at stake and still disagree on the application of the principle to a specific case problem. The gap between the abstract principle and the specific case can be large. Nurses and others reflecting on moral problems often find it helpful to turn to moral precepts that are intermediate in their specificity between principles and cases. Moral rules often play this role.[19] The rule "always get consent before surgery" bridges the gap between an abstract principle such as autonomy or respect for persons and the healthcare professional's decision at the bedside. For example, the nurse in a triage unit knows the moral rules of triage that bridge abstract principles of justice and nursing care decisions in specific disaster situations.

Instead of stating as a moral rule that the healthcare professional has a duty to get consent before surgery, one might say much the same thing by claiming that the candidate for surgery has a right to consent to the surgery. Moral rules and rights are often correlative in this way. Whether the language of rules or of rights is used, however, both normally provide guidelines for action or descriptions of moral practice at an intermediate level of generality. (For this reason, they are together sometimes called "middle axioms" of morality.)[20] The various moral rules pertaining to abortion are all examples of these middle-level moral rules expressed in different traditions what various abstract principles such as the principles of beneficence, autonomy, avoiding killing, or the sacredness of life might imply for the abortion situation.

Different social groups are likely to hold somewhat different and sometimes conflicting moral rules on a particular problem area. These disagreements about moral rules may take place even among people who do not disagree on the most general principles.

The nurse maintains relationships with many groups at any one time. The nurse may be a member of religious, ethnic, socioeconomic, political, and familial groups as well as a member of one or more professional groups. Each group may come to a different conclusion about any particular issue. The nurse's religious group may come to a moral conclusion (expressed in rules of conduct) on an issue such as abortion that may not be precisely the same as that reached by his or her professional group. The nurse thus experiences ethical conflict at the level of moral rules when a rule of the religious group prohibits him or her from participating in specific aspects of patient care, whereas the rules of some other social or professional group offer no such prohibition or even consider such participation morally required. This conflict is especially acute if one accepts as binding the claim of the ANA *Code of Ethics for Nurses* that "Nurses have a duty to remain consistent with both their personal and professional values."[21] The disagreement may or may not include differences regarding the more abstract ethical principle. It clearly, however, involves disagreement at the level of moral rules. The following case illustrates this problem.

Case 1-5

The Nurse Asked to Assist in an Abortion

Mrs. Betty Phelps worked part time in a small suburban hospital. Because she was familiar with the hospital's routines and the staff, she was often asked by the nursing supervisor to work in patient care areas that were short on nursing staff for that particular shift. Today, she was asked to work in the recovery room. Within an hour, however, the nursing supervisor called and asked her to report to A-4, the suite of rooms where elective abortions were usually performed. Hesitatingly, Mrs. Phelps told the supervisor that she did not believe in abortion. A devout Catholic, she considered abortion to be the killing of human life and a mortal sin. Would it be possible for the supervisor to find someone else to help out at A-4?

The supervisor said she understood and would try to find another nurse. In the meantime, however, Dr. Graham needed someone to prep his patient and set up the room for the abortion. Because Mrs. Phelps was not busy at the moment, the supervisor asked if she would go to A-4 and at least prep Dr. Graham's patient. Reluctantly, Mrs. Phelps agreed to this arrangement as long as the supervisor would send another nurse to replace her. The supervisor assured her that she would do this.

In A-4, after preparing the equipment and the room, Mrs. Phelps prepped Dr. Graham's patient, a 16-year-old unmarried teenager who was approximately 8 weeks pregnant. She then told the physician that his patient was ready but that she would not participate in the proceedings. Another nurse would arrive shortly who would assist him. Dr. Graham protested, saying in an annoyed tone of voice to Mrs. Phelps, "Do you think I have all day to wait while the nursing staff puts its moralism and emotions in order? Everyone—the patient, the fetus, and the community—will be better off not having to deal with one more illegitimate child requiring public support."

When Mrs. Phelps stated that her religious and moral beliefs did not allow her to participate in performing an abortion, Dr. Graham claimed that the fetus was really just "a piece of tissue" and not really human life. Thus, there was nothing morally wrong with performing abortions early in pregnancy. Now would Mrs. Phelps please come into the room and assist him? When Mrs. Phelps declined, Dr. Graham stalked angrily down the hallway claiming it was a sad day for patients when nurses decided they would not provide needed care.

Commentary

The question of participation in an abortion inevitably raises questions about the morality of abortion itself, including the surrounding issues of when life begins and the supposed right to life. These are the issues usually contained in any conflict over abortion. They are certainly present in this case, but there are other components as well.

It may seem, at first, that the ethical conflict in this case exists between the nurse and the physician: whether the nurse should "obey" the physician's request to assist in the abortion. But the issue is really one of conflicting moral rules that direct professional acts. Although it is not obvious, Dr. Graham is responding to his patient's request for an abortion out of a Hippocratic emphasis on benefiting the patient and, in this case, a calculation of the greatest benefit, on balance, to everyone concerned with the pregnancy. The unmarried teenager will benefit by not having an unwanted child at this stage of her life. Society will benefit by not having to support another person at public expense. On balance, the benefits of aborting the teenager's unwanted pregnancy are greater than any perceived harms to the patient, according to Dr. Graham.

Mrs. Phelps, however, is not responding to the situation solely out of a benefit-producing principle. She is responding out of a personal value structure influenced by religious belief, which claims that life begins at conception, the fetus is human life, and the destruction of human life is murder and therefore a sin. Thus abortion where the life of the mother is not in question is an unspeakable crime that the devout Catholic cannot participate in or support.[22] She may, in fact, agree that Dr. Graham is correct in his assessment of the amount of benefit to be produced by aborting this pregnancy. However, the mere production of benefit does not make abortion right, according to her religious beliefs and personal values. She may even believe that, as a professional, she should act in the interests of a patient's welfare in all circumstances. Yet she cannot do so, in good conscience, in the case of abortion. Her religious group has come to a conclusion on the issue of abortion that prohibits her participation in professional acts involving abortion.

Dr. Graham counters the nurse's objections by claiming that he does respect human life but that the fetus in this case is not human life, and therefore it is morally acceptable to abort the product of conception in this pregnancy. But for Mrs. Phelps, the act is still not right. In fact, it is irrelevant to Mrs. Phelps whether the age of the fetus is 8 weeks or 30 weeks. Fetal age is simply not important in the face of a personal belief that all fetal life is of value and should not be aborted.

We can well imagine how fervently Mrs. Phelps hopes that the nursing supervisor will soon send another nurse to assist Dr. Graham. Even though she agrees with the physician and the professional patient-benefiting ethic with respect to all other aspects of health care, deciding not to assist Dr. Graham in this procedure on the basis of religious-group-directed moral rules has placed her in a very uncomfortable position. The difference between her choice of nonparticipation in the act of abortion and participation in other healthcare acts for the benefit of patients lies within the strength of the moral rule generated and supported by religious beliefs. Whether the abortion will or should be performed, with or without Mrs. Phelps's assistance, is not the important question. What is important is: On what basis and to what extent do personal values and beliefs and preservation of the nurse's integrity influence professional acts in routine nursing care?

Research Brief 1.3

Source: Martin, P., Yarbrough, S., & Alfred, D. (2003). Professional values held by baccalaureate and associate degree nursing students. *Journal of Nursing Scholarship, 35*(3), 291–296.

Purpose: To determine whether differences exist in the value orientations of graduating students in baccalaureate and associate degree programs.

Method: A survey design was used with a convenience sample of 1450 graduating nursing students from 23 baccalaureate (BSN) and 16 associate degree nursing (ADN) programs in Texas. Complete data, both demographic and scale, were returned by 1325 graduating nursing students. Data were collected using the Nurses Professional Values Scale (NPVS), a 44-item, norm-referenced instrument with a Likert scale ranging from 5 (*most important*) to 1 (*not important*). The NPVS has 11 subscales, each representing 1 of the 11 position statements in the 1985 ANA's *Code of Ethics for Nurses*. Descriptive and parametric statistics were used for analysis.

Findings: ADN and BSN students did not differ significantly on the NPVS total score; however, ADN students scored higher on 5 of the 11 subscales (protecting patient confidentiality, accountability for nursing judgments and actions, accepting responsibilities and delegating them to others, participating in efforts to improve nursing standards, and collaborating with others to meet the health needs of the public) than did their BSN counterparts. Men from both programs scored significantly lower than did women on the total scale and on all subscales. Ethnic groups differed on the responses to three of the subscales (respect for human dignity, safeguarding the client and public, and collaborating to meet public health needs).

Implications: First, professional values in graduating nursing students are significantly related to sex and ethnicity, regardless of the educational program. Nursing faculty members are challenged to address these differences during the educational process and mentoring of students. Second, the current healthcare environment requires that professional nurses have the ability to manage complex ethical dilemmas. Awareness of the need for strong professional values is important to the preparation of nurses capable of managing ethical patient care in this environment. Third, teaching and mentoring strategies to meet the varied needs of a diverse student population should be reevaluated to ensure the retention and integration of essential professional values. Further research is needed to determine the values of entering and exiting nursing students and to identify the extent professional values are taught by nursing faculty.

Limits on Rights and Rules

The fact that a nurse may be a member of a religious group favoring one moral rule on abortion and simultaneously be a member of some other social or professional group favoring some other moral rule suggests that there must be some limit on moral rules. At least, when two moral rules come into conflict, the nurse has to decide how each is limited in order to resolve the conflict.

Sometimes the nurse may discover limits on certain moral rules or rights related to nursing care even when they do not come into direct conflict with other rules or rights. One kind of limit may be encountered when the nurse has been released from an obligation. If a nurse promises to keep confidential some information about the patient's sexual history, for instance, the nurse would normally be obliged to act on the moral rule requiring that the confidence be kept. The moral rule might be seen as being derived from the general principle of promise-keeping. What, however, if the nurse decides it would be very important to disclose the information to the consulting psychiatrist? If the nurse asks the patient for permission to disclose and the patient grants that permission, we would probably conclude that the nurse has been released from the rule of confidentiality.

The release might come, according to some interpretations, from the behavior of one of the parties rather than from a verbal release. If one of the parties to a contract fails to fulfill the specified part of the bargain, the other might thereby be released, at least in some circumstances.

A second kind of limit on a moral rule or a moral right may be built into the rule or right itself. Even if there has been no "release," most moral rules, if stated carefully, include within them exceptions. The confidentiality rule, for example, often carries with it the exception "unless breaking confidence is required by law." The rule that the nurse should provide nursing care that will benefit the patient probably includes some implied limits. The nurse may be expected to provide care "up to a reasonable level" or "within the nurse's competence."

In the following case, the nurse must determine what limits, if any, are placed on the duty to provide patient care.

Case 1-6

The Visiting Nurse and the Obstinate Patient: Limits on the Right to Nursing Care

Mr. Jeff Williams, a staff nurse with Home Care Services at the county health department, was preparing to visit Mr. Rufus Chisholm, a 59-year-old patient with emphysema who was recently discharged from the hospital after suffering pneumonia. Well known to the health department, Mr. Chisholm was unemployed as a result of a farming accident several years ago and was essentially homebound. Hypertensive as well as overweight, he was also a heavy cigarette smoker of long duration despite his decreased lung function. Mr. Williams's reason for visiting him today was to assess Mr. Chisholm's medication use—if there were any side effects, and how effective the medications were in clearing his lung congestion from the pneumonia.

As Mr. Williams parked his car in front of his patient's house, he could see Mr. Chisholm sitting on the front porch smoking a cigarette. He experienced a flash of anger as he wondered why he continually tried to teach Mr. Chisholm the reasons for not smoking and why he took the time out from his busy home care schedule to follow up on Mr. Chisholm's health. This patient certainly did not seem to care about his own health, at least not to the extent that he would give up smoking.

During the home visit, it was determined that Mr. Chisholm had discontinued the use of his antibiotic before the full course of treatment was completed and that he was not taking his expectorant and bronchodilator medication on a regular basis. In addition, his blood pressure was 210/114, and he coughed almost continuously. Although his lung sounds were improved, Mr. Chisholm said he tired easily and had no appetite. He politely listened to Mr. Williams's concerns about his respiratory function and the continued use of his medications, but he did not seem to be taking any responsibility for his health status. Mr. Williams told Mr. Chisholm that he would visit him again in 3 days.

As he drove to his next appointment, Mr. Williams wondered to what extent he was obligated as a nurse to provide care to patients who took no personal responsibility for their health. He also wondered if there was a limit to the amount of nursing care a noncooperative patient could expect from a community health service.

Commentary

Employed by a healthcare system whose goal is to provide nursing care services at public expense for those who need and desire them, the nurse is confronted with the occasional patient who fails to follow the recommended healthcare plan. When this happens, the nurse may experience moral conflict. The nurse who personally values health and the provision of quality nursing care may view the patient who continually engages in health-risky behaviors as a waste of personal time, professional skill, and public monies. Yet the nurse may also feel there is a professional obligation to provide nursing care in response to the patient's right to healthcare services.

One approach to this issue is to regard patients like Mr. Chisholm as having a limited claim on nursing care services. His claim may be limited because other patients have a claim on Mr. Williams's time and nursing services. In this case, benefits to others must be balanced against the benefit of nursing attention and care for Mr. Chisholm.

His claim may also be limited because he has failed to fulfill his part of the contractual relationship between patient and nurse. Failure on his part thus releases the nurse from the duty to provide care that would normally be required.

But there is one other reason why the patient's claim to care may be limited. It may be that personal interests of the nurse—to take a continuing education course or to receive a visit from a health product salesperson—may take precedence once certain levels of healthcare services have been provided. This may be true even when no failure in the contractual relationship on the part of the patient exists. But who sets the limit on how much nursing care a patient is entitled to receive, and who is to say when the nurse has fulfilled his or her obligations to the patient? It is the question of who has ethical authority in defining the moral requirements and moral limits of the practice of nursing that we will turn to in Chapter 2.

Critical Thinking Questions

Describe an ethical conflict that occurred in your nursing practice during the past year.

1. How did you know that this situation was an ethical conflict and not some other type of conflict?

2. To what extent do you think a nurse's personal values and beliefs should affect patient care? Why?

3. What signals to you this is an ethical challenge? Intellectual disconnect? Queasy feeling in the pit of your stomach? Discomfort or disappointment in the way you or your team is responding? Pay attention to *how you reason* as you think about how you *should* and *would* respond.

4. What informs your judgment? How do you calibrate your moral compass?

5. Are there moral "rules" or guidelines that apply?

6. Do you have a responsibility to respond? Are you personally *able and willing* to respond?

7. Are there institutional or other external variables making it difficult or impossible to respond?

8. Do you reach your decision competently? Are you *confident* in your ability to respond ethically?

9. What counts as a *good* response? What criteria/principles do you use to inform, justify, and evaluate your response?

   Able to put your head on your pillow and fall asleep peacefully
   Transparency
   Consistency
   Maximize good and minimize harm
   Just distribution of goods and harms
   Other

10. Are there any universal (nonnegotiable) moral obligations that obligate all healthcare professionals?

11. To whom would you turn if you were uncertain about how to proceed?

12. What agency/professional resources exist to help you think through and secure a good response?

A Systematic Process for Approaching an Ethics Case   We have now examined a series of cases that reveal how the normative dimensions can be recognized and distinguished from matters of fact. Then among the normative issues, we attempted to distinguish the ethical value issues from other kinds of evaluation that do not raise ethical questions. Some will find it helpful at this point at the end of

Chapter 1 to have available a systematic process for analyzing an ethics case. Answering the questions in Box 1-1 will provide such a process.

Box 1-1
A Systematic Process for Addressing Ethical Issues

1. Recognize and identify the *ethical* challenge.
   - Respond to the sense (intuitive, cognitive, or gut) that something is or may be wrong.
   - Clarify that this is an *ethical* challenge.
   - Gather information.
     - Who are the stakeholders?
     - What are their interests, beliefs, values?
     - Who is/are the decision maker(s)?
     - Is time a factor?
     - Are there pertinent contextual factors?
     - Are there ethical, legal, or professional standards that apply?

2. Identify and weigh alternative courses of action.
   - Apply pertinent action-guiding theories. (What makes one course of action more ethically right than another? Which courses of action are unethical? Are there ethical rules or principles that apply to this situation?)
   - Apply pertinent character-guiding theories. (How would an honest, competent, trustworthy, caring professional respond? Which course of action is most likely to promote the virtue of participants?)
   - Ask, "Does the nature of the relationships among participants in the situation (e.g., nurse-patient) make one course of action preferable to another?"
   - Are there unique contextual factors in this situation that make one course of action preferable to another?

3. Work with others to determine what ought to be done in this specific situation.

4. Ask the question, "Can we implement the ethically right course of action?"
   - If no, to what extent is this the fault of deficient moral agency (e.g., lack of courage)?
   - If no, to what extent is this a real instance of moral distress where external variables prevent our doing the right thing for the right reasons?

5. Take action and be sure to evaluate the action taken.

6. Preventive ethics: What needs to change at the level of individuals, the institution/profession, or society to prevent the recurrence of this ethically challenging situation?

ENDNOTES

1. Kluckhohn, F. R., & Strodtbeck, D. L. (1961). *Variations in value orientations.* Evanston, IL: Row, Patterson.

2. Anderson, R. E., & Murphy, P. A. (1995). Outcomes of 11,788 planned home births attended by certified nurse-midwives: A retrospective descriptive study. *Journal of Nurse-Midwifery, 40*(6), 483–492; Davidson, M. R. (2002). Outcomes of high-risk women cared for by certified nurse-midwives. *Journal of Midwifery & Women's Health, 47*(1), 46–49; Pang, J. W., Heffelfinder, J. D., Huang, G. J., Benefetti, T. J., & Weiss, N. S. (2002). Outcomes of planned home births in Washington state: 1989–1996. *Obstetrics & Gynecology, 100*(2), 253–259; Vedam, S., & Kolodji, Y. (1995). Guidelines for client selection in the home birth midwifery practice. *Journal of Nurse-Midwifery, 40*(6), 508–521.

3. Declercq, E. R., Paine, L. L., & Winter, M. R. (1995). Home birth in the United States: 1989–1992. *Journal of Nurse-Midwifery, 40*(6), 474–481; Gabay, M., & Wolfe, S. M. (1997). Nurse-midwifery: The beneficial alternative. *Public Health Reports, 112*(5), 386–394; Harvey, D., Rach, D., Stainton, M. C., Jarrell, J., & Brant, R. (2002). Evaluation of satisfaction with midwifery care. *Midwifery, 18*(4), 260–267; Janssen, P. A., Lee, S. K., Ryan, E. M., Etches, D. J., Farquharson, D. F., Peacock, D., et al. (2002). Outcomes of planned home births versus planned hospital births after regulation of midwifery in British Columbia. *Canadian Medical Association Journal, 166*(3), 315–323.

4. American College of Nurse-Midwives. Research and Statistics Committee. (1978). *Nurse midwifery in the United States: 1976–1977* (p. 18). Washington, DC: Author.

5. Kovner, C. T., & Burkhardt, P. (2001). Findings from the American College of Nurse-Midwives' annual membership survey, 1995–1999. *Journal of Midwifery and Women's Health, 46*(1), 24–29.

6. Curtin, S. C. (1999). Recent changes in birth attendant, place of birth, and the use of obstetric interventions, United States, 1989–1997. *Journal of Nurse Midwifery, 44*(4), 349–354; Curtin, S. C., & Park, M. M. (1999). Trends in the attendant, place, and timing of births, and in the use of obstetric interventions: United States, 1989–1997. *National Vital Statistics Report, 47*(27), 1–12.

7. MacDorman, M. F., & Singh, G. K. (1998). Midwifery care, social and medical risk factors, and birth outcomes in the USA. *Journal of Epidemiology and Community Health, 52*, 310–317; Murphy, P. A., & Fullerton, J. (1998). Outcomes of intended home births in nurse-midwifery practice: A prospective descriptive study. *Obstetrics and Gynecology, 92*, 461–470; Oakley, D., Murray, M. E., Murtland, T., Hayashi, R., Andersen, H. F., Mayes, F., et al. (1996). Comparisons of outcomes of maternity care by obstetricians and certified nurse-midwives. *Obstetrics & Gynecology, 88*(5), 823–829.

8. Clarke, S. C., Martin, J. A., & Taffel, S. M. (1997). Trends and characteristics of births attended by midwives. *Statistical Bulletin, 78*, 9–18; Janssen, P. A., Lee,

S. K., Ryan, E. M., Etches, D. J., Farquharson, D. F., Peacock, D., et al. (2002). Outcomes of planned home births versus planned hospital births after regulation of midwifery in British Columbia. *Canadian Medical Association Journal, 166*(3), 315–323.

9. Baldwin, L., Raine, T., Jenkins, L. D., Hart, L. G., & Rosenblatt, R. (1994). Do providers adhere to ACOG standards? The case of prenatal care. *Obstetrics & Gynecology, 84*(4), 549–556.

10. Oakley, D., Murray, M. E., Murtland, T., Hayashi, R., Andersen, H. F., Mayes, F., et al. (1996). Comparisons of outcomes of maternity care by obstetricians and certified nurse-midwives. *Obstetrics & Gynecology, 88*(5), 823–829; Pang, J. W., Heffelfinger, J. D., Huang, G. J., Benedetti, T. J., & Weiss, N. S. (2002). Outcomes of planned home births in Washington state: 1989–1996. *Obstetrics & Gynecology, 100*(2), 253–259.

11. Neuhaus, W., Piroth, C., Kiencke, P., Gohring, U. J., & Mallman, P. (2002). A psychosocial analysis of women planning birth outside hospital. *Obstetrics & Gynecology, 22*(2), 143–149.

12. The Boston Women's Health Book Collective. (1998). *Our bodies, ourselves for the new century: A book by and for women.* New York: Simon & Schuster.

13. American Nurses Association. (2001). *Code of ethics for nurses with interpretive statements* (p. 23). Washington, DC: Author.

14. Ibid.

15. Ibid., p. 14.

16. Beauchamp, T. L., & Childress, J. F. (2001). *Principles of biomedical ethics* (5th ed., p. 357). New York: Oxford University Press; Feinberg, J. (1980). *Rights, justice, and the bounds of liberty: Essays in social philosophy* (pp. 143–155). Princeton, NJ: Princeton University Press.

17. American Nurses Association. (2001). *Code of ethics for nurses with interpretive statements* (p. 8). Washington, DC: Author.

18. Dworkin, G. (1972). Paternalism. *Monist, 56,* 64–84; Gert, B., & Culver, C. M. (1976). Paternalistic behavior. *Philosophy and Public Affairs, 6,* 45–67; Gert, B., Culver, C. M., & Clouser, K. D. (1997). *Bioethics: A return to fundamentals.* New York: Oxford University Press; idem. (1971). Paternalism. In R. Wasserstrom (Ed.), *Morality and the law* (pp. 107–126). Belmont, CA: Wadsworth Publishing Company; idem. (1979). The justification of paternalism. In W. L. Robison & M. S. Pritchard (Eds.), *Medical responsibility: Paternalism, informed consent and euthanasia* (pp. 1–14). Clifton, NJ: The Human Press; idem. (1979). The justification of paternalism. *Ethics, 89,* 199–210.

19. Moral rules state, at a middle level of generality, what action is required of someone who has a duty to act. If one wanted to state what action is required of some other individual or group from the point of view of the one acted upon, the language of rights might be used to the same end.

20. Bennett, J. C. (1967). Principles and the context. In J. C. Bennett et al., (Eds.), *Storm over ethics* (pp. 1–25). Philadelphia: United Church Press; Feinberg, J. (1980). *Rights, justice, and the bounds of liberty: Essays in social philosophy.* Princeton, NJ: Princeton University Press; Gert, B. (1988). *Morality: A new justification of the moral rules.*

New York: Oxford University Press; Lyons, D. (1979). *Rights.* Belmont, CA: Wadsworth Publishing Company.

21. American Nurses Association. (2001). *Code of ethics for nurses with interpretive statements* (p. 19). Washington, DC: Author.

22. Cahill, L. S. (1995). Abortion: Roman Catholic perspectives. In W. T. Reich (Ed.), *The encyclopedia of bioethics* (pp. 30–34). New York: The Free Press.

Chapter 2

The Nurse and Moral Authority

Other Cases Involving Conceptions of Values

Case 13-1: The Psychotherapist Confronted by Different Values

Key Terms
Code of ethics
Conscience clause
Integrity
Integrity-preserving compromise
Moral authority

Objectives
1. Identify the influence of individual religious and other beliefs on the nurse's ethical judgments.
2. Describe the authority of personal, professional, institutional, societal, health-oriented, and patient-oriented sources as guides for ethical nursing practice.
3. Explain the limitations of the professional code of ethics as a guide to ethical nursing practice.

The nurse's ability to identify ethical and other value judgments in clinical or policy-making situations is a skill that may be sufficient to resolve many ethical problems. Some tensions may be relieved simply by recognizing that a dispute or a feeling of uneasiness arises because ethical or other value choices are at issue. In more difficult cases, however, the nurse may not know which of two or more options is the best or the most morally right to choose. At this point the nurse may turn to traditional sources for help. She or he may ask the opinion of colleagues, consult other health professionals, or turn to a **code of ethics** such as the American Nurses Association's (ANA) *Code of Ethics for Nurses*. Other possible sources of guidance for making these difficult judgments include institutional rules, the law, the broader mores of society, the nurse's religious tradition, or the patient's value system.

Although consulting one of these potential authorities may sometimes resolve tensions or reveal to the nurse what appears to be the right course of action, at other times, the nurse may still be perplexed. On these occasions the question inevitably arises: "By which of these authorities, if any, ought I to be influenced?" Which of them should be viewed as a legitimate source for clarifying and justifying ethical positions?

The problem is a classical one in ethics. Before we can determine which principles or rules for behavior are appropriate, we need to have some basis for assessing the various sources of such principles or rules. This is what philosophers often refer to as the problem of metaethics, or understanding the meaning and justification of our moral judgments.[1] Some have held, for example, that an action, rule, or principle is right when and only when it is approved by God or by one's religious tradition. This would constitute a religious basis for answering the question of *moral authority*. One of the advantages of such a basis of authority is that moral judgments are then usually thought of as universal in the sense that everyone has some common ultimate frame of reference. Everyone looking at the same problem ought to come to the same conclusion. There really is, for one operating from this kind of religious worldview, a right answer to our ethical questions.

Others, working in a more secular framework, also believe there really are right answers to our moral questions. They might be rationalists who, like Immanuel Kant, believe that reason will ultimately be the foundation of right judgments.[2] Still others think that there is a single right or wrong answer, but it must be known intuitively.[3]

By contrast, some people have given up the idea that there is a single ultimate source of moral authority. They may believe that expressions of moral judgment are merely expressions of the speaker's personal feelings or the judgments of society.[4] Medical professional groups have written codes for many years, sometimes implying that they themselves were the source of their moral rules or at least that they were the ones in the best position to know what the morally correct course was.[5]

Nurses often have been caught in a tension among the many groups who claim to be the correct or legitimate sources of moral authority. This chapter presents some cases designed to help think through these competing claims. For example, is it right to turn off a respirator because a physician says to do so? Because the hospital lawyer says to do so? Because the health insurer insists that it be stopped? Should the approval of society as a whole be a consideration? What if the nurse is a member of a professional association that specifies in its code of ethics that a particular behavior is called for or is categorically unethical? Does the fact that a code approves of the nurse's participation in research on children who cannot consent necessarily make that participation ethical?

What if the nurse is a member of a religious group? Does that provide a source of moral authority for his or her decisions in nursing? What if the religious group's judgment conflicts with some other judgments the nurse obtains when seeking advice? What if it conflicts with the physician's judgment, the judgment of the state licensing board, the consensus of the nurse's colleagues, or the ANA's code of ethics? It is the tension between a professional code and a religious tradition that creates the problem addressed in Case 2-1.

The Authority of the Profession

Case 2-1

The Nurse Who Thought the ANA *Code of Ethics for Nurses* Was Wrong

Martha Levy, staff nurse in a small nursing home in a Midwestern community, has just reviewed the physician's orders for Mr. Carson, an 84-year-old man who is being readmitted to the nursing home after a 2-week stay at the county medical center. Suffering from diabetes, chronic brain syndrome, frequent urinary tract infections, and heart disease, Mr. Carson had been admitted to the medical center for treatment of his gangrenous left foot. An amputation had been recommended to prevent additional deterioration of his condition and possible death, but the operation had been refused by Mr. Carson's niece, his only surviving relative and legal guardian. The niece, Mrs. Myers, refused to consent to the surgery on the basis that Mr. Carson would not have consented to the procedure if he were competent and able to state his wishes. The surgery was not performed and over a period of several days, Mr. Carson's condition improved to the point where he could be discharged to the nursing home, his residence for the past 6 years.

While Mr. Carson was in the medical center, a gastrostomy tube had been inserted to facilitate his feeding and nutritional intake. The physician's orders stated that he was to be fed a high-protein, low-sodium, tube feeding preparation. This order would not pose any problem in the nursing home, as several of the home's residents were on tube feedings via gastrostomy or jejunostomy tubes. Mr. Carson was largely unaware of his surroundings, but he did move his extremities and moaned loudly when the nursing staff tried to move him or give him small sips of liquids. There was no expectation that his condition would significantly improve.

During the first 24 hours after his return, the nursing staff noted that Mr. Carson apparently experienced some discomfort from the g-tube feedings. He frequently moaned and placed his hands over his abdomen. The nurses were not concerned by these behaviors because it was not unusual for patients to occasionally experience discomfort when receiving feedings via a g-tube.

The following day, Mrs. Myers visited her uncle and was visibly upset by his general condition, the presence of the g-tube, the feedings, and what she perceived as his discomfort during the procedure. She told the nurse that although she thought the g-tube might have been necessary in the hospital, she had presumed that it would be removed before Mr. Carson returned to the nursing home. She had not been aware that it was still in place. Mrs. Myers called her uncle's physician from the nursing home and asked that the feeding tube be removed. Even though it was doubtful that Mr. Carson would be able to take sufficient nutrition by mouth, the physician agreed to the removal of the g-tube. He then called Mrs. Levy and asked that she stop the feedings. He said he would come by the nursing home in the evening and remove the tube.

Mrs. Levy objected to the decision to stop Mr. Carson's feedings and remove the g-tube. She did not feel that Mr. Carson would be able to receive adequate nutrition without the tube and that removing the tube would contribute to a deterioration of his condition. Despite Mr. Carson's discomfort with the tube feedings and his niece's wishes to have the tube removed, Mrs. Levy did not want to participate in a procedure that, in her opinion, might contribute to his death. Her reasons, in part, stemmed from the fact that she was a strictly observant Orthodox Jew. She had learned that the Talmudic tradition places the highest emphasis on the duty to do what was necessary to preserve an identifiable, individual human life. She had, in discussions with her rabbi, debated on several occasions the ethics of maintaining terminally ill patients, especially those who were near death. She had gradually become convinced of the wisdom of her religious tradition, which had consistently taught that even moments of life should be preserved. Her religious commitment required her to do what she could to ensure that risk of death be avoided or at least minimized.

Other nursing staff members and Mr. Carson's physician sharply disagreed with Mrs. Levy, however. They cited the right of the patient to refuse treatment, as exercised by his legal guardian, and the obligation of the nurse not to prolong the dying process. When she consulted the ANA *Code of Ethics for Nurses* for direction, she discovered that the obligation of the nurse to practice "with compassion and respect for the inherent dignity, worth, and uniqueness of every individual . . ." had recently been interpreted by the profession in the following manner: "Nurses actively participate in assessing and assuring the responsible and appropriate use of interventions in order to minimize unwarranted or unwanted treatment and patient suffering . . . . The nurse should provide interventions to relieve pain and other symptoms in the dying patient even when those interventions entail risks of hastening death."[6] She took this statement to mean that nurses may withhold feedings from individuals even though this action would reduce adequate nutrition and hydration in the patient and might hasten death. This professional ethic apparently would agree with the niece's and the physician's decisions to stop the tube feedings.

Clearly, Mrs. Levy is facing a difficult moral dilemma: The ethics of her nurses' association pulls her in one direction, whereas her religious heritage pulls her in another. Her problem is to determine which, if either, should take precedence.

Commentary

Mrs. Levy is caught between two potential sources of moral help in resolving her dilemma, and as she understands them, they are in conflict. The ANA *Code of Ethics for Nurses* places great emphasis on the autonomy of the patient and the nurse's duty to respect the **integrity** of the patient's wishes. True, in this case, Mr. Carson's wishes are being transmitted by his niece, but his wishes appear to be clear and the ANA code specifically endorses the use of a surrogate decision maker.

On the other hand, Mrs. Levy's religious tradition, as she understands it with the help of her rabbi, insists on the moral obligation to preserve life, even for a terminally ill patient such as Mr. Carson.[7] In some cases the nurse might be able to resolve the conflict by appealing to the "conscience clause" of the ANA code.[8] The code says, "Where a particular treatment, intervention, activity, or practice is morally objectionable to the nurse, whether intrinsically so or because it is inappropriate for the specific patient, or where it may jeopardize both patients and nursing practice, the nurse is justified in refusing to participate on moral grounds."[9] In this case, however, the moral conflict is more difficult. Mrs. Levy is asked to withhold tube feeding, with the realization that Mr. Carson's life will be shortened. Withdrawing from the case would simply mean that some other nurse would withhold the tube feeding, which would not satisfy Mrs. Levy's religiously rooted obligation to preserve life. Mr. Carson would still die from lack of adequate nutrition and hydration.

A similar problem might occur if a decision not to attempt resuscitation were made by Mr. Carson or his niece and placed in the medical record. In this situation, it might be awkward for Mrs. Levy to withdraw from the case. She might be the only nurse on the unit for her shift, for example. But if she were to honor the decision not to resuscitate if he coded on her shift, she would be violating her religiously based duty.

The underlying issue raised by Mrs. Levy's dilemma is the question of the relative status of various codes and religious interpretations in helping the nurse formulate her ethical stand.[10] The two kinds of authority Mrs. Levy is considering seem to be quite different. One makes claims about what is ethically correct for all of one's life and will be accepted to the extent that one accepts the particular religious tradition. The other makes claims about a particular sphere of one's life—in this case, nursing. It will be accepted to the extent that one believes that professional groups actually invent the morality of their members or to the extent that one believes that the collective wisdom of the professional group is the best way of knowing what is right for its members.

Technically, professional associations' codes of ethics are binding on the members of those associations, but only to the extent that the association can censure the member for violations. The ultimate penalty, presumably, would be expulsion from the association. But should Mrs. Levy consider that her professional association has special authority in determining what is ethical for nurses? Historically, some health professionals have claimed that the professional group actually creates the ethical duties for its members. Insofar as one wants to be a member in good standing, one would consider the profession's judgment definitive. Others have argued, however, that ethics simply cannot be invented by any group of human beings, that what is ethically required must be grounded in some source beyond mere convention—in reason or universal moral law or divine authority.

If that is the case, then a professional association cannot be said to be authoritative just because it invents the moral norms of professional conduct. Still, even if the norms come from beyond a human professional group, it might be claimed that the profession is authoritative in knowing what the norms are. The issue then becomes one of whether the professional group is authoritative in understanding and articulating the moral obligations of professionals. It might be argued that clinical experience or socialization into the meaning and goals of the profession is essential before one can understand what a nurse ought to do.

There are also critics of this position, however. Surely, healthcare professionals have special duties that would not apply to people in other roles. Being uniquely dedicated to the patient is one of the most apparent of these duties. Just as police or military officials or parents have special ethical responsibilities, so do healthcare professionals. Yet the question is whether one has to be a member of one of these groups to understand what the group members' duties are. Presumably, both parents and nonparents understand why the role of parent includes a bias in favor of the welfare of one's own children. Both police and nonpolice recognize that police behave in special ways—that they use violence in ways not authorized for others, for example.

A similar question arises for the ethics of the professions. Do members of the professions have a special authority in deciding what the professional's duty is? If so, then the pronouncements of professional associations should be given special weight by Mrs. Levy and others wanting to know their professional obligations. If they do not, then Mrs. Levy might listen to what they say but not consider them definitive or authoritative. She would consider them to be merely the opinion of one group about the special duties of that group.

How should Mrs. Levy view the authority of her religious tradition and her rabbi in deciding what she ought to do in the face of a decision not to provide nutrition, hydration, or resuscitation? It is the nature of religious institutions that they claim to have authoritative ways of knowing. They know through revelation, reason, tradition, or inspired prophecy. They claim moral authority. Of course, not everyone accepts that authority as definitive, but its members do, at least to some extent. That is part of what it means to be a member of that group.

If Mrs. Levy considers herself a member of the Orthodox Jewish community, she presumably accepts the moral authority of her tradition. It is not that she will necessarily automatically accept what her rabbi says as definitive, but she should at least consider carefully the wisdom of her religious tradition, and to the extent that she considers herself a part of that tradition, she should consider its sources of moral knowledge authoritative. Mrs. Levy's question should be whether she feels that her professional group ought to be given the same status. If it should, she may be in the terrible situation of having two conflicting sources of moral insight that she considers authoritative. Does a professional group have claims to moral authority the way a religious tradition does?

Critical Thinking Questions

1. Can you think of a patient care situation where your own religious beliefs might influence your nursing practice? If so, describe the religious beliefs and their origins, and consider how they might or might not influence your nursing practice.

2. Is it ever permissible for the nurse to conscientiously object to participate in patient care? If so, under what condition(s)? What does the ANA *Code of Ethics for Nurses* have to say about this? Read Provision #5 carefully.

Research Brief 2-1

Source: Anthony, M. K. (1999). The relationship of authority to decision-making behavior: Implications for redesign. *Research in Nursing & Health, 22*, 388–398.

Purpose: To determine if two dimensions of structure (administrative/decentralization and professional authority/expertise) influence the process of participation in decision making for two kinds of decisions (caregiving and condition-of-work) that nurses make.

Method: For this correlational, cross-sectional study, a stratified random sampling technique and survey methodology were used. The study took place among 600 registered nurses (RNs) in 13 acute care hospitals within two zip codes of metropolitan Cleveland, Ohio, who had worked on their current general medical or surgical unit for at least 6 months and worked for at least 18 hours per week. Decentralization was defined as the extent to which staff nurses perceive that they have administrative authority for decision making and was measured by the Van deVen & Ferry (1980) 4-item Job Authority scale. Expertise was defined as the extent to which nurses have professional authority for decision making and was measured by the RNs' self-reported responses to three items. Participation was defined as the extent to which nurses have a say in decisions affecting their practice and was measured by the 42-item Participation in Decision Activities Questionnaire (PDAQ) developed for the study. Three hundred usable questionnaires were used in the data analysis, for a valid response rate of 50%. Descriptive and parametric statistics were used in data analysis.

Findings: There was greater nurse participation in identification, design, and selection for caregiving decisions than for condition-of-work decisions. Further testing confirmed that, for caregiving decisions, participation in the identification phase was greater than in the design phase, and participation in design was greater than participation in selection. Results were similar for condition-of-work decisions: participation in the identification phase was greater than in the design phase, and participation in design was greater than participation in selection. For condition-of-work decisions, full-time nurses participated significantly more in the identification, design, and selection phases than part-time nurses did. Nurses working on surgical floors participated more in the identification phase of condition-of-work decisions than nurses on medical floors did. These differences were found to be small and not practically important. For caregiving decisions, decentralization, expertise, and their interaction did not significantly affect participation in identification. For condition-of-work decisions, decentralization, expertise, and their interaction explained little of the variance in participation in the identification, design, and selection phases of decision making. A surprising finding was that expertise did not increase participation in the design phase of caregiving decisions.

Implications: First, although the nursing profession claims that greater control over practice is achieved through greater participation in decision making and that lack of participation in decision making is caused by lack of authority, this study does not support these claims. Nurses in the study perceived they had considerable administrative authority for decision making, yet it was not strongly associated with decision-making behavior. Thus, administrative authority may be necessary, but it is not sufficient to explain important variations in participation in decision making. Second, although nurses express the desire for more authority, some do not use it when they have it. Further study of organizational and individual nurse factors may be useful in understanding this finding. Third, nurses' failure to use their authority for decision making may also be related to their education and socialization in a profession dominated by women, lack of motivation, and lack of recognition of the kind of decisions that nurses want to make. Further research is needed to identify why providing nurses with authority may not lead to practically important variations in their participation in decision making. Finally, the study findings highlight the complexity of participation in decision making, supporting further testing of the conceptual disengagement of having authority for decision making from exercising that authority. Modeling techniques that target other factors responsible for inhibiting or facilitating participation are needed.

The Authority of the Physician

In many cases, the tension the nurse faces over the source of moral authority is not between the professional code and some other source of authority to which he or she is committed, such as his or her religion, but between the nurse's own sense of what is right and the viewpoints of other people involved in the case: the physician, the institutional authorities, society at large, or the patient. The next group of cases examines in turn each of these sources of conflict. In each case the nurse's problem is deciding whether to compromise his or her own ethical commitments and substitute the ethical framework of other people.

Case 2-2
Following the Physician's Orders: The Nurse as Moral Spectator

Gretchen Sears, a 20-year-old in midpregnancy, was admitted to a small community hospital early one evening when she developed signs of premature labor and delivery. Although Mrs. Sears had undergone two prenatal checkups, both she and her obstetrician, an elderly but well-respected practitioner in the community, were uncertain about her stage of pregnancy. Alerted by the labor room staff, the nurse in the special care nursery, Roger Simmons, prepared for the possible admission of an infant of unknown gestation. Mr. Simmons was a neonatal nurse specialist and had recently been employed by the hospital. He quickly alerted the pediatric associate, Dr. Frank Barnes, who was on call for the evening.

In the labor room, the obstetrician explained to Mrs. Sears that it was very unlikely that her infant would be alive when it was delivered. Both she and her husband were urged to reconcile themselves to the loss of the pregnancy. Within an hour, Mrs. Sears delivered the product of her first pregnancy, a very small female infant, in the labor room bed. The infant breathed spontaneously and was quickly rushed to the special care nursery. Mr. Simmons examined the tiny infant. Weighing 630 g, she was pink in color and had a heart rate of 140. No physical abnormalities were noted. From the infant's physical development, the nurse estimated its gestational age at 23 to 24 weeks. Based on this information, Mr. Simmons anticipated that the infant would be placed on respiratory support and transported to the nearest tertiary care facility.

He quickly called Dr. Barnes and began supporting the infant's respiratory efforts. After examining the infant, however, Dr. Barnes told Mr. Simmons, "I'm not sure we ought to be too aggressive with this infant. I'm going to talk with the obstetrician before we go any further." Mr. Simmons was surprised because he was accustomed to instituting treatment for infants of this size (and even smaller) in his previous position at a large medical center. He knew how important early treatment and quick transport to another facility might be to this infant's survival.

Within a few minutes, the obstetrician arrived to consult with Dr. Barnes. After some discussion, Dr. Barnes discontinued the ventilation support, telling Mr. Simmons that they would not be giving the infant any further treatment. In his opinion, the infant was too small to survive. Mr. Simmons disagreed with Dr. Barnes. He then asked if Mr. and Mrs. Sears were aware of their child's condition and her chances for survival if she were to be transported. Dr. Barnes stated that both he and the obstetrician were going out to talk with the parents. The obstetrician added, "Look, these parents are just young kids getting started with their lives. They don't have the resources or know-how to take care of the kind of problems this child will encounter. They'll have more babies." As the physicians left the nursery to inform the parents, Dr. Barnes told Mr. Simmons to keep the infant comfortable and to call him "when its heart stops beating."

Commentary

As in the previous case, the nurse in this situation may feel the tension between two different kinds of moral authority. Mr. Simmons does not feel moral ambivalence within himself forcing him to choose between religious and professional authority, however. He seems to be convinced of what is morally required. His problem is rather that someone else—a physician in a traditional position of authority—has made a choice, apparently based on some other set of moral principles.

Mr. Simmons presumably formed his own conclusion, drawing on important sources of moral authority: his religious and philosophic convictions, his sense of the commitments he has made as a professional nurse, and other information of significance to him.[11] On the other hand, Dr. Barnes apparently concluded that it is ethically appropriate, or at least ethically permissible, for him to decide on his own to let the Searses' baby die. Dr. Barnes may have had several reasons for his decision. He may have thought the baby would be sufficiently handicapped if it survived to justify his letting her die. He may have thought that the Searses were not capable of being adequate parents. He may have thought that the costs to society would not justify doing what was necessary to give the child a chance to live. For whatever reason, Dr. Barnes made a moral judgment, just as Mr. Simmons did. The critical question is whether there is any reason to assume that Dr. Barnes's judgment should automatically take precedence.

Were the choice based on technical medical knowledge, many would hold that Dr. Barnes's judgment has a special authority. After all, he is the one with the medical skill. By the same token, were the decision one that required nursing expertise, Mr. Simmons's judgment might be given special weight. Yet, there was no evidence in the case as presented that Dr. Barnes and Mr. Simmons disagreed over anything requiring either a physician's or a nurse's expertise. They appeared to disagree over the morality of letting a baby die who might live if treated but who then might live with some degree of debilitation. "Is it acceptable for a physician to let such a baby die?" is the first ethical question. If so, is it acceptable without the knowledge and permission of the parents?

Dr. Barnes has presumably drawn on his religious or philosophical belief system in deciding that it is acceptable to let the baby die. He may have been informed by the Hippocratic tradition, which urges the physician to use his own judgment to do what will benefit the patient.[12] Is there any reason, however, why the personal religious and philosophical views of the physician should be definitive? Presumably, some other physician, had he been on call that evening, would have brought to the case some other set of beliefs and values. It is hard to see why the fate of the patient should be decided by the luck of the draw as to who happens to be on call on a given evening. By the same token, it is hard to imagine why a professional code or professional consensus, should one exist among physicians, should be definitive in deciding the baby's fate. On the other hand, it is hard to see why Mr. Simmons's own beliefs and values or the code of his profession should be definitive either.

Critical Thinking Question

A number of avenues of response have been proposed for a nurse caught in the predicament where the physician or some other de facto decision maker has inappropriately claimed moral authority in patient care situations. Consider each of the following potential actions for the nurse. Do any of the persons to whom the nurse might appeal have any authority—moral or legal—to override the decision made by Dr. Barnes in Case 2-2?

A. Discuss with nursing colleagues the wisdom of the physician's treatment plan.

B. Discuss directly with the physician concerned whether the course he or she is following is ethically appropriate.

C. Appeal the physician's decision through nursing channels—for example, through the nursing supervisor.

D. Take the issue to a hospital ethics committee.

E. Discuss the situation with family members.

F. Report the situation to local child abuse or other legal authorities for review.

Research Brief 2-2

Source: Baggs, J. G., Schmitt, M. H., Mushlin, A. I., Mitchell, P. H., Eldredge, D. H., Oakes, D., & Hutson, A. D. (1999). Association between nurse–physician collaboration and patient outcomes in three intensive care units. *Critical Care Medicine, 27*(9), 1991–1998.

Purpose: To investigate the association of collaboration between intensive care unit (ICU) physicians and nurses, and patient outcomes.

Method: This was a prospective, descriptive, correlational study using self-report instruments. Unit-level data were collected through individual audio-taped and transcribed interviews of nurse and physician administrators. The participants included resident and attending physicians ($n = 156$) and staff nurses ($n = 150$) in the surgical and medical ICUs of three hospitals in upstate

New York. When patients were ready for transfer from the ICU to an area of less intensive care, questionnaires were used to assess care providers' reports of collaboration in making the transfer decision. Providers reported levels of collaboration, patient severity of illness and individual risk, patient outcomes of death or readmission to the ICU, unit-level collaboration, and unit patient risk of negative outcome. After controlling for severity of illness, the association between interprofessional collaboration and patient outcome was assessed. Unit-level organizational collaboration and patient outcomes were ranked.

Findings: Medical ICU nurses' reports of collaboration were associated positively with patient outcomes. No other associations between individual reports of collaboration and patient outcomes were found. There was perfect rank-order correlation between unit-level organizational collaboration and patient outcomes across the three units.

Implications: First, the selection of patients to be transferred from the ICU and the implementation of transfers might well be improved if nurses collaborated in the decision making. There are examples in the literature of situations in which nurses believed that they had not been involved in decision making and patient care suffered. Nurses, who typically link collaboration more closely with their satisfaction with decision making than do physicians, may be better judges of collaboration. They also may be more aware of when it does and does not occur. Thus nurses' reports, rather than physicians' reports, may be a more sensitive indicator of the variable. Second, this study offers some support for ICU staff nurse–physician collaboration as a variable associated with favorable ICU patient outcomes, particularly in units with complex patients at highest risk. The support was found both in the association between nurses' reports of collaboration and patient outcomes, and in the unit-level associations between collaboration and patient outcome risk. Third, further research is needed on units with very sick, complex patients and the use of patient outcomes in addition to mortality to maximize the opportunity to assess the relationship between collaboration and patient outcomes. Also, intervention studies are needed to assess the effects of collaboration on patient outcomes.

The Authority of the Institution

The profession, the nurse's religious tradition, and the physician are not the only entities proposing interpretations of moral duties for the nurse. At times the nurse's hospital or other healthcare institution may have moral commitments of its own by the authority of which it attempts to structure the nurse's obligations. This raises the question of whether the nurse's moral duty and that of the healthcare institution are always compatible.

Case 2-3

The Nurse Covering the Maternity Unit

Herma Gonzales was a nurse for a medical/surgical nursing unit of a small county hospital in the Midwest. She was a recent graduate of an undergraduate program in nursing and had worked on her unit for approximately 2 months. During this time she had become familiar with most of the unit's routines and felt confident about her nursing abilities. One Saturday evening the nursing supervisor came to her unit right at the beginning of the shift and stated that someone would need to be pulled to temporarily cover the 10-bed maternity unit. The regular evening nurse had experienced car trouble on the way to work and would be approximately 1 to 2 hours late getting to the hospital. Because the med/surg unit was relatively quiet, the supervisor thought that the licensed practical nurse (LPN) working with Mrs. Gonzales could handle that unit while Mrs. Gonzales covered the maternity unit. The emergency room nurse had just notified her of an impending admission to the maternity unit.

Mrs. Gonzales quickly went to the maternity unit, where she received a report from the waiting day-shift nurse. The report revealed nothing extraordinary except the anticipated new admission from the emergency room. They would be transporting the new admission to the maternity unit in a few minutes. The patient was a 24-year-old woman in her last trimester of pregnancy (36 weeks). She had two living children and a history of precipitous labor. The physician was concerned that she was in the early stages of labor. Because of her labor and delivery history and the fact that she lived 25 miles away from the hospital, she was being admitted for close observation.

As soon as she checked the maternity patients, Mrs. Gonzales called the nursing supervisor to let her know that she would need assistance with the newly admitted patient. She was not competent in maternity nursing and was concerned about the potential needs of the new patient. Did the supervisor have a more experienced RN who could cover the maternity ward? The supervisor said no and told her not to worry. An RN was needed on the ward to admit the patient but she (the supervisor) knew that the regular nurse would be arriving soon. As soon as she arrived, Mrs. Gonzales could go back to her regular unit.

Within minutes, the patient arrived from the emergency room (ER). Mrs. Gonzales assessed the patient and checked the fetal monitor. The patient was having irregular but moderately strong uterine contractions; her BP was 176/118; P 98; R 24. The patient seemed very anxious and restless. The fetal heart rate was 146, strong and regular. Mrs. Gonzales again called her supervisor. She wanted the supervisor to come to the floor immediately and relieve her of the responsibility for this patient. She simply did not feel competent to handle the situation, and it would be another 30 minutes at least before the regular nurse could be expected. How could hospital policy that required the presence of an RN for admissions from the ER override Mrs. Gonzales's obligation not to take on responsibilities for which she did not feel competent?

Commentary

Much like the physician in Case 2-2, Mrs. Gonzales's hospital had a moral position from which it was acting. The administrators felt obligated to make sure that RN coverage, which was in short supply because one RN was delayed, was sufficient in all units. To them, this meant letting the LPN cover the medical/surgical floor and shifting Mrs. Gonzales temporarily to the maternity unit. They argued, probably correctly, that this staffing would do more good for patients than any other arrangement would, given the emergency that had developed. The hospital administrators necessarily adopted a social ethic, one that was committed to moral treatment of all the persons within their institution. As such, they would appear to have the right and the responsibility to use their personnel in accord with their ethical obligation.

But Mrs. Gonzales and other nurses in clinical settings are not administrators. The nurse's obligation is normally thought to be directed to the health, welfare, and safety of the individual client. In addition, the ANA *Code of Ethics for Nurses*, the most recognized interpretation of the nurse's ethical obligations, warns against incompetent practice. Many nurses would hold that they have a duty not to practice in settings where they are not appropriately trained and competent and, therefore, might feel obligated to refuse to practice on a unit where they believe they cannot do an adequate job.

Some nurses might make an exception in an emergency when their refusal means that patients in need will not receive any nursing attention at all. Others might feel obligated, even in an emergency situation, to refuse to practice nursing under circumstances in which they are convinced they would not practice competently. Nurses should be open to the possibility that their ethical mandate and that of the administrators are quite different. This issue will be addressed in many of the cases in Chapters 4 and 5.

Critical Thinking Questions

1. The ANA *Code of Ethics for Nurses* points out that the nurse has a duty to preserve his or her own integrity. How does the ANA *Code of Ethics for Nurses* define integrity? How is Mrs. Gonzales's integrity being threatened by the patient care situation in Case 2-3?

2. Sometimes it is possible to preserve one's integrity through compromise. However, the ANA *Code of Ethics for Nurses* states, "Nurses have a duty to remain consistent with both their personal and professional values and to accept compromise only to the degree that it remains an ***integrity-preserving compromise***. An integrity-preserving compromise does not jeopardize the dignity or well-being of the nurse or others."[13] How might Mrs. Gonzales work out an integrity-preserving compromise in this patient care situation?

Research Brief 2-3

Source: Penticuff, J. H., & Walden, M. (2000). Influence of practice environment and nurse characteristics on perinatal nurses' responses to ethical dilemmas. *Nursing Research, 49*(2), 64–72.

Purpose: To explore the relative contributions of practice environment characteristics and nurse personal and professional characteristics to perinatal nurses' willingness (nurse activism) to be involved in activities to resolve ethical dilemmas.

Method: A descriptive correlational design and hierarchical multiple regression were used to examine responses of perinatal nurses to three instruments: the Nursing Ethical Involvement Scales (NEIS), Perinatal Values Questionnaire (PVQ), and Demographic Data Sheet (DDS). Of the 200 nurses solicited, 127 mailed back completed questionnaires, giving a return rate of 64%. The nurses in the study worked directly with patients at least 20 hours per week in obstetric or neonatal ICUs and had at least 6 months of experience in their current nursing unit. More than 80% of the sample were staff nurses; the remainder were in head nurse/assistant head nurse or clinical specialist/advanced practice roles.

Findings: The organizational variable, nursing influence, accounted for the greatest amount of variance in nurses' reported resolution actions, with nurses' concern about ethics and consequentialist values also contributing significantly. The three predictors (nursing influence, concern about ethics, and consequentialist values) together accounted for 31% (24% adjusted) of the variance in actions to resolve clinical ethical dilemmas. The level of nursing education was not a statistically significant influence.

Study findings support the contributions of both environmental and nurse personal systems to nurse activism. Nurses in the study were more likely to be involved in dilemma resolution activities when they perceived themselves as having influence in their practice environments, expressed concern about the ethical aspects of clinical situations, and reasoned about ethical dilemmas in ways that emphasize consideration of morally relevant aspects of individual patient situations and deemphasize adherence to abstract standards, rules, and policies. Findings indicated that nurses in this sample perceived themselves as limited in their ability to influence patient care, however. They did not have a strong sense of being valued by their institutions, and their willingness to take actions to resolve ethical dilemmas was often limited. Of particular concern was the fact that only about half of the nurses in the sample believed they were able to influence the quality of patient care, with 45% stating that staff nurses had little influence in their units.

The most frequently reported action to resolve a clinical ethical dilemma was to discuss the dilemma with other nurses (94%), the head nurse (79%), or physicians (72%). Nurses were reluctant to communicate their ethical concerns beyond their own units. Less than 25% would request an ethics committee meeting, and only 10% would go outside their unit to talk with hospital administration.

Implications: The study results lend support to the thesis that ethical practice in nursing is influenced not only by nurses' values and concerns about ethics, but also by the organizational characteristics of the particular unit in which they practice. Because few nurses in this study were willing to go outside their units to communicate about ethical dilemmas, their ethical concerns may remain unresolved if they are not resolved within the unit. Thus, it is important to: (1) increase nurses' motivation and abilities to engage in ethical reasoning, (2) develop organizational strategies that provide nurses with opportunities to discuss ethical concerns within the unit setting, and (3) increase nurses' perceptions that they can influence multidisciplinary team practices.

The Authority of the Health Insurer

In recent years, health insurers' policies have set limits on the number of days patients may remain hospitalized for specific illnesses or health events. These limitations may conflict with the nurse's perceived obligation to care for patients or to prevent patients from harm. The following case illustrates this conflict.

Case 2-4
When Health Insurers Put Newborns at Risk[1]

Terry Adams is a pediatric nurse in an urban medical center. Over the past few months, she has seen numerous admissions of newborn infants with dehydration and severe jaundice, often requiring weeks of intensive pediatric care. One infant was so dehydrated that he required a leg amputation. His inexperienced mother did not realize that he wasn't nursing properly and that she did not have an adequate supply of breast milk. Another infant was so severely jaundiced that permanent brain damage was suspected.

   Miss Adams knows that the infants and their mothers were discharged from the hospital within 24 hours following delivery because their insurer, Brooker Health Plan, does not

---

[1]Adapted from "Deliver, Then Depart," by S. Begley, K. Springen, and A. Duignan-Cabrera, (1995), *Newsweek, 126*(2), p. 62.

pay for more than a 24-hour stay after an uncomplicated vaginal delivery. If the mothers and their infants had remained in the hospital for 3 days, the feeding problems and the jaundice would undoubtedly have been noted and treated. She strongly believes that shorter hospital stays are placing the health of newborns at risk. She also suspects that shorter hospital stays are not cost-effective when one considers the number of infants readmitted for costly procedures and treatments, but she is not really sure about this. Do health insurers have the authority to create policies that place some infants at risk and that force nurses like Miss Adams to provide less than satisfactory nursing care for new mothers and their infants?

Commentary

As in Case 2-3, the nurse in this situation seems to be convinced of her moral responsibility. She believes that new mothers and their newborn infants should be kept in the hospital for a minimum of 3 days to detect newborn feeding problems and jaundice, which newborns frequently experience. She might also agree that these additional days would provide opportunities for the nurse to observe how new mothers were bonding with their infants and to look for any signs of postpartum depression that would place mother and child at risk. Miss Adams knows that watching for these problems in the neonatal period is a nursing responsibility. She has decided that this is her moral responsibility as well as her professional responsibility.

The problem is that another entity, Brooker Health Plan, has concluded that new mothers and their infants do not need nursing observation beyond the 24 hours following birth. They have become the authority by establishing that they will not pay for hospital expenses after this period of time. The insurer is basing its judgments on values other than the health of the mother and the infant. They have probably determined (using cost-benefit analyses) that the likelihood of health problems developing in the mother and the infant following an uncomplicated vaginal delivery is relatively low in the majority of cases. True, some mothers and infants will develop problems, but on balance, it is more cost-effective to deny continued hospitalization to all of them, rather than to keep them hospitalized to avoid problems in the few. This moral judgment considers that it is right to allow some people to experience illness and even disability or death, even though preventable, as long as the overall costs of health care are reduced.

It is not clear on what basis the insurer claims the authority to set these limits. It might, as a profit-making insurance company, do so without the knowledge or consent of its subscribers. It might, for instance, be following a mandate from its shareholders to sustain a particular profit margin. One might question, however, whether the health insurer should be making judgments that affect individuals' health and nursing practice. Is the health insurer the appropriate moral authority for the health of new mothers and their infants and for nursing responsibility in the neonatal period?

The picture might be yet more complex. Suppose that the insurer had a subscriber's advisory council that had been told of the cost-benefit analyses, understood the risks to mothers and infants of the 24-hour limit for normal childbirth, and approved of the company's effort to conserve subscriber resources in order to keep premiums to a minimum. Would that give the insurer more moral justification to rely on cost-benefit analyses to make these judgments? Or suppose that all patients were clearly told of the limit and at the same time told they could self-pay for a second or third day in the hospital, which the insurer was not willing to fund because of the low probability of benefit. Would that legitimate the insurer's decision to set limits that violate the nurse's understanding of morally appropriate care? Finally, suppose the limit is set not by a private insurer but by a public insurance agency such as Medicaid. Does a public, nonprofit insurance plan have more authority to make moral judgments of this kind? That leads to consideration of the next kind of conflict between the nurse and others who may be considered to be authorities in ethics.

The Authority of Society

There are times when it is not the physician, the hospital, or the health insurer, but society at large that places moral pressure on the nurse. Cases 2-5 and 2-6 examine the authority of society in articulating moral duties for the nurse and how the nurse should respond to those pressures.

Case 2-5
Medications by Unlicensed Technicians[2]

Rose McGovern, Director of Nursing of an 80-bed nursing home facility in an urban setting, has just learned that a bill has been introduced in the state legislature to allow medications to be given by unlicensed technicians in nursing homes throughout the state.

Mrs. McGovern is outraged. As a long-standing advocate of skilled nursing home care, she knows that administration of medications to elderly clients is much more than the mere giving of ordered dosages of chemical substances. Medication administration provides the best opportunity for the qualified nurse to assess the overall health status of the elderly person. Although medication technicians have been allowed by law to give medications in state-owned and psychiatric hospitals within her state for many years, the

---

[2]Adapted from "Ethical Issues: Politics, Power, and Change," by S. T. Fry. In S. Talbot and D. Mason (Eds.), 1985, *Political Actions: A Handbook for Nurses* (pp. 133–140). Reading, MA: Addison-Wesley. Used with permission.

practice has never been legislated for general hospitals or for nursing homes. In fact, the state nurses' association and the state association of nursing homes have always agreed that the administration of medicines in nursing homes is a nursing function and must be performed by licensed personnel (RNs and LPNs). Mrs. McGovern maintains that the ANA *Code of Ethics for Nurses* makes it clear that the health, well-being, and safety of the patient are the nurse's primary considerations. She is convinced that the state has no business authorizing unlicensed technicians to perform nursing functions and that such a proposal could easily compromise the health and safety of patients. Now that position is being challenged directly by the legislature.

After a few hurried telephone calls, Mrs. McGovern and her colleagues in the state nursing home association learn that the bill has been referred to committee. They also learn that the bill was introduced by a representative in support of a group of businessmen who are building a large nursing care facility for the elderly in his rural district. The businessmen argued that medication technicians in nursing homes are more cost-effective than licensed personnel, and if properly trained and supervised, they present no additional risk to nursing home residents. Because the number of elderly people needing nursing home care and the cost of employing licensed nursing personnel have both risen dramatically in the last few years, the bill is viewed as one means of providing low-cost nursing care for the state's elderly citizens. The bill has the support of the state medical association and the state pharmaceutical association.

Within 36 hours the bill comes out of committee, is passed, and is sent to the governor for signing. Mrs. McGovern, other directors of nursing homes, and officials of the state nursing home association send an urgent message to the governor opposing the potential legislation and requesting time to study the use of medication technicians in nursing homes. Mrs. McGovern wonders whether the state has the authority to risk patients' health and safety in this way. Because the bill grants nurses legal immunity from prosecution for the action of a technician unless the technician is acting directly under the nurse's supervision, the problem for the nurses is not strictly one of legal liability. Rather, their concern is that the nursing profession should have the authority to set the norms for nursing practice, in this case giving the health and safety of patients priority over the cost saving that seems to get priority in the legislature's plan.

Commentary

This case raises the problem of the relation of the nursing profession to society and what roles the profession and society ought to have in articulating norms of nurse conduct. The proposed legislation authorizing the use of medication technicians might, at first, appear to be grounded in an empirical disagreement. The supporters of the legislation claim that the unlicensed technicians would be cheaper and would pose no risk to patients. Mrs. McGovern is apparently convinced that patients would face at least some risk if unlicensed technicians administered medications.

The case would become more interesting ethically if both sides were to agree that there is probably some increased risk, even though that risk may be small. If this were admitted, then the dispute might really be over moral principles. Mrs. McGovern appeals to the ANA code to identify the most important ethical principle: protecting the health, well-being, and safety of patients. Presumably the state, if it accepts the arguments of the supporters of the bill, is operating under a somewhat different norm, something like the notion that small risks are worth taking if they will save significant amounts of money.

If this is not a simple dispute over the matter of whether the use of unlicensed medical technicians would lead to increased risks for patients, then it may be a dispute over the relative authority of the nursing profession and the state to determine moral norms for nursing practice. The registered nurse is usually responsible for all nursing functions performed by nonnursing staff, including nonlicensed technicians, who work under the RN's supervision. If the nurse will still be directly responsible for unlicensed technicians' administering of medications, the effects of those medications, and the potential harm to the patients under his or her care, then there is a dispute over the relative authority of the nursing profession and the state in deciding the acceptable limits of the RN's responsibility.

Some might argue that the nursing profession has legitimate authority for articulating moral norms for nurses but that the state has taken the task of administering medication in nursing homes out of the nurse's purview.

That argument might simply shift the issue to whether the profession or society as a whole has the authority to determine what is within the purview of nursing responsibility. In any case, the critical problem remaining is what the relation should be between the profession and the broader society in determining the scope of nurses' responsibilities.

Some would hold that when it comes to articulating moral norms for a professional group such as nurses, the profession is the only group with the experience, skill, and sensitivity to make that articulation. They would ask, "Why should state legislators tell nurses what the norms should be for the practice of their profession?"

The defenders of the involvement of the broader society in determining the norms for professionals reject this position. They may well concede that when it comes to matters requiring technical competence, only the members of the profession are adequately experienced to speak authoritatively. Only nurses can make judgments about the appropriate nursing interventions to take in response to actual or potential health problems of the patient.

However, they may not be disputing the technical, empirical question of whether patients are at risk (a question about which nurses might claim special expertise). Possibly, they are disputing which of two moral norms is appropriate for institutionalizing policy regarding the administration of medication. If the dispute is really one over moral norms, it is not clear that being a professional in a field gives one expertise in choosing moral norms for social practices. They might, in effect, be disputing how much risk to elderly patients' health is worth taking in order to save money.

If that is the nature of the argument, then it could be concluded that the authority of the broader society is substantial. Different groups within society are likely to have different preferences for moral norms. They are likely to have different views about how much risk is worth taking. Nurses may be more inclined against taking risks with patients than the general public is. Some other professional group, such as accountants, however, may be much more supportive of risk-taking than the general public is. The issue for debate is whether the expertise that one gains when one becomes a member of a profession has anything to do with the kinds of judgments required in determining moral norms governing the conduct of the profession as it interacts with the public. Society as a whole may well have authority to articulate moral norms of conduct, such as deciding that marginal risks are justified.

The position of society as the group articulating the norms for nursing is not exactly parallel to the position some other profession, such as that of physicians, would have. It seems clear that one professional group cannot claim the authority to determine what the norms shall be for the conduct of another professional group. It is more difficult to ascertain the extent to which society as a whole should be able to play an active role in determining what the norms of conduct should be for the professions.

Research Brief 2-4

Sources: Fry, S. T., Harvey, R. M., Hurley, A. C., & Foley, B. J. (2002). Development of a model of moral distress in military nursing. *Nursing Ethics, 9*(4), 373–387.

Fry, S. T., Duffy, M. E., Hurley, A. C., Harvey, R. M., & Foley, B. J. (2002). *The experience of moral distress among crisis-deployed and non-crisis-deployed military nurses*. Abstract delivered at Advancing Nursing Practice Excellence: State of the Science Congress, September 25–28, 2002, Washington, DC.)

Purpose: To identify the experience of moral distress among crisis-deployed and non–crisis-deployed military nurses.

Method: Phases I and II of the study involved the development of a model of military nursing moral distress from the "moral distress stories" of 13 Army Nurse Corps officers (6 = female; 7 = male), currently on active duty or retired, who had participated in a crisis military deployment to Somalia, Bosnia, Germany, El Salvador, Honduras, Saudi Arabia, the Persian Gulf, or Vietnam. Stories of moral distress were elicited from the participants by using a semi-structured interview guide. The transcribed interviews were read independently and coded by two members of the research team. Content analysis strategies were used to identify moral distress stories based on the characteristics of moral distress identified in the literature. A crisis military deployment was defined as a situation in which military personnel are suddenly ordered to duty to support an operation away from their home station and in a potentially dangerous environment. Such deployments are not always to overseas locations and may occur in defense of the homeland, as a result of war, or for peacekeeping or humanitarian missions by the military. Moral distress was defined as a feeling state experienced when a person makes a moral judgment about a situation in which he or she is involved but experiences a barrier to acting on that judgment. When experienced, moral distress has situational, cognitive, action, and feeling dimensions, as well as short- and long-term effects.

From the interview data, the process of developing moral distress as experienced by military nurses and the dimensions of initial military nursing moral distress and reactive military nursing moral distress were identified. A measure of moral distress, the 25-item Military Nursing Moral Distress (MNMD) Scale, was constructed and tested for its reliability and validity. Phase III of the study used a descriptive comparative study design to determine whether there were significant differences in the experience of moral distress between crisis-deployed and non–crisis-deployed military nurses. Data analysis was completed on 959 mailed questionnaires from Army Nurse Corps officers who had been crisis deployed ($n = 529$) and had not been crisis deployed ($n = 430$).

Findings: Military nurses who were crisis deployed experienced significantly higher levels of moral distress than non–crisis-deployed nurses did. The most significant difference between the two groups of nurses was for the effects and consequence of reactive moral distress. There were fewer differences between the two groups for the experience of initial moral distress.

Implications: First, MNMD is one factor that can affect the ability of the military nurse to practice effectively. Second, the presence of MNMD among military nurses, especially those who have been crisis deployed, may potentially affect military nursing readiness, the state of being prepared. Third, interventions to reduce the occurrence, effects, and consequences of MNMD may need to be developed so that military nurses can be ready to participate in crisis military deployments anywhere in the world and perform at peak efficiency for long periods of time under uncertain conditions. Further research is needed to (1) determine the disturbance levels of initial moral distress among military nurses, (2) identify the duration of reactive moral distress among military nurses following crisis deployments, and (3) determine whether nonmilitary nurses experience the same dimensions of moral distress that military nurses do.

The Authority of the Patient

Thus far in this chapter, we have explored the moral authority of a number of agents. The question being addressed is to whom might the nurse appropriately turn as an authority for deciding what morality requires. We have examined the authority of religious tradition, professional groups, physicians, health insurers, and society. There is yet one more possible source of authority that a nurse might consider: the patient. Every patient comes to a nurse with a set of beliefs and moral values. Patients have some sense of what is required of them ethically. They draw on their own religious or philosophical systems. They are influenced by others in society. They are capable of reaching moral conclusions about the kind of health care they desire and about how the nurse, physician, and other healthcare professionals ought to act. Those convictions may sometimes be at odds with the nurse's own judgments. In the following case, we explore the relation of the nurse's own moral convictions to those of the patient.

Case 2-6

The Patient Who Refused to Be Tested for a Genetic Disease

Doris Franklin is a nurse genetic specialist in a busy neurogenetics clinic at a large, urban hospital. Recently, a blood test to detect presence of the gene for neurofibromatosis-type II (NF2) had been developed using the techniques of molecular biology. Mrs. Franklin's clinic follows the families of 23 patients who have been diagnosed with NF2 in the past. Realizing that the children of a person with NF2 have a 50/50 chance of having the NF2 gene and that most persons with NF2 do not experience their first symptoms of the disease until their late teens or early 20s, the clinic has been offering the blood test for presence of the gene to parents with adolescent children and to young adults in affected families.

Several families have declined to have their children tested for the gene. The lack of an adequate treatment for the disease until brain tumors are detected is the most often cited reason for declining to have children tested. Other families and older teenagers have consented to having the test, however. They typically argue that they want to know if they have the gene so that they can undergo frequent MRI testing to identify tumors while the tumors are small and are not causing symptoms of the disease.

Kevin Hughes, a healthy 18-year-old boy, is the son of a 45-year-old woman who was recently diagnosed with NF2 at Mrs. Franklin's clinic. Mrs. Hughes began to experience mild hearing loss several years ago but did not know the reason for this until tumors on the vestibular nerve were detected and the diagnosis of NF2 was made. Three months ago, she underwent surgery to remove the tumors and has been comatose ever since. Kevin's two sisters (ages 13 and 10) were tested for the NF2 gene; the results were that one has it and the other does not. Kevin's father insists that Kevin also have the test, but Kevin has refused. Mr. Hughes asks Mrs. Franklin to help him convince Kevin that he should have the test.

Mrs. Franklin personally thinks that Kevin should have the test—after all, it would be in his best interest to know this information and to consider relevant changes in his bodily systems as he gets older. She also thinks that the earlier tumors are found, the better the results of brain surgery, although this does not eliminate the possibility of future tumor growth and surgery. Legally, however, Kevin is old enough to refuse the blood test. A talented athlete, Kevin plays on the varsity basketball team for his high school. He told

Mrs. Franklin that he would not want to be regarded as "sick" or to have anyone's opinion of him change were he to be found to have the gene. Should Mrs. Franklin rely on her own judgment in deciding whether to pressure him into being tested, or is this a matter in which the patient is morally authoritative?

[Note: NF2 is a rare, autosomal, dominant genetic trait that causes nervous system tumors, most commonly along the eighth cranial nerve. NF2 affects about 1 in 40,000 people, without regard to sex or race. The early symptoms of NF2 include hearing loss, ringing in the ears, and problems with balance. These symptoms usually appear during the late teen years or the early 20s. A few people with the disorder develop symptoms in childhood, and some do not have symptoms until their 40s or 50s. Presently, the only available treatments for NF2 tumors are surgery and radiation therapy including gamma knife treatment. Most persons with NF2 require at least one operation during their lifetime. Surgical removal of the tumors is not without risk because the tumors usually lie on nerves near the brain and spinal cord.]

Commentary

Once again, the initial question in this situation is whether it involves a moral dispute or merely a judgment of benefits and harms. Mrs. Franklin and Kevin Hughes may be disagreeing about who is the better judge of whether Kevin is at risk if he forgoes the blood test for NF2. Surely Mrs. Franklin has had much more experience than Kevin has in caring for patients with NF2 and their family members. Although she probably doesn't know as well as Kevin does how the disease has affected his family, she does have experience with other families struggling with the disease and is guided by professional standards about the management of genetic information.[14]

A more sophisticated assessment of the risks and benefits of knowing if Kevin carries the gene for the disease would, of course, include not only the risk of the disease but also the risks of psychologic stress from waiting for symptoms to appear.[15] It would also involve knowing how well Kevin can handle the waiting. All in all, it is hard to say for sure whether Mrs. Franklin or Kevin would be better at assessing the risks and benefits to Kevin of having the test.

It is not clear, however, that the dispute is merely one of assessing risks and benefits. It may well be that Mrs. Franklin and Kevin are operating according to different ethical principles. Mrs. Franklin's principle seems to be her duty to protect patients from harm and to place the individual patient's care and safety as the first consideration. She also considers that although, traditionally, parents make healthcare decisions for their children, this does not seem to be a firm standard for presymptomatic testing for genetic diseases in adolescents.[16] Kevin's principle is probably not as clearly defined. He may, if pressed, say that his goal is not his ultimate health but rather his overall well-being, including his happiness and other psychologic considerations. He may even, if pressed further, make another claim. He may say that he wants the freedom to live his own life, even if it puts him at risk and even if it turns out that his welfare is not as good as it otherwise might be. The dispute may be over which of two principles—ultimate patient health or patient autonomy—ought to govern Mrs. Franklin's actions.

If that is the case, then the nurse needs to know how to relate her own judgment about the right principle of action to Kevin's judgment.[17] When religious authority was a possible source of norms for nursing conduct, we saw that there was good reason for the nurse who was committed to a particular religious tradition to treat the religious tradition as authoritative. Likewise, in Case 2-5 we saw that arguments could be made concluding that society, as a whole, might be able to articulate moral norms governing nursing conduct. In contrast, the moral authority of professional groups was more complex. We examined arguments that concluded that neither individuals nor professional groups should be viewed as having special expertise in articulating moral norms.

The problem posed by Kevin is more complex. Surely, there is no particular reason to assume that this 18-year-old boy is an expert in picking moral norms. He might be a respected member of the adolescents in his community and provide moral leadership for other adolescents within that community. But nothing in this case suggests that he is a moral authority for the community at large. There seems to be no reason to assume that Kevin is any more of an authority in picking moral norms than Dr. Barnes was in Case 2-2 when he decided to let a premature infant die.

Is Kevin claiming to be an authority for the moral norms to be followed by the nursing profession? Probably not. He is perhaps making a much more simple claim: that in deciding about his own health, within certain limits he ought to be governed by his own values and ethical commitments. Kevin is probably not making the same claim that society seemed to be making through its legislature in the case involving the use of unlicensed medical technicians. He is not claiming that the whole nursing profession should be governed by some moral norms articulated from outside nursing. Rather, he is merely asking for the freedom to have his own care governed by his norms. If Mrs. Franklin ought to yield to Kevin with regard to blood testing, it is not because Kevin has general moral authority. It is because he is the patient and can rightfully claim that his health should be determined on his own terms.

At the same time, the limits of patient authority need to be assessed. What should happen, for example, if the nurse cannot participate in the patient's health care on the patient's terms without violating her own conscience? What do we make of Mrs. Franklin's continuing reservations after Kevin rejects the blood test? It seems unlikely that Mrs. Franklin's objections to Kevin's moral position are so great that she would choose this issue to take a stand on conscience. However, some patients' moral positions might so violate Mrs. Franklin's ethical framework that she ought not to cooperate. What, for example, if Kevin developed symptoms of the disease and said that the moral framework he wanted for his care was one that accepted active mercy killing? At some point, patients' authority must have its limits.

ENDNOTES

1. Brandt, R. B. (1959). *Ethical theory: The problems of normative and critical ethics* (pp. 151–294). Englewood Cliffs, NJ: Prentice Hall; Feldman, F. (1978). *Introductory ethics* (pp. 160–247). Englewood Cliffs, NJ: Prentice Hall; Frankena, W. (1973). *Ethics* (2nd ed., pp. 95–116). Englewood Cliffs, NJ: Prentice Hall; Taylor, P. W. (1975). *Principles of ethics: An introduction* (pp. 175–227). Encino, CA: Dickinson Publishing Company.

2. Kant, I. (1964). *Groundwork of the metaphysic of morals* (J. J. Paton, Trans.). New York: Harper & Row.

3. Ross, W. D. (1939). *The right and the good*. Oxford, UK: Oxford University Press.

4. Summer, W. G. (1906). *Folkways*. Boston: Ginn; Westermark, E. A. (1960). *Ethical relativity*. Patterson, NJ: Littlefield, Adams.

5. Veatch, R. M. (1981). *A theory of medical ethics* (pp. 79–107). New York: Basic Books.

6. American Nurses Association. (2001). *Code of ethics for nurses with interpretive statements* (p. 8). Washington, DC: Author.

7. Bleich, J. D. (1979). The obligation to heal in the Judaic tradition: A comparative analysis. In F. Rosner & J. D. Bleich (Eds.), *Jewish bioethics* (pp. 1–44). New York: Sanhedrin Press.

8. Jensen, A., & Lidell, E. (2009). The influence of conscience in nursing. *Nursing Ethics, 16*(1), 31–42.

9. American Nurses Association. (2001). *Code of ethics for nurses with interpretive statements* (p. 20). Washington, DC: Author.

10. Veatch, R. M. (2009, March 21–27). The sources of professional ethics: Why professions fail. *The Lancet, 373*(9668), 1000–1001.

11. Allen, M. C., Donahue, P. K., & Dusman, A. E. (1993). The limit of viability—Neonatal outcomes of infants born at 22 to 25 weeks gestation. *New England Journal of Medicine, 329*(22), 1597–1601.

12. Ludwig, E. (1967). The Hippocratic oath: Text, translation, and interpretation. In O. Temkin & C. L. Temkin (Eds.), *Ancient medicine: Selected papers of Ludwig Edelstein* (pp. 3–64). Baltimore: The Johns Hopkins Press.

13. American Nurses Association. (2001). *Code of ethics for nurses with interpretive statements* (p. 19). Washington, DC: Author.

14. Scanlon, C., & Fibison, W. (1995). *Managing genetic information: Implications for nursing practice*. Washington, DC: The American Nurses Association.

15. Kolata, G. (1994, September 26). Should children be told if genes predict illness? *New York Times,* pp. A1, A14; Harper, P. S., & Clarke, A. (1990). Should we test children for "adult" genetic diseases? *The Lancet, 335,* 1205–1206.

16. Wertz, D. C., Fanos, J. H., & Reilly, P. R. (1994). Genetic testing for children and adolescents: Who decides? *Journal of the American Medical Association, 272*(11), 875–881.

17. Botkin, J. R. (1995). Genetic counseling: Making room for beneficence. *The Journal of Clinical Ethics, 6*(2), 182–184; Hayry, M., & Takala, T. (2001). Genetic information, rights, and autonomy. *Theoretical Medicine and Bioethics, 22*(5), 403–414.

Chapter 3

Moral Integrity and Moral Distress

Other Cases Involving Integrity and Distress

Key Terms
Ethics environment
Moral integrity
Moral agency
Moral distress
Moral residue

Objectives
1. Define the terms moral agency, moral integrity and moral distress.
2. Analyze the relationship between an institution's ethics environment and the moral agency of nurses
3. Identify strategies for responding to situations that create moral distress in the workplace

As we have seen in Chapters 1 and 2, nurses confront ethical challenges in their professional practice daily. Before turning to Part II to explore the basic principles of ethical decisions in nursing, we need to address a problem particularly important to nurses: *moral integrity* and the related notion of moral distress. Nurses sometimes find themselves in positions in which they feel pressured to act in ways that do not fit with their understanding of what is morally required. Physicians, nurse supervisors, hospital administrators, insurance company managers, or the requirements of the law may demand behaviors that do not conform to the nurse's ethical standards. When this happens the nurse's integrity is challenged, leaving the nurse feeling in moral distress.

The accompanying table defines the types of ethical experiences and situations nurses encounter. Being able to recognize and name these experiences enables nurses to take action to address them. ***Moral agency*** is the capacity to habitually act in an ethical manner. It entails a certain set of ethical competencies as well as moral character and motivation. Among these are

1. **Moral Sensibility:** Ability to recognize the "moral moment" when a moral challenge presents itself.
2. **Moral Responsiveness:** Ability and willingness to respond to the moral challenge.
3. **Moral Reasoning:** Knowledge of and ability to use sound theoretical and practical approaches to "think through" moral challenges; these approaches are used to **inform** as well as to **justify** moral behavior.
4. **Moral Discernment:** The ability to select the best course of action in a particular situation after weighing competing alternatives.
5. **Moral Accountability:** Ability and willingness to accept responsibility for one's moral behavior and to learn from the experience of exercising moral agency.
6. **Moral Character:** Cultivated dispositions, which allow one to act as one believes one ought to act.
7. **Moral Valuing:** Valuing in a conscious and critical way that squares with good moral character and moral integrity.
8. **Transformative Moral Leadership:** Commitment and proven ability to create a culture that facilitates the exercise of moral agency, a culture in which people do the right thing because it is the right thing to do.[1]

Each of us, as a moral agent, is situated in a complex of relations, complicated by differences of all sorts, particularly differences in power. The differences that mark and distinguish these relationships may facilitate the moral agency of an individual, a group of individuals, or an institution, or these differences may constrain moral

Box 3-1

Who or What Exercises Moral Agency?

- an individual
- individuals in relation (the moral agency of collectives)
- individuals in relation within institutions (the moral agency of the healthcare community)
- individuals in relation within institutions within particular societies and cultures

agency. The cases in Chapter 2 illustrated the conflicts that resulted when the moral authority of different individuals or groups differed.

Why Does Moral Agency Matter?

Moral agency matters because it enables nurses to practice ethically and be trustworthy, and it promotes and safeguards the integrity of the nurse. **Integrity** can be defined as that condition of soundness or wholeness, that exists when there is a good fit between who I am (human being, spouse, parent, nurse) and what it is reasonable to expect of me given these identities. I can be a moral scoundrel with integrity if I identify myself as a scoundrel and behave as one would expect a scoundrel to behave. When we place the modifier "moral" in front of "integrity" we imply a positive ethical identity and behavior. There is a good fit between who one is and a particular vision of the good life. I have integrity as a nurse if I reliably discharge my nursing duties and obligations. Article 5 of the American Nurses Association (ANA) *Code of Ethics for Nurses* states that the nurse owes the same duties to self as to others; *including the responsibility to preserve integrity*, to maintain competence and to continue personal and professional growth (emphasis added).[2] Some have questioned whether nurses in modern healthcare settings can be ethical because of their dual responsibilities as employees as well as independent practitioners. We do know that nurses who regularly accept the inability to act ethically sacrifice their integrity and eventually develop *moral residue* that overtime can lead to disengagement.

Moral Distress

When what we think we *would* do differs from what we think we *should* do (i.e., the ethically right decision/course of action) either our moral agency is deficient, *moral distress* is present (we know the right thing to do but institutional or other variables are making it virtually impossible to do so), or some combination of deficient moral agency and moral distress are operative. There is a growing body of nursing literature on the concept of moral distress, a term first coined by philosopher Andrew Jameton, who spent hours listening to the stories of nurses who described the suffering they experienced when they were prevented from doing what they believed they should do and had to participate in activities they believed to be ethically wrong.[3] Additionally, there are now tools to measure moral distress.[4]

The American Association of Critical-Care Nurses (AACN), which has a position statement on and model of moral distress, describes moral distress as a serious problem in nursing.

> It results in significant physical and emotional stress, which contributes to nurses' feelings of loss of integrity and dissatisfaction with their work environment. Studies demonstrate that moral distress is a major contributor to nurses leaving the work setting and profession [See Research Brief 3.1]. It affects relationships with patients and others and can affect the quality, quantity, and cost of nursing care.

... Groups of people who work together in situations that cause distress may experience poor communication, lack of trust, high turnover rates, defensiveness, and lack of collaboration across disciplines.[5]

AACN calls upon employers to implement interdisciplinary strategies to recognize, name, and resolve the experience of moral distress. See their website for a list of practical recommendations (www.aacn.org).

Critical Thinking Questions

Reflect on a situation that commonly recurs in your practice setting that creates moral distress for you and your staff. Then think through the following questions.

1. Is the moral distress truly a situation where individuals know what is right to do but are prevented from doing so because of variables beyond their control? To what degree does deficient individual or corporate moral agency complicate the scenario?

2. Another way to think about the preceding question, is leaving this unit or hospital the only way to resolve the distress? What would need to change to resolve the distress and is such change possible? What would it take to bring about needed change and who might facilitate such changes?

Research Brief 3-1

Source: Ulrich, C. M., O'Donnell, P., Taylor, C., Farrar, A., Danis, M., & Grady, C. (2007). Ethical climate, ethics stress, and the job satisfaction of nurses and social workers in the United States. *Social Science & Medicine, 65,* 1708–1719.

Purpose: To describe how nurses and social workers in the United States view the ethical climate in which they work, including the degree of ethics stress they feel and the adequacy of organizational resources to address their ethical concerns

Method: A self-administered paper-and-pencil survey was mailed to a random sample of 3000 nurses and social workers chosen from the state licensing lists of four states in four census regions of the United States in 2004 (California, Maryland, Massachusetts, and Ohio). A single questionnaire was designed in conjunction with the Center for Survey Research at the University of Virginia and used for both professional groups. The questionnaire addressed the following domains: description of the workplace ethical climate, availability and type of organizational resources to assist with ethical issues, type and frequency of ethical issues encountered, ethics stress, job satisfaction and intent to leave, and sociodemographic and practice characteristics. Job satisfaction and intent to leave were the outcome variables.

Findings: Respondents reported feeling powerless (32.5%) and overwhelmed (34.7%) with ethical issues in the workplace, and frustration (52.8%) and fatigue (40%) when they cannot resolve ethical issues. In multivariate models, a positive ethical climate and job satisfaction protected against respondents' intentions to leave as did perceptions of adequate or extensive institutional support for dealing with ethical issues. Black nurses were 3.21 times more likely than white nurses to want to leave their position.

Implications: These data show the importance of a positive ethical climate and degree of ethics stress on nurses' and social workers' job satisfaction and intentions to leave their positions. Improving job satisfaction among these providers requires sustainable work-related interventions to allay ethics stress, increase ethics resources, and improve the ethical climate. Open dialogue on strategies for increasing respect within the workplace and the value of a positive ethical climate is warranted. Nearly two thirds of the sample reported that there are some ethical issues they can do nothing about, and many reported frustration and fatigue. Those without institutional support for handling ethical issues and stress were more likely to want to leave their jobs. This data suggests that investing in institutional ethics support and resources for employees and establishing a positive ethical climate for practice might lead to more job satisfaction of nurses and social workers, and possibly reduce turnover intentions. This could in turn have a positive effect on patient care and quality outcomes at a reasonably low cost.

Case 3-1
The Nurse Expected to Go Along with the Doctor's Deception

Ginger Berrian, registered nurse (RN) and the nurse manager, walks onto an oncology unit. Thelma Galinsky, a bedside nurse, comes up to her and screams, "I've had it! Dr. Little is telling Mr. Winter's family that all is well and ordering another round of chemo and everyone except Mr. Winter and his family know that he is dying! Besides, he is still a full code." Ms. Berrian knows that Dr. Little has a reputation for not knowing the limitations of medicine and for inappropriately treating those who are actively dying with life-sustaining medical technology. The words *hospice* and *palliative care* just do not seem to be in his lexicon—not to mention "dying". Unfortunately, Dr. Little has a huge practice (and generates *beaucoup* bucks for the hospital) and his patients seem to like his cheerful presence. Earlier efforts to get him to change his practice have been unfruitful. Thelma Galinsky, the nurse who just screamed, has been a passionate patient advocate, but you have noticed recently that her efforts to advocate for patients have been subdued. This time she tells you in no uncertain terms that she does not want to care for any of Dr. Little's patients—which would be a scheduling nightmare since there are so many.

Commentary

This case raises ethical issues at many levels. We might note first that Mr. Winter cannot possibly have given an acceptably informed consent to his chemotherapy if he does not know his true medical status. Thus the treatment Dr. Little is providing (and in which Ms. Galinsky is being asked to cooperate) is probably in violation of informed consent law as well as informed consent ethics. This raises issues we will examine further in Chapters 16 and 17. Moreover, Dr. Little has probably lied to the patient about his prognosis or at least spoken in a deceptive or misleading way. That raises questions about the ethics of truth telling that we will examine further in Chapter 8. It is not clear whether Mr. Winter remains mentally competent. If he is, there may be issues about why Dr. Little and the rest of the healthcare team are dealing with the family rather than the patient.

For now let us focus on the unpleasant dilemma of Ms. Galinsky and her supervisor, Ms. Berrian. They seem to understand that the patient, Mr. Winter, is not being treated in an ethically appropriate manner and that they are the victims of Dr. Little's expectation that they will cooperate in his approach. While that might have been the expectation in an earlier era, it no longer fits with the understanding of the nurse and other members of the healthcare team as professionals with responsibility for their actions. The challenge is trying to figure out an appropriate response.

In some ways, the problem of Ms. Galinsky and Ms. Berrian resembles that of the nurse in Chapter 2 who experienced decisions in which others claim a source of moral authority that leaves the nurse stranded without it. We saw in Case 2-2 and the critical thinking questions following the commentary that nurses have a number of channels to which they might appeal: In that case, a nurse also was challenged by a physician who presumed the authority to pick the moral norms. We considered that, in addition to confronting the physician directly, the nurse could turn to nursing colleagues, a hospital ethics committee or ethics consultation service, family members, or nursing supervisors. In this case, the supervisor, Ms. Berrian, is already aware of the issue and bears some responsibility in assisting to resolve the matter.

One approach, removing Ms. Galinsky from Dr. Little's cases, does not address the underlying issue of the patients who are being treated inappropriately. It merely shifts the burden to other nurse colleagues. Ms. Berrian, the supervisor, may have other resources available, including consultation with the physician colleagues of Dr. Little and the Director of Medicine. This particular case presents another option since it appears that the treatment of the patient may well be illegal as well as unethical. Ms. Galinsky, with the assistance of Ms. Berrian, might need to bring the case to the attention of the legal counsel for the hospital.

Creating and Sustaining Healthy and Ethical Work Environments

We have now seen that many factors in the workplace can compromise integrity and moral agency for nurses. To name but a few: inadequate staffing, lack of administrative support, power imbalances, disrespectful communication, and institutional policy. Nurses with adequate moral agency including strong leadership and management competencies and virtues like courage are taking on their employing institutions and partnering to improve outcomes for all. Resources available to nurses included *ethics environment* assessments, recommendations for creating and sustaining healthy environments, and change theory models.

Ethics Environment Assessments

In an early work, system ethicist, Jack Glaser, highlighted the relationship among what he termed the three realms of ethics: individual, institutional, and societal.[6] Today's attention to organizational ethics recognizes these relationships and is challenging leadership in our organizations to ensure that the ethical behaviors of the institution (e.g., values, decisions, policies) reflect the core mission and values. Experienced nurses can readily describe whether the culture in their work environment promotes or constrains their moral agency. There are now tools that provide data about whether an institution's culture promotes moral agency. One popular assessment tool is McDaniel's "Ethics Environment Questionnaire," which includes criteria like the following:

> Personnel decisions in this organization reflect ethical considerations. Administration provides their employees with ethics guidance when it is needed. When ethics violations occur, this organization has procedures to identify and to deal with them.[7]

Resources for Establishing and Sustaining Healthy Environments

The AACN's commitment *to actively promote the creation of healthy work environments that support and foster excellence in patient care* is a superb example of how a professional organization can use its moral agency to bring about needed change. Citing the mounting evidence that unhealthy work environments contribute to medical errors, ineffective delivery of care, and conflict and stress among health professionals, AACN President Kathleen M. McCauley wrote:

> Negative, demoralizing and unsafe conditions in workplaces cannot be allowed to continue. The creation of healthy work environments is imperative to ensure patient safety, enhance staff recruitment and retention, and maintain an organization's financial viability.
>
> … The public has repeatedly identified nurses as the profession most trusted to act honestly and ethically. Five times since 1999 nurses have topped Gallup's annual survey of honesty and ethics among professions…. The public relies on nurses to bring about bold

change that ensures safe patient care and sets a path toward excellence.[8]

The AACN's standards for establishing and sustaining healthy work environments are:

Skilled communication
Nurses must be as proficient in communication skills as they are in clinical skills.

True Collaboration
Nurses must be relentless in pursuing and fostering true collaboration.

Effective Decision Making
Nurses must be valued and committed partners in making policy, directing and evaluating clinical care, and leading organizational operations.

Appropriate Staffing
Staffing must ensure the effective match between patient needs and nurse competencies.

Meaningful Recognition
Nurses must be recognized and must recognize others for the value each brings to the work of the organization.

Authentic Leadership
Nurse leaders must fully embrace the imperative of a healthy work environment, authentically live it and engage others in its achievement.[9]

In 1982, the American Academy of Nursing's Task Force on Nursing Practice in Hospitals conducted a study of 41 hospitals to identify and describe variables that created an environment that attracted and retained well-qualified nurses who promoted quality patient care through providing excellence in nursing services. These institutions were called Magnet hospitals because they attracted and retained professional nurses who experienced a high degree of professional and personal satisfaction through their practice. These institutions used a decentralized decision-making process, self-governance at the unit level and a respect for and acknowledgment of professional autonomy. In 1990, the American Nurses Credentialing Center developed a formal process to recognize excellence in nursing service and to confer Magnet status. Characteristics of Magnet and non-Magnet hospitals follow. Nurses are more likely to find themselves in a healthy work environment in a Magnet facility.

Change Theory Models

There is some concern that nurses today are "using" the popularity of the concept of moral distress to accept unethical work environments without trying first to change them. In any human organization there are situations that require change in order to promote human flourishing. Many change theorists have offered models to

Box 3-2
Characteristics of Magnet and Non-Magnet Hospitals

Magnet Hospitals
- Self-scheduling
- Autonomous, accountable professional nursing practice
- Healthy, collaborative relationships with physicians
- Adequate numbers of competent, clinically expert peers
- Supportive nurse managers
- Control over practice environment
- Support and provision for education
- Culture that values concern for the patient

Non-Magnet Hospitals
- Centralized decision making
- Practice dominated, and in some instances controlled, by physicians and others
- Higher staff vacancy rates
- Higher staff turnover
- Higher levels of staff burnout and exodus from the bedside

effect desired change. One of the most practical is J. P. Kotter. He has articulated an eight-stage process of creating moral change as follows:

1. **Establishing a Sense of Urgency**
   - Examining the market and competitive realities
   - Identifying and discussing crises, potential crises, or major opportunities

2. **Creating the Guiding Coalition**
   - Putting together a group with enough power to lead the change
   - Getting the group to work together as a team

3. **Developing a Vision and Strategy**
   - Creating a vision to help direct the change effort
   - Developing strategies for achieving that vision

4. **Communicating the Change Vision**
   - Using every vehicle possible to constantly communicate the new vision and strategies
   - Having the guiding coalition role model the behavior expected of employees

5. **Empowering Broad-Based Action**
   - Getting rid of obstacles
   - Changing the systems or structures that undermine the change vision
   - Encouraging risk taking and nontraditional ideas, activities, and actions

6. Generating Short-Term Wins
- Planning for visible improvements in performance, or "wins"
- Creating those wins
- Visibly recognizing and rewarding people who made the wins possible

7. Consolidating Gains and Producing More Change
- Using increased credibility to change all systems, structures, and policies that do not fit together and do not fit the transformation vision
- Hiring, promoting, and developing people who can implement the change vision
- Reinvigorating the process with new projects, themes, and change agents

8. Anchoring New Approaches in the Culture
- Creating better performance through customer and productivity-oriented behavior, more and better leadership, and more effective management
- Articulating the connections between new behaviors and organizational success
- Developing means to ensure leadership development and succession[10]

If nurses use informal or formal processes to decide what needs to change in their practice environments to facilitate their moral agency, the accompanying worksheet can be helpful in bringing about and sustaining the needed change.

Case 3-2
Nurses Caught Between a Rock and a Hard Place

Nurses at Memorial Hospital, a 40-bed rural community hospital, are faced with what seems an impossible dilemma. Their best efforts to advocate for patients are routinely blocked by the hospital's physicians and senior leadership. Two recent examples: When Mr. Rodriguez, a seasoned surgical nurse, requested time to administer an analgesic before a patient's painful wound debridement, he was told by the surgeon that no pain medication was necessary. The patient was clearly in distress while the debridement was performed and so was his nurse. When Mr. Rodriquez reported this experience to his supervisor he was told that the nurse's job is to do what the physician orders. On another occasion, a woman presented to the emergency room with a fractured distal radius. Because a family member with a similar injury had unsatisfactory results (deformity and pain with movement) when treated by the doctor on call that evening, the woman and her husband requested transport to a larger hospital. The doctor on call insisted that it was important to set the fracture as soon as possible and convinced the couple that he could competently perform the procedure. The nurse had reservations about the doctor's competence and wanted to counsel the couple to be persistent in seeking transport to another facility, but knew that her job was on the line if she did. When she reports this to her supervisor she is told that her job is not to advocate for patients but to be a loyal employee.

Repeated efforts by nurses to address these sorts of challenges have resulted in the persistent message that they can accept the status quo or leave. The nursing supervisor is tightly allied with the medical director and CEO. The problem for the nurses is that it is a 2-hour drive over the mountain to the nearest hospital and there are no other employment options.

Commentary

This is a classic example of moral distress. The nurses at Memorial Hospital have been very clear that their primary obligation is to patients and they have repeatedly and unsuccessfully advocated for patients until their jobs were threatened. If they cannot find a champion in a position of authority willing to address their concerns and work with them to create and sustain a positive work environment, they will have two choices: They can either accept the status quo, sacrifice their personal and professional integrity, and endure the type of moral distress that leads to disengagement, or quit their jobs. If they leave this hospital and need to find employment elsewhere, the 4-hour commute will definitely compromise the time they have for their families and similarly constrain their integrity and result in moral distress. Provision 6 of the ANA *Code of Ethics for Nurses* reads, "The nurse participates in establishing, maintaining, and improving healthcare environments and conditions of employments conducive to the provision of quality health care and consistent with the values of the profession through individual and collective action." The interpretive statements for this provision are unequivocal.

Acquiescing and accepting unsafe or inappropriate practices, even if an individual does not participate in the specific practice, is equivalent to condoning unsafe practice. Nurses should not remain employed in facilities that routinely violate patient rights or require nurses to severely and repeatedly compromise standards of practice or personal morality.[11]

Ideally, the nurses working at Memorial Hospital could seek assistance from their State Board of Nursing and State Nurses Association. Collective action, such as collective bargaining or workplace advocacy, may be helpful in creating the desired change. Any agreement reached through such action would ideally be consistent with the profession's standards of practice, the state law regulating practice, and the ANA *Code of Ethics for Nurses*.[12]

Critical Thinking Questions

If you were able to survey your staff or team, how do you think they would collectively assess themselves with the following questions?

1. How would you describe your unit's/team's moral agency?

Zilch . . .   Prepared to address any challenge!
1 ------ 2 ------ 3 ------ 4 ------ 5 ------ 6 ------ 7

2. How would you describe the ethics environment in your practice setting?

   What ethics environment?   Darn near perfect!

   1 ------2 ------3 ------ 4------ 5 ------6 ------7

3. How would you describe the degree of moral distress you and your staff/team typically experience on a daily basis?

   None at all   Off the charts!

   1 ------2 ------3 ------ 4------ 5 ------6 ------7

4. How would you describe the degree to which your team's/staff's moral distress is negatively affecting morale on your unit?

   We have hit bottom!   Our morale is high!

   1 ------2 ------3 ------ 4------ 5 ------6 ------7

Share with your colleagues how this assessment makes you feel and what it indicates about the need for change.

Box 3-3
Types of Ethical Experiences and Situations

When nurses can name the type of ethical concern they are experiencing, they are better able to discuss it with colleagues and supervisors, take steps to address it at an early stage, and receive support and guidance in dealing with it. Identifying an ethical concern can often be a defining moment that allows positive outcomes to emerge from difficult experiences. There are a number of terms that can assist nurses in identifying and reflecting on their ethical experiences and discussing them with others:

Ethical problems involve situations where there are conflicts between one or more values and uncertainty about the correct course of action. Ethical problems involve questions about what is right or good to do at individual, interpersonal, organizational, and even societal levels.

Ethical (or moral) uncertainty occurs when a nurse feels indecision or a lack of clarity, or is unable to even know what the moral problem is, while feeling uneasy or uncomfortable.

Ethical dilemmas or questions arise when there are equally compelling reasons for and against two or more possible courses of action, and where choosing one course of action means that something else is relinquished or let go. True dilemmas are infrequent in health care. More often, there are complex ethical problems with multiple courses of actions from which to choose.

Ethical (or moral) distress arises in situations where nurses know or believe they know the right thing to do, but for various reasons (including fear or circumstances beyond their control) do not or cannot take the right action or prevent a particular harm. When values and commitments are compromised in this way, nurses' identity and **integrity** as moral agents are affected and they feel moral distress.

Ethical (or moral) residue is what nurses experience when they seriously compromise themselves or allow themselves to be compromised. The moral residue that nurses carry forward from these kinds of situations can help them reflect on z they would do differently in similar situations in the future.

Ethical (or moral) disengagement can occur if nurses begin to see the disregard of their ethical commitments as normal. A nurse may then become apathetic or disengage to the point of being unkind, noncompassionate, or even cruel to other healthcare workers and to persons receiving care.

Ethical violations involve actions or failures to act that breach fundamental duties to the persons receiving care or to colleagues and other healthcare providers.

Ethical (or moral) courage is exercised when a nurse stands firm on a point of moral principle or a particular decision about something in the face of overwhelming fear or threat to himself or herself.

Source: Canadian Nurses Association. (2008). *Code of ethics for registered nurses, 2008 centennial edition*. Ottawa, ON: Author. Used with permission.

RESOURCES FOR RESOLVING MORAL DISTRESS

- American Nurses Association *Code of Ethics for Nurses*
- Canadian Nurses Association *Code of Ethics for Registered Nurses*
- International Council of Nurses *Code of Ethics for Nurses*
- American Nurses Association Center for Ethics and Human Rights, Position Statements
- AACN *4 A's to Rise Above Moral Distress Handbook*
- AACN *4 A's to Rise Above Moral Distress Facilitators Toolkit*
- AACN *Standards for Establishing and Sustaining Healthy Work Environments*

ENDNOTES

1. Taylor, C. (2012). Values, ethics and advocacy. In C. Taylor, C. Lillis, P. LeMone, & P. Lynn (Eds.), *Fundamentals of nursing: The art and science of nursing care* (7th ed.). Philadelphia: Lippincott, Williams & Wilkins.
2. American Nurses Association. (2001). *Code of ethics for nurses, with interpretive statements*. Washington, DC: Author; See also Fowler, D. M. (Ed.). (2008). *Guide to the code of ethics for nurses: Interpretation and application*. Washington, DC: American Nurses Association.
3. Corley, M. C. (1995). Moral distress of critical care nurses. *American Journal of Critical Care, 4*(4), 280–285; Hamric, A. B. (2000). Moral distress in everyday ethics. *Nursing Outlook, 48*, 199–201; Jameton, A. (1984). *Nursing practice: The ethical issues*. Englewood Cliffs, NJ: Prentice-Hall; Wilkinson, J. M. (1987–1988). Moral distress in nursing practice: Experience and effect. *Nursing Forum, 23*(1), 16–29.

4. Corley, M. C., Elswick, R. K., Gorman, M., & Clor, T. (2001). Development and evaluation of a moral distress scale. *Journal of Advanced Nursing, 33*(2), 250–256; Corley, M. C., Minick, P., Elswick, R. K., & Jacobs, M. (2005). Nurse moral distress and ethical work environment. *Nursing Ethics, 12*(4), 381–390; Morris, P. E., & Dracup, K. (2008). Time for a tool to measure moral distress. *American Journal of Critical Care, 17*(5), 398–401.

5. *AACN Position Statement on Moral Distress.* Available at: www.aacn.org/WD/Practice/Docs/Moral_Distress.pdf. Accessed April 27, 2010. The AACN's *4 A's to Rise Above Moral Distress.* Available at: www.aacn.org/WD/Practice/Docs/4As_to_Rise_Above_Moral_Distress.pdf. Accessed April 27, 2010.

6. Glaser, J. (1994). *Three realms of ethics.* Kansas City, MO: Sheed & Ward.

7. McDaniel, C. (1997). Development and psychometric properties of the Ethics Environment Questionnaire. *Medical Care, 35*(9), 901–914.

8. McCauley, K. M. (2005). A message from the American Association of Critical-Care Nurses. *American Journal of Critical Care, 14*(3), 186.

9. American Association of Critical-Care Nurses. (2005). *AACN standards for establishing and sustaining healthy work environments.* Available at: http://www.aacn.org/WD/HWE/Docs/HWEStandards.pdf. Accessed April 27, 2010.

10. Kotter, J. P. (1996). *Leading change.* Boston: Harvard Business School Press.

11. American Nurses Association. (ANA). (2001). *Code of ethics for nurses, with interpretive statements* (pp. 20–21). Washington, DC: Author.

12. Ibid.

PART II

Ethical Issues in Nursing

The ability to recognize ethical and other value issues in nursing care situations and to understand proper sources of moral authority is the foundation of the analysis of ethical dilemmas in nursing. When used in conjunction with codes of ethics for nurses, these skills help build a framework for analyzing specific case problems in nursing care. Figure I-1, p. xxvi (Introduction) illustrates this framework as the stages of ethical analysis. For example, when considering specific case problems, intuition often provides perfectly adequate solutions to ethical problems. In fact, many of the ethical decisions a nurse must make during the course of the day are made on the basis of intuitive knowledge.

Many patient care problems are more serious, however. They require more than intuitive knowledge of their ethical dimensions. Our common sense intuition often does not provide clear answers. Sometimes what seems to the nurse to be the ethically obvious course is opposed by a colleague, a physician, an administrator, or a patient. In these situations other aspects of the framework may help the nurse think through the alternatives and the reasons for making various choices.

Beyond specific case decisions are rules or guidelines that, depending on one's view about how rigidly they should be adhered to, provide either guidelines or firm answers to the problem being faced. These rules are specific enough to apply to concrete situations but general enough to be used widely. "Always get informed consent before surgery" is an example. Another is: "It is wrong to kill a patient actively, even for mercy." Many of the provisions in the ANA *Code of Ethics for Nurses* state rules of this nature.

Sometimes rules are stated from the point of view of the person who has a claim rather than that of the person upon whom the claim is made. In these cases, the language of rights often is used. The claim that the patient always has the right to give informed consent before surgery is directly parallel to the rule that the nurse must always obtain the patient's informed consent before surgery. When the language of rights is used in this way, the rights are often thought to be derived from the rules.

At some point it may become necessary to call into question one of the rules—that is, to debate whether the rule is justified or properly formulated. For example, if we really are not sure whether it is always wrong to kill for mercy, we may feel a need to appeal to another aspect of the framework. It is widely accepted in ethics that moral rules reflect the ethical principles—principles such as doing good, avoiding evil, promoting justice, respecting autonomy, telling the truth, keeping promises, and respecting the sanctity of human life. These principles often are given the names, respectively, of beneficence, nonmaleficence, justice, autonomy, veracity, fidelity, and the sacredness of life. According to some ethical theories, additional ethical principles exist—the principle of reparation, for instance, which specifies that one should make amends for previous wrongs done. Other theorists, however, claim that all of ethics can be reduced to an even shorter list of principles—perhaps even just one principle, such as beneficence or utility (a single principle that combines doing good and avoiding harm).[1]

Regardless of the number of principles ascribed to, ethical principles make up an important aspect of the framework for analyzing ethical problems. One might ask if one ethical principle has greater authority than another. To ask which principle ought to be accepted over another principle is to grapple with the very basics of ethical theory. There are two dominant normative theories that apply here. One holds that the question of right and wrong is fundamentally a matter of producing good consequences and avoiding evil consequences. This approach—often called *consequentialism*—is illustrated by the ethical position referred to as *utilitarianism*, the idea that the ethically correct course is the one that produces the greatest good on balance. The alternative is to insist that right and wrong cannot be reduced to producing good consequences. There are many different varieties of this alternative theory; all agree that there are inherent right or wrong characteristics of actions or rules. For example, acts or rules that involve lying, breaking a promise, or distributing resources unfairly are often considered to have wrong-making characteristics. Theories that espouse this view are called *nonconsequentialistic* (or sometimes *formalist* or *deontological*). Consequentialist theories and nonconsequentialist theories, together with their variations, constitute what can be called *normative ethics*.

Finally, one may have to ask the most basic ethical questions when attempting to understand and justify one's patient care decisions. This aspect of the framework, called *metaethics*, deals with the source of ethics and the ways we know and justify ethical positions.

The cases in Part II all raise problems related to one or more general ethical principles. Chapter 4 looks at the two principles directly related to the consequences of ethical actions: the principles of producing good and avoiding evil, or what are sometimes called the principles of *beneficence* and *nonmaleficence*. Chapters 5 through 10 analyze cases involving the principles of justice, autonomy, veracity, fidelity, and the sanctity of human life.

Among the more well-known ethical theorists advocating this single-principle approach are the following Bentham, J. (1967). An introduction to the principles of morals and legislation. In A. I. Melden (Ed.), *Ethical theories: A book of readings* (pp. 376–390). Englewood Cliffs, NJ: Prentice Hall; Mill, J. S. (1967). Utilitarianism. In A. I. Melden (Ed.), *Ethical theories: A book of readings* (pp. 391–434). Englewood Cliffs, NJ: Prentice Hall; and Sidgwick, H. (1874/1966). *The methods of ethics*. New York: Dover Publications. Some contemporary writers in healthcare ethics also use this approach, such as Singer, P. (1975). *Animal liberation: A new ethics for our treatment of animals* . New York: Avon Books; Rachels, J. (1975). Active and passive euthanasia. *New England Journal of Medicine, 292*, 78–80; and Fletcher, J. (1974). *The ethics of genetic control: Ending reproductive roulette*. Garden City, NY: Anchor Books.

Chapter 4

Benefiting the Patient and Others: The Duty to Produce Good and Avoid Harm

Other Cases Involving Beneficence

Key Terms
Avoiding harm
Beneficence
Benefit
Florence Nightingale Pledge
Nonmaleficence
Patient advocate
Patient's well-being
Primum non nocere
Producing good
Role-specific duty
Rule consequentialism

Objectives
1. Define the principle of beneficence.
2. Define the principle of nonmaleficence.
3. Describe the nurse's primary commitment according to the professional code of ethics.
4. Identify potential ethical conflicts with the nurse's duty to benefit and avoid harm to the patient.
5. Identify limits to the nurse's duty to benefit and avoid harm to the patient.

Virtually everyone agrees that **producing good** and **avoiding harm** are relevant to ethics in some way. The ethics of healthcare professionals has given special emphasis to the consequences of actions. The Hippocratic oath says it twice. At one point in the oath, the physician pledges, "I will work for the benefit of the sick according to my ability and judgment; I will keep them from harm and injustice." At a later point in the oath, the physician pledges, "Whatever houses I may visit, I will come for the benefit of the sick."[1]

Nursing ethics has a similar emphasis. The **Florence Nightingale Pledge** includes the promise "I will abstain from whatever is deleterious and mischievous . . . and devote myself to the welfare of those committed to my care."[2] The American Nurses Association (ANA) *Code of Ethics for Nurses* has language that is similar in its moral impact. The explanation of the third provision of the code begins, "The nurse's primary commitment is to the health, well-being, and safety of the patient across the life span and in all settings in which health care needs are addressed."[3]

These code statements sound so benign that they appear uncontroversial, almost platitudinous. Yet, we begin to encounter some problems as we probe more deeply into some of the cases in this volume. Sometimes the duty to **benefit** the patient will come into direct conflict with some other ethical requirement, such as respecting the autonomy of the patient or distributing resources fairly. Conflicts between producing good consequences for the patient and fulfilling the requirements implicit in other ethical principles will be explored in later chapters.

Even when we focus exclusively on the consequences of nursing actions, unexpectedly, difficult problems arise in trying to decide exactly what it means to have a primary commitment to the patient's care and safety. There are also problems in trying to decide whether we ought to protect the patient if, when the impact on others in the society is taken into account, less good is done on balance.

One problem frequently encountered by the nurse is whether the nurse's responsibility is to benefit the patient, taking into account all the ways that he or she might be benefited. That is what the Hippocratic oath seems to ask of physicians. An account of all benefits to the patient can, however, lead into areas where the healthcare professional has little or no competence. It might include producing social, psychologic, economic, and religious benefits for the client—forcing the healthcare professional to overstep the limits of his or her ability. The ANA *Code of Ethics for Nurses* seems to ask this of the nurse as it states that the nurse's primary commitment is to the ***patient's well-being*** and safety as well as health. Here, "well-being" seems to be much broader than health.

A second problem that often occurs in deciding how to produce benefit and avoid harm concerns whether avoiding harm to the patient has a higher priority than benefiting the patient. Some ethical analysts have claimed that the duty of avoiding harm to the patient is more stringent than that of benefiting the patient.[4] That may explain why a nurse would feel more responsible if he or she injures a patient by giving a wrong medication than if he or she simply fails to benefit a patient (say, because the nurse is busy helping other patients). If it is more important to avoid harm than to benefit, the implications can lead to very conservative levels of patient care. The nurse could perfectly fulfill the ethical requirement of avoiding harm to patients by simply never doing anything for them. In the cases that follow, watch to see if the consequences involved stem from the nurse producing benefit or avoiding harm.

A third problem revolves around the two very different approaches to doing good and avoiding harm. Traditionally, utilitarians simply counted the net amount of good and harm for each person affected by a given action and added up the net good for each individual to find the total good produced.[5] Each action was considered separately, with an implicit calculation of harms and benefits produced each time. Within the past generation, many philosophers committed to an ethic of consequences have adopted a different strategy. They have proposed calculations of benefits and harms as a way of evaluating alternative rules of conduct. The rule (or set of rules) that the calculations indicate will produce the best consequences is then adopted. When decisions must be made about individual actions, no direct calculation of consequences is made. One simply applies the rule that previously has been determined to produce the best consequences. For example, the rule "Always get informed consent before surgery" might be adopted because it has better consequences than any alternative rule. (We shall see later that this is not the only reason to adopt it or necessarily even the best reason to do so.) Thus, when it comes to specific cases at the bedside, one simply would apply the rule rather than trying to calculate in the individual case whether consequences are better if consent is obtained. This position, referred to as *rule utilitarianism* or ***rule consequentialism***, has recently gained great favor among sophisticated consequentialists.[6]

Finally, there is a major tension between the consequences of nursing and other health professional ethics and more general ethical theories devoted to the principles of beneficence and nonmaleficence. Most consequentialist theories hold that the goal of ethics is to do as much good as possible, considering the benefits to all people affected by one's actions. Yet, many healthcare ethical theories put limits on the consequences that are to be considered. They limit the nurse or other health professional to consideration of benefits and harms for the patient. Remember, it is the patient's health, well-being, and safety that are the nurse's chief concerns according to the ANA *Code of Ethics for Nurses*.

On what basis are such limits placed, and how is the well-being of the patient traded off against the well-being of various other people about whom the nurse might be concerned? The ANA *Code of Ethics for Nurses*, for example, also talks about the nurse being concerned about the common good and participating in research that is not for the benefit of the patient. It speaks of the nurse's responsibility to the public. Does not the nurse have an obligation to benefit the institution, society at large, the profession, and especially, specific, identified persons who are not his or her patients, but who could be helped greatly by his or her efforts? Finally, are there ever times when the nurse can compromise the patient's care and safety in order to serve the nurse's own interests or those of the nurse's family? These are the issues presented in this chapter's cases.

Benefit to the Patient

Because it is widely accepted that the healthcare professional's duty is to benefit the patient and protect the patient from harm, it is best to begin with a series of cases that help clarify exactly what this means and that consider problems that arise in trying to benefit patients and protect them from harm. Later in the chapter we shall address the more complex issue of conflicts between benefit to the patient and benefit to others—the institution, the society, the profession, identified nonpatients, and oneself or one's family.

In trying to figure out how to benefit one's patients and protect them from harm, the following four separate problems arise:

1. How does the nurse determine what counts as a benefit when there is uncertainty or differences of opinion among the patient, family and/or other members of the professional caregiving team?

2. Should the nurse strive to produce the greatest possible general benefit for the patient, or should the nurse focus only on health benefits?

3. Should the nurse give special weight to protecting the patient from harm, or do benefits and harms get the same weight in calculating net benefits?

4. Should the nurse try to do what is most beneficial in each individual case, or should the nurse think in broader terms—say, by acting on a set of rules that will produce more good on balance than any other set of rules?

Uncertainty About What Is Actually Beneficial to a Patient

There are many examples of nurses being uncertain about whether a plan of care is benefitting a patient, as well as instances when we should be uncertain and may not be. Since nurses are responsible for their actions, they should question interventions they suspect of not being beneficial or of being harmful. History is full of nurses who implemented interventions that were not beneficial. Think only of how we have medicalized childbirth and dying and of our history of inappropriately using pharmacologic and physical restraints in nursing homes to "prevent falls."

Case 4-1

Is the "Ashley Treatment" Beneficial?

When the ethics committee at Seattle Children's Hospital approved the request of 6-year-old Ashley's parents to shorten and sterilize their daughter to improve her quality of life and make it easier to properly care for her, an international debate raged about the ethics of the desired interventions. Suffering from a developmental brain condition called static encephalopathy, Ashley had a normal birth but failed to develop mentally and physically. In a blog that can be accessed at http://ashleytreatment.spaces.live.com/blog, Ashley's parents write:

> "It was obvious to us that we could significantly elevate Ashley's adult quality of life by pursuing the following three goals:
>
> 1- Limiting final height using high-dose estrogen therapy.
> 2- Avoiding menstruation and cramps by removing the uterus (hysterectomy).
> 3- Limiting growth of the breasts by removing the early breast buds."

Disability rights advocates countered with the claim that this treatment might potentially lead to the violation of human rights for the disabled—especially since Ashley was not suffering and the treatment was untested. Dienhart and Gleezen, ethicists from Seattle University, asked the following questions: Are there uses of medical technology that are inconsistent with a dignified life? Could this decision lead us to endorse even more controversial procedures? Could we use other procedures to reduce the size or reproductive capacity of a severely demented adult patient at risk of receiving substandard care because of his or her size or vulnerability? And finally, if the treatment becomes standard medical practice, how will it affect insurance coverage or rates?[7]

Ms. Belanger is a pediatric nurse who has been caring for Jennie, a 6-year-old patient who shares Ashley's diagnosis. Ms. Belanger has worked with Jennie's parents on several of Jennie's hospital admissions and she has their trust. When they read about the "Ashley Treatment" they ask Ms. Belanger her thoughts about whether this would be beneficial for Jennie.

Ms. Belanger was dreading the question because she had followed the news reports about the "Ashley Treatment" carefully and honestly did not know what she thought about its benefits and harms. While she sympathized with all the parents who confronted overwhelming caregiving burdens as small children with permanent disabilities aged, she was not sure that these were good medical interventions that improved the child's quality of life and she knew her pediatric team was conflicted about this. She simultaneously knew that Jennie's parents valued her opinion and recognized that she had the potential to influence decisions they made about her care. Although Ms. Belanger knew that there were questions about family and societal benefits, her primary concern was whether the treatment would be beneficial for Jennie.

Commentary

It is not unusual for nurses to face uncertainty about which of an array of potential interventions are most likely to truly benefit a patient. When patients and their surrogates ask nurses for their opinions about benefits and burdens based on the nurse's expertise and experience, nurses are frequently challenged about how to respond. The standard reply in the past was "You should ask your doctor." One problem with that approach, however, is that the physician is not likely to be able to claim expertise on whether these interventions would produce benefit or harm. The physician probably has no experience with such "treatments" and, even if he or she had used them previously, the physician cannot really claim authority on deciding whether the new life envisioned is better for Jennie.

Today's nurses are willing to share their judgments and, ideally, do so in cases of uncertainty only after careful dialogue and reflection with other respected colleagues. In some cases, patients and families are not asking nurses what they think, and nurses are still responsible to question any interventions they believe to not be beneficial at best and harmful at worst. In this case, Ms. Belanger honestly reported to Jennie's parents that she had not yet made her mind up about the "Ashley Treatment" but asked them if they would like to be part of a dialogue with other members of the team who knew Jennie and were familiar with the "Ashley Treatment." Jennie's parents enthusiastically accepted the invitation, and Ms. Belanger began a review of the literature. She was careful to find articles that represented the diversity of opinions about the "Ashley Treatment." When the parents and team met, medical experts presented the medical facts of Jennie's condition and a local ethicist led an ethical analysis. An article by Clark and Vasta proved persuasive which concluded:

> ... it is clear that the Ashley Treatment does not minimize the risks incurred by this patient, but exposes her to unnecessary risks that have the potential for injury, harm, and even death. This is an experimental, non-lifesaving treatment with serious and even deadly unknowns. Arguably, this treatment not only fails the test of beneficence, but also fails the test of nonmaleficence.[8]

Jennie's parents decided not to request the "Ashley Treatment." Ms. Belanger believed that she was helpful to them in making their decision and with living with its consequences.

Health Benefits vs Overall Benefits

Case 4-2
The Patient Who Did Not Want to Be Clean[1]

Marion Downs, a community health nurse, must decide whether to refer her patient, 72-year-old Sadie Jenkins, to the community fiduciary for consideration of conservatorship and guardianship. Miss Jenkins has no living relatives and lives alone in a one-room apartment furnished with a bed, refrigerator, table, chair, lamp, and small sink. Because she does not have a stove, two meals per day are supplied by her landlord. With the support of her Social Security check and food stamps, she has adequate money for her needs and has lived for more than 10 years in these arrangements. She is in good physical health.

Ms. Downs has made three home visits to Miss Jenkins to check her vital signs and the effects of medication following recent treatment in the health center's hypertension clinic. Although Miss Jenkins has made excellent progress and visits from the community health nurse are no longer warranted, her landlord, the other residents of her small apartment building, and her immediate neighbors are urging the nurse to "do something" about Miss Jenkins. Admittedly, Miss Jenkins's apartment has a strong odor from the long-term accumulation of dust, dirt, and mold. Cockroaches can be seen in the apartment and an unemptied bedpan is often sitting next to Miss Jenkins's bed. (It is "too much trouble" to walk down the hallway to the bathroom shared by Miss Jenkins and two other tenants.) Ms. Downs has noticed that Miss Jenkins has worn the same soiled clothes every time she has been to her apartment. It is also obvious that Miss Jenkins has not bathed nor washed her hair for a long time, and she apparently does not clean her nails and dentures. In addition, her toenails are so long that they have perforated the canvas of her tennis shoes, apparently the only shoes that she likes to wear.

Yet, Miss Jenkins is comfortable with her lifestyle and does not want to change her living arrangements. Although Ms. Downs has offered to contact agencies to help Miss Jenkins—homemaker services, counseling professionals, and senior citizens' groups—Miss Jenkins says that she is comfortable and does not want (or need) help from anyone. Moreover, Ms. Downs is aware that she has several other patients who have severe needs for nursing care in the more traditional sense. She knows that if she interrupts her schedule of visits for the day to help place Miss Jenkins, she will not be able to use her skills as a nurse for these other patients as well as she might. Should Ms. Downs use her role of community health nurse to create an arrangement in which Miss Jenkins would lose the right to control her person, her financial resources, and her environment? Can an individual in the community be forced to be clean and to live in a clean environment? How far should a nurse go in providing "good" for a patient, and who determines what is "good" for Miss Jenkins?

---

[1]Adapted from Cross, L. (1983). The right to be wrong. *American Journal of Nursing, 83*, 1338.

Case 4-3

Is Leaving the Nursing Home Beneficial?

Mrs. Gertrude Swensen is 86 years old. She had been a resident of St. Luke's Village for slightly over a year. St. Luke's Village is a self-contained lifetime care community outside of a large Southern city. She decided to move in after the death of her husband and after surgery for a tumor behind her right ear. In the community, she has her own apartment, receives one hot meal a day in a common dining room, and has access to a full range of services, including a church, a library, a beauty shop, and many recreational activities. She is very happy in the community, which she considers an ideal environment for someone who has difficulty caring for herself. She has no immediate family, so the large one-time fee she paid in exchange for the commitment to lifetime support was no problem for her. Her mind was put at ease knowing there was long-term nursing care available within the community, should she ever need it.

Her medical problems were not severe. She had adult-onset diabetes requiring regular oral medication. Her main problem, however, was that the wound from her ear surgery had never healed properly. Two weeks ago, she began feeling weaker and had difficulty coming down to the dining room for dinner. She was having difficulty walking and often forgot to change the dressing on her surgical wound. Mrs. Lillian Feldman, the nurse from the community's nursing care unit, visited Mrs. Swensen in her apartment and advised her to move to the nursing care unit. There she would have 24-hour nursing care and supervision until she regained her strength.

Mrs. Swensen had gone reluctantly. Now 2 weeks later, she was beginning to feel a little stronger. She still had trouble walking and was forgetful, but she desperately wanted to be back in her own apartment. She wanted to be near her friends and to eat dinner with them instead of in her bedroom in the nursing care unit.

She complained to Mrs. Feldman that she was getting restless and wanted to go back to her apartment. Mrs. Feldman was concerned. She had seen Mrs. Swensen try to walk and nearly fall. She knew she would have difficulty remembering her medication and would not be able to change the dressing on her ear by herself. The relationship that had developed between Mrs. Swensen and Mrs. Feldman was a close one. Mrs. Feldman knew that her patient would do whatever she recommended. Mrs. Feldman was convinced that this patient's health required a further stay in the nursing care unit.

Commentary

Marion Downs and Lillian Feldman are two nurses facing a similar problem. They are committed to the health and welfare of their patients but are having difficulty determining exactly what that means. The ethic of the healthcare professions is traditionally committed to benefiting the patient, but it can be difficult to determine how health benefits relate to other goods that may be on the patients' agendas.

In the case of Sadie Jenkins, the nurse, Ms. Downs, appears to believe that Miss Jenkins would be better off in a nursing care facility. She might be better off medically and she would certainly be better off in other ways. At least she would be in a clean environment. She would get good meals and would have her clothes and personal hygiene attended to.

Still, Miss Jenkins might argue with Ms. Downs about whether, taking everything into account, she would be better off. Miss Jenkins might concede that medically she would be better off, but that does not appear to be Miss Jenkins's chief concern. She appears to prefer her familiar home environment and the control she exercises there, even if it is a less-than-ideal living situation.

Moreover, Ms. Downs is aware that other patients need her services, services that only she, as a skilled nurse, can provide. The problem is whether Ms. Downs should take as her responsibility the total well-being of the patient, including such tasks as house cleaning, grooming, and maintenance of clothing, which are not traditionally nursing responsibilities, or whether she should remain committed to nursing skills in the narrower sense.

The ANA *Code of Ethics for Nurses* commits her to the health, well-being, and safety of her patients. Does that limit her to traditional nursing care and medical safety? If so, she would have to justify institutionalizing Miss Jenkins on narrowly conceived health grounds. Moreover, she would have to give special attention to the health needs of her other patients rather than the nonhealth needs of Miss Jenkins.

On the other hand, if the ethical mandate of nurses is to benefit the client (without restriction to health benefits), Miss Jenkins may get very different treatment. Her house cleaning, grooming, and clothing needs could legitimately be included in the nurse's agenda. In addition, Miss Jenkins's psychologic well-being would also need to get full consideration, because Miss Jenkins does not appear to believe that she will be better off, on balance, if she moves to a nursing care facility.

A similar problem faces Mrs. Feldman. If the medical and health needs of Mrs. Swensen are the nurse's first consideration (i.e., if that is what commitment to her health, well-being, and safety means), then surely Mrs. Feldman should recommend that she stay longer in the community's nursing care unit. On the other hand, if Mrs. Swensen's total well-being is Mrs. Feldman's objective, then her care and safety might have to be compromised.

When Mrs. Feldman takes on the role of advisor to Mrs. Swensen, an interesting problem arises. If Mrs. Feldman makes her judgment focusing only on Mrs. Swensen's medical needs, health, and safety, then it would appear that health concerns would be a strong consideration. But no rational person would make such choices solely on the basis of what maximizes his or her health. People have their general well-being in mind, including many considerations that could lead to decisions that are risky to health.

If Mrs. Feldman tries to take into account not only Mrs. Swensen's health but also the other dimensions of her well-being (as Ms. Downs appeared to do), another problem arises. As a nurse, Mrs. Feldman has no particular skill in making decisions that promote the well-being of patients outside the health sphere. In fact, in comparing the health and nonhealth dimensions of the choice, she might reveal an overcommitment to the health aspect. She has, after all, committed herself to a health profession.

Thus, if by the principle of doing good (beneficence) nurses limit their attention to the health aspects of their patients' well-being, they are omitting what may be the most important concerns of their patients. If, on the other hand, they expand their horizons to attempt to promote the overall well-being of their patients, they venture into areas about which they have no special skill, they dilute their energies so that they spend relatively less time doing those things for which they are specially educated, and they run the risk of overlooking the unique ways in which their clients assess their own overall well-being.

One thing should be clear from these cases. Striving to maximize the health or medical well-being of clients cannot be the same thing as striving to maximize their overall well-being. Which agenda should Ms. Downs and Mrs. Feldman adopt?

Critical Thinking Questions

1. Who defines the well-being of the individual patient?
2. Who defines the well-being of patient populations (such as the elderly)?
3. To what extent should the nurse's judgment of patient well-being influence care for individual patients as well as for patient populations? Support your answer with sound reasoning using ethical principles and the ANA *Code of Ethics for Nurses*.

Research Brief 4-1

Source: Chafey, K., Rhea, M., Shannon, A. M., & Spencer, S. (1998). Characterizations of advocacy by practicing nurses. *Journal of Professional Nursing, 14*(1), 43–52.

Purpose: The purpose of this study was to describe how nurses define and characterize patient advocacy. Specifically, it asked nurses whether and how they exercised the advocacy role and what they believed to be the conditions, events, and values that promote or frustrate the practice of advocacy.

Method: The study employed a qualitative descriptive design to explore the characterizations of client advocacy by practicing nurses. A standardized, open-ended interview guide was used. At the conclusion of taped interviews, demographic information was collected. The study participants were 17 nurses recruited from 3 communities that varied in size and scope of healthcare delivery services. The taped interviews were transcribed and analyzed to capture the essence of the responses. Inductive analysis was used to identify themes and categories from the data. Coding of the data continued until three themes and three categories related to advocacy emerged.

Findings: Advocacy was defined by the participants as: (1) coordinating patient care within the system; (2) intervening with the system on the patient's behalf; (3) knowing the patient (i.e., being a listener, a confidante); and (4) empowering the patient (i.e., making sure the patient is informed enough to get the care he or she needs). Characteristics that influenced the nurse to advocate were the nurse's self-confidence and strength of personal conviction; recognizing that a patient was being ignored by the physician (i.e., had unanswered questions); and economic reasons that affected the patient's access to health care. Characteristics that influenced the nurse not to advocate for a patient were lack of workplace support; threats to job security; intimidation by the physician; violent behavior (yelling, throwing things) on the part of the physician; and a lack of nurse readiness to be an advocate (i.e., lack of experience, knowledge, dedication, self-confidence).

Implications: Advocacy is best practiced when the nurse has the knowledge, experience, and self-confidence to support her advocacy efforts and when a patient is unable to obtain satisfaction of his or her healthcare needs. Nurses need educational experiences to develop the necessary skills and knowledge to be effective advocates and to recognize when the healthcare needs of patients are not being met. Advocacy for the patient is a critical dimension of nursing practice that is changing rapidly and that may be diverging from the models of nurse advocacy in the professional literature and as currently taught in undergraduate nursing curricula.

Benefiting vs Avoiding Harm

Case 4-4

When "Doing Good" May Harm the Patient

The nurses in a critical care unit had been under a great deal of stress from very ill patients, a high census, and frequent staff illnesses during a 2-week period. On one particular evening, two nurses recognized that they were developing the symptoms of an upper respiratory infection that had been affecting other members of the staff. Because they had three post-op patients needing one-on-one care and were receiving another admission from the emergency room, the nurses solicited medication from the house staff in order to suppress their symptoms and "keep going." Although they were able to remain working on the unit and not contribute to an already critical staffing situation, they recognized that they might be causing harm by communicating their illnesses to already vulnerable patients and by risking making mistakes while under the influence of medications (antihistamines).

The two nurses contemplated the alternatives. They were convinced that the additional risk to the patients was quite small, and they believed that the patients were in real need of the one-on-one care that could only be provided if they remained on duty. They concluded that, on balance, the good they could do exceeded the risk of harm, but they wondered: Is there a special obligation for health professionals to avoid harm?

Commentary

Although this seems to be a very simple, routine problem for the two nurses, the ethical question the case raises is a fascinating one. In thinking about the ethics of nursing based on benefits and harms to patients, sometimes the formula used is derived from the Hippocratic Oath. The health professional's duty is to benefit the patient and protect the patient from harm. Under this formulation, the benefits and harms are on a par.

One standard way of approaching healthcare decisions is to anticipate the expected benefits and the expected harms of alternative courses (taking into account the probabilities in each case).[9] In this situation, the nurses would reflect on the good they could do if they cared for patients and on the harm that they could cause if they transmitted an infection or made mistakes because of the medication they had taken. They would also reflect on the benefits the patients would forgo if they were to go home sick. If benefits and harms are on a par, the nurses would simply compare the net benefits (the benefits minus the harms) of the alternatives. As long as the benefits from their nursing care exceeded the projected harms, they would be morally justified in covering up their illnesses in order to serve their patients.

There is an alternative way for health professionals to compare benefits and harms, however. It is expressed in the slogan *primum non nocere*, "first of all do no harm."[10] Many people believe that it is contained in the Hippocratic oath, but it is not. In fact, it is nowhere to be found in any Hippocratic writings or in any ancient writings on medical ethics. It appears to have emerged around the middle of the 19th century.[11]

The meaning of primum non nocere is as obscure as its origin. It may be just a careless way of saying that health professionals should maximize net benefits for their patients, but it may also have a very different meaning.

Some people hold that it is ethically worse to hurt people than to fail to help them.[12] They hold, for example, that it would be worse to take food away from a child so that he starves than it would be to fail to provide food for a child who was starving. In the first case, the one taking the food away is actually harming, whereas in the second case, he or she is only failing to help.

Some people maintain that health professionals have a special duty to avoid harming that is more stringent than the duty to help. They interpret "primum" in the slogan primum non nocere to mean exactly this. Not harming is a duty that is first in order of priority. To give a medical example: In deciding whether to perform a difficult, experimental operation that could cure the patient or injure him or her severely, they would feel a special obligation to at least avoid doing more harm to the patient. Only after these health professionals had assured themselves that they would not hurt the patient would they believe it was ethical to try to help.

The two nurses who are convinced that they will do more good than harm in hiding their illnesses so that they can provide intensive nursing care for their patients will decide differently what they ought to do depending on whether the duty to avoid harming is more stringent than the duty to help. If their duty is to maximize the expected net benefits for their patients and they are convinced that staying on the job will do more good than harm, then they are justified in staying. In fact, they have a duty to stay. If, on the other hand, they feel that avoiding harm is a duty with a special priority, they might feel obligated to avoid the risk of injuring the patients or giving them an additional medical problem, even if the benefits they anticipate from their continued nursing care exceed the amount of harm they think they would do.

Act vs Rule Consequentialism

A third complication in the ethics of doing what will benefit the patient arises when there are general rules in place covering nursing practices. Often, those rules can be justified on the grounds that they spell out practices that generally will benefit patients. As long as it appears that the rule will, in fact, produce behavior that will benefit the patient in the specific instance, no problem arises. What should happen, however, when a nurse believes that a particular patient presents an exception to the rule? If the moral mandate of the nurse is to act always so as to benefit the patient, then it would appear that the rule should be violated whenever violating the rule will do more good than following it. On the other hand, rules may serve important moral purposes. The next case poses the question of when rules governing nursing care ought to be violated.

Case 4-5

Do Patients Always Have to Be Turned?[2]

Bessie Watkins was a 5 ft 10 in., 70-year-old, white-haired, retired school teacher who was admitted to the hospice care unit of a small community hospital. She was diagnosed as having metastatic cancer that had spread from her left breast to her spinal column and ribs. She was a single woman and had been living in her own home with her only sister. She was admitted to the hospital because she had become too weak to walk and could barely feed herself. Upon the advice of her personal physician, she had decided not to have chemotherapy. Her admission orders noted that she was in the terminal stages of cancer and that she was to be kept comfortable with medication (narcotic) per continuous IV infusion.

---

[2]Case supplied by Marie E. Ridder, PhD, RN. Used with permission.

Miss Watkins had many friends on the unit. Staff and visitors delighted in her bright wit, charm, sparkling eyes, and stories. But as the cancer spread throughout her body, she would cry and beg the staff not to move her by turning her. Because Miss Watkins was tall and thin, her bony prominences became more pronounced as she became sicker. A special mattress was ordered to help prevent breakdown of her skin, but the staff still needed to turn her several times a day to prevent bedsores and to change the bed linens. When they did, Miss Watkins cried out from the pain so much that the staff wondered if they were really helping this patient by their nursing interventions.

Finally, the staff met to decide what they should do. Mrs. Twomey, the head nurse for 4 years, insisted that Miss Watkins be turned at least every 2 to 3 hours for linen changes and for observation of her skin. After all, she pointed out, that was routine and minimal nursing care for all bed-ridden patients, and this was the standard of the unit. Any skin breakdown and its necessary treatment would be a very serious problem for Miss Watkins in her already severely compromised condition. Mrs. Hanks, a nurse's aide on the unit for almost 15 years and a long-time acquaintance of Miss Watkins, said that she could not stand to see this patient cry every time she was turned. She said that she would prefer that Miss Watkins's sedation be increased to reduce her pain and facilitate linen changes. Miss Benson, a recent graduate, voiced her opinion that the patient should have some say regarding her care. After all, she had terminal cancer, and not turning her would hardly make a difference in the overall outcome of her illness. Mrs. Culver, the evening nurse, thought that her physician ought to be the one to decide how often Miss Watkins should be turned. Then the nurses would not have to make a decision and could just follow his orders. The rest of the nurses strongly objected to this suggestion. Turning a patient, changing linen, and observing for skin breakdown are nursing measures, they argued, and they should decide together the appropriate nursing interventions for this patient. Could everyone be comfortable not turning Miss Watkins unless it was absolutely necessary? How should they decide?

Commentary

Mrs. Hanks, the nurse's aide on the unit, is apparently convinced that turning Miss Watkins is doing more harm than good. To her, turning a patient is for the purpose of changing linen. She believes that the rule of turning the patient for linen changes should be followed but also that the amount of harm to the patient should be reduced by sedating her. If Mrs. Twomey's duty as a nurse is to benefit her patient (and especially if she should protect her patient from harm), Mrs. Hanks reasons that the nurse should follow the rules and produce good, but avoid harm through some alternative means—in this case, sedation.

Mrs. Twomey agrees that the patient should be turned, but her reasons for following the rule are different. In some cases, nurses may be more likely to do good by following the rule than by using their own judgment about when not to follow them. Many medicomoral choices are complex. They often are made under emotional circumstances and without the benefit of full information. In some cases, if people are free to use their judgment to over-turn existing rules, they will make mistakes. They may even make enough mistakes that, on balance, patients would be better off if the rule were always followed.

Consider the rule that informed consent should always be obtained before surgery. If surgeons were permitted to waive the rule whenever they thought patients would be better off without the consent process, they might waive it so often that more harm than good would result. That, after all, is the same principle that is used at traffic lights. We might have a policy of waiting at red lights if traffic is coming and proceeding on if the coast is clear. If drivers were infallible that would be a better policy, but in a world of fallible human beings we are probably better off if we always follow the rule.

Whether this reasoning would apply in the case of turning patients is hard to tell. Because turning patients who are suffering is a potentially unpleasant task, nurses might underestimate the harms of not turning the patient. Of course, there might be checks against such miscalculations. Some rules, how-ever, can be defended as appropriate even in cases where they appear to do greater harm than breaking them would. Mrs. Twomey may be in agreement with this reasoning.

Would the nursing staff be willing to substitute a new rule, one that had exceptions built into it? For instance, would they accept a rule that states that patients always should be turned except when the nurse believes the patient would be better off not being turned? If they accepted this (and if such a rule gained general acceptance), then a new rule would be created. If, however, the nurses feared that the modified rule would permit too many mistakes, then it would seem to follow that an exception should not be made.

A second defense of rule following is somewhat different. Mrs. Twomey may be what philosophers call a *rule utilitarian*. Such persons hold that the goal of moral conduct is to produce good, but that this criterion should be used only to choose a set of rules by which people should interact.[13] They would choose the rule that produces more good than any other rule and, in the individual case, simply follow that rule. That might mean that in indi-vidual actions the greatest good would not result, but over the course of time more good would come from following that rule than from following any other rule. Of course, if there seemed to be a group of cases in which excep-tion to the rule would always produce greater good, then the exception could be incorporated into the rule. "Never go through a red light except to turn right" is a relatively simple, easy-to-apply exception that could be incorpo-rated into the rule about traffic lights. However, rule utilitarians would insist that the rule be followed even when it looks like breaking it might do more good. Could one of the nurses propose a rule that contains such an easily applied exception?

Miss Benson seems to be suggesting another kind of exception. She might have in mind, "Always turn patients except when they protest." Mrs. Culver, on the other hand, seems to be proposing the alternative, "Always turn the patient except when the physician decides against it." It is conceivable that either of these variants could be defended on the grounds of being a rule that would do more good than any other rule. Honoring patients' wishes might increase the amount of good done (but it might not). Giving physicians decisive authority might work, but that assumes that physicians know more than nurses about the benefits and harms of turning (an unlikely assumption).

In fact, Miss Benson may have another basis for her proposed exception. She might believe that even though turning a patient does good, patients have a right to refuse such benefits. If that is her reasoning, then she is not basing her proposal on benefits and harms, but on rights grounded in autonomy, a principle taken up in Chapter 7.

When exploring alternative rules with and without exceptions, see if they would produce acceptable outcomes in other cases in which patients or their agents might oppose turning: after surgery, following childbirth, when the patient is comatose, and so forth.

Critical Thinking Questions

Nurses follow a number of rules in providing patient care.

1. List seven "clinical rules" that nurses typically follow in providing patient care.
2. List seven "ethical rules" that nurses often follow in providing patient care.
3. What makes some rules "ethical" and other rules "clinical"?

Benefit to the Institution

Thus far, the cases in this chapter deal with producing benefits when the good to be done is strictly for the patient. The issues presented have been whether to limit the horizon to health benefits or to take into account the total well-being of the patient; whether avoiding harm (nonmaleficence) takes precedence over benefiting (beneficence); and whether individual case decisions or operating rules should inform assessments of benefit and harm. In real-life nursing practice, the focus often cannot remain exclusively on the benefits and harms to the individual patient. Whereas the ethics of the health professions often demands that calculations of benefit and harm relate only to the patient, many other ethical systems that focus on consequences impose no such limits. Classical utilitarianism holds that actions (or rules) are assessed on the basis of their overall benefits and harms without any limit to who receives them. One possible conflict is between the well-being of the patient and the well-being of the institution. In the following case, the nurse is required to determine whether the welfare of the institution can ever justify an action that is not in the interest of the patient.

Case 4-6
Cost Cutting for the Indigent Patient

Cora Martin was a staff nurse at a small, church-supported pediatric rehabilitation hospital in a suburban community. One day, Mrs. Martin and the rest of the staff were informed that they would no longer be able to use the disposable, plastic-backed pads commonly used as "linensavers," as necessary for patients on Medicaid support. Each Medicaid patient would receive six pads per day and no more. Patients with private health insurance coverage could, of course, be charged for as many pads as were needed for their care. The staff was instructed to count the number of pads used for each patient and to submit the appropriate charges for those patients with private healthcare insurance.

The reason for the new policy related to the limitation of Medicaid funding for long-term care and to the need for all personnel to be aware of costs. The rehabilitation hospital had suffered serious financial deficits during the past 2 years. It was felt that eliminating unnecessary services and products would be the best way to bring finances into line without any real risks to patients.

Mrs. Martin wondered how the staff could adequately care for some of the Medicaid-supported patients in the home without free use of disposable pads. The pads were indispensable for the care of patients who suffered from frequent urinary and/or bowel incontinence, and for those who drooled onto their pillows. The use of the pads protected the linen and prevented frequent linen changes. Changing linen involved staff time and effort to move and position the patient in the bed. Frequent and fortuitous placement of the pads usually prevented linen changes and enabled the staff to keep patients clean and dry with minimal effort. For patients with private healthcare insurance, the new policy was not a problem. For the Medicaid patients, however, the new policy was a considerable burden. How could Mrs. Martin and the rest of the staff be expected to fulfill this policy of the institution without violating their commitment to nondiscriminatory care and the protection of the well-being of all patients? Should they, perhaps, bill the use of extra pads for the Medicaid patients to the patients with private insurance coverage?

Commentary

Cora Martin was asked by hospital management to engage in actions motivated primarily by concern for the well-being of the institution, not the welfare of the patient. It is not likely that Mrs. Martin's Medicaid patients would benefit from the new policy limiting access to disposable pads. The only way they would benefit would be if the money saved were used for something that would benefit all patients in the rehabilitation hospital.

The more likely explanation is that the institution will benefit from the new policy, but the patients will not. In addition, if the nurses' duty is to serve the health, well-being, and safety of their patients, fostering the new policy by carrying out these practices can hardly be on the nurses' agendas. Still, many healthcare institutions are in serious financial jeopardy today, and the high cost of providing care is related to the financial status of these institutions. If cost-saving measures and measures to increase revenues are not implemented, some hospitals will fail. If this happens, patients will be shifted to other hospitals, and some nurses will lose their jobs. One solution would be to modify the duty of the nurse-clinician. The ANA *Code of Ethics for Nurses*, for example, says,

> Individuals are interdependent members of the community. The nurse recognizes that there are situations in which the right to individual self-determination may be outweighed or limited by the rights, health and welfare of others, particularly in relation to public health considerations.[14]

Unfortunately, the code does not give any examples of where public health considerations may override individual rights to self-determination.

The financial crises hospitals are facing, however, are hardly akin to public health considerations such as exposure to toxic chemicals or violence. Changing the duty of the nurse so that he or she becomes a cost-containment agent for the hospital has radical implications. Nurses could be asked to eliminate staff education and health teaching or to delegate patient care to nonprofessional staff. In doing so, they would become the institution's agents rather than those of the patient. Some have made a good case for this, arguing that clinicians may be the ones who know exactly where cuts could be made or extra services could be billed while doing minimal harm to patients.

On the other hand, asking nurses to take on the institution's perspective amounts to a significant change in their traditional role. It means asking them to abandon the patient, at least at the margins, and to engage in a style of care that cannot be justified in the name of individual patient welfare. Recently, nurses have joined physicians in protesting this trend in the U.S. healthcare system.[15]

One possibility is that both nurses and administrators acknowledge that there are two separate moral roles involved. The administrator necessarily has to promote the more social perspective of the institution, whereas the nurse could be asked to remain in the role of **patient advocate**. This would mean serving the interests of the particular patient or at least doing what is possible to make sure that his or her rights are protected, even in cases when doing so is not promoting the welfare of the institution.

If the nurse is to remain an advocate for the patient, then Cora Martin would argue for the use of disposable pads as needed to benefit all her patients. She might, however, recognize that she ought not to win all these types of arguments. If she can show that it is in the institution's interest (as well as in the patient's) to use disposable pads, as needed, then she might hope that the problem can be resolved. If, however, the administrators are correct in believing they can serve institutional interests by reducing the use of the pads, then the administrator and the nurse may end up in different moral roles. The administrator might have to promote the welfare of the institution while the nurse remained an advocate for the patient. If that is the case, then they ought to disagree. The nurse ought, sometimes, to lose the argument.

Cora Martin and the nursing staff are also faced with the possibility of cheating an insurance company. As such, the ethical choice they must make may involve questions of honesty as well as the conflict between the patient and the institution. Mrs. Martin may feel that billing the Medicaid patients' use of extra pads to the patients with private healthcare coverage is immorally dishonest or even illegal. If she believes that she has a duty to avoid being part of such dishonesty or that she has a duty to be faithful to health insurance policies, she may feel an obligation to speak out against the practice of billing other patients for the pads—not only because it is not in her patients' interests, but also because the action would involve dishonesty or breaking faith. These latter questions will be addressed in the cases in Chapters 8 and 9. In any case, the nurses in Case 4-6 have confronted the potential conflict between the welfare of their institutions and the well-being of their patients. They will have to choose whether they will modify their roles so that they take into account the institution's agenda or whether they wish to remain advocates for their patients, recognizing that sometimes they will not be able to get everything they desire or need.

Benefit to Society

Similar problems arise when the conflict is between the patient's well-being and the well-being of society as a whole. Often a procedure's net benefits to a patient are clear, yet when the decision is viewed from the societal perspective, the benefits are not as great as those that would accrue from using resources in some other way. The tension often arises when cost containment is the issue. It also arises in research settings, where what is best for society may not be what is best for the individual patient.

Case 4-7

When Providing Benefit Might Be Costly

Samuel Tatum is a 6-year-old boy who has acute leukemia and has had several relapses while on chemotherapy. The possibility of undergoing a bone marrow transplant to improve his condition has been suggested. This procedure is the only treatment that offers him a reasonable hope of survival at this point. Although Samuel receives Medicaid assistance, the bone marrow transplant is a costly procedure that would involve the family's travel to a distant medical center and weeks of treatment. It is not an experimental treatment, but it is not expected to offer a chance of total cure for Samuel's disease. The estimated cost of treatment would represent a considerable portion of the annual Medicaid budget allotted for Samuel's entire state.

Samuel's family asks his primary nurse, Mrs. Compton, what she thinks they should do. What should she tell them? Should the nurse make a judgment about how much "doing good" should cost or what expense to others is acceptable?

Commentary

One might approach this case first by asking whether more good can be done by spending the funds on Samuel even though they represent a considerable portion of the state budget. If it should turn out that spending the state's resources this way does more good than any other use of them would, then there would be a convergence of the nurse's clinical commitment to be an advocate for the patient and the broader perspective of trying to maximize the good done overall with society's resources.

If that is the case, there may remain a conflict over whether it is fair for one citizen, even a desperately ill citizen, to command such a disproportionate share. If resources are distributed on the basis of need, he may have a claim, but if everyone is entitled to a more nearly equal share, he is surely getting more than his allowance. This problem—the problem of what is a fair allocation—is the subject matter for the cases in Chapter 5. The problem to be addressed at this point—the potential conflict between benefiting the patient and maximizing the benefit to society—disappears if it turns out that benefiting this patient also produces greater benefit in total than could be produced by other uses of society's resources.

The case becomes more difficult if Mrs. Compton concludes that giving Samuel the bone marrow transplant does not result in the greatest possible good the resources can produce. A large portion of the state's budget is a great deal to go to one patient. It seems quite likely that the good that could be done if those funds were spent for larger numbers of patients would be greater than the possible good done for Samuel, even if one admits that Samuel has great potential for benefiting from treatment. Spending the resources on immunizations, for example, might save many lives.

It is interesting to ask whether the fact that Mrs. Compton is Samuel's primary nurse is crucial to what her moral role ought to be in this case. Would Mrs. Compton's opinion be the same if she were administrator of the state's Medicaid program? Clearly, someone in the system must take the system's point of view. Someone must ask what is the morally appropriate way to spend state funds. Some people would say that the appropriate way to spend the funds is in the way that will produce the greatest overall benefit. Others would take more directly into account the question of what is the fair or equitable way to spend the resources, given the various needs of potential recipients. In either case, if Mrs. Compton were the administrator taking the system's point of view, she would give no special priority to Samuel's claim.

Mrs. Compton is not the Medicaid administrator, however; she is Samuel's primary nurse. We saw in the commentary on Case 4-6 that, when faced with the problem of scarce resources, the primary nurse might still take the broader perspective. She might ask herself the same kinds of questions the administrator would ask: Which use of the resources would produce the greatest benefit overall? What is the fairest way of allocating the resources? On the other hand, clinicians might be viewed as having a primary responsibility to be advocates for their patients. They might take on a special ***role-specific duty***, that of pressing their patient's case in the strongest possible manner. According to the ANA *Code of Ethics for Nurses*, "As an advocate for the patient, the nurse must be alert to and take appropriate action regarding . . . any action on the part of others that places the rights or best interests of the patient in jeopardy."[16] If they do this, clinicians should recognize that they will sometimes lose the battle—they ought to, in fact, in cases where their patient's claim is not a strong one. Nevertheless, they could take on the role of patient advocate for their patients.

This raises the question of why Samuel's family asks Mrs. Compton for advice. Are they asking her because they think of her as an advocate for Samuel? If so, Mrs. Compton is in a position not unlike the parents. Presumably, the parents should not be forced to deal with broader social issues such as whether Samuel should surrender his claim because someone else could benefit more from the resources. The parents should stand with their child, fighting for his interests and leaving it to someone else to set limits.

If Mrs. Compton, like the parents, is an advocate for Samuel, then the question she is asked is relatively straightforward. Mrs. Compton and the parents might be asking whether Samuel would be better off with the treatment than without it. That is a reasonable question for advocates to address. The question requires balancing the subjective considerations of Samuel's overall well-being, the burdens of the transplant, and the likelihood of success. Mrs. Compton might have a unique perspective that would assist the parents in answering this question.

Much more problematic is whether Mrs. Compton ought to be asked by the parents whether they should sacrifice Samuel's well-being for the good of society. Neither the parents nor Mrs. Compton (if she is an advocate for the patient) is in a good position to deal with that issue. They are in a fundamentally different position from the administrator whose task it is to make decisions about such social issues.

Benefit to Identified Nonclients

It might be argued that clinicians have a special duty to patients that, for them, takes precedence over consideration of the welfare of society as a whole because specific patients (such as Samuel in Case 4-7) are given moral priority over unidentified statistical persons who might benefit from alternative uses of resources. In fact, even bureaucrats and administrators might feel this pull toward "identifiable lives." They might, for example, have given Samuel a greater proportion of the state's Medicaid funds than considerations of overall benefit would justify simply because he was a concrete patient. The fact that he was a critically ill youngster who could generate public sympathy might lead them to give him even greater consideration.

The problem would be different if, in addition to Samuel, the administrator had to consider another identifiable person who needed state Medicaid funds.

If that were the administrator's dilemma, the dimension of whether the life was identified would cease to be a consideration. The administrator would have to balance the claims of the two identifiable persons in some fashion. Does a clinician have to do a similar balancing act? Does the nurse in the clinical role have the responsibility of comparing her own patient's needs with those of another patient who is not under her care? That is the issue addressed in the next two cases.

Case 4-8
When Benefit to the Client Is Constrained

Ginny Wilson, a community health nurse in a large urban area, has recently located Mrs. Burns, a tuberculosis patient who the health clinic had been following for many years. Mrs. Burns had moved several times during the past few years and had not had her yearly chest X-ray and sputum culture for quite some time. When Miss Wilson located Mrs. Burns, she encouraged her to attend the chest clinic at the local health hospital. Mrs. Burns agreed to an appointment despite her seeming reluctance to discuss her past health problems and her current health status.

As Miss Wilson left the row-house apartment building where Mrs. Burns lived, she noticed two small boys playing on the steps near the front door. The oldest child, about 4 to 5 years of age, was eating a raw potato. The younger child, about 2 years of age and wearing a very filthy and wet diaper, was crying and begging a bite of the potato from his brother. He held up a bandaged and swollen hand to wipe the tears from his eyes. Miss Wilson stopped to talk to the boys for a minute and encouraged the small boy to show her his hand. Underneath the crude bandage was an infected, angry-looking sore about the size of a quarter. The child was obviously in pain, and his skin was very warm.

Miss Wilson asked the older boy if his mother was at home. The boy showed her the apartment where he lived. Through the open door of the apartment, Miss Wilson could see a litter-filled room with a pot-bellied stove in the middle. She asked the boy what he had to eat that day. He said, "potatoes," and pointed to a 100-lb bag of potatoes in the corner of the room. She asked him again if he knew where his mother was. He took her to a second floor apartment where the mother was visiting a friend. Miss Wilson asked to talk with her and showed her the younger boy's hand. She advised the mother to seek medical attention as soon as possible. She also talked to the mother about child safety (leaving the boys outside the building on the steps without supervision) and nutrition.

The mother was not very receptive to Miss Wilson's advice and claimed that she was doing the best that she could and would see that the boys' nutrition and the infection were taken care of. Miss Wilson gave her the health clinic phone number and invited her to come in for the well-baby clinic and other services that would help her situation.

Several days later, Miss Wilson returned to Mrs. Burns's apartment to give her an appointment at the chest clinic. She also planned to check on the small boys in the other apartment. Mrs. Burns refused to open the door or talk to Miss Wilson because she had interfered in the business of the family downstairs.

Apparently, the children's mother blamed Mrs. Burns for the intervention of the community health nurse in her affairs. Mrs. Burns stated that if Miss Wilson did not leave the other family alone, she would move again, and this time "you'll never find me." Miss Wilson wondered whether her responsibility as a nurse was simply to Mrs. Burns or whether she should attempt to serve the mother and small children as well.

Case 4-9
Institutionalizing a Disabled Child: Benefit or Harm?

James is a 9-year-old, moderately mentally and physically disabled child. He has lived at home with his mother, Mrs. Hardy, since birth and has been well cared for. During the past year, however, his mother has developed rheumatoid arthritis and is finding it difficult to care for James by herself. James has made steady progress in achieving some motor and cognitive skills, yet his disabilities prevent him from taking advantage of group teaching and other services available in his community.

Mrs. Aikens, a nurse at the rehabilitation center that follows James's case, is attempting to help Mrs. Hardy make decisions for his long-term care. Although Mrs. Aikens recognizes the comfort and high level of care that James receives at home, she also recognizes that his mother may not be able to provide this care as her own disease progresses. Mrs. Hardy clearly relies on the information that Mrs. Aikens supplies and trusts her judgment because she has been James's nurse for several years. Mrs. Aikens finds it very difficult to advise Mrs. Hardy because any action that benefits Mrs. Hardy may result in harm to James and vice versa. Should Mrs. Aikens make it her responsibility to strive to do what will produce the most good for both Mrs. Hardy and James, or is her job limited to promoting James's welfare?

Commentary

In both of these cases, the nurse might ask exactly who her patient is and what difference it makes. In the case involving the mentally disabled James and his mother, Mrs. Aikens seems to think of James as her patient. She then faces the problem of reconciling the interests of the patient with those of someone who is not her patient, James's mother. In the case involving Miss Wilson, the community health nurse, Mrs. Burns is the original patient. At what point have the two boys and their mother also become Miss Wilson's patients?

Assuming that there is only one patient in each case, does the nurse have a primary responsibility to that patient? In the previous sections, we saw that some argue that when the nurse is in the clinical role, he or she should limit attention to the patient's well-being. That would mean, in this situation, that the two boys and their mother, as well as Mrs. Hardy, assuming they are not patients of the nurses involved, have no claim on the nurses' attention.

Both nurses are in positions in which they could expand their notion of who their patients are. Because Miss Wilson is a community health nurse and the two boys are part of the community, Miss Wilson might reason that they are also patients. Does the fact that the boys' mother appears to want nothing to do with Miss Wilson exclude them from patient status? If so, does that exclude them from Miss Wilson's agenda?

Mrs. Aikens, if she is working under a family care model of nursing, might decide that both James and his mother are her patients. If so, the traditional Hippocratic maxim that the healthcare professional should work for the good of the patient (in the singular) is irrelevant. The question becomes one of what to do when the interests of two patients conflict.

What happens if the nurse encounters clinical situations where the interest of another party clearly conflicts with the patient's interests and there is no plausible way that the nurse could conceptualize the other party as an additional patient? For example, what would happen if Miss Wilson was a hospital-based nurse caring for Mrs. Burns, and Mrs. Burns, while actively contagious with an infectious disease, wanted to go home? Miss Wilson might have never met the boys but just heard of them through Mrs. Burns. If the two boys were in close interaction with Mrs. Burns and Mrs. Burns had a strong psychologic need to return to her home, their interests would likely conflict with those of Mrs. Burns. It is very difficult to suppose that Miss Wilson could think of these two boys, whom she has never seen, as her patients. Certainly, neither they nor their mother has ever engaged Miss Wilson, and no nursing care has ever been rendered. If Miss Wilson, as primary nurse, has a special responsibility for the well-being of her patient and it is in her patient's interest to go home, does she then have a duty to block from her mind the well-being of the nonpatients who will be at risk? She would if her obligation is the well-being of her patient. Is it either permitted or required that the nurse consider the welfare of nonpatients in situations like these?

Benefit to the Profession

Another potential conflict the nurse faces when considering the morality of actions in terms of benefits and harms is between service to the patient and service to the profession. Whereas nurses may have no particular loyalty to the society at large or even to specific nonpatients, they surely do feel an obligation to their profession. Normally, the profession has as its goal the service to patients and the improvement of nursing care that they receive. In special circumstances, however, the profession's aim of improving patient care and improving its own position to serve patients may come into conflict with specific patients a nurse is serving. The following case illustrates the problem.

Case 4-10

The Duty to Participate in Collective Action[3]

As Mrs. Marge Tomlinson, the evening charge nurse on A-Wing, completed her charting, she wondered who would be taking her place during the remainder of the week. She and most of Memorial Hospital's nurses would be on strike starting at 8:00 A.M. the next morning. The decision to strike was reached several days ago by the nurses in this private, urban hospital after many hours of meetings, conferences with hospital administration, and heated discussion among fellow nurses.

Mrs. Tomlinson strongly supported her colleagues' efforts to increase salaries, fringe benefits, and general working conditions for all nurses employed by Memorial Hospital. She had experienced many frustrating evenings in recent months because of the loss of nursing staff dissatisfied with mandatory overtime and poor salaries. She had experienced decreased support services for the consistently high number of elderly patients assigned to her 35-bed unit. Yet, now that the strike was imminent, Mrs. Tomlinson wondered whether further reducing the available nursing services to her patients while the nurses were on strike was in the patients' immediate best interests.

During the past 2 days, some patients had been sent home early in preparation for the strike. Several others whose care was too involved for families to manage at home had been placed in nursing homes, much to the distress of the patients as well as their families. But other patients, like Mr. Ralph Osborn, a 63-year-old recent liver transplant recipient, could not be moved. Mr. Osborn and other patients without families or other resources were dependent on the specialized care provided by the hospital's nursing staff to meet their daily physiologic and physical needs. A patient on Mrs. Tomlinson's unit for 5 weeks, Mr. Osborn was just beginning to assume control of his physical care in preparation for his eventual discharge home. There was no means by which Mrs. Tomlinson could guarantee the availability of the kind and level of care he needed during the next few days or even weeks. Like the other nurses, she could only hope that the collective efforts of the nursing staff would quickly bring about improved working conditions for the benefit of future patients.

As some of her nurse colleagues often quoted, the sixth provision of the ANA *Code of Ethics for Nurses* stated that "the nurse participates in establishing, maintaining, and improving healthcare environments and conditions of employment conducive to the provision of quality nursing care . . . through individual and collective action."[17] Yet Mrs. Tomlinson questioned whether these efforts should be carried out when nursing services were already operating at minimum levels of care and safety for the identified patients, and whether the profession itself, through its ethical code, should direct the actions of individual nurses. The expectations of patients like Mr. Osborn and the nurse's obligation to provide the best possible care under any conditions caused her to think that the ANA *Code of Ethics for Nurses* was wrong in encouraging nurses to "participate in collective action . . . in order to address the terms and conditions of employment." Mrs. Tomlinson wondered what to do when the code called for service to the profession to maintain its high standards but also insisted that the health, well-being, and safety of patients should be the nurse's first consideration.

---

[3]Adapted from Fry, S. T. (1985). Ethical issues: Politics, power and change. In S. Talbott and D. Mason (Eds.), *Political action: A handbook for nurses* (pp. 133–140). Reading, MA: Addison-Wesley.

Commentary

The possibility that the nurse's obligation to the profession might conflict with his or her obligation to the present patient is a perplexing one. To some extent, the profession itself says that the primary ethical duty is to serve the patient. Yet, at least historically, the profession has made demands on the individual practitioner that go beyond serving the present patient.

For physicians, the Hippocratic oath placed many demands on members of the Hippocratic group. Hippocratic physicians were expected to show respect for their teachers, even to the point of giving them money if the need arose. They were to teach their teachers' offspring without fee. They were to keep the secret knowledge of the cult, revealing it only to fellow initiates. Clearly, none of these things could always work for the benefit of specific patients.

The Florence Nightingale Pledge, patterned after the oath of Hippocrates, drops all of these, but it does retain the pledge to "maintain and elevate the standards of my profession." In an era when many healthcare professionals are not even members of professional groups, does it make sense to place benefit to the profession on the nurse's agenda? If so, does it still make sense when working to benefit the profession will compromise the care given to patients like Mr. Osborn?

The strike is perhaps an ambiguous case. It involves working for the benefit of the profession and, in this particular example, very concrete issues of self-interest to nurses, such as long hours and poor salaries. And in an indirect sense, the strike being considered by Mrs. Tomlinson can be defended as being undertaken to improve conditions for future patients. Although the cynic might raise an eyebrow, even efforts to improve salaries and working conditions might be defended as eventually improving patient care. After all, if nurses cannot be recruited, then patients will suffer. To the extent that the strike is really about better patient care, Mrs. Tomlinson's problem reduces to one of comparing the welfare of present, identifiable patients with the welfare of future, unidentified patients, an issue addressed in earlier cases.

The case also raises another issue—whether the welfare of the profession itself has a claim on nurses and whether such a claim can ever compete with the obligation to provide patient care.

Research Brief 4-2

Source: Aiken, L. H., Clarke, S. P., Sloane, D. M., Sochalski, J., & Silber, J. H. (2002). Hospital staffing and patient mortality, nurse burnout, and job dissatisfaction. *Journal of the American Medical Association, 288*(16), 1987–1993.

Purpose: To determine the association between the patient-to-nurse ratio and patient mortality, failure-to-rescue (deaths following complications) among surgical patients, and factors related to nurse retention.

Methods: Cross-sectional analyses were completed of linked data from 10,184 staff nurses' surveys; 232,342 general, orthopedic, and vascular surgery patients discharged from the hospital between April 1, 1998, and November 30, 1999; and administrative data from 168 nonfederal adult general hospitals in Pennsylvania. Risk-adjusted patient mortality and failure-to-rescue within 30 days of admission, and nurse-reported job dissatisfaction and job-related burnout were measured.

Findings: After adjusting for patient and hospital characteristics, each additional patient per nurse was associated with a 7% increase in the likelihood of dying within 30 days of admission and a 7% increase in the odds of failure-to-rescue. After adjusting for nurse and hospital characteristics, each additional patient per nurse was associated with a 23% increase in the odds of burnout and a 15% increase in the odds of job dissatisfaction.

Implications: In hospitals with high patient-to-nurse ratios, surgical patients experience higher risk-adjusted 30-day mortality and failure-to-rescue rates, and nurses are more likely to experience burnout and job dissatisfaction. If nurses are morally obligated to "do good and avoid harm," then nurse staffing/patient care ratios may significantly influence whether good is done and harm is avoided.

Benefit to Oneself and One's Family

There is one final possible conflict between benefit to patients and benefit to others that ought to be considered: benefit to the nurse and the nurse's family. All of the professional codes speak as if the very essence of being a professional is commitment to the patient. We have explored several possible competing claims, including the institution, society, identified nonpatients, and the profession. At some point, however, all nurses sacrifice their patients for themselves and their loved ones. They go home at night, and they spend parts of their waking hours doing something other than caring for patients. They play other roles: parent, spouse, citizen, and friend. Each of these, in one way or another, is a competing claim on the nurse's time and energy. The final case in this chapter examines the limits of patients' justifiable claims.

Case 4-11
Is There a Limit to Benefiting the Patient?

Recent global events, such as 9/11, the SARS outbreak, the avian and H1N1 flu, hurricane Katrina, and other natural disasters, have focused attention on the healthcare professional's duty to treat. Chuck Held is an emergency room nurse and is finding himself being paged to report to the ER immediately because a more virulent form of H1N1 has "attacked" the city. He realizes that he may become quarantined after arriving at the hospital and has no way of predicting when he will be free to leave the hospital. He is married and has a 2-year-old autistic son and two golden retrievers. His spouse is a nurse who is currently working in another area hospital.

Commentary

When the ANA *Code of Ethics for Nurses* states that the patient's health, well-being, and safety should be the nurse's first consideration, does it really mean that it is immoral for nurses to spend any time taking care of themselves and their families whenever there are patients whose health, well-being, and safety could be served by the nurse being present on the hospital floor? Suddenly Chuck Held is exploring the limits of the nurse's commitment to the patient.

Is there ever a time when the nurse's other obligations justifiably compete with those to the patient? The question is really about the nature of those other obligations. Some of them—the obligations associated with the roles of parent, spouse, and family member—surely are as fundamental as some of those related to the nursing role. Other roles—such as those of citizen, church member, friend, and even pet owner—can hardly be placed categorically below that of health professional either.

It is striking that nurses and other professionals almost never discuss the nature of the conflicts inherent in the lives of persons who take on more than one fundamental commitment. Part of the answer may lie in the collective responsibility of the professional group to patients. A nurse who has been working for 12 hours can reasonably pass the nursing responsibility on to someone else. The nurse who must stay home with a sick child may be able to call on colleagues to help provide coverage. But it seems unrealistic to assume that colleagues can always provide the needed coverage—especially in a pandemic. Some nurses, such as Chuck Held, may have to sacrifice benefit to their patients for the well-being of other persons to whom they are deeply committed. On the other hand, Nurse Held's responsibilities in the emergency room may trump his other obligations provided that his employer has carefully planned in advance to how best to care for his son and pets in the event that he becomes quarantined.

Finally, Chuck Held's case forces us to examine the nature of the obligation the nurse owes to herself. The idea of duty to oneself is controversial. Some people see the duty as really to one's God or one's community, but the nurse must reflect upon the limits on her obligation to the patient when it is simply her own welfare that is competing. What should Chuck Held have done if he honestly believed his own health and future well-being had become so critical that they took precedence over the needs of patients in the emergency room? Suppose he was ready to get on a flight to South America when the page came. Would it matter if this was a vacation he had dreamed about for years or a health mission to an underserved population? Does Chuck have any claim for his own welfare that can compete with that of the patient?[18]

Critical Thinking Questions

1. Do you believe there are minimal obligations incumbent on all nurses to report for duty in a pandemic, and what, if anything, might mitigate these obligations for some nurses?

2. What is the source of these obligations: your nursing oath, standards articulated by the profession, tradition, contractual obligations, societal expectations, or personal expectations?

3. What clinical virtues are most likely to direct a good response from an ethical nurse, and are these elective?

ENDNOTES

1. Edelstein, L. (1967). The Hippocratic oath: Test, translation and interpretation. In O. Temkin & C. L. Temkin (Eds.), *Ancient medicine: Selected papers of Ludwig Edelstein* (pp. 3–64). Baltimore: The Johns Hopkins Press.

2. Tate, B. L. (1977). *The nurse's dilemma: Ethical considerations in nursing practice* (p. 72). Geneva, Switzerland: International Council of Nurses.

3. American Nurses Association. (ANA). (2001). *Code of ethics for nurses, with interpretive statements* (p. 14). Washington, DC: Author.

4. Feldman, F. (1978). *Introductory ethics* (p. 47). Englewood Cliffs, NJ: Prentice-Hall; Frankena, W. (1973). *Ethics* (2nd ed., p. 47). Englewood Cliffs, NJ: Prentice-Hall; Ross, W. D. (1939). *The right and the good* (p. 22). Oxford, UK: Oxford University Press.

5. Burns, J. H., & Hart, H. L. A. (Eds.). (1996). *The collected works of Jeremy Bentham: An introduction to the principles of morals and legislation.* New York: Oxford University Press.

6. Brandt, R. B. (1968). Toward a credible form of utilitarianism. In M. D. Bayles (Ed.), *Contemporary utilitarianism* (pp. 143–186). Garden City, NY: Doubleday; Rawls, J. (1955). Two concepts of rules. *The Philosophical Review, 44,* 3–32.

7. Dienhart, J. W., & Gleezen, P. (2007, January 14). On ethics: Ashley's treatment: Whose business? Which ethics? (Op Ed). *Seattlepi.com.* Available at: www.seattlepi .com/opinion/299518_ethics14.html. Accessed April 28, 2010.

8. Clark, P. A., & Vasta, L. (2007). The Ashley Treatment: An ethical analysis. *The Internet Journal of Law, Healthcare and Ethics, 5*(1). Available at: http://www .ispub.com/journal/the_internet_journal_of_law_healthcare_and_ethics /volume_5_number_1_45/article_printable/the_ashley_treatment_an_ethical _analysis.html. Accessed April 28, 2010.

9. Bentham, J. (1967). An introduction to the principles of moral and legislation. In A. I. Melden (Ed.), *Ethical Theories: A book of readings* (pp. 367–390). Englewood Cliffs, NJ: Prentice-Hall, Inc.

10. Jonsen, A. R. (1977). Do no harm: Axiom of medical ethics. In S. F. Spicker & H. T. Engelhardt, Jr. (Eds.), *Philosophical medical ethics: Its nature and significance* (pp. 27–41). Boston: D. Reidel Publishing Company; Veatch, R. M. (1981). *A theory of medical ethics* (pp. 159–164). New York: Basic Books.

11. Smith, C. M. (2005). Origin and uses of *Primum Non Nocere*—Above all, do no harm! *Journal of Clinical Pharmacology, 45,* 371–377.

12. See note 5.

13. Lyons, D. (1965). *Forms and limits of utilitarianism.* Oxford, UK: Oxford University Press; Ramsey, P. (1967). *Deeds and rules in Christian ethics.* New York: Charles Scribner's Sons; Rawls, J. (1955). Two concepts of rules. *The Philosophical Review, 64,* 3–32.

14. American Nurses Association. (ANA). (2001). *Code of ethics for nurses, with interpretive statements* (p. 9). Washington, DC: Author.

15. Ad Hoc Committee to Defend Health Care. (1997). For our patients, not for profit: A call to action. *Journal of the American Medical Association, 278*(21), 1733–1738; Shindul-Rothschild, J. (1998). Nurses' weak tribute: A nursing call to action. *American Journal of Nursing, 98*(5), 36.

16. American Nurses Association. (ANA). (2001). *Code of ethics for nurses, with interpretive statements* (p. 14). Washington, DC: Author.

17. Ibid, p. 20.

18. Sokol, D. K. (2006, August). Virulent epidemics and scope of healthcare workers' duty of care. *Emerging Infectious Diseases, 12*(8). Available at: http://www.cdc.gov/ncidod/EID/vol12no08/06-0360.htm. Accessed April 28, 2010.

Chapter 5

Justice: The Allocation of Health Resources

Other Cases Involving Justice

Key Terms

Allocation of health resources
Autonomy
Beneficence
Benefits and burdens
Egalitarianism
Libertarianism
Nonmaleficence
Justice
Utilitarianism

Objectives

1. Define the principle of justice.
2. Describe three major approaches to the allocation of resources.
3. Identify conflicts between the principle of justice and other ethical principles.
4. Apply the principle of justice in the distribution of nursing care resources.

Chapter 4, which introduced the possibility of taking the welfare of parties other than the nurse and patient into account, showed us that an ethic is in some sense social. The next question is likely to be how **benefits and burdens** ought to be distributed among the affected parties. Some of the most interesting problems recently arising in healthcare ethics have involved questions of justice, or equity, in the **allocation of health resources**. The cases in Chapter 4 posed problems of deciding between benefiting the individual patient and benefiting others—either society as a whole or certain other identified persons. Much of the debate in healthcare ethics, however, goes beyond this problem of the conflict between the individual patient and others. It deals with the question of how scarce resources—resources like the nurse's time and energy as well as nursing budgets—should be spread among those who could benefit from them.

One possibility is that the nurse should choose the course that will do the most total or combined good considering all the parties that might be affected. But that is not the only possibility. An intriguing debate rages over the proper meaning of the ethical principle of justice. That debate has direct implications for how the case problems of this chapter will be resolved. Several kinds of problems involving justice might arise.

In the first group of cases, the nurse is forced to choose how to allocate his or her time among the patients under the nurse's care. Here the question is: Once the nurse has made a commitment to serve the interests and protect the rights of more than one patient, what happens when those interests or rights conflict? In the second group of cases, the problem of allocating scarce resources is slightly different. This group involves conflicts between the nurse's obligation to a patient and the needs or interests of nonpatients. In this connection, we shall have to ask whether a right to health care exists for some or all who are not now getting care. Finally, a third group of cases involves more social health policy questions. These cases show that the nurse may sometimes have to deal with ethical problems at the policy level as well as at the level of the individual patient. In all three groups of cases, the critical ethical problem is whether producing as much good as possible (or avoiding as much harm as possible) is the only morally relevant factor in decisions about allocation of nursing resources.[1]

The Ethics of Allocating Resources

Two Meanings of the Word Justice

The debate about the proper basis for allocating resources is made more complicated by the fact that sometimes the word justice is used in two different ways. First, the word is used in the broad sense to describe an ethically correct allocation, even when the allocation is based on an ethical principle, such as ***beneficence*** or ***autonomy***. In other writings, the word justice is used in the narrow sense, referring to an independent principle of allocation (usually having to do with equality, need, or merit). According to those who use the term in this narrow way, determining the ethically right allocation may involve identifying the allocation that would best satisfy the specific principle of justice and then balancing the principle of justice against some or all of the other principles. For example, a nurse might conclude that the principle of justice (in the narrow sense) requires taking care of the sickest patient first, whereas the principle of beneficence would require giving attention to some patient who is not as sick but who can be helped much more.

Three Ways to Allocate Resources

Utilitarianism: Maximizing Net Benefits
Three more or less standard positions regarding the means of deciding how resources should be allocated have emerged. The most easily understood position simply answers the allocation question by reverting to the *principles of **beneficence*** and ***nonmaleficence***—of trying to produce the most good on balance. This is the answer given by the classical utilitarians such as Jeremy Bentham[2] and John Stuart Mill.[3] When trying to decide between two or more courses of action, the strategy of ***utilitarianism*** would be to count up the amount of good each course would do for each person and subtract the amount of harm it would do, thus producing a measure of each individual's net benefit. The sum of all of the individual's net benefits results in the overall net amount of benefit for each course of action. The decision maker is morally obligated to choose the course that produces the most overall good.

We have already seen in earlier chapters cases in which some people believe there are ethical principles that weigh against simply choosing the course that maximizes the good. If, for example, a nurse had promised to help one patient, but then realizes that he or she might do more good on balance by helping another one, some would argue that the promise counts as a reason for the nurse to proceed in the direction of helping the promisee, even though choosing the other course would do more good. Here we have a head-on conflict between maximizing benefit and keeping promises. Many people would not give promise keeping an absolute priority; they would see it as simply a moral factor countering the consideration of benefits and harms. On the other hand, if the extra net benefit that would come from breaking the commitment to the first patient is small, it may be that the promise should be kept. This conflict between keeping promises and doing as much good as possible will be the issue in the cases of Chapter 9. In other chapters, we shall see that the principles of truth-telling and respecting autonomy also pulls against the principles of benefiting and avoiding harm.

Libertarianism: Respecting Autonomous Choices   Whereas one group of ethical theorists insists that resource allocation questions should be answered simply by calculating benefits and harms, a second group, holding to **libertarianism**, believes that the principle of autonomy—or liberty, as they sometimes refer to it—provides an important alternative to allocating based on consequences. Libertarians believe that resources should be allocated according to the free choices of those who rightfully own or control them. The most important philosophical contributor to this viewpoint, Harvard philosopher Robert Nozick, argues that people are entitled to what they justly possess through acquiring it from resources not previously possessed or by trade, gift, or inheritance.[4] If health care is provided to those who are in need, it is not because they have a right to it. It is either because they have made an acceptable bargain with a provider willing to deliver the care or because the provider is willing to give the care out of a sense of charity. Either way, the free choices of those involved dominate the decision-making process. Whereas nurses in noninstitutional settings make such decisions all the time, those practicing in institutional settings are usually not in a position to make them. Rather it is the physician, hospital, or nursing home that decides policies about charity care. The nurse is expected to deliver on any such commitments.

The utilitarians and libertarians have in common the fact that they solve resource allocation problems by appealing to other ethical principles: beneficence and nonmaleficence in the case of the utilitarians (discussed in Chapter 4) and autonomy or liberty (discussed in Chapter 7) in the case of the libertarians.

Justice As an Independent Principle   A third important group of thinkers rejects both of those answers. These theorists believe that resources should be allocated according to another principle—the *principle of justice*. It is sometimes said that people have a right to health care, that health care should be allocated on the basis of need, or that increased equality of health status should be the goal of resource allocation decisions. These are all rather crude reflections of the belief that neither maximizing benefits nor granting total liberty is an adequate way to allocate resources. The most important recent holder of this position has been John Rawls. In an elaborate theoretical construction in a volume entitled *A Theory of Justice*, Rawls concludes that in the basic decisions establishing the practices of a society, resources should be allocated according to two basic principles. First, liberty is so fundamental that each person should have a right to equal basic liberties. Then, when it comes to allocating other basic social and economic goods, justice requires that there should be equality unless two conditions are met: (1) inequalities must be to the benefit of the least well off and (2) there must be equal opportunity for all to gain from the advantages of treating people unequally.[5]

Transferring those basic principles of justice to a specific healthcare decision made by a nurse standing at the bedside can be very difficult.[6] If, however, the idea can be used to establish some basic practices for nursing, the implications will be radical. The principle of justice would require allocations that are not necessarily those that produce the most good, nor those that most respect autonomy. Deciding whether to turn away from one patient to help another one or to help some nonpatient may be contingent not only on what will produce the most good and what commitments the nurse feels he or she has made to the first patient, but also which of the parties is least well off (that is, in greatest need).

Some defenders of the view that justice is an independent principle go even further. They go beyond merely trying to make the worst off people better off. They argue that justice is a principle that requires producing equality when possible. This theory is sometimes called **egalitarianism**, and its proponents agree with Rawls and his supporters that equality is a fundamental ethical requirement of practices in the healthcare sphere. They differ, however, in their interpretation of what should happen when everyone (or at least the least well off) will be better off if inequalities are tolerated.

A problem that illustrates the dilemma is determining, in the case of an airplane accident, what should happen if one of the injured is a physician or nurse, who can help other injured people, but only if given special priority attention from rescuers. In this case, should rescuers first help the injured health professional or the most badly injured passenger? The Rawlsian principle of justice, if extended to the specifics of a practice related to this allocation decision, would seem to say that justice permits (or even requires) treating the healthcare professional first because even the least well off will be better off if the healthcare professional is given this unequal advantage.

The more radical egalitarians might arrive at the same decision, but they would interpret it very differently. They would say that justice requires that resources go to the worst off person who can be helped. They might still, however, conclude that priority should go to the healthcare professional, but not in the name of justice. Because justice is only one among several ethical principles, when those principles conflict some trade-offs may have to be made; it may be necessary to set some priority rules. If treating the healthcare professional first maximizes the benefit (satisfies the principle of beneficence) while giving the worst off accident victims an opportunity for maximum benefit then perhaps justice can be overridden by beneficence. If so, the healthcare professional gets priority in spite of justice rather than in the name of it.

That is one way egalitarians might handle the problem. Another is to acknowledge that the right to equal treatment in the name of justice is a right that can be waived. A prudent accident victim who knew that giving someone else a special chance for priority care would increase his or her probability of being better off in the long run would waive the right to have an equal chance for first treatment. Using this logic, even if beneficence can never take precedence over justice when they conflict (a position held by some strongly committed to deontological or formalist principles), still justice can be overcome through the consent of the least well off.

Thus, the nurse has three major positions from which to choose when deciding how to allocate her or his time, energy, and other resources: The first position stresses maximizing net benefits, grounded in the principle of beneficence; the second position stresses the freedom of providers and patients to bargain for whatever they can get, grounded in the principle of autonomy; the third position stresses equality of outcomes, grounded in an independent principle of justice. Among those opting for the independent principle of justice, some (the Rawlsians) would sacrifice equality in the name of justice whenever it benefited the least well off. Others (the more radical egalitarians) might sacrifice equality, but never in the name of justice. These three major positions provide alternative frameworks for dealing with the case problems in this chapter.

Justice Among the Nurse's Patients

The clinician cannot avoid dealing with resource allocation in the situation where more than one of the nurse's patients need attention simultaneously. In almost every clinical nursing role (with the exception of full-time private duty nursing), this is a common situation. For the nurse to cite the traditional ethic that the health professional's duty is to the patient does not help. The word "patient" in the classical ethical codes is in the singular, yet "patients" is in the plural. Choosing among patients is the issue for the first group of cases in this chapter. In some cases, choice is necessary because two patients are making conflicting demands that cannot both be met or at least cannot be met well. Two patients coding at the same time is only one dramatic example. In other cases, time can be allocated among the nurse's patients, but there still remains a question of what the fairest allocation is. In either case, the nurse must appeal, at least implicitly, to some notion of allocation.

Case 5-1
Allocating Nursing Time According to Patient Benefit

After reviewing the needs of all patients on a med/surg nursing care unit, night nurse Cora Bingham decides that she must set priorities for her time among four needy patients. One, Mrs. Robertson, is an 83-year-old woman with a cerebrovascular accident who is semicomatose and inevitably dying but who needs suctioning every 15 to 20 minutes. The second, Mr. Jablowski, 47 years old, was admitted with gastrointestinal bleeding and has already had several bloody stools. The third, 52-year-old Mr. Hanson, is a recently diagnosed diabetic with unstable blood sugar levels receiving insulin per IV and requiring frequent vital sign checks. The fourth, 35-year-old Mr. Manfra, is a patient who learned today that he has inoperable cancer with metastasis to the spine. He has been suicidal in the past.

Ms. Bingham realizes that these patients have different needs. Moreover, the amount she can do to help is different in each case. Should her decision be based entirely on how much she can benefit each patient or on how much need each patient has? Should she spread her time equally among all the patients? How should she decide about allocating her time?

Commentary

Ms. Bingham knows that the traditional commitment of the nurse is to benefit her patient. She very much would like to do that. The trouble is that she has four patients, each of whom could benefit to some degree from her attention, and she simply cannot meet all of their needs fully. One strategy would be to spread her time evenly among each of her patients. Their needs for nursing care are very different, however. If she were to distribute her time equally, certainly the amount of good she would do for each patient would be unequal.

Another approach would be for Ms. Bingham to ask herself where she could do the most good. This necessarily gets into difficult subjective judgments. Is it a great benefit, for example, to prevent a suicide in a previously suicidal patient with inoperable metastasized cancer? How much good does she do suctioning an inevitably dying, semicomatose woman? Still some comparisons can be made. For instance, Mr. Jablowski, admitted with gastrointestinal bleeding, will probably benefit less from close supervision than Mr. Hanson, the unstable diabetic.

Comparing benefits requires some subtle, controversial judgments. For example, younger patients whose lives are saved will live longer statistically than older patients. If "years of life added" is the criterion of benefit, then younger patients will get much more benefit from a life-saving intervention than older patients. Moreover, if future contribution to the labor force or even more general contribution to society is the criterion, then younger patients will benefit more. By that standard, possibly Mr. Jablowski will benefit more from Ms. Bingham's attention than Mrs. Robertson, even though Mrs. Robertson's condition is much more critical at the time.

If Ms. Bingham approaches her problem by asking herself who will benefit most from her nursing care, she faces all of the questions addressed in the previous chapter. She might, however, ask a somewhat different question: Who has the greatest need, regardless of how much he or she will benefit? Sometimes those who have the greatest need will also benefit the most from a nurse's care; in other situations, however, patients with great need can be helped, but not as much as those with lesser needs. This is where the problem of justice arises.

Among the four patients, Mrs. Robertson's situation is probably the most desperate. She is facing imminent death. Failure to suction her could easily result in a mucus plug blockage of her bronchi and respiratory failure. Yet even with careful attention to suctioning, it is not clear how much benefit Ms. Bingham would be offering. Surely, she should do what she can. Humaneness seems to require that. Some additional facts might be relevant in determining exactly how much benefit Ms. Bingham can offer Mrs. Robertson with particularly rigorous nursing scrutiny. Is Mrs. Robertson suffering from her situation? Is the suctioning primarily to make her comfortable or to prolong her life? If it is to prolong life, did Mrs. Robertson (or her family, if she was not able to express her wishes earlier in the course of her illness) want interventions that prolong her life? It is possible that, although Mrs. Robertson's condition is very grave and therefore her needs are great, Ms. Bingham has relatively little to offer that will really benefit her. If so, using benefit as the criterion, Mrs. Robertson might not get as much of Ms. Bingham's attention as the other patients will.

Age is another complicating factor. Whereas age may help determine how much benefit will result, it can also be relevant to need. Eighty-three-year-old Mrs. Robertson, 52-year-old Mr. Hanson, 47-year-old Mr. Jablowski, and 35-year-old Mr. Manfra all seem to have great needs, yet they are of substantially different ages. If Ms. Bingham is to base her time allocation on need, should age be relevant in defining need, as it might be in defining possible benefits? On the one hand, all three patients can be said to have significant immediate nursing care needs. In that sense, their needs may be thought to be about equal, judged from a "moment-in-time" perspective. On the other hand, need might be viewed with an "over-a-lifetime" perspective. The older the patient, the more of a life plan has been completed. If Ms. Bingham is considering what is needed to complete a life plan, then the younger the patient, the greater the need.

One thing seems clear from these four patients: Meeting need and maximizing benefit are different moral tasks. If Ms. Bingham tries to do one, she may not be able to do the other.

Critical Thinking Questions

1. If you were Ms. Bingham, how would you allocate your time among these four patients?
2. Which approach to justice would guide your decisions and actions? Why?

Case 5-2

Choosing Between Two Infants with Multiple Handicaps

Baby J was a 16-hour-old neonate who had been transferred from a local medical facility to the neonatal intensive care unit (NICU) of a tertiary care center. She was the firstborn child of a state legislator and his wife and the product of in vitro fertilization (the couple had attempted to conceive three previous times unsuccessfully at $5000 an effort). At the time of transport, Baby J was having mild-to-moderate respiratory distress and had been anuric since birth. On examination, it was noted that the infant had an enlarged thymus, low-set ears, questionable lung size on X-ray, and a history of no amniotic fluid present upon delivery. Completed testing indicated that she had no kidneys, ureters, or bladder and that her small lung size was indicative of pulmonary hypoplasia. The pediatric staff offered the diagnosis of Potter's syndrome, a condition known to be fatal within a few weeks.

Consultation with infant renal transplant centers indicated that, because of pulmonary complications, there had never been a successful renal transplant done in an infant with Potter's syndrome. All but one center declined to offer treatment, stating that a renal transplant in such an infant would be purely experimental. The primary physician, Dr. A. Smith, after consulting with other health team members, discussed the prognosis with Baby J's parents. They wanted a few hours to think about whether they wanted their infant transported to the one center that offered to treat her on an experimental basis.

While the parents were making their decision, the unit was notified that they would be receiving another admission. There were no more beds in the unit unless, of course, one became free when Baby J was transported. But Baby J's parents were waiting for another neonatologist to visit their infant and give a second opinion about Baby J's prognosis. They did not plan to make any decisions about their daughter's care for several hours. When members of the healthcare team pressured Baby J's physician to speed up the decision-making process or to order Baby J's transport, he refused. According to him, Baby J's parents were "paying customers" and should be able to purchase the type of care they needed or, for that matter, wanted. There was also the fear of legal recourse if Baby J's condition should deteriorate when being transferred against her parents' wishes. If the unit needed to receive another admission, another infant would have to be moved; but not Baby J.

Within an hour, it was decided that the unit would transfer Baby T, an infant with Down syndrome and a hypoplastic left heart, to the pediatric step-down unit. Baby T was awaiting surgery, her only opportunity to survive. Baby T's mother, 18 years old and unmarried, lived 50 miles away in a rural community. Because she did not have a telephone, she could not be notified immediately of the decision to transfer her child. The mother had been discharged from the hospital 5 days earlier and had not called about her baby since leaving. There was a note on Baby T's chart that the mother would be placing the infant for adoption if she lived.

The decision to transfer Baby T demoralized the nursing staff, especially Becky Turner, Baby T's nurse. She knew that Baby T needed close cardiac monitoring and that the step-down unit would be hard pressed to provide close supervision of the infant. Even though Baby T had a very poor prognosis, even with surgery, Ms. Turner felt that the transfer would place this infant at greater risk than she was presently experiencing. Ms. Turner and the other nurses could not agree with the decision to transfer Baby T. Somehow it seemed that some infants, because of circumstances beyond their control, were not as "deserving" of care and services as other infants. Surely, this was not right.

Commentary

Both Baby J and Baby T had desperate need of care. From the standpoint of need alone, they seem equally critical. If need were the only criterion, it is hard to imagine how the person responsible for the NICU would choose. Even someone committed to using need rather than benefit as the criterion might, under such circumstances, be inclined to look at potential benefit as a possible "tiebreaker." Someone who believes the proper basis for allocating nursing care should be potential benefit would, of course, be even more comfortable with a benefits assessment.

In this case, Baby T seems to stand a much more obvious chance of benefiting. With intensive care until surgery, Baby T stands a chance of surviving. Without it, Baby T will die. On the other hand, the chances of Baby J benefiting from care in the NICU are remote. In fact, when the burdens of the experimental, heretofore unprecedented transplant surgery are taken into account, Baby J might actually be worse off with the temporary NICU care than without it.

If the benefits assessment is extended beyond the medical benefits, the judgment might become more complicated. Someone might argue that saving Baby T, with Down syndrome, would count for less benefit than saving a presumably more normal Baby J with Potter's syndrome. Such an assessment of benefits, however, requires the premise that a baby with Down syndrome is somehow less valuable than one without. Without that judgment, this conclusion would not be possible.

Dr. Smith adds another dimension to the decision. He appears to bring two assumptions to the cases. First, he accepts the idea that Baby J's parents, as "paying customers," should have the right to buy whatever care they need or desire. He seems to be committed to the notion that NICU care, including nursing care, can be sold as a commodity to anyone who has the ability to pay. He has a free-market view of allocation, in which persons should be able to buy whatever providers are willing to sell. This position is linked to the libertarian view. According to this view, autonomous individual buyers and sellers should be free to make whatever bargains they can. If other persons who are not blessed with equal resources cannot make such a deal for themselves or their children, it is unfortunate, but not unfair or unjust.[7]

Even if that view of allocation of resources were accepted, Dr. Smith brings to the case another assumption that needs to be examined. He seems to assume that he, as the attending physician for one patient, should be the one to make a deal with Baby J's parents on behalf of the hospital. Even given a libertarian outlook on allocating health resources, it is not clear that an individual physician is in a position to bargain away the hospital's NICU beds. Becky Turner, Baby T's nurse, by that logic might also have the authority to deal with Baby T's parent.

A good case can be made that neither Dr. Smith nor Ms. Turner should have absolute control over the NICU beds. Rather, that would appear to be an institutional decision under the control of the trustees of the hospital or its sponsoring agency and guided by certain moral standards.

If neither need nor potential benefit justifies "bumping" Ms. Turner's patient, and ability to pay is not acceptable as a basis for allocating the bed, then Ms. Turner may find herself in the position of being witness to what appears to be an immoral allocation decision. If she is to be an agent for her patient's rights and welfare, this would lead her to reflect on how she might intervene to attempt to serve her patient's interests, in this case, keeping Baby T in the NICU bed. Seeking discussion and review of the decision with Dr. Smith, other physicians, nursing colleagues, nursing supervisors, and administrators of the hospital is a possibility. Many institutions have hospital ethics committees that nursing staff can consult to help review such ethically controversial decisions. Finally, Ms. Turner may have to consider outside review: reporting the case to child abuse authorities under federal regulations governing such reporting or to other police authorities. What would be the effect of these alternative strategies?

Critical Thinking Questions

1. To what extent should obtaining a bed in any ICU be based on probable benefit from ICU care? On need? On ability to pay?

2. Do you think ICU nurses should have some decision-making authority on who stays in the ICU and who is transferred out of the ICU? Why?

Whereas in this case it appeared difficult to establish which infant had the greater need, often, as in the next case, it is much clearer.

Case 5-3

The Psychiatric Patient with Special Nursing Care Needs

Paula Kellerman, an experienced psychiatric nurse, was working the evening shift with two other nurses and two psychiatric technicians. The staff was responsible for 20 patients on the psych unit. One patient, 26-year-old Mr. Simchak, required close observation because of seizure precautions (seizures occurred about 3 to 4 times a day); three other patients were on suicide precautions. Unfortunately, even with the seizure and suicide precautions, these patients were not doing well. Mrs. Kellerman knew that the other nurses and technicians were doing about as well as she could with the patients. She believed that what she could add would be modest. One other patient (Mrs. Couch, a 56-year-old woman with a history of poorly controlled bipolar disorder), admitted 2 days before, was extremely delusional and disoriented. However, no new admissions were expected, and none of the patients required one-on-one nursing supervision.

After visiting hours ended, Mrs. Couch became agitated. She undressed in the nurses' station and ran from Mrs. Kellerman when she tried to calm her, but was finally led into seclusion. Mrs. Kellerman then gave Mrs. Couch an as-needed dose of Haloperidol, but when the nurse left the room, Mrs. Couch pounded on the door and shouted. Mrs. Kellerman went into the seclusion room and attempted to calm her; she seemed particularly effective in this.

After 20 minutes, one of the technicians asked Mrs. Kellerman to come out on the unit because one of her other patients was agitated and needed her. This patient, a middle-aged woman suffering from multiple neuroses, was worried about a day pass she would have the following day. Mrs. Kellerman talked briefly with this patient and promised to talk longer with her later. Although this patient was much worse off than Mrs. Couch, Mrs. Kellerman seemed to be able to accomplish more for her better-off patient. Stopping at the nurses' station to consult with the other nurses and the technicians, she learned that Mrs. Couch was pounding on the seclusion room door again.

Believing that Mrs. Kellerman could provide at least some benefit for the other patients and that their need was really much greater, the staff urged that Mrs. Couch be restrained in the seclusion room. Mrs. Kellerman knew that even though Mrs. Couch's problems were less severe, she could be more effective in benefiting her and thought she should stay where she could do the most good. She knew that her attention calmed Mrs. Couch and was therapeutic. She especially did not want to see Mrs. Couch regress to her condition on admission (taking her clothes off, urinating on the floor, smacking staff, being excessively fearful, and running away from staff). One of the technicians angrily said that staying in the room with Mrs. Couch and leaving the two technicians to control the other, worse-off patients was irresponsible of Mrs. Kellerman. She was uncertain whether she should spend her time with Mrs. Couch, where she knew she would be beneficial, or support the other staff in doing whatever she could to help the worse-off patients, even if the amount of good she could do seemed to be less.

Commentary

It may be helpful to ask how Mrs. Kellerman might analyze her moral problem by examining it in the light of each of the three positions about allocating resources outlined in the introduction to this chapter. If her goal is to produce as much benefit as possible—that is, if she approaches the problem as a utilitarian—it seems clear what she should do. Mrs. Couch could benefit greatly from her care, whereas the other patients, even though they suffer from more severe psychologic problems, would benefit less. If Mrs. Kellerman is a utilitarian, then the fact that the other patients are suffering from more severe problems does not count as long as she can do more good for Mrs. Couch. If Mrs. Kellerman could add significantly to what the technicians and other nurses can do to help the other patients, the case would require a different analysis, but assuming she can do more good by staying with her better-off patient, her responsibility from the utilitarian perspective is to stay with Mrs. Couch.

The analysis from the standpoint of need—that is, from a more egalitarian perspective—leads to a different conclusion. If Mrs. Kellerman's goal were to use her nurses to benefit the sickest or least well-off patients, then it seems likely that Mr. Simchak or the suicidal patients would have a higher priority than Mrs. Couch would, even if Mrs. Kellerman could add only modestly to what the other staff could do. Therefore, from the more egalitarian standpoint of distributing resources on the basis of need, Mrs. Kellerman should temporarily leave Mrs. Couch restrained in order to help the others.

Mrs. Kellerman might also consider the third basis for resource distribution outlined in the introduction to this chapter: the libertarian view. This view holds that autonomous people can make agreements using their financial and other resources to influence the choices as they see fit. A real libertarian supporting free-market mechanisms for allocating healthcare resources would, in the case of autonomous patients, let the medical resources go to those who could pay for them.

Even if some goods in society are allocated this way, most people find this unacceptable for allocating health care. For those who support a free market in health care for autonomous adults, it is hard to imagine how this approach would be meaningful in the case of a psychiatric hospital in which the patients are often not sufficiently autonomous to make their own healthcare decisions. The only possible way this approach could apply to a psychiatric patient who was presently mentally incompetent would be to base the allocation decisions on choices the patient made while competent. For example, if all of the patients in Case 5-3 had once been competent and had been presented choices about whether to buy health insurance with extensive psychiatric coverage or merely basic services, a libertarian might conclude that the patients who bought the more expensive and extensive coverage are entitled to better care.

In the mind of the libertarian, this might justify placing some patients in a higher quality, more attractive private facility while placing those who chose only basic coverage in less well-staffed state hospitals. The libertarian would have a harder time applying these notions to the allocation of a specific nurse's time when several patients need attention simultaneously. Is there any way libertarian principles could be applied to Mrs. Kellerman's problem?

For nonlibertarians (as well as for libertarians who would not apply their views to incompetent patients), the real issue in this case seems to be how a nurse should act when a patient who is already better off can be expected to get more benefit from the nurse than other, more seriously afflicted patients who are nevertheless less likely to be helped. For the utilitarian, Mrs. Kellerman should stay with Mrs. Couch even though her condition is not as severe, as long as she can do more good. Egalitarians, on the other hand, would hold that she should go to the worse-off patients even though she cannot help them as much.

Research Brief 5-1

Source: Bell, S. E. (2003). Nurses' ethical conflicts in performance of utilization reviews. *Nursing Ethics, 10*(5), 541–554.

Purpose: To identify the ethical conflicts of utilization review nurses and to test the hypothesis that a justice perspective would dominate the ethical orientations of these nurses.

Method: A cross-sectional survey research design was used. Participants were recruited from three Midwestern managed care organizations (1 = nonprofit; 2 = for profit) in which RNs were employed at least 20 hours per week as utilization reviewers. Participants completed a three-part questionnaire that previously had been tested for reliability and validity. Participants were asked to provide two ethical conflicts they had encountered while doing utilization reviews and to identify the ethical principles that were important to them as they made decisions and resolved conflicts in their work. Descriptive statistics and qualitative data analyses were completed on 97 returned questionnaires, a 51% return rate.

Findings: The majority of the examples of ethical conflicts provided by the participants involved distributing benefits, costs, and risks of health care fairly as opposed to providing good and preventing harm to patients. The conflicts often involved overutilization or inappropriate use of medical services and the fair distribution of limited healthcare resources. Other reported conflicts involved problems with the process of utilization review or questionable uses of power in the review setting by providers, employers, and managed care executives. Participants' primary ethical orientations were reported as "doing good" (46%), "distributing benefits, costs, and risks of health care fairly" (22%), "respecting self-determination" (6%), and "avoiding harm" (4%).

Implications: The role of utilization reviewer challenges nurses' traditional ethical orientations of respecting self-determination and providing care (fidelity). Because utilization reviewers make decisions about the appropriateness of medical care, nurses need to be educationally and practically prepared for the ethical conflicts they are likely to experience in the role. They also need to be aware of the power they exercise in balancing organizational goals, individual patient needs and wants, and the equitable distribution of existing medical resources. Sensitivity to ethical conflicts and conflict resolution skills are needed for success in the nurse utilization reviewer role.

Justice Between Patients and Others

In all of the cases in the first section of this chapter, the nurse faced the problem of allocating care among patients. The notion of doing what will benefit the patient (in the singular) was unhelpful, in fact irrelevant, because doing what would benefit one patient meant failing to do what would benefit another. Sometimes, however, the nurse must choose between his or her own patients and the interests of third parties who are not the nurse's patients. Whereas in the first group of cases the nurse had to determine some basis for choosing among patients—whether it was on the basis of meeting needs, maximizing benefits, respecting autonomy, or some combination of the three—in this section's cases the nurse could, in principle, always act to maximize the patients' welfare and rights. The question is whether the nurse ought always to do that, even when it means failing to meet greater needs of others who are not his or her patients or if it means failing to do as much good as possible considering the interests of both patients and nonpatients. This can arise when those who are not the nurse's patients are, in fact, patients or potential patients within the nurse's institution, or it can arise when the other parties are not patients at all.

Case 5-4
The Elderly Patient Who Was Transferred

Mrs. Sally Grissom, the day supervisor of a skilled nursing facility, has just learned that several of the home's patients will be transferred to other homes. Mrs. Grissom hates to tell one of the patients that this will occur. Seventy-four-year-old Mrs. Lewiston has lived at Ferndale Care Home for 3 years. Mrs. Lewiston has no relatives, is quite alert, and has assumed that Ferndale will be her home for the rest of her life. Although confined to a wheelchair, Mrs. Lewiston no longer requires skilled nursing care and therefore has been singled out for transfer as a means of controlling costs of patient care in higher priced skilled nursing homes across the state. Mrs. Lewiston is a recipient of public assistance. The administrators are insisting that care not be funded at a level beyond what is necessary.

After learning of the planned transfer, Mrs. Lewiston calls a public-assistance lawyer and asks him to represent her and other patients in a legal suit to block the move. She argues that the state has no right to move her and other patients without notice and without a hearing about the benefits of the present level of care and the potential harms and benefits of placement at another facility with a lower level of care.

Mrs. Grissom is undecided whether she should support the patients' legal suit. Aside from the detrimental effect such an action might have on her job, she is truly uncertain whether an elderly resident of a nursing home can select his or her nursing home and level of care when the state pays for all costs of the care. Certainly, each patient is entitled to some level of care, but who decides what level is appropriate for each patient, and how much input does the patient have in such decisions?

Case 5-5
The Noncompliant, Alcoholic Patient in the ER

Sue Munson is a staff nurse in a large (30-bed), inner-city emergency room. Currently, she is responsible for patients in four rooms and several patients on stretchers in the hallways waiting for laboratory results and physician disposition. While in Room #9 with a patient experiencing cardiac pain, she hears an approaching stretcher being pushed down the hall. The charge nurse tells her to pull the patient (a woman with lower back pain) from Room #10 into the hallway. A new patient (the one on the stretcher) is to be put into Room #10 for triage and a full workup by Miss Munson.

The new patient, Mr. Cooper, is familiar to Miss Munson. She has taken care of this 63-year-old, homeless man several times over the past 3 months and twice during the past week. Mr. Cooper is a chronic alcoholic and previously has been urged to enter a detoxification center where the needs of elderly persons are given attention. However, he left the ER at 5:00 A.M. that morning against medical advice. The ambulance driver tells Miss Munson that someone found Mr. Cooper lying face down in the gutter several blocks away from the hospital. A head injury is suspected.

On physical exam, Mr. Cooper is found to be undernourished, emaciated, and unkempt. His long gray hair and beard are tangled, and his fingernails have fecal material underneath them. He is wearing three layers of moist, dirty clothing that smell of urine, garbage, and alcohol. Although he is oriented and neurologically intact, he is also lethargic, his skin is pale with many healing abrasions and scabs, and his heart rate is slightly elevated (104 beats/min). Blood samples are drawn and sent to the laboratory for routine analysis. Essentially, Mr. Cooper receives the same attention and treatment as any patient with a possible head injury. Blood tests show that Mr. Cooper has a normal CBC but a low magnesium level and an alcohol level of 327 mg/dl, which is within the toxic range. Results of a chest X-ray, EKG, urinalysis, and head CT scan are within normal limits. Mr. Cooper remains in the ER for the remainder of Miss Munson's shift, receiving IV fluids with vitamins, two meal trays, and specialized nursing care, despite the duress Miss Munson is under in providing care to her other four patients.

During Mr. Cooper's workup, Miss Munson continually thinks about her other patients and other potential patients who might need treatment in the ER and who don't abuse the system like Mr. Cooper does. Are the needs of these other patients not more important than those of a noncompliant patient like Mr. Cooper? She wonders who pays for his expensive (and wasted) treatment. If the hospital has to absorb the costs of such treatment, perhaps it should have the right to refuse treatment to any patient like Mr. Cooper who signs himself out against medical advice once he is sober.

Commentary

Both of these cases pose ethical problems regarding resource allocation. In both cases it seems clear that the interests of patients are in conflict with the interests of those who are not patients. Seventy-four-year-old Mrs. Lewiston would prefer to stay in Ferndale Care, where she has lived for 3 years. But the economic interests of others, in this case the taxpayers providing the public assistance supporting Mrs. Lewiston's care, are quite different. Mr. Cooper, the alcoholic who signs out against advice, is draining staff time that could be used for other emergency room patients, but he is also consuming society's resources by generating costs that society must pay.

The three approaches to resource allocation presented in the introduction to this chapter each would have a unique way of handling these issues. The libertarian, who is willing to let free-market forces determine how resources are allocated, might not support public assistance programs such as those funding Mrs. Lewiston's or Mr. Cooper's care.

The utilitarian decision maker, who would approach the problem from the standpoint of trying to do as much good as possible with limited resources, would have an easy time justifying the transfer of Mrs. Lewiston. Skilled nursing care is not needed to provide adequate benefit to this patient. To be thorough, calculation of the benefits and harms would have to take into account Mrs. Lewiston's emotional distress from the move, but even so, it is not implausible to conclude that the funds for skilled nursing care could be better used elsewhere.

From this standpoint, Mr. Cooper probably would not fare well either. He is a chronic alcoholic and repeatedly signs out against advice—before the hospital system can have any hope of benefiting him. If the only goal is to use nursing time effectively, patients like Mr. Cooper probably would have low priority.

The egalitarian would ask not who is willing to pay or how benefits can be maximized, but rather who is in the greatest need. Both Mrs. Lewiston and the alcoholic Mr. Cooper seem to have significant claims of need. Mrs. Lewiston's need, however, is presumably not as great as that of patients requiring skilled nursing care. Mr. Cooper's need is more complicated to assess. He is surely in bad shape. His future prospects are dim, barring some radical change. He is thus a patient who, at least at first, might be seen as having weighty claims in the eyes of those who focus on need. But the problem is more subtle. Does needs-based justice in the healthcare system respond to all need no matter how personally culpable the patient may be for being in the condition he finds himself? Or is it reasonable to say that even though Mr. Cooper's need may be great, it is only because he has squandered his opportunity for health? Does needs-based justice focus on those in need regardless of whether they have brought the need upon themselves, or is it really only concerned with making sure people have had an opportunity for adequate health? Of course, this issue is relevant only if one believes that alcoholism results from voluntary choices made by the individual. If one believes that alcoholism is a disease caused by genetic or other factors beyond Mr. Cooper's control, then he has had no opportunity for health. But if one views alcoholism as a condition that to some extent is under the patient's voluntary control and believes that justice requires only an opportunity for adequate health, then even from a justice point of view, Mr. Cooper may not have a claim here.[8]

For the nurses in these cases, the real question may not necessarily be what counts as a just or fair allocation of resources. Mrs. Grissom and Miss Munson cannot help but be aware of the resource allocation question. It can be argued, however, that it may not be their job to solve the ethical and policy questions raised by such allocation issues. They have special obligations to their patients, and when their patients' interests conflict with others in the system, someone must deal with the allocation problem. But the nurses should ask themselves whether that is their responsibility. Some would argue that their first duty is to their patients. This would mean that they become advocates for their patients. Presumably someone else—the public assistance administrators in Mrs. Lewiston's case and the administrators or funders of care in Mr. Cooper's case—will advocate on behalf of the interests of the other parties.

If this notion of special role-specific duties is adopted—that is, if the clinician is an advocate for the patient—then it makes sense that sometimes the clinician ought to lose. Sometimes the advocates for the interests of other parties will be closer to being right. Mrs. Grissom, under this model, should not feel angry or distressed if Mrs. Lewiston is moved, even though as her nurse, she argued that the move was not in Mrs. Lewiston's interest.

If this special advocacy role is not assigned to clinicians, then Mrs. Grissom and Miss Munson would presumably be responsible for considering the broader question of fair limits on the use of the skilled nursing home or the emergency room. If they are to deal with these social ethical questions, they will have to be the ones who decide that each patient's interest must be sacrificed for the more weighty moral claims of other parties. In cases where there is a conflict of interest between a clinician's patients and other parties, one critical question is whether they should attempt to decide what the fair limits of care are for their patients or whether they simply should advocate for their patients and let someone else make the allocation decisions.

Critical Thinking Questions

1. The formal principle of justice counsels that we treat equals equally. What this frequently translates to for nurses are questions about what characteristics are morally relevant justifications for treating people differently. In Case 5-5, Miss Munson queries whether Mr. Cooper's history of nonadherence would justify treating him less aggressively than another patient with a possible head injury. Under what conditions, if any, might nurses use the following to justify different types or levels of care?

   Age
   Gender
   Race
   Socioeconomic status
   Degree of education
   Social worth
   Adherence to medical and nursing orders
   History of self-care
   Personal appearance
   Popularity
   "Niceness"

2. If people are unable to meet their own needs for care and have no family or other advocates, are they entitled to the same, less, or more care than others?

Justice in Public Policy

In the cases presented thus far in this chapter, the nurse is clearly paired with at least one identified patient. In the first group of cases, the problem was that more than one patient had needs and these needs were in conflict. In the second group, the patients' interests conflicted with those of other persons—stockholders or the public at large. In the latter cases, we raised the question of whether the nurse should be in the role of deciding how resources are allocated. The alternative was for the nurse to take on the role of advocate for the patient, leaving the allocation decisions to others. The cases in this section deal with nurses in other than clinical care giving roles where the nurse, by the very nature of the role she or he plays, must make allocation choices.

Case 5-6
Problems of Justice in Policy Decisions

Marcia Forsyth is the director of nursing at a community health nursing agency in a large Midwestern county. Periodically, she meets with her two associate directors to discuss the budget for agency programs for the next fiscal year. Together, they determine how the agency will allocate its nursing resources during the coming year and discuss the agency programs that will be initiated, terminated, or changed in order to meet the health needs of their community.

During the most recent meeting, one associate director, Jann Beech, requested that the agency give her the resources to initiate a primary care clinic for adults that would be staffed by nurse practitioners. Her data in support of this program included an increase in the adult population in the community over the past 5 years and a decrease in the number of family physicians serving the county during the same time period. She argued that care provided in adult care clinics had resulted in dramatic improvements in community health statistics where such programs had been tried.

The other associate director, Susan Chinn, also made a request at this meeting. She requested that the agency provide counseling services for pregnant teenagers. Citing increased numbers of teenage pregnancies in the county during the last 3 years, she argued persuasively that counseling pregnant teenagers would help prevent future pregnancies in this age group and that both the mothers and their children are potentially among the most needy residents of their community.

Mrs. Forsyth reminded her associate directors that there is a ceiling on the amount of agency funds available for new programs. Only one new program can be initiated this year and then only if the agency is willing to support the program for a minimum of 3 years. Therefore, she counseled the associate directors consider carefully the type of policies that might be formed as a result of the focus on specific programs and populations within the county. The amount of financial support that each program requests in order to be operative and the amount of nursing time and expertise that will be required by the residents of the county should also be carefully considered. Mrs. Forsyth was at a loss to move forward with a choice without further study. What should the determining factors be in deciding to fund one program and not the other?

Case 5-7

Screening School Girls for Urinary Tract Infections[1]

Sheila Goberman is a community health nurse. After receiving an advanced degree in child health care, she began working for the Warren County department of health and is now employed as the director of school health maintenance. She and others specializing in public health for school-age populations have been concerned about the high incidence of urinary tract infections in school-age girls in her county. Approximately 15% of girls with asymptomatic bacteriuria (ASB) are reported to have renal scarring when the infection is first detected. It is believed that early detection might prevent progressive renal damage. Ms. Goberman is in the process of developing a program to screen school girls in the county.

She is aware of two strategies for screening school-age populations. The first method involves sending an explanatory letter to parents a week before the screening. A health department nurse is then sent to the school. She distributes kits containing a dipslide and a letter of instructions, which each child takes home. At home the parent assists in collecting a midstream urine specimen on the slide. The slides are then returned to the school the following day and analyzed in the health department lab. The second strategy involves sending a health department mobile unit to the school, where the specimens are collected under the supervision of a health department nurse.

Ms. Goberman is aware that studies have shown that the first, home-administered tests, is considerably cheaper. One study in Britain reported that the cost per child screened under the first method was £0.26, whereas the cost of the second method, using the mobile unit and health department personnel, was £0.77 per child screened.

In addition to the fact that the cost of the home-administered method was about one third as expensive, Ms. Goberman is also aware that the home testing was not equally successful for all socioeconomic groups. Specifically, failure rates were three times as great for children in the lower socioeconomic classes as they were for children in the upper classes. This was attributed to both a greater incidence of failure to return the slide and a greater incidence of spoiled slides among families in the lower socioeconomic classes.

Ms. Goberman realizes she has an ethical choice to make. As a health officer for the county, is it her mission to find as many cases of ASB per dollar invested (in which case she would use the home-administered test), or is it to see that girls of all socioeconomic classes have an equal opportunity to have their ASB detected (in which case she would have to use the more expensive test or some mix of the two methods)? If resources were unlimited, Ms. Goberman would simply opt for the second method, but she knows that she will not have enough funds from the department to do the screening as often as would be desirable in any case.

---

[1]Adapted from Rich, G., Glass, N. J., & Selkon, J. B. (1976). Cost-effectiveness of two methods of screening for asymptomatic bacteriuria. *British Journal of Preventive and Social Medicine*, *30*, 54–59.

Commentary

Cases 5-6 and Case 5-7 both pose problems involving nurses in administrative positions rather than nurses with one-on-one patient relations. In both cases, the nurse is in a position to make ethical policy determinations in which the key question is what constitutes fair use of limited resources.

Marcia Forsyth is in the unenviable position of having to choose between two programs, both of which would be valuable but only one of which can be funded. She might notice that Jann Beech and Susan Chinn, the two associate directors, have made somewhat different appeals for their proposals. Ms. Beech based her appeal on data showing that aggregate community health statistics improved dramatically when nurse practitioners provided a primary care clinic for adults. Ms. Chinn, on the other hand, based her appeal on the fact that adolescent pregnant women and their children were among the most needy residents of the community. Both arguments are commonly heard in health resource allocation debates, but morally they are different appeals. In the first case, it is the amount of improvement in aggregate health statistics that is the basis of the argument. In the second case, it is not improvement in total community health that is being cited, but the health of one particular segment of the community—the most needy.

Possibly, each nurse-administrator could have reframed her argument in the terms that the other used. Ms. Beech might have argued that the patients of the adult primary care clinic were going to be among the most needy of the community, and Ms. Chinn might have argued that her adolescent pregnancy program might produce dramatic improvements in aggregate public health statistics such as rates of mortality and morbidity. The question here is: Which kind of appeal is ethically most appropriate? Is the goal to produce the most benefit in aggregate or to help the most needy?

A similar issue arises in the bacteriuria screening program. Ms. Goberman has no direct one-on-one patient relationships. Although her staff eventually will visit the schools, she will never see any of the patients herself. Case 5-4 and Case 5-5 posed problems of conflict between the nurse's patient and society, but in this case Ms. Goberman's patient, in a way, is society. She needs to know whether her ethical obligation is to find the highest possible number of cases in her population with the limited resources she has for the screening program or, alternatively, whether she should screen less efficiently, but in doing so give socially and economically deprived school girls a better chance of having their cases of ASB detected.

Because her funds for the project are limited, Ms. Goberman will have to compromise in some way. She will probably opt for an arrangement in which the testing is done at much less frequent intervals than would be desirable. If she opts for the second method in order to give the socially and economically deprived school girls an equal chance of having their cases identified, she will be able to screen even less frequently and will thus find fewer cases overall.

The three major alternative approaches to the ethics of resource allocation presented in the introduction to this chapter give three very different answers to Ms. Goberman's dilemma. The libertarian approach, insofar as it supports free-market policies, would simply make information about screening available so that any parents who wanted to and could afford it would have their daughters screened. Possibly, such a person would even have the health department offer the screening, but on a fee-for-service basis.

The approach that considers a fair distribution to be one that gets the most benefits in total for the investment would clearly favor the home-administered test. It is the essence of the approach that the distribution of benefits and burdens, in principle, does not count ethically. Because it is the community's health in aggregate that is the goal of the health department, the funds available should be used to lower the incidence of ASB regardless of the test's distribution.

The more egalitarian approach, on the other hand, is very concerned about matters of distribution. Who receives the benefits is ethically important. Each girl in the community ought to have an equal chance to have urinary tract infections diagnosed. That would mean spending extra money, if necessary, to detect cases among socially and economically deprived school girls.

Possibly a compromise strategy could be developed. In-school screening could be used for lower class students, whereas the home-administered test could be used for upper class girls. If, however, this were done on a school-by-school basis, with schools in upper class neighborhoods using the home-administered method, some lower class students in primarily upper class neighborhoods would still lose out. If the differentiation were done on a student-to-student basis, awkward, potentially stigmatizing discriminations would have to be made. Ms. Goberman has encountered a situation in which doing what is efficient in community health terms will be quite different from doing what will give people an equal opportunity to have their health problems addressed.

In fact, the problem faced by Ms. Goberman may not be critical any longer. The case originally arose when it was believed that great benefit would come from finding ASB in school girls. Although today it is considered less important, the general problem Ms. Goberman faces—deciding whether to maximize aggregate health benefit or spread benefit more equally—continues today.

Critical Thinking Questions

1. If you were Mrs. Forsyth, which factors would be most important to you in deciding which of the programs to fund?
2. If you were Ms. Goberman, which method of testing for ASB would you select? Why?

Justice and Other Ethical Principles

The cases in this chapter thus far have dealt exclusively with distribution of scarce nursing resources on the basis of the needs of the patient (egalitarian justice), the amount of benefit to be done (beneficence), and the freedom of persons to make agreements (autonomy). The final case suggests that occasionally there are other moral principles that may influence the morally right decision. In Case 5-8, a nurse has made a promise to one of her patients. She must decide how her duty to keep a promise is to be reconciled with her duty to be fair, to do good, and to respect autonomy. In this situation, it may turn out that doing what is right may be different from doing what is fair or what maximizes benefit or respects autonomy.

Case 5-8
When It Is Hard to Keep Promises[2]

Peter was a 15-year-old boy with acute myelocytic leukemia. As his condition deteriorated, Peter began to realize that he was dying. He was in pain, angry, afraid, and largely dependent on others to meet his physical needs. However, the nurses on his unit promised that he would not be allowed to suffer and that he would not be alone as he became sicker.

During a 6-month period, Peter was in and out of the hospital many times. Although Peter was often difficult to get along with, the nursing staff had begun to care about Peter, and he had learned to trust them. The fact that Peter had lived in foster homes most of his life explained some of his difficult behavior. Of greater concern was the fact that his natural parents had slowly withdrawn from him during his illness. Over time, the staff of the nursing care unit realized that they were, in many ways, Peter's "family" and that the nursing staff would be the ones to care for him and be with him when he died.

As Peter's condition worsened, his needs for physical and emotional care increased. The staff decided that he should be assigned a primary care nurse, Sheri Martin, RN, who would coordinate and plan the increasing amount of care that he would need. Within a few days, Peter could no longer walk because of the pain from the effects of his illness. He was often feverish, and he suffered from nausea, vomiting, and diarrhea. He experienced constant fear—of pain, of the effects of morphine, and of the possibility that he might not wake up once he fell asleep. Nighttime was especially difficult for Peter and his nurses. He was in near constant pain but often refused his morphine. Instead, he asked that his nurse stay in the room, talk to him, read to him, do anything to distract him from his pain.

One evening, he asked Miss Martin to stay with him even though she had already worked all day. She switched her hours with another nurse and stayed on the unit to take care of Peter. There was a real possibility that Peter was near death. Unfortunately, another staff nurse called in sick. There then was not enough staff to take care of all the patients,

---

[2]Adapted from Leff, E. (1982). Keeping a promise. *American Journal of Nursing, 82,* 1136–1138.

especially if Miss Martin spent the majority of her time with Peter. Miss Martin could not decide what to do. She had promised Peter that she or one of the other nurses would stay with him, especially when he died. Yet it did not seem fair to the other patients, some of whom needed careful preparation for diagnostic tests the following day, to forgo their needs in favor of Peter's needs. Yet if no one stayed with Peter, he would feel abandoned at the time when he needed someone the most. If this happened, the nurses would surely suffer the consequences of feeling guilt, frustration, and anger at being unable to respond to Peter's important needs. Should promises to Peter be kept when nursing resources were strained to the limit and other patients' needs were also important?

Commentary

The moral problem in this case seems to arise from the fact that Sheri Martin is convinced that there are other patients who could benefit greatly from her nursing care and yet she has made a promise to Peter to stay with him in his time of need.

We have already seen in the other cases in this chapter that not everyone is convinced that the morally correct thing to do is always to use resources in ways that do the most good in total. Some people would say that justice requires identifying the people with the greatest need and using resources to meet that need, even if some other use would do more good. If Peter has a very great need, and it appears that he does, then perhaps Sheri Martin, if she is governed by an egalitarian interpretation of the principle of justice in addition to or in place of beneficence, will conclude that she should go where the need is the greatest—quite possibly to Peter. That would mean that justice would require the same thing that keeping the promise would require. Her moral dilemma would disappear.

Some people hold, however, that it is morally more correct to do the most good than to help the people with the greatest need. If Sheri Martin is one of those people, then she still has a problem with Peter. If he has the greatest need, but she can do more good helping others, then she would normally have a moral duty to abandon Peter.

If she holds this view, then the fact that she had promised him that she would stay with him could become morally important. In effect, there are three moral dimensions to the case: doing good, serving the most needy, and keeping promises. The resolution could depend on how one ranks these various principles. If doing good counts as definitive, then the matter will be settled in favor of abandoning Peter and breaking her promise. That position would be the same as saying that normally needs should be met and promises should be kept, but only because usually that does the most good. In cases where it does not, one should do the most good anyway.

Others might give priority to the other principles. Someone like Immanuel Kant would hold that the duty to keep promises is unconditional. That might have settled the matter for Kant, in favor of staying with Peter in order to keep the promise. Still others might hold that the duty to serve the most needy is unconditional.

One final position is worth considering. Serving the needy and keeping promises are related duties in the sense that they are not based simply on the amount of consequences produced. Philosophers sometimes call such duties deontological or formalist, meaning that it is the form or nature of the action rather than its consequences that is morally important. One might hold that these duties take precedence over simply producing good consequences. Holders of that view would recognize that both serving the needy and keeping promises would bind Miss Martin to staying with Peter, whereas only the lower priority principle of doing good authorizes her to leave him. It is to these other principles that we turn in Chapters 7 through 10.

Case 5-9

Allocating Mechanical Ventilators During a Severe Influenza Pandemic

Marilee LeBon is an infectious disease nurse with a special interest in bioethics. She has served for years on her hospital's ethics committee and recently volunteered to represent the hospital on a statewide committee meeting to develop guidelines for allocating mechanical ventilators during a severe influenza pandemic. She understands that during a severe pandemic of influenza, many patients with respiratory failure who are able to receive mechanical ventilation may survive, while patients with respiratory failure who do not receive mechanical ventilation are likely to die. Importantly, it is possible that in the event of a severe pandemic of influenza, many hospitals and other healthcare facilities will not have adequate numbers of ventilators to support a major disaster response.

If a scarcity of ventilators occurs during a severe influenza pandemic, ventilators would need to be allocated according to different guidelines than during usual clinical care. During a public health emergency, there will be competing priorities for ventilator use from patients whose need for a ventilator is unrelated to influenza, including the need for chronic ventilator use. In addition, decisions will need to be made regarding whether patients should be removed from a ventilator to make way for others who may have a better chance of recovery and whether there should be suspension of nonemergency surgical procedures that might create a need for ventilator therapy.

Ms. LeBon's first challenge is to work on a subcommittee charged with articulating the ethical framework they will use. She reviews current guidelines.[9] What role should justice considerations play in dictating who should get access to the scarce ventilator therapy? What other principles are helpful?

Commentary

Ms. LeBon and the members of the committee will need to articulate some general guidelines for allocating ventilators. Almost certainly, they will want to take into account a range of moral principles including autonomy, justice, beneficence, and nonmaleficence, as well as perhaps the principle of promise keeping. They may also need to take into account a principle that it is wrong to kill (in Chapter 10 we will refer to this as the principle of the sanctity of human life). All of these seem morally relevant to the problem of allocating ventilators during a pandemic.

Justice, understood as giving resource priority to the worst off patients, would assign ventilators to the sickest patients—perhaps those with the highest priority of dying without the ventilator. This is likely to include both patients ventilator-dependent in ways unrelated to the pandemic and the sickest of the sick influenza patients. The problem with this justice-based priority rule is that it is likely to be very inefficient. Some influenza patients may have a good chance of survival, but could benefit significantly if they have access to a ventilator for a short period. Several such patients could be helped with the same ventilator time that would be needed for the chronic ventilator-dependent patient or the very sick influenza patient. Thus, it is realistic to expect that more good could be done targeting patients who are less ill and need the ventilator only temporarily. A good utilitarian would give priority to patients who could be helped a great deal with brief use of the ventilator even if that meant excluding the sickest influenza patients or withdrawing the ventilators from the chronically ill, ventilator-dependent patients. Thus, as we have seen in other cases in this chapter, the principle of beneficence (utility maximizing) may support a different set of priority rules than the principle of justice.

However, in this case, other principles may come into play as well. The principle of autonomy may be relevant in at least two ways. First, a pure libertarian autonomy advocate may support free-market notions even to the extreme of letting those with ability to pay negotiate access to the ventilators. Second, autonomy would support letting mentally competent patients (and perhaps surrogates for incompetent patients) refuse access to ventilators. This right to refuse treatment will be explored further in the chapter on autonomy (Chapter 7) and the chapter on consent (Chapter 16).

Still other ethical principles will be relevant when Ms. LeBon's committee meets. The principle of promise-keeping holds that commitments made ought to be kept. If we understand the decision to place a patient on a ventilator as a kind of promise that the patient will continue to have access, then the chronic ventilator-dependent patients as well as influenza patients already on ventilators may have a claim to continue. Also, some hold that withdrawing a patient from a ventilator would be killing the patient. We need to explore whether adopting a policy of intentionally removing patients from ventilators in order to use them more efficiently to save other patients would violate the duty to avoid killing. That will be explored in detail in Chapter 10, the chapter on the principle of the sacredness of human life.

Thus, Ms. LeBon's committee will have to develop an understanding of what they should do when many ethical principles arise at the same time and not all the principles can be satisfied simultaneously. In order to do so, she will need a clear understanding of the remaining ethical principles that impinge on health care. Those principles are examined in the chapters that follow.

ENDNOTES

1. For discussions on the role of nurses in allocation, see: Arries, E. J. (2009, March). Interactional justice in student-staff nurse encounters. *Nursing Ethics, 16*(2), 147–160; Crigger, N. J. (2008, January). Towards a viable and just global nursing ethics. *Nursing Ethics, 15*(1), 17–27; Halvorsen, K., Førde, R., & Nortvedt, P. (2009, August). The principle of justice in patient priorities in the intensive care unit: the role of significant others. *Journal of Medical Ethics, 35*(8), 483–487; Nortvedt, P., Pedersen, R., Grøthe, K. H., Nordhaug, M., Kirkevold, M., Slettebø, Å., et al. (2008, May) Clinical prioritisations of healthcare for the aged— Professional roles. *Journal of Medical Ethics, 34*(5), 332–335; Pacquiao, D. F. (2008, April). Nursing care of vulnerable populations using a framework of cultural competence, social justice and human rights. *Contemporary Nurse, 28*(1–2), 189–197.
2. Burns, J. H., & Hart, H. L. A. (Eds.). *The collected works of Jeremy Bentham: An introduction to the principles of morals and legislation.* New York: Oxford University Press.
3. Sidgwick, H. (1874/1966). *The methods of ethics.* New York: Dover Publications.
4. Nozick, R. (1974). *Anarchy, state, and utopia.* New York: Basic Books.
5. Rawls, J. (1971). *A theory of justice.* Cambridge, MA: Harvard University Press.
6. For a summary of the alternative approaches to allocating resources, see: Beauchamp, T. L., & Childress, J. F. (2009). *Principles of biomedical ethics* (6th ed., pp. 230–235). New York: Oxford University Press; Veatch, R. M. (2003). *The basics of bioethics* (2nd ed., pp. 126–134). Upper Saddle River, NJ: Prentice Hall.
7. Engelhardt, H. T. (1996). *The foundations of bioethics* (2nd ed.). New York: Oxford University Press.
8. Moss, A. H., & Siegler, M. (1991). Should alcoholics compete equally for liver transplantation? *Journal of the American Medical Association, 255*, 1295–1298.
9. Alabama Department of Public Health. (2008, July 3). *Final draft criteria for mechanical ventilator triage following proclamation of mass casualty respiratory emergency.* Birmingham, AL: Author; New York State Department of Health. (2007, March 15). *Allocation of ventilators in an influenza pandemic: Planning document* (Draft for public comment). Available at: http://www.health.state.ny.us/diseases/communicable/influenza/pandemic/ventilators/docs/ventilator_guidance.pdf. Accessed November 12, 2008; Ventilator Guidance Workgroup for the Ethics Subcommittee of the Advisory Committee to the Director (CCD). (2009, October 30). *Ethical considerations for decision making regarding allocation of mechanical ventilators during a severe influenza pandemic.* Available at: http://s3.amazonaws.com/propublica/assets/docs/Vent_Guidance_.draftoc 2008pdf.pdf. Accessed April 28, 2010; White House. (2006). *National strategy for pandemic influenza: Implementation plan.* Washington, DC: U.S. Government Printing Office. Available at: http://hosted.ap.org/specials/interactive/wdc/documents/pandemicinfluenza.pdf. Accessed April 28, 2010.

Chapter 6

Respect

Other Cases Involving Respect

Case 1-6: The Visiting Nurse and the Obstinate Patient: Limits on the Right to Nursing Care

Case 3-2: Nurses Caught Between a Rock and a Hard Place

Case 9-2: Is There a Duty to Abandon Illegal Immigrants

Case 12-11: Questioning the Purposes of Surrogate Motherhood Requests

Case 13-6: Sedating and Restraining the Disturbed Patient

Key Terms
Deontology
Formalism
Principle
Respect
Respect for persons

Objectives
1. Define the principle respect for persons.
2. Affirm or challenge the claim that nurses are obligated to practice with compassion and respect in all professional relationships.
3. Apply the principle respect for persons in situations where the dignity and worth of patients, family members, and staff is being undermined.

In the previous chapter we saw that the principle of justice provides a moral reason why someone might resist distributing scarce resources so as to produce the greatest net benefit in aggregate. Justice is a principle that affirms the distribution of good as morally relevant, not just the total amount of good. In this chapter and the four that follow we will look at another moral consideration that many believe constrains doing good and avoiding harm. In contrast to justice, which is only relevant when more than one person's welfare is at stake, the principles we take up now apply even if one's actions affect only one individual. The moral consideration we now want to consider is sometimes referred to as *respect*.

Many ethical views hold that there is more to ethics than merely doing good and avoiding evil. Often these additional considerations are presented under the heading of **respect for persons**. Immanuel Kant is an example of an ethical thinker who focuses his ethics on respect for persons. He holds that there are certain moral norms or maxims that spell out what we owe people that are not based on doing good for them. He holds that it is simply our moral duty to treat people in certain ways. Because it is the formal characteristics of these norms that determines what is morally right rather than the consequences, these views are sometimes called **formalism**. Others refer to this view as **deontology**, meaning that certain behaviors are simply our *duty* even if they do not produce benefit. Respecting autonomy, telling the truth, keeping promises, or avoiding killing people are all examples of duties that many hold we owe people regardless of the consequences. Each of these can be expressed as a **principle** of ethics: autonomy, veracity, fidelity, and avoidance of killing or the sacredness of life. These four principles are the subject of the following four chapters of this book.

Often this collection of formalist or deontological principles gets grouped together under the heading of respect for persons. Respect for persons can be taken as kind of a super-principle that directs our attention to the intrinsic moral worth of people. It requires that we treat them as ends in themselves, not mere means to good consequences. In fact some important ethical theories simply list respect for persons as the principle. The first U.S. official government report on ethics, The Belmont Report of the National Commission for the Protection of Human Subjects,[1] for example, lists respect for persons as one of its three principles (along with beneficence and justice, the two principles of the previous chapters in this book). Those who refer to the over-arching principle of respect for persons then derive the duty to respect autonomy, to tell the truth, and to keep promises, and avoid killing people from it.

Other theorists accomplish something similar by somewhat different language. Tom Beauchamp and James Childress, for example, in their influential book, *The Principles of Biomedical Ethics*, include the "principle of respect for autonomy" as one of their four principles (along with beneficence, nonmaleficence, and justice). They then derive veracity and fidelity from respect for autonomy.[2] This leaves open the question of whether duties like telling the truth and keeping promises are owed to people who are nonautonomous.

These approaches are all similar. They recognize an independent duty to respect persons and several related more specific duties such as respecting autonomy, veracity, fidelity, and perhaps avoidance of killing. Our approach in previous editions of this book was simply to include four chapters on these principles that do not focus on maximizing good consequences: autonomy, veracity, fidelity, and the sanctity of life. In doing so we implied, but perhaps did not sufficiently emphasize, that they are all aspects of what we are calling the super-principle of respect, usually referred to as *respect for persons*.

That name, respect for persons, raises another complicated issue: is it only "persons" who command respect or are there others requiring it as well. This, of course, depends on the precise meaning of "person." Many secular commentators define a "person" as a being who is self-aware or self-conscious. By that definition, many living humans (babies and individuals with advanced Alzheimer's disease, for example) are not persons. To make matters more complicated others refer to any being who deserves maximum moral standing as a "person" in which case some persons may not be self-aware or self-conscious. Babies or even fetuses could be thought of as persons under this usage.

It seems to us arguable that some living humans who are not persons in the sense of being self-aware or self-conscious nevertheless deserve maximum respect and that moral duties derived from our super-principle of respect apply. Moreover, in this edition for the first time we specifically recognize that this principle of respect may be particularly important in nursing even in situations in which none of the traditional principles of autonomy, veracity, fidelity, or avoidance of killing arise.

Respect for the inherent worth, dignity, and human rights of every individual is a fundamental concern underlying all nursing practice. The first statement in the American Nurses Association (ANA) *Code of Ethics* reads:

> The nurse, in all professional relationships, practices with compassion and respect for the inherent dignity, worth and uniqueness of every individual, unrestricted by considerations of social or economic status, personal attributes, or the nature of health problems.[3]

Nurse ethicist Barbara Jacobs recommends respect for, or the restoration of, human dignity,[4] as a common central phenomenon to unite and reflect nursing theory and practice.[5] By virtue of their daily intimate encounters with patients and their caregivers, nurses have tremendous power to influence the well-being of others. In each clinical encounter, a nurse verbally and nonverbally communicates one of three messages: you are a person of worth and I care, you are an object and you mean nothing to me, or you are vile and despicable and inspire disgust, or worse. The nurse's capacity to reduce humans to objects or worse can profoundly influence others' sense of well-being and healing.

Critical Thinking Question

Reflect on the fundamental assumptions about people you bring to practice and check those with which you agree. Compare your list with a colleague and explore any differences.

_____ Every human being by virtue of being human, merits my equal and full respect.

_____ Only those persons who are self-aware and self-conscious merit my equal and full respect.

_____ The more vulnerable people are because of illness, frailty, or other marginalizing factors, the *more* they command my compassion and respect.

_____ The more vulnerable people are because of illness, frailty, or other marginalizing factors, the *less* they command my compassion and respect.

___ I need to be compassionate and respectful to those innocently affected by disease, injury or frailty—so long as self-abusive behaviors did not cause the disease or infirmity.

___ People need to earn my respect.

___ It is only human and ethically justifiable to respect people differently according to their uniqueness.[6]

In this chapter we take up some troubling cases in which nurses confront dramatic examples of a lack of respect—respect for patients, family members, and health professionals. We identify three kinds of behaviors that suggest a lack of respect, focusing on pathology to the exclusion of the person with the pathology, arrogant decision making, and humiliation of subordinates.

Ignoring a Person as a Person and Focusing Only on the Pathology or "Task" to be Performed

We turn first to a rather common practice in the clinical setting: focusing on the pathology or task to be performed to the exclusion of the person who has the pathology or upon whom the task is to be performed. We hear of "the broken leg in room 234" or "the central line on floor 2 West" without realizing that these speech patterns seemingly ignore that there is a patient connected to that leg or receiving the central line. The two cases in the first section of this chapter present patients who seem reduced to their pathologies. The first involves an AIDS patient whose hostility leads to the use of restraints and the second involves ignoring the person in the emergency room.

Case 6-1
Humanity Lost in the Bed

Elmer Miller is a 42-year-old African American with AIDS, newly admitted to a hospital for treatment of a cerebellar tumor. Friendly, gregarious, and eager to please, he is liked by the hospital staff. As his tumor progresses, however, he becomes hostile and combative and after he attacks a nurse with an IV pole and pharmacologic management of his combativeness fails, he is placed in four point leather restraints according to hospital policy. Twice an MRI is cancelled because of his inability to cooperate during the procedure. The nurses caring for Mr. Miller call an ethics consult because they are troubled by their increasing inability to recognize and respond to his humanity. "When we walk into his room what we see is an animal tethered to a bed. His patient gown is often awry because of his restlessness, and he lies there in glorious nakedness. His Texas catheter often comes off, and his sheets are urine soaked. He moans ... It's hard to think of him as a person. Somehow we lost the man we knew and love."

Commentary

This is perhaps the simplest of challenges to respect but it is significant that the nurses involved recognized that they were in danger of violating their obligation to respect Mr. Miller's inherent worth, dignity, and human rights—merely because a change in his status resulted in their naturally responding to him differently. Aware of the challenge, they regrouped and strategized with a nurse ethicist about how they might respond differently. One newly graduated nurse shared with the group that she knew the patient loved to be massaged. "When I wash him up in the morning I warm some lotion in my hands and then massage him from the crown of head to his toes. I can feel his muscles relax. It's my way of saying, 'You are a person of worth and I care.'" Nurses often find themselves in clinical encounters with patients and their family caregivers who prompt negative responses: frustration, disgust, horror, anger, and anxiety. Aware of these human responses, nurses can focus their energies on responding professionally, realizing that their profession calls them to a higher ethic. The centrality of advocacy to nursing's core identity underscores the importance of nurses being witness to the humanity of patients to the healthcare team at large. At times, being an advocate for patients will mean finding constructive ways to challenge other caregivers who are disrespecting patients

Case 6-2
The Heel Wound in the ER Bed

Gretl Hochstettler, a student nurse doing a clinical rotation in an emergency room, hears a scream from behind the curtains in a patient bay in the ER. Pulling back the curtain she sees a resident and medical student examining a wound in a patient's heel. The patient is an 89-year-old contracted nursing home resident with advanced dementia who arrived in the ER an hour earlier without a family member or advocate. The patient's gown is awry, the medical student is holding the patient's leg straight up in the air with her perineal area clearly exposed, and the resident has his gloved finger probing the wound. The resident and medical student are clearly focused on the wound and not the patient—in fact they seem oblivious to her screams.

Ms. Hochstettler wants to "rescue" the patient but hesitates, being unsure of her position and not wanting to be laughed at by her colleagues for being tenderhearted. When she finds her clinical mentor and reports what is going on she is told "not to sweat" this, that many nursing home residents are "screamers" and that the doctors have to learn on someone. As an afterthought she tells Ms. Hochstettler to see if the patient has anything ordered for pain. Is Ms. Hochstettler obligated to come to the patient's defense? Did the student's clinical mentor respond appropriately? Are the resident and medical student acting competently, safely, ethically, and legally? Should their behavior be reported, and if so, to whom?

Commentary

Ms. Hochstettler is getting a crude and unfortunate introduction to her nursing career. Two separate problems arise, each of which needs attention. First, the resident and the medical student are seriously deficient in their clinical skills and need help. Even if we assume that the physical examination of the wound is being done properly, the care of the patient is surely not. There may be times in the ER in which timely access is so critical that compromise with patient privacy is essential. In this case, however, taking a few seconds to show respect for the patient would not jeopardize the examination. The initial problem is that the medical student and resident seem insensitive to the need for respect. While it would ideally be the resident's job to mentor the medical student so that disrespectful patterns of practice are not learned, the harsh reality is that the physician and medical student may not take this responsibility. This puts Ms. Hochstettler in the awkward position of being the only one who seems concerned.

The second problem arises when Ms. Hochstettler reports to her clinical mentor, who seems no more sensitive to the patient than the medical personnel. The nurse supervisor seems to think that this is normal behavior. She demeans the patient by suggesting that many nursing home residents are "screamers." When she did offer a suggestion, it was directed at a pharmacologic fix for the patient's pain, totally ignoring the humane responses—closing the gown, covering the patient, and expressing sympathetic concern for the suffering the patient was experiencing.

Ms. Hochstettler's problem seems to be that she is not yet desensitized to these attacks on the patient's dignity. She seems to understand all too well the need for an intervention, but, as a nursing student, she does not know what to do. Her first response seemed correct: She talked with her supervisor. However, in this case, the supervisor was part of the problem, not the solution. She may feel compelled to talk with fellow students or perhaps nursing faculty. She may have the strength to raise the issue with the resident or a more sensitive physician on the staff. She may, at least, treat this as a learning experience in which she will be more aware of the patient connected to the pathology when she takes on the full responsibilities as a registered nurse.

A final note: Nurses who work in teaching hospitals frequently encounter situations where the focus is more on educating the next generation of healthcare professionals than on patient care. When a patient becomes primarily or merely a teaching or research opportunity, the patient is being disrespected. Ideally Ms. Hochstettler's experience will be the catalyst for her learning how to advocate for patients in similar situations as her professional development advances.

Arrogant Decision Making

A second kind of disrespect that needs attention appears in the making of clinical decisions. It is not necessarily the decisions themselves that are disrespectful, but the way in which they are made and the presumptions of the decision maker about his or her authority to make the choices involved. Although the example in the case that follows involves a physician who usurps decision-making authority in a manner that is so inappropriate that it is disrespectful, nurses can also be guilty. Increasingly, we are recognizing that healthcare decision making is a shared responsibility in which many members of the health professional team will share the task with the patient and family who may be supporting the patient. In the following case, a surgeon seems to believe that the authority to continue or stop life support on a terminal patient is his and his alone. Note that it is not merely the usurping of the decision making that is disrespectful, but also the communication with the patient's wife.

Case 6-3
May a Surgeon Order the Patient to Survive?

Mr. Valdez is a 30-year-old male who had a liver/small bowel transplant 2 years ago. In the interim, he has been in and out of the hospital for multiple complications. At present, he is on the 45th day of this hospitalization and is in the surgical intensive care unit. He is well-known to the nursing staff and there is strong consensus among the critical care team that it is long overdue for this patient's treatment goals to transition to purely palliative goals. He is receiving ventilatory support, is on total parental nutrition, is being dialyzed, and receives numerous medications. Mr. Valdez's wife, Regina, has been vocal for 2 weeks about wanting a "no code" order for her husband, but the transplant surgeon repeatedly tells her that when he received the scarce organs he sacrificed his "right" to "give up." Recently the surgeon told Mrs. Valdez, "I spend my nights trying to think of how to save your husband and you are trying to kill him."

Mrs. Valdez has frequently been reduced to tears by these exchanges, and she confided to a nurse, "They are making me feel like a monster. I love my husband, and I am only trying to make the requests he would make if he could speak for himself. I can't stand to see him suffer like this."

This morning Mr. Kimura is the patient's nurse. He finds the patient actively dying. When he contacts the transplant surgeon reporting that the wife wants her husband extubated and the goals of care changed to comfort, the transplant surgeon states he cannot agree with this change. Mr. Kimura gives the phone to Mrs. Valdez who begs the surgeon to allow her husband to die in peace. She asks, "What else do I have to do to get you to honor our wishes?" Ultimately the surgeon "allows" the medical intensivist to wean the patient from the ventilator. Mr. Kimura and other nurses try to make Mr. Valdez comfortable, and his wife is able to spend about 2 hours with him before he dies. As she leaves the unit she tells Mr. Kimura, "I don't know how I'm going to live with myself. I feel like I killed my husband." How should Mr. Kimura and the other nurses address the disrespect Mrs. Valdez experienced from the transplant surgeon?

Commentary

This case raises many legal and ethical issues about consent and the right to refuse treatment. It is now generally established that, especially when patients are terminally ill, patients and their valid surrogates have the legal and ethical right to refuse consent to life-supporting interventions. Those issues will be the topic of Chapters 7 and 16.

Here the discussion should focus on a somewhat more subtle problem—the disrespect shown by the surgeon and how Mr. Kimura might respond. The notion that receiving organs implies sacrificing a right to "give up" not only mistakes the legal and ethical obligations of a transplant recipient, it does so in a particularly offensive manner, implying that the patient (who has undertaken a long list of aggressive treatments) is merely not willing to do the work needed to survive. It is as if the surgeon believes the patient owes him a debt that is beyond reason. Even more offensively, he accuses the wife of wanting to kill her husband, a description of what she is doing that we shall see in Chapter 10 is not only an inaccurate description of what the wife is attempting to do, but also a particularly pejorative way of expressing it. The surgeon clearly thinks this patient and his wife owe him something.

Thus, in addition to the significant legal and ethical mistakes made by the surgeon, he is also making the mistake of inexcusable arrogance. Arrogance involves expressing a sense of superiority in an overbearing manner. This surgeon has a particularly bad case. In the end, he thinks he is "allowing" the patient to be weaned. The same behavior could be described as the surgeon reluctantly recognizing the right of the patient and the surrogate to refuse to consent to the treatment that the surgeon has the authority only to recommend, not to command.

Mr. Kimura's problem is how to respond. Since the surgeon's usurpation of authority violates both legal and ethical norms of the hospital, Mr. Kimura has some resources available. He can turn not only to fellow nurses or sympathetic physicians, but also to the legal authorities and ethics consultation service of the hospital. Failure to report illegal treatment without consent would, in fact, expose Mr. Kimura himself to legal risks. When Mr. Kimura informed the transplant surgeon that he was calling the hospital's legal counsel the surgeon suddenly acquiesced to the medical intensivist changing the treatment goals to palliation. He remained adamant that he believed this was a wrong decision. Taking advantage of the ethics consultation service of the hospital also provided Mr. Kimura with valuable support for his advocacy.

Confronting the arrogance of the surgeon may be a more difficult task. If Mr. Kimura values his own worth and that of the patient and his wife, he is obligated to challenge the transplant surgeon's disrespect, especially if this behavior is chronic. Many factors can make such a challenge seem impossible. In the actual situation from which this case was derived, there is not a positive work environment in the surgical intensive care unit. The transplant surgeon has made no effort to get to know the nurses caring for his patients in spite of their efforts to initiate collaborative dialogue. Moreover, since this surgeon is rapidly growing the hospital's transplant program, he is viewed with great respect by the hospital's administration. Mr. Kimura can continue to experience the moral distress engendered by this and similar situations and ultimately disengage or work with nursing and medical leadership to address problematic behaviors. Since this is not an isolated breach, much is at stake for all involved. Ideally the hospital's ethics committee or consultant would be helpful in strategizing how best to achieve valued outcomes. In the end, the hospital's leadership will have to make a judgment about their core values and the importance of patient care and respect.

Humiliating Others

A third aspect of disrespect arises in relation to other members of the healthcare team, some of whom will be thought of as "subordinates," and between patients and nurses. There are basic conceptual problems in the use of the term "superiors" and "subordinates" in describing members of the healthcare team. For example, nurses have traditionally been thought of as subordinates of a team in which the physician is the "captain of the ship." The very use of such metaphors as "captain" are problematic, especially in modern health care in which many members of the team are highly trained professionals with specialized skills and authority. The hospital pharmacist, for example, may know more about the pharmacology of a medication than the physician. The radiologic therapist may know more about radiation exposure. Likewise, the nurse is increasingly seen as a professional with unique set of skills over which he or she has legal and ethical responsibility. Thus, the concept of the collaborative interdisciplinary team exercising open communication and mutual respect is the reigning paradigm.

Likewise, within a health profession, there will exist authority relations that can create moral problems of respect. The director of nursing does have legitimate authority over the nurses on the staff. The nursing supervisor has authority over various nursing personnel. The issue in this section of the chapter is not over the legitimacy of this authority. It is over the way in which that authority is exercised. It can be used to build up or tear down one who is in the subordinate position. The following two cases raise issues of humiliation.

Case 6-4
"Reaming Out" Subordinates

Phyllis Dukakis is an associate degree–prepared nurse who is orienting to her responsibilities as charge nurse in a skilled nursing facility. After only 10 days on the job she is appalled by the interactions she observes between the nursing supervisor and several of the charge nurses and the licensed practical nurses and nursing aides. It is not uncommon for an aide to be "reamed out" publicly in the hall for not having all her residents into the dining hall on time or some other transgression. Additionally, the nursing leadership frequently gossip and complain about the staff they have to work with. Having worked as an aide in a nursing home several summers she knows that staff workloads are heavy and a little bit of encouragement can go a long way to lightening the load. Conversely, she can see how the sniping and put-downs coming from leadership are affecting morale. Ironically, nursing leadership has high expectations that all frontline caregivers will demonstrate great compassion and respect for residents of the facility and their families. "Remember, Residents are our Number One Priority." She is surprised that leadership does not understand that you cannot give what you do not have. If staff do not experience compassion and respect it is difficult to "dish it out, day in and day out, shift by shift." She is wondering if she should accept the challenge of remaining in this job.

Case 6-5
On-the-Job Abuse of Nurses by Patients and Physicians

Xiamei Hu is a family nurse practitioner who works in a not-for-profit adult and pediatric clinic serving an inner-city–impoverished community. Most of the families served are African American and Latino. She was happy with her practice until about 8 months ago when a new medical director was hired to address the alarming financial status of the clinic, which was hopelessly in the red. With unemployment rates rising in the city and fewer families with employment linked health insurance, the clinic population had tripled over the last year and everyone was trying to do "more with less." What Ms. Hu had most liked about her practice was the clinic's commitment to its patients and to literally "moving mountains" to see that their complex and, at times, overwhelming healthcare needs were met. A cohesive interdisciplinary team was available to work with individuals and families.

Recently, however, every time she tried to advocate for someone who needed help getting medications, medical equipment, food, or shelter she was berated by the director who told her to stop trying to be Santa Claus and to just "get her job done. Move them in and move them out and do it quickly!" Recently she learned that the director was trying to eliminate the positions of two social workers who were invaluable members of the team. When she went to the director on their behalf he stood up, pointed his finger in her face, and screamed at her, "Don't try to do my job, missy! If you value your own job you'll shut your mouth!" Ignoring his condescension was one thing, but the abusive anger was another. She can appreciate the difficult task he has of balancing revenues and expenses—but she cannot accept this behavior. It is bad enough that many of the patients vent their anger on the staff and some, in spite of the team's heroic efforts on their behalf, leave ungrateful and angry. Even more problematic are the family members who accompany many of the patients to the clinic. Often overwhelmed themselves by life in general and the burden of caring for sick family members, they frequently "dump" their frustration and anger on the clinic staff becoming verbally and, in a few cases, physically abusive. How should Ms. Hu respond? Until now she has not personalized the abuse but she fears that it will begin to compromise her own mental health and practice. Is she being disrespectful of herself if she puts up with these behaviors?

Commentary

Cases 6-4 and Case 6-5 both deal with aspects of disrespect that comes in the form of humiliation. Case 6-4 involves behavior of higher status nurses—supervisors and charge nurses—as they interact with lower status members of the team—licensed practical nurses and nursing aides. It is crucial here to separate the potential problems that aroused the supervisor hostility—failure to get patients to the dining hall on time—from the way in which the supervisors express their dissatisfaction. It is sometimes difficult to tell whether a problem, such as the failure to get patients to their proper places on time, is the result of impossible work loads or failures on the part of the nurse to do what easily should have been done. Regardless, however, there are more respectful ways to intervene to address the issue. Asking the nurses who are responsible for locating patients in their proper places why there is a problem might, for example, be a way of starting a needed conversation. That leaves open the question of whether it was the nurse's fault or was beyond the nurse's control.

Dressing down one who is supervised is rarely the right way to go, especially if it occurs in public in front of patients, colleagues, and other members of the healthcare team. Juxtaposing humiliation of the nurse with an expectation of compassion and respect for patients or residents of the facility is particularly problematic.

Case 6-5 raises similar issues, except that the humiliation of the nurse comes from the director of the facility, someone with even more power and authority than the nursing supervisor in the previous case. Moreover, the nurse also is on the receiving end from the patients who are venting their anger on the staff for the compromises in patient care required by the facility director.

Critical Thinking Question

Your hospital is located near a large penitentiary and it is not unusual for pregnant inmates to deliver in your obstetric department. Hospital policy requires that these women be handcuffed to the bed to prevent their escape. You and other nurses question the humanity of the policy and are wondering whether to try to change the policy. In all but a very few instances, the women were not a danger to themselves or others and were not a flight risk. An officer was always in attendance in the room. Labor is never a comfortable experience and the lack of mobility with the handcuffs made the experience excruciating for these women. Which of the following assumptions, if any, do you bring to your reasoning?

A female inmate has lost the basic rights of other citizens.

A female inmate is, first, a person with the basic right to be respected.

Better safe than sorry.

Restraints should only be used if the risk of harm (including flight) is significant.

Best obstetric practices may legitimately be compromised for inmates.

Other:

In the Research Brief that follows, Shields and Wilkins report that: (1) health-care providers commonly experience violence or verbal abuse from patients in their care; (2) nurses who experience on-the-job abuse are at risk of physical and psychologic problems, and (3) there is also some evidence of a link between on-the-job abuse of nurses and diminished quality of patient care.[7]

Research Brief 6-1

Source: Shields, M., & Wilkins, K. (2009). Factors related to on-the-job abuse of nurses by patients. *Health Reports, 20*(2), 1–13.

Purpose: To examine physical and emotional abuse from patients in nurses working in hospitals or long-term care facilities.

Method: Data are from the 2005 *National (Canadian) Survey of Work and Health of Nurses*. Cross-tabulations were used to examine abuse in relation to personal characteristics of the nurse, job characteristics, and workplace climate factors. Multiple logistic regression modeling was used to examine abuse in relation to staffing and resource adequacy and relations among colleagues, controlling for personal and job characteristics.

Findings: In 2005, 34% of Canadian nurses providing direct care in hospitals or long-term care facilities reported physical assault by a patient in the previous year; 47% reported emotional abuse. Abuse was related to being male, having less experience, usually working non-day shifts, and perceiving staffing or resources as inadequate, nurse–physician relations as poor, and coworker and supervisor support as low. Associations between abuse and staffing or resource inadequacy and poor working relations persisted when controlling for personal and job characteristics.

Implications: Modifiable factors are important to nurses' on-the-job safety.

ENDNOTES

1. National Commission for the Protection of Human Subjects of Biomedical and Behavioral Research. (1978). *The Belmont report: Ethical principles and guidelines for the protection of human subjects of research*. Washington, DC: U.S. Government Printing Office.
2. Beauchamp, T. L., & Childress, J. F. (2009). *Principles of biomedical ethics* (6th ed., pp. 99–140, 288–295, 311–314). New York: Oxford University Press.
3. American Nurses Association. (2005). *Code of ethics for nurses with interpretive statements* (p. 7). Washington, DC: Author.
4. Here we intentionally connect "respect" and "dignity." We use the term "dignity" to refer to the properties that humans (and perhaps other beings) have that causes them to command respect.

5. Jacobs, B. (2001). Respect for human dignity: A central phenomenon to philosophically unite nursing theory and practice through consilience of knowledge. *Advances in Nursing Science, 24*(1), 17-35.

6. Taylor, C. (2008). Provision one. In M. D. M. Fowler (Ed.), *Guide to the code of ethics for nurses: Interpretation and application* (pp. 1–10), Silver Spring, MD: American Nurses Association.

7. Shields, M., & Wilkins, K. (2009). Factors related to on-the-job abuse of nurses by patients. *Health Reports, 20*(2), 1–13.

Chapter 7

The Principle of Autonomy

Other Cases Involving Autonomy

Key Terms

Autonomy

Competency

Capacity for autonomous decision making

Existential advocacy

Incompetency

Paternalism

Objectives

1. Define the principle of autonomy.
2. Describe two types of constraints on individual autonomy.
3. Identify conflicts between the principle of autonomy and other ethical principles.
4. Apply the principle of autonomy in patient care situations.

In the two previous chapters, we examined ways in which the morally correct course might not simply be a matter of producing as much good as possible. Chapter 5, which focused on the principle of justice, presented cases in which the distribution of the good among patients or between patients and nonpatients was seen by many as morally relevant. Chapter 6 introduced the notion of respect, suggesting that morality was a matter of showing respect as well as producing good.

The idea that morality requires respect for people has been central to contemporary biomedical ethics. Often respect is addressed by appealing to one or more principles that suggest ways that people can be respected. This chapter and the three that follow take up four specific principles that signify ways of showing respect. In this chapter, we take up respect for autonomy. In the three that follow we consider the principles of veracity, fidelity, as well as the principle that we call the sanctity of life (the idea that there is something intrinsically immoral with the intentional killing of another).

One of the most important of these is the principle of **autonomy**. Here the claim is that we owe others respect for their autonomy and that showing such respect may be as important or even more important that producing benefits for others. If the nurse could persuade, pressure, coerce, or trick the patient into staying, should he or she do so? Suppose the nurse, by lying or deceiving the patient, could change the patient's mind and thus make him or her better off. Would that be acceptable behavior simply because it would make the patient better off?

Often the goals of doing good and avoiding harm for the patient—the principles of beneficence and nonmaleficence—come into conflict with such other ethical principles as respect for autonomy, truth-telling, promise-keeping, or avoiding killing. The cases presented in this chapter raise problems related to the first of these additional principles: the principle of autonomy. The principle of autonomy affirms that individuals are to be permitted personal liberty to determine their own actions according to plans they themselves have chosen. Respecting autonomy means that persons with decision-making capacity have the right to make these decisions. A patient has decision-making capacity "when the patient has: (a) the ability to comprehend information relevant to the decision at hand, (b) the ability to deliberate in accordance with his or her own values and goals, and (c) the ability to communicate with caregivers."[1] Any determination of capacity must address the individual abilities of the patient, the requirement of the task at hand, and the consequences likely to flow from the decision. Medical ethicists generally recommend a sliding scale model of capacity determination with more stringent capacity standards for consent or refusal as the consequences that result from such a decision become more serious.[2] Confusion persists about usage of the terms "competence" and "capacity." Strictly speaking, only the courts have the authority to declare a person "incompetent." Individuals who lack capacity to make treatment decisions should be referred to as someone who lacks decision-making capacity rather than as a person who is incompetent.[3]

Part of what is entailed in the idea of respect for persons, according to those who support the principle of autonomy, is an acceptance of individuals' own choices regardless of whether such choices are in their interests.[4]

Respect for autonomy is a central principle in U.S. bioethics, which developed when abuses of paternalistic medicine were rampant. In times when it was common for physicians to make decisions for patients who were then expected to comply, nurses often played a strong patient advocacy role, championing the patient's right to be self-determining. Today, it is more common for patients to be harmed by abuses at the opposite end of the spectrum. Too many clinicians all too quickly accede to a patient (or her surrogate's) wishes—even when these wishes are misinformed, ill-advised, and are unlikely to benefit the patient. Patients (first called clients) are now customers, and "the customer is always right." In an early work, nurse ethicist Sally Gadow, offered a classic definition of ***existential advocacy***, which is an ideal that continues to be a challenge.

> The ideal which existential advocacy expresses is this: that individuals be assisted by nursing to authentically exercise their freedom of self-determination. By authentic is meant a way of reaching decisions which are truly one's own—decisions that express all that one believes important about oneself and the world, the entire complexity of one's values.
>
> Individuals can express their wholeness and uniqueness as valuing beings only if their full complexity of values—including contradictions and conflicts is clearly in mind, having been reexamined and clarified in context. Yet that clarification is the most difficult especially when it is most needed, when a situation arises, which threatens to overturn previously stable values.

... [Advocacy] is not based on an assumption about what individuals *should want* to do, nor does it consist in protecting individuals' *rights to do* what they want. It is the effort to help persons become clear about what they want to do, by helping them discern and clarify their values in the situation, and on the basis of that self-examination, to reach decisions which express their reaffirmed, perhaps recreated, complex values. Only in this way, when the valuing self is engaged and expressed in its entirety, can a person's decision be actually self-determined instead of being a decision, which is not determined by others.[5]

Of course, not all persons are capable of autonomous choice, and some, such as small children or the severely retarded, have never had that capacity. These can be referred to as "internal constraints" on autonomy. The first case in this chapter examines the conflict between autonomy and patient welfare for a patient with diminished capacity for autonomy—an aging person who can no longer live alone. The second case involves an adult whose religious beliefs raise questions about her ***capacity for autonomous decision-making***.

Other persons, although they may not lack the capacity for autonomous choice, are nevertheless in environments that make autonomous decision making very difficult. We refer to these as "external constraints." Cases 7-3 and 7-4 deal with clients in such environments—persons in nursing homes and the military.

Cases 7-5, 7-6, and 7-7 explore the grounds upon which a nurse might decide to override the client's autonomy because it would be in the patient's interest to do so. Case 7-8 presents the situation where the welfare of other parties may lead to a constraint on patient autonomy.

Internal Constraints on Autonomy

Several of the cases presented in earlier chapters involved a conflict between the autonomy of the patient and the welfare of the patient. It is now widely accepted that autonomy, like justice, is an independent principle that helps determine whether actions are right or wrong. It stands alongside the principles of beneficence and nonmaleficence. Anyone who holds this position would be prepared to say that an intervention could benefit the patient but still be wrong because it violates the patient's autonomy.

One problem that arises in analyzing autonomy is that persons appear to be autonomous in varying degrees. No one is perfectly autonomous—perfectly capable of choosing a plan for himself or herself free from internal and external constraints. However, some persons are capable of being substantially autonomous in their decisions. Others clearly are not capable of such inner direction. If persons who are capable of substantial inner direction are able to act on their own plans, then it is important to explore the limits of the capacity for autonomous choice.[6] Case 7-1 poses this problem.

Case 7-1

When Aging Parents Can No Longer Live Independently[1]

Joyce Fisher, a home health agency nurse, has just received a telephone call from the daughter of a patient, 82-year-old Mr. Sims, whom she had visited some months before. The daughter was very distraught, telling Ms. Fisher that her father had fallen at home but refused to be seen by a physician. Mrs. Sims, her mother, had called the daughter at her place of business and pleaded with her to come to their home and stay with them. The daughter was exasperated by the frequency of these calls from her parents in recent weeks and was appealing to Ms. Fisher for help in making some long-term decisions for the care (and safety) of her parents.

Ms. Fisher remembers well the conversations she had with Mr. and Mrs. Sims and their daughter several months ago, following Mr. Sims's last hospitalization. The Simses live alone in a small home and are frequently visited by their married daughter, who buys their groceries and takes them to their various health appointments. Mr. Sims has always been the decision maker of the family, but he allows this amount of assistance from the daughter "for Mama's sake." Another daughter lives in a nearby city, but she has chronic health problems that prohibit her active involvement in the affairs of her parents. A son lives on the West Coast and travels constantly in his line of business. He supports his parents by sending money for their expenses to his sister (Mr. Sims has refused direct financial aid from any of the children). All three children are concerned about the future welfare of their parents, but they have been unsuccessful in persuading them to change their mode of living.

The present problem is caused by the fact that Mr. and Mrs. Sims are losing their ability to live independently and make their own decisions. Mr. Sims's unexplained falls are also increasing, a constant source of worry for Mrs. Sims and a genuine concern for their married daughter. They all look toward Joyce Fisher as the person who can help them make and support a decision that will preserve some autonomy for the aging parents and respect their choices and lifestyle. Yet Ms. Fisher doubts that what is best for all concerned (parents as well as children) can avoid infringing upon the choices and self-respect of the older Simses. Is there no happy medium for aging parents when they can no longer live independently? What is the role of the home health nurse in assisting individuals in reaching decisions with which they can live?

Commentary

When thinking about healthcare decisions made by one member of a family that have implications for other family members, it is important to note that bioethics in the United States has been criticized for its "rugged individualism." There is no pat answer about the degree to which family members should participate in

[1]*Source*: Mullins, L. C., & Hartley, T. M. (2002). Residents' autonomy: Nursing home personnel's perceptions. *Journal of Gerontological Nursing, 28*(2), 35–44.

healthcare decisions but clearly they have a role to play.[7] Moreover, in some cultures, authority for decision making rests with a male elder or wise leader, with the family, or with the community at large.

Mr. and Mrs. Sims both are people whose capacities for autonomous decision making are beginning to be compromised. The critical decision, both for Ms. Fisher and for the Simses' daughters and son, is whether they will treat the Simses as autonomous agents. If they do and if they are convinced that it is in the Simses' interest to change their living arrangements, they may try to persuade them of the wisdom of a change. They will present reasons why a change would be appropriate; they may try to argue with them. If they are to respect their autonomy, however, they will not make decisions against their will. They will not coerce them into a living arrangement to which they do not consent.

If Ms. Fisher and the children have doubts about the parents' **competency** or capacity to be substantially autonomous decision makers, they may try to test them. They may try to determine if the Simses comprehend the risks of their current situation, the alternatives, and the advantages and disadvantages of their possible choices.

If one or both parents seem incapable of making reasonably autonomous choices, Ms. Fisher and the children will face a critical point. They might simply take over the decision making, but even though they might get away with it, that kind of unilateral "declaration of incompetency" is problematic both legally and ethically.[8]

Legally, the children have no authority to take over decisions for their parents, even if they are well-motivated in wanting to do so. Certainly, a healthcare professional has no such authority. If there is to be a declaration of **incompetency**, the only agency with the legal authority to make that declaration is a court of proper jurisdiction. Where does that leave the children and Ms. Fisher ethically?

They might first approach the problem by looking at the consequences of going beyond persuasion and offering reasons for the alternative they favor. The children might argue that they have seen the dangers increasing and know their parents well enough to realize that they are at risk. Ms. Fisher might argue that she has seen elderly people similarly situated so that she knows the risks they are taking.

The consequentialist argument for respecting the liberty of the parents to make their own decisions rests on at least two considerations.[9] First, probably neither the children nor the nurse is in a particularly good position to know the disadvantages of a more protected living arrangement. The parents are probably in a better position than anyone else to know the psychic trauma of a major lifestyle change. Second, the mere fact that they would be losing control would appear to be an important disadvantage of a more protected arrangement. Mr. Sims appears particularly distressed by that possibility. Thus, even on consequentialist grounds alone, there are good reasons for the Simses to retain their freedom of choice.

Added to this is the fact that a general practice of permitting adult children and/or health professionals to take over decision making for elderly persons would run the risk that some people authorized under such a policy would not be as caring as Ms. Fisher and the Simses' married daughter seem to be. A general policy would have to determine the authority of the second daughter and the son. In some cases, and the Simses' case may be one, not all people of equal degree of kinship are equally committed to the elderly persons' welfare. In some cases, there might be not only a single nurse, but several health professionals, each with a unique idea about what would best serve the welfare of the persons who were being made their wards. A general policy that permitted relatives or health professionals to take over decision making without the benefit of judicial review could lead to serious problems.

Finally, even if these hurdles could be overcome by the argument that some mixture of family and healthcare professionals could do what is best for persons who have never been declared incompetent, those committed to an ethical principle of autonomy would still argue that it would be wrong to take over the decision making. According to the principle of autonomy, an action is wrong insofar as persons with substantial capacities for autonomous decision making are not permitted to exercise that autonomy.

Critical Thinking Questions

1. If you were Ms. Fisher, what recommendation would you make about the care and safety of Mr. and Mrs. Sims? Why?

2. If Ms. Fisher is committed to Gadow's ideal of existential advocacy, how would this inform her judgment about how best to get involved with the Sims?

Research Brief 7-1

Source: Mullins, L. C., & Hartley, T. M. (2002). Residents' autonomy: Nursing home personnel's perceptions. *Journal of Gerontological Nursing, 28*(2), 35–44.

Purpose: To examine the perceptions of nursing home personnel about the scope and limits of residents' autonomous decision making and the extent to which their decision making should be facilitated while also adhering to nursing home standards.

Method: A series of six case studies was provided to 310 employees of 15 Florida nursing homes. Each case study focused on one autonomy dimension. Study participants included registered nurses (RNs; $n = 61$), certified nursing assistants (CNAs; $n = 129$), and department heads ($n = 120$).

For each of the six case studies, respondents were asked the following question: "If Mr. or Mrs. X were at your facility, what would have been decided?" Responses were recorded along a continuum that indicated whether the resident would be allowed to make his or her own decisions or whether the nursing home staff would decide for the resident. Demographic and attitudinal questionnaires were utilized to provide background information on the respondents.

Findings: Findings indicated that staff members' education and race had the greatest effect on their perceptions of personal autonomy. Somewhat surprisingly, staffing levels, turnover rates, and restraint usage did not affect the participants' views of autonomy. The distinction between the views of CNAs and RNs was meaningful for all autonomy dimensions except decisional/executional (i.e., making and implementing decisions freely). CNAs, in contrast to RNs, were more likely to believe that it is the facility's responsibility to make choices for residents.

Implications: Further research is recommended to more completely examine the complex dimensions of autonomy and to identify the changes nursing home staff and administrators can implement to improve residents' quality of life where decision making is concerned. Continuing education about ethical issues, conflicts involving autonomy, and ethical decision making in the nursing home is recommended for all nursing home staff, especially CNAs.

In the previous case, the elderly couple retained some capacity to act autonomously. What should happen, however, in cases involving persons who are clearly totally lacking in autonomy—infants, the profoundly retarded, chronically senile, or comatose, for example? Where capacity for autonomy is lacking, it cannot be a violation of autonomy to take over decision making. There still may be very good arguments that the interests of the nonautonomous one can best be served by using rigorous due process, but no one can seriously dispute that the goal must be to designate a decision maker whose assignment is to promote the welfare of the nonautonomous person. Several questions are worthy of debate. At what point along the continuum of capacity for autonomous decision making ought decision-making authority be taken from the one whose autonomy is compromised? Is there some identifiable point at which autonomy is so obviously lacking that transfer of decision-making authority can legitimately take place without due process of court review? If so, who ought to be given that authority? Are there any circumstances under which it would be acceptable for a nurse or physician to take over that role? By law, parents already have that authority for their minor children. Several states now also have given that responsibility to the next of kin, even in cases where the nonautonomous one is not a child.[10] What is the justification for such a policy, and what are the potential dangers? Are there adequate safeguards (such as court reviews) to protect against those dangers?

One of the earliest controversies regarding the capacity of patients to exercise their autonomy arose over Jehovah's Witnesses who are committed to refusing to "eat" blood. They consider transfusions included in the prohibition. In the United States, the courts generally have recognized the right of mentally competent adults to refuse any medical treatments, even those that would save their lives. The problem becomes more complex, however, when the capacity of the patient to make autonomous choices is in question. It is even more complex when the welfare of others, such as children, is at stake, as in Case 7-2.

Case 7-2
The Jehovah's Witness Patient Who Refused Blood Products

Mrs. Lyons was a 27-year-old woman who had recently given premature birth to a set of twins. The infants were doing well, but Mrs. Lyons suffered hemorrhage and required emergency surgery resulting in a hysterectomy. Severe loss of blood dropped her hemoglobin to 6.0 gm/dl. Because the patient and her husband were Jehovah's Witnesses, they refused blood transfusions as treatment for the low hemoglobin level.

Christina Moore was the nurse caring for Mrs. Lyons after her surgery. Although she did not personally believe that patients should refuse blood transfusions, especially new mothers with dependent infants, she supported the rights of others to decide their health care in accordance with their religious beliefs.

Shortly after admission to Ms. Moore's unit, Mrs. Lyons's hemoglobin began to drop. It was suspected that the patient was hemorrhaging from an unknown site in her body. Vasoactive drug therapy was begun to help maintain adequate perfusion of her body tissues, and her cardiac output was constantly monitored. Mr. Lyons remained at his wife's bedside and supported her repeated desire not to be transfused, even though to not do so might result in his wife's death.

Over the next 24 hours, Mrs. Lyons drifted in and out of consciousness and remained very close to death, despite a slight rise in her hemoglobin level. As Ms. Moore was leaning over the patient adjusting the intravenous tubing, she heard Mrs. Lyons whisper, "Please, I don't want to die—please don't let me die." Ms. Moore quickly asked Mr. Lyons if he had heard what his wife said. He was on the other side of the room and had not heard his wife's words. Even though the nurse believed that his wife was apparently changing her mind about receiving blood products, Mr. Lyons was reluctant to believe this and did not want to reverse her previous decisions. Ms. Moore knew that the patient's condition required a rapid response to avert her death. Should she notify the physician that the patient had changed her wishes, over the objections of the husband?

Commentary

When there is doubt about whether a patient's decision to refuse treatment remains valid, it is wise for any health professional to consult other members of the healthcare team. This is true for a physician or a nurse. When the decision is literally a life-and-death matter, the imperative to consult becomes even greater. Whether the consultation is with other members of the team, a hospital ethics committee, or the hospital's attorney, it makes sense to obtain it.

The critical question is whether the patient's apparent change of mind should prevail. If Mrs. Lyons is substantially autonomous, then her refusal generally would be accepted.[11] Imagine that the patient's position had originally been to accept treatment, then while mentally compromised to the point of moving in and out of consciousness, the patient uttered a refusal of life-saving treatment. Certainly, the nurse would be tempted to argue that the patient's latest decision was not a substantially autonomous one. The earlier prolife choice made while lucid would seem decisive. If the patient's change of heart during a time when she is of suspect competence is to be rejected, that would seem to count against accepting her apparent change in the present case.

If decisions are uttered in moments where autonomy is suspect, should Mrs. Lyons's apparent change of treatment choice be given credence? Is it the more lucid decision that should prevail? The more recent decision? Or the one that is more reversible?

Competent adults are given the authority to refuse treatment, even life-saving treatment; however, if Mrs. Lyons is no longer considered competent to make her own decisions, that authority would normally pass to Mr. Lyons, her next of kin, who would be expected to make decisions based on the views his wife held while she was competent.

Such decision making becomes even more complex when the welfare of others who are incompetent is involved. This could provide a basis for treating Mrs. Lyons, even if her husband's refusal of blood on her behalf is considered valid. Mrs. Lyons is now the parent of twins. Her death affects not only her own and her husband's welfare, but also that of her children. Parents refusing life-saving blood transfusions may place the welfare of their children in jeopardy. In some cases, parents have been ordered to undergo treatment against their wills in order to protect the welfare of their children.[12] In one case, however, the spouse argued that relatives would be able to fulfill caregiving responsibilities if a parent died from refusal of treatment believed life saving. The court supported the refusal of the transfusion.[13]

Critical Thinking Questions

1. Should Ms. Moore, in asking for consultation, press for treating Mrs. Lyons only if she believes Mrs. Lyons was making an adequately autonomous choice when she appeared to reverse her choice? Or should she press for treatment regardless of her assessment of Mrs. Lyons's mental status because she believes the welfare of the recently born twins is in jeopardy?

2. If you were Ms. Moore, would you notify the physician that Mrs. Lyons had changed her wishes? Why or why not?

3. If you were Ms. Moore, would you refer this case to your patient care ethics committee or ethics consult service? Why or why not?

External Constraints on Autonomy

The capacity for autonomy of the elderly couple in Case 7-1 was questioned because of doubts about their inherent abilities to act on their own agendas. What limits there were arose from organic and psychologic factors that posed internal constraints on their autonomy. Similarly, the Jehovah's Witness patient in Case 7-2 was influenced by her religious beliefs. Neither was seriously constrained by external factors. That is not to say that persons with compromised capacities for autonomy cannot have what capacity there is enhanced. Careful explanation of alternatives, efforts to overcome limitations in vision and hearing, and support with financial and physical resources all may increase a person's capacity to act autonomously. Other persons have no internal constraints but are still unable to act as autonomous agents because of external constraints. The next two cases illustrate the problem.

Case 7-3
The Patient Who Wanted to Eat Alone

Sylvia Gambino, nursing supervisor of Bayside Elderly Care, gives a quick look at the dining room where the majority of Bayside's 30 residents are eating lunch. She notices that Miss Phoebe Merryweather is gazing out the window and has not touched her lunch. A quiet, dignified woman of 78 years, Miss Merryweather has been living at Bayside for 2.5 months. In recent weeks, Mrs. Gambino and the rest of the staff have noticed that Miss Merryweather is becoming withdrawn, does not eat much of her food, and is noticeably thinner. Mrs. Gambino is troubled by Miss Merryweather's behavior and concerned about her nutritional status. Although this patient has some left-sided weakness due to a mild stroke she suffered some 12 years earlier, she had seemed alert and in good health for her age until recent weeks.

Miss Merryweather apparently had lived an active life as an interior decorator in a southern city until her retirement. About 2 years ago, she came to Brooklyn to live with her one remaining relative, an unmarried sister. When the sister died quite suddenly, members of her sister's church persuaded Miss Merryweather to live at Bayside Elderly Care. Well known for its small resident population, excellent facilities, and the fact that most of the residents needed minimal nursing supervision, Bayside seemed to be the ideal place for Miss Merryweather to live. The residents of Bayside are almost entirely drawn from the large Italian/American community surrounding Bayside, seem to know one another's families, and receive excellent community support.

Miss Merryweather, however, has not joined in the activities and comradery of Bayside. She seems to prefer reading, crocheting, watching a few select TV programs, and eating alone in her room. In fact, she strongly objects to eating her meals in the main dining room with the other residents. On several occasions, she has even wrapped her food from her tray in a napkin and surreptitiously carried it to her room. When this practice was discovered, the staff scolded Miss Merryweather for bringing food to her room. She was told to "count her blessings" in that she could walk to the dining room and eat her meals with other people and did not have to eat all alone in her room like some of the elderly residents did.

It seems that Mrs. Gambino and her staff firmly believe that the health of elderly persons is directly related to opportunities for community involvement, contact with other people, and shared daily activities such as eating meals. Bayside operates its daily activities on a partnership model, which fosters partnerships between residents, residents and staff, and residents and community members. Having been educated in the community near Bayside, Mrs. Gambino considers the partnership model in resident elderly care to be a close approximation to the kind of lifestyle Bayside's residents enjoyed in earlier days. Thus, the partnership model is heartily supported by the residents, the staff, and community groups. Yet, Miss Merryweather does not seem interested in this overall plan and the goal of resident involvement.

Deciding to talk directly with Miss Merryweather about her eating behavior, Mrs. Gambino learns that this elderly woman detests eating meals with the other residents. As Miss Merryweather states, "I lose my appetite when I see others drop their food all over their trays and clothes. Some have suffered strokes like me and cannot help but be messy eaters. Others have trouble guiding forks and spoons to their mouths. I cannot stand to watch others eat like this. So I prefer to eat alone. Is that too much to ask?"

Mrs. Gambino is stunned by the vehemence behind Miss Merryweather's words. Certainly this elderly patient could be more tolerant toward others and learn something from them, despite their low feeding skills. After all, one of the goals of the partnership model is to increase social opportunities for elderly residents, and in Bayside's community, mealtime is considered the major social activity of the day. Because Miss Merryweather has no friends or relatives in Brooklyn, her social involvement is entirely dependent on activities at Bayside. Moreover, the Bayside administration has had serious maintenance and sanitation problems from residents keeping food in their rooms. The administration has had to adopt a policy of permitting food in rooms only for patients who are too ill to come to the dining room, and even then, food is permitted only under the strict supervision of the staff. Should Mrs. Gambino continue to enforce Bayside's requirement of eating meals in the dining room for all residents who are able to walk, including Miss Merryweather, or should she give up some of her beliefs about resident elderly care in this patient's case?

Case 7-4
The Recruit Hospitalized for Weight Control

Phyllis Somerville is a civilian nurse who works in a U.S. Naval hospital. A 19-year-old patient, Private Barnes, has just been admitted to the medical ward for enlisted personnel with the diagnosis of obesity. He is moderately overweight, weighing 225 lbs and measuring 5 ft 10 in. in height. While admitting the patient, Mrs. Somerville learns that Pvt. Barnes has a long-standing weight problem, predating adolescence. He managed to survive basic training after losing 60 lbs in a 4-month period. Now that he has been assigned to his first duty station, he has relaxed the near-starvation diet imposed on him during basic training. Unfortunately, he has gained 40 lbs and has been unable to keep up with the rest of his platoon during morning marches and forced runs. His platoon leader, Second Lieutenant Harris, desperately wants his platoon to excel in platoon competition and basic military skills. Because of Pvt. Barnes's previous weight problem, 2d Lt. Harris has ordered him to lose weight, a feat that Pvt. Barnes has not been able to accomplish in the last few weeks.

At today's early-morning formation, Pvt. Barnes wondered how much longer he could endure 2d Lt. Harris's belittling comments and the inevitable 100 pushups he was assigned each time he blinked an eye. To his surprise, his name was called to check in for sick call. He soon learned that 2d Lt. Harris wanted him to be hospitalized for the purpose of weight reduction. Pvt. Barnes was adamantly opposed to the plan because he was to begin his specialized training—for him the entire reason for enlisting in the military—within a few days. It soon became apparent that Pvt. Barnes really did not have any choice in the matter. Because he had not lost the required weight in recent weeks, 2d Lt. Harris had the power to admit him to the hospital for weight reduction. Pvt. Barnes would thereby lose the opportunity for the specialized training, an opportunity that might not occur again during his 3-year enlistment. In discussing with him the rigor of the diet ordered by the admitting physician, Mrs. Somerville could not help but feel sorry for Pvt. Barnes and the fact that he had absolutely no control over his present situation and future success in the military because of a very basic life mechanism such as eating. Even more disturbing, she would be the agent to enforce the regulation imposed on Pvt. Barnes and to deny his choices on a day-to-day basis.

Commentary

Both Miss Merryweather and Pvt. Barnes lack the capacity to choose lifestyles based on their own internalized norms. They lack autonomy. However, unlike Mr. and Mrs. Sims in Case 7-1, they have no inherent physical and mental limitations that constrain their autonomy. Rather, they are constrained by living in institutional environments where their choices are limited. Like many residents in what are sometimes called "total institutions" (that is, institutions that involve one's total life, such as prisons, boarding schools, and religious communities), they are confronted with institutional policies that shift many aspects of decision making away from the individual and toward supervisory figures vested with authority to make decisions.

The first question faced by nurses Gambino and Somerville is whether there is any justification for them to practice their profession in an environment where external constraints on autonomy are part of the fabric of everyday existence. In both cases, especially in Mrs. Gambino's case, one might argue that part of the duty of the nurse is to be an advocate for the patient. In more traditional times, that probably would have meant that the nurse was to be an advocate for the medical well-being of patients—that is, for their care and safety. More recently, however, the nurse, in taking on the role of patient advocate, has focused on patients' rights as well as their well-being. If one of the rights of patients is to act as autonomous decision makers within their inherent capacities, the nurse may sometimes find herself or himself advocating for decision-making freedom for patients rather than merely for their care and safety.

Mrs. Gambino might have some leeway to do just that in the case of Miss Merryweather. Have institutional policies been too rigid? Has commitment to the partnership model been overdone? Should exceptions be made in institutional policies about residents having food in their rooms? If she is an advocate for the autonomy of the client as well as for her medical welfare, then these are all legitimate questions for Mrs. Gambino.

Mrs. Somerville must face similar questions. For at least some of her patients, institutional policies may be unnecessarily constraining. If the policies are unreasonably depriving participants in the institution of their freedom to make basic lifestyle decisions, perhaps the only answer, if she is unsuccessful in advocating for changes in those policies, is for Mrs. Somerville to resign her position and seek a more acceptable institution in which to practice her profession.

At least some policies in some institutions make sense, however. The institutions are serving legitimate purposes and their policies plausibly are necessary to accomplishing those purposes. Whereas Bayside Elderly Care may not need to be quite as rigid in imposing its partnership model, some limitations on food in rooms may be reasonable in some environments. Certainly, some limits on personal choice are reasonable for those in the military, especially when the requirements are necessary to accomplish important institutional objectives. Placing some limits on weight gain may be such a limit.

One way to analyze the relationship between autonomy and such external institutional constraints on freedom of choice is to ask whether the participants in such total institutions have freely waived their personal decision-making freedom. If Miss Merryweather and Pvt. Barnes can meaningfully be said to have waived their freedoms in the relevant decision-making areas as part of the price for being in the institution, it makes no sense for them to complain or for the nurses to worry about their complaints. The real question, of course, is whether the clients in either case really consented in any way to the policies under which they are now suffering.

The notion of persons autonomously relinquishing their autonomy has puzzled philosophers at least since the time that Ulysses agreed to have himself bound to the mast of his ship to enable him to resist the temptations of the Sirens. The idea that one can autonomously surrender one's autonomy is generally believed to have some moral limits.[14] It is often held to be morally unacceptable, for example, to voluntarily sell oneself into slavery or other forms of permanent servitude. Miss Merryweather's decision to enter Bayside, however, is hardly a surrendering of autonomy of that order of magnitude. Even Pvt. Barnes would appear to be within what most people would consider reasonable limits of surrendering one's autonomy. Thus, if Miss Merryweather or Pvt. Barnes has knowingly consented to limits and those limits serve some reasonable purpose, it is questionable whether the nurses involved have any reason to pursue the matter further.

There is one additional issue raised by these two cases. The limits placed on these people are both at the fringes of what could be called medical decisions. It is because they are vaguely related to health care that nurses find themselves in the decision-making position in the first place. Yet, the choice of where one eats, even if it means challenging the partnership model, is not normally considered a medical choice. Likewise, obesity is a problem having health implications, but the rigid diet proposed for Pvt. Barnes is not exactly a core medical intervention.

This can become important when one realizes that the right of refusal of medical intervention, which we shall explore more fully in Chapter 16, is often considered to be preserved even in total institutions where other constraints are the norm.[15] Medical interventions are normally offered for the good of the patient. To the extent that the interventions are only for the patient's good, they are plausibly seen as subject to the autonomous decision making of the client. Thus, even in prisons and in military institutions, persons are often seen as having freedom of choice regarding medical intervention even if they are severely constrained in many of their other choices.

What is interesting about the policies that are constraining Miss Merryweather and Pvt. Barnes is that it is not clear that either policy is being enforced for the client's welfare. The extra costs and other risks of having food in residents' rooms are surely institutional concerns and not driven by concern for Miss Merryweather's welfare. Even more so, the concern driving 2d Lt. Harris is a U.S. Marine Corps concern, not one exclusively about the health and well-being of the private.

In both cases, nurses find themselves in awkward positions. If the only concerns were the rights, health, and welfare of their clients and if the nurses were committed to maintaining their clients' autonomy, no problem would exist in respecting the clients' wishes. In both cases, however, the nurses are caught in situations where agendas unrelated to the clients' health are driving policies that constrain the nurses as well as the clients. Nurses in such situations must recognize that they are being asked to use their nursing skills for nontraditional purposes. If they cannot resolve the tension by having policies changed (in such a way that does not jeopardize important institutional objectives), the nurses will have to determine whether they are willing to work in programs having objectives well outside traditional nursing.

Critical Thinking Questions

1. When policies constrain respect for patient autonomy, what should the nurse do? Try to change the policies? Ignore the policies? Let someone else handle the problem?
2. What would you do if you were the nurse caring for Miss Phoebe Merryweather or Pvt. Barnes? Why?
3. What institutional ethics resources would you use to help guide your response?

Overriding Autonomy

If autonomy is accepted as an independent principle of ethics in addition to the principles of beneficence and nonmaleficence, it is inevitable that eventually it will come into conflict with those principles. There will be circumstances in which the nurse is convinced that what is best for the patient and what the patient is choosing are not the same. In such circumstances, the critical question is how autonomy and beneficence (as well as nonmaleficence, if it is a separate principle) relate to each other. Any ethic for nursing must address the question of how these two ethical considerations are weighted in cases of conflict between them.

One strategy is to give one of them priority over the other. Philosophers sometimes refer to this as *lexical ordering* (as in a dictionary, where all As come before any Bs). A full lexical ordering would make the principle of doing good always superior to or subordinate to autonomy. An alternative strategy is to hold that both are legitimate moral concerns, neither of which can be totally subordinated to the other. Holders of the latter view might insist that the two concerns be balanced depending on the circumstances of the case.

Paternalistic Overriding of Autonomy

The problem of relating beneficence to autonomy is sometimes avoided because it often turns out that granting persons the freedom to act on their own plans, in fact, also does the most good. That, at least, is what liberal philosophers such as John Stuart Mill have maintained. The interesting cases, however, are those where it is plausible that granting the client a free hand to act on his or her own agenda will end up doing more harm than good. In health care, professionals have traditionally given high priority to acting so as to benefit the patient. Great moral controversy arises when benefit to the patient comes at the price of overriding the patient's autonomy. The following cases illustrate this problem.

Case 7-5
The Patient Who Refuses His Pills

Jesse Hodges is a 21-year-old young man who resides in a halfway house for psychiatric patients. The home has nine residents in a family-type arrangement (men, women, and young adults) and is under the direction of Abe Brown, a social worker, and Mimi Donaldson, a registered nurse. All residents attend school or have jobs and have high potential to be fully productive members of the community. Mr. Hodges is very pleased to be a member of the home and is receiving technical training at a local job training center.

Ordinarily, Mr. Hodges presents few problems for Mr. Brown and Ms. Donaldson. He is well-mannered and manages his training and financial allowance with minimal assistance. In fact, he might soon be able to live in a less protected environment. During the past few weeks, however, Mr. Hodges has had several agitated outbursts directed at the other residents. And one night, he picked a fight with Mr. Brown that resulted in Mr. Brown physically restraining him and taking him to his room to "cool off."

When questioned, Jesse admitted that he was not taking his medication, a mild tranquilizer that had been prescribed to help combat the anxiety that he experienced when he first started living at the home and traveling to the training center. Because taking the medication was a condition of his continued placement in the home, Ms. Donaldson was surprised to learn that Jesse had not been following through with this seemingly routine procedure. Apparently, Jesse did not like the idea that he had to take the medication and did not want his newfound friends at the training center to think that he was "on something" or had a "mental problem."

Ms. Donaldson tried to explain to Jesse why it was necessary that he take the medication, but she could not get him to agree that he would take it in the future. When Jesse continued to have agitated spells at home as well as at school, Ms. Donaldson considered limiting Jesse's movie privileges until he could demonstrate his willingness to cooperate with his prescribed regimen. It is obvious to Ms. Donaldson that Jesse needs to take the medication until he has adjusted to living in the home. Jesse, however, feels that he should decide whether he takes his medication. Does the nurse have the right to limit Jesse's privileges in this manner?

Case 7-6
The Elderly Patient Who Fears Constipation[2]

Mr. Johnstone, a mentally alert 82-year-old man, was admitted with the diagnosis of pneumonia. During the course of his recovery, Mr. Johnstone experienced an uncomfortable episode of constipation. The problem was corrected, and the patient soon returned to his normal state of good health.

---

[2]Adapted from Morreim, H., Donovan, A., Huey, R., Brimigion, J., & Fine, E. (1982). The patient's right to privacy. *Nursing Life, 2*, 35–38.

When it was time to prepare Mr. Johnstone to leave the hospital, Janis Forsyth, his primary nurse, noticed that Mr. Johnstone was having frequent diarrheal bowel movements. When questioned, Mr. Johnstone just chuckled and said it was no problem. "Better this than being constipated," he stated. Miss Forsyth and his physician were not convinced that he was entirely well.

The physician suspected that Mr. Johnstone might be causing the diarrhea by taking laxatives. Mr. Johnstone denied the charge. Miss Forsyth, however, thought that the physician's suspicion might be correct. In fact, she had noticed that Mr. Johnstone had a small bag that he kept in his suitcase in the closet. The previous day, he had quickly closed the suitcase and put it in the closet when she walked into the room. When she asked if he needed anything, he was quite defensive and quickly turned on the TV.

After relating this episode to the physician, Miss Forsyth was asked to "do a little detective work" and search for laxatives when Mr. Johnstone was out of his room. Should she search Mr. Johnstone's personal belongings? If she finds any laxatives, can she take them from Mr. Johnstone or prohibit him from taking them? After all, doesn't the patient have some choice over his bowel functions? Or does the fact that one is hospitalized take away this type of choice?

Case 7-7
Inflicting Agony to Save a Life

Sally Morganthau was an experienced nurse specializing in the care and treatment of patients suffering from body burns. She was newly assigned as the primary nurse for James Tobias, a 32-year-old man who had been on the burn unit of Parsons County Hospital for 4 weeks. He had suffered 60% body burns (40% first and second degree and 20% third degree) as a result of being trapped in a house fire.

It was clear to the staff that Mr. Tobias would survive his injuries but that his treatment process would be a long and painful one. He would be hospitalized for months and would face a number of operations. He would probably lose his eyesight and have limited mobility due to extensive muscle damage in the lower extremities. Of greater concern to the staff was Mr. Tobias's mental distress associated with his tankings and dressing changes. He often screamed with agony as the staff worked on his dressings. He demanded that they stop, but the team, used to the screams of its patients, continued their efforts day after day. Because of the excellent performance of this particular burn team, patients for whom survival would have been unprecedented only a few years ago now often pulled through.

One day after his daily tanking and dressing changes had been completed and he had been returned to his room, Mr. Tobias asked for Ms. Morganthau. He insisted that no further treatment be performed. He made it clear that he understood that this would mean his possibilities of surviving his injuries would decrease and that if he did survive, his contractures would be worse and his problems even more severe. Yet he insisted that the agony was too much for him, and he did not want any further treatment.

Ms. Morganthau spoke with her nursing colleagues and discovered that Mr. Tobias had been demanding that they stop the treatments for over a week. A psychiatric consult had confirmed that Mr. Tobias was mentally competent and understood the significance of his decision. Dr. Albertson, the attending resident, was well aware of Mr. Tobias's feelings. He had seen patients like Mr. Tobias before. Some who had considered refusing further treatment thanked Dr. Albertson and the staff years later for going on. Dr. Albertson knew that Mr. Tobias's life was on the line. He was not going to lose a patient he knew he could save. What should Ms. Morganthau do?

Commentary

All three of these cases pose problems for nurses who are considering overriding the autonomy of their clients. The first question to be faced by each of them is whether they are dealing with substantially autonomous clients. If they are not, then whatever the ethical problem is, it is not one involving the conflict of autonomy with other ethical principles such as beneficence.

It is clear that all three patients have made choices that many rational people would not make. Omitting the tranquilizer seems unreasonable, especially if doing so contributes to the disruptions in living that Jesse Hodges is facing. Mr. Johnstone's behavior, although it involves a relatively trivial problem, does not seem to make much sense. James Tobias's treatment refusal could be a literal matter of life and death, and most reasonable people probably would not make the decision he has made.

Moreover, all three of them are facing conditions that call their mental capacities into question. Jesse Hodges is a psychiatric patient. Mr. Johnstone is elderly, perhaps facing the confusion and disorientation that trouble some people in his age group. James Tobias has recently experienced a major, life-disrupting trauma. It would not be surprising if depression, anxiety, and loss of hope clouded his ability to reason about his treatment. The severe pain his treatment causes may make it impossible for Mr. Tobias to compare short-term suffering with the long-term benefits of the tankings and dressing changes. For all these reasons the quality of the relationship developed between these patients and their nurses is critical. Gadow's ideal of existential advocacy is meaningless unless nurses know patients well enough to talk with them about the values and meanings behind their choices.

It is possible that each of these patients suffers from debilities that make him less than a substantially autonomous decision maker, but there is nothing in any of the case reports that supports that conjecture. Jesse Hodges has not been committed to a mental institution. He has not been adjudicated incompetent. In fact, he is living in a halfway house with reasonable hope of gaining even more independence. Mr. Johnstone has not been diagnosed as experiencing any problems of senility or other mental debilitation that might accompany age. James Tobias has been found mentally competent by a psychiatrist.

Furthermore, no effort has been made on the behalf of any of these patients to seek court intervention to remove his presumption of competence.

It might be argued that the substantive decision that each has made is good evidence that he is not acting autonomously. The choices are seriously disruptive of their life plans. In Mr. Tobias's case, the choice could result in his death. The fact that persons make unusual choices, choices that most reasonable people similarly situated would not make, however, is not grounds for presuming that they cannot act autonomously. They may, in fact, be incapable of autonomous choice, but there is nothing in any of the case reports to support that conclusion. If Mr. Brown and Ms. Donaldson limit Jesse Hodges's privileges in order to pressure him into taking his medication, they are acting so as to infringe upon his autonomy; they are acting paternalistically. If Ms. Forsyth cooperates in a plan to determine whether Mr. Johnstone is taking laxatives and then takes them from him, she is infringing upon his autonomy and acting paternalistically. If Ms. Morganthau cooperates with Dr. Albertson over the wishes of Mr. Tobias, then Mr. Tobias's autonomy is being infringed upon, and she is acting paternalistically.

That does not necessarily mean that any of these nurses would be doing the morally wrong thing. That would be the proper conclusion if it is always wrong to infringe upon a person's autonomy. If autonomy is the more stringent principle, if it trumps beneficence, there seems to be no justification for the actions the nurses are contemplating. If, on the other hand, promoting the client's welfare is the dominant moral principle, or even if beneficence and autonomy need to be counterbalanced against each other, presumably on some occasions infringing upon autonomy is acceptable. What conditions must be met for autonomy to be overridden?[16]

The most obvious condition is that there must be good reason for the nurse to be convinced that the patient will really be better off with the paternalistic action. But in each of our cases there is some reason to doubt that the patient would be better off. Jesse Hodges may feel stigmatized if he is forced to take his medication. Although the medication would appear to help him, it is not absolutely clear that he will benefit socially from his caretakers' planned intervention. Likewise, Mr. Johnstone might benefit from being separated from the means to perform inappropriate self-medication. On the other hand, he may discover the clandestine search and feel infringed upon. He may obtain a new supply and simply continue taking the medication he thinks he needs. Mr. Tobias seems to have the most to gain from Dr. Albertson's and nurse Morganthau's paternalistic forced treatment. He would, in all likelihood, live because of it, whereas without it he might die. However, with compulsory tankings and dressing changes, he will live in great agony. We shall see in the cases in Chapter 17 that many people hold that it is morally acceptable to refuse treatments that are gravely burdensome, even if the result of such refusal is death. Mr. Tobias will be better off with the forced tankings and dressing changes, provided living is always better than dying, but that is a controversial, evaluative judgment. In all cases, the judgments that the patients will be better off with the nurses' intervention need careful assessment.

Even if the patient will be better off with the intervention, it is not immediately clear that the intervention is justified. If the patient is only slightly better off, while his or her autonomy is infringed upon, then those who balance the competing principles might not consider the additional benefit sufficient to tip the scales in favor of violating autonomy. Given the controversial and subjective nature of the judgments involved and the fact that a patient's freedom is being infringed upon, many would argue that the ***paternalism*** is unjustified.

Even if the paternalism is justified, we must ask whether it can be carried out solely on the basis of the private assessment of a private citizen. Even if that citizen happens to be a physician or a nurse, some more formal process may be needed to justify paternalism. The concern is not primarily over the good intentions of the decision makers; it is more over the high risk of error in making very complicated, very subjective judgments. Perhaps those who have given their lives to health care and preserving life are not in a good position to judge whether health benefits justify infringing upon patients' autonomy. Many would insist that there be some due process, some formal review, before overriding a patient's autonomy.

That review might be conducted by a group like a hospital ethics committee, but such committees normally have no more authority to override autonomy than individual physicians or nurses do. Committees might have biases as a group, especially biases associated with the healthcare professions, such as commitment to the preservation of life. Should a more public review, such as a court review, be necessary before the autonomy of a patient is overridden?

The final question the nurses in these cases face is whether, even given the best possible conditions, it is justifiable to override autonomy. Suppose that in each case careful assessment of patient benefit and harm was made and that assessment could be confirmed by some due process (such as judicial review). Assuming no further evidence that the patients involved are incompetent, would a decisive judgment made with formal due process that the patients would be better off if their autonomy were infringed upon justify overriding the patients' wishes? On what grounds?

Overriding Autonomy to Benefit Others

Even if one finally concludes that the welfare of the patient never justifies overriding a substantially autonomous person's decisions about medical treatment, there is still the possibility that the welfare of others could justify limits on autonomy. Even people who are strongly antipaternalistic sometimes hold that when the welfare of other parties is at stake, autonomy may have to be constrained. Consider the problem faced by the nurse in the following case.

Case 7-8
When Should Parental Rights Be Overridden?

Delores Castle is an experienced genetic testing nurse counselor and is often asked to discuss testing options with expectant parents. She has been asked to meet with Mr. Roger and Mrs. Melanie Burroughs because Mrs. Burroughs was recently diagnosed as a gene carrier for Li Fraumeni syndrome, which is known to result in early age onset breast cancer in 85% of people who inherit a cancer-specific gene from each parent. Mrs. Burroughs is 7-weeks pregnant, and this is her first pregnancy. She and her husband waited 9 years after marriage before having children. It is obvious that they are delighted with the pregnancy and look forward to being parents.

During the first counseling session with the Burroughs, Mrs. Castle learns that Mr. Burroughs has a strong family history of a variety of different types of cancers over three generations of relatives. Given this history and the fact that Mrs. Burroughs is a gene carrier for Li Fraumeni syndrome, prenatal testing of the fetus is strongly recommended. The Burroughses, however, are reluctant to undergo testing of their fetus. They would rather not know this information because termination of the fetus is not an option for them due to religious beliefs.

The situation presents a moral dilemma for Mrs. Castle. On one hand, she believes that, given the information that is already known, the Burroughses have a moral duty to test the fetus and find out whether it has inherited cancer-specific genes from both parents. She believes that expectant parents should use whatever technology is available to prevent harm from occurring to their fetus. On the other hand, she recognizes that parents have a right to decide for or against prenatal diagnostic procedures. But is the likelihood of harm to the fetus one situation where parental right to decide should be overridden?

Commentary

Here, Mrs. Castle believes that Mr. and Mrs. Burroughs have a moral duty to undergo a genetic test to obtain information about the status of their fetus. But she also recognizes that, as autonomous adults, they have certain rights to lead their lives according to the life plan they choose. In this case, that seems to mean living without the knowledge of their fetus's genetic status. Autonomy appears to conflict with benefit to the fetus.

Antipaternalists hold that the welfare of the patient does not justify violating the autonomy of individuals, but even they recognize that sometimes the welfare of others can generate moral claims that conflict with respect for autonomy. Still, however, those who, in principle, are willing to compromise autonomy to protect the welfare of others must make a realistic judgment about how likely it is that the other party really will benefit from autonomy infringement. In this case, Mrs. Castle appears concerned about protecting the future child from the burdens of early-onset breast cancer, but forcing the parents to have their fetus tested for Li Fraumeni syndrome seems unlikely, by itself, to do the fetus much good. Knowing that the child has the syndrome probably will result in frequent testing to detect breast cancer. Early detection would, of course, increase the child's survival from breast cancer. Another option appears to be terminating the pregnancy, but Mr. and Mrs. Burroughs have ruled that out. Unless one contemplates compulsory abortion, the fetus's immediate status will not be affected by the test, and compulsory abortion is an infringement on parental autonomy that almost no one would contemplate. Mrs. Castle can only claim that the parents will benefit immediately by a negative test or, in the case of a positive test result, the fetus will benefit from early detection in the future.

A more fundamental question is: When can benefit to third parties justify overriding autonomy? Although most people believe that in some cases autonomy must give way to third-party welfare, they also tend to believe that not just any third-party welfare justifies infringing autonomy. For some, the amount of good that can be done is the deciding factor. Suppose that for some other condition a fetus could be treated if early testing revealed a pathologic condition. If the potential condition were serious and easily treated, would compulsory testing (and perhaps compulsory treatment as well) be justified?

Others believe that it is not so much the amount of good that can be done for others, but rather the nature of their claim that potentially justifies overriding autonomy. For example, parents have a duty of fidelity to care for and nurture their children, duties that go beyond those they have toward friends or strangers.[17] (These claims of fidelity will be examined more closely in the cases in Chapter 9.) In other cases, we might believe that it is not so much the amount of benefit, but how poorly off the one is who stands to benefit that makes the difference. In Chapter 5, we saw that the moral principle of justice is different from and sometimes at odds with the principle of beneficence. Beneficence focuses on the amount of benefit, whereas justice focuses on the special claim that people might have because of the position they are in. For example, defenders of egalitarian justice claim that those who are worst off may have special claims to have their needs met. According to this view, if the fetus can be seen as potentially suffering from a particularly serious condition, then it might have a claim of justice against the parents in addition to a claim of fidelity that would extend beyond considerations of beneficence.

Critical Thinking Questions

1. Do you think that Mr. and Mrs. Burroughs owe it to their fetus to undergo the test and to act on the information that ensues? Why or why not?
2. Do you think that the Burroughses' parental rights should be overridden in this case? Why or why not?

ENDNOTES

1. The Hastings Center. (1987). *Guidelines on the termination of life-sustaining treatment and the care of the dying* (p. 7). Bloomington and Indianapolis, IN: Indiana University Press.

2. Drane, J. (1985). The many faces of competency. *Hastings Center Report, 15,* 17.

3. The Hastings Center. (1987). *Guidelines on the termination of life-sustaining treatment and the care of the dying* (p. 7). Bloomington and Indianapolis, IN: Indiana University Press.

4. Beauchamp, T. L., & Childress, J. F. (Eds.). (2001). *Principles of biomedical ethics* (5th ed., pp. 57–104). New York: Oxford University Press; Childress, J. F. (1982). *Paternalism in health care.* New York: Oxford University Press; Dworkin, G. (1978). Moral autonomy. In H. T. Engelhardt & D. Callahan (Eds.), *Morals, science, and sociality* (pp. 156–171). Hastings-on-Hudson, NY: The Hastings Center; Faden, R., Beauchamp, T. L., & King, N. N. P. (1986). *A history and theory of informed consent* (pp. 235–273). New York: Oxford University Press.

5. Gadow, S. (1980). Existential advocacy: Philosophical foundation of nursing. In S. F. Spicker & S. Gadow (Eds.), *Nursing images and ideals* (p. 85). New York: Springer Publishing Company.

6. Faden, R., & Beauchamp, T. L. (1986). *A history and theory of informed consent* (pp. 274–297). New York: Oxford University Press.

7. Blustein, J. (1993, May/June). The family in medical decisionmaking. *Hastings Center Report, 23*(3), 6–13; Hardwig, J. (1990, March/April). What about the family? *Hastings Center Report, 20*(2), 5–10; Nelson, H. L., & Nelson, J. L. (1995). *The patient in the family: An ethics of medicine and families.* New York: Routledge.

8. Allen, R. C., Ferster, E. A., & Weihofen, H. (1968). *Mental impairment and legal incompetency.* Englewood Cliffs, NJ: Prentice Hall; Roth, L., Meisel, A., & Lidz, C. (1977). Tests of competency to consent to treatment. *American Journal of Psychiatry, 134*(3), 279–285.

9. Mill, J. S. (1869/1956). *On liberty.* New York: The Liberal Arts Press.

10. Choice in Dying, Inc. (n.d.). *Right to die law digest statutes.* New York: Author.

11. Moore, M. L. (1983). Their life is in the blood: Jehovah's Witnesses, blood transfusions and the courts. *Northern Kentucky Law Review, 10*(2), 281–304.

12. In re President and Directors of Georgetown College, Inc., 331 F.2d 1000 (D.D. Cir.), cert. denied sub nom; Jones v. President and Directors of Georgetown College, Inc., 377 U.S. 978 (1964); Raleigh Fitkin–Paul Morgan Memorial Hospital v. Anderson, 42 N.J. 421, 201 A.2d 537 (1964) cert. denied, 337 U.S. 985 (1964).

13. Erickson v. Dilard, 44 Misc 2d 27, 252 NY S.2d 705 (Sup. Ct. 1962).

14. Winston, M. E., Winston, S. M., Appelbaum, P. S., & Rhoden, N. K. (1982). Can a subject consent to a "Ulysses Contract"? *Hastings Center Rep, 12*(4), 26–28.

15. Gobert, J. J. (1975). Psychosurgery, conditioning, and the prisoner's right to refuse "Rehabilitation." *Virginia Law Review, 61,* 155–196.

16. Dworkin, G. (1972). Paternalism. In R. Wasserstrom (Ed.), *Morality and the law* (pp. 17–126). Belmont, CA: Wadsworth; Gert, B., & Culver, C. M. (1979). The justification of paternalism. *Ethics, 89,* 199–210.
17. Blustein, J. (1982). *Parents and children: The ethics of the family.* New York: Oxford University Press; Levine, C., & Murray, T. H. (Eds.). (2004). *The cultures of caregiving: Conflict and common ground among families, health professionals, and policy makers.* Baltimore: Johns Hopkins University Press.

Veracity

Other Cases Involving Veracity

Key Terms
Deception
Disclosure
Honesty
Lying
Moral dilemma
Nondisclosure
Truth telling
Veracity

Objectives
1. Define the principle of veracity.
2. Identify ethical problems of truth telling.
3. Describe patient care situations where not telling the truth may seem ethical.
4. Describe potential consequences of not telling the truth to a patient or his or her family.

Telling the truth in personal communication with patients is another characteristic of actions that many people believe is morally required for reasons other than just producing good consequences. Just as the principle of autonomy requires that there be respect for the self-determination of substantially autonomous individuals— independent of the fact that such respect will often have good consequences—so the principle of **truth telling** requires that the nurse assess whether communication is honest. If truth telling is a right-making characteristic of actions independent of the consequences of those actions, then we may have to face situations where being honest will be inconvenient to the nurse, distressing to other health professionals, and even harmful to patients. The cases in this chapter raise problems of **honesty** in communication.

The nurses in Cases 8-1 and 8-2 encounter problems of what to do when they have information that they are not yet sure is accurate. Assuming that the nurses would feel they have a moral obligation to disclose a piece of information once they are sure about it, what should they say during that period when they are still in doubt? Are there guidelines that indicate the point at which nurses should feel confident enough about their information that they should act on the duty to disclose?

Other cases directly tackle the problem of situations where telling the truth may lead to consequences that are bad for the client. It is sometimes argued that withholding information is morally different from **lying**.[1] We say, "I didn't lie; I just didn't tell the whole truth." In these cases, we shall see whether omitting the truth can be morally different from outright lying.

Two special complications arise in the debate over the ethics of telling the truth in healthcare situations. One is the case where the competent adult patient makes a specific request of the healthcare professional not to be told a piece of information that most patients would want to know about or might find material to their decision about participating in a course of treatment. The patient may plead that he does not have the time for the detailed discussion of the complicated research protocol being proposed. He may say that he trusts the research team and is willing to proceed without the details. Or another patient may, when having a breast mass diagnosed, say she would rather not know the details of what is found. She may simply authorize the medical staff to go about treatment in the way they think is reasonable. Should the patient be permitted to waive his or her right to know? If so, does this not violate the duty to deal truthfully with the patient?

The other complication is when family members—often of an elderly patient who is perhaps still competent but not fully in charge of his or her day-to-day critical living decisions—ask the nurse or other health professional not to disclose to their ill family member the true gravity of his or her disease. Does the family have the right to waive the requirements of the principle of truth telling? If so, what does the nurse say to the patient who then asks about his or her condition?

Finally, we shall look at the truth-telling problem from the patient's perspective. How should the nurse respond to the patient who wants to know his or her pathology report? Does the patient have the right to the truthful and immediate communication of this kind of information? In many jurisdictions, hospital charts are, by law, available for patients to read.[2] Is there a right to health record information, and what should a nurse do who observes a nonfamily member reading the patient's chart?

The Condition of Doubt

Before tackling the difficult substantive issues related to the ethics of truth telling, a preliminary issue must be addressed. Even if one were to acknowledge a duty to be truthful with well-established and confirmed information, in health care there is a constant evolution of suspicions, trial diagnoses, hunches, and speculations. Information about diagnoses and prognoses gradually evolves and different members of the healthcare team have different knowledge during the time of that evolution. There is often a period when the physician, the nurse, and others are in doubt about what the truth is. This period of uncertainty might be called "the condition of doubt." The following cases show problems the nurse may face when confronted with new, preliminary, and uncertain information.

Case 8-1

Assessing the Impact of Replacing RNs with Nonlicensed Personnel

Joyce Follins, the director of nursing of a community hospital, found it necessary to cut the size of her RN staff in half as a result of cost-cutting measures imposed by the hospital. Nonlicensed personnel (nursing aides) became the main providers of direct care to patients in the majority of the medical, surgical, and OB/GYN units, and technicians replaced 60% of the RN staff in the operating room and other specialized units.

Six months after these changes were implemented, Mrs. Follins compared the number of incident reports involving patient care during that period to the number that occurred before the changes were implemented. She found that the number of incident reports had increased by 40%. Because changes in nursing organization, medication administration, requests for lab work, and meal delivery had also been made during the same period of time, however, she was uncertain whether the increased number of incident reports involving patient care was the result of the reduction in RN staff or of other changes. She was also uncertain whether the increased number of incident reports represented increased risks to patients under the new nursing care delivery system. In reporting her findings to hospital administrators, she emphasized the need for further study of the incident reports and the types of risks to patients that might be involved. She worried, however, that while these studies were being completed, risks to patients' safety and health might occur and these risks might be of a serious nature.

Case 8-2

The Nurse Discovering a Ventricular Dysrhythmia

Mortimer Haley, 51 years old, had recently joined the North Country HMO through his employer. He was scheduled for a routine intake physical examination with his primary physician. An EKG and laboratory tests were completed by a technician. One week later, Mr. Haley was physically examined by nurse practitioner Jennifer Spandler. Reviewing the results of the lab tests, EKG, blood pressure readings, and physical, Ms. Spandler noticed several EKG abnormalities. She took Mr. Haley's blood pressure again, listened carefully to his heart sounds a second time, and asked him several questions. How had he been feeling lately? Did he feel any different than he had several months ago? Did he experience any dizziness? Any diaphoresis? Chest pain?

Mr. Haley denied having any of these symptoms, saying he had been healthy and felt no different than he had for several years. He realized, however, that something in his EKG or lab reports had alerted Ms. Spandler and prompted her to ask the questions and to listen carefully to his heart a second time. He asked her, "Is anything wrong?" She felt fairly sure there was and had been planning to bring her concerns to the attention of his primary physician. But what should she say right now to Mr. Haley in response to his questions?

Commentary

These cases present problems of nurses who have reason to suspect that something is wrong. Were they completely certain, they might very well know what to do. They would apparently not be afraid to speak up if they were certain of their facts and their judgments, but in both cases the nurses were in the process of discovery. Mrs. Follins began to be convinced that she had discovered a pattern of increased incidence reports related to patient care by unlicensed personnel. Ms. Spandler was the first to discover the electrocardiogram (EKG) abnormalities and ventricular dysrhythmia.

In Ms. Spandler's case, when she was asked by Mr. Haley if there was anything wrong, the easiest response would have been "No, nothing at all." It would also have been untruthful. Ms. Spandler was suspicious that something unusual was taking place. On the other hand, were she to come right out and say to the patient "You have a serious cardiac problem," she would be saying more than she was technically able to say. The reality of the situation was that she was in doubt. She could not have been expected to make a definitive diagnosis on the basis of her physical examination and the EKG. Yet she knew that something was evident in Mr. Haley's physical condition that was unexpected.

The cases reveal various ways in which nurses can be in doubt. Mrs. Follins was in doubt primarily because the new nursing care delivery plan had not been in place long enough to say with certainty that it was creating certain effects. The emerging pattern might even have disappeared as more data were collected. Presumably, Mrs. Follins had the capacity to understand and interpret the data such as they were. The problem was that preliminary data were inherently ambiguous. Had she reported her preliminary findings too early, she would have caused needless alarm, damaged the integrity of the new plan of delivery, and looked foolish in the process. If, on the other hand, she had avoided speaking up even when the pattern became clearer, she might have exposed more patients to substantial risk.

It is interesting to note that there are truthful statements that could have been made throughout the entire process of data gathering from the very first discovery of an increased number of patient care incidence reports to the point where the data were confirmed and reconfirmed by additional investigation. One argument often heard when data are ambiguous is that, because the health professional cannot know for sure, it is wrong to say anything. It is surely wrong to say more than one knows. It would have been wrong for Mrs. Follins to report that the new delivery plan was causing injury to a large number of patients when she had not established that fact. She could, however, have spoken truthfully by describing the appearance of the pattern together with the degree of uncertainty that existed. Because she had calculated before and after rates of incident reports, she could honestly have said, for example, that the rate was higher than expected and that the rate was unlikely to have occurred by chance. Whether it would have been morally correct for her to do so is another matter, but she could not have relied on the fact that the data were not certain to justify saying nothing. Uncertain data justify avoiding a claim of certainty, but only some other kind of moral argument would justify withholding the statement of the facts, such as they are.

Mrs. Follins might argue that the duty to be truthful is subordinate to an assessment of the benefits and harms that are likely to come from speaking up and remaining silent. We shall see in the next sections that it is ethically problematic to subordinate the duty of **veracity** to a calculation of consequences. Mrs. Follins might claim that although she has a duty to be honest, that does not include a duty to speak up if she is not asked. She might say, "I didn't lie. I simply withheld the truth." Whether this justification of **nondisclosure** works will depend on whether one believes that withholding the truth is different ethically from actually telling a falsehood. If that is the basis of Mrs. Follins's willingness to remain silent, then she would be in a predicament if anyone, for example a reporter, should happen to ask her if she has found anything unusual in patient care following the implementation of the new nursing care delivery plan.

Ms. Spandler is in a slightly different position. The data she has are preliminary, but they will never be subject to a definitive statistical analysis that would confer a level of confidence in the findings. Rather, they will be subject to a much more vague clinical judgment. Part of Ms. Spandler's problem is that she has limited information upon which to base a finding, but equally important is the fact that Ms. Spandler is not the person charged with interpreting the data. At the same time, she knows enough about EKGs to know that what she sees is not right and that the abnormality is probably coming from the patient rather than from the EKG equipment. It is simply not truthful to say to

Mr. Haley that nothing is wrong. When asked by him if anything is the matter, if Ms. Spandler is to be honest, she has to avoid saying that everything is fine. She might make any of the following statements:

1. "There is a pattern in your heart rhythm that needs to be called to your physician's attention."
2. "I think I see some ventricular dysrhythmia. I am going to have your physician do further tests."
3. "I am not sure what is happening here. I'll bring it to your physician's attention."
4. "I know a serious cardiac problem when I see it, and you have it."

Which answer is the most honest? Which is the most appropriate morally? On what moral grounds, if any, could Ms. Spandler convey that nothing is wrong? What would be the result if she simply refuses to answer Mr. Haley's question?

Duties and Consequences in Truth Telling

Lying and Patient Well-Being

In some cases the ethical problem regarding truth telling is trying to figure out what the truth is and when it should be disclosed. In many other cases, the truth is only too apparent. The patient is dying, has a serious genetic disease, is diagnosed as being mentally ill, or is facing a future of pain and suffering. The traditional ethical mandate in the health professions has been to do what will benefit patients and protect them from harm. That is what the Hippocratic Oath and the *Florence Nightingale Pledge* tell us. Sometimes clinical professionals have believed that the way they can best benefit patients or protect them from harm is to withhold the truth or tell an outright lie.

More recently, this belief has been challenged on two grounds. First, there has been increasing doubt that withholding information from patients really benefits them.[3] Second, even if it would benefit them, some people maintain that persons have the "right to the truth."[4] The following cases explore these controversies.

Case 8-3

Lying to Protect the Patient[1]

Cleo Wimmers, a 70-year-old diabetic, developed a small ulcer on a toe (left extremity) following a recent below-knee amputation (BKA) of the right extremity. Because of his depression and sense of hopelessness prior to the BKA, the nursing staff decided not to tell

---

[1]Adapted from Harris, E., Schirger-Krebs, M. J., Dericks, V., & Donovan, C. (1983). Nothing but the truth? *American Journal of Nursing, 83*, 121–122.

him the results of the wound culture report of pseudomonas (it was unclear whether the culture report referred to the BKA wound or the toe). They placed an "infection control" sign over his bed and told him that he had "an infection." They reasoned that because he had been through a great deal of stress, they did not want to contribute to his fears of losing his other leg. It soon became apparent that the infection was definitely in the toe of the left extremity. The nursing staff wondered if and when they should tell him the truth. They decided not to tell him anything. Eventually his left toe became gangrenous and required amputation.

Several months later, the nurses decided to present the incident to the ethics committee. Mr. Wimmers was invited to tell how he felt once he learned that the nurses had withheld information from him. The patient described how his nurses and doctors had reacted when he asked them direct questions about his left extremity and the infection. He claimed that they "hid behind their medical authority" and that he experienced fear and false impressions about what was really going on. He stated, "If I had been told, 'Yes, there is some infection in the toe of your left foot but we are going to treat it,' it would have been easier for me." Instead, he worried that he had a terrible infection throughout his body that was going to get progressively worse. He understood that the nurses were keeping the truth from him out of a desire to help, but their actions were not helpful. They just made him feel alone and scared.

Case 8-4
When the Physician Asks Not to Tell

Nurse Patricia Alexander admits patient Donald Vespucci to his room following surgery. His diagnosis is metastatic colon cancer. The patient's family members have apparently talked with the physician, Dr. Ernest Hester, and know the diagnosis. However, the physician advises the nursing staff that he will not be telling the patient his diagnosis until he is on antidepressants for a few days because Mr. Vespucci has a history of severe depression.

During the first 2 days following surgery, the patient frequently asks the nursing staff about the results of the surgery, results of lab reports, and so on. The physician visits the patient twice, but still does not tell him his diagnosis. The wife and children are finding it difficult to avoid the questions Mr. Vespucci asks. They keep asking the nurse when the patient will be told his diagnosis (they want the physician to tell him), and the nurse feels caught between the patient's requests, the family's requests, and the physician's plan. The nurse firmly believes that the patient has a right to know his condition but does not believe that it is her responsibility to tell him. Should the nurse be put in a situation that requires her to lie when others on the healthcare team do not follow through with their responsibilities?

Commentary

Both of these cases involve what are sometimes called "benevolent *deceptions*." Both patients are told lies (or at least not told the truth), but the motivations of the liars are benevolent. In both cases, the health professional wanted to protect the patient from the trauma of bad news. The central ethical question is whether either good motive or accurate judgment that the patient would be better off not knowing the news justifies the deception.

It is important in analyzing these cases to distinguish between good motive and right action. Benevolence is acting out of a will to do good. If we were asked to assess the intentions of each of the healthcare teams, we would surely find them to be well motivated. But beneficence is a principle of action, not motive. It holds that one characteristic of actions that tends to make them right is that they will do good.

In the case of Cleo Wimmers, the 70-year-old diabetic suffering from an infected ulcer on his toe, the nurses were sensitive to the trauma Mr. Wimmers had experienced from the BKA of the other extremity. They clearly were motivated by a concern that he be spared the agony of anticipating another amputation. They were clearly benevolent. It is not as clear that they were beneficent, that they were acting so as to really benefit him. He claimed during the ethics committee meeting that he experienced fear and "false impressions about what was really going on." He said that if he had been told the truth about the infection, it would have been easier for him. He imagined that something even worse was happening. All of these statements by Mr. Wimmers suggest that even if a nurse is benevolently motivated, she can still end up harming the patient by withholding the truth.

The same empirical questions arise in the case of Donald Vespucci (the colon cancer patient). Calculating the full range of possible consequences from disclosing or withholding information is terribly complicated. It is increasingly recognized that even well-motivated health professionals are likely to err in making such calculations. Because either of these *disclosures* would be emotionally difficult for physicians or nurses to make, the health professional has a vested interest in having the calculation of consequences come out favoring nondisclosure. Perhaps it explains why controversial decisions often come out against disclosure.

There are other compounding factors in calculating whether disclosure does more harm than good. Health professionals often are inclined to apply the so-called golden rule. They ask, "If I were in the patient's position, would I want to be told this bad news?" The golden rule, applied in this way, can be very dangerous. At best, it discloses what the healthcare professional would want to happen. Health professionals may have very different values than patients do, however. They may have different psychologic makeups. For instance, it is reported that physicians may have an unusually high fear of death. That might have led Dr. Hester to decide against immediately disclosing the diagnosis to Mr. Vespucci. He might have truthfully been able to say, "If I were in the patient's position, I would not want to be told."

One problem with the golden rule, therefore, is that in adopting the patient's position, one must be certain to adopt the value system, the psychologic profile, and the social characteristics of the patient. That, of course, is difficult, perhaps impossible, to do. On the other hand, asking what a person with the physician's or nurse's values would want done about a disclosure is clearly not the right question.

Aside from the difficulties of resolving these issues by calculating what would do the most good for the patient, many people would argue that this is not really the relevant question in the first place. Some would hold that the patients in these cases have a right to the truth regardless of whether the truth makes them better or worse off. If truth telling is a characteristic of actions that makes them right, then perhaps it is wrong to lie even if it were granted that in a particular instance it would do good. Many philosophers (Immanuel Kant is probably the most famous of them) hold that one's ethical duty in such situations cannot be determined solely by the consequences. They give various accounts of why it would be wrong to lie even for good consequences. Some say, for example, that there is an implied promise when relationships are established that communication will be honest and open. Purposeful deception, such as that experienced by Cleo Wimmers when he was told he had "an infection," violates the trust that is presumed by both parties in a communication.

Health professionals are shifting in their assessment of this problem. Physicians, for example, used to hold that deceiving the patient is acceptable, even required, provided it will benefit the patient. Increasingly, however, they are shifting in the direction of recognizing that there is an ethical duty to tell the truth independent of consequences. The American Medical Association's (AMA) 1980 revision of its principles of ethics, for example, says boldly, "A physician shall deal honestly with patients. . . ."

Nurses have been more committed than physicians to providing patients with honest information. The first provision of the American Nurses Association (ANA) *Code of Ethics for Nurses* includes the following in its interpretation: "Patients have the moral and legal right . . . to be given accurate, complete, and understandable information in a manner that facilitates an informed judgment; . . . to accept, refuse, or terminate treatment without deceit . . ."[5] Although the professional codes of physicians and nurses do not necessarily settle the question of what is morally right for members of each group, the codes do raise questions that are worth addressing in conjunction with these cases.

Even if the nurse does not accept the trend in the direction of honoring the principle of veracity, a more pragmatic problem arises when patients such as Cleo Wimmers and Donald Vespucci are not given significant information about their cases. Nurses and physicians have legal obligations as well as ethical ones. Among these is a requirement that patients be afforded informed consent. Had either of these patients given an adequate consent to the treatment they were receiving? When Dr. Hester advised withholding the cancer diagnosis from Donald Vespucci, he not only treated the patient without an adequately informed consent, but he required Patricia Alexander and her colleagues to do so as well. There probably are times when treatment of patients that is in violation of the law is called for and ethically justified. Do these cases fall into such a category? If not, what responses are available to the nurses in these cases?

Critical Thinking Question

1. Reflect on a patient care situation in which you thought it might be beneficial to withhold the truth from the patient or to deceive the patient about the truth. What were the ethical justifications for these actions? Would you do the same today? Why or why not?

Research Brief 8-1

Source: Sullivan, R. J., Menapace, L. W., & White, R. M. (2001). Truth telling and patient diagnoses. *Journal of Medical Ethics, 27*, 192–197.

Purpose: To gather information about what patients want to be told about their illnesses; to explore the standards used by physicians when making decisions about information given to patients; and to investigate the opinions and observations of nurses on these topics.

Method: This was a descriptive, correlational study using self-report instruments. The participants were patients ($n = 337$) who visited a same-day surgery outpatient facility of a mid-sized hospital in New York during a 3-month period, their physicians ($n = 72$), and their nurses ($n = 66$). Separate questionnaires for each group of participants with overlapping questions were used. Descriptive and parametric statistics were used for data analysis.

Findings: The majority of the patients wanted to know about their condition (99%), thought their physician was obliged to tell them (99%), and wanted to know if they had a life-threatening illness (97%). Only 72% of patients wanted to know all of the details, whereas 85% wanted their family members to be informed. There was a statistically significant relationship between wanting family members to know one's exact condition and patient age. Of those over 60 years of age, 94% wanted family members to know details, compared to only 68% of those 18 to 30 years of age. In general, patients with higher levels of education wanted to be told more information.

Twenty-four percent of physicians reported that they inform patients of the major implications of their diagnosis and treatment 50% to 90% of the time, 39% of physicians inform patients 95% to 99% of the time, and only 37% of physicians inform patients 100% of the time. Only 42% of physicians thought that patients want to be told all the details about their illness. Fifty-seven percent said patients want to be told only in general terms, and 1% said patients want no information. The majority of physicians (58%) believed that patients want their family members to be informed of their illness, whereas 40% believed this is true only sometimes. There was no relationship between physician age or country of medical education with these findings.

The majority of nurses (99%) thought patients want to be told all the details concerning their illnesses and that physicians have an obligation to provide this information. However, 60% of nurses believed that patients expect only general explanations of their illnesses. There was a statistically significant difference between patients and nurses on whether patients want to be told all the details of their illnesses and a less significant difference between patients and physicians on this question. Physicians (58%) and nurses (33%) differed on whether patients want family members to be notified of the patient's illness. More nurses (79%) than physicians (52%) wanted to participate in structured discussions about the information that should be told to patients about their illnesses.

Implications: Physicians and nurses tend to underestimate the amount of information that patients want concerning their conditions and possible treatments. This is especially true for well-educated patients. However, patients of all ages should be told the truth about their medical conditions and the treatment options available to them. Patients also should be asked about the amount of information they want to know about their conditions and whether they want family members to know full details or only general information. For the elderly patient, specific efforts should be made to involve family members in discussions of the patient's condition.

Lying and the Well-Being of Others

Cases 8-3 and 8-4 dealt with the problems of lying for the well-being of the patient, a goal clearly central to the traditional ethics of the healthcare professions. Sometimes problems of telling the truth arise when one is motivated not out of concern for the well-being of the patient but rather the well-being of other parties. The next three cases examine, in turn, lying to protect a fellow student, a colleague, and oneself.

Case 8-5

Covering Up for a Fellow Student[2]

Student A is the team leader on a medical unit. Student B is a part of Student A's clinical group. Newly divorced and the mother of two children, Student B has experienced a personality conflict with the nursing instructor during the clinical rotation. Student B was advised that she was in danger of failing her clinical experience.

On the day that Student A is Team Leader, Student B is assigned to an elderly man with a history of cardiovascular disease and poor venous access. He is now hospitalized for treatment of diabetes mellitus. During the day, he is scheduled for an oral glucose tolerance

[2]Case supplied by Leslie G. Potter, RN, BSN. Used with permission.

test requiring five blood samples at intervals of 30 minutes, 1 hour, 2 hours, 3 hours, and 4 hours. Because the hospital lacks transportation services for this type of testing, the nurse is responsible for taking the patient to the lab for the appointed blood samples. Student B fails to remember to bring the patient to the lab for the 1-hour and the 3-hour samples. She does not inform anyone of this fact until the end of the day.

When reporting to Student A, Student B begs her friend not to inform the clinical instructor about the forgotten blood samples and the fact that the test would have to be repeated the following day. Student A agrees not to tell the instructor because the students are friends and she does not want Student B to be open to any more criticism from the instructor. When the instructor asks Student A for her final report of the day, she specifically asks if the patient's test had been completed without incident. Should Student A tell the truth?

Case 8-6
Telling the Family of the Deceased About a Mistake

Miss Hodges, the night-shift nurse, pages the resident on call when a newly admitted female patient (for observation following a car accident, age 46, history of asthma) develops anxiety, wheezing, increased blood pressure, and tachycardia. By the time the sleepy and somewhat disoriented resident comes to the unit, the patient has severe shortness of breath. Miss Hodges has alerted the ICU and is prepared to intubate the patient. The resident takes over and decides to do a hasty tracheotomy before transporting the patient to the ICU. While doing the tracheotomy, he severs a major blood vessel, and the patient loses a great deal of blood. A trach tube is put in place, however, and the patient is quickly prepared for transportation to the ICU. At this point, Miss Hodges realizes that the portable oxygen tank does not seem to be functioning properly. The patient remains oxygen deprived and is brought to the ICU. The patient never gains consciousness and dies 6 hours later. The death is not related to injuries from the car accident.

When the husband comes to the unit to pick up the deceased's belongings, Miss Hodges struggles with whether she should tell him the truth about the mistakes that were made in the care and treatment of his wife.

Case 8-7
Lying to Cover Up Your Past

Janet Miller has recently completed a 6-month rehabilitation program for substance abuse (cocaine). She has been an experienced and competent critical care nurse at Memorial Hospital for many years, but now she decides to seek employment elsewhere where coworkers will not know about her addiction problem. Janet applies for a position at another hospital in the city. She is aware that she is under investigation for her substance abuse by the license registration council in her state, but she also knows that while the investigation is in progress, she is still regarded as an RN and fully licensed.

In speaking to potential employers, Janet is open about her reasons for leaving her previous place of employment and her treatment for substance abuse. However, she experiences difficulty securing employment due to the reference being given by her previous employer. She begins to wonder if she should lie about her substance abuse problem and her employment at Memorial Hospital.

Commentary

Unlike the cases in the previous section, the nondisclosures in these three cases are not contemplated for the benefit of patients. The student who asks that her fellow student withhold information about her failure to send a patient to the lab was motivated by her own interests, possibly even to the detriment of the patient whose omitted tests might go unnoticed. When Miss Hodges contemplates withholding the truth about the resident's mistakes, it is surely not for the benefit of the deceased patient. Conceivably it could be argued that it was for the benefit of the patient's husband, because it would spare him the agony of knowing the truth about the irreversible disaster that had taken place. Realistically, it is primarily for the benefit of the resident. Withholding the information from the husband could, in fact, prohibit him from taking actions that are very much in his interest, such as suing for damages. Janet Miller's proposed plan to lie about her history of substance abuse is obviously for her welfare, not for that of patients.

None of these dishonesties and nondisclosures is open to the most obvious defense of the earlier cases. It cannot realistically be argued that at least the lies were for the benefit of the patients. The question then becomes one of whether nurses have the right or even the duty to violate the principle of veracity when the welfare of parties other than the patient is at stake.

One possible justification of dishonesty is that the people to whom the lies were told are not deserving of the truth. Kant and many other philosophers have contemplated the dilemma of whether a Nazi-era German hiding a Jew in his house should respond truthfully when asked about it by a Nazi. Some have argued that lying is acceptable in such a case because the Nazi has no right to the truth. There has been no bond established in which truthfulness is expected. There is no right to information that will be used for evil purposes.

Whether one accepts this qualification of the truth-telling principle, it is hard to see that it would apply in any of our cases. Possibly the student could argue that she was unfairly in jeopardy because the clinical instructor "had it in for her." It would be hard to introduce a similar argument in the other two cases.

That would leave the defender of the deceptions in these three cases only with arguments based exclusively on consequences. We have already seen that even if it could be shown that the consequences would be better, on balance, with the deception than with the truth, many people hold that there is a duty to be truthful.

Of the three examples of deception for the benefit of fellow health professionals, the lack of honesty about a clinical error is the most common. In 2006, the National Quality Forum endorsed a new guideline on disclosure of serious unanticipated outcomes to patients. The following year, it summarized some "Key Elements of the Safe Practice for Disclosing Unanticipated Outcomes to Patients."[3] Most are in agreement that disclosures should include:

- An explicit statement that an error occurred
- What the error was and the error's clinical implications
- Why the error occurred
- How recurrences will be prevented
- An apology

Thirty-five states have adopted legislation protecting apologies from being used as evidence of liability and eight states require disclosure of serious adverse events to patients.[6]

Complications in Truth Telling

When the Patient Asks for Dishonesty

Case 8-8

Should the Nurse Agree to Deceive?

Ronald Dawson, a 46-year-old father of three being treated in employee health for high blood pressure and diabetes, schedules a visit with Elizabeth McMahon, the nurse practitioner he generally sees. He tells Ms. McMahon that his wife who is currently deployed to Afghanistan, is scheduled for leave next week and he desperately wants to take at least 2 days off to maximize their time together. Finances are a huge issue for the Dawson family. Mr. Dawson needs this job and cannot just call in sick without a note. He begs Ms. McMahon to write a note documenting medical need for the absence.

She knows and likes Mr. Dawson and has great sympathy for his situation. She has met his wife and in her heart supports his desire to spend as much time together as possible. She knows that trying to hold the family together during her absence has not been easy for Mr. Dawson. Should she lie to the company to help Mr. Dawson? In what ways are her commitments to the patient complicated by her responsibilities to the employer?

Commentary

The situation in which the patient himself requests nondisclosure or dishonest disclosure requires reassessment of both reasons for supporting disclosure. Those who argue for disclosure on the grounds that it will normally produce better consequences need to take into account that Mr. Dawson has some reason for wanting dishonest information about him to be provided to his employer. If the

---

[3]The National Quality Forum disclosure guidelines may be found at: http://www.quality forum.org/. Retrieved May 17, 2010.

patient says that he does not want his employer to know the truth, there is good reason to suspect that the consequences of the disclosure will not be good.

The remarkable thing about this situation is that, if Ms. McMahon accepts the traditional ethic of the health professional—the norm that actions should be directed only for the benefit of the patient—then the obvious conclusion is that she has a duty to lie to the employer. It seems that the lie would clearly benefit her patient. The idea that the nurse should be a party to cheating the employer is more problematic than that. The request from Mr. Dawson is essentially a proposal to obtain 2 days pay without using vacation time. It comes down to whether it is right to make the employer use its funds to provide 2 extra days pay rather than have Mr. Dawson use vacation time to be with his wife and to have the nurse force this outcome without the employer knowing it.

Those who insist that telling the truth is a right-making characteristic that is morally relevant regardless of the consequences, of course, will not be convinced that this is morally acceptable. Is there a duty to be honest that derives from the principle of truth telling in such cases?

The duty to be truthful, if it exists independent of the consequences, is based on the expectations of the relationship among people. One philosopher argues that lying is a breaking of the implied commitment that persons normally make when they communicate with one another. If that is so, then the duty to tell the truth exists when honesty is the expectation. In certain unusual situations, people actually do not expect honest and reasonably complete disclosure. No one would accuse a magician of violating the norms of truth telling when he deceives his audience. Many would argue, however, that health professionals are violating the expectation of veracity if they fail to be honest when the one with whom they are communicating expects honesty. Even if a principle of autonomy permits one to choose what will be known about oneself and by whom, it does not follow that it is right for the patient to ask the nurse to lie or deceive others on his behalf. Autonomy gives people the freedom to act, even if their actions are not always the most conscientious or appropriate. But the patient may still have to face the question of whether it is morally appropriate to present false information about his condition to his employer.

When the Family Asks Not to Tell

Case 8-9

Fetal Death in the Labor Room: Should the Nurse Tell the Patient?[4]

Nurse Sally Majeski has admitted a new patient: Mrs. Feedham, a 36-year-old woman (G-2, P-1) of 22 weeks' gestation. The admitting diagnosis is eclampsia, acute glomerulo-nephritis, and IUGR. Mrs. Feedham is placed in a quiet room and given a parenteral

---

[4]Case supplied by Christine Way, PhD, RN. Used with permission.

administration of magnesium sulfate. The admission assessment reveals that Mrs. Feedham has hypertension, proteinuria, epigastric pain, a severe headache, and blurred vision. Abdominal palpation reveals a soft but irritable abdomen, a uterus small for gestation date, and a faint and rapid fetal heart rate. The patient is easily startled and appears tense, restless, and unable to concentrate.

Ms. Majeski learns that the patient and her husband have been planning for this baby for a long time. They have a 6-year-old daughter who eagerly looks forward to having a brother or sister. From reading the physician's notes, Ms. Majeski learns that the physician hopes that conservative treatment will stabilize Mrs. Feedham's renal condition. If the renal condition does not stabilize, he will propose a treatment that is, unfortunately, potentially detrimental to the survival of the fetus. Mrs. Feedham expresses concern about her baby, but she does not seem to realize that the treatment of her renal condition may require medication that could be harmful to the fetus.

On the following day, Ms. Majeski is again assigned to care for Mrs. Feedham. Her condition has not improved since admission. The physician has discussed Mrs. Feedham's condition with her husband, and he has consented to the treatment of the renal condition. He understands that the medication used will greatly diminish the chances of the fetus's survival. The husband has agreed not to discuss the matter with his wife—additional stress would only increase the danger of her condition.

Ms. Majeski remains in the labor room with Mrs. Feedham during most of the day, checking on the treatment per IV infusion and checking on her vital signs and the vital signs of the fetus. Mrs. Feedham, although heavily sedated, repeatedly asks, "How is the baby doing?" Ms. Majeski can see the erratic heart beats of the fetus on the fetal monitor, but she does not tell this to the patient. Instead, she urges her to rest and not to worry. Finally, the fetal heart rate tracings on the monitor become a flat line. Soon after this, Mrs. Feedham arouses from her semistuporous state and specifically asks, "What is the baby's heartbeat?" Ms. Majeski replies, "Sh-h-h, just try to rest." When she informs the head nurse that she does not think she can remain in the room any longer and deceive the patient, the head nurse replies, "I know that this situation is difficult, but we must do what is best for the mother regardless of the guilt that we might feel." Ms. Majeski does not find this to be an adequate response to the moral distress she is experiencing.

Commentary

The case of Mrs. Feedham is similar to Case 8-8, the case of Mr. Dawson, who asks that his employer be deceived, in that someone has decided what information about the patient will be known and by whom. In this case, however, it is not the patient but a family member, Mrs. Feedham's husband, who has made the request. Thus, the question becomes one of whether the family has the authority to decide what the patient should know.

As with previous case, in analyzing the ethical issues we might first assess the consequences of disclosure and nondisclosure. Even though in some cases in which health professionals contemplate withholding information from patients we have good reason to expect the patient would be harmed, it is not obvious what the effect will be on Mrs. Feedham if she learns her fetus has died. To be sure, this would be traumatic for her, but the consequences of her learning this at a later time could also be devastating. We saw in earlier cases that there is a great deal of room for error in the assessment of consequences. The same problem exists when family members are the ones deciding whether the patient would be better off not knowing. The only difference to consider is whether family members might be better able to assess the impact of the bad news on their loved ones than health professionals would.

Next, we should assess the possible impact of the principle of truth telling. Do family members have the authority to waive rights claims of the patient? In some cases they might. For example, if the patient were totally incompetent, many would argue that the family has not only the right but also the duty to serve the incompetent one's interests. It might be argued that totally incompetent persons have no right to disclosure of information at all. If they do, could family members waive it on their behalf on the grounds that it was in their best interests?

In the case of Mrs. Feedham, there is no evidence that she is in any way incompetent. She is in the midst of the late stages of pregnancy but apparently not rendered incapable of making autonomous choices. If the information is needed to help make those choices, then the role of the family in waiving the patient's rights is suspect. Both autonomy and truth telling appear to count against permitting family members a role in granting nurses or other health professionals the right to withhold or disclose information, or to deceive patients.

Mrs. Feedham's case is complicated by the fact that the life and welfare of a 22-week fetus is also at stake. Would the interests of the fetus justify treating Mrs. Feedham differently from other competent adults? Several factors need to be taken into account in making this judgment. First, Mrs. Feedham apparently has the legal right to abort her fetus, assuming this action was necessary to protect Mrs. Feedham's health. Second, even if the medical staff could get a court order to treat Mrs. Feedham in some special manner against her consent in order to protect the fetus, the resulting order would not be one of authorizing the risky treatment. It would more likely be one blocking it. In fact, Mrs. Feedham might actually have preferred to take the risk of more conservative therapy in an effort to save the fetus. Without knowing the choices being made about her care, that is a choice she cannot make. Withholding the information about the more aggressive treatment being a risk to the fetus deprives Mrs. Feedham not only of her right to consent to the treatment, but also of her right to determine what should be done to protect her fetus.

If nurse Majeski does continue, she should realize that she is providing nursing care for her patient without her consent. She might well find that not only unethical, but also illegal. She may, therefore, want to appeal not only to her supervisors but to the legal authorities within her institution. They may feel obliged to point out that such behavior is not consistent with the ANA *Code of Ethics for Nurses* or other ethics codes they consider authoritative. Ultimately, they simply may have to refuse to participate in the nondisclosure scheme.

There is one final moral dimension to cases of familial requests for nondisclosure. Traditionally, the health professions have been bound by the principle of confidentiality, a principle we shall examine in Chapter 9. There are various inter-pretations of that principle. Most bind the health professional, with certain limi-tations, to avoid revealing information about the patient to others. Mrs. Feedham's physician has broken confidentiality by disclosing her condition to her husband without her permission. It is conceivable that this was a justifiable breech of confidence given her condition, but it was a breech nevertheless. If that is the case, the nurses who cooperate in such circumstances are not only caring for patients without their consent and potentially violating the norms of truth tell-ing, but they are also collaborating in a breech of the duty of confidentiality.

Research Brief 8-2

Source: Gallagher, T. H., Waterman, A. D., Ebers, A. G., Fraser, V. J., & Levinson, W. (2003). Patients' and physicians' attitudes regarding the disclosure of medical errors. *Journal of the American Medical Association, 289*(8), 1001–1007.

Purpose: To determine patients' and physicians' attitudes about error disclosure.

Method: Thirteen focus groups were organized, including six groups of adult patients, four groups of academic and community physicians, and three groups of both physicians and patients. A total of 52 patients and 46 physicians participated. Qualitative analysis of focus groups' audiotaped transcripts elicited themes related to the attitudes of patients and physicians about medical error disclosures, whether physicians disclose the information patients desire, and patients' and physicians' emotional needs when an error occurs and whether these needs are met.

Findings: Both patients and physicians had unmet needs following the com-mission of errors. Patients wanted disclosure of all harmful errors and sought information about what happened, why the error happened, how the error's consequences would be mitigated, and how recurrences will be prevented. Physicians agreed that harmful errors should be disclosed but said that they chose their words carefully when telling patients about errors. Although phy-sicians disclosed the adverse event, they often avoided stating that an error occurred, why the error happened, or how recurrences would be prevented. Patients also desired emotional support from physicians following errors, including an apology for the error. Physicians, however, worried that an apol-ogy might create legal liability. Physicians were also upset when errors hap-pened, but they were unsure where to seek emotional support.

Implications: Physicians may not be providing the information or emotional support that patients seek following harmful medical errors. Physicians should strive to meet patients' desires for an apology and for information on the nature, cause, and prevention of errors. Institutions should address the emotional needs of practitioners who are involved in medical errors.

The Right to Health Records

In the cases presented thus far in this chapter, we have examined the consequences of disclosure and nondisclosure and the possible inherent duty to be truthful. We have seen that sometimes it is difficult to determine the exact point at which the nurse has enough information to disclose (she may be in a condition of doubt), but that once she reaches that point, the **moral dilemma** is approached by assessing both consequences and the implications of the principle of veracity. Furthermore, patients may at times waive their right to information, in part because the duty to disclose is based on the expectations of the relationship and in part because patients should be free to act autonomously. It is much harder to establish a similar right of waiver on the part of the family of the patient. If, in some sense, patients are entitled to information about their conditions so that, among other things, they may make intelligent choices about their care, important and controversial issues come into play about the handling of health records. The following case raises the issue of who is the moral "owner" of the information in a nursing chart.

Case 8-10

When Friends Want to Read the Patient's Health Record

Mr. Ellwood Berry had been hospitalized six times in the previous 2 years for treatment of cancer of the prostate that had metastasized to the pelvis. He was often in great pain and had serious red blood cell loss. He had experienced fainting spells that had led to the current hospitalization. When he was hospitalized this time, his blood pressure was 90/50. He was stabilized by a transfusion of two units of packed cells but was very weak and sometimes confused.

Over the years, Mr. Berry's friend and proxy decision maker, Mr. George Davis, had become quite knowledgeable about his condition. He knew that Mr. Berry's vital signs and red blood cell counts were important clinical indicators of Mr. Berry's condition. When nurse Charlene MacPherson made her routine rounds, she took Mr. Berry's vital signs, measured his intake and output, and recorded this information on Mr. Berry's chart. She did not give this information to Mr. Davis. Mr. Davis then asked Ms. MacPherson about his friend's vital signs, general condition, and blood work. Ms. MacPherson reported the general nature of Mr. Berry's condition and lab test results, but she was not specific.

One day, Ms. MacPherson came into Mr. Berry's room and found Mr. Davis reading his friend's chart, which had been left on the bedside stand. She scolded Mr. Davis, telling him that it was against the law for unauthorized persons to see a patient's chart and that it was an invasion of a patient's privacy. Mr. Davis apologized but explained that he was just trying to find out the specifics about Mr. Berry's condition, lab test results, medications, and the physician's thoughts. In his mind he thought, "Who is she to tell me I can't know my friend's medical status? It's his information, and I am responsible for him. I even help pay for the cost of his care. Why can't I know this information?" Who does health record information belong to?

Commentary

This case follows naturally from the earlier ones dealing with the patient's or family's right to information. The evidence is quite good in the case that Mr. Davis desired the information on behalf of his friend, that he had some basic understanding of its meaning, and that he was distressed about not getting it. On grounds of consequences, Mr. Davis's case seems to be a good one. On the other hand, other patients or their proxy decision makers might not understand as clearly the meaning of the information on the chart. They might become needlessly upset, especially if the nurse cannot adequately explain some of the findings. From the point of view of benefits and harms, the case for a general rule letting patients and proxies see their charts is more controversial.

What steps might be taken to overcome the potential harms of patients and proxies getting information from the charts? Some in the movement for more active patient or proxy participation have suggested that it ought to become routine practice for patients and proxies to have access to the health record together with an explanation of the meaning of what is in it. In fact, in many jurisdictions, state law requires giving patients and sometimes proxies access to charts when they request it. The federal HIPAA (Health Insurance Portability and Accountability Act) specifically affirms that patients have the right to see a copy of their medical records. While it is less clear about the rights of proxies, most would recognize a similar right of proxies especially when access is important in making healthcare decisions for the patient.

Advocates of reform want to go even further. They maintain that patients would be better off if all patients and proxies, not just the curious ones, received an explanation of what was in the health record. Upon request, most healthcare institutions now give the patient a copy of his or her health record so that the patient can carry it with him or her, in case the patient moves or changes practitioners.

Regardless of the consequences of withholding the health record information from the patient's proxy, Mr. Davis might be suggesting that he ought to have a right to the information, that it is his friend's health information, and that they are paying to have the information produced. Although a case can be made that friends do not generally have a right to information about a patient, in the case of an incompetent patient whose friend is functioning in a legal capacity as a surrogate, morally and legally that surrogate may need the information and have a right to it that is analogous to the right of the patient.

The model Mr. Davis is operating under suggests that the patient has engaged the healthcare team for services while the patient or his proxy remains in charge—a radical contrast to the traditional, more paternalistic model. There clearly is a breakdown in understanding between Ms. MacPherson and Mr. Davis. Ms. MacPherson must now face several critical questions. First, under this model, is there any good reason that Mr. Davis should not be able to get his friend's healthcare information? Second, if there is not, should he be able to get it in Ms. MacPherson's hospital? Assuming the hospital has no principled objections to this model, is there any reason that Ms. MacPherson should not be willing to cooperate? If she insists on the more traditional understanding of communication between nurse and patient, should she prevent Mr. Davis from seeing the information until Mr. Berry is clearly incompetent? What should the nurse do if she is willing to cooperate with Mr. Berry's proxy, but Mr. Berry's physician is not?

Sometimes the question of a right of access to medical information may arise when the one who might want the information is not the patient from whom it was obtained. In some cases, the person who could make use of the information might not even have reason to know it exists. The following case poses this question in the case of paternity testing.

Case 8-11
When the Nurse Has Information of Mixed Benefit to a Family

Jorn Bulger is an oncology nurse practitioner working for a bone marrow treatment program. He also sits on the hospital ethics committee. Recently the BMT staff have had repeated conversations about what to do when testing family members for matches reveal that the paternity of all or some of the children is not what has been presented. Do you tell the patient, the children, or other family? Surprisingly there is no policy on this matter and it seems that individual clinicians do different things. Some have a conversation up front with families prior to the testing and ask how they want this information handled should in occur with their testing. Others just hold the information private and simply inform family that there is not a match.

Mr. Bulger decides to seek the counsel of the hospital ethics committee. He asks if there is any obligation to provide families with information about paternity. One of the committee members points out that there has been some case law faulting physicians for not sharing information on cancer genes such as colon or breast based on the high risk to the family member who does not know about the gene and fails to get close follow-up. Another mentions that a child who has a parent who is someone other than the presumed parent faces potentially significant medical issues such as not being at risk for the genetic diseases of the presumed parent while unknowingly being at risk for genetic problems inherited from the actual biological parent.

Commentary

Until recently, we could usually presume that a patient's medical information was of legitimate interest only to the patient and those responsible for that person's medical care. In the era of genetic disease, in which we increasingly can know a great deal about others solely on the basis of our own medical information, the question arises of whether others have a right of access. Especially, when they can take clinical actions based on another person's medical information, there will increasingly be a claim of a right of access.

It is the nature of the testing necessary for organ and tissue transplant such as bone marrow transplant, that important and sometimes controversial information can be learned. This is not the purpose of the testing, but, once the information is generated, the question arises of whether those who could use the information have a right of access.

Establishing unexpected paternity is one such example. The spouse who is not the biologic parent may have an interest in this information. Even more critically, the child who is not the offspring of one of his or her presumed parents may have an interest. For example, if the presumed parent has a genetic disease, the child could be very interested in knowing that his or her risk should not be calculated presuming inheritance from that parent. On the other hand, establishing who the real biological parent is could be medically useful.

Thus, spouses and children have a real interest in the medical information gratuitously learned. Needless to say, great harm can come from dissemination of this information as well.

One strategy anticipated by some of the clinicians at Mr. Bulger's hospital would be to ask in advance the patient being tested what should be done with such information. The problem with that approach is that it ignores the question of the right of the offspring to the potentially important information. Another approach is to inform the person being tested in advance that such information would be shared with the spouse or the one believed to be the other parent, leaving to that person the decision about whether to inform the offspring. That, of course, also fails to address the question of whether the offspring have a right of access. What policy should Mr. Bulger's hospital adopt?

ENDNOTES

1. Beauchamp, T. L., & Childress, J. F. (2001). *Principles of biomedical ethics* (5th ed.). New York: Oxford University Press.
2. Hayes, J. (1978). The patient's right of access to his hospital and medical records. *Medical Trial Technique Quarterly, 24*(3), 295–305; Tucker, G. (1978). Patient access to medical records. *Legal Aspects of Medical Practice, 6*, 45–50.
3. Bok, S. (1978). *Lying: Moral choice in public and private life.* New York: Pantheon Books; Novack, D. H., Plumer, R., Smith, R. L., Ochitil, H., Morrow, G. R., & Bennett, J. M. (1979). Changes in physicians' attitudes toward telling the cancer patient. *Journal of the American Medical Association, 241*, 897–900; Veatch, R. M., & Tai, E. (1980). Talking about death: Patterns of lay and professional change. *Annals of the American Academy of Political and Social Science, 447*, 29–45.
4. Kant, I. (1797). On the supposed right to tell lies from benevolent motives. In T. Abbott (Trans.). (1909). *Critique of practical reason and other works on the theory of ethics* (pp. 361–365). London: Longmans.
5. American Nurses Association. (2001). *Code of ethics for nurses with interpretive statements* (p. 8). Washington, DC: Author.
6. McDonnell, W. M., & Guenther, E. (2008). Narrative review: Do state laws make it easier to say "I'm sorry"? *Annals of Internal Medicine, 149*, 811–816.

Chapter 9

Fidelity

Other Cases Involving Fidelity

Key Terms
Confidentiality
Fidelity
Privacy
Promise keeping
Respect for persons

Objectives
1. Define the principle of fidelity.
2. Describe the types of commitments typically made by nurses in patient care.
3. Describe two patient care situations in which it is morally permissible for the nurse to break a promise made to a patient.
4. Describe two patient care situations in which it is morally permissible to break a patient's confidentiality.

Both autonomy and veracity are principles that involve respect for other persons. Sometimes they are treated as aspects of the same moral requirement, what in Chapter 6 we called the superprinciple of **respect for persons. Fidelity** is another aspect of respecting persons. When commitments are made to others, other things being equal, most people recognize that there is a moral obligation to keep those commitments. To fail to do so would be a sign of lack of respect. Commitments can take many forms, one of which is making a promise. Insofar as the promise is made, there is an ethical obligation to keep it, according to people who include a principle of fidelity in their ethics.

This does not necessarily mean that the duty of fidelity is rigid and without exception. In some cases, such as when remaining faithful to one's commitments would result in serious harm being done to another, the requirements of doing good and avoiding harm may conflict with those of fidelity. If keeping a promise means that serious harm will be done, then the principle of beneficence would pull in the direction of breaking the promise, whereas the principle of fidelity would pull in the direction of keeping it. Here, these partial or prima facie duties pull in opposite directions. Whether the commitment is kept or broken will depend on how one relates the demands of the two principles. If, for example, one uses only calculations of benefit and harm as the criteria for resolving such conflicts of principle, then promises would never be kept when breaking them does more good than harm.[1] Other philosophers, however, give priority to the principle of fidelity, leading to the conclusion that the promise should be kept even if breaking it would do more good.[2] Still others argue that neither principle can take absolute priority, giving rise to an approach in which one "balances" the competing claims and is guided by how weighty the demands of each principle are in a particular case.[3]

The cases in this chapter all raise problems of what it means for the nurse to be faithful. The first group of cases deals with promises made to patients. Sometimes those promises are explicit; sometimes they are implied. One implied promise is the promise to keep information that is disclosed during the course of providing nursing care confidential. If there has been an explicit or implied promise—through the well-established practices of the nursing profession and through the codes of ethics to which nurses adhere—then the nurse has a duty of fidelity to keep such information confidential. That is the issue in the second group of cases in this chapter.

Promise Keeping

It is widely recognized that acting morally includes keeping promises. At least, if there is not a good reason to break a promise, it is normally recognized that promises should be kept. Some people would hold that this principle derives from the consideration of consequences. If people did not generally have an obligation to keep promises, then the very act of making a promise would be meaningless. **Promise keeping**, then, may simply be an aspect of our duty to act on the rules that will generally produce good consequences.

Other people take promise keeping more seriously. They believe that it is a duty that has independent moral status. It is not just that keeping promises tends to produce good results. Rather, keeping promises is like respecting autonomy and telling the truth—it is inherently a right-making characteristic of actions.

Although most people acknowledge that promises should not be broken trivially, they face a moral conflict when faced with a situation in which keeping the promise will lead to much worse consequences than breaking it would. They ask whether, in that situation, it is morally permitted (or even morally required) to break the promise.

Explicit Promises

We normally think of promises as explicit commitments made to another. Some people also speak, however, of "implicit promises," that is, commitments that all parties assume to exist even if no specific and explicit act of promising has taken place. Many social practices in health care and in other spheres of life are shaped by such implicit promises. We present one case of each kind here. In the first case presented, a nurse has promised explicitly to protect her patient from harm.

Case 9-1
When Breaking a Promise Might Do Good[1]

Helene Shifflett is a 79-year-old woman who had been admitted to the hospital on three different occasions during the past year for her "nerves." Now she was complaining of dizziness, weakness, multiple awakenings during the night as well as early morning awakenings and generalized pain. Mrs. Shifflett's internist notified the psychiatrist, Dr. Muller, and Mrs. Shifflett was admitted to the psychiatric unit of a large county medical center. Brought to the unit by her son and daughter-in-law, Mrs. Shifflett was obviously quite anxious and wanted to make sure that one of her family members was within touching distance during the initial nursing assessment. Her posture was slightly slumped, and she walked with a shuffling gait. Except for mild diabetes controlled by diet and mild hypertension controlled by medication, she seemed in good physical condition. She was, however, confused and very frightened of being admitted to the psychiatric unit.

Judith Broughton, an experienced psychiatric nurse, admitted Mrs. Shifflett to the unit and obtained some important psychosocial information about her patient. It seemed that Mrs. Shifflett had experienced several losses in recent times, including the death of her husband just over a year ago. She had also been rejected by her middle child, who had always been her favorite. She currently cared for her oldest daughter, who was disabled. She had also raised her granddaughter, but this child had recently moved away to a distant

---

[1]Case supplied by Nancy L. Hazard, RN. Used with permission.

city. She had no living siblings and expressed special concern about a younger sister who had been in a state mental hospital for many years and had died there. Apparently, this sister and Mrs. Shifflett had been very close.

An extensive medical workup was completed, and the results of all tests were essentially within normal range. Mrs. Shifflett was started on low doses of norpramin and clonazepam, without good results. Although she did respond when spoken to by others, she took little interest in her appearance and refused to participate in unit activities. Given her continued depression, Dr. Muller thought that a course of electroconvulsive therapy (ECT) should be considered. He asked the social worker to discuss ECT with the family while he and the nurses attempted to discuss it with Mrs. Shifflett.

Mrs. Broughton had established a good relationship with Mrs. Shifflett and felt confident that her patient could benefit from ECT. She believed in the overall effects of the therapy for depressed elderly patients who also had good family support and care. Mrs. Shifflett, however, strongly opposed any discussion of a potential course of ECT. After both Mrs. Broughton and Dr. Muller had discussed it with her, she became very agitated and began to show marked signs of mental decompensation, making it clear she was no longer competent to make her own decisions. She begged Mrs. Broughton to promise her that she would not "let them do that to me." Mrs. Broughton assured her that they would not harm her and that she had nothing to fear.

In discussing the matter with Mrs. Shifflett's son, it was learned that his mother had signed a power of attorney shortly before admission to the hospital, giving him the authority to handle all her affairs. Because she was still the sole provider for her disabled daughter, this had seemed a wise thing to do while she was in the hospital. The social worker had informed the son that he could authorize the ECT for his mother, based on the legal powers that he already had for her care and her affairs. Yet the son was reluctant to sign for the therapy, knowing how much it frightened his mother. He also realized, however, that the ECT would probably improve her mental status to the point where she could return home and live without fears. He was convinced that the procedure was safe and promised great benefit to his mother. He decided to seek the advice of Mrs. Broughton in helping him decide whether he should agree to the treatment for his mother. He told her, "If you and Dr. Muller think that ECT will help my mother, then I will sign the papers agreeing to the therapy. What do you think is best for my mother?"

Mrs. Broughton was torn between her promise to the patient that she would not let anything harm her and her knowledge of the beneficial effects of ECT. Although Mrs. Broughton did not think ECT was harmful, Mrs. Shifflett certainly perceived it as something harmful. Consequently, Mrs. Broughton was very uncomfortable with the son's questions. She also realized that her comments would more than likely sway the son to sign or not to sign the forms. At the same time, however, she could see Mrs. Shifflett's mental condition deteriorating more each day. Mrs. Broughton was uncertain how she should respond to the son.

Commentary

Several strategies of moral reasoning are available to Mrs. Broughton. One conspicuous possibility is that she could finesse the problem of keeping the promise if she reasoned that she was not breaking the promise she made. She did not promise Mrs. Shifflett that she would keep the medical staff from doing the ECT. She promised that she would not let them harm her. Assuming that Mrs. Broughton concurs with Dr. Muller and Mrs. Shifflett's son that the ECT will help rather than harm, she might try to convince herself that she would not be breaking her promise if she failed to speak up against the ECT.

This may not be an accurate approach to the problem, even on its face. Mrs. Broughton realizes that Mrs. Shifflett perceives the ECT as harmful. She would at least be upset. So it may not really be accurate to say that she will not be harmed. Mrs. Broughton would also need to face the question of what "keeping her patient from harm" really means. We saw in Chapter 4 that some people, when they speak of not harming, have in mind the net amount of benefits over harms, so that a person who receives more benefit than harm could be said not to be harmed. Others, however, distinguish between harming and helping in such a way that if there were some harm (such as the discomfort of the ECT), they would say that harm was done (even though more good was done on balance). If Mrs. Broughton were to take the latter stance, she would have to admit that harm was to be done even if the end result would be good on balance. It is going to be hard for Mrs. Broughton to argue that she is not breaking her promise to avoid harm.

More critically, she may be obliged to take into account the spirit of the promise. It appears that what Mrs. Shifflett really wanted (and what she probably thought she received) was a promise to protect her against ECT. If that was what was implied, it is deceptive and hardly respecting of persons for Mrs. Broughton to rationalize her way out of a moral dilemma by arguing that, technically, she never promised to prevent the ECT, only to protect Mrs. Shifflett from harm.

The core moral problem faced by Mrs. Broughton is really whether it is justifiable to break a promise (or at least an implied promise). It might be that it is acceptable to break promises when (and only when) more good will come from breaking the promise than from keeping it. If that is the case, then Mrs. Broughton would be justified in calculating carefully all the good that could come from breaking her promise. She would, of course, also have to take into account all the evils that could result from breaking the promise: the possibility that Mrs. Shifflett would no longer trust the staff, that she would never return to the institution in the future, and that she might suffer physical harm from the ECT.

True consequentialists who focus on individual acts would say that promises can morally be broken whenever the benefit outweighs the harm on balance (taking into account all of the subtle harms). On the other hand, some consequentialists use another approach, one that makes promise breaking more difficult. These consequentialists say that consequentialism should be used to assess moral rules and that the rule that should be adopted is the one that produces more good consequences than another. These consequentialists could consider two possible rules—one that requires keeping promises unless more good would come from breaking the promise and another that requires keeping promises regardless. They might conclude that the latter rule actually would lead to more good than the former even though the former appears to permit more good. They could reach this conclusion if they hold that people are likely to make errors in calculations so that the rule "Keep promises unless you believe more good would come from breaking them" would actually lead to less good than the simpler rule "Always keep promises." This would be one way that Mrs. Broughton could conclude that, on grounds of consequences, the promise should be kept even if she believed it would do more good for her patient to break it.

Still another approach is to acknowledge the duty of promise keeping grounded in the principle of fidelity as a duty independent of consequences. Just as some people hold that there is a duty to respect autonomy or to tell the truth, so they also may hold that it is simply wrong to break promises. Although other considerations may be so overwhelming that the promise could be broken in a particular instance, there is still an inclination to regard breaking a promise as wrong. Some overwhelming counterconsideration would have to be brought into play to offset this. The question then becomes whether Mrs. Broughton made a promise to protect her patient against ECT in the first place and, if so, whether she has any duty to keep that promise when she believes her patient would be better off if it were broken.

Implicit Promises and the Right of Access to Health Care

Promises are sometimes not as overtly made as in Case 9-1. It is widely held among health professionals that they have made a commitment to their patients that requires providing care, at least once they are in a relation with the patient. Although this kind of promise might be only implicit, it shapes the very fabric of health care and poses serious problems for nurses if they are asked to withdraw from caring for a patient. Laws placing limits on access to health care for illegal immigrants poses this problem starkly.

Case 9-2
Is There a Duty to Abandon Illegal Immigrants?

In November 1994, California voters approved Proposition 187, which required publicly funded healthcare facilities to deny care to illegal immigrants and to report them to government officials. Supporters argued that "an invasion of illegal aliens" was bankrupting California and that free health care and education were magnets attracting illegal immigrants. In arguing for the measure, proponents declared, "While our own citizens and legal residents go wanting, those who choose to enter our country ILLEGALLY get royal treatment at the expense of the California taxpayer."

According to Proposition 187, publicly funded healthcare facilities must ensure that "a person shall not receive any healthcare services from a publicly-funded healthcare facility to which he or she is otherwise entitled until the legal status of that person has been verified." If the facility "determines or reasonably suspects" that a patient is an illegal immigrant, it must deny nonemergency care and report the patient to the Immigration and Naturalization Service, the state attorney general, and the state director of health services. The healthcare facility must provide "any additional information that may be requested by any other public entity."[4]

More recently, vocal critics of U.S. healthcare reform raised similar concerns. A study released September 8, 2009, by the Center for Immigration Studies stated "Because of the lack of immigration verification requirements in the House healthcare bill, an estimated 6.6 million illegal aliens could be covered because they meet the financial criteria. Those 6.6 million currently cost the public $4.3 billion in emergency rooms and free health clinics but would cost $31 billion under the House healthcare system."[5]

In the emergency room, true emergencies would be treated regardless of immigration status. Many ER patients, however, are not really emergencies; they are merely coming for needed care. While clerks may handle routine administrative tasks, it is typical that the ER nurse would encounter such patients while providing triage to determine if an emergency exists. They would then be left to decide appropriate disposition of patients who were considered nonemergencies and would therefore be excluded according to Proposition 187.

How should emergency room nurses respond to mandates to report illegal immigrants and to deny them needed care? Is there a professional obligation for emergency room healthcare professionals to commit civil disobedience and or face institutional censure/discipline for failing to comply with a state or national mandate? Finally, if you were a member of your state or national professional nurses association and were charged with writing a position paper on denying care to illegal immigrants what would your position be and why?

Commentary

Many nurses would accept the claim that traditional professional ethics includes an implicit promise that the nurse will provide competent care to their patients and not abandon them. They will not fail to provide needed nursing services without making appropriate arrangements to transfer care to a competent colleague. Many nurses would also accept the claim that they have made an implicit promise to live by the laws of the land in which they live.

In Case 9-2, we appear to have a situation in which nurses have made two implicit promises that can come into conflict with each other. It is possible that some illegal immigrants would be screened out of the healthcare system before they ever reach a nurse or other healthcare professional. That should not happen in the emergency room, however. Even Proposition 187 makes clear that illegal immigrants are permitted to receive emergency treatment. It is only care that is deemed not to rise to an emergency that is to be excluded. The clerk at the ER door should not have the capacity or authority to determine whether the patient presents an emergency. Even if the clerk can establish that the patient is an illegal immigrant, that person should not be able to definitively determine that the patient presents no emergency. That should not occur until the patient is seen by a nurse or other health professional.

That means that there will be at least a temporary professional–patient relationship established before it can be determined whether an emergency exists. If the nurse is the one making that determination, then obeying the law that requires exclusion of illegal immigrants would require abandoning the patient, which seems to be a violation of the promise made by the nurse to stay with their patient. Thus, the nurse may have made two conflicting implicit promises—to obey the law and to stay with the patient that the law requires him or her to abandon. How do nurses extricate themselves from this inherent conflict?

Critical Thinking Questions

1. What explicit and implicit promises do psychiatric and emergency room nurses make to their patients by merely presenting themselves as professional caregivers?
2. Reflect on the numerous promises nurses make daily ("I'll be right back"; "I'll look into that for you"; "You can trust me"; "I know what I am doing.") and the consequences of these promises being fulfilled or unfulfilled.

Confidentiality

One aspect of fidelity is the keeping of confidences, that is the commitment not to disclose information learned in the course of the clinical relation. This is one of the classical requirements of professional healthcare ethics. In virtually all of the codes of ethics for the healthcare professions, some form of **confidentiality** requirement is included. The content of those codes is more variable and controversial than might be expected, however. The key provisions are summarized in Table 9-1. Note that the Hippocratic Oath is very ambiguous. It calls for confidentiality only in reference to those things "which ought not be spoken abroad."

The code of the World Medical Association and the *Florence Nightingale Pledge* seem to require keeping all confidences without exception. The 2002 *Code of Professional Conduct* of the United Kingdom Nursing and Midwifery Council, however, allows the nurse to share confidential patient information with the patient's consent.[6] The International Council of Nurses' (ICN) *Code of Ethics for Nurses*, while stating that "the nurse holds in confidence personal information," acknowledges that the nurse may also use his or her judgment "in sharing this (personal) information."[7]

Other codes allow for certain kinds of exceptions. The most frequently cited exception, especially in the older professional codes, is breaking confidence when it is in the interests of the patient to do so. The early American Medical Association (AMA) *Principles of Ethics* and early codes of the British Medical Association

Table 9-1
Confidentiality in Codes of Medical Ethics

I . . . will hold in confidence all personal matters committed to my knowledge in the practice of my calling.

Florence Nightingale Pledge[a]

The nurse holds in confidence personal information and uses judgment in sharing this information.

International Council of Nurses, *Code of Ethics for Nurses*, 2000[b]

The standard of nursing practice and the nurse's responsibility to provide quality care require that relevant data be shared with those members of the healthcare team who have a need to know. Only information pertinent to a patient's treatment and welfare is disclosed, and only to those directly involved with the patient's care.

ANA, *Code of Ethics for Nurses with Interpretive Statements*, 2001[c]

The nurse safeguards the patient's right to privacy. The need for health care does not justify unwanted intrusions into the patient's life . . . Associated with the right to privacy, the nurse has a duty to maintain confidentiality of all patient information . . . The rights, well-being, and safety of the individual patient should be the primary factors in arriving at any professional judgment concerning the disposition of confidential information received from or about the patient, whether oral, written or electronic . . . Duties of confidentiality, however, are not absolute and may need to be modified in order to protect the patient, other innocent parties, and in circumstances of mandatory disclosure for public health reasons.

ANA, *Code of Ethics for Nurses with Interpretive Statements*, 2001[d]

Whatever, in connection with my professional practice, or not in connection with it, I see or hear, in the life of men, which ought not to be spoken abroad, I will not divulge, as reckoning that all such should be kept secret.

Hippocratic Oath[e]

A physician may not reveal the confidences entrusted to him in the course of medical attendance, or the deficiencies he may observe in the character of his patients, unless he is required to do so by law or unless it becomes necessary in order to protect the welfare of the individual or of the society.

AMA, *Principles of Medical Ethics*, 1971[f]

A physician shall respect the rights of patients, of colleagues, and of other health professionals, and shall safeguard patient confidences ["and privacy" added in 2001] within the constraints of the law.

AMA, *Principles of Medical Ethics*, 1980 and 2001[g]

5. As a registered nurse . . . you must protect confidential information. (5.1) You must treat information about patients and clients as confidential and use it only for the purposes for which it was given. . . .You must guard against breaches of confidentiality by protecting information from improper disclosure at all times. (5.2) You should seek

patients' and clients' wishes regarding the sharing of information with their families and others. (5.3) If you are required to disclose information outside the team that will have personal consequences for patients or clients, you must obtain their consent. Disclosures may be made only where they can be justified in the public interest or they are required by law or by order of a court.

United Kingdom Nursing & Midwifery Council, *Code of Professional Conduct*, 2002[h]

Too great intimacy between the patient and the nurse is not to be encouraged, but the confidential intercourse to which nurses are admitted should be used with the utmost discretion and with the most scrupulous regard to fidelity and honor. The obligation of secrecy extends beyond the period of professional services. . . . Patients and their affairs should not be made a subject for conversation or discussion between nurses; silence is even more binding upon the nurse than upon the physician, as the opportunities of the former for knowing her patient's affairs are often greater than those of the latter.

Alumnae Association, *The Johns Hopkins Hospital Training School for Nurses*, 1896[i]

[The nurse] has obligated herself in the choice of her profession: to preserve the confidence of the patient and his family by keeping inviolate disclosures made by them or through her own observations. None of the privacies of personal and domestic life, the nature of the patient's illness or adverse personality attributes, should ever be disclosed to others, except the patient's physician and nurse co-workers who are cooperating in the patient's care, or under circumstances that render such action an imperative duty.

The Johns Hopkins Hospital Nurses' Alumnae Association, Inc., 1953[j]

---

[a]Tate, B. L. (1977). *The nurse's dilemma: Ethical considerations in nursing practice* (p. 72). Geneva: International Council of Nursing.

[b]International Council of Nurses. (2000). *Code of ethics for nurses*. Geneva: Author.

[c]American Nurses Association. (2001). *Code of ethics for nurses with interpretive statements* (p. 12). Washington, DC: Author.

[d]Ibid.

[e]Edelstein, L. (1967). The Hippocratic oath: Text, translation and interpretation. In O. Temkin & C. L. Temkin (Eds.), *Ancient medicine: Selected papers of Ludwig Edelstein* (p. 6). Baltimore, MD: The Johns Hopkins Press.

[f]American Medical Association. (1971). *Judicial Council opinions and reports* (p. 53). Chicago: American Medical Association.

[g]American Medical Association. (1984). *Current opinions of the Judicial Council of the American Medical Association* (p. ix). Chicago: American Medical Association.

American Medical Association. (2001). *Health and ethics policies of the AMA* (p. 681). Chicago: American Medical Association.

[h]United Kingdom Nursing & Midwifery Council. (2002). *Code of professional conduct* (pp. 4–5). London: UKCC.

[i]The Johns Hopkins Hospital Nurses' Alumnae Association, Inc. (1896). *The code of ethics of the Alumnae Association* (p. 26). Baltimore: The Johns Hopkins Hospital Training School for Nurses.

[j]The Johns Hopkins Hospital Nurses' Alumnae Association, Inc. (1953). *Some ethical concepts for nurses* (p. 10). Baltimore: The Johns Hopkins Hospital.

Research Brief 9-1

Source: Kennard, M. J., Speroff, T., Puopolo, A. L., Follen, M. A., Mallatratt, L., Phillips, R., et al. (1996). Participation of nurses in decision making for seriously ill adults. *Clinical Nursing Research, 5*(2), 199–219.

Purpose: To describe the involvement of nurses in the decision-making process concerning seriously ill hospitalized adults as perceived by the patient, surrogate, physician, and nurse; specifically, the nurses' influence on decision making, their contributions to the decision-making process, and the association of specific nurse characteristics (education, clinical experience, area of practice, age, and hours worked per week) with nurse participation in decision making.

Method: This was a prospective cohort study involving patients ($n = 4301$) at five hospital sites across the United States from June 1989 to June 1991. Called the SUPPORT (Study to Understand Prognoses and Preferences for Outcomes and Risks of Treatments) study, data collection methods included patient chart reviews, interviews with patients and their surrogate decision makers, interviews with physicians, interviews with nurses ($n = 696$), and self-administered questionnaires (physicians and nurses). Descriptive statistics were computed to describe the sample; nurses' self-reports of their role in decision making; and patients', surrogates', and physicians' reports of the nurses' role. Chi-square and t-tests were used to examine univariate relationships between nurses' reported role in decision making (i.e., knowledge of patient preferences, advocating for patient preferences, discussing prognoses) and specific nurse characteristics. Multivariate associations between nurses' reported role in decision making and nurse characteristics were examined using ordinal logistic regression.

Findings: More than 50% of the patients and surrogates reported that conversations with the nurses were "very much" or "quite a bit" helpful in making healthcare decisions, whereas about 25% reported that conversations were "not at all" helpful. Approximately 25% of the patients and surrogates perceived that nurses' preferences had "quite a bit" or "very much" influence on the choice of treatment, and about 60% reported nurses had "no" influence on the choice of treatment. The majority of patients and surrogates reported that: (1) nurses were "very good" to "excellent" in being attentive and listening to what they had to say, and (2) they were very satisfied with the information they received about their medical condition and about alternative treatments. The majority of physicians and nurses reported that nurses had "no" or "little" influence on the choice of treatment. The majority of nurses also reported that they had "little" or "no" knowledge of their patients' preferences for care and had "little" or "no" influence on the plan of care. However, about 64% of the nurses perceived themselves as "always" or "usually" offering recommendations to physicians regarding treatment options. Nurses' clinical experience, age, and education level had significant relationships with their advocating for patient preferences.

Implications: Nurses do not appear to be as involved in the decision-making process regarding seriously ill hospitalized adults as they might be. On the other hand, the majority of patients and surrogates found conversations with nurses helpful in deciding on the kinds of care to receive. They also perceived nurses as being more influential than the nurses saw themselves. However, they apparently would like to have more conversations and to be provided with more information by the nurses. Because nurses employed longer than 5 years were less likely to be involved in decision making than those employed for lesser periods of time, lack of involvement could be a sign of nurse burnout syndrome. Physicians felt nurses were less influential than patients or nurses did, and nurses felt excluded from patient care decisions, both of which could lead to lower self-esteem, feelings of frustration, and dissatisfaction. Further research is needed to define the role nurses identify for themselves in the decision-making process and how this role changes with increasing age, education, and experience. Research is also needed to help nurses learn how to communicate with patients about their preferences for care and to further investigate the relationship between nurse burnout syndrome and the institutional culture of the hospital on participation of the nurse in decision making.

included such an authorization. Both have been revised, however, and have dropped this exception. In doing so, they may have run the risk that no client-centered reasons are sufficient to permit breaking confidences. This leaves anyone guided by these codes with a dilemma when, for example, he or she might break a confidence to report clients that appear to be so severely mentally ill that they are a serious danger to themselves.

The ANA *Code of Ethics for Nurses* clearly states that "the nurse has a duty to maintain confidentiality of all patient information." However, the code permits breaking confidentiality "in order to protect the patient, other innocent parties, and in circumstances of mandatory disclosure for public health reasons." The code says, "The rights, well-being, and safety of the individual patient should be the primary factors in arriving at any professional judgment concerning the disposition of confidential information."[8] The use of rights language indicates that the right of **privacy** cannot be overridden simply because of consideration of benefits and harms. This statement also indicates that "Only information pertinent to a client's treatment and welfare is disclosed, and only to those directly involved with the patient's care."[9] Unfortunately, these statements seem to leave the nurse in an ambiguous position if the patient's rights require confidentiality and her or his well-being and safety require disclosure. The Johns Hopkins Hospital Nurses' Alumnae Association, Inc., was also quite vague about whether an exception to the confidentiality rule should be made in order to benefit a patient.[10] Cases 9-3, 9-4, and 9-5 look at problems of confidentiality when the welfare of the patient is at stake.

A second possible exception to the duty of confidentiality arises when the welfare of other parties is seriously jeopardized by keeping a confidence. Is it clear, for example, that the nurse should break confidence if he or she knows that the patient is a carrier of a serious contagious disease or is a parent engaged in child abuse? The earlier version of the AMA's *Principles of Medical Ethics* permitted breaking confidence when it would protect the welfare of the patient. When the AMA rewrote its code in 1980, it dropped this exception entirely, leaving the problem of what to do if your client confesses to you a plan to commit a mass murder and there is no exception for disclosure to protect others. The ANA *Code of Ethics for Nurses*, by contrast, holds that "duties of confidentiality . . . are not absolute and may need to be modified in order to protect the patient" and "other innocent parties."[11] Cases 9-5 through 9-8 deal with breaking confidentiality to benefit other identifiable persons or to benefit society in general.

There is a third possible exception: breaking confidentiality when required by law. The interpretive statements of the 1976 ANA *Code for Nurses* permitted breaking confidentiality when required by law. But this provision was dropped from the 1985 and 2001 interpretive statements. Case 9-9 deals with problems of confidentiality in the face of laws that may require disclosure.

The moral basis of the duty of confidentiality is not always clear. Often, keeping information confidential will benefit the patient. In those cases, it might be called for by the traditional professional ethical principles that require the nurse to benefit the patient and protect him or her from harm. That implies, however, that in cases where the nurse believes that a patient could be benefited by a disclosure, the nurse would be justified in disclosing. Moreover, if the welfare of the patient is the criterion for deciding when to keep and break confidences, then the interests of society are excluded. The requirements of law are also excluded.

The ANA *Code of Ethics for Nurses* suggests a second possibility. It implies—in an ambiguous manner, to be sure—that confidentiality is a right, perhaps a right that is independent of judgments about benefit and harm to the client. According to the *Code of Ethics for Nurses*, confidentiality is grounded in a principle of privacy—a principle requiring that people not have information disclosed about them without their consent. If confidentiality is a right, then benefits to the client would not justify the disclosure.

Grounding confidentiality in a principle of privacy may lead to a strong confidentiality requirement—perhaps too strong. It would seem not to allow for breaking confidence under any circumstances, either to protect the client (e.g., initiating commitment hearings for a suicidal patient) or others (e.g., reporting child abuse).

Another possibility is that confidentiality should be grounded in the ethics of promise keeping. Fidelity is a principle in many ethical systems. It, like autonomy and truth telling, may be a right-making characteristic of ethical action, binding on a person independent of the consequences. If that is the basis, then the critical question is: What should healthcare professionals and clients promise one another regarding confidentiality? Should they promise confidentiality of the patient's health record information? Should they promise that they will not discuss the patient in a public place without his or her permission? Many would agree that the obligation of confidentiality includes these latter promises. They are supported by the ANA *Code of Ethics for Nurses* and expected by the public, although, as research has shown, such promises are often broken.[12]

Should healthcare professionals promise to keep confidences even though, under certain circumstances, the law may require that they break them? To do so would require breaking another promise—the promise to obey the laws of the land. They probably would not promise to keep confidences when there were serious threats of bodily harm to others at stake (although they might promise to keep information confidential when only minor interests of others were involved). Whether they would promise to keep confidences when it was thought to be in the interests of the one to whom the promise was being made—the patient in the case of the nurse—is not clear. If they refused to make such a promise, patients would reasonably be reluctant to disclose important information. If they did make such a promise, then it would impose a moral obligation even when the significant welfare of the patient was at stake, such as in commitment proceedings.

When the Patient May Be Harmed

Being faithful to a patient normally requires that information transmitted during the course of professional contact be kept confidential. In the traditions of medical ethics, however, health professionals have also been seen as having a duty to benefit the patient and protect the patient from harm. For the nurse, the pledge is to the health, well-being, and safety of the patient. That means that the nurse has a serious ethical problem whenever he or she is convinced that the only way to protect a patient from harm is to disclose a piece of information that was transmitted with the assumption of a pledge of confidentiality. The next cases in this chapter illustrate the problem.

Case 9-3
The Pregnant Teenager with Other Health Problems

Vickie Simpson, the pediatric nurse practitioner (PNP) in an ambulatory health clinic, called 15-year-old Melinda into her office. Melinda had been referred to the PNP by the fracture clinic. At her 6-month checkup for a difficult ankle fracture, it was discovered that Melinda's hemoglobin was below normal. Because her fracture had healed without complications and would require no further follow-up, the fracture clinic nurse had referred Melinda and her mother to Ms. Simpson for evaluation of the low hemoglobin and nutritional counseling.

During the nutrition-counseling session, Melinda confided to Ms. Simpson that she was 6-weeks pregnant. She also told Ms. Simpson that she was scheduled to have an abortion the following week and did not want her mother to know. At the close of the session, Ms. Simpson invited Melinda's mother into her office to explain the diet and follow-up planned for the low hemoglobin. Melinda's mother expressed concern about her daughter—she seemed so tired lately, has had nausea, has not been eating well, and so on. Were these symptoms caused by her daughter's low hemoglobin?

Ms. Simpson is concerned about Melinda. She is convinced that Melinda should not be facing her abortion on her own. She believes that Melinda's mother would be understanding and that Melinda would be much better off if her mother were told about her real problem, but she is also committed to confidentiality. They live in a state that does not require parental notification for a minor's abortion, so Ms. Simpson fears that Melinda's mother will never be told.

Case 9-4

When "Doing Good" May Harm the Patient

Joan Schuller, an OB nurse on the night shift, has received an admission from labor and delivery. The patient, Miss Timmons, a 23-year-old unmarried woman, has delivered a healthy female. While getting Miss Timmons settled for the night, she learns that Miss Timmons is planning to give up her child for adoption. Mrs. Schuller is surprised, as mothers who do not keep their babies are usually admitted to the medical unit rather than the obstetrics unit. Miss Timmons assures the nurse that she knows what she is doing— she has read about the beneficial effects of the bonding process between mother and child immediately after birth, and she wants to give the child everything she can before giving her up for adoption. There is no indication that Miss Timmons will change her mind about giving the child up for adoption—her life situation simply does not include the care of a child. Yet, she wants to care for and breast-feed her infant during her 48-hour stay in the hospital. She asks the nurse how soon she can see her infant and get started.

Mrs. Schuller pleads for some time while she quickly reviews Miss Timmons's chart. The possibility of adoption is not included on the chart, and Miss Timmons quickly explains that she has not told anyone because she was afraid she would not be able to see and hold her infant if her plan were known. Mrs. Schuller explains that it is very unlikely that she will be allowed to see her infant, let alone breast-feed the child, during the brief hospital stay if she plans to give the child up for adoption. The hospital strongly discourages visits between children up for adoption and their natural mothers. She also expresses concern for the psychologic harm that Miss Timmons might experience from the process. Giving a child up for adoption is always a difficult process for women, regardless of their circumstances. Once bonding has occurred, giving the child up for adoption often leaves deep psychologic scars on the mother that persist for many years. Mrs. Schuller urges Miss Timmons to reconsider her request.

Miss Timmons insists on carrying through with her plan to breast-feed the infant. She asks the nurse to keep her secret. Mrs. Schuller realizes that she is in a very awkward position. She recognizes that early contact and bonding between mother and child are beneficial to both. It is especially important for children given up for adoption, because they are often moved from one foster home to another while an adoptive family is sought. If she keeps Miss Timmons's secret, much good can result in terms of the health of the child, and keeping the secret will also respect the wishes of the mother. However, considerable harm could result in the long run, as well. Mrs. Schuller is not sure whether to keep Miss Timmons's secret.

Case 9-5
Breaking Confidentiality to a Colleague[2]

Rebecca Fein and Sarah Goldman were staff nurses on the night shift in a pediatric surgical unit. One night, as they neared the completion of their work, Miss Fein noted that a 6-year-old diabetic patient recovering from minor surgery looked very pale and was perspiring. When she was unable to awaken the patient, she notified her colleague and best friend, Miss Goldman, and together they tested the patient's blood sugar. The results confirmed Miss Fein's fears: The child was extremely hypoglycemic. She called the resident and assisted her in stabilizing the patient. The child recovered and was discharged home 2 days later.

The next day, Miss Fein reviewed the incident, stating how surprised she was to find the child hypoglycemic. At first, Miss Goldman did not say much, but finally she admitted that it was all her fault. She had mistakenly given the child too much insulin. She had not gone back to check on the child and realized her mistake only when Miss Fein found the child unresponsive.

Miss Fein was surprised and asked her friend whether she had completed an incident report or notified the child's physician afterward. Miss Goldman said she had decided not to report the mistake because it would create an inquiry and undoubtedly make trouble for her. "I can do without that right now," she stated. She was being reviewed for promotion to the next step in the clinical ladder program of the nursing division and feared that the incident would prevent her promotion and the financial benefit it would bring. She looked at Miss Fein and said pointedly, "And I hope you're not going to report it, either. I told you this in confidence and as a friend. It would be unethical for you to do anything about the mistake. After all, it was just a mistake, and the patient recovered. I'll be more careful in the future." What should Miss Fein do?

---

[2]Adapted from Fry, S. T., & Johnstone, M. (2002). *Ethics in nursing practice: A guide to ethical decision making* (2nd ed., p. 158). Oxford, UK: Blackwell Sciences.

Commentary

Ms. Simpson, the nurse in Case 9-3 who learns of a young patient's plan for an abortion, seems to be caught in a moral dilemma because her judgment about what is in her client's interest leads her to want to disclose, whereas her commitment to a promise of confidentiality leads her to want to keep Melinda's trust by remaining silent.

One approach to this case involves an assessment of Ms. Simpson's judgment that Melinda would be better off in the long run if her mother knew about her real problem. Perhaps Ms. Simpson is wrong. Possibly, Melinda knows what her mother's reaction would be better than Ms. Simpson does. One problem with ethical codes that authorize breaking confidence whenever the health professional judges it to be in the patient's interest is that it depends on a very difficult, subjective, possibly idiosyncratic assessment by the individual practitioner.

In Ms. Simpson's case, however, her judgment is not unreasonable. Although Melinda might find it uncomfortable for her mother to know, in the long run she might really be better off. That raises the question of whether correct judgments of patient welfare justify breaking confidentiality. Suppose, for example, that Ms. Simpson took her case to her hospital ethics committee and that the committee confirmed her judgment. Suppose she did everything possible to make sure her judgment was a good one. Would she then be justified in breaking confidence, or would Melinda still have a right to confidentiality? If she would, why?

One basis for viewing confidentiality as a right is that it rests on a promise made (at least an implied promise) by health professionals that information disclosed in the course of professional communication will be held confidential. Any nurse who is a member of the ANA has made an implicit promise to abide by the ANA's *Code of Ethics for Nurses*. Breaking confidentiality involves more than preventing potential injury to the patient. It also involves breaking a promise, a promise that is important to the lay–professional relationship.

Breaking the confidence may also be viewed as violating the autonomy of the patient. If the patient is an autonomous person capable of making choices about medical and nursing care, it is paternalistic to disclose to others information about the patient on the grounds that it would be in the patient's interest to do so.

Some would argue that Ms. Simpson should seek Melinda's permission to disclose her pregnancy to her mother. If Melinda agrees, then Ms. Simpson would no longer be bound by a promise of confidentiality and she would not be acting paternalistically. But what if Melinda refuses to grant to Ms. Simpson permission to tell her mother? Then Ms. Simpson would be back in the same moral bind. If she is committed to doing what she thinks will benefit Melinda, she may feel obliged to break confidence. If she is committed to a morality that insists that promises (such as the promise of confidentiality) should be kept even when breaking them would be beneficial, then she will feel a moral obligation not to disclose.

Some people might argue that Melinda, being 15 years old, is, in fact, not an autonomous person who should have the right to insist upon or to waive confidentiality. If she is a minor whose parents must consent to medical treatment, then do the normal rules of confidentiality apply?

There is a complicating factor. Some states have laws permitting minors to obtain abortions without the permission of the parent. Some states do not require parental approval yet require that parents be notified, but many of those jurisdictions permit a judge's approval when informing a parent is believed to pose a problem for the minor seeking the abortion. If Melinda is in such a state and can, therefore, get the abortion without informing her mother, does that imply that she also has a right to demand confidentiality (or to waive it)?

Anyone who concludes that Ms. Simpson has a right or a duty to break confidence in Melinda's case because of her age should turn to Case 9-4, the case in which Miss Timmons wanted to bond with her baby before placing it for adoption. Miss Timmons is an adult, and presumably, she could be asked to waive any right to confidentiality she might have. But it seems clear that, if asked, she would not give Mrs. Schuller, the nurse in her case, permission to disclose the fact that she is planning to place her child for adoption. When age is no longer a factor, does Mrs. Schuller have the right to disclose, even against Miss Timmons's wishes?

Mrs. Schuller is perplexed, in part, because it is possible that good can come of keeping her patient's secret. On the other hand, harm can come of it as well. Miss Timmons might be injured psychologically by bonding with the infant she would eventually place for adoption. If Mrs. Schuller concludes that the patients would both be better off if the secret were kept, then there is no real confidentiality problem. There remains the moral problem of whether Mrs. Schuller should be a party to the deception, but that is another matter.

The interesting problem arises if Mrs. Schuller concludes that one or both of her patients would be better off if the disclosure were made. She might possibly conclude that Miss Timmons would be better off if she did not bond with the infant she is going to place for adoption. In that case, Mrs. Schuller will have to go through the same reasoning that Melinda's nurse did. It is also possible that Mrs. Schuller could conclude that the infant would be the one who would be better off if the bonding did not take place. In that case, she might be inclined to break confidence for the benefit of the infant. However, it can be hard to determine who would be better off and the significance of the benefit.

In Case 9-5, involving the drug error with respect to the diabetic child, it is clear that the patient suffered harm from Miss Goldman's mistake. Miss Fein learns about the mistake the next day, but Miss Goldman uses their friendship as the basis for a claiming Miss Fine has a duty to keep the information in confidence. If Miss Fein does not keep the information in confidence, harm will likely occur to Miss Goldman. Given that the patient suffered no residual harm and, in fact, has been discharged home, how much benefit would the patient receive by reporting the incident?

Yet, if there is ever a situation in which the nurse should break confidence to protect future patients, this is it. Nurses have a responsibility to safeguard patients from incompetent and unethical care provided by other members of the healthcare team. Conflicting loyalties are involved when mistakes that cause patient harm are made by personal friends, but the obligation to protect patients from harm overrides any claims to friendship between colleagues.

Is Miss Goldman's medication error evidence of incompetent or unethical practice, or perhaps both? Some consider the incompetent healthcare worker to be someone who suffers from impairment (i.e., physical or mental illness, or substance abuse) or from ignorance of standards of care, whereas the unethical healthcare worker "knowingly and willingly violates fundamental norms of conduct toward others, especially his or her own patients."[13] Was Miss Goldman's error a simple mistake, or was it something else (incompetent and/or unethical practice) that warrants further action by Miss Fein?

Regardless of how Miss Fein now regards the situation, she may still experience difficulty in reporting what happened in this patient's care. No reporting or charting was done about a medication error, and the patient has recovered and has been discharged to home. Furthermore, bringing it up now may appear to be an uncomfortable situation of "professional tattling." It also might be one nurse's word against the other's word. If there is a usual duty of confidentiality between colleagues, should the confidence be kept when no residual harm has occurred to the patient? Does the amount and type of harm resulting from an error determine whether confidentiality between colleagues should be kept? Or does it depend on whether Miss Goldman's error is judged to be merely an accident rather than an instance of incompetent and/or unethical practice? If the error is judged to be incompetent or unethical practice, the *Code of Ethics for Nurses* suggests that the nurse has a duty to prevent the recurrence of such practices: "As an advocate for the patient, the nurse must be alert to and take appropriate action regarding any instances of incompetent, unethical, illegal, or impaired practice by any member of the healthcare team . . ."[14] To the extent that the nurse relies on the *Code of Ethics for Nurses* as a basis for determining what is ethical, the nurse's duty may include one of several levels of actions—from reporting the mistake to censuring the colleague's practice.

If the error is believed not to constitute incompetent, unethical practice, but nevertheless was a mistake that unfortunately caused harm to the patient, Miss Fein's duty to her colleague is more controversial. Although health professionals can be assumed to have promised confidentiality to their patients, it is not clear they have ever made such a promise—or even an implied promise—to colleagues. Moreover, patients (or their surrogates) may have a legitimate interest in the fact that a mistake occurred, even if it did no lasting damage. There may be claims for pain and suffering or for expenses generated. Some patients may simply want to know about such events. To the extent that the doctrine of informed consent requires that patients be told information they want to know, do patients or their surrogates have a right to such information? This brings us to the problem of breaking confidences for the benefit of other parties, which is the subject of our next group of cases.

Critical Thinking Question

Describe a patient care situation in which you wanted to break confidentiality to protect the patient from a perceived harm. What action(s) did you take? What were the reasons for your action(s)? Were your actions ethically justifiable? If so, why?

When Others May Be Harmed

In some cases, the nurse may consider breaking the promise of confidentiality not to benefit the patient but to benefit third parties. The nurse may feel that the patient's family needs to know some important information about the patient's medical condition. The patient may, for example, be a carrier of a genetic disease, a fact that could be important to others in his or her family. If the patient refused to disclose the genetic disorder, the nurse would need to consider whether she has a duty to disclose.

In the first case in this section, a son might benefit from learning of his father's terminal illness. In other situations, the potential beneficiaries may be much more distant from the patient. The second case in this section deals with a nurse with a drug problem and whether confidential communication between her and another nurse should be disclosed to protect future patients. The third case deals with information that a nurse learns when an elderly patient confides in her but the patient believes she might be harmed if the police know this information. Finally, privacy sometimes may be invaded for educational purposes, research, or other benefits to others when there is nothing unique to the patient's condition that is crucial. That is the focus of the fourth case in this section.

Breaking Confidences to Benefit Another Individual

Case 9-6

The Dying Father and His Son

Mr. Burns is dying. His large bowel is riddled with metastatic, cancerous lesions that have been unresponsive to treatment, and the staff fear that a massive hemorrhage could develop at any time. A widower, Mr. Burns is fully aware of his condition and has decided not to tell his grown children. He does not want to be a burden to them and has told them that he will be coming home in a few weeks.

One evening, he confides to Martha Spencer, the regular evening shift nurse, that one of his biggest disappointments in life occurred when his youngest son dropped out of college and adopted a deviant lifestyle several years ago. Although he is proud of all his other children, his disappointment in the youngest son is quite noticeable and has disrupted their relationship. He expresses hope that the son will be able to straighten out his life in the future, although he will probably not be alive to see this happen.

A week later, one of the family members confides to Ms. Spencer that they have a big surprise for Mr. Burns when he comes home. Mr. Burns's youngest son, who lives in another state and has been estranged from his father for several years, will be coming home to visit his father. The surprise is that the son has been attending college part-time for the last 2 years and will graduate in a few weeks. He plans to surprise his father with his diploma for Mr. Burns's 65th birthday, 3 months from now.

Realizing that Mr. Burns may not live long enough to learn of the surprise and that his son might be deprived of winning his father's approval before he dies, Ms. Spencer wonders whether she should break one of her confidences. Or should she keep all of them?

Breaking Confidences to Benefit Society

Case 9-7
The Case of the Nurse Addict

Judy Boise and Claire Temple have been colleagues for a long time—they have worked together at the same hospital for 6 years. Since obtaining a divorce, however, Ms. Temple's personality has changed. She often makes silly comments or giggles at inappropriate times. At other times, Ms. Temple is very irritable and resorts to taking medication for her "nerves." Ms. Boise suspects that her friend is developing a drug dependency. Her suspicion is confirmed one day when Ms. Temple asks Ms. Boise to work for her while she sleeps off the effects of some medication. Ms. Boise confronts her friend with her suspicions. Ms. Temple acknowledges that she has been taking cocaine but asks Ms. Boise not to tell other nurses about the nature of her problem. Ms. Boise promises not to tell.

The next day, however, Ms. Boise finds Ms. Temple asleep in a chair in an empty room when she should be taking care of a patient. Does Ms. Boise have an obligation to break the promise she made to Ms. Temple in order to protect their patients from unsatisfactory levels of nursing care? How much respect for confidentiality can one expect from a fellow nurse?

Case 9-8
The Elderly Patient Who Claims She Was Sexually Assaulted

Emma Green, 62 years old, is brought to the ER with an MI, having been found unconscious in her home. Mrs. Green is a widow who lives alone and has no previous history of cardiac anomalies. While in the ER, she codes and is resuscitated. When she regains consciousness, the nurse attempts to gain some information about the patient. Mrs. Green denies any knowledge of how she wound up on the floor in her home. Eventually though, she asks the nurse if she can keep a secret. When the nurse says she can, the patient tells her that a man entered her (the patient's) house after breakfast, sexually assaulted her, and told her he would kill her if she told anybody. She asks the nurse not to tell the police because she is afraid of the man and thinks he will come back and kill her. In order to calm Mrs. Green and help her to rest, the nurse promises that she will not tell anyone about the assault. The nurse then became busy with another patient, and Mrs. Green was transferred to the CCU.

The next day, the ER nurse finds out that Mrs. Green required CPR again in the CCU. The CCU nurse tells the ER nurse that when Mrs. Green is conscious, she yells out in terror when anyone approaches her bed. But a neighbor has told the physician that Mrs. Green was once hospitalized for psychiatric reasons. Does the ER nurse have a responsibility to tell others what Mrs. Green said about being assaulted by a strange man?

Case 9-9
The Supervisor's Dilemma

Mrs. Phyllis Brock is the supervisor of emergency room and critical care facilities in a large, urban, teaching hospital with a famous medical school. She is informed by ER nurses that on weekends, several physicians on the faculty of the medical school are setting up closed-circuit videotaping of medical students doing admissions, histories, physical exams, and so on, in the ER. The tapes are being used for teaching purposes to allow students an opportunity to evaluate their own mistakes. The physicians assure nursing staff that no one else ever sees the films and that the films help medical students give better medical care. However, the nursing staff feel they are being coerced into participating in the physical exposure of the clients as well as giving personal information without their consent.

The ER nurses appeal to the supervisor, who intercedes with the physicians. She is told that the hospital is a teaching institution and that the films will continue to be taken. If the ER nurses are uncomfortable with the practice, they can refrain from entering the room. But the nurses still know that the practice is going on. The supervisor finds that the practice of taking training films on weekends has been going on for several years. The previous nurse supervisor did not find anything objectionable to the practice. The supervisor feels caught between furthering the goals of medical education in a teaching institution and upholding her nurses' obligations to protect the privacy and confidentiality of their clients.

Commentary

In none of these four cases does the question of breaking confidentiality strictly bear on benefiting the patient. In some sense, Claire Temple, the drug-abusing nurse in Case 9-7, is a "patient," but even in this situation, an important reason for breaking confidence is that the welfare of future patients is jeopardized if her problem is not addressed. Likewise, the nurse who took care of Mrs. Green in Case 9-8 may find the welfare of other women who might be at risk for sexual assault in their homes an important reason to break confidence.

The ANA *Code of Ethics for Nurses* apparently is open to the possibility that a nurse may break confidence for the benefit of others. The code says that the patient has a "right to privacy" and that "the nurse has a duty to maintain confidentiality of all patient information," but then adds that "duties of confidentiality are not absolute and may need to be modified to protect other innocent parties."[15] The nurse trying to follow the code may be confused about which circumstances justify breaking confidentiality for the benefit of other parties.

The situation in which an identifiable individual, such as a family member, has a real interest in having confidentiality broken perhaps represents the most powerful rationale for breaking confidences. Would one stand by with information that a patient is planning to murder a family member, for example? Mr. Burns, the man in Case 9-6 who is dying from cancer, poses one version of the problem. He might well benefit from the disclosure to his children that he is dying. He would surely be made happy by the news of his youngest son's progress. Martha Spencer, the nurse in the case, is also concerned about the welfare of the younger son and the fact that, without disclosure, he would be deprived of winning his father's approval before his father dies.

This concern for the son's welfare is admittedly not quite like the concern for the potential victim of someone planning murder, but it does point to an important benefit that predictably would come from breaking the confidence. Are there ways that Ms. Spencer could accomplish the good she is pursuing without disclosing Mr. Burns's condition?

The situation in Case 9-7, involving the nurse taking cocaine, is different in that the potential beneficiaries of the disclosure are not easily identified (aside from Claire Temple herself). It could be that no one would ever benefit. On the other hand, many people could experience substantial benefit in the form of being protected from a dangerously incapacitated nurse.

Claire Temple's scenario is different in another respect, as well. The duty of confidentiality is, in effect, a promise made to the patient. A right is something that the patient may exercise or waive. The relationship between Claire Temple and her nursing colleague is not necessarily governed by the same moral rules as that between patient and professional. Presumably, there is some kind of promise implied between professional colleagues that generates an expectation of confidentiality, but it is not the same explicit commitment that is made to patients in codes of ethics and rules of professional conduct of various state licensing boards. Confidentiality with regard to patient communications is justified, in part, by therapeutic necessity—without an expectation of confidentiality, patients would be reluctant to disclose. This is not present in communications among colleagues, at least not in the same way.

The promise to the patient is present in Case 9-9, in which patients are being videotaped without their consent for the training of medical students. In contrast with all of the previous cases in this chapter, the condition of the patient does not raise the concern about breaking confidence. In fact, nothing about these particular patients generates the invasion of privacy. Other patients would work just as well. It is hard to see what moral reasons would be given for failing to ask permission for the videotaping. Although not every patient would approve, probably enough would to successfully fulfill the objective of helping students learn interviewing techniques.

A promise has also been made to Mrs. Green, the woman who suffered an MI and confided that she was sexually assaulted. However, she could be asked if, for her own good, she would agree to having her confidence broken. There is a good chance she would refuse, however. On the other hand, keeping the fear of being killed by her assailant bottled up inside her could well be life-threatening. If the sexual assault is part of the patient's psychiatric problems, that information could be essential to her treatment. If the sexual assault did, in fact, occur, then other women might be at risk for sexual assault in their homes. Perhaps this case is the best test for determining whether the nurse is willing to be paternalistic or whether she will stick to the duty of confidentiality even though there is good reason to believe that breaking confidence would benefit the patient. On the other hand, if her motivation for breaking confidence is to protect the welfare of third parties and she really believes others are at serious risk, she could justify the breaking of the confidence by citing the welfare of others, thus avoiding the paternalism of disclosure for the purpose of protecting her patient. Doing so, however, would commit her to subordinating the rights of her patient to the welfare of others who are not her patients.

One method of assessing the legitimacy of such practices is sometimes referred to as the "criterion of publicity." One asks, "Would we be willing to announce publicly the rule under which we are acting?" Regarding Case 9-9, one would ask, "Would we be willing to announce that some patients in the emergency room are being taped for teaching purposes without their knowledge?" The physicians argued, in defense of the taping, that their hospital was a teaching institution and that patients should be willing to contribute to the medical students' education through the taping. If, in fact, that is their position, they should be willing to announce the practice to patients entering the emergency room. That way, if patients would prefer not to receive care on those terms, they could go elsewhere or simply decline the care. Lack of willingness to announce the moral rule under which one is acting is a sign of a moral problem.

The issue is whether there is a commitment made to the patient to protect privacy and confidentiality and, if so, under what circumstances. A promise without exception would commit the professional to withholding information—even information about anticipated major crimes and even when reporting is required by law. This seems extreme. On the other hand, a promise that would permit breaking of confidence whenever the individual clinician believed it would benefit the patient or benefit some other party (no matter how trivial the benefit) probably would not gain the support of either lay persons or health professionals. One plausible exception to the confidentiality promise might be made when the welfare of other parties would be significantly threatened if the information were kept confidential. Some people limit the threat to others to "grave bodily harm." Others might include substantial psychologic threats as well. Would breaking of confidence be justified under these criteria in the four cases in this section?

When Required by Law

To overcome the problems raised by having too many exceptions to the confidentiality requirement, the AMA *Principles of Medical Ethics* of 1980 (unlike the ANA *Code of Ethics for Nurses*, which would permit breaking confidence to benefit innocent parties) appears to permit only one exception: when breaking confidence is required by law. Presumably, the AMA has in mind such requirements as reporting gunshot wounds, venereal diseases, and infectious diseases. If the moral community has gathered together and passed a law requiring specifically that certain information be reported, then clearly any implied promise of confidentiality is overturned. Patients have no right to expect confidentiality when a public law requires that information be disclosed. There may also be cases where nurses are required by law to disclose information about a patient. The following case presents one example.

Case 9-10
Minor Children of the Dying Cancer Patient Who Refuses Treatment

A 38-year-old divorced mother of two girls, ages 8 and 10 years, refuses further treatment for metastatic cancer of the larynx. She remains at home and manages quite well with occasional visits from the home health nurse to check on her medications and nutrition. Over a period of weeks, the nurse begins to notice that the patient is losing weight and seems to require more medication to relieve the almost constant pain. She begins to worry about the two daughters, particularly their supervision and their understanding of their mother's condition.

The older child tells the nurse that her mother's appearance and growing dependency on physical assistance scares her. She also mentions that the school has contacted the home about her sister's poor work during recent weeks. Before their mother's illness, apparently both girls were good students. Should the nurse contact the school nurse and let her know about the situation at home? The nurse is not sure if the information she has learned about the patient, her daughters, and the home is confidential. She is aware that local law in her jurisdiction requires that health professionals (nurses as well as physicians) report cases of suspected child abuse or neglect. She suspects that what she is witnessing amounts to child abuse or neglect.

Commentary

The home health nurse who visits this mother with two daughters sees what she fears may constitute child abuse. It is presumably not malicious; rather, it can be explained by the illness of the mother. Nevertheless, the daughters seem to be suffering. It may be that child protective agencies may need to be contacted. Health professionals have obligations to report child abuse in other contexts as well. For example, the Baby Doe regulations, designed to protect disabled infants subject to parental nontreatment decisions require that mechanisms for reporting child abuse be established.[16]

If there is a specific law requiring the reporting of child abuse, the ethics of confidentiality becomes somewhat different than it was in earlier cases. In those cases, a decision to break confidence was contemplated on the basis of the nurse's judgment that the patient or others would benefit substantially from the disclosure. Patients might have no reason to anticipate the nurse's judgment. In fact, the nurse's judgment may be idiosyncratic, one that colleagues would not share. When a specific law requires reporting, however, lay persons have reason to anticipate that confidences may have to be broken. Moreover, the judgment justifying the disclosure is made in public with due process. It cannot be idiosyncratic. This suggests that in cases where disclosure is required by law, the disclosure will be easier to justify than it was in the earlier cases.

This leaves the nurse with one remaining problem: What should happen in the case where the disclosure is required by law, but the nurse is convinced that it nevertheless violates the duties of the clinical relationship? For example, if the law requires reporting child abuse and the nurse is convinced that such reporting would be a deterrent to the parent's willingness to accept treatment and might result in removal of the child from his or her home, the nurse who believes that his or her duty is to the patient rather than to society may be convinced that it would be immoral to report. The situation may be one in which the clinician is willing to promise confidentiality even though society does not approve of that promise. If a nurse makes such a promise, is it morally or legally binding? If confidentiality is rooted in the ethics of the principle of promise keeping, the nurse may find himself or herself occasionally in the bind of having made two contradictory promises: one to protect confidential information and the other to obey the law that requires reporting. What should a nurse do when two contradictory promises are made?

ENDNOTES

1. This is the position of many utilitarians.
2. For an example, see Veatch, R. M. (1995). Resolving conflict among principles: Ranking, balancing, and specifying. *Kennedy Institute of Ethics Journal, 5,* 199–218.
3. This is the position of T. L. Beauchamp & J. F. Childress (Eds.). (2001). *Principles of biomedical ethics* (5th ed.). New York: Oxford University Press.
4. Ziv, T. A. & Lo, B. (1995). Denial of care to illegal immigrants—Proposition 187 in California. *The New England Journal of Medicine, 332*(16), 1095–1098.
5. Available at: http://cis.org. Accessed January 3, 2010.
6. United Kingdom Nursing & Midwifery Council. (2002). *Code of professional conduct.* London: UKCC.
7. International Council of Nurses. (2000). *Code of ethics for nurses.* Geneva, Switzerland: International Council of Nurses.
8. American Nurses Association. (2001). *Code of ethics for nurses with interpretive statements* (p. 12). Washington, DC: Author.
9. Ibid.
10. The Johns Hopkins Hospital Nurses' Alumnae Association, Inc. (1953). *Some ethical concepts for nurses.* Baltimore: The Johns Hopkins Hospital.
11. American Nurses Association. (2001). *Code of ethics for nurses with interpretive statements* (p. 12). Washington, DC: Author.
12. Ubel, P. A., Zell, M. M., Miller, D. J., Fischer, G. S., Peters-Stefani, D., & Arnold, R. M. (1995). Elevator talk: Observational study of inappropriate comments in a public space. *American Journal of Medicine, 99,* 190–194.
13. Morreim, E. H. (1993). Am I my brother's warden? Responding to the unethical or incompetent colleague. *Hastings Center Report, 23*(3), 19–27.
14. American Nurses Association. (2001). *Code of ethics for nurses with interpretive statements* (p. 14). Washington, DC: Author.
15. American Nurses Association. (2001). *Code of ethics for nurses with interpretive statements* (p. 12). Washington, DC: Author.
16. U.S. Department of Health and Human Services. (1985, April 15). Child abuse and neglect prevention and treatment program. Final Rule: 45 CFR 1340. *Federal Register: Rules and Regulations, 50*(72), 14878–14892.

Chapter 10

The Sanctity of Human Life

Other Cases Involving Sanctity of Life

Key Terms
Advance directive
Assistance in suicide
Doctrine of double effect
Euthanasia
Sanctity of human life
Withdrawing treatment
Withholding treatment

Objectives
1. Define the principle of the sanctity of human life.
2. Identify the differences between actions and omissions.
3. Describe the benefits and potential harms of advance directives.

4. Apply the doctrine of double effect to a patient care situation in which withdrawal of treatment is being considered.
5. Apply the principle of the sanctity of human life in a patient care situation involving a request for assisted suicide.

Many cultural and religious traditions, especially those influenced by Judeo-Christianity, Islam, Hinduism, and Buddhism, view human life as sacred. Holders of this view maintain that human life, especially innocent human life, should not be taken even for noble motives. When life is taken in conditions of war or even capital punishment, such action is often justified on the grounds that the people being killed are not innocent. In health care, the problem of taking life emerges in a number of contexts—abortion, suicide, and decisions about ending the lives of terminally ill or intractably suffering patients. However, in these cases, the lives under consideration are innocent, and justifications for taking life are not as easily made. For example, the person whose life is at stake may be pleading for death; in other cases, such as abortion, the individual is in no condition to plead. In some cases, such as suicide, the individual may be contemplating taking his or her own life. Recently, **assistance in suicide** in health care has become a heated public policy and clinical controversy.

The reasons for contemplation of killing in the healthcare sphere are usually related to mercy. Someone makes a judgment that the patient (or perhaps other persons) would be "better off dead." If it is the health professional's duty, at least in certain circumstances, to benefit patients and protect them from harm, may health professionals assist in putting a suffering patient out of his or her misery by hastening death? May they kill patients who are incapable of making such decisions on their own? May they withhold or withdraw treatment knowing that these actions will surely hasten death?

Some people argue that these issues can be resolved by making use of the ethical principles already addressed in earlier chapters. The principles of beneficence and nonmaleficence, of doing good and avoiding evil, provide ready arguments to support those who wish to defend merciful killing as well as decisions to withhold or withdraw treatment. In the case of patients who are competent and capable of making their own choices, the principle of autonomy also provides a moral basis for approving of or at least tolerating treatment-refusal decisions by patients. It also helps explain our great reluctance to approve of killing a person who does not want to be killed, even if we have good reason to believe that the person would be better off dead.

There are other arguments against merciful killing, although, that do not require abandoning traditional intuitions about the morality of killing. Some will argue that the principles of doing good and avoiding evil themselves, if carefully applied, lead to policies of respect for the **sanctity of human life**.[1] They point to the risk of well-intentioned persons making erroneous judgments about whether death would benefit the patient. They also point to the danger of malicious persons using such reasoning as a rationalization for killing the patient who is difficult to care for. Some people who believe ethics is a matter of consequences nevertheless maintain that consequences should be used to judge rules of conduct involving killing rather than individual actions of killing. They argue that a rule against killing, even for mercy, will have better consequences than any other rule, including a rule that would permit killing when it appears merciful. These people, then, believe they can explain the intuition against killing on the basis of consequences.

One other possibility might help explain the intuition that killing is wrong. Perhaps there is an ethical principle of the sanctity of human life. Analogous to the position that it is simply wrong to lie or break a promise, it might be that it is simply wrong to kill. This view would be congruent with certain religious traditions (Judaism, for example) that proscribe killing or limit it to special conditions demanded by retributive justice or self-protection.

If one accepts some moral reservations about killing, even in cases where it appears that the patient wants to be killed or that the patient would benefit from being killed, a number of issues become important. Does the avoidance of killing apply only to active killing, or does it also extend to decisions to let a person die? Is there a difference between actions and omissions? If so, do cases of **withdrawing treatment** count as actions or omissions? Does a prohibition against killing proscribe behaviors in cases where the intent is not the death of the patient but it is known that death is a risk (risky treatment or research, for example)? And does the request or consent of the person who might be killed justify killing that would otherwise be proscribed? The cases in this chapter are designed to help clarify these issues.

Actions and Omissions

One of the classic problems in biomedical ethics is that of whether there is a difference between actions and omissions, especially when the result will be the death of the patient. If a patient is inevitably dying (for example, a comatose patient who is terminally ill), many people believe that it is morally preferable to withhold or withdraw treatment than to intervene actively to kill that patient. They would prefer simply omitting treatment in order to let the patient die, other things being equal. On the other hand, other things are not always equal. The patient may not be in a coma. He or she may be suffering intractable pain. If the patient is inevitably dying, would it not be morally preferable, under these circumstances, to actively intervene to hasten the death and end the agony? The cases in this section help analyze these issues.

Case 10-1
Mercy Killing in the Newborn Nursery[1]

In 1985, Carol Frances Morris, a former nurse at Central Memorial Hospital in North Carolina, pleaded guilty to the 1983 murder of an infant in Central's neonatal intensive care unit. The infant had been born with anencephaly, or lack of cranial development. The infant's skull was an open sore that the nurses packed and layered with gauze to give his

[1]The names of the nurses have been changed to protect their privacy.

face a round appearance. Because of lack of cerebral hemispheres, the infant was incapable of any conscious activity. After his birth, the infant was admitted to the neonatal intensive care unit and placed in a bassinet. He was reported to be kicking and breathing, and his heart was beating. The hospital issued him a live birth certificate.

Months after the infant's death, Ms. Morris was heard to say that she once "terminated" a dying infant at Central's neonatal unit. An investigation ensued. Following exhumation of the infant's body, an autopsy revealed a quarter-inch bruise over the infant's left chest. The autopsy report was changed to read "death by mechanical compression of the chest."

Central County prosecutors argued that Ms. Morris and another nurse, Tanya Jean Simmons, killed the infant. Ms. Morris admitted to compression of the infant's chest in order to stop him from breathing. She pleaded guilty to manslaughter and faced a possible 20 years, imprisonment at sentencing. Prosecutors charged that Ms. Simmons assisted Ms. Morris by covering the infant's mouth and nose while Morris compressed his tiny chest. Simmons stood trial for murder and refused to plea bargain, testifying that she did not attempt to suffocate the child. Apparently, she had discussed the hopelessness of the child's condition with Morris and had expressed concern over the trauma and strain the infant was bringing to his family. Simmons, Morris, and other nurses had also apparently debated the morality of mercy killing. Testimony in the case revolved around the state's definition of "death" and whether Simmons could reasonably be charged with murder when some people claimed that the infant in question did not have a brain and was, therefore, legally "brain dead" according to state law. Also at issue was whether Simmons's actions could be seen as active killing or simply helping the infant complete the dying process.

After less than 2 hours of deliberation, the six-man, six-woman jury found Simmons not guilty of first-degree murder. Morris, however, because she pleaded guilty to voluntary manslaughter, was sentenced to 4 years imprisonment.

Commentary

Increasingly, there is a consensus that not all severely afflicted infants must have all treatments provided that could preserve their lives. Federal regulations that took effect on May 15, 1985,[2] allow that infants need not receive life-prolonging medical treatment when:

1. The infant is chronically and irreversibly comatose;
2. The provision of such treatment would merely prolong dying, not be effective in ameliorating or correcting all of the infant's life-threatening conditions, or otherwise be futile in terms of the survival of the infant; or
3. The provision of such treatment would be virtually futile in terms of the survival of the infant and the treatment itself under such circumstances would be inhumane.

Presumably, the baby under the care of Carol Frances Morris and Tanya Jean Simmons would have qualified under either of the first two criteria so that, if the parents had asked that treatment not be rendered, withdrawal of medical support would have been acceptable under those regulations. The infant with anencephaly was irreversibly comatose and inevitably dying. Nothing could have been done to preserve the life beyond some additional, apparently useless, extra hours, days, or weeks. If "humaneness" refers to pain or suffering, it is hard to argue that the baby would qualify under the third clause because, lacking capacity for consciousness, the infant could not feel pain or suffer.

These nurses, however, chose a different course. They actively intervened and were later accused of manslaughter and first-degree murder for their actions. Presumably, because the infant's brain had not developed the capacity for consciousness, it felt nothing; it apparently did not suffer a painful death. One of the nurses pleaded guilty to an illegal death. In the United States and also all other legal jurisdictions, it is illegal to kill even if the motive is mercy. Was the action of these nurses ethically different, however, from simply stepping aside and letting the baby die?

Those defending the nurses could use two approaches. They could argue that the baby was already dead or that, under special conditions, it is acceptable to end the life of such infants. Some might argue that the baby was already dead because it had no brain function. In all U.S. jurisdictions and most of the rest of the world, brain criteria can be used for pronouncing death. If the infant was already dead, presumably the nurses could not be charged with murder.

That approach to the case raises several problems, however. First, many anencephalic infants do, in fact, have lower brain function. Thus, they would not meet the criterion for death based on irreversible loss of all brain activity. Although some people have proposed defining newborns with anencephaly as being dead based on absence of brain function,[3] many anencephalic infants retain brain stem activity. For instance, some breathe spontaneously, which reveals that they have intact brain stem functions. Unless the law is changed, legally, such infants are living human beings. Causing the death of an anencephalic infant who maintains some brain function is thus still a homicide in all legal jurisdictions. Even if there were no brain activity, this baby had apparently not been pronounced dead. No nurse can assume a patient is dead if death has not been pronounced. Finally, even if they were certain the infant was dead, it would be very hard to explain why the nurses had compressed the chest of a dead infant.

If the baby cannot be treated as dead, defenders of the nurses' behavior might still argue that ending the baby's life was acceptable. People who defend such behavior sometimes distinguish between active killing and omissions that allow a dying process to continue. One puzzling problem in this case is whether the nurses considered simply allowing the infant to die. Many believe that such a course would be morally different from actively intervening in the dying process. Sometimes active intervention to end life is defended as better than merely omitting life support because it ends suffering more quickly. If the nurses' position was that the infant would suffer less from the active killing, they might have considered showing mercy and hastening the process along. They might, for example, have given emphasis to the ethical principle of beneficence—the principle that they should do good and avoid evil. The problem with that argument in this case, however, is that an anencephalic infant is not conscious and cannot experience suffering.

Even in cases in which active killing will end suffering, concluding that killing would do more good than simply letting the patient die would take some argument. It would first of all require the belief that killing the infant was itself not a harm (or at least not any more of a harm than if death resulted from simply stepping aside).

Another possible consideration is benefit to other parties—the suffering parents; the other patients, who were not getting the attention of the nursing staff; or the nurses themselves, who might otherwise have to exert energies expending pointless care for the patient. The moral question, especially for a clinical professional, is whether the benefits to any of these other parties count. If they do not, then killing on those grounds would not be acceptable. If they do (or if it were the patient who would benefit from the killing), we then would face the question of whether active killing is wrong when the justifiably considered benefits exceed the harms.

Two types of responses might be offered by critics of the notion that patients can be killed morally when the justifiably considered benefits exceed the harms. The first is called the "rule-utilitarian position." Some critics would argue that benefit and harms are the right bases for the moral judgment but that benefits and harms should be used to assess the moral rules for conduct rather than individual actions. They would say that the expected benefits and harms should be used to choose among alternative possible rules but that the rules should then be applied without regard to benefit/harm calculations in every case. They might support this approach out of fear that if individuals did the calculations every time they acted, they might make too many mistakes. They could conclude that following the rule that tends to produce the best consequences will result in more good overall than having fallible humans make their own judgments in individual cases, especially when the conditions are emotionally stressful and when the result is irreversible (as would be the case in a mercy killing). After all, we do not permit individual judgments at traffic lights for similar reasons. Another version of the rule-utilitarian position is that it is simply the nature of morality that people should live by rules. Once the rules are established (based on the assessment of the consequences), they should be followed even in cases where the consequences in the individual case might not be the best.

Other critics of active killing might argue that there is a straightforward moral principle opposing the killing of another human being (even in cases where, hypothetically, it would result in more good than harm). Just as it is simply wrong to break a promise or tell a lie or distribute goods unjustly, so it might be wrong to kill human beings (or possibly even any living creature).

Killing another human being simply is a wrong-making characteristic of actions. If that were the case, it might explain why many hold that it is wrong to kill.

This explanation would require, of course, that we reassess the alternative of simply letting the baby die rather than actively killing it. If the moral principle that opposes killing also includes letting humans die as a wrong-making characteristic, then it would not explain our intuitive belief that killing is worse. It is hard to imagine that the prohibition could be extended to letting people die, however. No human could possibly act on a principle that says it is always wrong to let people die. Inevitably, many people die from causes that we could take no action to prevent. However, people could act on the principle that it is always wrong to kill people (at least innocent people) actively. If one holds that there is a principle that identifies killing as something that always ought to be avoided and that it does not extend to instances where people are allowed to die, then that would help explain the widely held intuition that active killing is morally worse than letting die.

The nurses in this case apparently believed that their criterion for action was to do good, that the good of the family counted even when the patient's welfare was not at stake, and that no general rule or principle against killing prohibited their actions.

Critical Thinking Questions

1. What are the reasons you would give for not killing a patient?
2. Have you ever thought a patient might be better off dead? If so, what were your reasons?
3. A physician, Dr. Anna Pou, and two nurses, Lori L. Budo and Cheri Landry, were charged with second degree murder following an investigation into mercy killings during the chaos after Hurricane Katrina. The three allegedly administered lethal doses of morphine and another drug to four New Orleans hospital patients. At the time, temperatures inside the hospital rose to 100°F, the generators did not work, toilets backed up, and nurses had to improvise care. How would you judge the nurses if they intended the best for the frail patients who were unable to be evacuated and did knowingly administer lethal overdoses? If you were a member of the state board of nurses reviewing their case what would you rule?[4]

Criteria for Justifiable Omission

Most cases confronting a nurse do not involve proposals for actively killing a patient. Rather, they involve treatments that the patient or others deem unacceptable. What is proposed is an omission. Presumably, not every possible treatment should be provided for every patient. What is needed is a set of criteria for justifiable treat-ment refusal by the patient or her or his agent. From the standpoint of the nurse, the critical question is often, "Am I justified in going along with a decision to treat or omit treatment?" The problem is illustrated by the following case.

Case 10-2
The Patient Who Was Not Allowed to Die[2]

Mr. John Corbett was newly retired after 30 years of managing a small truck transport company. He had never married and had no children. His only brother had died the year before his own health problems occurred, and he did not have many friends. Originally hospitalized for resection of the colon and a colostomy following a bout with cancer of the colon, Mr. Corbett was readmitted several months later with pneumonia following a severe case of the flu. Adult-onset diabetes was also diagnosed on his admission, and he became hypertensive. Now, Mr. Corbett was being admitted again—he apparently tripped on his dog's leash and suffered a broken hip.

Gretchen Kerns was assigned as Mr. Corbett's primary nurse. Over several days, they developed a bantering, congenial relationship. Mr. Corbett frequently referred to himself as "a disaster that found a place to happen" and commented that "Jolly Jack, the Grim Reaper, is coming to get me—the slow way. That is sure not the way I want to go."

Soon he was well enough to return home. He did well at home for several weeks with a walker and occasional visits from a home health nurse. Then Mr. Corbett suffered a stroke and was readmitted to the hospital. This time, there were no jokes or bantering. When Ms. Kerns inserted the IV to provide antibiotics for a bladder infection (a three-nurse fight), Mr. Corbett made loud guttural noises, wept, and fought the familiar nurses with flailing arms. When he refused to eat, clenching his jaws, and moving his head from side to side, he was force-fed a pureed diet from a syringe until a nasogastric tube was inserted (a four-nurse fight). When Mr. Corbett developed congestive heart failure, his hands were restrained and he was sedated so that nasal oxygen could be administered. It was almost a relief to the nursing staff when he became semicomatose.

Still, it took some juggling to keep Mr. Corbett going. Ms. Kerns regulated his blood sugar, fought multiple bladder infections from his indwelling Foley, replaced infiltrated IVs, and packed pressure sores that multiplied despite turning and massages. His blood pres-sure dipped and soared, the liquid diet caused diarrhea, and his arthritis caused contrac-tures. When he suffered a respiratory arrest, he was resuscitated. The nurses were praised for their fine work. When he suffered a second arrest 3 days later, some of the members of the care-giving team began to doubt the wisdom of their efforts. Yet, Mr. Corbett improved to the point where he could shout guttural sounds again and fight off Ms. Kerns and the other nurses with his fists. Then his kidneys began to fail, and he was dialyzed. Eventually

---

[2]Adapted from Huttman, B. (1984). The bitter end. *American Journal of Nursing, 84,* 1366–1367.

he "stabilized" with dialysis three times a week, although his blood gases, electrolytes, cardiac enzymes, urine cultures, and whatever else was tested were always abnormal.

One day when Mr. Corbett's blood pressure dropped steadily, his physician indicated that they should "let nature take its course." A do not resuscitate (DNR) order was written, and the physician said "goodbye" to the patient. Ms. Kerns, however, refused to follow the order. "You can't do that. We've brought him back before—twice. We can pull him through again. Let's give him some dopamine," she said. She argued with the physician, the rest of the staff, and her supervisor, claiming that everyone deserves to be resuscitated and that she could not participate in euthanasia. "It is morally and legally wrong," she said. The physician obliged Ms. Kerns and rescinded the DNR order. Two days later, Mr. Corbett had a third arrest. Ms. Kerns and the resuscitation team performed expertly. "God gave us the technology to preserve the life of our patients," she said. Two months after the first arrest, the sixth resuscitation attempt failed, and Mr. Corbett died. "We did the best we could," Ms. Kerns said proudly. "We gave him the benefit of everything we had to offer." Other members of the nursing staff were bitter. One said, "When I get to heaven, I'll explain to God that I did the best I could for every patient. But who's going to explain it to Mr. Corbett?"

Commentary

Ms. Kerns was clearly opposed to euthanasia, and she apparently believed that withdrawal of treatment from Mr. Corbett constituted euthanasia. The term *euthanasia*, however, is an ambiguous one. Sometimes it means, based on its Greek root, "any good death." Sometimes its use is limited to decisions that hasten the death of a critically or terminally ill patient. Some people limit the term to active killing for mercy, whereas others use it more broadly to include decisions to withhold or withdraw treatment, such as was contemplated in Mr. Corbett's case.

Legally, there is a clear difference between active killing and simply letting a patient die.[5] Whether there is an ethical difference is a matter of debate.[6] That is the ethical question Ms. Kerns ought to be addressing, however. It may be that although omissions are legal even though they can be predicted to hasten death, Ms. Kerns would nonetheless find them morally objectionable. If so, she is within her right to protest omissions and, if necessary, to withdraw from involvement in this patient's care. Should Ms. Kerns consider withholding or withdrawing treatment for Mr. Corbett to be unethical?

Several different treatments were being considered for Mr. Corbett: an IV for antibiotics, force-feeding, a nasogastric tube, nasal oxygen, an indwelling Foley, CPR, and hemodialysis. Each might have to be assessed separately. Some people label treatments that are required "ordinary" and those that are expendable "extraordinary." That terminology increasingly has been called into question because it is so ambiguous. Many clinicians equate "ordinary" with "statistically common" and "extraordinary" with "unusual," as the terms might apply in everyday usage. In the moral and legal debate over withholding and withdrawing treatment, however, that is not what the terms have meant. Others have equated "ordinary" with "simple" and "extraordinary" with "complex." Under that usage, the hemodialysis for Mr. Corbett might be expendable because it involves a complex machine, whereas the CPR and nasogastric tube might be viewed as more simple.

The President's Commission for the Study of Ethical Problems in Medicine and Biomedical and Behavioral Research considered the distinctions between usual and unusual, and between simple and complex, as bases for distinguishing between morally required and morally expendable treatments, and rejected them.[7] Instead, it adopted a pair of criteria that were originally developed in Roman Catholic moral theology.[8] Treatments are expendable, according to the President's Commission, if they are useless or if the burdens exceed the benefits.[9] This means that a very simple treatment, such as Mr. Corbett's IV or nasogastric tube, could be expendable, just as is his hemodialysis, if such treatments were burdensome to him; so could antibiotics and other medications.

Patients increasingly are signaling their own views about which treatments are morally expendable by writing *advance directives*—legally effective documents indicating their views about which treatments should be provided and which should be forgone. Unfortunately, Mr. Corbett, like many patients, had not prepared an advance directive. The ethics of withholding IVs and nasogastric tubes will be explored more fully in the cases at the end of this chapter. In any case, not everyone agrees that withholding and withdrawing treatment are morally the same as active killing. It is clear that in the American legal system they are not the same.

It is for Ms. Kerns to determine whether she is willing to accept withholding or withdrawing treatment as moral, at least in cases where the patient's wishes are that it be forgone. If she is willing, she would be in agreement with the President's Commission and many, but not all, of our religious traditions. However, should she decide that even though withholding or withdrawing treatment is legal, at least if the patient clearly refuses the treatment in an advance directive, she would still have to face the question of her own conscience. If her conscience tells her that withholding or withdrawing treatment is not moral, then she might decide that she must withdraw from the case. If she makes this choice and other provisions can be made for the nursing care of her patient, her rights need to be respected.

She might be particularly concerned about the fact that the nasogastric tube, the IV, and several other treatments being provided for Mr. Corbett are already in place, so that withdrawing them would appear to be closer to actively killing him. The problem of withdrawing treatments already begun is the subject of the next case.

Critical Thinking Questions

1. In your opinion, what went wrong in the case of Mr. Corbett?
2. Would having an advance directive have made a difference in planning care for Mr. Corbett? Why or why not?

Withholding and Withdrawing

If withholding certain treatments—those that are useless or disproportionately burdensome—is not considered by everyone to be the same as active killing, and therefore might not be prohibited under the principle of the sanctity of human life, what about withdrawing a treatment once begun? In that case, the nurse or someone else must actively turn off a switch, remove a tube, or turn off a medication drip. If the critical distinction is based on whether someone actually makes a movement, then is withdrawing a treatment proscribed under the principle of the sanctity of human life?

Case 10-3
Is This Nurse a Killer?[3]

Mary Rose Robaczynski, a nurse at Maryland General Hospital in Baltimore, was charged with murder for disconnecting the respirator of a comatose patient, 48-year-old Harry Gessner. Mr. Gessner, a former taxi-cab driver, had been hospitalized with bladder cancer, cirrhosis of the liver, and pneumonia. He suffered heart failure while in the hospital and had stopped breathing. It was claimed during the nurse's trial that he would have died in any case within hours. Asked during the trial if she disconnected the respirator, she said, "Yes, after I felt he had no pulse and no blood pressure." Later, pressed on why she did it, she said, "I was trying to act in the best interest of the patient. I felt helpless. I don't know exactly why I did it." At another point, she was quoted as saying, "I only do it to GORKs (patients for whom 'God only really knows' whether they are alive)."

Others, commenting on Ms. Robaczynski's actions, observed that if they were Mr. Gessner and had a terrible array of fatal conditions, they would not have wanted further treatment. They would have wanted their respirators disconnected. One critic, however, said, "She was not willing to just wait for him to die. She had to kill him. She murdered him." Testimony was introduced during the trial that Ms. Robaczynski had spoken in favor of mercy killing in cases of comatose patients who had little or no hope of recovery. Was disconnecting the machine a "mercy killing"? Was it morally different from simply failing to resuscitate Mr. Gessner when he had his next respiratory arrest?

Commentary

Something seems very wrong with Ms. Robaczynski's action. Was the problem here that Ms. Robaczynski had crossed the line between the decision to let the patient die and active killing? We have seen that even for reasons of mercy, active killing is illegal. It is morally condemned by many, but not all. She disconnected a respirator, the result of which was the death of her patient. Should that be classified as active killing?

---

[3]Saperstein, S. (March 20, 1979). Unhooked system, nurse says. Washington Post, p. C3; Nurse, on trial for murder, called compassionate. (March 14, 1979). New York Times, p. A17

Traditionally, many clinicians have thought of withdrawing treatment as a kind of action. If the withdrawal resulted in the death of the patient, it would then be considered active killing. Withdrawal of treatment requires an action. Switches must be thrown; tubes must be removed. Psychologically, the nurse or physician engaging in the withdrawal of an ongoing medical treatment might feel like he or she is taking an action.

On the other hand, those outside the clinical setting have tended to classify withdrawing treatment as more akin to not starting treatment in the first place. Part of this argument is pragmatic. Ongoing treatments can be viewed as the continual repetition or administration of individual units of treatment. An indwelling IV supplying continuous medication is akin to repeated injections. A respirator is akin to continual compressions supplying air. Stopping a treatment is like deciding not to supply the next dose. Moreover, almost any ongoing intervention is stopped from time to time—to place a new line or to clear an airway, for example. If it is deemed unacceptable to stop a treatment in order to let the patient die but acceptable not to start it again once it has been stopped, we could simply wait until that moment when the intervention has been discontinued and then exercise the option of not restarting. There seems to be no significant moral reason to go through that fiction.

Moreover, if it is policy that treatments can be omitted, but once begun, they must be continued, there would be a strong incentive to refuse to start procedures. This would be true even if, as in Mr. Gessner's case, when they were begun it would have been imprudent to have omitted them.

Some of those who favor classifying withdrawing treatment as more akin to not starting it ask that we examine the moral basis of the right of refusal of treatment. It rests, in part, on the principle of autonomy, which gives people the right to consent or refuse to consent to treatment. The decision to forgo treatment follows from the right of persons to be left alone. The person with authority for Mr. Gessner's care would have the right to refuse treatment when that judgment is plausibly in Mr. Gessner's best interest. The authority to make that judgment, however, does not imply the right to have Mr. Gessner killed. The principle of autonomy could never be used as the basis for authorizing someone else to actively kill another person. Some people have concluded that if there is a moral principle of the sanctity of human life, it does not extend to all decisions to omit life-prolonging treatments. They are not considered active killings, which can remain morally prohibited.

The President's Commission for the Study of Ethical Problems in Medicine and Biomedical and Behavioral Research reached a similar conclusion. It says, "Neither law nor public policy should mark a difference in moral seriousness between stopping and not starting treatment."[10]

Still, it appears that Ms. Robaczynski did something wrong. If she did not engage in an action that can be thought of as being the same as actively killing Mr. Gessner, then has she committed no moral offense? One possible response is that, even though she withdrew a respirator and that withdrawal is morally akin to omitting, there are circumstances when it is morally wrong either to withhold or withdraw treatment. In some cases, forgoing treatment can even be the equivalent of murder. Withholding or withdrawing food from a starving, but otherwise healthy child for whom one is responsible would be an example. If Mr. Gessner's case were such a circumstance, Ms. Robaczynski might be guilty of murder by forgoing treatment.

It is clearly wrong for health professionals (nurses or physicians) to forgo treatment when there is a presumption in favor of treatment and the patient or agent for the patient has not decided to refuse treatment. The presumption in favor of treatment is present in Mr. Gessner's case. There is no evidence that he had refused the respirator nor that he had a relative or anyone else speaking for him who had refused the treatment. Had he offered such a refusal, forgoing treatment would have been plausible, but without it there is an abandonment. In this case, it was an abandonment that resulted in death. Those who follow this line of argument might conclude that even though withdrawing a respirator is morally like an omission and, therefore, is as morally acceptable as omissions, it is wrong to forgo life-prolonging treatment when the patient or agent for the patient has not refused the treatment. The alternative way of accounting for our intuition that Ms. Robaczynski did wrong is simply to classify what she did as an active killing. That would mean, however, that withdrawals of treatment even upon the refusal of the patient would also be so classified.

Critical Thinking Questions

1. Do you think Ms. Robaczynski killed Mr. Gessner? Why or why not?
2. Would you view Ms. Robaczynski's actions differently if Mr. Gessner had asked to be disconnected from his respirator? Why or why not?

Case 10-4
The Patient Who Might Have an Advance Directive[4]

Jerry Packard was a staff nurse in the coronary care unit (CCU) of a large medical center. One morning, he was informed that a patient from the recovery room (RR) would soon be admitted to the CCU and that the new admission would be assigned to him. The patient, a 66-year-old male with a known history of myocardial infarction (MI), also had cancer of the prostate. This hospital admission was for a transurethral resection (TUR), which had been aborted in the operating room when the patient developed cardiac changes following spinal anesthesia. The patient had been transported to the RR with the diagnosis of possible MI and was being transferred to the CCU for management and evaluation.

---

[4]Case supplied by Albert L. Scheckterman, RN. Used with permission.

Mr. Packard went to the RR with a bed to pick up the patient. When he arrived, the patient was coding. Apparently, he had gone into ventricular tachycardia/ventricular failure (VT/VF) in the RR and had required countershock ×3, cardiopulmonary resuscitation (CPR), intubation, lidocaine, and vasopressors to maintain his blood pressure. A Swan Ganz catheter was put in place. Recovery rhythm was sinus bradycardia to sinus tachycardia, with occasional pauses. The patient was acidotic, in pulmonary edema by chest x-ray with a PaO_2 of 50–60, on FIO_2 of 100%.

During the events of the code, an attending cardiologist (Dr. Diamond) passed by, observed the code, and made the following statements to the RR staff and the CCU resident: "Say, that's Mr. Sawyer. I know him from his last hospitalization a month ago when I was attending in CCU. I believe he has an advance directive." While the patient was being stabilized, Dr. Diamond called the patient's relative, who happened to work in another part of the medical center. The relative also expressed the belief that Mr. Sawyer had an advance directive and did not want to receive extraordinary support measures. Dr. Diamond relayed this information to the other physicians, and there was general agreement that conservative measures to ensure support were indicated while the advance directive was located.

The CCU resident and Mr. Packard transported Mr. Sawyer to the CCU. When admitted, the patient's systolic blood pressure was in the 70s while on dobutamine, 8 micrograms per kg and dopamine, 26 micrograms per kg. The patient occasionally responded to verbal commands, opened his eyes, gripped Mr. Packard's hands, and responded to pain in the upper extremities (his lower extremities were still under the effects of the spinal anesthesia). Cardiac monitoring showed that the patient was still having sinus tachycardia (130), C.O. 6.8, SVR800, PCWP28, temp. 35.5. Resp. ABG was improving with 730/42/60 on 100%; IMV 12, Peep5.

At this point, the CCU resident and an intern approached Mr. Packard and informed him that they believed the present treatment of the patient was cruel. In reading the medical record chart, they had learned that the patient had been designated "do not resuscitate" (DNR) on his last admission. In addition, the patient was supposed to have an advance directive, although it was not yet located. They told Mr. Packard to slowly turn off the IV drip of dopamine and dobutamine. What should Mr. Packard do?

Commentary

Mr. Packard's situation is somewhat similar to Ms. Robaczynski's. He also must contemplate withdrawing treatment, and the treatment to be withdrawn is basic and simple. Ms. Robaczynski withdrew a ventilator, whereas Mr. Packard would withdraw an IV. Some people might be inclined to say that the hospital team missed its chance when it failed to act decisively when it had a chance to omit the resuscitation. The team members might now feel that they have to continue the supportive care that had been started.

Two reasons for that position might be offered. First, it might be argued that aggressive resuscitation is "extraordinary," whereas an IV drip is "ordinary." We saw in Case 10-2 that these terms are ambiguous and that many people would make judgments not on the basis of the complexity of the treatment but rather on whether they fit with the patient's wishes. Then the question would become one of whether the patient saw the IV as serving a useful purpose any more than the CPR does. That is a question we shall address later in this chapter.

The other possible explanation of the difference between omitting the CPR and stopping the IV drip is that one is an omission and the other is a withdrawal. Just as in the Robaczynski case (Case 10-3), we need to determine if it makes a difference whether a treatment is stopped or never started. Maintaining such a distinction might incline caregivers to be reluctant to start treatments such as the IV drip. Defenders of the view that there is no legitimate moral distinction believe it is better to start a treatment when there is doubt about the correctness of the course and then withdraw if the time comes when it is clear that the patient would not have wanted the treatment to continue.

Here, however, Mr. Packard is being told by the resident and intern to turn off the IV drip on the basis of an unconfirmed belief that the patient has an advance directive and the fact that he reportedly had been designated for nonresuscitation on his last hospital admission. Mr. Packard must face the question of whether that is sufficient reason to stop the treatment, even with the apparent approval of Mr. Sawyer's relative.

It is likely that the next of kin's judgment would be sufficient in the case where the patient's wishes cannot be determined, but that does not seem to lead to a clear answer here. First, we are not sure if the relative is Mr. Sawyer's next of kin. Moreover, even if he or she is, it seems possible that Mr. Sawyer has expressed his own wishes and those wishes would surely take precedence. Although the rumor is that he has an advance directive, no one seems to know exactly what it says. Some living wills are written for the purpose of insisting that treatment continue. Unless Mr. Packard and the physicians know the content of the document and can confirm that it, in fact, exists, they are taking considerable liberty.

As for the existence of a nonresuscitation instruction during the previous admission, that does not provide definitive guidance for Mr. Packard either. First, even if Mr. Sawyer was willing not to be resuscitated at that time, it is not clear those remain his wishes today under somewhat different medical and social circumstances. Second, Mr. Packard does not know whether the decision against resuscitation during the previous admission was made by Mr. Sawyer or by other parties. There are increasing incidents of physicians writing nonresuscitation instructions on their own without confirming that they are supported by the patient or the patient's surrogate. Deciding to let the patient die under such circumstances is morally controversial. It may be that Mr. Packard is being asked to omit treatment on the basis of a rumor that Mr. Sawyer has an advance directive and the purported fact that someone decided during a previous admission that Mr. Sawyer should not be resuscitated. Is either an adequate basis for Mr. Packard to withdraw treatment? If not, what are his options?

Direct and Indirect Killing

In trying to understand a principle that requires respect for the sanctity of human life, there is another distinction that sometimes comes into play. Sometimes persons are killed although there is no intention to kill. Persons are killed in surgery because of anesthesia accidents. They are killed by risky research protocols where a feared, but undesired side effect occurs. In Catholic moral theology[11] and in some secular philosophic debate as well,[12] a distinction is made between killings that are directly intended and those that are unintended.

The doctrine, sometimes referred to as the ***doctrine of double effect***, holds that evil consequences of actions, even deaths, are morally permissible provided that four conditions are met.[13]

1. The action is good or indifferent in itself.
2. The intention of the agent is upright; that is, the evil effect is sincerely not intended.
3. The evil effect must be equally immediate causally with the good effect; that is, it is not a means to the good effect.
4. There must be a proportionally grave reason for allowing the evil to occur.

Sometimes the direct/indirect distinction is confused with the action/omission distinction. We have already seen, however, that sometimes omissions can result in deaths that are direct and intended (see the previous discussion of Mr. Sawyer in Case 10-4). We shall now examine an action that results in a death but that is arguably not direct or intended.

Case 10-5
Sedating the Dying Patient[5]

Jennifer Lincoln was back at work on her oncology nursing unit after a week's vacation. As she received her report, she could hear moans of pain coming from the room of Leonard Wilson, a 28-year-old man suffering the effects of metastatic bone cancer. This patient had been one of her favorites when he was hospitalized several months ago for chemotherapy. Now he was back to die. The metastatic growths in his spine were causing him excruciating pain at the same time as brain stem metastases were threatening death.

The goal of Mr. Wilson's nursing care was to keep him as comfortable as possible. But as Ms. Lincoln checked his chart for his narcotic order, she stared in disbelief. She called

---

[5]Adapted from A question of ethics: Sedating the dying [editorial column]. (1981, November/December). *Nursing Life, 1,* 41–43.

the head nurse: Had Mr. Wilson really received 780 mg of morphine by continuous infusion during the last 8 hours, plus 20-mg boosters every 4 hours, prn? That was enough to cause respiratory depression, even in a 180-pound man.

The head nurse confirmed the dose and explained that Mr. Wilson's tolerance was extremely high, probably because he had been addicted to heroin as a teenager. "Give him another 20-mg booster," she told Ms. Lincoln. "We have to relieve his pain." Ms. Lincoln agreed that his pain should be relieved, but she wondered whether she should give him another dose on top of the amount of medication that he had already received. What if he stopped breathing after she gave him the booster? What should she do?

Commentary

Ms. Lincoln is concerned that she might kill her patient. She knows that a well-recognized side effect of morphine is respiratory depression and that Mr. Wilson's dose is extremely high. She also knows that patients develop tolerances to morphine and that increased dosages are then needed to produce the analgesic effect. Should she be willing to run the risk of killing her patient to get the desired analgesia? If she is governed solely out of a duty to benefit her patient, she will relieve his pain and give the injection. But if there is an independent moral principle that requires respect for the sanctity of human life, she has a conflict.

In the previous case, the nurse might have been able to avoid the implications of the principle of the sanctity of human life by arguing that withdrawing a ventilator is not to be classified as an active killing. Ms. Lincoln's therapeutic mission, however, is giving an injection that may kill. It is not withdrawing a treatment.

It is impossible to escape the fact that many interventions in health care are somewhat dangerous. Administering a blood transfusion, weaning a patient from a ventilator, even administering penicillin all have a risk of serious complications, including death. If it is always wrong to actively kill, should physicians and nurses avoid all of these normally helpful interventions in order to avoid running the risk of killing the patient?

The doctrine of double effect provides one answer. If the death is not intended and is not a means to the good effect, it is tolerable provided it is for a proportionally good objective. The objective in this case was relieving severe pain, pain great enough that Ms. Lincoln could hear Mr. Wilson moaning down the hall. According to the doctrine of double effect, killings are not necessarily wrong if they are not intended, which this one clearly would not be. The goal of the nursing care plan was to "keep him as comfortable as possible."

Some people question the adequacy of the doctrine of double effect because it establishes a qualification on the principle of the sanctity of human life. One question centers on the role of intention in determining whether an action is right or wrong. Some people maintain that the morality of an action can be distinguished from the blameworthiness of the actor. They hold that someone can do the right act out of a bad intention. The nurse who provides impeccable nursing care solely to gain a promotion would be an example. Conversely, one can do the wrong thing out of a good motive. Someone who actively kills for mercy may be an example.

However, if that is the case, questioners ask whether intention is critical in deciding whether giving the pain-killing medication is wrong. In some cases, an actor may know with great certainty that death will result from an action, but still not intend the death. In the textbooks dealing with the doctrine of double effect, the example is sometimes given of a military officer who decides to bomb a munitions factory knowing that innocent children in a school yard next door will be killed. The intention might apply only to destroying the munitions, but there may be certain knowledge that the children will be killed as an indirect effect. According to the doctrine of double effect, the bombing could be licit if the intention did not include killing the children (and there would be proportionally great good resulting from the bombing). Critics argue, however, that if it is known with certainty that the indirect evil will result, the good intention of the actor should not matter.

Applied to the healthcare sphere, giving a narcotic analgesic when resulting death is a certainty would be as great (or as little) a wrong as an act in which the intention was to kill the patient. The assessment of the moral character of the actor might be different, but the assessment of the act itself would be the same.

In Ms. Lincoln's case, however, the death of her patient is not a certainty. Patients with tolerance can withstand very high doses of morphine. It is reasonable to give higher than normal dosages to relieve pain.[14] If death is an unexpected and unintended side effect, it is acceptable. According to this view, active killings are acceptable only if they are not expected and not intended. By contrast, according to the defenders of the double effect position, good intention makes such killings acceptable even if there is foreknowledge that death is a certainty. Thus the critical question raised is whether good intention makes the killing morally a more acceptable action (i.e., makes it more right, as the double effect position suggests) or whether it is wrong to take an action the likely result of which will be death, even if the intention is good. If there is an independent moral principle of the sanctity of human life, then there is a moral force pulling Ms. Lincoln away from giving the injection, to the extent she believes it will kill her patient—even if her intention is a good one.

One of the groups that has expressed a view on this issue is the American Nurses Association (ANA). The *Code of Ethics for Nurses* includes the following statements:

> The nurse should provide interventions to relieve pain and other symptoms in the dying patient even when those interventions entail risks of hastening death. However, nurses may not act with the sole intent of ending a patient's life even though such action may be motivated by compassion, respect for patient autonomy and quality of life considerations.[15]

Thus the ANA appears to recognize the distinction between direct and indirect killing. Although it does not condone direct active killing, it explicitly recognizes that it is appropriate to take the risk of killing a patient provided the nurse's intention is to prevent or relieve suffering associated with the dying process.[16] The ANA thus supports the double effect position as well as the principle of the sanctity of human life.

Critical Thinking Questions

1. Think of a patient care situation in which you hesitated to give frequent or high doses of morphine to a patient. Why were you hesitant to give the morphine in this situation?

2. Do you continue to hesitate before giving frequent or high doses of morphine? Why or why not?

The issues raised by the doctrine of direct and indirect effect have recently emerged in the dramatic and controversial cases of attempts to separate conjoined twins. Especially in the situation in which one twin is not as well developed and is destined to die, a decision may be made to do what is necessary to save the other twin, even if that means that the less developed one will have its life shortened in the process. The following case is an example.

Case 10-6
Bound Together in Life and Death[6]

Born only hours earlier at a distant community hospital in New Jersey, the twins looked surprisingly strong when they arrived by helicopter on September 15. They were joined at the chest, and they seemed to be hugging each other, with their wizened newborn faces only a few inches apart. Their respiration rate and their color were comparatively good, indicating that their blood was getting adequate oxygen. Special x-ray studies the next day showed that the twin designated Baby Girl B has an essentially normal, four-chambered heart that was fused to the stunted two-chambered heart of her sister, Baby Girl A. The hearts were joined along the walls of the left ventricles. The connecting wall was only one tenth of an inch thick—far too thin to be neatly divided in order to give each twin what belonged to her. And even if this were possible, the stunted heart of Baby Girl A would not be able to support the child for long. The doctors felt that they could not leave the babies the way they were, either. They knew it would be only a matter of time before

---

[6]Adapted from Drake, D. C. (1977, October 16). One must die so that the other might live. *The Philadelphia Inquirer.*

the overworked hearts would start to fail, killing both babies. No twins joined at the heart like this had ever lived for more than 9 months.

The twins had been born to a deeply religious, Orthodox Jewish family of rabbinical scholars. The father himself is a rabbinical student to whom nothing matters more—not even life itself—than God, the teachings of his religion, and biblical ethics. One axiom of biblical ethics is the infinite worth of human life. Since this ethic implies that all human life is equal—that one life is worth no more or less than another—would he consider it moral to kill Baby Girl A so that Baby Girl B could live? Several rabbis and other learned men met 4–5 hours every night for 11 days discussing the ethical issues.

Word spread through Children's Hospital that the surgeons were planning to sacrifice one of the conjoined twins. The hospital had said little, so the rumors were sometimes inaccurate. Mrs. Jane Barnsteiner, who is Catholic and the associate director for clinical nursing, was asked about the twins by the head nurse as she went about the hospital every day on her rounds. The Catholic nurses, of whom there were many, were particularly concerned that the surgeons might be doing something that violated the teachings of their church. The word "sacrifice" was used so much by the nurses in discussing the matter that Mrs. Barnsteiner herself became concerned and decided to consult a priest.

At the same time, the nurses in the operating room were becoming particularly uneasy because they knew they would be called upon to participate in the surgery if it took place. Miss Betsch [assistant director of the operating room complex] said that she would consult a priest. A Catholic herself, she would not want to participate in the surgery if it went against her church.

How should nursing leadership respond to the nurses' concerns about "sacrificing" one of the twins? What would actually happen in the operating room? A justified killing? Something else?

Commentary

This tragic situation of conjoined twins in which only one can live poses several moral issues. Of greatest concern to Ms. Barnsteiner and Ms. Betsch, both of whom are Roman Catholic, is whether it is ethical to intervene in such a way that the healthcare team, of which nurses would be a part, would actively cause the death of one of the twins.

Roman Catholic moral theology accepts the doctrine of indirect effect whereby it is morally tolerable to cause a harm provided certain conditions are met including the following requirements: (1) that the action taken is itself morally good or at least neutral (surgery to repair Baby Girl B's defect) and (2) that the harm (Baby Girl A's death) not be intended, but merely permitted. The question they must face, then, is whether the proposed surgery is to be thought of as an intentional killing of Baby Girl A so that her sister, Baby Girl B, can live or is better thought of as providing the medically necessary and appropriate surgery on Baby Girl B so that she can live even though the unintended consequence will be the death of her sister.

Clearly, all involved know that the death of Baby Girl A will be inevitable. The surgery will hasten that outcome, but not change it. Moreover, some would hold that they sincerely do not intend the death even though they foresee it. If that is a legitimate account of what is happening, then traditional Roman Catholic thought would find the surgery acceptable.

Even if this is an acceptable account from the Catholic perspective of the nurses, there is another problem. The twins were born into a family of Orthodox Jews. It is likely that they, with the guidance of their rabbinical advisors, will conclude that the lives of both girls are of infinite worth and should not be shortened even by a brief time. It is entirely possible that the parents will refuse to consent to the surgery anticipated by the physicians and perhaps accepted by the Catholic nurses.

If that is the situation, a new moral issue arises. Should the hospital seek legal intervention to authorize the surgery against the parents' wishes? Doing so would plausibly save one of the twins when, otherwise, both will certainly die. As we shall see in the cases of Chapter 17, we would not seek judicial intervention against the parents' wishes for trivial gain for the patients, but here, the gain for Baby Girl B will be dramatic—life rather than death—while the harm to Baby Girl A is modest—a slightly earlier death—and arguably an unintended (but foreseen) outcome. Should the nurses agree to participate in the surgery and should they support efforts to obtain a court order?

Voluntary and Involuntary Killing

At this point, we have explored several possible qualifications to the notion that life is sacred and that killing should be avoided. We have seen that some people limit the principle to active killing, permitting omissions, and treatment refusals; some people include withdrawing of treatment as active killing, whereas others classify it as an omission; and some people exclude unintended killings that are the indirect result of a good action. There is yet another qualification to be explored: Some people argue that the prohibition on killing applies only to actions that bring about the deaths of others against their will. Because most people do not normally desire to be killed, the question of whether killing is desired is not very important in most cases. Actions that bring about deaths are considered wrong. In the care of severely ill patients, the question of the desire of the patient can be critical.

Some people are now advocating the legalization of assistance in suicide, or mercy killing, when the patient, while mentally competent, voluntarily wants his or her life ended. For a number of years the Netherlands has had a policy of not prosecuting physicians who commit euthanasia, that is, killing the patient at the patient's request.[17] Such active killings have now been legalized in the Netherlands, Switzerland, Luxembourg, and Belgium. Efforts are also underway to legalize euthanasia in other countries.[18] In the United States, people in a number of states have tried to legalize physician-assisted suicide upon the voluntary request of a terminally ill patient. Jack Kevorkian, a no-longer-licensed physician in Michigan, has admitted to assisting in a number of suicides and has sought to challenge the laws making such practice illegal.[19] Although he was never convicted of assisting in a suicide, he very publicly injected an ALS patient with a lethal agent. He was convicted of that homicide, even though the patient clearly appeared to be competent and was explicitly requesting to be killed. Dr. Kevorkian served a long prison term for that killing.[20] In New York, Dr. Timothy Quill has publicly admitted to prescribing barbiturates for one of his patients in order to assist her in killing herself.[21] He was brought before a grand jury, which failed to indict him. After the states of Washington and California attempted without success to pass state referenda to legalize physician-assisted suicide, Oregon passed such a bill in 1994.[22] It was challenged in the courts, but in October 1997, Oregon became the first jurisdiction in the United States to legalize any form of professional-assisted dying. In the first 6 years the law was in effect, 171 people ended their lives in Oregon with physician assistance.[23] Physician-assisted suicide is also now legal in Washington state. Nurses in these states have had to think carefully about whether they can participate in physician-assisted suicide without sacrificing their personal and professional integrity. As this edition goes to press, the ANA is working on a new position statement on end-of-life care. The current position statement on assisted suicide reads:

> The American Nurses Association (ANA) believes that the nurse should not participate in assisted suicide. Such an act is in violation of the Code for Nurses with Interpretive Statements (Code for Nurses) and the ethical traditions of the profession. Nurses, individually and collectively, have an obligation to provide comprehensive and compassionate end-of-life care which includes the promotion of comfort and the relief of pain, and at times, forgoing life-sustaining treatments.[24]

The issue of voluntary active mercy killing arises in Case 10-7 that involves a patient who may be ready to die and who may voluntarily undertake a course leading to his death. The question is whether the prohibition against killing ought to apply to patients who are voluntarily ready to end their lives.

Case 10-7
The Suicidal Patient Who Went Unrecognized[7]

Ralph Baxter, 52 years old, had chronic lymphocytic leukemia. He was weak and tired, and he lay listlessly in bed most of the time. Despite his disorder, however, he maintained a good appetite and enjoyed the fresh fruit that his wife brought to the hospital every day. As the weeks passed, however, Mr. Baxter's condition declined. He was started on a series of chemotherapy treatments that soon left him nauseated. Even after the treatments ended, he was nauseated and would vomit whenever he tried to eat. His thin body became thinner, and his energy level fell. He became reconciled to the fact that everything that could be done for him had been done; he and his wife decided that it would be best if he were to spend his last few weeks at home.

---

[7]Adapted from Thielemann, P. (1984, May). Suicide: Two views: A chilling encounter. *American Journal of Nursing, 84,* 597–598.

Pamela Sorrenson was the nurse on the night shift the night before Mr. Baxter's scheduled discharge home. About 2:00 A.M., Ms. Sorrenson discovered Mr. Baxter walking slowly in the hall. He seemed to want company and was talkative about his concerns for his family: whether he would be a burden to his family, whether his wife could care for him as he got weaker, whether he would be able to keep food down, among other questions. Ms. Sorrenson talked to Mr. Baxter, assuring him that her own impressions of his family led her to believe that they would never regard him as an encumbrance. In the course of the conversation, Mr. Baxter sounded depressed. He said he was not sure that it was worth fighting any longer. After escorting him back to his room, she quickly went on to her other duties and the needs of other patients.

At 4:30 A.M., the nursing assistant checked on Mr. Baxter and found him sitting on the toilet. She told him to ring the call light when he was through, and she would help him back to bed. When she went back to check on him 15 minutes later, she found him in the bathroom, slumped over the washbasin. She thought he had fallen asleep, but as she approached him, she realized that he was dead. She quickly called Ms. Sorrenson. When the nurse straightened Mr. Baxter's shoulders, she noticed that he had cut his wrists with the little pocketknife that he usually used to cut up his fresh fruit. The pocketknife lay in the bloody washbasin. Ms. Sorrenson was at first shocked at what had happened, but the more she thought about it the more she wondered if Mr. Baxter's decision was not the best possible one for him under the circumstances. Although at first she felt guilty for failing to intervene, she began to wonder whether the next time she encountered a similarly depressed, terminally ill patient she should act differently.

Commentary

The case of Mr. Baxter, who committed suicide in the face of a lingering terminal illness with a bleak prognosis, raises the question of whether respect for the sanctity of human life includes initiation of actions that would prevent someone from taking one's own life.

Suicide in the face of terminal illness raises some technical questions. First, was Mr. Baxter really competent? The argument that free, rational choice on the part of the individual justifies suicide or even homicide upon request rests on the premise that persons deciding that they should be allowed to kill themselves or be killed can, in fact, be rational. Some persons who are suicidal clearly are not rational. They are not free agents making voluntary choices, so any possible exception to the prohibition against killing based on voluntariness would not apply to them.

However, Mr. Baxter showed no obvious signs of mental incompetence. Some people now acknowledge that it is possible for individuals to make a rational choice that the best course for them is to end their lives. At least, persons should not be necessarily considered irrational when they make such a choice.

Second, could the nursing staff have proposed other alternatives for Mr. Baxter that would have made his remaining days more meaningful? They might have investigated home nursing care. They might have urged medical assessments to modify future chemotherapy, provided antinausea and antipain medication, and explored the use of antidepressants. If a decision for suicide was based on an inadequate exploration of options, or if modifications could have improved Mr. Baxter's life, then the suicide decision was questionable on its face.

Suppose, however, that all of those options had been explored and Mr. Baxter still felt that suicide was the best way out. Two arguments are given to support an exception to a rule to avoiding killing in the case where the one being killed has consented (or does the killing himself or herself). Some people might approach the problem strictly in terms of the consequences. Although killing normally has bad consequences, situations where the individual voluntarily chooses to die might be the exception. David Hume has defended suicide on consequentialist grounds.[25] Alternatively, anyone committed to the priority of autonomy as a separate moral principle might argue that individuals have the right to dispose of their own bodies as they see fit, even if the consequences of doing so are not the best.[26]

By contrast, there are arguments based on consequences that weigh against suicide. In some cases the community will lose a valued member. Loved ones may have their interests jeopardized. These consequences, however, become less critical when applied to a terminally ill patient and compared with the suffering he or she may well endure under any other course. The most important argument against suicide may be that it violates some moral obligation. St. Thomas expressed this view in terms of the natural law and the duties the human owes to his God.[27] Secular persons may also hold that there is a duty to avoid killing that applies even to killing oneself.[28] If such a duty is recognized, it must be compared with the arguments in favor of self-killing. Mr. Baxter and Ms. Sorrenson might well conclude that there is something wrong with killing, even if the patient consents to it and the patient benefits more than under any other course of action.

Research Brief 10-1

Source: Ganzini, L., Harvath, T. A., Jackson, A., Goy, E. R., Miller, L. L., & Delorit, M. A. (2002). Experiences of Oregon nurses and social workers with hospice patients who requested assistance with suicide. *New England Journal of Medicine, 347*(8), 582–588.

Purpose: To describe the experiences of hospice practitioners with Oregon patients who have requested legalized physician-assisted suicide.

Method: This was a descriptive study using a survey design that included a questionnaire mailed to all hospice nurses and social workers in Oregon.

Findings: Of 545 eligible hospice nurses and social workers, 397 (73%) returned the survey, including 71% of nurses and 78% of social workers. Since November 1997, 179 of the respondents (45%) had cared for a patient who requested assistance with suicide. Hospice nurses reported on 82 patients who had received prescriptions for lethal medication. Ninety-eight percent of the nurses had discussed the request with a coworker, and 77% of the requests had been presented at hospice interdisciplinary conferences on patient care. A predominant reason for the patients' requests was that they wished to control the circumstances of death. The least important reasons included depression, lack of social support, and fear of being a financial drain on family members. Although the patients were concerned about burdening others, only 11% of hospice nurses rated their family caregivers as more burdened than those of other hospice patients.

Implications: Since assisted suicide was legalized in Oregon in 1997, many hospice nurses and social workers have provided care for patients who requested assistance with suicide. They rated patients' desires to control how they died as a very important reason for these requests. Support and continuing education for nurses and social workers in Oregon should focus on how to respond to requests for assistance for suicide and how to help terminally ill patients maintain control of the circumstances of their deaths.

Is Withholding Food and Water Killing?

The most controversial decisions about ***withholding treatment*** are those involving very simple, routine treatments. We have already seen that some people consider any treatment that is simple or common to be morally required. This has generated controversy over withholding antibiotics and other medications, CPR, and especially medically supplied nutrition and hydration as the 2005 Terri Schiavo case illustrated. The following cases illustrate the controversy first with a competent patient expressing her refusal for medically supplied nutrition and hydration and then with an incompetent patient, one of whose nurses objected to orders to discontinue the patients IVs and nasogastric tube.

Case 10-8

Removing a Feeding Tube: Starvation or Withdrawing an Extraordinary Mean?[8]

Ms. Anderson was a frail, 80-year-old woman with severe kyphosis who had recently been diagnosed with mycosis fungoids, or cutaneous T-cell lymphoma (CTCL), a malignancy that begins as a skin lesion and ends as a lymphoma with lymph and visceral involvement. Treatment for the disorder is palliative, and the life expectancy is only about 3 years from the time enlarged lymph nodes appear.

---

[8]Adapted from Reiley, P. J., Strecker, L., Perna, K., Burton, C., & Janeco, D. (1985, July). Letting go. *American Journal of Nursing, 85,* 776.

At the time she was admitted to Beth Reardon's oncology unit, Ms. Anderson had skin lesions on more than 10% of her body. Her pain was so extreme that she cried and moaned when Mrs. Reardon performed even the simplest procedure. Her nutritional status was very poor because eating was an ordeal. Even when her pain appeared to be under control, she adamantly refused to eat. A gastrostomy tube was inserted, despite Ms. Anderson's protests, and tube feedings were instituted. Ms. Anderson tried to pull the tube out, however, saying that she just wanted to die. After repeated attempts on the patient's part to pull out the tube (despite being restrained).

Mrs. Reardon and the other nurses assessed the situation. Clinically, Ms. Anderson was getting worse. Her prognosis was extremely poor. Yet all of the nursing interventions seemed to make her uncomfortable and unhappy. If the nurses established her comfort as the main nursing goal, then it would seem reasonable to not force any artificial feeding on her. Clearly, Ms. Anderson wanted to die, and her family did not want to continue watching her suffer. Yet the nurses held back from performing only comfort measures for Ms. Anderson. Wouldn't they be contributing to the hastening of death rather than the preservation of life?

Commentary

Ms. Anderson's agony presses us to the limits in determining what treatments morally may be refused. We have recognized that, at least at the level of law, competent persons have the right to refuse medical treatments being offered for their own good. Moreover, many individuals believe it is also morally right for them to refuse treatments that they find are serving no useful purpose or are gravely burdensome. It is evident that Ms. Anderson finds the gastrostomy tube burdensome. Does the use of the gastronomy tube, like any other medical treatment, fall under the rules that permit treatment refusal, or would removing it be "hastening death" as Mrs. Reardon asks?

It seems to be a matter of medical fact that removing the tube would hasten Ms. Anderson's death. That, of course, does not mean that her death would be intended or that removing the tube would constitute active killing. In fact, removing the tube would be a withdrawal of treatment, which, as we have seen earlier in this chapter, many people consider morally to be the equivalent of not starting treatment in the first place. Of course, Ms. Anderson could refuse to have the tube reinserted after it had been removed, in which case she might be said to be refusing consent to treatment rather than withdrawing treatment. If withdrawing and withholding are not significantly different morally, it will make no difference anyway.

The real issue seems to be whether food and fluids are so basic that they must be provided even if they are serving no useful purpose or are gravely burdensome or, on the other hand, whether they are expendable on the same grounds as other treatments such as ventilators and CPR.

Several philosophical commentators[29] and several legal cases[30] have concluded that nutrition and hydration may be withheld on the same grounds as other treatments. The ANA also concludes that artificially provided nutrition and hydration may be forgone.[31] Once one acknowledges that it is not the complexity nor the statistical commonness of the treatment that is morally critical but rather whether the treatment is fitting for the patient, then even something as routine as medically administered food and fluids can sometimes be expendable when patients do not want them or when they would not be fitting for the patient in the eyes of the patient's surrogate.

Sometimes a comparison is made between the withholding of medically administered oxygen through a ventilator and medically administered nutrition through a feeding tube. Oxygen is as basic to life support as nutrition or hydration, so the argument goes, so if one is expendable, then the others should be as well.

Nevertheless, many critics are reluctant to accept the withholding of the basics of nutrition and hydration, even upon the instruction of the patient as appears to be the case with Ms. Anderson. Several state "natural death acts" explicitly exclude nutrition and hydration from the treatments that can be refused. The Baby Doe regulations require that infants receive "appropriate nutrition and hydration," even in cases where other treatments can be withheld.[32] Some scholars are beginning to express concern that provision of food and fluids is not really a medical procedure but rather basic caring that should always be required.[33] Others are viewing provision of food and fluids as symbolic of our care of the hungry.[34] The question remains whether this would require provision of food and fluids even in cases where patients are not hungry or thirsty and, in fact, they suffer when nutrition and hydration are maintained.[35]

The latest wrinkle in the nutrition and hydration controversies is being raised by surrogates who request that patients with dementia who are physically capable of eating but who need assistance getting food and fluids to their mouths not be provided such assistance. "Bring their trays to them but don't help them eat." These requests are usually accompanied by the statement that the patient would not want to live the life he or she is living. Many nurses who have no difficulty withholding or withdrawing medically supplied nutrition and hydration judged to be disproportionately burdensome have great difficulty acceding to the request to not handfeed a patient who can eat, arguing that this is basic care like bathing or turning a patient. On the other hand, there are nurses who believe that this is a legitimate, autonomous request that should be honored and some individuals have begun to write this preference in their advance directives.

Critical Thinking Questions

1. If you were one of the nurses caring for Ms. Anderson, would you have continued to feed her? Why or why not? Do you believe that medically supplied nutrition/hydration is a medical intervention subject to general ethical guidelines for initiation, withholding or withdrawing of life-sustaining treatment, or is it basic care that must always be provided when it is possible to do so?

2. How would you respond to a request not to hand feed a patient with dementia who is able to eat and swallow but whose spouse wants no feeding assistance because "my husband wouldn't want to live this way"? Is this being complicit in killing by neglect or an example of good nursing care?

Research Brief 10-2

Source: Schwartz, J. K. (2003). Understanding and responding to patients' requests for assistance in dying. *Journal of Nursing Scholarship, 35*(4), 377–384.

Purpose: To explore how nurses experience and respond to patients' requests for assistance in dying (AID).

Method: This was a qualitative study of 10 self-selected nurses who worked in hospice home care ($n = 4$), with AIDS patients ($n = 3$), in critical care ($n = 2$), and with spinal-cord-injured patients ($n = 1$). The nurse participants were asked: "Tell me about a time when a patient asked you for help in dying." The nurses' stories were gathered in 2-hour audiotaped interviews conducted in the participants' homes; repeat interviews were held 2 weeks after the initial interviews, to clarify details and meanings. Analysis of interview data was based on van Manen's methodologic approach for interpretive phenomenology. Once individual thematic summaries were written, recurring aspects of the experience common to all participants were identified and described. An auditor reviewed interview transcripts, themes, and the organization, description, and interpretation of findings.

Findings: The four major themes identified from the data were: (1) being open to hear and hearing, (2) interpreting and responding to the meanings, (3) responding to the persistent requests for AID, and (4) reflections. The first theme revealed how nurses experienced hearing a request for AID. The six non-hospice nurses described the experience as upsetting, unusual, and sometimes life altering. Each plea for help in dying was experienced within the participants' personal cultures, personal and professional values, and spiritual or religious beliefs. The second theme included steps the nurses took to explore what patients meant by the request for AID. Most nurses said requests for AID were not associated with unmanageable physical pain, but often with the suffering related to existential or spiritual distress, weariness with the prolonged process of dying, or determination to control the circumstances of dying. Patients frequently wanted help in achieving a "good" death, as they defined it. Most participants distinguished "opiate-related hastened" death from "opiate-caused" death; they accepted the possibility of opiate-related hastened death because they believed that effective pain management for dying patients was a moral imperative. Participants explicitly or implicitly appealed to the principle of double effect as moral justification for assuming the risk of secondarily and unintentionally hastened death. The third theme concerned how far the participants would travel on their journey with dying patients requesting AID, and where they recognized or drew a line on their commitment to help patients die well. Most participants described a moral line that limited their responses to persistent requests for AID and that was based on strongly held personal values, moral or spiritual beliefs, a sense of professional responsibility or duty, and fears of legal or professional liability. They did not consider or consult their professional code of ethics or written position statements on end-of-life care. Participants' responses ranged on a continuum from refusal, not interfering with patient or family plans to hasten or cause death, to providing varying degrees and kinds of assistance. Two nurses explicitly acknowledged providing direct AID.

Implications: Few nurses in this study unequivocally agreed or refused to participate in helping patients die. Most struggled alone and in silence to find another way to respond, such as providing good end-of-life care and remaining present when patients and families suffered. When the goal of care was to help patients die well, these nurses experienced difficulty identifying a reliable moral line that distinguished among palliative interventions that allowed, hastened, or caused death. They described unspoken understandings and covert agreements with family members, and collusion with physician colleagues. When acts of secrecy and collusion become routine, they undermine the important role of collaboration and consultation in good hospice and palliative end-of-life care. This study's findings indicate a need to further explore nurses' understanding of the meaning of intentions when providing palliative care to dying patients.

Case 10-9
The Nurse Who Blew the Whistle on the Clarence Herbert Case[9]

Sandy Bardenilla, nursing supervisor of the intensive care unit (ICU) at Kaiser Foundation Hospital, Harbor City, California, reviewed the chart of Clarence LeRoy Herbert, a 55-year-old racetrack security guard and father of eight children. Mr. Herbert, a familiar patient to the ICU staff, had been resuscitated in the recovery room 2 days prior (August

---

[9]Adapted from Smith, L. (1983). Zero intake. *Nursing Life, 3*, 18–25; Annas, G. J. (1983, December). Non-feeding: Lawful killing in CA, homicide in NJ. *The Hastings Center Report, 13*, 19–20; Steinbock, B. (1983, October). The removal of Mr. Herbert's feeding tube. *The Hastings Center Report, 13*, 13–16. For the various legal actions, see Superior Court of the State of California for the County of Los Angeles. People of the State of California v. Neil Barber and Robert Nejdl. Tentative Decision. May 5, 1983; Court of Appeals of the State of California. Second Appellate District, Division Two. Barber and Nejdl v. Sup. Ct., 2 Civil No. 69350, 69351, Ct. of Appl. 2d Dist., Div. 2, Oct. 12, 1983. Barber v. Superior Court of California, 147 Cal. Appl. 3d 10006, 195 Cal. Rptr. 484 (1983).

26, 1981) after he suffered respiratory arrest following the uneventful closure of an ileostomy. Upon admission to the ICU, Mr. Herbert's endotracheal tube had been connected to a Bennett MA-1 ventilator, and the previously placed nasogastric tube and intravenous lines were maintained. Although his vital signs remained stable, Mr. Herbert had remained unconscious since his admission to the unit.

In reading Mr. Herbert's chart, Mrs. Bardenilla noticed that Mr. Herbert's physician had written a note that Herbert's wife had requested "no heroics" the day following his arrest. There had also been controversy over whether to remove Mr. Herbert's ventilator. When the ventilator was withdrawn by Dr. Barber, however, Mr. Herbert continued breathing on his own. His respirations improved and his vital signs restabilized with a normal sinus rhythm and a heart rate in the 70s. The physician in charge of the ICU subsequently wrote orders to withhold treatment for hypotension, hypertension, and arrhythmias and to give supportive care. As part of the supportive care, the nurses attached a misting device to Mr. Herbert's endotracheal tube to prevent the formation of mucus plugs.

On Monday, August 31, 5 days after Mr. Herbert had arrested in the recovery room and Mrs. Bardenilla's day off, Dr. Barber discontinued all the patient's IV fluids and the nasogastric tube. One of the nurses removed the IVs and the nasogastric tube, and the patient was transferred from the ICU to a room in the surgical unit. Dr. Barber also wrote an order to stop all blood work.

When Mrs. Bardenilla returned to work the following day, she found that all fluids had been discontinued on Mr. Herbert. Six days later, September 6, 1981, Mr. Herbert died. The preliminary autopsy report listed anoxia and dehydration as two of the causes of death. During subsequent weeks, Mrs. Bardenilla attempted to obtain written hospital guidelines defining "heroic" and "supportive" care as well as criteria for deciding how much care a patient should get and who should make that decision. She asked for the guidelines that provided for peer review of the care given in the ICU. Her efforts were rewarded by a sharp warning from the director of nursing. She was advised to adopt a more realistic attitude about the hospital system, and she was warned against taking her concerns outside the hospital. Several days later, Mrs. Bardenilla met with the chief of staff, who then promised to take her requests to the medical executive meeting. Several weeks later, Mrs. Bardenilla learned that her requests were never mentioned at the meeting and that no action had been taken to discuss or implement the guidelines she sought.

By this time, Mrs. Bardenilla was thoroughly demoralized. She was undecided as to whether she ought to go "outside" to find anyone willing to investigate and evaluate the care and treatment that Mr. Herbert had received. Also, what impact would going "outside" have on her employment and her family? Her indecision ended, however, when she learned that two other patients had been removed from life-support systems under conditions as unclear as Mr. Herbert's. On September 23, she resigned her position at Kaiser Foundation Hospital. On September 25, Mrs. Bardenilla called the county health department and made a formal complaint about the management of Mr. Herbert's care.

After a year of investigation by the health department, police department, and Los Angeles district attorney's office, Dr. Barber and another physician, were charged with murder and conspiracy to commit murder. Following 6 weeks of testimony, Municipal

Court Judge B. D. Crahan decided there was no evidence that Drs. Barber and Nejdl had acted in a "malicious, selfish, or foolhardy manner" in treating Mr. Herbert. The case was dropped without a trial. On appeal by the district attorney's office, Judge Crahan's decision was reversed and the original charges against Drs. Barber and Nedjl were reinstated. In the meantime, Clarence Herbert's widow filed a malpractice suit against the two doctors and the hospital. She claimed that she had been told by the doctors that her husband was brain dead; she would not have authorized the removal of life-support systems if she had known he was not brain dead.

Sandy Bardenilla eventually moved from California and continues to work in nursing. She still has questions about the care Mr. Herbert received and what a nurse realistically can do, without institutional support, when following a doctor's orders goes against her or his conscience.

Commentary

The decision to remove the ventilator and then the IV from Mr. Herbert raises all of the issues that emerged in Case 10-8, plus many others. It is clouded by the clear tensions between Mrs. Bardenilla, the director of nursing, and the physician chief of staff. It is complicated by the absence of any clear sign of the patient's wishes. The problems of guardian decision making will be addressed more fully in the cases in Chapter 16. The issue raised here, however, is whether there is any acceptable reason—beyond the patient's clearly expressed wishes—to remove such basic treatments as ventilators, IVs, and nasogastric tubes.

A similar court case involving a woman being maintained on a nasogastric tube led a New Jersey court to hold that such interventions could be removed under three conditions.[36]

1. It is clear the patient would have refused.
2. There is some indication that the patient would have refused, and continuing would only prolong suffering.
3. The burdens of continuing clearly and markedly outweigh the benefits.

It is not clear that Mr. Herbert would meet any of these conditions. He never expressed himself explicitly on withdrawing hydration. Even if it could be deduced that those would be his wishes, he is not suffering because he is in a coma. Finally, because he is comatose, it is not clear that the burdens of the treatments clearly and markedly outweigh the benefits.

Of course, the fact that these are the conditions under which one court says that it is legal to remove such treatments does not necessarily resolve the complex ethical questions at stake. Several religious and philosophic commentators, for example, approach these issues applying exactly the same reasoning as for any other medical treatments; those treatments that are useless or gravely burdensome are expendable, whereas those where the benefits exceed the burdens are required.

Regardless of these legal and ethical complexities, Mrs. Bardenilla had strong objections to the decisions that were made. What other options were open to her under the circumstances? How do you assess the course she finally took?

ENDNOTES

1. Beauchamp, T. L. (1979). A reply to Rachels on active and passive euthanasia. In W. L. Robison & M. S. Pritchard (Eds.), *Medical responsibility: Paternalism, informed consent, and euthanasia* (pp. 181–194). Clifton, NJ: The Humana Press.
2. U.S. Department of Health and Human Services. (1985, April 15). Child abuse and neglect prevention and treatment program. Final Rule: 45 CFR 1340. *Federal Register: Rules and Regulations, 50*(72), 14878–14892.
3. Beller, F. K., & Reeve, J. (1989). Brain life and brain death—The anencephalic as an explanatory example. A contribution to transplantation. *Journal of Medicine and Philosophy, 14*(1), 5–23; Sass, H. M. (1989). Brain life and brain death: A proposal for normative agreement. *Journal of Medicine and Philosophy, 14*(1), 45–59.
4. Detailed information is available at: http://www.nytimes.com/2009/08/30 /magazine/30doctors.html?_r=1&pagewanted=2. Accessed May 6, 2010.
5. Fletcher, G. P. (1967). Prolonging life. *Washington Law Review, 42,* 999–1016.
6. Beauchamp, T. L. (1979). A reply to Rachels on active and passive euthanasia. In W. L. Robison & M. S. Pritchard (Eds.), *Medical responsibility: Paternalism, informed consent, and euthanasia* (pp. 181–194). Clifton, NJ: The Humana Press; Beauchamp, T. L. (1996). *Intending death: The ethics of assisted suicide and euthanasia.* Upper Saddle River, NJ: Prentice Hall; Menzel, P. J. (1979). Are killing and letting die morally different in medical contexts? *Journal of Medicine and Philosophy, 4,* 269–293; Rachels, J. (1975). Active and passive euthanasia. *New England Journal of Medicine, 292,* 78–80; Thomson, J. J. (1976). Killing, letting die and the trolley problem. *The Monist, 59,* 204–217.
7. President's Commission for the Study of Ethical Problems in Medicine and Biomedical and Behavioral Research. (1983). *Deciding to forego life-sustaining treatment: Ethical, medical, and legal issues in treatment decisions* (p. 84). Washington, DC: U.S. Government Printing Office.
8. Pope Pius XII. (1958). The prolongation of life: An address of Pope Pius XII to an international congress of anesthesiologists. *The Pope Speaks, 4,* 393–398; Vatican Congregation for the Doctrine of the Faith. (May 5, 1980). *Declaration on euthanasia.* Rome, Italy: Vatican Congregation for the Doctrine of the Faith.
9. President's Commission for the Study of Ethical Problems in Medicine and Biomedical and Behavioral Research. (1983). *Deciding to forego life-sustaining treatment: Ethical, medical, and legal issues in treatment decisions* (pp. 84–87). Washington, DC: U.S. Government Printing Office.
10. President's Commission for the Study of Ethical Problems in Medicine and Biomedical and Behavioral Research. (1983). *Deciding to forego life-sustaining treatment: Ethical, medical, and legal issues in treatment decisions* (p. 77). Washington, DC: U.S. Government Printing Office.
11. Ramsey, P., & McCormick, R. A. (Eds.). (1978). *Doing evil to achieve good: Moral choice in conflict situations.* Chicago: Loyola University Press; Vatican Congregation for the Doctrine of the Faith. (1980, May 5). *Declaration on euthanasia.* Available

at: http://www.vatican.va/roman_curia/congregations/cfaith/documents/rc_con _cfaith_doc_19800505_euthanasia_en.html. Accessed May 6, 2010.

12. Foot, P. (1967). The problem of abortion and the doctrine of the double effect. *Oxford Review, 5,* 5–15; Graber, G. C. (1979). Some questions about double effect. *Ethics in Science and Medicine, 6*(1), 65–84.

13. McCormick, R. A. (1978). Ambiguity in moral choice. In R. A. McCormick & P. Ramsey (Eds.), *Doing evil to achieve good: Moral choice in conflict situations* (p. 7). Chicago: Loyola University Press.

14. See, for example, Agency for Health Care Policy and Research [AHCPR]. (1994). *Management of cancer pain.* Clinical Practice Guideline Number 9. Publication no. 94-0592; also, Foley, K. M. (1993). Changing concepts of tolerance to opioids: What the cancer patient has taught us. In D. R. Chapman and K. M. Foley (Eds.), *Current and emerging issues in cancer pain: Research and practice* (pp. 331–350). New York: Raven Press.

15. American Nurses Association. (2001). *Code of ethics for nurses with interpretive statements* (p. 8). Washington, DC: Author.

16. American Nurses Association. (1991). *Position statement: Promotion of comfort and relief of pain in dying patients.* Washington, DC: Author.

17. van der Maas, P. J., van der Wal, G., Haverkate, I., de Graaff, C. L. M., Kester, J. G. C., Philipsen, O., et al. (1996). Euthanasia, physician-assisted suicide, and other medical practices involving the end of life in the Netherlands, 1990–1995. *New England Journal of Medicine, 335*(22), 1699–1705.

18. Anon. Eutha Law. Actesparlementaries du Sénat de Belgigue 2001–2002, Bruxelles, 2002, number 2-244/26; Review procedures of termination of life on request and assisted suicide and amendment to the Penal Code and the Burial and Cremation Act. Senate session 2000–2002, 26 691, number 137 [Netherlands Euthanasia Law]

19. Kevorkian, J. (1991). *Prescription medicide: The goodness of planned death.* Buffalo, NY: Prometheus Books.

20. Johnson, D. (1999, April 14). Kevorkian sentenced to 10–25 years in prison. *The New York Times,* p. A1.

21. Quill, T. (1993). *Death and dignity: Making choices and taking charge.* New York: Norton.

22. The Oregon Death with Dignity Act. (1996). In T. L. Beauchamp & R. M. Veatch (Eds.), *Ethical issues in death and dying* (2nd ed., pp. 199–206). Upper Saddle River, NJ: Prentice Hall.

23. Oregon Department of Human Services. (2004, March 10). *Sixth annual report on Oregon's Death with Dignity Act* (p. 5). Available at: http://egov.oregon.gov/DHS /ph/pas/docs/year6.pdf. Accessed May 6, 2010.

24. American Nurses Association. (1994, December 8). *Position statement on assisted suicide.* Available at: http://www.nursingworld.org/MainMenuCategories /HealthcareandPolicyIssues/ANAPositionStatements/EthicsandHumanRights. aspx. Accessed January 5, 2010.

25. Hume, D. (1777). *On suicide.* Edinburgh, Scotland. See also Brandt, R. (1975). The morality and rationality of suicide. In S. Perlin (Ed.), *A handbook for the study of suicide* (pp. 61–75). New York: Oxford University Press.

26. Szasz, T. (1971). The ethics of suicide. *The Antioch Review, 31,* 7–17.

27. The Dominican Fathers of the English Province (Trans.), T. Gilbey (Ed.). (1966). Thomas Aquinas, *Summa theologica* I–II (Q. 91, Art. 2, Vol. 28, pp. 21–24). Cambridge, UK: Blackfriars.

28. Feinberg, J. (1978). Voluntary euthanasia and the unalienable right to life. *Philosophy and Public Affairs, 7,* 93–123.

29. Lynn, J. (1986). *By no extraordinary means: The choice to forgo life-sustaining food and water: Medical, ethical, and legal considerations.* Bloomington, IN: Indiana University Press; Lynn, L., & Childress, J. F. (1983). Must patients always be given food and water? *The Hastings Center Report, 13,* 17–21; Micetich, K., Steinecker, P., & Thomasma, D. (1983). Are intravenous fluids morally required for a dying patient? *Archives of Internal Medicine, 143,* 975–978; Paris, J. J., & Fletcher, A. B. (1983). Infant Doe regulations and the absolute requirement to use nourishment and fluids for the dying infant. *Law, Medicine and Health Care, 11*(5), 210–213; Paris, J. J., & Fletcher, A. B. (1983). Infant Doe regulations and the absolute requirement to use nourishment and fluids for the dying infant. *Law, Medicine and Health Care, 11*(5), 210–213.

30. Court of Appeal of the State of California, Second Appellate District, Division Two. Neil Barber and Robert Nejdl v. Superior Court of the State of California for the County of Los Angeles. October 12, 1983; Cruzan, by Cruzan v. Harmon, 760 S.W.2d 408 (Mo.banc 1988); Cruzan v. Director, Missouri Department of Health, 110 S.Ct. 2841 (1990); In Re Plaza Health and Rehabilitation Center, Sup. Ct., Onodaga County, New York, Feb. 2, 1984. In the Matter of Claire C. Conroy, Syllabus, Prepared by the Office of the Clerk, Supreme Court of New Jersey, A-108, September Term 1983; In the Matter of Mary Hier, 464 N.E.2d Series 959, Mass. App. 1984.

31. American Nurses Association. (1992). *Position statement: Forgoing nutrition and hydration.* Washington, DC: Author; See also American Nurses Association. (2001). *Code of ethics for nurses with interpretive statements* (provision 1.3). Washington, DC: Author.

32. U.S. Department of Health and Human Services. (1985, April 15). Child abuse and neglect prevention and treatment program: Final Rule: 45 CFR 1340. *Federal Register: Rules and Regulations, 50*(72), 14878–14892.

33. Meilaender, G. (1984). On removing food and water: Against the stream. *The Hastings Center Report, 14*(6), 11–13.

34. Callahan, D. (1983). On feeding the dying. *The Hastings Center Report, 13*(5), 22.

35. May, W. E. (1987). Feeding and hydrating the permanently unconscious and other vulnerable persons. *Issues in Law and Medicine, 3*(3), 203–217.

36. In Re Conroy, No. A-108 (NJ Sup. Ct. Jan. 17, 1985).

PART III

Special Problem Areas in Nursing Practice

The cases in Part I dealt with problems of identifying ethical and other values and how to adjudicate ethical disputes in nursing practice, including reflection on the role of professional codes in ethical decision making. Those in Part II provided a framework of general ethical principles that can be applied to a wide range of dilemmas faced in nursing. There still remain some specific problem areas to which these general principles can be applied. The nurse readily recognizes certain issues that are likely to pose particularly difficult ethical conflicts—abortion, sterilization, contraception, genetics, HIV/AIDS care, psychiatric care, human experimentation, consent, and death and dying decisions. The cases in Part III present these issues and give an opportunity to apply the general principles to some of the most critical ethical conflicts the nurse faces in day-to-day practice. The boxes at the beginning of each chapter point to other cases elsewhere in the book that are relevant to these problem areas.

Chapter 11

Abortion, Contraception, and Sterilization

Other Cases Involving Abortion, Contraception, and Sterilization

Key Terms
Abortion
Contraception
Implantation
Moral standing
Sterilization
Viability

Objectives
1. Identify three arguments for moral standing in the community.
2. Defend a moral position on abortion.
3. Identify the ethical role of the nurse in discussing contraceptive use with the patient.
4. Describe the ethical issues relevant to sterilizing incompetent individuals.

One of the classical areas in healthcare ethics deals with issues concerning abortion, contraception, and sterilization. Whereas for some people, some of the decisions surrounding these issues are not as difficult as they once were, many important decisions remain for the nurse.

A woman's legal right to decide in favor of an abortion has not resolved many of the ethical issues surrounding the procedure. Every woman is now legally free to obtain an abortion, but the ability to exercise this freedom does not necessarily render abortion ethically acceptable. That is, the legal right does not necessarily imply the moral right. Even for those who decide that abortion is, in principle, acceptable in certain circumstances, the ethical decision must still be made as to which circumstances those are. In addition, a nurse, if she is to be a responsible moral agent, must also decide what her role in abortion procedures ought to be. Even if a patient decides in favor of an abortion, it remains an open question whether healthcare personnel will and should choose to participate.

Cases 11-1, 11-2, and 11-3 present ethical conflicts involving specific problematic abortion decisions: cultural and religious differences regarding abortion, the woman's right to make the decision on her own, the unmarried teenager, and abortion because the fetus is not the sex the parents wanted.

Cases 11-4 and 11-5 involve contraception. Again, many newer, more subtle issues have emerged recently.

The final section of the chapter involves the related ethical issue of sterilization. Although, like abortion, sterilization is not as controversial as it once was, many ethical conflicts remain, even for nurses who do not object, in principle, to the procedure. Serious issues of consent arise when a nurse believes a young patient has been sterilized without the patient or her parents being informed.

Abortion

On January 22, 1973, the U.S. Supreme Court issued a ruling that, in effect, legalized most *abortions*.[1] Although the ruling resolved many legal controversies (at least for the time being), it did not solve the ethical dilemmas faced by many women and many healthcare professionals who still had to make critical choices about whether to interrupt pregnancies.

Abortion is a difficult moral issue, in part because the abortion decision rests on the moral status of the fetus, a question that is not easily resolved by appeals to ethical principles of the sort introduced in previous chapters. For example, the principle of avoiding killing seems clear enough in its implications, but at some point the applicability of the principle needs to be specified. Does it cover animals or only humans? Does it apply to all humans or only those who possess what could be called *moral standing*? Most critically, does it apply to prenatal humans?

The notion of moral standing conveys who it is who has moral claims on the rest of the community. Several positions are argued in the philosophic and religious literature.[2] Some people argue that the fact that living tissue is endowed with human genetic material is enough to make it the bearer of the rights that normally accrue to humans. Holders of such positions normally exclude human egg and sperm cells before conception, but they argue that with the combining of the genetic material of the two parents, a new life is created that bears full moral standing.[3] This position, sometimes referred to as the "biologic" or "genetic" position, is based on what appears to be a biologic fact: That a new individual with a new and fixed genetic endowment begins at conception.

Others disagree with this position because they disagree with the scientific claim on which it is based. Some biologists have pointed out that the genetic code is not always unchangeably fixed at conception. When twinning occurs, some switching of genetic material might take place. These critics imply that the critical point at which moral standing accrues is more like the second week after conception, the last time at which twinning can take place.[4] Although they adopt the genetic position, they simply disagree over when the genetic code is unchangeable.

Some individuals disagree on a more fundamental basis. They question whether the issue of moral standing can be determined solely on a biologic, especially genetic, basis. There are many other events in fetal and postnatal development that might be seen as significant, including any of the following:

- Implantation
- Pumping of the heart
- Development of neurological activity of brain cells
- Spontaneous movement
- "Quickening"
- Development of circulatory system function
- Development of integrated neurological activity
- Viability
- Development of the capacity for consciousness
- Birth
- Breathing of air
- Development of speech
- Development of capacity for rational thinking
- Acceptance by others

This is a long and complicated list. More controversial capacities could also be named. Some people might argue that certain social and cultural events are necessary for moral standing. Holders of these positions, sometimes referred to as "social" positions, claim that capacities for speech and rationality, as well as events involving the responses of other parties (e.g., the perception of movement by the pregnant woman) and acceptance by others, are required for moral standing.[5]

In addition to those who identify one biologic, social, or cultural event as definitive for moral standing, a third group of individuals, called "incrementalists," hold that many of these events are important and that the fetus gains more and more of a moral claim on others as it develops. This position requires a much more rigorous justification for the abortion of a fetus at 18 weeks than it does at 5 or 6 weeks because more of the purportedly critical events have taken place, giving the fetus more of a claim. Most people, whether they are incrementalists or committed to either the genetic or social position, hold that at some point "full standing of personhood" accrues. At that point, the organism with human genetic endowment has full moral claims, including all of those based on the principles discussed in Part II.

The nurse encounters many moral questions pertaining to abortion. In addition to facing them as a lay person making personal and public policy choices, he or she must face them as a clinical professional. For some nurses, all abortion is morally unacceptable, no matter what the reason. Presumably, a nurse with this belief would face a serious ethical conflict if asked to participate in performing an abortion. But for others, those who are open to at least some abortions, difficult choices may have to be made on a case-by-case basis.

Critical Thinking Question

The Freedom of Choice Act (which was introduced into Congress but never enacted) declares that it is the policy of the United States that every woman has the fundamental right to choose to: (1) bear a child; (2) terminate a pregnancy prior to fetal *viability*; or (3) terminate a pregnancy after fetal viability when necessary to protect her life or her health. It prohibits a federal, state, or local governmental entity from: (1) denying or interfering with a woman's right to exercise such choices; or (2) discriminating against the exercise of those rights in the regulation or provision of benefits, facilities, services, or information. Many claims have been made about the consequences of this or similar legislation and among them is the concern that physicians and nurses would be obligated to, at the very least, provide abortion counseling and referrals to women wanting such.[1] How do you think a country should address conflicts between respecting a woman's reproductive freedoms and the conscience protections of healthcare professionals?

---

[1]For more information on FOCA see the FactCheck website: http://www.factcheck.org/2009/02/freedom-of-choice-act/

The nurse who is prepared to assess the reasons for abortion will face several types of abortions that may be problematic. The "hard case" abortions include those performed for the health of the pregnant woman and in the cases of rape, incest, and fetal deformity, as well as those where the woman simply does not want to carry a child for social or economic reasons. Abortions being considered by adolescents and others whose capacity to make well-thought-out choices is questionable are also controversial. Abortions for the health of the pregnant woman are not often performed. The other indications are all likely to be faced by any nurse working in a hospital or clinic performing abortions. Cases 11-1 and 11-2 raise problems of possible fetal deformity and pregnancy in an adolescent. Case 11-3 involves what some would consider an abortion for trivial reasons.

Case 11-1
When Cultural Differences Limit the Patient's Choice

Nao Vang Xiong, his wife Sheng, and their two small children, ages 1 and 2, were Southeast Asian refugees. Their resettlement in the United States was being sponsored by an agency of the Catholic Church. After settling into their new community, the Xiongs visited the county health department for individual health evaluations. To their dismay, chest x-rays and other tests revealed that Mrs. Xiong had active tuberculosis. The clinic nurse, Miss Jane Murphy, explained with the help of an interpreter that Mrs. Xiong must take medications for an extended period of time and should have lots of rest and nutritious food. She was placed on antituberculosis medications, referred to a home care agency, and scheduled for follow-up clinic visits.

At a repeat visit to the clinic 3 months later, it was determined that Mrs. Xiong was approximately 10 weeks pregnant. Because of the high risk of fetal abnormality from taking the antituberculosis drugs during the first trimester of pregnancy, the clinic physician suggested that Mrs. Xiong consider an abortion. As Buddhists, she and her husband were not opposed to abortion. Arrangements for the procedure were made easily through the health department and the county hospital. The matter seemed settled.

To Miss Murphy's surprise, the Xiongs and Mr. James Walsh, a representative of the church-sponsored agency, visited the clinic the very next day. The Xiongs appeared very upset and said, through the interpreter, that they had changed their minds about the abortion. When Miss Murphy asked why they had changed their minds, Mr. Walsh pointed out that it was directly contrary to the sponsoring agency's religious viewpoint for Mrs. Xiong to have an abortion. He adamantly objected to the clinic's recommendation in this regard, given that her life was not directly threatened by the pregnancy. Through the interpreter, Miss Murphy also learned that Mrs. Xiong was under the impression that she and her family would lose the agency's support if she had the abortion. Although Miss Murphy tried to reassure Mrs. Xiong and her husband that she had the right to make this decision regardless of the sponsoring agency's position, Mrs. Xiong was not convinced. The young family was completely dependent on the sponsoring agency and very fearful of what might happen to them without this support.

Miss Murphy explained to Mr. Walsh the reasons that abortion was suggested in this case and supported Mrs. Xiong's right to make this choice without influence from the sponsoring agency. Mr. Walsh, however, insisted that abortion was morally unacceptable to the sponsoring agency. Because the agency's representatives were supporting the Xiongs, they could not permit them to make such a choice. He stated that he and his agency would arrange other healthcare follow-up for Mrs. Xiong and her family if the health department continued to suggest that Mrs. Xiong have an abortion.

At this point, Miss Murphy was not sure what she should do. She could decide that the Xiongs' lack of proficiency in English and limited understanding of Mrs. Xiong's right to choose abortion were cultural problems beyond her expertise or intervention. On the other hand, she could decide to be an advocate for the patient by communicating with the International Refugee Service and requesting another sponsor for the Xiong family. This intervention could take many weeks, however, and Mrs. Xiong would be well into the second trimester of pregnancy before the abortion could be performed. Because Mrs. Xiong's general physical condition was weakened by her tuberculosis, Miss Murphy wondered if this choice of action would, in the long run, be in her patient's best interests.

Case 11-2
The Unmarried Teenager and Abortion

Mrs. Miriam Dwyer, a family planning nurse at the county health department, was reviewing the health records of patients seen for birth control counseling or pregnancy tests during the morning's clinic. With surprise, she noted that Karen Ferguson, the 16-year-old daughter of a long-time friend and neighbor, had visited the clinic for a pregnancy test. The test was positive and, from personal history and physical findings, Karen was judged to be 10 to 12 weeks pregnant.

The clinic record noted that Karen had specifically asked about available abortion services. It also noted that her parents did not know she was pregnant. In discussing with Karen all the options open to her, the clinic nurse had advised that any decision for abortion would need to be made within 1 to 2 weeks because her stage of pregnancy was at the upper limits of acceptable risk for elective abortions. Although parental notification was not required in this state for first trimester abortions requested by minors, most abortion services would not perform a late abortion on someone of Karen's age without it. Before she left the clinic, Karen was given the names, addresses, and costs of abortion services available throughout the state.

Mrs. Dwyer was faced with a dilemma. As a parent of teenage children, she was horrified that Karen must face this kind of choice at her age. Her concern took several forms: first, the physical hazards of an abortion this late in pregnancy; second, the moral and psychologic hazards or potential sense of guilt that could harm Karen emotionally; and third, the fact that 16-year-old Karen—a minor—could make this decision, which involved considerable risk, without parental knowledge. As a friend of Karen's parents for more than 15 years, she felt they should know about Karen's pregnancy. They were understanding parents and were, in Mrs. Dwyer's view, in the best position to counsel and support Karen in her decision. As a family planning nurse, however, she knew that Karen had the legal right to make this decision herself and that, generally, such information should be kept confidential. She struggled with the problem for several days and was still uncertain what she should do.

Case 11-3
When the Fetus Is the Wrong Sex

Elena Hanchett is the nurse manager of a busy obstetric unit in a well-known eastern medical center. Today, she is providing direct nursing care to a newly admitted patient, 37-year-old Mrs. Ostrum. The patient is being admitted for an elective abortion, and two other nurses in the unit have asked not to be assigned to this patient. Their reasons stem from the fact that Mrs. Ostrum and her husband have decided to abort her fetus because the fetus is not the sex that they want. The nurses feel that it is wrong for people like the Ostrums, who can afford children and are economically stable, to abort a fetus solely on the basis of sex, especially when other patients undergo difficult fertility drug treatments and attempt desperately to become pregnant at great personal cost and marital stress. Ms. Hanchett seems to be the only nurse in the unit who does not have any particular feelings about Mrs. Ostrum's elective abortion. Thus, she thinks that she should be the primary nurse for Mrs. Ostrum.

While completing the admission assessment and prepping her patient, Ms. Hanchett learns more about the Ostrums's choice to discontinue this pregnancy. The Ostrums have three girls, 3, 5, and 9 years of age. They would like to have one more child if they could be assured it was a boy. Because of her age, Mrs. Ostrum does not feel that she wants to have any more pregnancies after this one.

A week ago, Mrs. Ostrum underwent chorionic villus testing, which revealed that the sex of her fetus is female. Deeply disappointed, the Ostrums decided not to continue the pregnancy. They both would rather interrupt the pregnancy at an early stage and try again in a few months. Even though they are distressed by the thought of aborting the fetus, they simply do not want another female child.

Although she does not usually question the reasons her patients choose abortion, Ms. Hanchett is becoming uncertain whether this particular choice is morally right. Is it right not to continue a willingly initiated pregnancy simply because of the sex of the fetus? Would it make any difference in the nursing care she provided if the abortion choice was morally wrong? Ms. Hanchett is not sure.

Commentary

These three cases involve tragically difficult choices, but they are tragic for quite different reasons. Mrs. Xiong's pregnancy, described in Case 11-1, apparently, was originally desired. Thus, the substantive question is whether a pregnancy to which the prospective parents would otherwise be committed may be aborted because the fetus might be injured as a result of the effect of the drugs taken during early pregnancy.

One line of argument in the abortion debate holds that in order for a woman to be obligated to carry a fetus to term, she must have made some commitment to the pregnancy, or at least the risk of pregnancy.[6] This suggests that a woman who is pregnant, as the result of a rape, for example, would have no definitive obligation to the fetus even if abortion is otherwise a serious infringement— even if the fetus has what is sometimes called a "right to life." In such a circumstance, if the fetus could be saved without imposing on the mother, then perhaps society would have a responsibility to save it. That, however, is impossible, and according to this line of argument, the woman would have no obligation to contribute against her will to bringing the fetus to term.

Conceivably, the same argument could be used for an adolescent (such as Karen Ferguson in Case 11-2), a mentally retarded woman, or anyone else who had no real understanding of the risk of pregnancy. One moral factor in the abortion debate is whether the consent of the woman to the risk of pregnancy is relevant.

In Mrs. Xiong's case, however, this would not be the basis for accepting the patient's decision to abort. She apparently accepted the idea of pregnancy. Although she did not accept the notion of carrying a possibly deformed fetus, she at least accepted the pregnancy. Then the question becomes whether the fact that the fetus may be deformed would justify her decision to abort.

Of course, for those who accept a very late event in fetal (or even postnatal) development as the basis for giving moral standing, this would not be an issue. Even a fetus that is definitely healthy could be aborted. Any reason would do. For those adopting the genetic position, the fact that there is an injury would hardly justify killing the fetus (any more than it would justify killing a postnatal human who is handicapped). Of those who are incrementalists, however, some consider the risk of fetal deformity to be enough of a consideration to tip the balance. Is it the burden to the potential parents that justifies this reasoning? If so, would the abortion be less justified when competent institutional caregivers were available to accept the deformed child or when other adults were standing by willing to adopt the handicapped child? On the other hand, is it presumed trauma to the fetus that justifies the abortion? In that case, an assessment of the likelihood of injury and suffering would be required. Abortion in this circumstance would involve the risk of aborting a normal, healthy infant. Does that make a decision for abortion less acceptable?

Miss Murphy, the nurse in this situation, faces two questions. First, is she willing to participate in abortions for these reasons? Presumably if she opposed all abortion, she could and should refuse assignment to any patient care involving abortion or at least seek reassignment, so she would not have to participate. She might decide—if she is more of an incrementalist on abortion—that she can participate in certain abortions, but not others. Then she would have to seek selective exemption from nursing services where abortion was considered.

Second, she has the unique problem in this case of what her role should be in responding to the pressure that Mr. Walsh is exerting on Mrs. Xiong and her husband. If we accept the right of Mr. Walsh and his agency to adopt a moral position opposing all abortions, including those for fetal deformity, should they not also have the right to extend aid only to persons who are willing to follow such a policy judgment?

Critical Thinking Questions

What are Miss Murphy's options?

1. Should she try to help the Xiongs find alternative sponsorship? Does a nurse's obligation extend that far?

2. Should she ask the hospital to assume the immediate medical costs with the hope of finding another sponsor in the future or persuading the existing sponsor to continue support?

3. Should she turn to a patient care ethics committee for assistance?

4. Should she propose to the obstetrician that they (misleadingly) announce that Mrs. Xiong's health required the abortion? Should they rationalize such an announcement as truthful on the grounds that she would be upset if she delivered a deformed infant and so her health (i.e., her mental health) required the abortion?

5. What other options might Miss Murphy consider? Or should she simply stay out of the situation altogether?

Miriam Dwyer (the family planning nurse in Case 11-2 who discovered that her teenage neighbor, Karen Ferguson, received pregnancy and abortion counseling in her clinic) faces similar questions. She would first have to face the substantive question: Is abortion in these circumstances acceptable? If so, it would not be because of the compromised condition of the fetus. One could argue that it would be acceptable either because Karen Ferguson really did not consent to the pregnancy or because, even if she did, she has the right to abort. If abortion is acceptable only because she did not consent to the pregnancy, it implies that Mrs. Dwyer is committed to the position that for other women who did consent to their pregnancies, abortion would not be morally appropriate.

On the other hand, if her position is that essentially autonomous women have the right to abort in such circumstances, another set of problems emerges. If Mrs. Dwyer believes that the moral claims of the fetus can be compromised for good reason (or the claims do not exist at all), then she would be willing to accept abortions chosen by women who are reasonably capable of making such choices autonomously. The problem then is whether Karen Ferguson is in such a position. It cannot be denied that some 16-year-olds are capable of making autonomous choices even in complex situations involving long-term implications. On the other hand, it is not clear that all females capable of becoming pregnant are capable of making such decisions. As a society, we have made a policy judgment that adolescents under a certain age (usually 18 years) are presumed to be incapable of rational, autonomous actions. Although in individual cases minors may be capable of such actions, they may have to go to court to establish their competence. They are referred to in the legal literature as "mature minors."[7]

For certain medical interventions, however, state laws permit minors to agree to treatment without parental involvement. Treatment of venereal disease and contraceptive and abortion services are sometimes included in such laws. The state may take the position that adolescents are mature, competent persons in these areas whereas they are incompetent in other areas. The more likely explanation of these laws, however, is that adults (including parents) believe that the interests of their minors are better served if they get treatment without parental supervision than if parental permission is required. In these areas of treatment, requiring parental permission might deter many adolescents from getting any treatment. If that is the basis for the laws in this area, then it is a special case by which minors can be treated without real consent (that is, consent based on substantially autonomous, informed decisions). Although this argument continues to be accepted and applied to matters of treatment of venereal disease and contraception, it is increasingly controversial when applied to abortion. Some states now have adopted laws requiring parental consent for abortions for minors, and others have required notifying a parent even if parental consent is not required. Some jurisdictions, however, continue to permit minors to obtain abortions without parental involvement.[8]

Is that what is happening here? If so, how should Mrs. Dwyer respond if she remains convinced that, in this case, Karen Ferguson would be better off if her parents were involved? If the nurse is committed to doing what she thinks will benefit the patient, she might well inform the parents. If, however, she believes that minors are permitted to have access to abortion and other treatments because they are capable of making autonomous choices and, furthermore, she believes that autonomy is a principle that takes priority, she will refrain from informing the parents. She might want to speak with Karen to see if she could be persuaded to involve her parents, but she would not infringe on her autonomy to choose abortion without consulting her parents. If she believes that Karen cannot be presumed to be autonomous but that the law is written because it will generally do more good for minors than any other rule, then she has to face the question of whether she feels obliged to follow such rules. If she does, once again, she may try to persuade Karen to involve her parents, but she will not violate the rule simply because she believes that, in this case, it would be better for Karen if she did.

Similar analysis is appropriate for the dilemma faced by Elena Hanchett, the nurse in Case 11-3 who is confronted with the couple who want to abort because they have learned that their fetus is a girl. It is now possible, with great accuracy, to determine the sex of the unborn child using sophisticated prenatal diagnostic techniques.[9] The evidence is clear that many people have preference for a child of a particular sex, especially when, as in the case of Mr. and Mrs. Ostrum, they already have several children who are all of the same sex.[10] Is it acceptable, however, to ask health professionals to use their skills to bring this about by aborting an otherwise perfectly healthy fetus simply because it is not the preferred sex?[11]

For those who grant full moral standing to fetuses at all stages of development, there is hardly any question. Likewise, for those who give no standing at all to unborn children, there is hardly a moral issue. A nurse such as Ms. Hanchett might have reservations because she is diverting her attention from other patients, but she would not likely question the ethics of the abortion per se.

If Ms. Hanchett adopts a more incrementalist position, however, in which the fetus's claims are justifiably compared with other moral claims based on the stage of development of the fetus, then her decision is a more complex one. For one thing, by the time the abortion is performed (at 10 to 12 weeks), the fetus would be fairly far along in development. For an incrementalist, that would suggest that a fairly strong argument would be needed to offset any claim of the fetus. The undesirability of the fetus's sex is not normally considered to be a very strong consideration. Is it appropriate for Ms. Hanchett to be an incrementalist about this?

Critical Thinking Questions

1. If Ms. Hanchett were an incrementalist, would the stage of fetal development, together with the relative weakness of the reason for the abortion, lead Ms. Hanchett to oppose the abortion? If so, would determination of fetal sex at an earlier time make it easier for her to participate?

2. Can you think of circumstances in which fetal sex determination has greater moral acceptability than in the case involving the Ostrums? How about when the fetus is at risk for carrying a sex-linked genetic disease?

Research Brief 11-1

Source: Marek, M. J. (2004). Nurses' attitudes toward pregnancy termination in the labor and delivery setting. *Journal of Obstetric, Gynecologic, & Neonatal Nursing, 33*(4), 472–479.

Purpose: To examine nurses' attitudes toward pregnancy termination in the labor and delivery settings and to determine the frequency of nurse refusal to care for patients undergoing pregnancy termination.

Method: This was a descriptive study using a survey design. The questionnaire was mailed to 75 labor and delivery registered nurses working at six central and northern California hospitals, including Level 1, 2, and 3 facilities.

Findings: Of the nurses, 95% indicated they would agree to care for patients terminating a pregnancy because of fetal demise. There were 77% would care for patients terminating a fetus with anomalies that were incompatible with life. And 37% would care for patients terminating for serious but nonlethal anomalies, with a significant drop in agreement as gestation advanced. Few nurses would agree to care for patients undergoing termination for sex selection, selective reduction of a pregnancy, or personal reasons. Nurses who accepted and refused some patient care assignments were criticized by coworkers.

Implications: Clear guidelines should be established in advance on how to handle nurse refusal to care for patients terminating pregnancies. Open discussions should be encouraged between staff and management to minimize criticism of nurses who accept or refuse patient assignments.

Contraception

Closely linked to the ethics of abortion is the ethics of **contraception**. Some of the same issues of sexual morality are raised, including the moral legitimacy of manipulation of the procreative process. In contrast to abortion, however, contraception does not usually raise the issue of conflict between two entities (i.e., the pregnant woman and her fetus) with potential or actual moral standing.

Two basic moral arguments against contraception have existed historically. The classical argument, especially within the tradition of Roman Catholic moral theology, is that contraception is morally unacceptable because it artificially interrupts the natural process of conception. Those reasoning from natural law considerations hold that there are natural ends of bodily processes that cannot be disrupted without moral impunity.[12]

A second argument against contraception is that the toleration of contraception will encourage illicit sexual activity. Some people who do not find the first argument convincing nevertheless oppose contraception, especially for unmarried people, because they find that condoning contraception implies condoning unacceptable sexual contact. Case 11-4 suggests both of these themes. Case 11-5, however, questions whether these arguments against contraception can and should be overridden to protect others from harm.

Case 11-4
The Nurse as Contraceptive Salesperson

Rosetta Meeks had visited the abortion clinic for her fourth abortion. She was 18 years old, had dropped out of school, and was unmarried. To Donna Tallson, the clinic nurse, Rosetta Meeks was a walking set of paradoxes. She was a devout Catholic. She argued vociferously about the immorality of contraceptives, yet she clearly made moral compromises with her church's teachings with regard to both premarital sexual activity and abortion.

Rosetta would not listen to any suggestion that oral contraceptives would be better than abortion. She said she did not believe in birth control and would use abortion only as a last resort.

Ms. Tallson considered two approaches. She could initiate a direct moral argument with the patient and try to convince her that oral contraceptives are morally acceptable, in fact morally obligatory, if Rosetta were to remain sexually active. Ms. Tallson knew that such a confrontation far exceeded the traditional role of the nurse. She also knew that some people considered contraception ethically unacceptable because of their religious beliefs and that, as a nurse, she should respect those beliefs and not try to override them. Nothing in her education really prepared her to be a moral advisor.

Another approach would be to support Rosetta through the abortion and not pressure her to consider some form of contraception. This approach would respect Rosetta's choice based on religious beliefs and would be consistent with the advocacy role of the nurse. Somehow, this approach did not seem to be in Rosetta's best long-term interests, however, and Ms. Tallson thought it supported Rosetta's illicit sexual activities. What should she do?

Case 11-5
When Contraception Is Punitive

Doreen Smalls, a 26-year-old, unwed, African American mother of four children, was referred to a family-planning clinic by the local county jail. She had recently been convicted of child abuse (she had publicly beat two of her children with a belt) and, as a condition for her probation, had been ordered by the court judge to undergo Norplant[2] *implantation* for 4 years.

When Megan Riley, the family-planning clinic nurse, calls Ms. Smalls into her office, she learns that the patient does not believe in contraception and has not previously used contraceptives to prevent pregnancy. She rejects contraceptives based on her religious beliefs and because she thinks that white people are trying to limit the birth of black children throughout the world for racist reasons.[3] She does not want the Norplant but has accepted it as a condition of her release from jail and probation. She wants to be with her children and is afraid that the county will take them away from her if she does not agree to the procedure. Ms. Smalls is very angry about this but does not feel she has any other recourse.

---

[2]Norplant is a contraceptive that is delivered via six soft, match-stick-sized rubber tubes that are placed under the skin of a woman's upper arm in a minor surgical procedure under local anesthesia. The tubes release the female hormone progestin and can suppress ovulation for as long as 5 years.

[3]Caron, Simone M. (2008). "Race Suicide, Eugenics, and Contraception, 1900–1930" In her: *Who Chooses?: American Reproductive History Since 1830*. Gainesville: University Press of Florida, pp. 44–80.

Ms. Riley is a devout Catholic who does not believe in abortion but does accept contraception for those who desire to avoid pregnancy for good reasons, such as when married couples already have several children and are financially unable to care for any more or when an unmarried woman is unprepared for the responsibilities of parenthood. She respects an individual's choice for contraception as part of being a responsible adult. But she is having problems with enforced contraception in Ms. Smalls's case. She realizes that Ms. Smalls and society would probably be better off without any more illegitimate children. She also considers it wise for Ms. Smalls to receive counseling as a child abuser to prevent harm to her children. But to enforce contraception via Norplant on Ms. Smalls seems to go beyond what Ms. Riley can accept. She does not want to participate in the implantation process and does not want to be Ms. Smalls's nurse for the 4 years of follow-up visits. She believes that she should be an advocate for Ms. Smalls and her procreative rights rather than the enforcer of punitive contraception on this patient, but she is not certain what she can realistically do when the law has put limitations on Ms. Smalls's procreative rights. Does a nurse have to accept and practice within this court-imposed directive?

Commentary

A complex mixture of ethical and psychologic issues is posed by Case 11-4. The nurse, Ms. Tallson, may be skeptical about the moral basis of Rosetta's objection to contraceptives because she is clearly engaging in other actions that are in violation of the moral tradition that she claims to be relevant. Perhaps there are deep psychologic reasons that Rosetta appears to object to contraception but is willing to engage in premarital sexual activity and to have abortions when an unwanted pregnancy results. There are psychiatrists who claim that some women, especially adolescents, willfully expose themselves to apparently unwanted pregnancies. Such attempts to use psychology to rationalize apparently inconsistent behaviors are themselves morally questionable, however. It is as if the patient cannot be taken at her word. An abortion may become morally tolerable as a last resort emergency measure. It is known that many persons subscribing to religious traditions opposing abortion do, in fact, have abortions in such emergencies. Perhaps that is an adequate explanation of Rosetta's behavior.

Ms. Tallson's dilemma is somewhat different. She apparently has no moral objections to contraception herself but faces a patient who, at least purportedly, refuses contraceptives on moral grounds. Convinced that contraception is at least acceptable, and in fact probably morally required, for someone in Rosetta's position, does Ms. Tallson become a moral advisor of a controversial position in the name of patient welfare, or does she retreat to a more traditional professional role of accepting the patient's ethical stance as a given and working to further the patient's interests within that framework?

Ms. Tallson might consider some other options. For instance, she might attempt to recruit others to convince Rosetta of the acceptability of contraception.

If she knew a Catholic priest who supported birth control, would it be acceptable for Ms. Tallson to ask the priest to discuss the matter with the patient? Could family members or friends be recruited for this task? Does recruiting some other moral advisor leave Ms. Tallson in the more traditional nursing role, or is she still indirectly attempting to persuade Rosetta to change her moral stance? Even if the nurse herself no longer has any moral problems with contraception, occasionally the patient may pose such a problem.

Some of the same issues occur in Case 11-5, that of Ms. Smalls and court-ordered contraception via Norplant. Ms. Riley, the nurse, is very uncomfortable with her nursing role in this situation. She accepts contraception, in principle, for good reasons, and she agrees that it would be better for Ms. Smalls to use birth control. But Ms. Smalls judges contraception to be wrong. If she were not in this situation, she would not use it. Should Ms. Riley try to persuade her that she is better off with the contraception? If Ms. Riley is successful and Ms. Smalls agrees to contraception, would implanting the Norplant on court order be less offensive?

Critical Thinking Questions

1. What is the ethical issue in Case 11-5? Is the issue the patient's right to choose whether to become pregnant, or is it the degree of invasiveness of the contraception method?

2. Some would argue that the right to procreate is so fundamental that any interference with the exercise of that right is unethical. Furthermore, nurses have a particular obligation to make sure that a patient's contraceptive choice is voluntary, informed, and in the best interests of the patient. If you were in Ms. Riley's position, what would you do?

Research Brief 11-2

Source: Chuang, C. H., Freund, K. M., & Massachusetts Emergency Contraception Network. (2005). Emergency contraception knowledge among women in a Boston community. *Contraception, 71*(2), 157–160.

Purpose: To assess the baseline knowledge of emergency contraception (EC) in a Boston neighborhood.

Method: This was a descriptive study using a survey design. A written questionnaire was distributed to women ages 18–44 years in the Boston neighborhood of Jamaica Plain.

Findings: Of the 188 participants who returned questionnaires, 82% had heard of EC. Knowledge disparities by race/ethnicity groups were seen with only 51% of Latina women and 75% of black women having heard of EC compared with 99% of white women (p < .001 and p = .002, respectively). Of the entire cohort, 39% knew that EC works by preventing pregnancy, 48% knew that EC should be taken within 72–120 hours of unprotected intercourse, and 44% knew that EC is only available by prescription in Massachusetts. Only 25% of women had ever discussed EC with a healthcare provider, and only 12% had ever received an advance prescription for EC.

Implications: A community education campaign aimed at reproductive-age women, healthcare providers, and pharmacists should be provided to address these knowledge deficits.

Sterilization

Sterilization raises all of the ethical questions of contraception and then some. Anyone who has objections to contraception will certainly object to sterilization. In addition, however, many people find sterilization particularly objectionable because it is usually presumed irreversible. Thus, many healthcare workers who are committed to rational planning and "keeping one's options open" have traditionally been unwilling to participate in sterilizations, even when they have no objections to contraception per se. In fact, they have been known to refuse to consider sterilization— especially for younger women and women who have not borne many children.[13]

Even for those who generally approve of sterilization, certain situations pose particular problems. One example, sterilization of a mentally retarded person, is illustrated in the following case.

Case 11-6
Sterilizing the Mentally Retarded Patient

Mary Ellen Thompson, a skilled maternal-child nurse, has recently been employed by a public hospital in a large southwestern city. Because she speaks fluent Spanish, she has been asked to serve as a translator for the scheduled C-section on a 14-year-old, mildly mentally retarded Hispanic teenager. The patient undergoes epidural anesthesia without incident and is delivered of a small but healthy 6 lb. 4 oz. infant girl. While completing the C-section, Mrs. Thompson suddenly realizes that the surgeon is going to perform a tubal ligation (TL). Checking the patient's chart, Mrs. Thompson does not find any specific consent for the TL and asks the physician if the procedure was anticipated and whether the patient was informed of its possibility. The physician tells Mrs. Thompson that he believes the procedure is "medically necessary" and that he will record it as such in his operative report.

Several days later, Mrs. Thompson visits the patient and her parents. The parents are concerned about their daughter's ability to care for her child, but they have made a commitment to shoulder the responsibility for both the mother and the child. In talking to them, Mrs. Thompson realizes that they have no awareness that a TL was performed on their daughter. They are economically indigent and poorly educated, yet Mrs. Thompson does not think that these circumstances warrant the involuntary sterilization of a mildly retarded individual without parental consent. What should she do?

Commentary

Sterilization of the low-income patient, the poorly educated, and the person with mental retardation has occurred in the past with less controversy than it now generates.[14] Several problems are worthy of discussion. First, one might question the ethics of sterilizing those who cannot consent, such as mentally retarded persons or any adolescent, even with parental approval. It is increasingly debated whether parents have any legal or moral authority to approve a permanent blockage of fertility for an incompetent person such as a minor. The problem is particularly controversial when the incompetent is mentally retarded. In contrast with contraceptive methods, sterilization must be presumed to be irreversible. Is Mrs. Thompson on morally safe ground when she implies that the situation involving this 14-year-old would have been different if the parents had given their approval? Some argue that mentally retarded persons have the right to retain their capacity to reproduce even if their parents approve of sterilization.

The obligation of the parents is to do what they believe is in their child's interest. On the other hand, there are limits to what parents can choose, even if they sincerely believe that their choice is in the child's best interest. Is this one of those cases where a parent who opts for sterilization rather than some less permanent method of contraception should be prohibited from acting? Or, would the parent's choice be sufficiently reasonable that parental approval would make the procedure acceptable?

In Case 11-6, the parents' approval was not sought, so different issues are raised. The physician states that he will record on the chart that the tubal ligation was "medically necessary." What would that mean in this case? There is one sense in which no procedure is medically necessary—if one is willing to accept the consequences. Even life-prolonging procedures cannot be termed "medically necessary" if patients are willing to accept more rapid death as the alternative (as some terminally ill patients are willing to do when faced with heroic surgical interventions). Presumably, the physician really means that he believes that a terrible, unacceptable consequence will result if this 14-year-old is not sterilized now. That seems hard to justify given the fact that she could be placed on some form of contraceptive until she had matured further. Alternatively, she could have been sterilized after her mother was asked. The physician could have discussed his plan with the mother, if not the daughter, prior to the delivery. It is not as if the physician could not have anticipated the issue before entering the delivery room.

More fundamentally, anyone contemplating this case must directly address the issue of whether it is acceptable to sterilize a nonconsenting, mentally retarded person. Even if it makes no sense to label the sterilization as medically indicated, and even if the wishes of the mother are not definitive, are there reasons that mentally retarded persons should be sterilized? Are there reasons that their reproductive capacities should be protected?

Mrs. Thompson seems to be on firm ground in questioning what has taken place. Her moral dilemma is, in part, one of deciding how to respond to what she is convinced is an unacceptable practice.

Critical Thinking Questions

If you were Mrs. Thompson, which of the following actions would you consider and why?

1. Speak to the physician and ask him to inform the girl and her mother of what had happened.
2. Speak to nursing staff about taking collective action against the physician.
3. Report to administrators that a surgical procedure was done without adequate consent.
4. Ask not to be assigned to work with that physician again.
5. Explain to the mother what took place.
6. Speak to a public advocacy group about the ethical issue of sterilization without consent.

ENDNOTES

1. Roe v. Wade, 410 U.S. 113, 93 S.Ct. 705, 1973.
2. Bayles, M.D. (1984). *Reproductive ethics.* Englewood Cliffs, NJ: Prentice Hall; Callahan, D. (1970). *Abortion: Law, choice, and morality.* New York: Macmillan; DeGrazia, D. (2005). *Human identity and bioethics.* New York: Cambridge University Press; Feinberg, J. (Ed.). (1973). *The problem of abortion.* Belmont, CA: Wadsworth; Martinelli-Fernandez, S. A., Baker-Sperry, L., & McIlvaine-Newsad, H. (Eds.). (2009). *Interdisciplinary views on abortion: Essays from philosophical, sociological, anthropological, political, health and other perspectives.* Jefferson, NC: McFarland; Noonan, J. T. (1970). *The morality of abortion: Legal and historical perspective.* Cambridge, MA: Harvard University Press; Rosen, H. (1967). *Abortion in America: Medical, psychiatric, legal, anthropological, and religious considerations.* Boston: Beacon Press.
3. Granfield, D. (1969). *The abortion decision.* Garden City, NY: Doubleday; Grisez, G. G. (1970). *Abortion: The myths, the realities, and the arguments.* New York: Corpus Books.

4. McCormick, R. A. (1991). Who or what is the preembryo? *Kennedy Institute of Ethics Journal, 1,* 1–15; Ford, N. M. (1988). *When did I begin? Conception of the human individual in history, philosophy, and science.* New York: Cambridge University Press.

5. Fletcher, J. (1979). *Humanhood: Essays in biomedical ethics.* Buffalo, NY: Prometheus Books; Tooley, M. (1972). Abortion and infanticide. *Philosophy and Public Affairs, 2,* 37–65.

6. Thomson, J. J. (1971). A defense of abortion. *Philosophy and Public Affairs, 1*(1), 47–66.

7. Holder, A. R. (1987). Minors' rights to consent to medical care. *Journal of the American Medical Association, 257*(24), 3400–3402; Stuhlbarg, S. F. (1992). When is a pregnant minor mature? When is an abortion in her best interests? The Ohio Supreme Court applies Ohio's abortion parental notification law: In Re Jane Doe 1. *University of Cincinnati Law Review, 60*(3), 907–961; Supreme Court upholds right of mature minor to obtain abortion without parental consent. (1979). *Family Planning Perspectives, 11*(4), 252–253.

8. Annas, G. J. (1992). The Supreme Court, liberty, and abortion. *New England Journal of Medicine, 327*(9), 651–654; Benshoof, J. (1993). Planned Parenthood v. Casey: The impact of the new undue burden standard on reproductive health care. *Journal of the American Medical Association, 269*(17), 2249–2257; Capron, A. M. (1992). Privacy: Dead and gone? *The Hastings Center Report, 22* (1), 43–45; Moskowitz, E. (1994). Parental control and teenage rights. *The Hastings Center Report, 24*(2), 4. U.S. Supreme Court. (June 29, 1992). Planned Parenthood of Southeastern Pennsylvania v. Casey. *U.S. Supreme Court Reporter, 112,* 2791–2885; Schmidt, C. G. (1993). Where privacy fails: Equal protection and the abortion rights of minors. *New York University Law Review, 68*(3), 597–638; Worthington, E. L., Larson, D. B., Lyons, J. S., Brubaker, M. W., Colecchi, C. A., Berry, J. T., et al. (1991). Mandatory parental involvement prior to adolescent abortion. *Journal of Adolescent Health, 12*(2), 138–142.

9. Wertz, D. C. (1995). Reproductive technologies: II. Sex selection. In W. Reich (Ed.), *Encyclopedia of Bioethics* (rev. ed., pp. 2212–2216). New York: Simon and Schuster Macmillan.

10. Williamson, N. E. (1978, January). Boys or girls? Parents' preferences and sex control. *Population Bulletin, 33,* 3–35.

11. Fletcher, J. C. (1979). The morality and ethics of prenatal diagnosis. In A. Milunsky (Ed.), *Genetic disorders and the fetus* (pp. 621–635). New York: Plenum Press.

12. Noonan, J. T. (1966). *Contraception: A history of its treatment by the Catholic theologians and canonists.* Cambridge, MA: Harvard University Press.

13. Scrimshaw, S. C., & Pasquariella, B. (1970). Obstacles to sterilization in one community. *Family Planning Perspectives, 2,* 40–42.

14. Buck v. Bell, 274 U.S. 200 (1927); In Re Grady 426 A. 2d 467 (N.J. Sup. Ct., Feb. 18, 1981); Relf v. Weinberger, 565 F.2d 722 (D.C. Cir. Sept. 13, 1977).

Chapter 12

Genetics, Birth, and the Biologic Revolution

Other Cases Involving Genetics and Birth Technologies

Case 2-6:   The Patient Who Refused to Be Tested for a Genetic Disease
Case 5-2:   Choosing Between Two Infants with Multiple Handicaps
Case 7-8:   When Should Parental Rights Be Overridden?
Case 8-9:   Fetal Death in the Labor Room: Should the Nurse Tell the Patient?
Case 9-4:   When "Doing Good" May Harm the Patient

Key Terms
Artificial insemination
Assisted reproduction
Genetic counseling
Genetic engineering
Genetic screening
In vitro fertilization
Selective abortion
Surrogate motherhood

Objectives
1. Describe three ethical issues concerning genetic screening.
2. Identify the nurse's ethical role in supporting patients making assisted-reproduction decisions.
3. Identify the role of the nurse in discussing and proposing policies for gene manipulation in treating health problems.
4. Describe the ethical issues generated by the uses of assisted reproduction.

New developments in genetics and the growing potential for human intervention in the process of procreation and birth are truly the cutting edges of the biologic revolution. They pose a wide range of new value conflicts for nurses. The conflicts may be as mundane as whether to discuss a patient's general fears that her baby may have a genetic problem and as exotic as contemplating the nurse's role in experimental efforts to manipulate the genetic endowment of an embryo conceived in the laboratory.

Expanded practice roles for nurses have created nursing responsibility for genetics case finding and referral, patient education, and counseling. Nurses are often the first ones asked by patients about the risks of having a genetically abnormal child. During prenatal and neonatal clinical encounters, the nurse may be the one who confronts ethical dilemmas such as whether to alarm parents by discussing small but real risks of genetic anomalies. The nurse may also be the one who discovers that a patient is a carrier of a recessive gene and is refusing to disclose that fact to the patient's brothers and sisters. The nurse may counsel a patient who makes an unpopular decision such as deciding not to abort a seriously malformed fetus. The issues here tend to raise conflicts between the principles of autonomy and truth-telling as well as difficult decisions about what will benefit patients—whether they be future parents or their offspring. These are the issues of *genetic counseling* and are presented in Cases 12-1 through 12-4.

Historically, the next group of issues to emerge centered around mass *genetic screening* programs. Here, a conflict between the welfare of the patient and others within the society can be critical. The nurse may find herself pressured into the role of protector of society's interests rather than the traditional role of advocate for the patient. Case 12-5 begins to raise problems of whether the nurse should be advocating a test in order to prevent the birth of a seriously afflicted infant, thereby saving society, as well as the parents, considerable money. Case 12-6 pushes the idea of mass genetic screening more into the future. It envisions the day when the nurse might be asked to cooperate in a systematic mass screening program to identify fetuses that may be expendable members of society.

The remaining cases in the chapter deal with the ethical problems connected to newer technologies of birth and the biologic revolution. *In vitro fertilization* (IVF; the process of fertilizing a surgically removed human egg in a laboratory dish) and related technologies such as GIFT (gamete intrafollicular transfer), ZIFT (zygote intrafollicular transfer), and ICSI (intracytoplasmic sperm injection) are attractive procedures of last resort for some of the millions of infertile couples throughout the world. The nurse participating in programs using these technologies faces a wide range of ethical issues—from such basic questions as whether the entire process is an immoral tampering with nature to more specific ethical controversies of whether embryos fertilized in vitro can ethically be implanted for gestation in a woman who did not provide the ova. The process of multiple fertilizations also gives rise to the problems of intentionally creating large numbers of simultaneous pregnancies and leftover embryos—embryos that are of great interest both to researchers, who might want to attempt brief gestation for scientific investigation, and infertile couples, who either may not be physiologically capable of supplying their own gametes or simply may not wish to go through the inconvenience and expense of a pregnancy. Cases 12-7, 12-8, 12-9 and 12-10 take up these issues.

Case 12-11 stems from another manifestation of newer birth technologies. *Artificial insemination* has been both technically feasible and ethically controversial for many years. Traditionally, artificial insemination involved inseminating a wife with either her husband's or a donor's sperm. However, there has never been any technical barrier to using the technique to fertilize some woman other than a wife either because the wife was incapable of bearing a child or simply because she preferred not to do so. Recently, **surrogate motherhood** arrangements have taken new forms that raise difficult ethical questions about parenthood. Our case studies explore the role of the nurse in these arrangements.

The final case, Case 12-12, explores the ethics of the most dramatic and innovative birth technology to date. Until recently, all genetic and reproductive interventions simply manipulated the existing genetic material, providing prospective parents with opportunities to refrain from getting pregnant, to abort if the woman does become pregnant, or to manipulate the fertilization process through IVF or artificial insemination. Now, it is rapidly becoming possible to change the genetic material itself through what has come to be called **genetic engineering**. The first attempts at genetic engineering will certainly be considered quite crude in the future. Nursing personnel will play a number of roles in such genetic manipulations—from providing information to performing clinical nursing services. Case 12-12 presents the problems faced by a nurse asked to participate in an experimental effort to manipulate the human genetic code.

Genetic Counseling

Genetic counseling issues have been with us since people first recognized that specific medical problems occur frequently in some families. However, the rapid development of technologies for diagnosing genetic anomalies has made genetic counseling a much more significant and controversial enterprise. We now not only understand the science of genetics, but we also can detect carrier status of a recessive gene/trait, detect an inherited genetic disease (caused by a dominant gene), and do predictive testing for risks of certain diseases (such as cancer) in postnatal humans as well as fetuses. We can detect fetal anomalies with varying degrees of reliability through the use of FISH (fluorescent in situ hybridization), which detects changes in the number of chromosomes present in a fetus's cells, chorionic villus sampling (biochemical and chromosomal analysis of the chorionic villi), amniocentesis (biochemical and chromosomal analysis of fetal cells obtained from the amniotic fluid), ultrasound, and analysis of fetal blood samples. Newer techniques are now making possible preimplantation diagnosis, following IVF and before the embryo is transferred to the uterus, and the isolation of fetal cells in maternal circulation during the first trimester of pregnancy. We can detect disease or carrier status in postnatal humans through biochemical and genetic tests that measure the genes themselves (which do not change over time) or the protein products of genes (which do change over time).

The importance of this field increased when abortion became legal and potentially available to cope with detected fetal anomalies. This is not the only reason that parents might want genetic information about their fetus, however. They might also want to know whether they are carrying a fetus afflicted with a genetic condition in order to plan for its birth or to put their minds at ease should the fetus not be affected. Genetic counseling also involves issues of clarifying complex scientific information, encouraging discussion with family members who may also be carriers of or at risk for a disease, and of learning to deal with the fact that our bodies carry the potential of harmful genetic information.[1]

Although most nurses do not have primary responsibility for genetic counseling, all nurses can expect to encounter genetic information about their patients. Determining what constitutes appropriate informed consent for genetic testing, conveying genetic information, and helping patients and their families understand genetic information are just a few nursing roles in this area.[2] A nurse's knowledge of new genetic diagnostics and therapeutics can also benefit individuals who are at risk for commercial exploitation by new biotech companies. Some nurses working in departments of obstetrics, pediatrics, or genetics may be educated specifically for these responsibilities. Others need at least to be able to recognize the issues of potential controversy so that they can refer patients for counseling, consult with other members of the healthcare team, and discuss issues with patients. A new text, *Genetics and Ethics in Health Care,* laments "the possibility of inadequate preparation of healthcare professionals to utilize gene-based diagnostics and therapeutics appropriately for the improvement of health and quality of life of entire societies."[3] Important resources for nurses are identified in Box 12-1.

Box 12-1

Genomic Health Resources for Nurses

Jenkins, J., Calzone, K., Lean, D. H., & Prows, C. (2008). *Essential nursing competencies and curricula guidelines for genetics and genomics.* Available at: http://www. genome.gov/Pages/Careers/HealthProfessionalEducation/geneticscompetency.pdf. Accessed February 3, 2010.

Jenkins, J., & Lea, D. H. (2005). *Nursing care in the genomic era: A case-based approach.* Sudbury, MA: Jones and Bartlett.

Monsen, R. B. (2009). *Genetics and ethics in health care: New questions in the age of genomic health.* Silver Spring, MD: Nursebooks.org.

Genetics Home Reference is the National Library of Medicine's website for consumer information about genetic conditions and the genes or chromosomes related to those conditions. Available at: http://ghr.nlm.nih.gov. Accessed February 3, 2010.

National Coalition for Health Professional Education in Genetics (NCHPEG) is a coalition of organizations and individuals promoting health professional education and access to information about advances in human genetics. Available at: http://www.nchpeg.org. Accessed May 10, 2010.

American Nurses Association Consensus Panel on Genetic/Genomic Nursing Competencies. (2009). *Essentials of genetic and genomic nursing: Competencies, curricula guidelines, and outcome indicators* (2nd ed.). Silver Spring, MD: Author.

Baily, M. A., & Murray, T. H. (Eds.). (2009). *Ethics and newborn genetic screening: New technologies, new challenges.* Baltimore: Johns Hopkins University Press.

Haugen, D. M., & Musser, S. (Eds.). (2009). *Genetic engineering.* Detroit, MI: Greenhaven Press/Gale Cengage Learning.

The following case reveals how a nurse may be called upon to initiate conversations about genetic counseling when other members of the health team have not done so.

Case 12-1
When the Risk of Genetic Abnormality Is Uncertain

Vivian Torrance works as the staff nurse in a busy OB/GYN clinic in an urban HMO. She has noticed that more women are delaying their pregnancies until their mid-30s and early 40s. This childbearing trend is documented in the literature and evidenced particularly in urban areas and clinic settings servicing professional women. Ordinarily, this trend would pose no particular conflict for Mrs. Torrance, but she is becoming increasingly concerned about the risk to older women of bearing disabled or handicapped children. The risks are being studied, and appropriate counseling, prenatal diagnostic procedures, and genetic testing are recommended for pregnant women 35 years of age and older.

The issue becomes acute for Mrs. Torrance one day when Stacy Carmichael, a 34-year-old administrator, visits the clinic for her routine pregnancy checkup. It is Mrs. Carmichael's first pregnancy, and she and her husband have planned it to coincide with their purchase of a townhouse in a restored part of the city. As Mrs. Carmichael leaves the clinic, Mrs. Torrance overhears a parting conversation between the patient and her obstetrician. Mrs. Carmichael asks the physician if she has any risk of bearing an abnormal child at her age. Her physician tells her, "Don't worry your pretty head about such matters. Rest, eat well, and exercise every day—you and your baby will be just fine!" Mrs. Carmichael beams at her physician and leaves the clinic under the assumption that she has nothing to worry about.

Even though Mrs. Carmichael does not technically fall under the "35 years of age and older" policy strongly urging an amniocentesis for the older pregnant woman, Mrs. Torrance believes that some risks exist and that they should be discussed with this patient. Should she take the initiative to mention the availability of prenatal testing while making the appointment for Mrs. Carmichael's next visit? Is the risk great enough to merit creating concern in the patient and possibly arousing a problem with the physician? Mrs. Torrance is not sure.

Commentary

Because of her age, Mrs. Carmichael is at higher risk than younger women are of bearing a child with a genetic abnormality, such as Down syndrome. The nurse, Mrs. Torrance, is aware of this. Mrs. Carmichael apparently has some suspicion, but she has been reassured by her physician. The justification for that reassurance is suspect. It involves some complex ethical judgments that Mrs. Torrance and Mrs. Carmichael may not share.

The medical literature today generally recommends amniocentesis for pregnant women who are 35 years of age and older. The reason for that is controversial. When data relating maternal age to risk of Down syndrome were first gathered, they were collected at 5-year intervals.[4] A substantial increase in risk was noted for women in the 35–39 age group, as compared with younger women. When the risks of the amniocentesis itself and the scarcity of the resources available to perform the tests were considered, many believed that age 35 was a reasonable cutoff point. That judgment, however, involved controversial value issues. On one hand, someone who opposed abortion of a fetus with Down syndrome might consider the expense and risks of the tests unjustifiable at any age. On the other hand, if someone had an extreme fear of carrying an infant with Down syndrome and desperately wanted a baby, she might be more than willing to bear the risks and the expense of the test, even at a very young age.

From the individual's point of view, deciding the level of risk of Down syndrome that justifies the test involves an ethical and value judgment. From the point of view of a society concerned about scarce resources, it would seem prudent to offer the tests more readily to those women at higher risk, but even then, some consideration might be given to the unusual concerns of younger pregnant women. Recent data make clear that the risk of Down syndrome increases gradually with age, with no major change at age 35.[5] This suggests that Mrs. Torrance would have a potential problem if she witnessed even a younger patient, say a 32-year-old, being denied information about fetal risks and prenatal tests that could be performed. The problem is more acute with a 34-year-old patient, such as Mrs. Carmichael. The physician has clearly decided that, at age 34, the patient does not warrant information about potential risks up front. This may be the standard of practice in the HMO—diagnostic testing may not be authorized for those younger than 35 years of age, unless other risk factors are present. However, the patient asked for a discussion of potential risks regardless of whether the HMO would authorize an amniocentesis. After learning of potential risks, she might have elected to obtain and pay for prenatal testing on her own.

This leaves Mrs. Torrance in the position of being forced to make a judgment. Even though she is not specifically trained in genetic counseling and has not sought out the role of genetic testing advocate, if she believes that Mrs. Carmichael has a right to the information to make an informed choice about her prenatal care, she will have to take some action. Preferably, she will discuss the matter with Mrs. Carmichael's physician. She might also discuss the matter with the patient directly or call the matter to the attention of other members of the healthcare team.

A more intriguing problem arises if Mrs. Torrance realizes all of this but believes that an abortion, the most probable outcome of a test revealing Down syndrome or some other serious genetic abnormality of the fetus, is morally wrong. If she believes that abortion is so wrong that it is murder, can she take action to alert Mrs. Carmichael to the potential risks associated with advanced maternal age and the possibility of amniocentesis to diagnose Down syndrome? She might even believe that referring the patient for counseling would be aiding and abetting a murder if, in the process, a serious genetic abnormality were found and Mrs. Carmichael aborted her fetus. That may have been the stance of the physician who decided not to counsel Mrs. Carmichael. If Mrs. Torrance recognizes that the physician's behavior is undesirable but not illegal, but also does not want to make the slightest contribution to what she believes to be a seriously immoral action, should she follow the physician's course and just finesse the entire discussion?

Case 12-2
Counseling the Pregnant Woman with Sickle Cell Disease

The County Hospital prenatal clinic, serving a largely African American, inner-city population, does routine sickle cell preps on all its patients. Audrey Brown, a 23-year-old, unmarried, African American patient, tested positive. She was at least 16 weeks pregnant, and she had sickle cell disease. Moreover, she had taken antinausea medication early in her pregnancy that has been reported to be teratogenic.

Gail Siegler, the nurse practitioner in the clinic, saw an array of troublesome problems. Because Audrey Brown was not just a carrier of sickle cell but actually had the disease, the pregnancy could cause her some problems. The exposure to a known teratogen, along with the risk of the pregnancy, led her to explore alternatives carefully with her patient. Ms. Brown was quite resistant to discussion of abortion as an alternative to giving birth to an impaired child. She seemed to want to have a baby regardless of any risks to its health. Moreover, she was a very devout Christian for whom abortion was morally suspect. Although she did not rule out the possibility of an abortion, it was clear she would find it a difficult decision to make.

The issues clearly troubled Ms. Siegler. Since Ms. Brown was already 16 weeks pregnant, Ms. Siegler realized that an abortion would require admission to the high-risk pregnancy clinic for a saline abortion. Audrey Brown would go through labor and experience a delivery; the fetus would be delivered formed. She envisioned the trauma the young woman would suffer from this procedure, sometimes called a "partial birth abortion."

Then she considered the genetic issues. Because Ms. Brown had sickle cell disease, the infant would be at least a carrier. Although virtually no medical problems accompany carrier status, it would increase the chances of the infant's offspring having sickle cell disease. Furthermore, since Ms. Brown's boyfriend was African American, there was about one chance in ten that he was a carrier, in which case there would be one chance in four of the baby also having sickle cell disease. Do these probabilities increase the justification for an abortion? Should this possibility be raised for Ms. Brown to consider? Should Ms. Siegler initiate action to have the boyfriend screened for sickle cell carrier status? How should this genetic information affect Ms. Siegler's approach to her patient?

Case 12-3
The Pregnant Teenager with a Genetic Problem

Melinda Eades was a 14-year-old adolescent diagnosed at an outpatient neurology clinic with the gene for neurofibromatosis–type 2 (NF2), an autosomal-dominant disorder that causes nervous system tumors that usually demonstrate symptoms during the late-teen years or early 20s. At the time of diagnosis, genetic counseling was recommended to Melinda's mother because any children born to Melinda would have a 50% chance of also carrying the NF2 gene. Melinda was quite upset by the genetic testing results and did not seem to comprehend the information, so Mrs. Eades decided to wait a few weeks before making the appointment with the genetic counselor to discuss future issues, such as child-bearing decisions, with Melinda. There was no reason to believe that Melinda was sexually active, so it was agreed that Mrs. Eades would contact the clinic for genetic counseling in a month or so.

Before this appointment was made, however, Melinda went to an OB/GYN clinic on her own for problems with menstruation. Testing revealed that she was approximately 7 weeks pregnant. She was counseled by the clinic nurse about abortion options and was advised to discuss her pregnancy with her parents. When Melinda mentioned that she was recently identified as having the gene for a genetic disorder, the clinic nurse recommended that she return to the neurology clinic for follow up and counseling. Melinda did not seem to understand that her disease was genetically transmissible to her offspring.

After several days of agonizing over her pregnancy, Melinda told her mother. Mrs. Eades was very upset with Melinda and immediately decided that Melinda should have an abortion. When Melinda seemed uncertain whether she wanted to abort the pregnancy, Mrs. Eades told her that any of her offspring would have a 50% chance of having NF2. Melinda was surprised by this information but was still uncertain what she should do. She also wondered why she had not been informed of this earlier.

When Melinda showed up for her appointment at the neurology clinic, she was very confused. She asked Janice Goldstein, the nurse practitioner she previously saw in the clinic, why someone did not tell her that she needed to be careful about becoming pregnant. When she realized that her mother had decided to withhold this information from her for a period of time, Melinda became angry. Did she not have a right to know this information, even though she was a minor? Also, why had the nurse conveyed this information to her mother and not to her? Could her mother control her in that manner, even to the point of forcing her to have an abortion, a course of action that Melinda would not likely choose under other circumstances? How should Ms. Goldstein proceed with this situation?

Case 12-4
Telling the Patient About an Unexpected Finding of Genetic Testing

Monica Boyd, nurse practitioner for a genetic testing and counseling clinic at an urban hospital, has just made an interesting discovery. Family members of a patient recently diagnosed with Huntington's Disease (HD) have been coming in for genetic testing to determine whether they also have the HD gene. After examining the test results of Roger Jr., the 12-year-old son of the HD patient's brother (Roger Sr.), it is obvious that Roger Sr. is not Roger Jr.'s biological father. Is Mrs. Boyd obliged to report this incidental finding, and if so, to whom? Or should the information simply be recorded in Roger Jr.'s health record without explanation?

Commentary

Two of these latter cases, like Case 12-1, raise questions about whether genetic anomalies provide justifiable grounds for abortion. The case of Audrey Brown, the 23-year-old patient with sickle cell disease, suggests several links between genetic conditions and abortion. First, Ms. Brown is at special risk in her pregnancy because of her disease, regardless of the condition of the fetus. Is this a case of abortion justified by maternal health risk?

Second, Ms. Brown was exposed to a known teratogen during her pregnancy. Teratogens, especially early in pregnancy, cause genetic changes in some fetuses, some so serious that they produce serious genetic abnormalities. The risks, however, are very difficult to assess. No precise risk figures are available. Is abortion justified by merely a threat of risk to the fetus? Ms. Brown would need to undergo some form of prenatal diagnosis testing to determine whether her fetus has the disease or has undergone genetic change from the teratogen. Once this information is known, aborting to avoid a serious known genetic affliction might be justifiable.

Third, it is conceivable that Ms. Brown would choose to abort because of what already is known about the fetal genetic composition. Her child will definitely be a sickle cell carrier. Some might argue that the abortion should be performed to avoid passing the sickle cell gene along in the gene pool. The problems to the patient of possessing a single sickle cell gene (of being a carrier rather than actually having the disease) are minor, however. Few people would be so committed to the purity of the gene pool that they would advocate aborting a known carrier just to protect the societal genetic make-up. The fact that Ms. Brown, like many sickle cell patients, is African American could easily lead to racist implications if an abortion were suggested simply to eliminate a fetus with sickle cell carrier status.

The possibility that the baby could get two sickle cell genes might also be considered. In that case, the baby would actually have the disease. Having sickle cell disease causes problems in life—pain from sickle cell crisis and even potentially life-threatening risks. Much of the time, however, patients with sickle cell disease live reasonably normal lives. Deciding to abort a fetus because it actually has the disease could be controversial, but not nearly as controversial as aborting a baby with carrier status.

To give Audrey Brown a chance to consider all of this, it might be necessary to begin asking questions about the father of her child. Should the father be identified? Should he be screened to see if he is a sickle cell carrier? Being an African American, he has about one chance in ten of being a carrier. If he is found to be a carrier, the pregnancy would have a one in four chance of resulting in a fetus with two sickle cell genes—that is, with the actual disease. Prenatal diagnostic testing can determine whether Ms. Brown's fetus has the disease. But because of the risks involved, this would be done only if both parents were carriers and the baby could potentially have the disease.

Critical Thinking Questions

1. Should Gail Siegler become involved in all the complexities of this case?

2. If Ms. Siegler is not adequately educated in genetics, would it be better if she simply kept quiet?

3. Does Ms. Siegler have a moral responsibility to see that the network of scientific, ethical, and racial issues raised by Ms. Brown's pregnancy is addressed? If so, why? If not, why not?

The case of Melinda Eades, the 14-year-old with NF2, is in some ways similar. It involves a pregnant woman with a known genetic disorder. Yet, Ms. Eades's case involves a disease that is transmitted by a single gene; NF2 is an autosomal-dominant condition. That means that even regardless of the absence of the gene in the father, each of Ms. Eades's offspring has a 50% chance of having the disease. Does this significant risk make the abortion easier to justify, and therefore is it easier for nurse

Janice Goldstein to support the abortion than it was for Gail Siegler in Case 12-2? Does the seriousness of neurofibromatosis compared with sickle cell disease make recommending an abortion easier?

There is another factor to consider. Whereas sickle cell disease might potentially be diagnosed in utero, this is not the case with NF2. This means that if an abortion is pursued, it would be based on the 50% chance of the fetus being affected. Does the fact that there is an equal chance of the child being normal make supporting abortion more difficult for Ms. Goldstein?

One complication of this case is that information was withheld from Melinda about the implications of her disease for childbearing. Believing that her daughter was not sexually active, Mrs. Eades decided to wait a month or two before taking Melinda to the genetic counselor. Melinda's confusion and anger upon learning that information was withheld from her are understandable. She is at the age of formal operational thought and therefore can be expected to have the cognitive ability to understand the implications of genetic testing but perhaps needs help in making choices based on that information.[6] Advanced practice nurses like Ms. Goldstein can help in determining a minor's capacity to request or consent to genetic testing, particularly the minor's capacity to understand the results of testing. Whereas parents are presumed to know how best to prepare their children to make important choices, nurses are presumed to have an obligation to be truthful where genetic information is concerned.

Critical Thinking Question

Given Melinda's anger and confusion about her situation, what actions should Ms. Goldstein take to provide Melinda with the information she needs to make important choices about her pregnancy?

Case 12-4, involving the discovery of nonpaternity in the genetic testing of 12-year-old Roger Jr., presents some interesting conflicts for Monica Boyd. Roger Jr.'s presumed father and family members are already concerned about the possibility of having the gene for HD, a progressive disorder for which there is no effective treatment and that results in death 15 to 20 years after onset. If she follows the rule to tell the truth about genetic information, Mrs. Boyd could give this information to Roger Jr., his mother, or even his presumed father. Clearly, providing this information to either Roger Jr. or his father could cause considerable harm to both and disrupt the entire family unit. Usually, in cases involving nonpaternity findings, the mother is given the genetic information and the father is not told unless the mother requests it. Regardless, the child is not told.[7] This approach protects the family unit and avoids emotional harm to the child. The nurse can always truthfully report that Roger Jr. does not have the HD gene, which was, of course, the reason for the testing. On the other hand, Roger Jr. does have a right to his genetic information, and such information may be important to his future decision making regarding health and life events. For instance, he may at some point be worried about inheriting some other health problem from his father, a concern that is unwarranted given the situation.

Critical Thinking Questions

1. At what point should Roger Jr. be given his genetic information? Why?
2. What role does the advanced-practice nurse have in providing genetic information to patients?
3. Some are now suggesting that paternity tests be mandated at birth to determine a child's biological father since every child has the right to this knowledge growing up. Some think as many as 10% of first children have biological fathers other than the man to whom their mother is married. Would you support such a policy? Why or why not?

Genetic Screening

Genetic screening raises all the issues related to genetic counseling and then some. Screening is done, usually in infancy, to detect serious genetic diseases that can be treated early to prevent debilitating health consequences or death. Tests identify whether an individual has a gene or a chromosome abnormality that may be harmful to himself or herself or to offspring. Normally, a positive test leads to further, more careful assessments and individual counseling. Sometimes screening is done in the community as, for example, when a Jewish community organization organizes screening for carrier status of Tay-Sachs, a condition that frequently occurs in Jewish populations. In the future, it will be possible to screen populations for numerous genetic markers simultaneously, not only to identify disorders and carrier status, but also to determine whether individuals have a susceptibility to some diseases. In such community-based screening programs, nurses may be the only healthcare professionals with direct responsibility for case finding and referral and counseling.

In the first case in this section, a nurse conducts genetic screening to measure alpha-fetoprotein levels, a preliminary diagnostic test for neural tube defects and Down syndrome. The second case, one of the few purely hypothetical cases in this volume, anticipates future mass screening programs for a genetic marker that correlates with low intelligence.

Case 12-5

The Pregnant Patient in an Alpha-Fetoprotein Screening Program

Polly Barnes is a new graduate nurse in a community-based prenatal care program that serves a low-income, immigrant population. She has just been informed that all new patients admitted to the program are to become part of the clinic's new maternal serum alpha-fetoprotein (MSAFP) screening project. Each patient will have a small amount of blood drawn by finger stick at 6 to 7 weeks of pregnancy to determine her serum level of alpha-fetoprotein (AFP). High levels of AFP suggest that the pregnant patient is at risk for bearing an infant affected by a neural tube defect. Low levels of AFP could indicate that the pregnant woman is at risk for bearing an infant with Down syndrome or some other genetic disorder. Additional testing—repeat MSAFP levels, sonogram, amniocentesis, as well as genetic counseling—will be provided for the patient who demonstrates abnormal levels of MSAFP.

When Ms. Barnes asks why this screening program is being performed on all patients, she is told that it is believed that most pregnant woman who know they are at risk for bearing a fetus with a neural tube defect, Down syndrome, or some other genetic disorder will want to abort the fetus rather than continue the pregnancy. The test is provided as a community service to help reduce the public cost of supporting infants born with these defects and the potential for long-term disability. Because the initial cost of the MSAFP test is low, the potential cost saving to the community is considerable, even if only 1 to 2 affected pregnancies per 1000 births are aborted. Thus, the screening program is of considerable value to the community in terms of reduced future costs for supporting disabled children.

Ms. Barnes understands why the community might want to require the performance of this test on all pregnant women in the immigrant population. However, she also realizes that the test might result in false positive reports, particularly for the initial screening test levels. The results of the tests might cause mental trauma to patients who already have a reduced ability to understand the test results due to language and cultural barriers. It is also possible that abnormal test results might alarm some patients to the extent that they would abort their otherwise normal pregnancy before undergoing further testing. Because the nurse's primary goal is to serve the patient, Ms. Barnes is not sure that she should participate in this MSAFP screening program. To do so seems to support the goals of society over those of the pregnant woman and the fetus. What is the nurse's obligation in this type of situation?

Case 12-6
Screening for Expendables: Nursing in the 21st Century

Mary Jane Manning will be participating in a community-based mass screening program scheduled to begin in June 2020. As a result of fetal cell sorting techniques developed in the late 1990s, it is now possible to isolate fetal cells from a sample of the pregnant woman's blood early in the first trimester and then to perform tests on the fetal cells to identify about 1000 disease-causing genes. Moreover, test results can not only identify a range of conditions that affect intelligence, but they can also be used as a reasonably accurate predictor of significant mental function deficits in the child. Although the tests are not 100% accurate, they are reliable enough that many individuals use them to make procreation decisions, including decisions about abortion. Because many mental function deficits are now clearly linked to genetic anomalies, pressures are being generated to make the diagnostic tests mandatory for all citizens, to make healthcare insurance unavailable for children born with mental deficits, and to fine individuals who elect to continue a pregnancy after test results indicate significant genetically linked mental deficits in the fetus.

The goals of the screening program are to prevent the suffering and expenses generated by the birth of mentally impaired children and, secondarily, to decrease the frequency in the gene pool of the genes responsible for the impairments. Participation in the screening program initially will be voluntary, but if significant cost benefits of the program are found, as is anticipated, the screening test will be mandatory for all pregnant women in the community.

Although social values have changed dramatically in recent years, Ms. Manning is uncomfortable about participating in this type of screening program. The results of the screening program will identify fetuses considered expendable both for the good of the individuals involved and for the good of the community. The obligation to avoid killing is still strongly held by most members of the nursing profession, but increasingly it is recognized that the nurse has an obligation both to prevent suffering when it can be avoided and to serve the community. In addition, there is increasing political pressure on the nursing profession to adopt ethical and practice standards more consistent with the changing needs of society. Indeed, a major revision of the American Nurses Association *Code of Ethics for Nurses* in 2017 made it evident that nurses' ethical judgments should be more responsive to social values and the needs of the community.

Assuming that the screening test is reasonably accurate, should Ms. Manning participate in the project while it remains voluntary? Should she continue to participate if the tests become mandatory?

Commentary

Polly Barnes, the nurse working in the community-based prenatal care program in Case 12-5, faces an array of ethical questions. She must decide whether she wants to be a part of a program that would almost certainly result in an increase in the rate of abortions for neural tube defects, Down syndrome, and other disorders. If she believes that abortion because of these conditions is not justified, she may well have a hard time working in the program. She must also face the more subtle effects of any genetic counseling program on family relationships, particularly the parent–child bond. She is understandably concerned about anxiety produced in her patients, the incidence of false positives, the precipitous increase in abortions of normal fetuses, and the obligation to disclose information to the patient's relatives who may also be at risk of disease. She is also concerned about the level of understanding that can realistically be expected on the part of the pregnant women of the immigrant population served by the clinic.

Beyond these concerns, Ms. Barnes faces additional difficulties because she is participating in a screening program that will potentially involve additional tests.[8] Although she may have the most noble objectives and be committed to her patients' welfare, she will have only limited contact with the patients who test positively in the initial screen. She will have to rely on other members of the healthcare team to carry out the follow-up counseling on a one-on-one basis. She may unwittingly be referring her patients into a network that could eventually lead to contact with some other practitioner who is unrealistically zealous in promoting abortion (or in keeping the implications of the tests from patients in order to foreclose abortion).

Ms. Barnes might also consider that participating in any genetic screening project is potentially forgoing the traditional clinical relationship with patients when they become part of a larger, more bureaucratic delivery system. A nurse should be concerned about how test results will be documented and what other uses will eventually be made of the test information.[9] There is probably little Ms. Barnes can do to influence the ultimate uses of the information, but she can ask questions on behalf of patients and ascertain the moral acceptability of the procedures involved. She is troubled by some who have claimed that the program is an example of Nazi eugenics by abortion.

One example of how genetic testing information may be used in ways incompatible with traditional nursing ethics is seen in the stated or implied agenda of the sponsors of the program. Although Ms. Barnes may participate in administering the screening for the purpose of benefiting the individual client (i.e., providing information on which to base choices), it seems clear that the sponsors of the program have a different, social objective: reducing the public costs of supporting infants born with certain disabling defects. Ms. Barnes, as well as other nurses, recognizes that the nurse has social as well as individual patient obligations. As long as the goals of the individual patient (avoiding the mental and physical suffering resulting from the birth of an afflicted child) and society (cutting costs) converge, there is no conflict. But suppose the sponsoring agency's announced agenda is to promote the abortion of fetuses with defects? The agency might at least expect her to make known the possibility of abortion and perhaps to encourage the patient with positive tests to pursue this course. Although participating in a screening project to identify genetic defects in unborn children initially seems consistent with the nursing role, it is the implications of the test results that ultimately determine the moral acceptability of the nurse's participation in a screening project.

The issue of implications of test results is projected into the future in the hypothetical case (Case 12-6), which is set in the year 2020. By that time, the use of screening tests has been perfected to the point that mental function deficiencies can be predicted with substantial accuracy. If deficits in intelligence can be predicted accurately and it is agreed that most rational people would prefer not to have a child with such a deficit, would it not make sense to make diagnostic tests mandatory? And, if so, would not other implications follow, such as unavailability of healthcare insurance for afflicted children, fining of women who continue pregnancy after testing indicated significant genetically linked mental deficits in their fetuses, and perhaps even mandatory abortion of such children?

Critical Thinking Questions

1. Do you think that in the future nurses will be expected to use their nursing knowledge and skills to identify patients at risk for disease, such as breast or colon cancer, so that the offending body parts (breasts or colons) can be closely monitored?

2. Do you think that such procedures will become mandatory so as to reduce the costs of caring for certain diseases in society?

3. Is it possible that it will become a role of the nurse to identify individuals at greatest risk so that they can be made to undergo involuntary surgical procedures (removal of breasts or colons) for the purpose of the aggregate good?

At the heart of these issues is the question of whether nurses have a responsibility to anticipate potential future uses of the technologies they are currently supporting. May nurses justifiably say that the use of social controls to foster elimination of children with some disorders is so much a violation of their understanding of morality that they should not participate in even the first stages of testing? If they are willing to participate in the initial screening test to identify women at risk but find the later uses of test results unacceptable, may they stop participating at that point? What is it about the envisioned later use that might give them pause? Is it the involvement of the government in promoting social purposes? If so, that has already occurred in the earlier use of AFP screening. Is it the rejection of children with disabling conditions? If so, that also is implied in the earlier use. Is it the potential involuntary removal of body parts from individuals at risk of disease, or involuntary abortion? Is there anything morally different about the screening project in the year 2020 that is not implied in the MSAFP screening project involving Ms. Barnes?

Research Brief 12-1

Source: Greco, K. E., & Salveson, C. (2009). Identifying genetics and genomics nursing competencies common among published recommendations. *Journal of Nursing Education, 48*(10), 557–565.

Purpose: To identify published recommendations for genetics and genomics competencies or curriculum for nurses in the United States and to summarize genetic and genomic nursing competencies based on common themes among these documents.

Method: A review of the literature between January 1998 and June 2008 was conducted. Efforts were also made to access the gray literature. Five consensus documents describing recommendations for genetics and genomics competencies for nurses meeting inclusion criteria were analyzed. Twelve genetics and genomics competencies were created based on common themes among the recommendations.

Findings: These competencies include: demonstrate an understanding of basic genetic and genomic concepts, provide and explain genetic and genomic information, refer to appropriate genetics professionals and services, and identify the limits of one's own genetics and genomics expertise. The competencies represent fundamental genetics and genomics competencies for nurses on the basis of common themes among several consensus recommendations identified in the literature.

Implications: Future research will be needed to document the implementation of core genetics and genomics competencies into undergraduate nursing programs. This will need to include preparing faculty to teach the content, identifying where within basic curricula genetic competencies fit most effectively, and determining how students' development of competence is evaluated. The commitment to genetics and genomics education of healthcare professionals at all levels will help assure that future nurses have the competence in genetics and genomics their patients and colleagues expect.

In Vitro Fertilization and Artificial Insemination

The detection of genetic status and using genetic information to make decisions about fertility are just the beginning stages of the birth technology revolution. Many individuals who are concerned about the birth process are not concerned about genetic problems but about infertility or other problems with normal conception. It is now technically possible to deal with many of these problems using the techniques of IVF, *assisted reproduction* in which fertilization is accomplished outside the body.[10]

Once fertilization is separated from the human body, it is technically possible to manipulate the process in different ways. The fertilization process can be assisted by injecting sperm directly into the egg, a technique known as intracytoplasmic sperm injection (ICSI), or by transferring healthy-appearing gametes directly into the fallopian tube, a procedure known as gamete intrafollicular transfer (GIFT).[11] The egg removed from a woman, after being fertilized by her husband's sperm, could be implanted in the womb of some other woman. A woman with an intact uterus, but no ovaries, could become pregnant after her husband's sperm were used to fertilize an egg cell removed from some other woman, perhaps one undergoing the procedure so that she herself could become pregnant. Beyond these variations, it is also technically possible to fertilize several ova at the same time, storing the extra embryos for later use if the first implantation is unsuccessful.

This method is preferred by clinicians as a way of reducing the extent of trauma to the woman providing the eggs. These extra embryos, however, can have other potential uses, including research and the production of stem cells. Implantation itself can also be enhanced by transferring a healthy-appearing zygote (the fertilized egg) into a fallopian tube of the woman, a procedure known as zygote intrafollicular transfer (ZIFT).[12]

Once a pregnancy is achieved through assisted reproductive techniques, there may be embryos left that the couple no longer needs to use.[13] Nurses involved in assisted reproductive treatment programs have to decide the extent to which their values will allow them to participate in such programs and how to use their nursing role to prevent harm to individuals while supporting their efforts to become pregnant. The next four cases, all involving the same nurse working at an infertility clinic, illustrate various conflicts that can be encountered while caring for individuals seeking help to bear a child.

Case 12-7
Frozen Embryos

Doris Clemmons has worked in a private clinic specializing in assisted reproduction for childless couples for several years. She finds her work rewarding and believes that the clinic provides a wonderful service to individuals who sincerely desire to bear and nurture a child. During the past few years, however, a few situations have tested her beliefs about the benefits of IVF and her role in assisting couples to achieve pregnancy.

Mrs. Clemmons had a close relationship with Ron and Tricia Spencer, a couple whose efforts to become pregnant had not yet been successful. Mrs. Spencer had suffered several tubal pregnancies 6 years ago, and surgery to open up her one remaining tube had been unsuccessful. Mr. and Mrs. Spencer then turned to IVF, although it was not covered by their healthcare insurance. Mrs. Spencer's menstrual cycle was regulated using Pergonal, and eventually 15 eggs were harvested from her ovaries. The eggs were mixed with her husband's sperm in a petri dish, resulting in 12 embryos. Two attempts to induce pregnancy by transferring the embryos to Mrs. Spencer's uterus were not successful, much to everyone's disappointment.

After taking a year to recover from the disappointing episode, the Spencers came back to the clinic to try IVF again. This time, 18 embryos resulted. Six were placed into Mrs. Spencer, but again, she did not become pregnant. Seven of the remaining embryos were thawed and 4 (3 did not survive) were placed into Mrs. Spencer. This attempt was also not successful. There were 5 remaining frozen embryos, but the Spencers decided to wait awhile before making another attempt to become pregnant.

Throughout the Spencers' attempts to become pregnant, Mrs. Clemmons had become quite close to Mrs. Spencer, sharing her ups and downs, hopes and fears. It was her job to calm and support women undergoing hormone treatments to stimulate egg production and to listen carefully to their concerns and reported symptoms. It was not unusual for Mrs. Clemmons's patients to confide in her and to share their concerns about all aspects of their married life. Thus, Mrs. Clemmons was not surprised when Mrs. Spencer called and tearfully asked if she could stop by to talk to her.

She was surprised to learn that Mr. and Mrs. Spencer had separated and were obtaining a divorce. Their marriage had not survived the childlessness, the stress of the IVF procedures, and the repeated disappointments when pregnancy did not result. Mrs. Spencer, however, wanted to try IVF again with the remaining embryos. To her, they were her "children" and represented her only hope of becoming pregnant. Mr. Spencer, on the other hand, was adamantly opposed to having the embryos placed into Mrs. Spencer. He did not want to be the father of any children born to Mrs. Spencer or want the embryos used by any other woman. He wanted the clinic to discard them.

Mrs. Spencer was pursuing legal action to block Mr. Spencer's attempt to discard the embryos, and she wanted Mrs. Clemmons to make sure that the embryos were safely stored. It was also clear that Mrs. Spencer expected Mrs. Clemmons to support her "side of the story" and her wish to have the remaining embryos placed into her uterus. How far did Mrs. Clemmons's support for her patients extend—and what about her own thoughts regarding using the frozen embryos against the wishes of Mr. Spencer?

Case 12-8
An IVF Request from an Unmarried Woman

Mrs. Clemmons, the nurse in the IVF clinic encountered in Case 12-7, found it difficult to develop a warm, supportive relationship with Jennifer Munro, a single woman who wanted to bear a child without the involvement of a husband or male partner. Miss Munro was the first single woman for whom the clinic was willing to provide IVF, despite several requests from single women over the past year. The clinic physicians considered Miss Munro a good risk because she was intelligent, owned her own business, and had elderly parents living with her in a spacious home. She would use her own ova and donated sperm, and was in excellent health. Mrs. Clemmons, however, was not certain that IVF should be available to single women or even lesbian couples. Just because a technology for assisted reproduction was available, was the clinic obligated to offer the service to anyone who requested it?

Case 12-9
Selective Abortion and IVF

Greg and Abigail Grossman, an older couple who were also patients of Mrs. Clemmons (the nurse encountered in the previous two cases), were finally successful in their third attempt at IVF. Mrs. Grossman's pregnancy test was positive 2 weeks after the procedure, and her hormone levels were very high, indicating that more than one embryo was growing. Indeed, by the fourth month of pregnancy, five fetuses could be seen on ultrasound and all seemed to be developing normally. The clinic had followed the usual procedure of implanting more than one embryo in order to increase the chance that at least some would survive. Although implanting as many as five is uncommon, some people wanting to increase the probability of at least one successful pregnancy do transfer that many, especially if the woman is older and previous attempts have failed.

At this point, the clinic physician recommended that the Grossmans reduce the pregnancy to two fetuses to ensure their survival, to prevent the birth of premature infants needing costly neonatal nursery services for weeks after the birth, and to avoid potential harm (cardiac overload) to Mrs. Grossman. The procedure would be a selective abortion of three of the fetuses.

The Grossmans were horrified by this information and did not know what to do. They asked Mrs. Clemmons to help them make their decision. To be honest, she found it very hard to see couples faced with this type of choice. She shared their grief when they failed to become pregnant through sometimes several IVF procedures. Each IVF attempt was hard on the woman's health, hard on the marriage relationship, and expensive. Many couples used their retirement savings or took huge loans to pay for the treatment and then had no idea how they would pay for the child's college education. Once a woman did become pregnant, it seemed a cruel twist to then recommend killing some of the fetuses so that others would have a better chance at healthy births—especially when it took such a great effort to have any fetuses in the first place! She found the potential for selective abortion one of the most undesirable aspects of IVF. Even though this possibility was explained to couples before beginning IVF, she had not observed one case in which a couple who made the decision to selectively abort did not experience serious emotional trauma and did not later question their decision. Two of the clinic's couples had, in fact, lost their remaining fetuses a few weeks after selective abortion procedures. How could Mrs. Clemmons best help the Grossmans through this difficult decision?

Case 12-10
The Risks of Egg Donation

Mrs. Clemmons's IVF clinic actively recruits egg donors. This is becoming a concern for her. Increasingly the women who present to "donate" are young, healthy, and in need of cash. While the clinic does disclose the risks of egg donation, which include the risks of using fertility drugs and the risks of egg retrieval itself, Mrs. Clemmons is not sure that most of the women donors fully comprehend how their decision might impact their own future reproductive decisions.

Commentary

The questions Mrs. Clemmons raises about the benefits of IVF have been raised by others. Some of the early commentators on IVF questioned the "demystification" of the birth process, taking what was once procreation and converting it into the "manufacture" of babies.[14] Some of these commentators grounded their objections in what amounted to natural law positions, arguing that certain biological processes constitute the naturally appropriate way of procreating and that artificial manipulations of something as fundamental as human germ cells violates the natural order.

They also objected on the basis that IVF constituted an experiment on a nonconsenting subject (the fetus), exposing it to risks that technically cannot be for its own benefit. Because the being upon whom the experiment of in vitro manipulation would be conducted would not otherwise exist, it would be impossible for the intervention to be for the new being's own good.

In reality, IVF is undertaken for the good of adults who perceive a child as beneficial to them.[15] As IVF has become more commonplace, concern about possible risks to the child has diminished. Evidence seems to show that babies born through IVF are not at any greater risk than those conceived more traditionally. In 2002, the most recent year for which data are available, there were over 45,000 babies born in the United States from assisted reproduction technologies. Almost all of these births are from IVF.[16] As many as a million births have occurred using this technique throughout the world since it was first introduced in 1978. Still, underlying ethical questions remain.

Whereas many ethics commentators have raised these questions, others have defended the process, some even calling IVF more ethical than traditional conception because it is a "more human" way to reproduce.[17] They have argued that the human is a rational animal and that traditional reproduction simply leaves matters to chance. According to them, rational planning of a pregnancy—overcoming the limits of nature, if necessary—is more human and therefore more ethical.

Some nurses may continue to struggle with these now-traditional issues about the risks of IVF and the morality of manipulating human embryos. Other nurses, like Mrs. Clemmons, may be raising newer, more specific questions, such as the ethical disposition of leftover embryos, decisions about who has access to the technology, and the morality of aborting healthy fetuses that were obtained by IVF.

One approach to the issue of extra embryos is to view the extra embryos as essentially the property of the man and woman who produced them. Because couples have the right to control their joint personal property, they have the right to control their embryos, even to destroy them. However, even if one grants couples the right to control or destroy their embryos, it does not necessarily follow that they have the right to do other things with them. In particular, they might not have the right to maintain them to the point that they live to be more mature. For this reason, many commentators have held that either no research should be permitted on embryos or that such research should be limited to the very early stages of life, say the first 14 days.[18]

Even if such research manipulations are prohibited, there is still a problem of what to do with extra embryos. Many couples report struggling with this decision.[19] If the couple dissolves their relationship, which partner should retain custody of stored embryos? Can one partner decide to use or dispose of the embryos without the consent of the other partner? Other options for the Spencers are to donate the embryos for embryo adoption or to authorize their use in stem cell research.

These are the issues facing the Spencers. The courts have tended to rule that the couple must make joint decisions about the disposition of their embryos and that the embryos should remain stored until the couple, even if no longer married, decides.[20]

Once the path of decision making for leftover embryos is settled, what if the decision is made to dispose of them? Must the couple carry out the disposal, or can someone else act on their behalf? Should there be norms of proper disposal, and if so, how should these norms be enforced? If the decision is not to dispose of the embryos, are there limits to the amount of time they can be stored? If the couple no longer wants to use the embryos but does not want them to be disposed of, should other couples wanting to conceive but unable to supply gametes be permitted access to stored but no longer wanted embryos? If so, does the couple that was the original source of the embryos have to consent to their use by others? Should they be compensated? The recipient couple is, after all, saving the expense, risk, and discomfort of IVF that was necessary to obtain the viable embryos.

Now that IVF is easily obtained, is covered by many healthcare insurance plans, and is beginning to have a higher rate of success than it did 10 years ago, questions arise as to whether access to the technology can justifiably be limited. Until recently, IVF clinics tended to limit their services to married couples who were unable to achieve pregnancy and a child without IVF assistance. But is there any moral reason that others should not have access to the technology? Are a marital relationship and a long-standing inability to become pregnant the appropriate prerequisites for IVF services? A presumption that they are prerequisites seems to be the reason Mrs. Clemmons has difficulty accepting Jennifer Munro as a patient at the IVF clinic. Ms. Munro's reasons for selecting IVF are not the same as other patients' reasons. It has always been clear to Mrs. Clemmons that she enjoys her work and values IVF for the same reasons that her married patients do. Access to assisted reproduction technologies was a hot topic in 2009 when Nadya Suleman, a single mother with 6 children gave birth to octuplets after having six embryos implanted, two or which resulted in twins. At the time Ms. Suleman was living with her parents and receiving disability payments from the state of California. She said that she always dreamed of having a big family as a result of being an only child.[21]

Critical Thinking Questions

1. Is there something immoral about Jennifer Munro's request for IVF because she eschews marriage and does not have a diagnosis of infertility? If so, why? If not, why not?

2. Why should any woman, even one who can achieve pregnancy the usual way but does not want to have sex, not be able to purchase IVF services as the means to having a child?

3. If unmarried couples are permitted to use IVF services, why shouldn't a single unmarried woman or a gay or lesbian couple have access to IVF if their goal is to achieve pregnancy and have a child?

A more difficult ethical issue is generated by one of IVF's consequences: a multifetal pregnancy resulting from the implanting of multiple embryos. On average, about three embryos are implanted hoping that at least one will survive.[22] Implanting fewer embryos decreases the chance of at least one live birth, but implanting more embryos increases the risk of multiple fetuses. Although the percentage varies with the age of the woman undergoing implantation, in 2002 about 35% of all the live births following IVF resulted in multiple infants.[23] In the case of a multifetal pregnancy, some physicians advise the woman to undergo a *selective abortion* in order to reduce risks to the fetuses' and to her health. This is morally controversial because it involves intentional termination of apparently normal fetuses and the procedure itself is not without risk. The loss of an entire pregnancy following selective abortion has been a significant problem.[24]

If Mrs. Clemmons is opposed to abortion in principle, it will be almost impossible for her to continue to work in an IVF clinic where selective abortion of a multifetal pregnancy is a common occurrence. If she is not opposed to abortion in principle, then she must evaluate what it is about selective abortion that is bothersome to her. It may be that she does not believe that couples are fully informed about the potential consequences of successful IVF and future decisions that may need to be made. The desire to have a child may be so powerful that couples are willing to try anything that promises success and thus underestimate potential risks when contemplating the overwhelming benefit of a successful pregnancy. If this is the case, then Mrs. Clemmons can assist couples by providing more information before they undergo IVF. That could be a very important part of her nursing role in the IVF clinic.

Mrs. Clemmons may also be questioning the morality of aborting some fetuses to enhance the survival of others. For example, if the Grossmans knew that Mrs. Grossman was carrying four female fetuses and one male fetus and decided to selectively abort three of the female fetuses in order to deliver one boy and one girl, Mrs. Clemmons might find the intent to abort female fetuses troublesome.

On the other hand, Mrs. Clemmons might not find it troublesome to choose selective abortion if the reason is to preserve Mrs. Grossman's cardiac health. Clearly, the various reasons for selective abortion of a multifetal pregnancy are not morally equal and need to be carefully considered, not only by couples faced with making such a decision, but also by the health professionals who support them through the decision-making process.

Critical Thinking Questions

1. If a couple could make a selective abortion choice based on sexual prefer-ence, what would prohibit some other couple from making a selective abor-tion choice based on genetic endowments such as blue eyes and blond hair, or mental intelligence?
2. What role should nurses have in discussing the limits of technological advances and the morality of their uses?

Case 12-10 raises the issue of the nurse's role in advocating for the wellbeing of women who come to the clinic to donate eggs. While some of these women know the individuals desiring to become parents and are motivated to help, most simply wish to sell something they do not need that has a value to someone else. Moreover, while they listen to the risks associated with using fertility drugs and egg retrieval, many do not seem to comprehend that in some cases, these risks might be serious. This case illustrates the conflict between the nurse's obligation to promote the health and well-being of the patient versus the obligation to respect the autono-mous preferences of the patient. If Mrs. Clemmons suspects that the process of informed consent is being compromised by the clinic's need for donor eggs or for donor eggs of a particular type, her obligation to intervene is clear.

Critical Thinking Questions

1. In what ways are the language and reality of the marketplace influencing nursing and medical practice in the fertility clinic? Are these positive or neg-ative influences?
2. What besides a "satisfied customer" ought to be the concerns of healthcare professionals working in the IVF clinic?
3. Is there anything wrong with a black market that makes "high quality" eggs, sperm, embryos, and wombs available for a price?

Case 12-11
Questioning the Purposes of Surrogate Motherhood Requests

Janice Collins works in the office of Dr. Ellis, a private physician who specializes in assisted reproduction approaches. Although the majority of Dr. Ellis's patients use their own gametes in assisted reproduction, some couples, because of a variety of problems, choose to use donor ova or sperm. During the past 3 years, Dr. Ellis has employed the services of several surrogate mothers for female patients incapable of carrying a pregnancy to term. Ms. Collins has been supportive of these surrogacy arrangements, but a few recent requests have caused her to question surrogacy.

The Merino Family: Stan and Lillian Merino contacted Dr. Ellis because they knew he was amenable to surrogate motherhood arrangements. Mrs. Merino is a healthy woman in her mid-30s and is capable of bearing a child (the Merinos have a 3-year-old daughter). The couple wants to have another child, but Mrs. Merino does not want to take the time from her career to undergo hormonal stimulation of her ovaries to harvest ova nor to undergo a pregnancy in the foreseeable future. Instead, she would like to employ a surrogate mother who will donate her own ova and agree to be artificially inseminated with Mr. Merino's sperm. The Merinos can afford to pay for the services of the surrogate and actually prefer this approach so that there will not be a large age difference between their children. They feel that a surrogacy arrangement is the best way for them to meet their social, career, and parenting needs.

The Beall Family: Crissy and John Beall are a childless couple who thought they could never have a genetic child until they heard about surrogate motherhood. Mrs. Beall was diagnosed with CA of the uterus while in her mid-20s and had a total hysterectomy, which included removal of her ovaries. They have asked Dr. Ellis if he would artificially inseminate Mrs. Beall's 51-year-old widowed mother with Mr. Beall's sperm, so that they can have a child that is genetically linked to both of them. Mrs. Beall's mother, Mrs. Hoffman, is willing to undergo the procedure and has no health reasons that would prohibit her from carrying a child to term. Mrs. Beall is her only daughter, and she views her role in this arrangement as an act of love.

The Murray Family: Sam and Anne Murray have been married for 23 years and have two children, 21-year-old Sam Jr., and 19-year-old Joan. The Murrays are requesting the services of a surrogate mother to help them have another child, a very special child, who will be used to donate bone marrow for Joan, who was diagnosed with leukemia 4 years earlier. Joan's leukemia has resisted treatment. Her only hope for survival is to have a bone marrow transplant. Unfortunately, no acceptable donor has been found after months of searching, and the Murrays believe that time is running out for Joan. Doctors have mentioned that the best bone marrow match for Joan would probably come from her own family members, but no match has been found. Because Anne has developed a kidney disorder that will not permit her to undergo pregnancy at her age, but she is not yet menopausal, she and Sam want a surrogate mother to carry their genetic child. Using IVF and preimplantation genetic testing techniques, the Murrays want Dr. Ellis to select embryos that can be suitable donors for the bone marrow procedure and then implant them into the surrogate mother's uterus. They are desperate to do whatever they can to help their daughter survive, even though it will mean creating this child for the purpose of using its bone marrow for Joan. They stress that they are committed to continuing to raise the child and that the objective of bone marrow donation will not interfere with their love and nurturing of another offspring.

Commentary

Ms. Collins and Dr. Ellis have apparently already answered some of the ethical questions about assisted reproduction to their satisfaction. They have confronted the traditional ethical questions about the artificiality of manipulating human germ cells that were discussed in conjunction with the previous cases. They have no insurmountable ethical conflict about the transfer of germ cells to someone outside of a marriage; they have previously accepted the use of donated ova or sperm in assisting a couple's reproductive efforts.

What they now confront are newer variations on this theme. To be sure, the involvement of a female gamete donor for the Merinos is more substantial. The surrogate mother will serve as the host for the pregnancy as well as supplying her ova. In reflecting on the ethics involved, Ms. Collins and Dr. Ellis might ask themselves whether there is a significant moral difference between a situation in which a woman simply donates ova and one in which a woman serves not only as the ova donor but also as the surrogate mother. In the latter case, the woman's involvement includes substantially more physical and emotional commitment. It will be much more difficult for the relationship to be anonymous than if only donor ova were used. Some surrogate mothers have developed unanticipated attachments to a fetus that is biologically, but not socially, partly theirs.

Because the surrogate mother is necessarily involved for a long period of time, other problems might arise that would not appear in traditional assisted reproduction. Would Stan and Lillian Merino, for instance, have the right to insist that the surrogate mother maintain good prenatal practices: avoid alcohol and smoking, take vitamins, exercise regularly, and make regular visits to the prenatal clinic? Would they have the right to insist upon prenatal diagnosis to detect possible fetal anomalies? If so, would they have the right to insist upon an abortion if some undesirable pattern of fetal development emerged? Would the Merinos be able to insist on abortion if a risk occurred that was unacceptable to them, or would the risk have to be unacceptable to the surrogate mother or to the "reasonable person"? Would the husband of the surrogate mother have any rights—for instance, the right to consent to the involvement of his wife in what would seriously disrupt the traditional marital relationship or the right to veto an abortion if he were willing to accept responsibility for a child the Merinos no longer wanted? All these questions need to be answered before Dr. Ellis and Ms. Collins recommend one of their surrogate mothers for the Merinos' request.

Critical Thinking Questions

1. Is there any moral difference between the situation in which a surrogate mother serves as a substitute for a woman unable to carry a child to term and the situation in which a surrogate serves as a substitute for a woman, like Lillian Merino, who simply finds it inconvenient to undergo a pregnancy? If so, why? If not, why not?

2. Is surrogate motherhood a last-resort arrangement reserved only for those incapable of bearing a child, or should it be an arrangement accessible and acceptable under any circumstances, as long as all parties consent? Why?

In some sense, not allowing surrogate motherhood unless it is necessitated by physical inability to bear a child includes a value judgment about the priorities of the woman who will eventually have the nurturing responsibilities for the child. Do the circumstances that prompt the Merinos to request surrogate motherhood make their situation less acceptable than other situations? With an increasing acceptance of nontraditional roles for women, some women are bound to want parenthood without pregnancy. Some women may desire a child for other reasons, as well. This seems to be the case for the Murrays, whose reasons for creating a child are very different from the Merinos'. Is the Murrays' desire to have another child in order to obtain a bone marrow transplant for their daughter Joan of a lower priority than desiring the child for its own sake? How morally relevant is desiring a child for its own sake or the physical inability to bear a child to Dr. Ellis in recommending a surrogate mother for either the Merinos or the Murrays?

The Murray case also involves a request for preimplantation genetic diagnosis (PGD), a procedure where, following IVF, cells are removed from the blastocyst and analyzed using various techniques.[25] Presumably, PGD can determine whether a fetus possesses the capacity to be a bone marrow donor for Joan. Usually, this kind of testing is done to determine whether a fetus is affected by a genetic disorder. It is a desirable testing procedure because it can eliminate abortion decisions taken for reasons of possible genetic disorder. The Murrays, however, want to use PGD for reasons that currently fall outside medical use of the technology.[26] There are no technical reasons why PGD cannot be done in this situation, however.

Critical Thinking Questions

1. Are the Murrays' reasons for requesting PGD morally acceptable? If so, why? If not, why not?

2. Who should be making this judgment?

At the present time, most PGD programs operate under the guidance of an ethics advisory board. Should the Murrays' request be reviewed by such a group, or should Dr. Ellis make the decision to honor or reject their request?

On the one hand, it certainly seems prudent to determine which of the Murrays' embryos could be donors for Joan before implanting them into the surrogate mother. This seems better than waiting until later in the pregnancy and then requesting selective abortion of the nondonor fetuses. After all, the Murrays want only one child or, at best, one child and a spare for their purposes. Because time is relevant to Joan's survival, PGD also offers the quickest route to obtaining a donor child. But what about the otherwise healthy embryos that are not judged to be acceptable donors? Should the Murrays be required to freeze these embryos and offer them to childless couples? Or could the Murrays dispose of the embryos according to the standards set by society? PGD, when combined with surrogate motherhood, becomes a variation that can take on some interesting dimensions. Again, Dr. Ellis and Ms. Collins will need to decide what is ethically acceptable to them before agreeing to the Murrays' request.

One final ethical issue about surrogate motherhood concerns its tendency to redefine what we mean by parenthood and family. Once it is possible for a surrogate to bear a child that is genetically hers, who is really the mother of the child? Is the genetic mother the real mother? Or is the woman who nurtures and cares for the child after it is born the real mother? If the surrogate is married and has other children, what is the relationship of this new child, borne for the sake of the genetic father and his wife, to her other children? Are families merely social units in society, or are they groups of individuals with genetic as well as social and emotional ties? Should the role of the original understanding and agreement of the parties be binding morally and legally or are there circumstances in which society should override them?

These concerns become especially troublesome when one family member (like Mrs. Hoffman) contributes her ova, is artificially inseminated with her son-in-law's sperm, and carries the child to term for the sake of her childless daughter. Mrs. Hoffman will essentially bear her own grandchild and Mrs. Beall will be the mother to her own half brother or sister. Does surrogate motherhood in this situation create future conflicts within the family about the guidance of and responsibility for the child? On the other hand, is surrogate motherhood more acceptable in this situation because it is done for altruistic reasons and uses genes within the family unit? Some might argue that such an arrangement is immoral because it tampers with traditional family relationships. Mrs. Beall will essentially be the mother to a child that her mother and husband created together. Is the joining of her husband's sperm with her mother's ova morally wrong?

There are no easy answers to these questions. But Dr. Ellis and Ms. Collins must come to some agreement about which surrogate motherhood arrangements they find justifiable and will work with in their practice. Technically, there are no barriers to the potential uses of surrogate motherhood arrangements.

> ## Critical Thinking Questions
>
> 1. Should our society have moral barriers to surrogate motherhood arrangements?
> 2. Should society be willing to let the marketplace and the willingness of potential host mothers dictate the practice?

Genetic Engineering

The newest and, in many ways, most controversial birth technology the nurse may encounter is what is often referred to as "genetic engineering" or "gene therapy." Genetic counseling and genetic screening focus on determining the existence of genetic conditions and helping the patient accommodate this information through psychologic interventions, support systems, and in some cases, abortion. They take the actual genetic endowment as a given. Genetic engineering, however, involves techniques that change the genetic makeup of an individual. It has been on the horizon since the 1970s.[27]

Recently, two procedures involving genetic engineering techniques entered clinical trials. One procedure, somatic cell gene therapy, involves the insertion of a functioning gene into the somatic cells of an individual to correct an inborn error of metabolism or to provide a new function for a cell. In the trials, researchers are investigating how this procedure works for genetic disorders such as adenosine deaminase deficiency, familial hypercholesterolimia, and cystic fibrosis.[1] It is predicted that the most common application of this procedure in the future will be for the treatment of cancer. The second procedure is germline gene therapy, altering the DNA in germline cells (that is, sperm or ova). The DNA alteration would, of course, be passed onto future generations and thus raises many ethical and social issues.

The technical ability to attempt changes in the genetic endowment is developing rapidly and promises to create remarkable possibilities as well as troublesome ethical questions. Nursing personnel will be called upon to engage in discussion about these questions and analysis of the social and ethical issues involved. They will also be asked to provide clinical and research support for efforts to manipulate genes. The following case, based on the current state of the field, presents some of the questions that might arise in the nursing care of patients undergoing experimental genetic engineering.

---

[1]Adenosine deaminase deficiency (ADA) is an autosomal-recessive disorder that results in the accumulation of deoxyadenosine and its metabolites. This inhibits DNA synthesis in cells and is especially toxic to T lymphocytes. It produces a severe immune deficiency that, if untreated, is usually fatal by the age of 2. Familial hypercholesterolemia results from a monogenic defect that causes elevated LDL cholesterol levels, leading to heart attack in 50% of male heterozygotes by the age of 50 years and in 50% of female heterozygotes by the age of 65 years. It has a frequency of about 1 in 500. Cystic fibrosis (CF) is one of the most common single-gene disorders in North America, affecting approximately 1 in 2500 white newborns. It results in thick secretions in the lungs and pancreas and leads to chronic pulmonary and digestive disease.

Case 12-12
The Nurse in Experimental Genetic Engineering[2]

Louise McHenry is a staff nurse at the Clinical Research Center at University Hospital, a major research center affiliated with a leading medical school. Two of the major lines of research that have been pursued at the center are converging toward a bold experiment. The molecular biology group, under the direction of Dr. Horrace Windover, has for years been conducting research on the basic processes of gene manipulation. Using techniques involving recombinant DNA, they have become proficient in the basic science and laboratory techniques known to make possible the addition of genetic material into living cells. Using partially inactivated retroviruses as vectors, bits of genetic material can be carried into cells and become incorporated into them.

Collaborating in the proposed research is a group of scientists that has conducted a long line of studies of metabolic processes under the direction of Dr. Max Kleindorf. The Windover team and Dr. Kleindorf are already conducting clinical trials of their techniques in the treatment of adenosine deaminase deficiency (ADA), a serious, otherwise untreatable metabolic disorder. Some months ago, Dr. Windover approached Dr. Kleindorf about collaborating on an attempt to become the first lab to provide a formally approved method of treating familial polyposis coli (FPC), a disorder that confers a nearly 100% risk of colon cancer unless surgically prevented by colorectomy.

Their approach would involve removing bone marrow from an affected individual and exposing it to gene splicing techniques developed by Dr. Windover's group and others from around the world working on recombinant DNA. If all went well, the treated bone marrow would take up the missing genetic material and be reintroduced into the patient. That patient would then have a new-found capacity to resist colon cancer.

Louise McHenry, as a nurse in the clinical center, would be called upon to provide the now-standard nursing services involved in helping patients comprehend the detailed information in the informed-consent-to-treatment protocols and in preparing patients for the bone marrow transplantation. She and the other personnel in the center have attended several meetings at which the new project was explained. She would be asked to do nothing different from what she has done for patients in the clinical trials for the treatment of ADA. The bone marrow would be reimplanted in the patient from whom it was taken, with new genetic material incorporated—hopefully the genetic material needed by the patient.

The researchers were candid in their announcement of the project to clinical staff. The technologies are new and potentially controversial. The same technologies could be used to make other changes in the basic genetic structure of human beings. Moreover, once fairly simple genetic manipulations are successful for patients with various kinds of cancer, the way would be cleared for more controversial interventions. Although the present project would involve attempts to modify somatic cells only, follow-up projects could involve the modification of germ cells, making it possible to transmit, from one generation to the next,

---

[2]This case was constructed with the assistance of LeRoy Walters, former chairman of the Working Group on Human Gene Therapy of the NIH Recombinant DNA Advisory Committee.

new genetic material introduced into the species. Indeed, studies were already under way testing various techniques that might be used in the treatment of Fragile X Syndrome, the most common form of mental retardation, accounting for up to 5% of the mentally impaired population. The mutation that causes this disorder is located on the X chromosome. Once perfected, the techniques will eventually be applied to other sex-linked disorders.

Ms. McHenry is being asked whether she is willing to be part of the team for the new research project to treat those with FPC at risk for colon cancer. Ms. McHenry has had experience assessing various features of research protocols in the past. She is familiar with both the national standards and the local standards used by the research center's institutional review board (IRB). She knows that the IRB will review the proposed research and that, because part of the work will be supported by NIH funds, a national-level panel will also review the work. She has no doubts that the proposed research will meet the highest technical standards and that the investigators are acting in good conscience. Still she needs to decide whether, ethically, she can be a part of a proposed project the future uses and implications of which are as yet unknown.

Commentary

In making her decision, Ms. McHenry will have to take into account all of the standard questions regarding the ethics of research involving patients. She should consult the American Nurses Association (ANA) *Ethical Guidelines in the Conduct, Dissemination, and Implementation of Nursing Research*, which recommends that, "the investigator ensure the ethical integrity of the research process by use of appropriate checks and balances throughout the conduct, dissemination, and implementation of the research."[28] In addition, she should be familiar with the recommendations for the participation of nurses in genetic research and the management of genetic information, which address various practice, education, research, and policy issues.[29] She might also familiarize herself with NIH documents addressing human somatic cell gene therapy.[30]

Questions remain that she must answer. In the assessment of risks, several that are unique to gene therapy should be considered.[31] The retroviruses used could recombine with other DNA material, produce deleterious effects, disrupt other genes, or produce carcinogenic effects. It is conceivable that the viruses could affect other persons—either workers in the laboratory or members of the public. Although steps would undoubtedly be taken to minimize these risks, they cannot be completely ruled out.

The most fundamental question Ms. McHenry has to face is whether there is something in principle that is morally questionable about human efforts to manipulate genetic material and to incorporate new genes into the cells of human beings. Genetic engineering has been compared to manipulation of the atom. These two scientific efforts have created the capacity to change the nature of the universe in ways that some people find more dramatic than the effects of any other previous scientific and medical endeavors in history. DNA, the genetic material, makes individual living species what they are.

Until recently, medical efforts have, by and large, left the nature of the species intact. To be sure, over extremely long periods, medical interventions might cause the evolution of infinitesimal, incremental changes in the nature of the human; over time, however, the species itself would remain constant. Now we have the knowledge and the capacity to make wholesale changes in the genetic composition of the species.[32] Established in 1990, the National Center for Human Genome Research at NIH, part of the Human Genome Project, began producing a map to identify the location of all genes in the human genome and determine the chemical sequence of DNA. In 2003, the center announced that an accurate and complete human genome sequence was finished. In addition, about 900 of the mapped genes have been identified as disease-causing genes for conditions such as sickle cell anemia. Discovery of these genes has been followed quickly by tests to assess the risks of developing certain disorders and to assess the potential to screen large populations for the presence or risk of the disease. Then gene therapy developments have followed, with the ability to substitute a normal gene for an altered gene, to provide a product of a normal gene, and to modify an individual's genotype.[33]

Nurses, like Ms. McHenry, and research teams, like the one described in this case, will increasingly be making choices about how they will participate in the new gene therapies created by these discoveries and considering what their involvement will be in efforts to improve upon the already normal human genetic endowment. They will need to reflect on whether it is important to limit experimental gene therapy treatments to changes in somatic cells. Changes such as the one contemplated in the proposed research in Case 12-12 would have their impact only in the individual patient. The patients' reproductive cells would remain as before. This has two implications. On the one hand, if the subjects of this experiment are treated successfully, they will survive to produce offspring who are also at risk of developing colon cancer. On the other hand, if something unexpected were to happen, if some harmful genetic material were incorporated into the treated patient, the effect would be limited to that patient.

Ms. McHenry should realize, however, that this research project will involve not only decisions to treat individual patients at risk for FPC, but it will also have a few long-term impacts. The same technologies—the retroviruses and the techniques of gene transfer developed in this experiment—will also be available for use by others in other settings to transfer other genetic material. Ms. McHenry must decide not only whether she is willing to participate in this first attempt to change the human genetic endowment; she must also decide whether she is willing to participate in starting what is likely to be a long line of experiments with impacts far more dramatic than those involving patients at risk of developing FPC. Her question is whether humans are rational agents with the rights and responsibilities for reshaping their very nature or, alternatively, whether they ought not to be tampering with matters so fundamental.

Critical Thinking Question

What types of roles should nurses play in the development and use of technologies that affect genetic endowments?

ENDNOTES

1. Bieesecker, B. B., Boenke, M., Calzone, K., Markel, D., Garber, J., Collins, F. S., et al. (1973). Genetic counseling for families with inherited susceptibility to breast and ovarian cancer. *Journal of the American Medical Association, 269*, 1970–1974; Elsas, L. J. (1990). A clinical approach to legal and ethical problems in human genetics. *Emory Law Journal, 39*(3), 811–853; Peterson, G. M. (1995). Genetic counseling and predictive genetic testing in familial adenomatous polyposis. *Seminars in Colon and Rectal Surgery, 6*(1), 55–60; President's Commission for the Study of Ethical Problems in Medicine and Biomedical and Behavioral Research. (1983). *Screening and counseling for genetic conditions: The ethical, social, and legal implications of genetic screening, counseling, and education programs.* Washington, DC: U.S. Government Printing Office; Weatherall, D. J. (Ed.). (1991). Ethical issues and related problems arising from the application of the new genetics to clinical practice. In *The new genetics and clinical practice* (3rd ed., pp. 347–368). New York: Oxford University Press; Wertz, D. C. (1992). Ethical and legal implications of the new genetics: Issues for discussion. *Social Science and Medicine, 35*(4), 495–505; Wertz, D. C., & Fletcher, J. C. (1993). Proposed: An international code of ethics for medical genetics. *Clinical Genetics, 44*(1), 37–43.

2. Scanlon, C., & Fibison, W. (1995). *Managing genetic information: Implications for nursing practice.* Washington, DC: The American Nurses Association.

3. Monsen, R. B. (2009). *Genetics and ethics in health care: New questions in the age of genomic health.* Silver Spring, MD: Nursebooks.org.

4. President's Commission for the Study of Ethical Problems in Medicine and Biomedical and Behavioral Research. (1983). *Screening and counseling for genetic conditions: The ethical, social, and legal implications of genetic screening, counseling, and education programs* (pp. 76–81). Washington, DC: U.S. Government Printing Office.

5. Ibid.

6. The American Society of Human Genetics Board of Directors and the American College of Medical Genetics Board of Directors. (1995). ASHG/ACMG report: Points to consider: Ethical, legal, and psychosocial implications of genetic testing in children and adolescents. *American Journal of Human Genetics, 57*, 1233–1241; Wertz, D. C., Fanos, J. H., & Reilly, P. R. (1994). Genetic testing for children and adolescents: Who decides? *Journal of the American Medical Association, 272*(11), 875–881.

7. Scanlon, C., & Fibison, W. (1995). Managing genetic information: Implications for nursing practice. *Nursing Ethics, 7*(3), 262–268.

8. Fry, S. T. (1987). The ethical dimensions of policy for prenatal diagnostic technologies: The case of maternal serum alpha-fetoprotein screening. *Advances in Nursing Science, 9*(3), 44–55.

9. Gostin, L. O. (1995). Genetic privacy. *Journal of Law, Medicine & Ethics, 23*, 320–330.

10. Dyson, A. (1995). *The ethics of IVF*. New York: Mowbray; Lauritzen, P. (1993). *Pursuing parenthood: Ethical issues in assisted reproduction*. Bloomington, IN: Indiana University Press; Holmes, H.-B. (Ed.). (1992). *Issues in reproductive technology: An anthology*. New York: Garland; Stephenson, P., & Wagner, M. G. (Eds.). (1993). *Tough choices: In vitro fertilization and the reproductive technologies*. Philadelphia: Temple University Press; Weber, L. J. (1996). In vitro fertilization and the just use of health care resources. In J. Humber & R. F. Almeder (Eds.), *Biomedical ethics reviews* (pp. 75–89). Totowa, NJ: Humana Press; Winston, R. M. L., & Handyside, A. H. (1993). New challenges in human in vitro fertilization. *Science, 260*(5110), 932–936.

11. Kong, D. (1996, August 4). What price pregnancy? The painful quest for fertility. *Boston Sunday Globe*, pp. A1, A34.

12. Ibid.

13. Bodin, M. M. (July 28, 1997). My turn: The eggs, embryos and I. *Newsweek*, pp. 14–15.

14. Kass, L. R. (1972, Winter). Making babies—the new biology and the "old" morality. *The Public Interest*, 18–56; Kass, L. R. (1979, Winter). "Making babies" revisited. *The Public Interest*, 32–60; Ramsey, P. (1972). Shall we "reproduce"? *Journal of the American Medical Association, 220*, 1346–1350, 1480–1485.

15. Kong, D. (1996, August 4). What price pregnancy? The painful quest for fertility. *Boston Sunday Globe*, pp. A1, A34.

16. Centers for Disease Control and Prevention. (2002). *Assisted reproductive technology success rates. National summary and fertility clinic reports, Introduction*. Available at: http://www.cdc.gov/reproductivehealth/ART02/nation.htm. Accessed April 3, 2005.

17. Fletcher, J. (1974). *The ethics of genetic control: Ending reproductive roulette*. Garden City, NY: Anchor Books.

18. U.S. National Institutes of Health, Human Embryo Research Panel. (1994). *Report, volumes I, II*. Bethesda, MD: Author.

19. Bodin, M. M. (1997, July 28). My turn: The eggs, embryos and I. *Newsweek*, pp. 14–15.

20. Capron, A. M. (1992). Parenthood and frozen embryos: More than property and privacy. *The Hastings Center Report, 22*(5), 32–33; Davis v. Davis. 842 S.W.2d 588 (Tenn. 1992), cert. Denied 113 S.Ct. 1259 (1993); Muller, R. J. (1993). Davis v. Davis: The applicability of privacy and property rights to the disposition of frozen preembryos in intrafamilial disputes. *University of Toledo Law Review, 24*(3), 763–804.

21. For an interview with Ms. Suleman, see: http://today.msnbc.msn.com/id/29038814/#29050752.

22. U. S. Centers for Disease Control. (2002). *Assisted Reproductive Technology (ART) report: 2002 fertility clinic report by state: Accessible national summary*. Available at: http://apps.nccd.cdc.gov/ART2002/ nation02acc.asp. Accessed April 3, 2005.

23. Ibid.

24. Antsaklis, A., Souka, A. P., Daskalakis, G., Papantoniou, N., Kantra, P., Kavalakis, Y., et al. (2004). Pregnancy outcome after multifetal pregnancy reduction. *Journal of Maternity-Fetal and Neonatal Medicine, 16*(1), 27–31.

25. Zilberstein, M., & Seibel, M. M. (1996). Preimplantation diagnosis: What can be done? *The Genetic Resource, 10*(1), 14–16.

26. Wertz, D. C. (1996). Ethical and social issues in preimplantation genetic diagnosis. *The Genetic Resource, 10*(1), 17–26.

27. Ross, G., Erickson, R., Knorr, D., Motulsky, A. G., Parkman, R., Samulski, J., et al. (1996). Gene therapy in the United States: A five-year status report. *Human Gene Therapy, 7*, 1781–1790.

28. Silva, M. (1995). *Ethical guidelines in the conduct, dissemination, and implementation of nursing research* (p. 35). Washington, DC: The American Nurses Association.

29. Scanlon, C., & Fibison, W. (1995). Managing genetic information: Implications for nursing practice. *American Nurses Association Publications*, 1–50.

30. U.S. National Institutes of Health. (1987). Recombinant DNA research: Actions under guidelines: Notice. *Federal Register, 52*(163), 31848–31850; U.S. National Institutes of Health. (1988). Recombinant DNA research: Proposed actions under guidelines: Notice. *Federal Register, 53*(251), 53262–53269; U.S. National Institutes of Health. (1996). Recombinant DNA research: Notice of intent to propose amendments to the NIH guidelines for research involving recombinant DNA molecules (NIH guidelines) regarding enhanced mechanisms for NIH oversight of recombinant DNA activities. *Federal Register, 61*(131), 35774–35777; U.S. National Institutes of Health, Recombinant DNA Advisory Committee, Human Gene Therapy/Points to Consider Subcommittee. (1990). The revised "points to consider" document. *Human Gene Therapy, 1*(1), 93–103; U.S. National Institutes of Health, Recombinant DNA Advisory Committee, Working Group on Human Gene Therapy. (1985). Points to consider in the design and submission of human somatic cell gene therapy protocols. *Recombinant DNA Technical Bulletin, 8*(4), 181–196; Wilson, D. J. (1993). NIH guidelines for research involving recombinant DNA molecules. *Accountability in Research, 3*(2–3), 177–185.

31. Elias, S., & Annas, G. J. (1992). Somatic and germline therapy. In G. J. Annas & S. Elias (Eds.), *Gene mapping: Using law and ethics as guides*. New York: Oxford University Press.

32. Bonnicksen, A. L. (1994, February). National and international approaches to human germline gene therapy. *Politics and the Life Sciences*, 1–9.

33. Scanlon, C., & Fibison, W. (1995). Managing genetic information: Implications for nursing practice. *American Nurses Association Publications*, 1–50.

Chapter 13

Psychiatry and the Control of Human Behavior

Other Cases Involving Psychiatry and Behavior Control

Key Terms
Behavior control
Psychosurgery
Psychotherapy

Objectives

1. Identify ethical issues associated with the control of human behavior.
2. Describe one ethical conflict between the principles of autonomy and beneficence in caring for a patient with mental illness.
3. Apply ethical principles in the nursing care of mentally ill patients.

A third area of healthcare practice presenting ethical challenges for the nurse is that of psychiatric nursing and the control of human behavior.[1] The problem of the meaning and justification of ethical claims—such as an argument over whether homosexuality or aggressive violence is a genetically determined natural variant of the human condition, an immoral behavior, or a manifestation of an illness—arise here with great regularity. Serious conceptual problems are at stake in deciding whether a generally unacceptable behavior should be considered the result of natural biology, mental illness or some moral deviance.

The *Diagnostic and Statistical Manual of Mental Disorders,* Fourth Edition (DSM-IV)[2] is the manual physicians, psychiatrists, psychologists, therapists, and social workers use in order to diagnose mental illness. Illustrative of the present day challenges in defining illness in general and mental illness specifically, are the challenges in determining what should be included in the *DSM-IV* as a mental disorder. For example, homosexuality, included in earlier versions of the *DSM*, is no longer in the present manual. A 2007 editorial in *The American Journal of Psychiatry* argued for the inclusion of relational disorders in the revised *DSM* and defined relational disorders as "persistent and painful patterns of feelings, behavior and perception involving two or more partners in an important personal relationship."[3] The author, Dr. Wayne Denton, argued,

> It is becoming increasingly clear that advances in brain science will eventually render the symptomatic approach to diagnosis embodied in DSM-IV obsolete and that the 'intellectual straitjacket' of the current DSM system will have to be loosened . . . Such loosening can open the way to fresh approaches that would include the description of relational disorders."[4]

But not everyone agrees that the *DSM* categories should be "loosened." An article by Walter Kirn and Sora Song in *Time* magazine laments that

> Every year there are new ways to be crazy. Until recently, being driven mad by others and driving others mad was known as life. It didn't have a name—at least not a medically sanctioned name that could be listed on insurance forms and used in advertisements for pharmaceuticals.[5]

It is immediately apparent that there are serious benefits and harms associated with diagnostic labels: changes in self-image, access to treatment, the costs of health care are just a few. Nurses who have first-hand experience of individuals experiencing the debilitating effects of the human condition and who can appreciate the benefits and limitations of medical treatment ought to have a voice in determining what counts as a "mental disorder" meriting a diagnostic label.

Critical Thinking Questions

1. How confident are you in your ability to define mental disorder and articulate the necessary and sufficient criteria for diagnostic categories?

2. Do you agree with Dr. Denton that it is time to "loosen" the current *DSM* system? If yes, how should it be changed to better account for advances in brain science and be a more accurate reflection of the biopsychosocial model?

3. Do you think obesity should be medical diagnosis? Why or why not? What are the advantages and disadvantaged of such labeling?

4. What is nursing's role in establishing diagnostic categories?

The second challenge raised in Part I of this book—who or what is the authority in making these moral judgments—also arises in cases involving psychiatry and other forms of **behavior control**. Should experts, for example, be the ones who decide for society whether a behavior such as drug addiction is a crime, an immorality, a disease, or acceptable behavior? If so, which experts? What should happen if psychiatrists claim that aggressive violence is a mental illness, whereas prosecuting attorneys claim it is a crime, moral philosophers claim it is unethical voluntary behavior, and the clergy claim it is a sin? Just as intriguing, what should happen if each of these groups of experts insists that, however they characterize a particular act of aggressive violence, it is not a manifestation of the type of behavior about which they claim expertise—psychiatrists saying it is not a mental illness, prosecutors saying it is not a crime, and so forth? The cases in this chapter provide an opportunity to examine these issues.

These cases also raise some of the most basic conflicts among the ethical principles introduced in Part II of this volume. Often the initial problem in cases involving psychiatry and other forms of behavior control is not an ethical one at all. It is one of determining the extent to which the behavior in question should be thought of as voluntary or autonomous. As we saw in the cases in Chapter 7, whether the client is considered autonomous may make a great deal of difference in determining whether a particular ethical principle applies. For example, it is often argued that the principle of autonomy should dominate in evaluating behaviors that may involve harm to the individual but no risk to other parties. This is so especially when the person engaging in the behavior is thought to be substantially autonomous. If the client engaging in the behavior is not substantially autonomous, then the principle of beneficence—benefiting the client—should prevail in some way. Nurses dealing with suicidal patients face these problems in a particularly dramatic way.

After looking at several cases involving psychiatry and psychology, we look at a case involving another mental health intervention—**psychosurgery**. The same range of ethical principles applies to this case, but several new conceptual issues basic to the ethics of behavior control are presented as well. The case involves questions such as whether a physical intervention—surgery—is more controversial than "merely talking with the patient." It asks whether the fact that an intervention is presumably permanent (as psychosurgery may be) makes it more suspect than one that is reversible (such as a pharmacological intervention). If this factor of permanency is morally relevant, the next question is an empirical one: Just how reversible are various interventions? Some have argued that psychologic interventions, particularly those experienced at an early age, may leave impressions that are just as irreversible as psychosurgery.

Still another question raised by the use of behavior-controlling interventions is whether finding identifiable physical evidence of pathology—a lesion or an abnormal electroencephalogram (EEG) pattern, for example—makes intervention more justifiable. Is it more acceptable to do pinpoint destruction of brain tissue when it is known that the tissue is generating abnormal EEG patterns than when there is documented evidence of a positive behavioral change with such ablation but no evidence of abnormal electrical activity? The case in the last section of the chapter provides a chance for the nurse to struggle with patient care involving behavior-controlling interventions and his or her role in these interventions.

Research Brief 13-1

Source: Grace, P. G., Fry, S. T., & Schultz, G. S. (2003). Ethics and human rights issues experienced by psychiatric-mental health and substance abuse registered nurses. *Journal of the American Psychiatric Nurses Association, 9*(1), 17–23.

Purpose: To identify the frequency of ethics and human rights issues experienced by psychiatric-mental health (P-MH) and substance abuse (SA) registered nurses (RNs), and how disturbing the issues are to them.

Method: Using Dillman's Total Design Method, a survey of more than 8000 RNs in six New England states was conducted. From the final sample size of 2090 New England RN participants, responses from 162 participants who completed the 32-item Ethical Issues Scale (EIS) and identified themselves as P-MH ($n = 145$) or SA ($n = 17$) RNs were further analyzed using descriptive statistics.

Findings: "Protecting patients' rights and human dignity" and "providing nursing care with possible health risks to the RN" were identified as the most frequently experienced ethics and human rights issues. "Staffing patterns that limit patient access to nursing care" and "implementing managed care policies that threaten the quality of patient care" were identified as the most disturbing issues. Of the RNs, 41% reported experiencing ethics and human right issues "daily" or "one to four times" per week in their clinical practices.

Implications: P-MH and SA RNs in New England encounter ethics and human rights issues in practice more frequently than all other RNs practicing in New England. In-service education programs should give priority consideration to the ethics and human rights issues most frequently experienced by and personally disturbing to P-MH and SA RNs. These issues are ones these nurses find difficult to manage and also may be the most resistant to resolution in practice. The effects on nurses of confronting disturbing issues that recur or prove resistant to resolution are known to contribute to nurse dissatisfaction with her or his job or job setting. Appropriate in-service education can provide P-MH and SA RNs with tools to gain clarity about the issues and help them address the ethics and human rights issues in clinical practice. Further research is needed to determine how workplace and patient characteristics affect P-MH and SA RNs' abilities to recognize, identify, and handle ethics and human rights issues in patient care, especially those identified in this study.

Psychotherapy

Many of the philosophic problems related to human behavior faced by the nurse arise in the context of ***psychotherapy***. For psychotherapy to be appropriate, there must be a judgment that the behavior or experience to be changed is undesirable. One does not try to change behavior or experience if it is good. Even if the behavior is undesirable, however, there can be varying interpretations of why the behavior exists and why it is undesirable. When the nurse participates in psychotherapy, he or she is making judgments involving these issues. For example, the nurse is determining that psychologic rather than religious or legal intervention is called for. Other problems also emerge in the psychotherapeutic context, including the conflicts between patient welfare and the interests of others (examined in Chapters 3 and 4) and between patient welfare and autonomy (examined in Chapter 5).

The Concept of Mental Health

The first case in this section demonstrates how the nurse must make conceptual distinctions in deciding whether a patient has a problem within the health sphere.[6] First, the judgment must be made that a problem exists; second, the judgment must be made that the problem is one that lends itself to the mental health model.

Case 13-1

The Psychotherapist Confronted by Different Values

Lorna Shettler had 15 years of experience working with patients with various psychologic disorders. In addition to undergraduate and graduate degrees in nursing with a focus on mental health nursing, she had advanced degrees and experience in clinical psychology. She was now a partner in a private community mental health clinic and carried a full caseload of outpatients requesting therapy for behavioral disorders. Recently, however, a patient challenged her expertise and experience to a far greater degree than any patient she had ever seen.

The patient was Rosalind Torrance, a successful executive in sales merchandising. Ms. Torrance was a lesbian deeply troubled by her sexual orientation and her present life-style. Ms. Torrance described her life as extremely lonely and isolated. Having lived in a small but prosperous southern city for 4 years, she wanted to initiate a relationship with another woman but was afraid to do so. She was afraid of discovery, of losing her job in a conservative business operation, and of being rejected.

She had had one brief lesbian relationship immediately after finishing her college education, but it had ended when her partner started dating a man and eventually married him. Her own dating experience with men had been limited, painfully embarrassing, and stressful. She liked the company of women much better but had not attempted to form a sexual relationship until after college. Having lost that relationship and moved to another city, she was uncertain whether she had the emotional energy and psychologic fortitude to initiate another relationship.

Because her own experience as a lesbian was so limited, she was even wondering if she could overcome her sexual orientation. The strain of trying to conceal her orientation was becoming very troublesome; yet, she was very reluctant to visit singles bars and sport clubs to find a lesbian partner. Could Dr. Shettler help her? She would try anything—shock therapy, behavior therapy, anything—if she could be helped to overcome her anxieties.

Dr. Shettler knew that she could follow several strategies in trying to help Ms. Torrance. One strategy often used by behavioral therapists was popularly called a "hetero-strategy." It enjoyed a high rate of success if the patient really wanted to change her sexual orientation. It included instruction on heterosocial and heterosexual techniques, and covert sensitization, an aversive conditioning procedure in which the client imagines lesbian situations while being induced to feelings of nausea and disgust.

A second strategy often used by behavior therapists was a "homo-strategy." This strategy assumed that sexual preference probably cannot be eliminated, the patient can be better helped by raising her self-esteem and reducing her social anxiety, the patient can be helped to find support systems such as gay liberation groups, and there is nothing inherently wrong with sexual fulfillment between consenting adults in any form, as long as it does not generate self-hate or psychologic or physical injury. Dr. Shettler was uncertain which strategy she would employ with Ms. Torrance. Because she was the first lesbian that Dr. Shettler had ever treated, either strategy seemed to create value conflicts that Dr. Shettler had not experienced before.

Commentary

Dr. Shettler's first task is to determine whether there is, in fact, a problem and if so, what it is. She is aware that many homosexuals are able to function quite well and that they take offense at being labeled "sick" or "pathological."[7] On the other hand, some people, like Ms. Torrance, are suffering with their homosexuality. Does the decision about whether there is a problem reduce to the question of whether the patient is suffering? Does the fact that one does not suffer mean there is no problem? Does the fact that one is suffering mean there must be a problem?

Some mental health professionals believe that persons may have problems and yet not be aware of them. A condition may be seen as a problem because it is likely to lead to something the individual will find undesirable in the future. Undiagnosed hypertension could be an example. By analogy, there may be unperceived problems in other spheres. People could have conditions that do not presently trouble them but that they nevertheless will find troubling in the future. Even more puzzling, there may be states that will never be troubling to the individual but that nevertheless ought to be perceived as troubling. A man who goes through his entire life never troubled by the fact that he infantilizes women is an example.

In Ms. Torrance's case, she clearly perceives a problem. Does Dr. Shettler automatically accept the patient's definition of the problem, or does the real difficulty remain an open question? In this case, the problem can be defined in at least two very different ways. It can be defined as having a desire to engage in a behavior that is morally unacceptable in a particular community. Formulating it that way places the problem in the sphere of morality, which would require several assumptions on Dr. Shettler's part. First, she would have to view the homosexuality as in some sense voluntary. It makes no sense to make use of moral categories if the behavior is totally beyond human control. This assumption is supported by the fact that both Ms. Torrance and her partner had engaged in heterosexual experiences, although in her case they were not particularly satisfactory. Second, even if Ms. Torrance has made a voluntary choice, in order for the homosexuality to be a moral problem, a judgment needs to be made about the morality of the behavior. It could be viewed as voluntary but praiseworthy. More plausibly, it could be viewed as voluntary but neutral. In either case, it would not be a moral problem because it is not viewed as morally wrong.

If the behavior is not voluntary, then some other model might be invoked. Dr. Shettler might view the behavior as caused by social, organic, or psychologic forces beyond Ms. Torrance's control. Again, it would only be a problem if the behavior is evaluated negatively. One difficulty in dealing with complex psychosocial situations such as this is that professionals in various fields are likely to vary systematically in the way they formulate the situation. Priests might view the lesbian behavior as a sin, law enforcement officers as illegal, ethicists as immoral, psychologists as psychopathology, and organic medical specialists as organically determined. Clearly, the fact that a specialist in psychology interprets the situation psychologically cannot settle the matter.

Dr. Shettler appears to interpret the problem psychologically; she sees it as open to psychologic intervention. She perceives two strategies of intervention. One assumes there is nothing wrong with the behavior—that the only problem is Ms. Torrance's psychologic response attached to the behavior. That may lead to "homo-strategy." The other strategy assumes that homosexuality is wrong, leading to "hetero-strategy." Hetero-strategy can also be adopted on strictly pragmatic grounds. If the only problem is the anxiety attached to the behavior, however, Dr. Shettler can either remove the anxiety, leaving the behavior minus the anxiety, or she can change the behavior, eliminating the cause of the anxiety.

What Dr. Shettler will choose to do depends first on some assumptions she will make about the voluntariness of the behavior and then on what she perceives to be the nature of the problem. She cannot help but make evaluative judgments about what kinds of outcomes will be desirable as well as what kinds of outcomes are most easily achievable.

Mental Illness and Autonomous Behavior

Even if the nurse successfully determines that the problem presented is in the healthcare sphere and is amenable to nursing intervention, problems still remain. One is determining if the patient is autonomous and, if so, whether the therapeutic strategy for reducing the problem comes at the expense of overriding that autonomy. The ethical tension is between the principles of autonomy and patient welfare. The next two cases illustrate this tension.

Case 13-2
Force-Feeding the Psychiatric Patient

Rosalind Jacuzek was newly employed on the psychiatric ward of a large county hospital. One of her patients was Daniel Forester, a 47-year-old man admitted for severe depression. A once successful owner of a small business, Mr. Forester had became depressed following the failure of his business and a messy divorce from his wife of 18 years. His wife and children now lived in another city. His only visitor was a younger sister, who seemed concerned about her brother's condition out of a sense of family obligation rather than genuine concern for him. His depression was complicated by the recent diagnosis of a rare form of leukemia for which there was only palliative treatment and no demonstrated cure. Burdened by the failure of his business, the loss of his family, and his illness, Mr. Forester's depression had progressed to the point where he was refusing all medications, food, and water in hopes that he would die.

Intravenous (IV) therapy had been instituted, and he was receiving electroconvulsive therapy (ECT). It was hoped that Mr. Forester's nutrition could be maintained by forced feedings and his hydration maintained by the IV until the ECT treatments began to effect some change in his alarming state of depression and his desire to die.

Force-feeding Mr. Forester, however, was distasteful to Ms. Jacuzek. Whenever she attempted to put food into Mr. Forester's mouth, he spit it out and moved his head away from the food offered on a spoon. A nasogastric (NG) tube was finally passed and a liquid supplement given to Mr. Forester. Despite the fact that his hands were tied and he was restrained in bed, he always managed to dislodge the NG tube, necessitating that the tube be passed anew each time he was fed. This procedure was a real nuisance to the nurses and required additional sedating of the patient. Each time she offered food to him, Ms. Jacuzek tried to force it into his mouth but eventually wound up passing the NG tube in order to get some nutrition into his body. The ordeal usually required the assistance of three or four individuals to hold Mr. Forester while the NG tube was passed and he was fed. After a few days of this procedure, Ms. Jacuzek noticed that Mr. Forester's face, jaw, neck, and arms were bruised from the manner in which the nurses were gripping him while trying to force-feed him.

Sickened by the treatment of Mr. Forester and the marks on his body, Ms. Jacuzek discussed the situation with her supervisor. An experienced psychiatric nurse, the nurse supervisor acknowledged the difficulty of feeding a severely depressed patient like Mr. Forester. But she urged Ms. Jacuzek to cooperate in the temporary feeding plan developed by the nurses. She assured the younger nurse that Mr. Forester would thank her and the other nurses when he got over his depression. The bruises were inconsequential considering the necessary nutrition that was being supplied. Ms. Jacuzek was not sure this was adequate moral justification for physical coercion of a very sick psychiatric patient.

Case 13-3
Lying to Benefit the Patient with a Psychosis

Elvira Perkins is a 59-year-old woman with paranoid schizophrenia, cardiomyopathy, and diabetes mellitus, who was admitted to the hospital 3 weeks ago for resolution of urgent hypertension. She has consistently refused oral medications stating that they make her neuropathies worse. At present, her hypertension is being managed by intravenous medications and she is also being administered antipsychotic medications via the intravenous route. She cannot be moved to the in-patient mental health unit until her medical condition is stabilized, and they will not accept her while she is receiving intravenous medications. She has been seen by two psychiatrists who have assessed her to lack decision-making capacity, and she has a court-appointed guardian who has authorized crushing medication to be administered in her food. Nurses are concerned about the need to hide medication from her and to lie when she queries, "Is there any medicine in this food or drink?" They are also concerned, as is hospital administration, about how long intravenous therapy must be continued while she refuses optimal treatment.

Case 13-4
Must Suicide Always Be Stopped?

Cynthia Morgan was an attractive, 26-year-old woman admitted to a psychiatric unit following an unsuccessful attempt at suicide. She had made the attempt several weeks after radical neck surgery to remove a highly malignant tumor from her lower jaw. Disfigured and faced with months of therapy and reconstructive surgery, she had decided that her life was no longer meaningful or worth living. Unmarried and with no living family members that seemed to care about her, she was extremely depressed about her future, the cost of her medical bills, and her ability to become gainfully employed again. She had been an advertising agent for a growing cosmetic company. Given the results of the disfiguring surgery, she would not be able to return to employment that placed her in the public eye. She simply felt that it was better to die than live with her disabilities.

One of her nurses, Beth Amos, tended to sympathize with Ms. Morgan. Although Ms. Amos was obligated to prevent the patient from attempting to commit suicide again, she thought that Ms. Morgan was making a rational choice and that it was wrong to interfere in this choice. Yet, Ms. Amos did interfere in the choice by searching Ms. Morgan for any implements by which she could harm herself and by not allowing her to wear a belt, stockings, a bra, or a slip. She also made Ms. Morgan open her mouth following the administration of each medication, limited the types of objects that could be taken into her room, and forced her to take tranquilizing medications that she did not want to take. Yet she wondered why it was "wrong" for a patient to end his or her life when no other parties would be affected and the patient would avoid the unpleasantness and pain that continued life created. Why could a patient not make this choice?

Commentary

One solution to the first and third case would be to find each of the patients incompetent or lacking in autonomy to make choices about his or her own care. Both are suffering from conditions that are traditionally associated with incompetency: depression in the case of Daniel Forester and suicidal behavior in the case of Cynthia Morgan. If they are not substantially autonomous agents, then there can be no conflict between patient autonomy and doing what is in the interest of the patient. The problem would seem to disappear.

Even if Mr. Forester and Ms. Morgan are not autonomous, the nurses in these cases (or the patients' physicians) do not necessarily have the right to treat these patients in ways that they perceive as beneficial to the patients—as in the case of Ms. Perkins. If the patients are believed to be incompetent, then someone ought to be designated as their agents for purposes of accepting or refusing treatment. The problems that can arise if guardians make what appear to be unreasonable choices will be discussed in the cases in Chapters 15 and 16. The judgment that these patients are incompetent, however, may simply put the nurses in the position of having to get someone else to make decisions for them.

The other alternative is that Ms. Jacuzek and Ms. Amos conclude that Mr. Forester and Ms. Morgan really are substantially autonomous. Especially in Ms. Morgan's case, she seems to understand the nature of the situation and to have made a choice about whether it is worth continuing life. Her nurse, Ms. Amos, seems to believe that Ms. Morgan's judgment is quite rational. Then the ethical problem reduces to how the principle of autonomy should relate to promotion of the patient's welfare.

There are other differences between the two patients besides the fact that Ms. Morgan's judgment seems more rational than Mr. Forester's. For one, Ms. Morgan's condition is not necessarily terminal, whereas Mr. Forester's is apparently irreversible. For another, the interventions in Ms. Morgan's case (forced tranquilization and constraints placed on normal living, dressing, and privacy) seem less invasive than the physical restraints, forced feeding, and bruising in Mr. Forester's case. Are these differences adequate to justify a different moral judgment about the interventions in the two cases, assuming that both patients are substantially autonomous? Does a judgment about incompetence justify deception on the part of the nurses?

In the past decade or two, it has become more common to recognize that patients cannot automatically be presumed to be incompetent just because they make judgments that most other people would not make. To the contrary, adults are presumed competent until found otherwise by a court. Because both these patients are adults who have never been found incompetent, they have the same rights as other adults. Forcing treatment against their consent is a legal violation, and many would consider the overriding of autonomy morally unacceptable as well. Unless the nurses or others at these institutions are prepared to seek to have the patients declared incompetent, they will face severe moral and legal difficulties if they treat against the patients' consent.

Critical Thinking Question

If you were the nurse caring for Ms. Morgan, Ms. Perkins, or Mr. Forester, which nursing interventions would you have recommended? Why?

Case 13-5
Should This Patient Be Admitted?

Al Rattigan is a 27-year-old, single white advertising executive who is brought to the emergency room by police after someone called in with a charge of disorderly conduct. His blood alcohol level is 1.4. He admits to a history of bipolar disease and to heavy drinking that evening but states "this is no big deal" and wants to sign himself out after "sobering up." He also admits to not taking his lithium for the last 3 months because he did not like the way it was making him feel. The medical and nursing consensus is that he should be admitted to the voluntary inpatient mental health unit. Jorge Ochoa, the emergency room nurse who admitted Mr. Rattigan, is wondering how strongly he should attempt to persuade Mr. Rattigan to admit himself to the unit.

Commentary

Questions about consent will be explored in Chapter 16. For now we simply want to highlight the fact that assessments of decision-making capacity are particularly challenging for patients with mental health disorders. All too frequently, nurses are challenged by balancing the obligation to respect the autonomous preferences of individuals to live life as they see fit, with the obligation to strongly advocate for choices that advance health and well-being. In this case, Mr. Ochoa strongly believed that Mr. Rattigan's well-being would be seriously compromised if he did not get his drinking under control and his bipolar disorder better managed pharmacologically. While manipulation and coercion are off-limits, how persuasive can Mr. Ochoa be? Each nurse in a similar situation must decide what professional response is obligatory for competent, caring, and morally responsible professionals.

Critical Thinking Questions

If you were caring for Mr. Rattigan, how would you intervene and why? What criteria would you use to evaluate a good outcome?

Mental Illness and Third-Party Interests

Sometimes patients with psychiatric illness pose not only conflict between the principles of autonomy and patient welfare but also conflict between the welfare of patients and the welfare of third parties. The next two cases pose these problems.

Case 13-6

Sedating and Restraining the Disturbed Patient

Percival Guthrie was a 58-year-old man with a history of organic brain syndrome. In good physical health, Mr. Guthrie had been admitted to a nursing home by his family. Because of his forgetfulness, wandering behavior, sleep pattern disturbances, and inability to care for himself, his family wanted him to be in a care center that would meet his growing needs for supervision and personal care. Family members had tried to care for him themselves during the past year, but they were exhausted from all the supervision that Mr. Guthrie needed. Despite the expense, they hoped that their relative would be happy in the nursing home and that he would receive the care that they could no longer give him.

Sandra Mooney was the day nursing supervisor of the nursing home. Recognizing the extent of the care that Mr. Guthrie would need, she agreed to place him in a room near the nurses' station and to observe him while he adjusted to the routine of the nursing home. Adjustment, however, seemed an impossibility for Mr. Guthrie. It soon became apparent that his wandering into other patients' rooms was disturbing to them. During meals, he talked loudly and frequently called for his relatives. When sedated with a mild tranquilizer, Mr. Guthrie became more agitated and spent all night roaming the halls, wandering into the rooms of sleeping patients, and generally exhibiting loud and boisterous behavior, much to the dismay of the nursing staff. Within a few days, it became apparent that mild medication was not going to affect Mr. Guthrie's behavior. He was also becoming very dirty and refused to change his clothes. Once, he sat in his armchair all night and failed to use the bathroom to urinate. His clothes and the chair were soaked with urine, and this became a daily occurrence.

Faced with the constant odor emanating from Mr. Guthrie's room, his wandering behavior, his unkempt appearance, and his loud talking, Mrs. Mooney considered confining the patient to a room at the end of the hall. She discussed the problem with the nursing staff, and they decided to use a combination of sedation and confinement, recognizing that their one attempt at confining Mr. Guthrie to his room had resulted in loud behavior that disturbed the other patients and the staff and alarmed visitors. It was a course of action that Mrs. Mooney chose reluctantly, given the good physical condition of Mr. Guthrie. Yet it seemed that his liberty would have to be restricted if the staff and the other patients were to have a satisfying nursing home atmosphere.

Case 13-7

Choosing a "Better" Patient Than the Elderly Schizophrenic

Shannon McFee, a student nurse in her final year of undergraduate study, was starting a new clinical rotation with a focus on psychiatric/mental health nursing. She and five of her classmates were assigned to a small unit housing female patients at a state mental health facility. On her first day of clinical, Miss McFee was encouraged to talk with all the patients in the day room and to select two patients with whom she would like to work during her 7-week clinical rotation. After spending most of the morning talking with various patients, playing cards with a few of the more outgoing patients, and even accompanying two patients to occupational therapy, she realized that a few of the patients on the unit did not seem to participate in unit activities. On the pretense of checking whether these patients had received their midmorning snack, she visited their rooms.

In one room, she found a well-groomed, 48-year-old woman, Willie Mae Chisholm, rocking in her chair and humming to herself. Miss McFee attempted to start a conversation with the woman but soon realized that this patient was quite paranoid, referring repeatedly to secret microphones concealed on her body that were recording her thoughts and her speech. In checking the patient's chart, Miss McFee learned that Ms. Chisholm had lived in mental institutions for over 16 years. Her diagnosis was chronic paranoid schizophrenia. She had been released to her family 2 years ago but had been readmitted after only 2 months. The patient was fairly likable, but she slipped into her paranoia whenever Miss McFee tried to converse with her.

In checking another patient's room, Miss McFee discovered Ella Peacham, a 56-year-old woman admitted 2 days ago, completely wrapped up in her bedsheet, including her head, and lying across the bed. Miss McFee talked to the enshrouded patient for a few moments until Mrs. Peacham slowly removed the sheet from her head and cautiously began to glance at Miss McFee. After being coaxed into talking for half an hour, Mrs. Peacham agreed to accompany Miss McFee to the day room, where she sat watching television but would not interact with other patients.

In checking this patient's chart, Miss McFee found that Mrs. Peacham had been hospitalized for a "nervous breakdown" over 30 years ago but had returned home after 6 years of institutionalization. She had four children, most of whom were reared by her husband and her sister. She had been rehospitalized for a short period of time 8 years ago, following the death of her husband. Since that time, she had lived in a trailer next to her youngest son's house. She had been able to take care of herself with minimal supervision until just recently, when she became reclusive, failing to eat, bathe, and care for herself or her trailer. When she began to complain to her son of hearing "voices" outside her trailer all the time, he contacted the state facility and admitted her for treatment. Her diagnosis was chronic undifferentiated schizophrenia.

At the end of the day, Miss McFee and her classmates met with their nursing instructor. After they talked about their experiences of the day and the unit's patients, the instructor asked the students if they had decided which patients they would follow during the clinical rotation. Miss McFee indicated that she would like to follow Miss Chisholm and Mrs. Peacham. The instructor asked Miss McFee why she had picked those particular patients. Miss McFee was not sure why she had picked them except for the fact that she was interested in their histories and diagnoses of chronic schizophrenia. After the post-conference, the instructor privately advised Miss McFee to select other patients. There were quite a few patients diagnosed with adolescent adjustment problems on the unit; also, there were other patients with disorders that would respond rapidly to medication and therapy. She advised Miss McFee to invest her time in these patients because they had greater potential of returning to the community. Both Miss Chisholm and Mrs. Peacham were chronically ill individuals, and it was unlikely that they would ever leave the hospital setting and live productive lives apart from it.

Miss McFee saw the wisdom of selecting patients in whom she could observe the results of psychopharmacology and therapy because she was a student and could benefit from the experiences. But she was not sure that a nurse should selectively distribute herself or himself, as a resource, to those who would benefit the most. She was especially troubled by what she perceived as the attitude that chronically mentally ill patients were not as deserving of nursing time and energy as other patients. Was she obligated to invest her time in those patients who could obviously benefit the most from her attention and services?

Commentary

Percival Guthrie, the man with organic brain syndrome who was sedated and confined to his room by nurse Sandra Mooney, is in some ways like the patients in the previous section. Like them, Mr. Guthrie's autonomy is in question. In such situations, nurses often decide to confine patients—in possible violation of their autonomy but for what appears to be the production of the greater good. Mr. Guthrie may well be less autonomous than the earlier patients. That is one possible difference in the cases. However, there is another important difference. Mrs. Mooney decided in favor of physical and chemical restraints not primarily for Mr. Guthrie's benefit but for the benefit of other patients, who were being disturbed by Mr. Guthrie's wandering and his erratic lifestyle.

We saw in Chapters 4 and 5 that even those who believe that patients have an autonomy-based right to make treatment choices (even when such choices appear to be contrary to their own interests) tend to agree there are some instances in which the welfare of third parties justifies interventions against the patient's wishes. In Mr. Guthrie's case, Mrs. Mooney might have sought to intervene against Mr. Guthrie's wishes to benefit him. In that case, she would be acting on grounds of patient welfare. She also, however, might intervene to protect others, such as the other patients in the center.

This poses a problem for Mrs. Mooney, however. Clinicians, including nurses, are traditionally committed to the welfare of their patients, not to promoting the overall greatest good. Mrs. Mooney might avoid this problem by considering all of the patients in the facility her patients, thus maintaining her clinical perspective. She might also conclude that the intervention serves not only other patients, but also Mr. Guthrie himself, thus turning the case back into one of patient welfare.

Many nurses, however, are increasingly willing to take at least certain third-party interests into account, as we saw in the cases in Chapters 4 and 5. The questions for Mrs. Mooney are whether just any benefits to others justify constraining Mr. Guthrie with physical and chemical restraints, or only certain benefits—and if only certain ones, whether such benefits are present in this case.

The second case, in which student nurse Shannon McFee is asked to choose patients for her clinical experience, may help shed light on the problem. She chose two chronic schizophrenics, patients her instructor believed would not improve dramatically during the 7-week rotation.

It is not clear exactly what the instructor's reasoning was when she recommended that Miss McFee choose patients other than Ms. Chisholm and Mrs. Peacham. She may have been expressing the goals of nursing education. She may have been advising Miss McFee that she would learn more if she chose other patients. That reason seems to be grounded in the ethical assumption that the student nurse should choose her patients on the basis of how much she will learn from working with them. Although that seems to make sense insofar as the objective is student education, it is debatable whether it is compatible with the moral mandate of nurses to benefit their patients.

It sounds, however, like the nursing instructor was applying a moral calculus to the choice based on which patients would benefit the most. She may be saying that, at least when choosing among those who are one's patients (or among those who are candidates to be patients), the nurse should choose the ones who will gain the most benefit from nursing interventions.

That is not her only option, however. As we saw in the cases in Chapter 5, Miss McFee might have decided to devote her time to those who she thought were the worst off. Ms. Chisholm and Mrs. Peacham may well qualify as being worst off, at least when compared with other patients with more acute and reversible disorders. Both Mrs. Mooney and Miss McFee must decide when, if ever, the welfare of others justifies a decision not to maximize the welfare of the individual patient. They will also have to decide whether the amount of good they could do to other patients justifies sacrificing their patients or whether how well off other patients are is decisive for the distribution of nursing expertise.

Research Brief 13-2

Source: Rose, L. E., Mallinson, R. K., & Walton-Moss, B. (2004). Barriers to family care in psychiatric settings. *Journal of Nursing Scholarship, 36*(1), 39–47.

Purpose: To identify barriers to family care in psychiatric settings and to describe family and provider perspectives about what constitutes effective family care.

Method: This study used a qualitative exploratory approach with focus groups. Seventy-eight people participated in 11 audiotaped group discussions conducted with families, patients, and health professionals. Group discussions focused on the need for family care, including helping families deal with feelings of helplessness, anger, guilt, and loss; barriers to provision of family care; access to and options for family care; and possible targets for improving family care, including communication and collaboration between families and professionals. Focus group transcripts were first read with a concentration on the answers to the research questions. Second, a more in-depth analysis procedure was conducted to identify critical issues not identified in the first reading. Trustworthiness of the findings was addressed by multiple readings of the transcripts, comparison of themes with group moderator notes, and coding of themes until consensus was reached.

Findings: Families identified poor quality care, conflict with health professionals about treatment, and lack of a role for families in treatment as barriers to family care. African American families also identified isolation of their communities from the mental healthcare system. Adolescents emphasized their role as caregivers and their need for support. Health professionals conveyed concerns about system-based barriers, professional practice–based barriers, and family-based barriers to care. Patients stated the need for their families to be better educated about mental illness.

Implications: The lack of family care in psychiatric settings is a multifaceted problem. Current health polices do not show endorsement of a family care approach. Responses from families and health professionals reported that health professionals often lacked training and resources to deal with complex family issues. Families believed that lengthy and intensive interventions were neither necessary nor desired to address their concerns. Family care can be improved by focusing on building rapport, and communicating problems and concerns, between families and health professionals. Further research is needed to identify the experiences of African American families regarding their access to mental healthcare services.

Other Behavior-Controlling Therapies

Whereas many of the ethical issues the nurse faces in the area of psychiatry and the control of behavior arise around psychotherapy and psychoactive drug interventions, other emergent technologies may raise somewhat different issues. These involve surgical interventions, electroshock, electrical stimulation of the brain, and unconventional therapies. A nurse dealing with these therapies faces such questions as whether physical interventions into the brain are morally any different than psychotherapeutic interventions and whether irreversible procedures are more controversial than reversible ones. The following case involves possible psychosurgical intervention.

Case 13-8
Psychosurgery for the Wealthy Demented Patient

Gail Conover was a staff nurse on a surgical unit of a small private hospital in the South. One of her patients was Regina Dinsworth, a 49-year-old woman admitted for treatment of minor injuries sustained in a fall. Miss Dinsworth was the sister of Rex Dinsworth, a wealthy philanthropist in the city and the president of the Dinsworth Foundation. The Dinsworth Foundation had contributed a great deal of money to develop social and cultural resources in the city over the years, and many of the results of its investments bore the Dinsworth family name: Dinsworth Park, the Dinsworth Museum of Modern Art, Frances Dinsworth High School, and so on.

Regina Dinsworth, however, was apparently sheltered by the family because of mental illness and many previous hospitalizations. She lived in the Dinsworths' spacious family home in the middle of the city and was cared for at home by a private nurse. In recent months, however, she had become very difficult to care for at home. She wandered away from the house on several occasions, was in constant physical activity, and rarely slept. Her family was becoming exhausted by her level of activity and was increasingly embarrassed by her escapes from the house to other areas of the city. During her latest escape, she had apparently wandered into a high-crime neighborhood of the city and had been attacked by two men. She was saved from more serious injury by an off-duty policeman, but she did sustain several broken ribs, cuts, and bruises.

The Dinsworths were considering psychosurgery for their relative as an alternative to permanent hospitalization. It seemed to be the easiest way for them to control Regina Dinsworth and would lessen the burden of caring for her. The family realized that the psychosurgery would alter her personality, produce irreversible physical changes, and probably make her dependent on the family for the rest of her life. But this seemed a small price to pay for alleviating the constant worry and embarrassment that her mental illness caused the family. Mrs. Conover, however, did not agree that this might be the best alternative for Miss Dinsworth. Surely there were important considerations here other than the family's reputation and ease of custodianship.

Commentary

The proposed treatment of Regina Dinsworth is controversial on several grounds. It is no wonder that the nurse, Gail Conover, would have doubts. The case report, however, does not tell us why she has concluded that psychosurgical intervention is not the best treatment for Miss Dinsworth.

One major problem in this case is the apparent motivation of the family. Its members appear to be more concerned about the disruption and embarrassment Miss Dinsworth is causing than about her welfare. On the other hand, Miss Dinsworth's life does not appear to be very pleasant. Agitation, wandering, sleeplessness, and physical assault is not much to look forward to, nor is permanent hospitalization. Is it possible that, in spite of the family's motivation, the surgical intervention is in Miss Dinsworth's interest? If so, should a nurse or any other caring professional object simply because the family is not well motivated?

If Mrs. Conover is not objecting solely on the basis of the family's motivation—that is, if she really believes some other treatment is better for Miss Dinsworth—what is the basis of her belief? Does she believe that there are other techniques available that can relieve Miss Dinsworth's symptoms more effectively? Is that the sort of issue about which a nurse should appropriately object, or is that a technical question better left to other authorities?

Possibly Mrs. Conover objects not so much on technical grounds as on moral grounds. Cutting into the human brain is an unusually controversial thing to do.[8] It conjures up the prefrontal lobotomies of earlier decades. It suggests blunting the human personality, irreversible physiological change, and dehumanization. Is it valid for Mrs. Conover to object on these grounds? Some people hold that physical interventions such as psychosurgery should be avoided, at least when psychotherapies such as counseling and behavior modification could be used. Is there a moral basis for such a preference?

One possible basis for this difference is that psychosurgery is believed to be irreversible whereas other psychotherapeutic interventions are not. That is an empirical claim worthy of exploration. Some counseling interventions may also turn out to be irreversible; surgery actually may be reversed in some cases, such as by having other brain tissues take on some of the functions originally performed by the excised tissue.

Critical Thinking Questions

1. Is there any valid reason that reversible procedures are morally preferable to irreversible procedures? If so, is it only because otherwise we may make mistakes that we want to reverse?
2. If Miss Dinsworth's behavior is as debilitating as it appears to be, would it not be preferable that the change was irrevocable?

Mrs. Conover needs to be clear on why she objects to the proposed surgery, even if the procedure seems intuitively revolting to her. Obviously, there are a number of reasons why she might object, and different reasons may have different implications for her. If, after sorting out her reasons, she still is convinced that psychosurgery would not be in Miss Dinsworth's interest, how should Mrs. Conover respond?

This case and the previous cases in this chapter reveal how the problems of conceptualizing rewards and punishments as well as disease and health shape how we judge people should be treated. Whether we are dealing with psychotherapy or other behavior-controlling therapies, labeling a condition a mental "disease" helps us attribute blame (or lack thereof). If the patient with a mental condition is deemed not to be acting in a substantially autonomous manner, our moral assessment will reflect this status. These problems are among those faced in caring for patients with HIV, to which we turn in Chapter 14.

ENDNOTES

1. American Psychiatric Association Ethics Committee. (2001). *Ethics primer of the American Psychiatric Association.* Washington, DC: Author; Radden, J. (2002). Psychiatric ethics. *Bioethics, 16*(5), 397–411; Bloch, S., Chodoff, P., & Green, S. A. (Eds.). (1999). *Psychiatric ethics* (3rd ed.). New York: Oxford University Press.
2. American Psychiatric Association. (2000). *Diagnostic and statistical manual of mental disorders: DSM-IV-TR,* (4th ed., text rev.). Washington, DC: Author.
3. First, M. B., Bell, C. C., Cuthbert, B., Krystal, J. H., Malison, R., Offord, D. R., et al. (2002). *Personality disorders and relational disorders: A research agenda for addressing crucial gaps in DSM* (pp. 123–195). Washington, DC: American Psychiatric Association.

4. Denton, W. H. (2007, August). Issues for DSM-IV: Relational diagnosis: An essential component of biopsychosocial assessment. *The American Journal of Psychiatry, 164*, 1146.

5. Kirn, W., & Song, S. (2002, September 16). I'm O.K. You're O.K. We're Not O.K. *Time Magazine, 160*(12). Available at: http://www.time.com/time/magazine/article/0,9171,1003247-2,00.html. Accessed February 4, 2010.

6. Caplan, A. L., Engelhardt, H. T., & McCartney, J. J. (1981). *Concepts of health and disease: Interdisciplinary perspectives.* Reading, MA: Addison-Wesley; Flew, A. (Ed.). (1973). Disease and mental illness. In *Crime or disease?* (pp. 26–94). London: Macmillan Press, Ltd; Scheurich, N. (2002). Moral attitudes and mental disorders. *The Hastings Center Report, 32*(2),14–21.

7. Bayer, R. (1980). *Homosexuality and American psychology: The politics of diagnosis.* New York: Basic Books.

8. Gaylin, W., Meister, J. S., & Neville, R. C. (1975). *Operating on the mind.* New York: Basic Books; Mersky, H. (1999). *Ethical aspects of the physical manipulation of the brain.* In S. Bloch, P. Chodoff, & S. A. Green (Eds.), *Psychiatric ethics* (3rd ed., pp. 275–299). New York: Oxford University Press.

Chapter 14

HIV/AIDS Care

Other Cases Involving HIV

Case 6-1:   Humanity Lost in the Bed

Key Terms
Confidentiality
Duty to warn
Justice
Libertarianism
Social beneficence

Objectives
1. Describe two ethical problems that may be experienced by the nurse caring for patients with HIV/AIDs.
2. Describe how conflicts of rights might occur when testing for HIV infection.
3. Describe an HIV/AIDS nursing care situation in which the nurse's duty to protect confidentiality conflicts with the nurse's duty to protect others from harm.
4. Discuss the moral relevance of treatment costs in the nursing care of HIV/AIDS patients.
5. Identify one ethical problem that may arise when an HIV/AIDS patient becomes a research subject.

Another area of nursing practice that presents ethical challenges is the care and treatment of patients with human immunodeficiency virus (HIV) and acquired immunodeficiency syndrome (AIDS).[1] The transmission of HIV is a major concern throughout the world. According to the Joint United Nations Programme on HIV/AIDS (UNAIDS) and World Health Organization (WHO)'s *2009 AIDS Epidemic Update*, the number of people living with HIV worldwide continued to grow in 2008, reaching an estimated 33.4 million. The total number of people living with the virus in 2008 was more than 20% higher than the number in 2000, and the prevalence was roughly threefold higher than in 1990.[2] At the end of 2006, an estimated 1.1 million persons in the United States were living with HIV infection, with 21% undiagnosed.[3] In 2008, the Centers for Disease Control and Prevention estimated that approximately

56,300 people were newly infected with HIV in 2006[4] (the most recent year that data are available). More than half (53%) of these new infections occurred in gay and bisexual men. African American men and women were also strongly affected and were estimated to have an incidence rate that was seven times as high as the incidence rate among whites. The cumulative estimated number of diagnoses of AIDS through 2007 in the United States and dependent areas was 1,051,875. In the 50 states and the District of Columbia, adult and adolescent AIDS cases totaled 1,009,220 with 810,676 cases in males and 198,544 cases in females, and 9209 cases estimated in children younger than 13 years old.[5]

Just as in previous chapters, the problems of the meaning and justification of ethical claims arise frequently in the care of HIV/AIDS patients. The nurse may wonder whether patients can justifiably request that their HIV infection be kept confidential when others, especially sexual partners, may be at risk. Likewise, should a pregnant woman, at high risk for HIV infection, be allowed to refuse testing and thereby endanger her unborn child? At issue in these questions are the reasons that HIV infection has not been managed like other public health infectious diseases, such as other sexually transmitted diseases or tuberculosis, during the past century. Traditional public health measures have given way to individual rights where HIV infection is concerned. Cases 14-1 through 14-8 involve various issues surrounding individual rights claims in HIV/AIDS care.

Cases 14-9, 14-10, and 14-11 involve two other troubling issues in HIV/AIDS care: the costs of treatment and who should receive it. Highly active antiretroviral therapy (HAART) combines three or more anti-HIV medications in a daily regimen and is the recommended treatment for HIV infection.[6] The choice of drugs can depend on multiple factors including the availability and price of drugs, the financial resources of the patient, the number of pills, the side effects of drugs, and laboratory monitoring requirements. When the mean cost of in-patient care is added to outpatient care, monitoring, potent antiretroviral therapy, and community care costs, the average annual costs was estimated at $17,600 per patient for those in pre-AIDS states versus $24,900 for a patient with AIDS.[7] In some states, AIDS drug assistance programs virtually run out of money and can no longer provide combination therapy by the midpoint of their yearly funding cycle. Nurses advocating for patients needing antiretroviral therapy are often challenged to find the resources. Given that AIDS cannot currently be cured but only treated, despite recent advances in treatment modalities, should costly medications and technologies be used to prolong the lives of those who most likely will only die anyway? Should healthcare workers be the ones to decide who is treated and which treatment will be provided? Or should healthcare insurers make these decisions?

Cases 14-12 and 14-13 raise questions about HIV research and the availability of new drugs or even a vaccine to patients. Should patients who have contracted HIV through contaminated blood supplies or those unknowingly infected by their spouses be able to benefit from research results before those infected through homosexual behavior or injectable drug abuse? Is more risk acceptable for HIV patients than other patients in clinical drug trials because of the threat of HIV infection worldwide and the likelihood that the patients will die anyway?

Should testing of potential vaccines be targeted toward prompt eradication of the disease at considerable risk to individual health, or should testing be aimed at slower control of the disease at less risk to already-infected individuals? These are some of the issues that nurses might encounter in HIV research.

Conflicts Between Rights and Duties

Some of the ethical problems experienced by the nurse caring for HIV-infected or AIDS patients arise when there are perceived conflicts between patients' rights, nurses' rights, or the rights of other individuals. Conflicts can also arise between the nurse's duties to protect privacy, ensure *confidentiality*, or provide care to patients. People with AIDS have individual and civil rights like anyone else. Many questions have been raised, however, about limitations on the rights of persons with AIDS when they conflict with the rights of others.

Screening/Testing for HIV

Some conflict-of-rights problems arise in the context of testing for HIV infection. For testing to occur, the patient must give his or her permission to be tested. Mothers must also give permission for their newborn children to be tested for HIV. The following cases demonstrate how two nurses have experienced conflicts between the rights of people with AIDS and the rights of other individuals.

Case 14-1
When a Mother Refuses HIV Testing for Her Newborn

Nurse Auriel Morris was caring for a young woman, Maria Sanchez, on a maternity unit when significant questions came up about the young mother's risk of HIV infection. By reading Ms. Sanchez's chart, Mrs. Morris learned that the patient was 18 years old, unmarried, and had a history of IV drug abuse. She had received no prenatal care until 3 weeks ago and had delivered her 6 lb., 9 oz. healthy child (her second living child) after an uneventful labor in the emergency room. Given Ms. Sanchez's history, the emergency room physician had requested that she be tested for HIV, but the patient had refused. Now, Ms. Sanchez's child is being brought out to her to begin breast-feeding.

Mrs. Morris asks Ms. Sanchez about her drug abuse background. The patient claims that she had undergone a drug treatment program after her last pregnancy and remained "clean" during this pregnancy. She also states that the father of this child has never used IV drugs, although her previous sexual partners did. She informs Mrs. Morris that she was tested for HIV after her previous pregnancy and that the results were negative. Because she has not used IV drugs in over 18 months, she sees no reason to be tested again.

Mrs. Morris, however, is concerned about Ms. Sanchez's infant. The mother could be HIV positive and could pass along the HIV virus to the child in her breast milk. There is also the possibility that the infant could already be infected with HIV; unless the infant is tested, no treatment will be initiated, significantly reducing the child's chance for survival. She asks the young mother for permission to test her infant. Ms. Sanchez refuses. She then tries to persuade Ms. Sanchez to bottle-feed her infant, because there is a possibility that she could be HIV positive and not know it. Ms. Sanchez becomes very angry, asserting her rights to make decisions for herself and her child.

Mrs. Morris silently disagrees and thinks that this is one situation where the rights of the newborn should outweigh the rights of the parents. She wonders whether she can persuade someone in the newborn nursery to send off a sample of baby Sanchez's blood for HIV testing without Ms. Sanchez's knowledge. She feels that this is the least that ought to be done to promote the child's best interests, given that mother and baby will undoubtedly be discharged within the next 24 hours and lost to follow-up.

Case 14-2

When the Patient Does Not Know That He Is Being Tested for HIV

Tanesha Coombs works in a well-known research hospital. She is the primary nurse assigned to care for Mr. Rivers, a 32-year-old neurologically impaired individual who was recently started on a multiple sclerosis research protocol. The protocol requires that many blood specimens be collected by the primary nurse and sent to the neuro research laboratory of Dr. Toliver and his colleagues, who are doing ground-breaking research on a new treatment for multiple sclerosis. Mr. Rivers was informed about the necessity of frequent blood samples being drawn and the tests that would be performed on his blood. Dr. Toliver assured Mr. Rivers that they would tell him about the reports on all the blood tests being performed. Ms. Coombs subsequently drew the blood samples according to the protocol and sent them to the laboratory.

A few days later, Ms. Coombs was reading the lab reports on the first round of blood specimens collected from Mr. Rivers. She wanted to be informed about their results when Dr. Toliver and his research team came to the unit later that day. She was surprised to find a report of an HIV blood test performed on Mr. Rivers's blood. She knew that such a test was not part of the research protocol; furthermore, the test was positive, which meant that Mr. Rivers should be moved to another suite on the unit, where it was easier to carry out universal precaution procedures for HIV-positive patients.

When Dr. Toliver and his team came to the unit, Ms. Coombs asked about the HIV test. Dr. Toliver stated that the lab would be doing HIV testing on all patients in the study as part of an in-hospital study on HIV infection among all patients and risks to lab personnel. It was not part of the study protocol because informed consent was not being obtained for the testing. She then asked whether Mr. Rivers would be told about the results of the HIV test. Dr. Toliver said that he would not be telling Mr. Rivers about the test results until the study protocol was completed (in about 4 months). Dr. Toliver also stated, "HIV testing is now a standard test in our laboratory for a number of research protocols so that the lab assistants can protect themselves from HIV transmission. They do a number of tests on patients' blood where transmission could easily occur, even with standard precautions being followed. We are doing the testing for the assistants' protection and will inform patients of test results at the end of studies."

Ms. Coombs could easily see the risk to the lab assistants, but she strongly objected to not telling patients about the test being performed on their blood and withholding test results from them for several months. Because she was the person who drew the blood samples from Mr. Rivers, she felt that she was directly deceiving him and that this was wrong.

Dr. Toliver commiserated with her concerns but explained that if the patients in this protocol were told that they would be tested for HIV, a significant number of them would likely refuse the test. He cited the results of several studies at other research centers as well as the results of an in-house study where patients were informed about having an HIV test as part of their protocol—a significant number refused to have the test. Because the lab tests being done for this research posed substantial risk of HIV exposure to lab assistants, it had been decided by the research team to do the HIV test on all blood specimens and not to inform the patients that the test was being done. He stated that the probable number of patients who would test positive was small enough that not informing them was preferable to running the risk of HIV exposure to the lab assistants and losing patients for this particular research protocol.

Certainly, Ms. Coombs could see the wisdom of conducting the protocol in this manner and the importance of the research, could she not? Ms. Coombs was not sure what "wisdom" meant in this situation, but she did know that she did not like being used to help the research team deceive patients, and she told this to Dr. Toliver in no uncertain terms. Dr. Toliver agreed that Mr. Rivers could be transferred to another suite on the unit to protect staff and other patients. However, he appealed to Ms. Coombs to "just work with me on this one, OK?" Ms. Coombs did not like the entire situation. Mr. Rivers was already neurologically impaired, and waiting 4 months might expose him to other risks. But she was uncertain what she should and could do under the circumstances. After all, this was a research facility and the research process was usually given highest priority. What was the "right" thing for her to do?

Commentary

Testing for HIV infection provokes ethical questions about rights to privacy, potential discrimination, and the rights of others not to be put at risk for HIV infection. Early in the AIDS epidemic, those at risk for infection were often urged to be cautious about seeking testing because of a possible loss of rights if they should be found to be infected. In recent years, however, the availability of new and effective treatments for HIV infection, clinical trials, and legislated protections for those infected with the virus have encouraged those at risk to seek testing.[7] Such testing is voluntary and can even be anonymous, protecting rights to self-determination and privacy.

Informed consent has always been a requirement for HIV testing because those at risk for infection are considered to be competent persons with rights to self-determination. As self-determining individuals, they also need to consider the risks and benefits of knowing their HIV antibody status carefully. As we shall learn in Chapters 15 and 16, an adequate informed consent for testing must include receipt of information, comprehension of the information, and voluntariness on the part of the person to be tested. Information that might be conveyed includes the availability and cost of treatment for HIV infection, the lack of a cure for AIDS, the possible stigma and discrimination that might threaten the well-being of a person found to be infected with HIV, and the availability of counseling for the HIV infected. Only when the person voluntarily agrees to testing can the test be done. If the test is found to be positive, the individual can exercise his or her rights to begin therapy or to enter an available clinical trial for treatment.

The rights of the individual to consent to HIV testing are at issue in the cases involving Mrs. Morris and Ms. Coombs. Mrs. Morris's patient refuses to give consent for HIV testing for herself or her infant, whereas Ms. Coombs' patient has already been tested without his consent. The concerns of the two nurses, however, are different. Mrs. Morris is primarily concerned about the health of the newborn child. She undoubtedly knows that 25–30% of HIV-positive pregnant women give birth to HIV-positive babies and that some infants acquire the virus through breast milk.[8] She is trying to protect the interests of the child by urging the mother to have the child tested and not to breast-feed unless the mother's own HIV antibody status is determined.

Mrs. Morris's opinion that the rights of the child not to be harmed should outweigh parental rights to decide for or against HIV testing is shared by many, but only two states—New York and Connecticut—require HIV testing of newborns whose mothers were not tested during pregnancy.[9] Recent federal legislation, however, mandates that states demonstrate a 50% reduction in AIDS cases resulting from perinatal transmission to receive federal funding for AIDS treatment.[10,11] States are implementing several different prenatal HIV-testing approaches to achieve this goal.[12]

But should Mrs. Morris arrange for testing of the infant without the mother's consent? If she does, she might find herself in the same situation Ms. Coombs is in—struggling with how to communicate a test result that has been obtained without the knowledge and consent of the individual.

Ms. Coombs is concerned about her role in deceiving Mr. Rivers about the use of the blood samples she has drawn. Her ethics tells her that testing without the informed consent of the individual is simply wrong. She must also be concerned about the risks for HIV infection to other patients and staff. Her primary concern, however, is the risk to the patient, who is already neurologically impaired and is now known to be HIV positive. *Not* informing him of his positive HIV status until the research study is completed prevents him from making informed decisions about starting treatment. Ms. Coombs knows that early treatment by antiretroviral drugs and protease inhibitors is effective in preventing a fall in CD4 counts to levels at which opportunistic infections and other conditions appear.[13] With his other health problems, Mr. Rivers is at significant risk of rapid proliferation of the infection in his body. These are reasons that Ms. Coombs might consider cooperating in the testing in order to benefit the patient. If her primary objective is benefit to patients like Mr. Rivers and if she is willing to act paternalistically toward him, she might agree to go ahead with the testing. That would mean sacrificing the patient's right to consent in order to benefit the patient and would leave Ms. Coombs with the problem of how to inform him of the results of a test he did not know he had received. If that is her goal, however, it is hard to imagine what would justify withholding the results for 4 months.

On the other hand, if her objective is to protect the welfare of researchers, the clandestine testing is easier to understand. Doing so, however, seems a clear violation of the patient's right to consent to the procedures of the research project. An alternative strategy would be to inform subjects of the screening test for HIV and to exclude patients from the study who, once adequately informed, refuse to consent.

Critical Thinking Questions

1. At what point does risk of harm to patients and concern about violating their rights outweigh the benefits gained from research results?

2. If a nurse experiences a needlestick injury from a patient whose HIV status is unknown, should an HIV test be done and is the patient's consent necessary? Should the patient be informed that such a test is being done, and, if the patient then refuses, does the nurse have recourse?

Balancing Confidentiality Protection and the Duty to Warn

The protection of confidentiality has been considered important to HIV testing in that it encourages people at risk for HIV to come forward for testing, counseling, and treatment. Preserving confidentiality, however, can test the duties of health professionals to protect others, especially sexual partners of those with HIV or AIDS, from harm. As we saw in Chapter 9, professionals have both a moral and legal **duty to warn** others who might be harmed significantly by a patient's actions.[14] Applying this standard for the duty to warn in regards to HIV infection and AIDS treatment, however, has not been easy. The actual risk of HIV transmission between sexual partners (thus, the "foreseeability of harm") is hard to quantify in each case.[15] In the final analysis, the health professional is expected to weigh the likelihood of harm to other parties against his or her duty to keep confidentiality and to act accordingly.

The following two cases demonstrate how conflicts between the protection of confidentiality and the duty to warn can arise in nursing practice.

Case 14-3
When the Transmission of HIV Is Uncertain[1]

Susan Jones is a home health nurse making visits to an elderly woman dying of metastatic breast cancer. The patient's daughter, a 32-year-old divorced mother of two small children, lives in the home and is the primary caregiver for her dying mother. One day, the daughter tells Mrs. Jones that she has a new boyfriend who is planning to move into the house and help care for her mother and the children. On a subsequent visit, Mrs. Jones meets the boyfriend and recognizes him as a patient she previously cared for at an inner-city drug rehabilitation program under her previous employer. She is fairly certain that he tested HIV positive after entering the drug treatment program.

Mrs. Jones asks the daughter about the boyfriend and learns that she knows about his former drug abuse problem but has no knowledge of his HIV status. Mrs. Jones manages to speak to the boyfriend alone. He acknowledges that he was a patient in the drug rehabilitation program but denies that he ever tested positive for HIV. Surely, Mrs. Jones must have him confused with some other patient. Mrs. Jones does not think this is the case, but she decides to do nothing under the circumstances.

Two months later, the daughter tells Mrs. Jones that she is pregnant. Should Mrs. Jones share her concerns about the boyfriend's possible HIV status with the daughter? Should she confirm her suspicions by asking a former colleague at the drug rehabilitation program to look up the boyfriend's treatment record? She could easily do this and no one would ever know. Does Mrs. Jones have any obligation to the daughter and her fetus with regard to the possible transmission of HIV and the prevention of AIDS? After all, the purpose of her home visits is to care for the woman dying of cancer and not her daughter, isn't it?

Commentary

Mrs. Jones has a justifiable ethical concern about the threat of HIV transmission from the boyfriend to her patient's daughter. She can determine whether her suspicion that the boyfriend is HIV positive is, in fact, true by having her colleague gain access to his treatment record at the drug rehabilitation program. Ought Mrs. Jones to do this?

If she were to gain access herself to his record, she clearly would be engaging in illegal and unethical behavior as a nurse. Because she is no longer employed by the agency sponsoring the drug rehabilitation program, she does not have legal access to his record; in addition, accessing it herself would be a clear invasion of his privacy and a violation of his right to self-determine who will have access to information about him and for what purposes. If she were

---

[1]Adapted from Fry, S. T., & Johnstone, M. J. (2002). *Ethics in nursing practice: A guideline to ethical decision making* (2nd ed., pp. 78–79). Oxford, UK: Blackwell Science, Ltd.

successful in having a former nurse colleague at the rehabilitation program look up the information for her, the action would be more complicated. Health professionals normally have access to the patient's record, but it should be on a need-to-know basis only. We would ordinarily understand "need to know" to mean "necessary for the care of that patient." Therefore, because the boyfriend's care is not at play here, even if the colleague could gain access to this record, it would be unethical to do so and would probably be illegal as well.

Moreover, even if the colleague did have the information about the boyfriend's HIV status (perhaps by remembering it), her disclosure of that information to a third party would be a breach of confidentiality. If the duty to keep confidences is governed by the patient's interest, it is hard to understand how she could justify such a breach. However, if she accepts the idea that confidences may (or must) be broken to protect third parties from a credible threat of grave bodily harm and she perceives that the pregnant woman or the fetus is at such a risk, then perhaps the colleague could justify such a disclosure. That, at least, is what the law is understood to require.

If Mrs. Jones cannot get the information from her colleague, she could consider telling the daughter about her suspicion that the boyfriend is HIV positive. Her action would depend not only on her assessment of the severity of the risk to the pregnant woman and her daughter but also on her understanding of the nature of the duty of confidentiality. Under the traditional understanding, her primary duty is to the welfare of her patient. Even though she no longer works at her former agency, she was in a professional–client relationship with the boyfriend, and her obligation to protect the confidentiality of the patients she treated while she was employed there would still continue. As we learned in Chapter 9, protecting patient confidentiality is one of the most fundamental ethical obligations of the nurse. There is also a possibility that she is simply wrong about the boyfriend testing positive for HIV. In that case, she would be relaying information that is untrue and could cause considerable harm to the daughter's and boyfriend's relationship and ultimately cast doubt on her credibility as a professional nurse.

If, however, she were quite confident that she remembered correctly that the boyfriend was HIV positive and that he posed a serious threat of bodily harm to the pregnant woman or her fetus, the case would be more complicated. As we saw in Chapter 9, newer understandings of confidentiality find it necessary to take into account the serious interests of third parties. The law requires disclosure provided the professional believes that the patient is a serious danger to others and that disclosure would likely prevent the risk.

Some would argue, however, that the most ethical action Mrs. Jones can take in this situation is to educate the daughter about HIV infection and safe sexual practices, encourage her to be tested for HIV, and urge her to persuade the boyfriend to undergo HIV testing with her. These actions are supported by the ANA *Position Statement on HIV/AIDS Care* as well as other published guidelines.[16,17]

Case 14-4

When Protecting Confidentiality Seems Wrong

Deborah Aaronson was an attractive, 32-year-old elementary school teacher who had recently returned, with her new husband, from their honeymoon, a 2-week Colorado skiing trip. Mrs. Aaronson developed a dry, nonproductive cough and fever on the trip, which left her tired and sometimes short of breath. During the initial physical by her HMO clinic physician, she admitted to a history of IV drug abuse 6 years previously. She explained that she had undergone a private drug rehabilitation program and had never told her husband about this "dark" side of her past. Her well-to-do, church-going family, embarrassed by her past "wild life," had never discussed it, either. Given Mrs. Aaronson's drug abuse history, Dr. Conroy, her physician, ordered HIV testing with his patient's knowledge and consent.

Mrs. Soames, nurse practitioner, was present when Dr. Conroy told Mrs. Aaronson that the HIV test results were positive. After the physician left the room, Mrs. Soames continued to talk to a distressed and tearful Mrs. Aaronson about the test results and the need to discuss her HIV status with her husband. Mrs. Aaronson said that she did not want anyone to be informed about her HIV status, least of all her husband. She wanted a few days to think everything over and agreed to further testing to determine her CD4 count and to a pregnancy test because she had not used birth control on her honeymoon trip. Mrs. Soames advised her about safe sexual practices and urged her to return to the clinic in a few days.

On the return visit, Mrs. Aaronson learned that her CD4 count was borderline, making her vulnerable to opportunistic infections such as Pneumocystis carinii pneumonia and candidiasis. The pregnancy test also was positive. Again, Mrs. Soames counseled Mrs. Aaronson—about the risk of HIV that her husband had already incurred, the potential for HIV transmission to her fetus, and the need to begin a drug treatment program. She encouraged her to discuss the test results with her husband and to bring him in for testing and counseling. Again, Mrs. Aaronson strongly rejected telling her husband.

During their engagement, they had had a domestic argument, and her husband (then boyfriend) had pushed Mrs. Aaronson into some furniture, resulting in minor injuries to her. Mrs. Aaronson moved out of their apartment and had broken the engagement. Several months later, the couple had resolved their differences and married. Although no similar incidents had occurred, Mrs. Aaronson said that her husband had a violent temper. She feared his reaction if he knew she was HIV positive.

When Mrs. Soames discussed this information with Dr. Conroy, he told her that the best thing for them to do was to tell Mrs. Aaronson that if she did not inform her husband about her HIV status, they would do so. State law permitted breaking confidentiality to report positive HIV status to a spouse and protected physicians from legal liability when they did so. On balance, he said, it was the best action to take, despite the potential of violent behavior toward Mrs. Aaronson on the part of her husband. Mrs. Soames, however, was uncomfortable with this decision. Did the potential harm to the husband (HIV infection) outweigh the potential harm to Mrs. Aaronson and her fetus (violence)?

Commentary

In this case, conflict between the protection of confidentiality and the duty to warn take a different turn. Patients with HIV infection should expect confidential treatment of their HIV test results by all health professionals, except under certain conditions. Even in states where it is required by law to report HIV infection to local health officials, such reporting is done without names or identifiers, to protect individual privacy. Although this practice may change in the near future because of increased public pressure for mandatory reporting policies and regulations, confidential reporting of HIV infection (as well as AIDS) is the present norm.[18]

However, if the HIV-infected person has a spouse and refuses to tell that spouse of the risk to him or her of HIV, the condition exists for a justifiable break in patient confidentiality. It is permissible in some states for health professionals to disclose HIV status to a spouse, especially when the HIV-infected partner refuses to do so. The physician is not required to warn the partner of an HIV-infected person but is merely allowed to do so based on professional judgment.[19] This, apparently, is the position of Dr. Conroy in this case. Mrs. Soames, on the other hand, is concerned about the risk of the husband's violent behavior toward Mrs. Aaronson. Her concern is appropriate.

The usual scenario involving confidentiality and risks to third parties does not include the possibility that the patient may be in danger from the one warned if the information is disclosed. The issue here is whether the risk to Mrs. Aaronson that her husband may assault her provides an exemption from any right or duty of the health professional to warn her husband. In the usual scenario, the main issue is determining whether the threat to the third party is credible enough and serious enough to permit or require breaking confidence. But the special circumstance of the one being warned himself posing a threat complicates the case, perhaps providing justification for nondisclosure.

Critical Thinking Questions

1. If you were Mrs. Soames, would you continue to encourage Mrs. Aaronson to inform her husband of her HIV status, knowing of the potential for violence on his part? Why or why not?

2. Should the nurse in the examples that follow respect patient requests for not disclosing HIV status? Why or why not?

   - A woman originally from the Middle East calls pediatrics hematology/oncology and tells the nurse that her 16-year-old son has both an HIV-infection and is recovering from chemotherapy for lymphoma. He needs a new pediatrics' infectious disease specialist and she wants to know if we agree to treat this young man without telling him he is HIV infected. He knows about the cancer but not the HIV infection acquired by transfusion as a newborn in the United States.

- A man presents for preoperative testing prior to a same day surgery arthroscopic procedure and tells the nurse practitioner doing his history that he is HIV positive but he does not want this fact recorded in his medical record. She is at liberty to verbally inform the orthopedic and OR teams but he wants *no written documentation* of his HIV status.

Research Brief 14-1

Source: Gielen, A. C., McDonnel, K. A., Burke, J. G., & O'Campo, P. (2000). Women's lives after an HIV-positive diagnosis: Disclosure and violence. *Maternal and Child Health Journal, 4*(2), 111–120.

Purpose: The purpose of this study was to examine: (1) the relationships between HIV risk and violence and (2) the role of HIV disclosure among women attending an outpatient HIV primary care clinic. The disclosure-related research questions were:

1. What role do healthcare providers play in women's disclosure to others of their HIV-positive status?
2. What are women's concerns and experiences with disclosure?
3. How is violence related to their diagnosis and disclosures?

Method: Participants included 310 HIV-positive women older than the age of 18 years. All of the women completed a quantitative interview, and a subgroup (those who reported violence) participated in in-depth qualitative interviews.

Findings: More than 46% of the sample reported that a healthcare provider offered to help her disclose her HIV status to a partner, and 57.1% were encouraged by a healthcare provider to tell their sexual partners about their HIV status. Fears of discrimination, infecting others, and losing someone's love or acceptance were important disclosure concerns expressed by the research participants. Of the sample, 12% experienced violence at the time their HIV status was disclosed. Risk factors for experiencing violence after disclosure included a prior history of violence, drug use, low income, young age, length of time since the HIV diagnosis, and having a partner whose HIV status was negative or unknown.

Implications: This information is important for nurses when counseling patients about HIV disclosure. First, it is important for nurses to discuss disclosure with their patients. In this study, only about one half of the participants reported that healthcare providers either offered to help the patient disclose or encouraged the patient to tell her sexual partner about her HIV status. Additionally, the risk of violence after HIV disclosure is a real concern. Therefore, the nurse must work with the patient to assess the degree of risk for violence and to make plans for disclosure that minimize that risk. For example, anonymous partner notification programs are available in many states. These programs are designed to notify potentially "at risk" individuals without disclosing the name of the person with HIV infection.

The Rights of HIV-Infected Individuals

In addition to the nurse's obligation to protect the rights of individuals to HIV testing, counseling, treatment, and privacy (provided by protection of confidentiality) is the obligation not to discriminate against those who are HIV-infected or who have AIDS. This obligation may, however, conflict with the nurse's duties to do good and to warn or prevent harm to others. The following cases involve some of these conflicts.

Case 14-5
When Reporting an HIV State Can Harm You

Debbie Monan was a junior in college when she found out that she was HIV positive. She was in the undergraduate nursing program and was an excellent student. The problem for Debbie was that she had signed a statement when she started the nursing program that said that she had read the HIV and Other Diseases Exposure Policy of the School of Nursing and would abide by its tenets. One tenet was that she would inform an official of the school if she became exposed to HIV, ever was stuck by a needle that was used on a patient, or had any communicable disease that would put patients at risk of disease. If she did not report her HIV status and someone found out about it, Debbie might be dismissed from the nursing program and the university.

Debbie knows that she contracted the disease from having unprotected sex and not from other causes. But she is uncertain what she should do. She is in good health, practices a very healthy lifestyle, and is not taking any antiretroviral drugs at the present time. She knows that if she is careful and uses universal precautions in her care of patients, it is unlikely that she will expose patients to HIV. Thus, Debbie thinks that she can keep her HIV status to herself until graduation. On the other hand, she is worried that she might suffer stress and fatigue in the nursing program, which could cause her to be sick and her "secret" to be known. How can she protect her rights to her education? Did she waive those rights when she became a student in a nursing program of study?

Case 14-6

When Not Reporting an HIV Infection Might Harm Others

Tanya Morris works at a day surgery clinic run by three surgeons. One of the gastroenterology surgeons, Dr. Mooney, is a known homosexual and has recently been ill. He was hospitalized briefly for pneumonia and is now experiencing frequent upper respiratory illnesses, weight loss, weakness, and fatigue. When Ms. Morris asks him about his health, he tells her that he has been HIV positive for about 10 years and that his physician colleagues know this. He now has AIDS that is not responding to treatment. He plans to work for as long as he can and then to take an extended "vacation." He does not think it is necessary for any of the patients to know about his AIDS status. He is careful about his procedures and does not believe that the patients run any risk of contracting HIV from him. He asks Ms. Morris to not think any differently of him than she has in the past.

Ms. Morris is, of course, concerned about Dr. Mooney. He has always been her favorite physician to work with. But she does not think it is right for patients to undergo endoscopic procedures without knowing that their surgeon is HIV positive. Don't patients' rights not to be infected with HIV override a surgeon's right to privacy regarding his personal HIV status?

Commentary

In both of the preceding cases, individual rights of HIV patients are in conflict with the rights of others not to be infected. Debbie Monan, a college student, has a right to her education. The right, however, is potentially in conflict with the rights of patients not to be infected. Likewise, Dr. Mooney has a right to pursue his occupation, but one might argue that his patients have a right to be informed about his HIV status and to choose whether they want to have surgical procedures performed on them by a person with AIDS. We shall see in Chapter 16 that the doctrine of informed consent gives patients the right to information that could be meaningful to them in making decisions about their medical care. Some patients would certainly find Dr. Mooney's HIV status to be "meaningful information."

Debbie's situation is difficult because she signed a statement when she entered the nursing program. She has, in effect, made a promise to disclose her HIV status. Therefore, she has to consider not only her duty to protect patients from harm but also her duty to keep her promise. It is unclear whether she would be dropped from the program if she reported her HIV status to an official of the school of nursing. The statement is designed to protect the university from liability if a student should put a patient at risk by transmitting a communicable disease. If she were not dropped from the program, it is quite possible that she would be prevented from participating in clinical experiences until she received treatment or her viral count was at a level that would preclude transmission of HIV. Without the approved number of hours of clinical experiences, Debbie would not be able to graduate and take her licensing exam. Delays in her program of study certainly would be harms to her. Are they more significant than the harms of HIV infection to unsuspecting and vulnerable patients? Do they override her duty to keep the commitment she made when she signed the policy statement?

As we have already learned, federal legislation and state statutes protect persons with AIDS from discrimination and from loss of employment and health insurance. Physicians and nurses, however, have a special relationship with patients. Because of this, they incur special obligations to protect patients' health, as stated in the position statements of professional organizations. For example, the American Nurses Association asserts that the health and safety of patients are the primary foci for nursing assessment and intervention.[20] In providing care to some HIV-positive patients, nurses may question the extent of the obligation to protect the health of others when doing so places nurses at risk of infection. That is the issue in the next two cases.

Case 14-7
When Nobody Wants to Care for an AIDS Patient

Kent Holmes is the evening supervisor in a 230-bed, acute care hospital. The emergency room nurse calls to tell him that they are going to admit an AIDS patient with pneumonia to West Four. The patient, Rosie Green, is well-known to the nurses. She has AIDS dementia complex (ADC), and during her last admission, she attempted to bite nurses and aides when they gave her treatments or medications.

When Kent calls Jean Atwater, the P.M. nurse on West Four, to tell her about Ms. Green's admission, Jean states that she will not take care of Ms. Green. She is afraid of being bitten, and she does not want to put herself at risk of contracting HIV—all the more so because she might be pregnant. When Kent goes to the unit to talk to Jean and the other nurse, he finds that the other nurse and the two nursing aides are also reluctant to take care of Rosie Green. Kent does not have another medical bed for this patient. What should he do to help the staff be willing to care for Ms. Green? What options does he have if they continue to refuse to care for her?

Case 14-8
When Treating an AIDS Patient Puts Other, Noninfected Patients at Risk

Joseph Giacobbi is a 60-year-old former drug addict with AIDS dementia. He has recently been admitted to an outpatient renal dialysis service for dialysis treatments three times per week. Maggie Cohen, the nurse in charge of the dialysis service, is finding it hard to give Mr. Giacobbi nondiscriminatory nursing care. He is verbally abusive to the staff and other patients. He threatens the staff and has knocked over equipment and hit several of the nurses when they have tried to restrain him during the dialysis process. He has required a police escort from the hospital on several occasions. Several of the local transportation services have denied him transportation to the center because of his abusive behavior. Yet, Miss Cohen has been told that she must provide care to this patient, regardless of what he does. She wonders, however, whether the rights of a terminally ill (but abusive) patient should really take precedence over the other patients' rights to comfort, safety, and nursing attention.

Commentary

Cases 14-7 and 14-8 both involve nurses who are at real risk from patients. The patient in Case 14-8 poses risks to other patients as well. Because both patients have AIDS dementia, it seems reasonable not to blame the patients for the threat they pose. Moreover, their behaviors do not decrease their need for skilled, compassionate nursing care. But none of this can justify overlooking the fact that Jean Atwater and Maggie Cohen are in real danger and reluctant to provide care to patients known to be HIV positive. Despite increased education about HIV infection, nurses continue to express fearful attitudes about being exposed to HIV and report that they frequently avoid caring for HIV-infected patients.[21] Their fears are understandable given that 51 healthcare workers had documented occupational acquisition of HIV infection through June 1996 and 20 of them were nurses.[22] All of the workers' HIV infections involved exposure to HIV-infected blood or visible bloody fluids, and 86% of the infections resulted from percutaneous exposures. Being bitten by Rosie Green or being exposed to Mr. Giacobbi's blood could place nurses at risk of infection. The issue is whether that danger gives nurses the right to refuse to care for their HIV-infected patients.

Increasingly, we are viewing lay–professional relationships in health care as contractual. Physicians have long insisted that they have the right to choose whether to enter into relationships with potential patients. Nurses could well make similar claims.

At least two issues need to be considered. First, is there a difference between independent practitioners choosing whether to take someone as a patient and hospital employees, who have accepted assignment to a particular role, making such decisions? Just as a physician in private practice may decide not to take on certain patients, so may nurses in private practice do the same. Likewise, it is probably the case that physicians on a hospital service may not legally refuse to treat certain patients who need their services.[23] If so, nurses on a service may be in a similar position of being required, legally and ethically, to deliver care. It seems clear that they could not refuse to treat patients on grounds of race, for instance.

Critical Thinking Question

What types of risks to the nurse would justify refusal to care for a patient? Certainly, a nurse could refuse to provide care if the patient needed something beyond the nurse's skill. But can risks to the nurse justify refusal to provide care?

It should be clear that health professionals are in a position that is quite different from that of ordinary citizens. Lifeguards cannot refuse to attempt to rescue a drowning swimmer, whereas the ordinary bystander could. This is because lifeguards have assumed a role of being responsible for rescues. They are professionally committed by way of a contract or covenant with society to perform this function, even though it puts them at risk.

Likewise, healthcare professionals contract or covenant with society to deliver certain healthcare services. The fact that providing such services puts the professional at risk does not automatically permit him or her to flee the scene, even though a lay person would have every right to do so. From the time of the plagues of the Middle Ages, physicians have been morally obliged to stay with their patients, even if doing so puts them in harm's way. Nurses assume a similar burden when they take on roles as health professionals. This suggests that morally, if not legally, they would have a duty to provide at least some level of care, even if they were independent, freestanding practitioners with a general right to pick whom they will serve.

The real issue is whether there are limits to such obligations to serve patients— especially patients who are of real danger to others through no fault of their own. If a nurse might be or is known to be pregnant, like Jean Atwater in Case 14-7, she usually is exempted, by hospital policy, from caring for HIV-infected or AIDS patients. Certainly, any nurse would have the right to insist on maximal safeguards in delivering care to patients like Rosie Green and Joseph Giacobbi. They should be entitled to extra security and perhaps even the use of physical and chemical restraints while they are serving the patient. At least one nurse has been awarded damages ($4.25 million to the nurse and $1 million to her husband) by a court for testing HIV positive less than a year after being stuck by an IV needle that disconnected from an AIDS patient's body during a seizure. Security personnel standing nearby refused to assist the nurse during the patient's seizure, resulting in a legal judgment against the nurse's and security personnel's employer.[24] There are few other circumstances in which the risk to the nurse or other patients would permit refusing to care for a patient because he or she is "too dangerous."

Conflicts Involving the Cost of Treatment and Allocation of Resources

Cost represents one of the most troublesome dilemmas in the care of HIV-positive and AIDS patients. A study by Bruce Schackman and others reports that an American diagnosed with the AIDS virus can expect to live for about 24 years on average, and the cost of health care over those decades is more than $600,000. Schackman credits expensive and effective drug therapies for the increases in life expectancy and the cost of care.[25]

Viewed from a global perspective, only those with unusually good health insurance or enormous wealth can afford the highest quality care. Even for those who have the best insurance, the question of whether all the expenditures are worth it is bound to arise.

Similar problems arise at the clinical level. Nurses who include AIDS patients in their caseloads could devote endless efforts to providing care to them and, in the process, compromise the attention they give other patients. They may also wonder whether providing costly life-preserving treatments to AIDS patients is a good use of healthcare resources. In the early days of AIDS treatment, these concerns stemmed from the reality that an AIDS diagnosis was often shortly followed by death. Today, with AIDS more of a chronic condition than terminal, questions are often related to determinations about life-sustaining treatments for other conditions and the relevance of AIDS in this context.

The general problems related to allocating medical resources were addressed in Chapter 5. There we saw that the traditional Hippocratic ideal of paying attention only to what is best for the individual patient fails to provide adequate guidance for the nurse who is forced to choose among patients making competing claims. We also saw that two principles provide guidance on how to allocate scarce medical resources. General **social beneficence** or utility would have the nurse allocate resources so as to produce as much good as possible taking into account the sum total of possible benefits for all patients involved. This principle implies that certain hard-to-treat or inefficient-to-treat patients will be left out. The second social principle, **justice**, pays more attention to the way the benefits are distributed. One commonly held form of justice would allocate resources to those who have the greatest need, even if doing so is inefficient and therefore sacrifices some of the aggregate benefit that could possibly be achieved.

AIDS patients are frequently among the "worst off" citizens and therefore would have strong claims under certain interpretations of the principle of justice. On the other hand, some persons with AIDS may be so critically ill that extensive efforts to care for them would produce only marginal benefits. A utility-maximizing approach would require that these patients be sacrificed for the good of others.

The following three cases present perspectives on these problems.

Case 14-9
Is a Life with AIDS a Life Worth Saving?

Dottie James is a nurse working for a large HMO. She follows up on patients' care after they have been seen in the clinic and is personally committed to close telephone contact with the six AIDS patients that she follows. She discusses advance directives with the patients and their families and often witnesses their statements. She is troubled, however, by one AIDS patient, 27-year-old Bill Simmons, who has not responded well to drug treatment. Mr. Simmons has insisted that he wants full resuscitation when he needs it and does not want to remain at home to die. He knows that he will soon be terminally ill, but he wants to remain alive as long as possible. He has undergone several surgical procedures (to reduce his pain and enable adequate nutrition) and has asked his long-time companion, Larry, to be his healthcare proxy when he can no longer make his own choices. Larry is committed to doing whatever Mr. Simmons wants, including resuscitation and all life-sustaining procedures.

Ms. James thinks it is wrong for Mr. Simmons to demand, as his right, full resuscitation services when they will not prolong his life in any significant manner. She thinks he is doing this just to make a "statement" for AIDS care treatment without regard for the cost of the resources that will be involved. She wonders why any terminally ill patient can demand such costly services when he or she will not benefit from them.

Commentary

The issues raised in this case are often referred to as the "futile care" problem. Mr. Simmons, for whatever reason of his own, is asking for resuscitation that makes no sense to Ms. James. From her perspective, resuscitation is bound to fail. Moreover, it will consume professional time and energy and other resources that could be used more valuably for other patients.

The "futile care" problem will be explored in more detail in Chapter 17. There we shall see that there are good reasons that some patients, particularly those with unusual value systems or special religious beliefs, may want treatments that other people deem useless. In Mr. Simmons's case, he may value highly even a few extra hours or days. He may recognize that through such care he is able to make a public statement about the rights of AIDS patients.

Whatever the logic behind such patient demands for care that some would consider futile, the core problem for Ms. James is whether patients have a right of access to any treatment they feel serves some purpose they consider worthwhile and, if not, whether she is the one who should worry about setting limits. Our discussion of justice and *allocation of scarce resources* in Chapter 5 suggested that in a world of finite medical resources some limits have to be placed on access to expensive, marginal services. At the very least, physicians, nurses, and insurers ought to have the right to refuse to provide expensive services when there is no evidence the intervention will achieve what the patient seeks.

The problem with Mr. Simmons's demand is that resuscitation may actually achieve what he is seeking. If he is realistic about recognizing that resuscitation is likely only to extend life briefly, he may be right in claiming that resuscitation will change somewhat the way he dies, prolonging his life a bit. If Mr. Simmons recognizes these limits and says he wants the care, it is dishonest to refuse to provide it with the argument that it would be without any effect. The real dispute is over whether the expected effect is of any value, not over whether resuscitation has a chance of temporarily reversing a cardiac arrest.

To set limits on access to care that has a realistic chance of achieving some modest effect that the patient deems valuable, society will have to claim straightforwardly that, even though the care might have the modest effect the patient desires, the patient's claim is not morally legitimate—that is, that others have a prior claim on those resources.

If one holds that the goal of a health policy is to get as much benefit as possible out of scarce resources, it may not be hard to show that the resources will do more good if they are used for other patients. Social beneficence or utility maximizing provides a moral basis for arguing that Mr. Simmons's demand must be subordinated to other claims that have higher priority.

On the other hand, if one holds that the prevailing moral principle is justice, then one will not be interested in the claim that more overall good will be done by spending the resources elsewhere. The focus will be on how poorly off Mr. Simmons is compared to others for whom those resources could be used. Because a terminally ill AIDS patient is generally considered to be in pretty bad shape, it will probably be hard to show that alternative uses of the resources would benefit worse off persons.

Whichever moral principle one uses for resolving this problem, there is a second-level issue that Ms. James must consider: whether she as Mr. Simmons's nurse should be the one worrying about the resources used in his care. Some have argued that bedside clinicians must abandon their single-minded focus on the welfare of their patients in order to make sure resources are used responsibly. This means clinical professionals should abandon their patient-centered focus and become society's resource allocators. Others claim that this approach ought to be resisted and a moral division of labor should be recognized. Bedside clinicians should remain focused on their individual patients, leaving it to others—public policymakers, administrators, or the public at large—to determine how scarce resources are allocated.

Case 14-10

How Much Money Should Be Spent Treating Children with AIDS?[2]

Joyce Hingham is a pediatric nurse practitioner (PNP) working on a unit that cares for pediatric AIDS patients. Miss Hingham questions the amount of resources and time spent caring for these children, who will inevitably die. She is not opposed to comfort care for these children, but she wonders why expensive treatment modalities and surgery, usually at public expense, are recommended for the majority of the patients. The health team members often discuss these issues, but they have never reached consensus about an ethical position. Each child has different needs, and each family has a different capacity to take care of their child. The only factor that is certain in all cases is that treatment for these children is expensive for their communities. The following two pediatric AIDS patients of Miss Hingham illustrate how difficult (and expensive) decisions about care for these children often are.

Mary was a 7-year-old child with AIDS who had been hospitalized for many months. She had experienced several complications of her disease, including multiple gastrointestinal tract

---

[2]Libman, M. (1995). Ethics column: In the child's best interests. *Massachusetts Nurse, 65*(5), 9–11.

fistulas. Mary underwent a bowel resection and the creation of a colostomy. The goals of surgery were to decrease the chance of infection and bleeding and, most important, to allow Mary the chance to be able to eat normally and be discharged to her home. Unfortunately, Mary was unable to maintain adequate oral intake, despite her surgical procedure.

Miss Hingham presented Mary's situation at the unit's team meeting, the members of which advised giving Mary total parenteral nutrition (TPN). Mary's mother, a chronic drug abuser living at her mother's home with two other children, was initially against TPN because it would require home nursing services for which she could not pay. She finally agreed to home TPN under the condition that she and her mother be allowed to manage Mary's home care. The team reluctantly agreed to a revised plan of care that included daily VNA (visiting nurse association) visits instead of blocks of home nursing care.

Mary's family, however, never came to the hospital to learn how to administer her TPN. After much agonizing and discussion, the team again revised its plan for home care. Mary was discharged without TPN. Hydration was administered on a daily basis by a VNA nurse, at public expense. Mary had frequent hospital admissions and more surgery over the next 18 months before she died. Although Mary never had optimal nutrition during this time, the team thought Mary enjoyed being at home more than being in the hospital.

Lucy was a 5-year-old child also cared for by Miss Hingham. She was admitted with seizures that were complications of AIDS. Neurological studies revealed central nervous system lesions that could only be treated palliatively. Because Lucy was unable to take adequate oral food, the team was concerned about nutrition and dehydration as well as adequate access for the administration of medication to keep Lucy comfortable and seizure free. Lucy's mother refused to consent to placement of a gastrostomy tube for Lucy's feeding and medication. While the team was trying to persuade her to change her mind, Lucy's mother was hospitalized with complications of her own disease (AIDS).

Finally, Lucy's mother did consent to the placement of a central venous line for her daughter so that she could begin TPN. It was her wish to have Lucy come home so that they could share their final days together. The home had very limited resources for the care of both Lucy and her mother, so home care services were provided. Lucy's mother even came to the hospital to learn how to administer the TPN and other IV medications. Miss Hingham and the team members agonized over whether this discharge plan for Lucy was realistic. They also wondered if they were using the community's limited home care resources effectively. Lucy required 16 hours per day of home nursing care. She did well at home, however, gaining weight and experiencing a slower progression of her neurologic problem than was initially expected. She lived at home for 6 months before she died. Her mother died several months later.

Did Miss Hingham and the healthcare team use healthcare resources wisely in caring for Mary and Lucy?

Commentary

The patients considered by Miss Hingham raise issues that are very similar to those in Case 14-9. The commentary for that case should be reviewed for consideration of these issues. Miss Hingham's case is even more complicated, however, because the patients involved are children. They are not competent to make their own choices. For each of the patients, the parents were in the position to make the choices.

Whereas in Case 14-9 the patient, to his mind, was competent to decide whether the benefits of the treatment outweighed the burdens, for Miss Hingham's patients, the parents make the choices. It is possible that they are imposing terrible burdens on their children for no good reason. In Chapter 17 we shall see that parents and other familial surrogates are given considerable discretion in deciding what counts as a benefit for their children, but they do not have unlimited discretion.

Miss Hingham may have to consider whether Mary and Lucy are being burdened significantly and, if so, whether she has any responsibility to initiate review of the parents' decisions. In an extreme case, a court order overruling the parents might be obtained if a judge determines that another course—including refusal of treatment—is in the patient's best interest. Is either Mary's or Lucy's case one in which such an order should be sought?

Miss Hingham seems to be worried not only about whether the treatment is harmful to her patients but also about whether their care is an unwise use of resources. In Case 14-9 we saw that the resource question depended on whether the proper principle is social utility or justice and also on whether bedside clinicians should exclude such social resource allocation questions from their care plan judgments. The same issues are at stake here.

Critical Thinking Questions

1. If you were Miss Hingham, how would you have addressed the cost-of-care issue in the cases of Mary and Lucy?
2. Should RNs consider costs in providing care to patients? If so, under what conditions? If not, why not?

Case 14-11
Are HIV Patients Being Treated Unfairly?[3]

Mary Ellen Dunn is the unit coordinator for an outpatient renal dialysis unit at an acute care hospital. The unit offers high-flux dialysis with canister reuse. High-flux dialysis is a form of dialysis that pulls increased amounts of fluid from a patient at an increased rate, resulting in a shorter time for dialysis to be completed. A canister, which contains the capillaries that filter out impurities in the patient's blood, is reused by the same patient at

---

[3]The authors acknowledge the consultation of Lucy M. Feild, PhD, RN, in the construction of this case.

each dialysis session. The canister is cleaned and sterilized between each dialysis session and can be used 10 to 15 times (or about 1 month) by the patient before it loses effectiveness and requires replacement. The canister for high-flux dialysis costs twice as much as the canister for conventional dialysis. In conventional dialysis, canisters can also be reused for each dialysis session but not as many times as in high-flux dialysis.

Miss Dunn was asked to write a unit policy and design an implementation procedure that denies high-flux dialysis to HIV-positive patients. She was told that the policy was needed to protect patients and staff from being infected with HIV. Even though the nurses followed universal precautions in their handling and sterilization of the canisters used in high-flux dialysis and each patient's canister was carefully stored for reuse by only that patient, the hospital wanted to reduce staff exposure to HIV-infected materials and act responsibly where risk to other, non–HIV-infected patients was concerned.

Miss Dunn suspects that HIV patients are being discriminated against. First, if the hospital was really concerned about transmission of HIV to staff from cleaning of canisters or to patients by a mix-up among the canisters, then the policy under consideration should extend to all patients with bloodborne diseases (such as hepatitis B, which is more prevalent than HIV infection). Yet, she is being asked to implement the policy for HIV-infected patients only. Second, Miss Dunn recognizes that implementation of the policy will mean that HIV-positive patients will be dialyzed on conventional dialyzers, which is less expensive than high-flux dialysis but is less convenient to patients because it takes more time. She thinks the hospital is trying to reduce the costs of dialysis overall by denying HIV patients access to a new technology that is more costly. How should Miss Dunn respond to her employer's request, and how might she best advocate for HIV patients needing renal dialysis at her institution?

Commentary

This case differs significantly from the previous two cases because it involves a nurse in a policy-making role. She is not in the clinician's position, in which she could say it is her sole duty to benefit her patient and the duty of others to decide how resources should be allocated among patients. Even if we distinguish between making the policy that excludes HIV-infected patients from high-flux dialysis (which Miss Dunn apparently did not make) and creating a unit policy to implement that decision, Miss Dunn is clearly involved at the policy level, not at the level of patient care.

If we assume that there is some risk to staff from cleaning the canisters for reuse and a definite risk to patients if a canister used by an HIV-infected patient is improperly labeled or stored and then inadvertently used for the dialysis of a non-HIV-infected patient,[26] would excluding HIV patients from high-flux dialysis with reuse reduce these risks? The answer seems to be that risks of HIV infection would be reduced, but Miss Dunn reasons that if there is a real risk to staff or patients, then the policy should exclude all patients with bloodborne diseases, not just HIV-infected patients, from use of the technology. In fact, one might argue that staff and patients are at less risk for HIV transmission from high-flux dialysis with reuse than they are for other more virulent bloodborne diseases, such as hepatitis B or C. Miss Dunn seems to have grounds for challenging this rationale for the new policy.

It is more complicated to argue against the hospital's policy on the basis of the costs of high-flux dialysis. Hospitals do have the option of making policies that conserve costs.

Critical Thinking Question

Is it ethically justifiable to target HIV-infected patients by denying them (and only them) access to a technology solely on the basis of costs? Why or why not?

One approach examines the decision using the principles of social beneficence. This approach would ask which policies will do the most good overall and how to use resources most efficiently. Because the canisters pose somewhat more risk when used for HIV patients, a benefit-harm analysis would identify that the net benefit is less. (An alternative of using new canisters each time would perhaps be even more costly.) From the perspective of efficient use of resources, a case can be made for requiring the more conventional, slower dialysis for the HIV-positive patients (and others with bloodborne infections). On the other hand, if the goal is to use resources so as to maximize the benefit to the worst-off patients, accepting the small extra risk for the nurses and the other patients by using high-flux dialysis might be more defensible. Justice requires doing what is necessary to benefit the patients who are worst off. Assuming that those who need dialysis and also have HIV infection are worse off than those without the infection, then taking a small risk with those who are better off in order to make the life of the worst off more convenient might fit this requirement of justice. Alternatively, spending extra resources to use new canisters each time might also fit the demands of justice. Either way, doing what is best for the HIV patients seems to require a different course of action than doing what is most efficient.

Research Brief 14-2

Source: Erlen, J. A., Sereika, S. M., Cook, R. L., & Hunt, S. C. (2002). Adherence to antiretroviral therapy among women with HIV infection. *Journal of Obstetric, Gynecologic, & Neonatal Nursing, 31*(4), 470–477.

Purpose: The purpose of this study was to describe self-reported adherence to antiretroviral therapy and to understand beliefs or perceptions about these medicines in a sample of women with HIV infection.

Method: A secondary analysis of data from a larger study of adherence to protease inhibitors was conducted to understand the issues of adherence among women. The sample included 61 HIV-infected women.

Findings: Only 26.2% of the participants reported that they had taken all of their HIV medications within the past week. The most common reasons for missed doses included forgetting (39.3%), going out and not taking medication with them (34.4%), and falling asleep (23%). Regarding beliefs and perceptions about the medications, 66% of the participants believed that the antiretrovirals were helping them, whereas 16.4% were unsure that these medications were helping them. Only 57.4% of the women thought it was dangerous to miss an antiretroviral dose, and an additional 23% of the women were uncertain about the danger of missing a dose.

Implications: This study highlights the need for nurses to educate HIV-infected patients about the importance of taking their antiretroviral regimen as prescribed. Missed doses are a frequent occurrence and can lead to clinical deterioration and the development of a resistant virus. Interventions that help women remember to take their medications when they are away from home (e.g., pillboxes, alarms) can be used to help women achieve improved adherence.

Research on HIV

As the major lethal infection of the late 20th and early 21st centuries, AIDS has generated a massive research enterprise. It is the very nature of medical research that it produces ethical controversies. By definition, research is activity undertaken with the intention of producing generalizable knowledge. It, therefore, is not conducted primarily for the benefit of the patient. In much medical research involving sick patients, especially critically ill patients such as those with HIV, research may be comparing a standard treatment with one that offers promise to be a better treatment but that may also be more harmful. Randomized clinical trials are ethical only if there is no reason to believe in advance that one of the treatments is better than the other. Hence, the randomization is never used for the benefit of the patient.

The ethical issues of research involving human subjects will be explored more fully in Chapter 15. There we will examine issues of determination of risks and benefit, protecting privacy, equity, and informed consent. In this chapter we shall introduce those issues by examining two cases involving research in the AIDS context.

Case 14-12

Excluding an IV Drug User from the Research Study

Fred Cameron is a 36-year-old, self-employed carpenter with a 10-year history of heroin use. He was tested for HIV after his older brother (with whom he had shared needles in the past) died of AIDS 6 months ago. Found to be HIV positive, he was advised to begin antiretroviral therapy because his CD4 count was 280.

Mr. Cameron requested to be considered for a research drug trial because he did not have health insurance to pay for his medications or office visits. He also said it would give his life some meaning if he helped researchers find the best combination therapy against HIV infection. His primary physician referred him to the research office, and Sandy Morrell, an adult nurse practitioner, met with Mr. Cameron to discuss aspects of a study currently under way. He met all of the entry criteria except one: He was still using small amounts of heroin every day. Mrs. Morrell called the company sponsoring the drug trial and asked for an exception from the "no active substance use" study criterion in Mr. Cameron's case. She said he was highly motivated to participate in the study, was compliant with his appointments, and met all other study criteria. She was given verbal permission to enroll Mr. Cameron in the study. She obtained his informed consent to participate, and he completed various laboratory blood and urine tests, a chest x-ray, an EKG, a physical exam, and a complete history.

Prior to beginning drug administration, Mrs. Morrell contacted the study sponsor and requested the exemption from the "no active substance use" criterion in writing. To her surprise, written response from the sponsor indicated that the exemption was denied. Apparently, the sponsor was concerned that Mr. Cameron would not be a reliable study participant if he was still an IV drug user. For example, he might be committing illegal acts, stealing, or infecting others, and he might be unable to keep his appointments because of being in jail. The sponsor did state, however, that it would reconsider the situation if Mr. Cameron gave satisfactory answers to the following questions:

1. Is he sharing needles? If not, where does he get the needles?
2. How much does his habit cost? Where does he get the money for this?
3. How much heroin is he actually using per day?
4. Does he have reliable transportation to the clinic?

Mrs. Morrell was reluctant to ask Mr. Cameron these questions. She did not think the sponsor had a right to request this type of information, and the informed consent form had had not indicated that it would be required. She suspected that the sponsor was evaluating Mr. Cameron's participation in the study on moral grounds rather than on scientific principles and essentially considering him, as an HIV-positive person who was also an IV drug user, to be less entitled to privacy than the usual research subject. It also seemed that the study was rejecting the people who most needed to participate in it.

Commentary

Mrs. Morrell is taking the perspective of a clinician concerned about maximizing the welfare of her patient. She makes a good case that, because Mr. Cameron seems to have no other means of getting medication, Mr. Cameron's interest would be served if he were in the trial. Moreover, she has good reason to be concerned about the invasive questions to which the research sponsor is seeking answers. Some of the questions do not even seem to relate plausibly to the likelihood Mr. Cameron will complete the study.

On the other hand, the purpose of research is not to get needed treatments to patients; it is to produce generalizable knowledge. For that reason, such research follows a protocol. The protocol in this case calls for an exclusion of those who are currently heroin users. The good reason for that exclusion is the risk that such subjects will fail to comply with the study regimen. Some physicians report a reluctance to give protease inhibitors to "IV drug users who get high, have unprotected sex, and who may potentially infect others with drug-resistant strains of HIV."[27] Thus, from the point of view of the sponsor of the study, enforcing the protocol exclusion seems justified. In fact, granting an exception is hard to justify.

Assuming that the sponsors concluded that the continued use of heroin would not interfere with the study's medication (or they decided to add a subgroup of active heroin users), would they be justified in screening such persons to eliminate those they thought would not be able to comply with the protocol? Some drug regimens involve ingesting 20 to 40 pills a day—some on an empty stomach, some with food, some with large amounts of fluid. These regimens can be very strenuous.[28] Investigators and research sponsors are not in the business of providing clinical care and do not have an obligation to enter any person into their trials. Is requiring that Mr. Cameron answer additional questions an invasion of his privacy or an unjustified departure from the informed consent requirements for participation in the trial?

Critical Thinking Questions

1. If the protocol were redesigned so that heroin users could be included in the trial, would the sponsor be justified in asking all the questions listed in Case 14-12? Which ones best serve study-related purposes?

2. Should heroin users have a different informed consent form for their participation in the drug trial than others do?

Case 14-13
When Vaccine Testing May Be Risky[4]

Mona Dubbins, RN, works for a profit-making biologicals development firm (SciTec) that has recently collaborated with Robert DeSalle, a vaccine researcher at a well-known medical school in the Northeast. DeSalle has been working on developing a vaccine against AIDS that uses live HIV virus, arguing that whole, weakened viruses have been very effective with such diseases as polio and smallpox in the past. By deleting certain genes from simian AIDS viruses, DeSalle has created a highly effective monkey vaccine. He is now

---

[4]This fictitious case is based on Crowley, G. (1998, July 6). Is AIDS forever? *Newsweek*, pp. 60–66.

eager to use the same principles in the development of a vaccine for people. Working with SciTec, he has engineered a type of HIV that can infect human cells but lacks three of the real virus' nine genes. He claims that this vaccine, once available to the masses, will out-perform all other vaccines in development. AIDS experts agree.

Miss Dubbins and other members of the research development team, however, are concerned that a vaccine using live but weakened HIV virus might cause AIDS in people with impaired immune systems or help the HIV virus evolve toward more virulent forms once it is in wide use. Should SciTec become involved in producing an effective vaccine that will undoubtedly make some people sick? Or should SciTec work toward developing a vaccine that is safe but not as effective in protecting people from disease?

Commentary

A libertarian might argue that there is really no ethical problem raised by this case. Because recruiting subjects for the eventual testing of the new vaccine requires obtaining adequately informed consent, either type of vaccine could be developed provided there are informed subjects willing to consent to the risks. Of course, subjects in each case would have to be told about the risks. Those on whom the testing of the live-virus vaccine is tried would have to be told that there is a chance of producing an HIV infection, but they could also be told that eventually this version could prove more effective. The investigators would then have to see if willing, informed volunteers step forward to be subjects. Because many people are deeply committed to overcoming the disease, an adequate number might be willing to take the risk for the good of science and their fellow human beings. But informed voluntary consent would be needed. For this approach to be used respon-sibly, consenting subjects would have to be screened to eliminate those with psy-chologic problems that might make their consent involuntary.

Critics of **libertarianism** would most likely not be convinced that getting ade-quately informed consent for trials of the attenuated live vaccine settles the mat-ter. They might first point out that developing a safe, relatively effective version of the vaccine, that is, one using a safer, killed virus, would be an enormous contribu-tion to humankind. In fact, if the vaccine were effective enough, it could reduce the incidence of the disease sufficiently that transmission would become much less likely, eventually reducing the incidence to the point that "herd immunity" could be established. They might also point out that it is not only the volunteer subjects who would be put at risk from the live virus. Presumably, many volunteers would be sexually active, exposing sex partners and offspring to the disease.

Finally, critics might argue that there is some research that is so dangerous that it would be immoral to engage in it even if willing, adequately informed volunteers were found. They might argue that it should bother the conscience of the investigator, even if it does not trouble the subjects, to engage in research that is too dangerous.

The ethics of human subjects research raises all of these questions and more. In Chapter 15 these questions are examined more thoroughly.

Research Brief 14-3

Source: Gifford, A. L., Cunningham, W. E., Heslin, K. C., Andersen, R. M., Nakazono, T., Lieu, D. K., et al. (2002). Participation in research and access to experimental treatments by HIV-infected patients. *New England Journal of Medicine, 346*(18), 1373–1382.

Purpose: To identify whether minority groups and women are underrepresented in research involving patients with HIV infection.

Method: Nationally represented data from the HIV Cost and Services Utilization Study were used to determine the characteristics of participants and nonparticipants in trials of medications for HIV infection and whether patients had access to experimental treatments. A probability sample of 2864 persons representing all 231,400 adults with known HIV infection who are cared for in the contiguous United States were interviewed on three occasions between 1996 and 1998. They were asked about participation in clinical research studies of medications and past receipt of experimental medications for HIV.

Findings: Approximately 14% of adults receiving care for HIV infection participated in a medication trial or study, whereas 24% had received experimental medications, and 8% had tried and failed to obtain experimental treatments. According to multivariate models, non-Hispanic blacks and Hispanics were less likely to participate in trials than non-Hispanic whites (odds ratio for participation among non-Hispanic blacks, 0.50 [95% confidence interval, 0.28 to 0.91]; odds ratio among Hispanics, 0.58 [95% confidence interval, 0.37 to 0.93]) and to have received experimental medications (odds ratios, 0.41 [95% confidence interval, 0.32 to 0.54] and 0.56 [95% confidence interval, 0.41 to 0.78], respectively). Patients who were cared for in private health maintenance organizations were less likely to participate in trials than those with fee-for-service insurance (odds ratio, 0.43 [95% confidence interval, 0.21 to 0.88]). Women were not underrepresented in research trials and had a similar likelihood of receiving experimental treatments as men did.

Implications: Among patients with HIV infection, participation in research trials and access to experimental treatment is influenced by race or ethnic group and by type of health insurance.

ENDNOTES

1. For some good sources on the ethical issues of HIV and AIDS see: Cameron, M. E. (1993). *Living with AIDS: Experiencing ethical problems*. Newbury Park, CA: Sage Publications; Cohen, E. D., & Davis, M. (Eds.). (1994). *AIDS: Crisis in professional ethics*. Philadelphia: Temple University Press; Faden, R., Geller, G., & Powers, M. (Eds.). (1991). *AIDS, women and the next generation*. New York: Oxford University

Press; Gostin, L. O. (Ed.). (1990). *AIDS and the health care system.* New Haven, CT: Yale University Press; Gostin, L. O., & Lazzarini, Z. (1997). *Human rights and public health in the AIDS pandemic.* New York: Oxford University Press; Mack, A. (Ed.). (1991). *In time of plague: The history and social consequences of lethal epidemic disease.* New York: New York University Press; Murphy, T. F. (1994). *Ethics in an epidemic: AIDS, morality, and culture.* Berkeley, CA: University of California Press; Reamer, F. C. (Ed.). (1991). *AIDS and ethics.* New York: Columbia University Press.

2. Joint United Nations Programme on HIV/AIDS & World Health Organization. (2009, December*). AIDS epidemic update* (p. 7). Available at: http://data.unaids.org/pub /Report/2009/JC1700_Epi_Update_2009_en.pdf. Accessed February 6, 2010.

3. Centers for Disease Control and Prevention. (2008). HIV prevalence estimates— United States, 2006. *Morbidity and Mortality Weekly Report, 57*(39), 1073–1076.

4. Hall H. I., Song, R., Rhodes P., Prejean, J., An, Q., Lee, L., et al. (2008). Estimation of HIV incidence in the United States. *Journal of the American Medical Association, 300*, 520–529.

5. Available at: http://www.cdc.gov/hiv/topics/surveillance/basic.htm#international. Accessed February 6, 2010.

6. HIV/AIDS Treatment Information Service. (2008, December). *Approved medications to treat HIV infection.* Available at: www.thebody.com/content/treat/art50165 .html. Accessed May 10, 2010.

7. O'Brien, J. A., Cutter, T., Pierce, D., Kavanagh, P. L., & Caro, J. J. (1999, September). *The economic burden of AIDS management: Annual direct medical costs in the United States* (abstract 461). Abstract presented at the 39th Interscience Conference on Antimicrobial Agents and Chemotherapy, San Francisco, CA.

8. Bayer, R. (1997). AIDS and ethics. In R. M. Veatch (Ed.), *Medical ethics* (2nd ed., pp. 395–413). Sudbury, MA: Jones and Bartlett.

9. Cassetta, R. (1993). The new faces of the epidemic. *The American Nurse, 25*(3), 16.

10. Centers for Disease Control and Prevention. (2002, November 15). HIV testing among pregnant women—United States and Canada, 1998–2001. *Morbidity and Mortality Weekly Report, 51*(45), 1013–1016.

11. Ryan White Comprehensive AIDS Resource Emergency Act, Pub. L. No. 101–381, 104 Stat. 576 (1990). Ryan White CARE Act Amendments of 1996.

12. Schneider, C. D. (1997). Testing, testing. *The Hastings Center Report, 23*(4), 22–23.

13. U.S. Department of Health and Human Services, Public Health Service, Centers for Disease Control. (2001). Revised recommendations for HIV screening of pregnant women. *Morbidity and Mortality Weekly Report, 50*(RR19).

14. Lisanti, P., & Swolski, K. (1997). Understanding the devastation of AIDS. *American Journal of Nursing, 97*(7), 27–34.

15. Tarasoff v. Regents of the State of California, 17 Cal. 3d 425, 55, 2d 334, 131 Cal. Rptr. 14 (1976).

16. Rothenberg, K. H., & North, R. L. (1991). The duty to warn "dilemma" and women with AIDS. *Courts, Health Science and the Law, 2*, 90–94, 96–98.

17. American Nurses Association. (1991). *Position statement: HIV testing.* Washington, DC: Author; American Nurses Association. (1992). *Position statement: HIV disease and women.* Washington, DC: Author.

18. Working Group on HIV Testing of Pregnant Women and Newborns. (1990). HIV infection, pregnant women and newborns: A policy proposal for information and testing. *Journal of the American Medical Association, 264,* 2416–2420.
19. Available at: www.thebody.com/govt/reporting.html. Accessed September 24, 2004.
20. Rothenberg, K. H., & North, R. L. (1991). The duty to warn "dilemma" and women with AIDS. *Courts, Health Science and the Law, 2,* 90–94, 96–98.
21. American Nurses Association. (1992). *Position statement: HIV infection and nursing students.* Washington, DC: Author; American Nurses Association. (2001). *Code of ethics for nurses with interpretative statements.* Washington, DC: Author.
22. Reeder, J. M., Hamblet, J. L., Killen, A. R., King, C. A., & Uroburu, A. (1994). Nurses' knowledge, attitudes about HIV, AIDS: A replication study. *Association of periOperative Registered Nurses Journal, 59*(2), 450–465.
23. U.S. Department of Health and Human Services, Public Health Service, Centers for Disease Control and Prevention. (1996). *HIV/AIDS Surveillance Report, 8*(1), 9.
24. Angoff, N. (1991). Do physicians have an ethical obligation to care for patients with AIDS? *Yale Journal of Biology and Medicine, 64,* 207–246.
24. Carson, W. (1993). AIDS and the nurse: A legal update. *The American Nurse, 25*(3), 12.
25. Schackman, B. R., Gebo, K. A., Walensky, R. P., Losina, E., Muccio, T., Sax, P. E., et al. (2006). The lifetime cost of current HIV care in the United States. *Medical Care, 44*(11), 990–997.
26. FDA raises dialysis concerns. (1999, May 12). *Boston Globe,* p. A8.
27. Nyhan, D. (1997, October 8). New AIDS drugs, new ethical issues. *Boston Globe,* p. A23.
28. Knox, R. A. (1998, June 28). AIDS patients struggle to cope with daunting drug regimens. *Boston Globe,* pp. A1, A4. See also Cowley, G. (1998, June 29). Sobering up about AIDS. *Newsweek,* p. 60.

Chapter 15

Experimentation on Human Beings

Other Cases Involving Experimentation on Human Beings

Key Terms
Equity
Informed consent
Institutional review board (IRB)
Privacy protections
Risks and benefits

Objectives
1. Describe seven criteria that must be met before research can be approved.
2. Describe three ways that questions of equity can arise in the conduct of research.
3. Describe the basic elements of informed consent for the conduct of research with human subjects.
4. Identify limits to the protections of privacy in research contexts.
5. Apply ethical principles in the calculation of risks and benefits of research.

The nurse often participates in medical and behavioral research involving human subjects—sometimes as a principal investigator and other times as a research team member or advocate for the research subject. Systematic research designed to test hypotheses and generate statistically significant generalizable results is a quite modern phenomenon. Traditionally, the primary objective of trying new interventions was to benefit the particular patient, especially when the usual remedies were not producing satisfactory results. Since about the middle of the 19th century, however, we have seen a change. Healthcare professionals now attempt to conduct systematically designed studies for the purpose of gaining knowledge to benefit society or specific groups within society, as well as the individual subjects of the investigation.

When this new purpose is added to the agenda, a new group of moral problems arises. The most conspicuous problem is the potential conflict between the healthcare professional's traditional duty to serve the individual patient—to benefit the patient or, as holders of newer, more rights-oriented biomedical ethical positions would say, to protect the rights of the patient—and the newer interest in benefiting others.

Since the post–World War II Nuremberg trials, researchers, potential subjects, and society at large have been concerned about the possibility that research agendas might conflict with traditional patient-centered obligations. At Nuremberg, after all, it became conspicuously clear that any investigator who approaches a human being as a subject for the purpose of gaining generalizable knowledge was abandoning, at least partially, the traditional focus on the welfare and rights of the patient. There were two major options: return to the ethic that required the healthcare professional to work only out of concern for the patient, or develop an ethic of research that would permit a limited shift of attention and, at the same time, protect the rights and interests of the potential subject.

At Nuremberg, the second option was chosen. The primary strategy for protecting subjects was a strong requirement that subjects give voluntary consent to participation, with no exception. As the Nuremberg Code puts it in its first provision:

> The voluntary consent of the human subject is absolutely essential. This means that the person involved should have legal capacity to give consent; should be so situated as to be able to exercise free power of choice, without the intervention of any element of force, fraud, deceit, duress, overreaching or other ulterior form of constraint or coercion; and should have sufficient knowledge and comprehension of the elements of the subject matter involved as to enable him to make an understanding and enlightened decision. This latter element requires that before the acceptance of an affirmative decision by the experimental subject there should be made known to him the nature, duration, and purpose of the experiment; the method and means by which it is to be conducted; all inconveniences and hazards reasonably to be expected; and the effects upon his health or person which may possibly come from his participation in the experiments.[1]

Although this strategy made possible research interventions that were not primarily for the benefit of the subject, it was soon discovered that it made impossible many kinds of research that were considered important. Research involving children, the mentally incompetent, and anyone else who could not exercise voluntary consent; research on emergency care where there was no possibility of getting consent; and psychologic studies involving deception were just a few of the types of research that could not possibly conform to the Nuremberg requirement.

Although the U.S. government had made policies governing human subjects research even in the World War II period, in the mid-1960s it began more forcefully and publicly to express concern for the protection of subjects of research conducted at major government research centers or conducted with government funds. The result has been a system of **institutional review boards** (**IRBs**) that review all research to ensure that it conforms with a set of regulations established nationally as well as any additional state, local, and hospital requirements.[2] It is not uncommon to have one or more nurses serving on these IRBs.

The Institute of Medicine (IOM) issued a report in 2002 emphasizing the responsibilities and functions of human research participant protection programs (HRPPPs) providing substantive descriptions of the activities intrinsic to a robust protection program.[3] More recently, the IOM issued a new set of recommendations aimed at addressing the growing concern among lawmakers, government agencies, and the public over extensive conflicts of interest in medicine, requiring stronger policies and procedures.[4]

The current regulations now apply to virtually all federal government agencies engaged in research with human subjects and are supported by the nursing profession.[5] Because of their use by virtually all of the federal government, they are referred to as the Common Rule. They require that seven criteria be met before any research can be approved. These criteria are as follows:

1. Risks to subjects are minimized: (i) by using procedures which are consistent with sound research design and which do not unnecessarily expose subjects to risk, and (ii) whenever appropriate, by using procedures already being performed on the subjects for diagnostic or treatment purposes.

2. Risks to subjects are reasonable in relation to anticipated benefits, if any, to subjects, and the importance of the knowledge that may reasonably be expected to result. In evaluating risks and benefits, the IRB should consider only those risks and benefits that may result from the research (as distinguished from risks and benefits of therapies subjects would receive even if not participating in the research). The IRB should not consider possible long-range effects of applying knowledge gained in the research (for example, the possible effects of the research on public policy) as among those research risks that fall within the purview of its responsibility.

3. Selection of subjects is equitable. In making this assessment the IRB should take into account the purposes of the research and the setting in which the research will be conducted and should be particularly cognizant of the special problems of research involving vulnerable populations, such as children, prisoners, pregnant women, mentally disabled persons, or economically or educationally disadvantaged persons.

4. Informed consent will be sought from each prospective subject or the subject's legally authorized representative, in accordance with,

and to the extent required by 46.116 [the requirements for informed consent].

5. Informed consent will be appropriately documented, in accordance with, and to the extent required by 46.117 [the consent documentation requirements].

6. When appropriate, the research plan makes adequate provision for monitoring the data collected to ensure the safety of subjects.

7. When appropriate, there are adequate provisions to protect the privacy of subjects and to maintain the confidentiality of data.[6]

These seven criteria can be seen as falling into four categories. This chapter is structured with sections on each of these categories. The first, most obvious requirement of any ethically acceptable research is derived from the principles of beneficence and nonmaleficence. Any investigator, research team member, IRB member, or nurse concerned about the protection of patients must make sure the risks to the subjects are minimized and that the benefits anticipated are reasonable in proportion to those risks. This requires sound research design and an assessment of the importance of the knowledge expected to result. It also calls for an assessment of risks and benefits specifically to the research subject. The criterion calling for adequate provision for the monitoring of data to ensure subject safety can also be seen as stemming from the ethical principles of beneficence and nonmaleficence.

One of the critical ethical problems in research is whether risk can justifiably be increased proportionally to the importance of the knowledge to be gained so that extreme risk—even certain death—might be justified if the expected benefits of the knowledge to be gained were great enough. A pure ethic of benefits and harms in which the ethical goal is to maximize the aggregate good would seem to permit, even require, such high risk–high gain experiments. Yet many IRBs and many philosophers object to this possibility. The alternative they would suggest is to impose additional ethical requirements. One such requirement would be that, in addition to expected benefits to society proportional to the risks to the subject, there must also be a reasonable balance between the benefits and risks to the subject himself or herself. Sometimes, especially with subjects who cannot consent, such as children, this requirement is expressed as the insistence that the risks to the subject be minimal regardless of the anticipated social benefits. The federal regulations dealing with research on children permit risks slightly beyond minimal under special cases, but under no circumstances can the risks exceed those limits, even if the benefits to society would be enormous.[7] The cases in the first section of this chapter, Cases 15-1, 15-2, and 15-3, present situations in which the nurse is required to assess the relation of subject risks to anticipated benefits to society and the subject.

In addition to requiring that subject risks be compared specifically to the potential benefits to the specific subject, several more ethical criteria are imposed on research under the Common Rule. In addition to considerations of benefit and harm, there must be adequate provision for protecting subject privacy and assuring confidentiality of data. This means that even if great benefit could come from conducting a study in a manner that required violating privacy or breaking confidentiality, that is not sufficient to override the privacy requirement. Subjects may, under normal circumstances, waive their right to privacy and confidentiality, but the promise of confidentiality generates an independent moral requirement of research, not capable of being overridden simply because great benefit would come of it. The case in the second section of this chapter (Case 15-4) presents the problems of privacy and confidentiality in research.

A third requirement for research in the federal regulations is that the selection of subjects be equitable. We have known for some time that research subjects have come disproportionately from oppressed groups—the poor, the institutionalized, and clinic patients. The principle of justice is now understood by many as having direct implications for research. The most obvious impact is on subject selection. Although at this time the regulations apply the criterion of equity only to subject selection, other aspects of research, such as experimental design, may also be affected by interpretations of justice. The widely held opinion that burdens to subjects must be reasonable in proportion to the expected benefits to the subject is evidence of this concern. Justice requires that benefits and burdens be distributed fairly. That means that even if great benefit could come to others it may be unjust to impose serious risks to subjects, at least without their consent. The cases in the third section of this chapter (Cases 15-5 and 15-6) present these problems of equity.

The remaining criteria for research under the federal regulations all deal in one way or another with the notion of consent. Whereas, as we saw, the Nuremberg Code makes voluntary consent an absolute requirement, the federal regulations are more complex. According to these regulations, consent can come from the subject's legally authorized representative as well as from the subject. In either case, the consent must be documented appropriately, and special safeguards must be established when some or all of the subjects are likely to be vulnerable to coercion or undue influence. In 1998, the National Bioethics Advisory Commission released a report specifically addressing research involving persons with mental disorders that may impair decision-making capacity.[8]

The ethical basis of the consent requirement has been the subject of considerable debate. In some cases it may function to protect the subject, thus being an application of the principle of beneficence.[9] This is especially true in cases in which a proxy consent is obtained. Often, however, the real basis for the consent requirement is not protection of the subject from risks, but protection of the subject's autonomy. Especially with competent subjects, the ethical goal is to preserve the subject's self-determination even if it does not maximize his or her welfare according to an outsider's assessment. Some of the most interesting cases are those in which preserving the autonomy of the subject conflicts with doing what will most reasonably promote the subject's welfare. In this chapter, five cases involving consent issues are presented. They set the stage for a larger group of cases involving consent that is presented in Chapter 16.

In these cases it is important to keep the research separate from various interventions that are justified solely on the grounds of the welfare of the patient.

Whereas some people designate research as therapeutic or nontherapeutic, we, following Robert Levine and the National Commission for the Protection of Human Subjects,[10] speak of interventions justified for research and interventions justified on grounds of patient welfare. Research interventions include anything done to normal persons for the purpose of gathering systematic data but also include some things done to patients while undergoing therapy (e.g., conducting an extra interview, drawing a blood sample that would not be drawn except to get research data, or performing a formal randomization to determine which of two treatments the patient will receive).

When, and only when, two treatments are approximately equal in value might the patient plausibly choose either one. In such circumstances, random choice sometimes makes sense. In such cases as well as in cases where no recognized treatment is available, patients may receive what is referred to as "innovative therapy"—that is, therapy that is not well accepted as standard practice (such as a new surgical procedure). That a therapy is innovative does not by itself make the intervention research (although lay people might sometimes refer to the therapy as "an experiment"). When therapy is innovative, however, it is often reasonable to gather information about the impact of the treatment. Systematically gathering information for the purposes of creating generalizable knowledge is what makes the activity research. Some would argue that gathering such information is, in fact, morally required.

One practical guide to evaluating the ethics of a proposed clinical research trial is offered by Emanuel, Wendler, and Grady. They recommend seven necessary and sufficient criteria for an ethical study:

Valuable scientific question

Valid scientific methodology

Fair subject selection

Favorable risk-benefit evaluation

Independent review

Informed consent

Respect for enrolled subjects[11]

Nurses interested in research ethics will find the *Oxford Textbook of Clinical Research Ethics* helpful.[12]

A final note before ending this general introduction: The contemporary interest in research ethics resulted from well publicized instances of public harms resulting from unethical research studies and a desire to protect vulnerable populations.[13] With the advent of AIDS, many individuals clamored to be able to participate in research trials because it was often the only way they could access highly desirable experimental treatments. Their focus was on the perceived benefits of research, not possible harms. At the same time, women, who previously had been underrepresented in clinical trials, and minorities advocated for greater participation hoping for a more equitable distribution of research benefits. As the cases in this chapter will illustrate, nurses play an increasingly valuable role in ensuring an equitable balancing of benefits and harms at every level of the research enterprise, from policy, to research review, to the monitoring of specific studies, and recruitment and retention of subjects.

Calculating Risks and Benefits

The first and most obvious task in assessing the ethics of research on human subjects is to assure that the risks are justified by the potential benefits. The federal regulatory mandate for IRBs requires that they determine that "risks to subjects are reasonable in relation to anticipated benefits, if any, to subjects, and the importance of the knowledge that may reasonably be expected to result."[14] Figuring out what the **risks and benefits** are is only the first problem. The decision maker must also judge how the impact on the subject is to be related to the impact on others. Presumably if all the risks taken together (considering both their magnitude and their likelihood) exceed the anticipated benefits, then the intervention is not justified.

Often, however, the projected harms to the subject are at least as great as the projected subject benefits, but the projected *total* benefits—including the benefits to others of the knowledge to be gained—tip the balance so that benefits reasonably outweigh harms. The following cases pose questions of assessing benefits and harms, including the question of what should be done when benefits to society are potentially great but the harms to the subject plausibly outweigh the benefits to him or her.

Case 15-1
When a Parent Says "No"

Charles Sutter was born with a large lumbar meningomyelocele, kyphosis, and bilateral dislocated hips. Shortly after birth, his parents were told that there was little hope for Charles and that they should be prepared to "let him go." They took him home from the hospital at 5 days of age and were determined to care for him themselves. Within a few weeks, Mr. Sutter contacted another physician, who told him about a new treatment for meningomyelocele being performed at a university research medical center in a nearby state. Mr. Sutter called Dr. H. Kron, the surgeon performing the treatment, and was invited to bring Charles to the medical center for examination and potential admission to the treatment program.

Becky Paxton, a pediatric nurse practitioner, admitted Charles Sutter to the research unit and conducted the initial assessment. She was impressed by Charles's physical condition, despite his deformities, and the positive outlook of his parents. After a few days of examinations and testing, Charles was offered admission to the treatment program. His parents were informed about the experimental nature of the treatment and about risks and benefits. Because there was limited hope for Charles with conventional treatment and no hope without any treatment, the Sutters agreed to Charles's participation in the treatment program. Within a few days, Charles's meningomyelocele was closed and a partial kyphectomy was performed.

Complications developed, however, when cerebrospinal fluid (CSF) started to leak through the closure site, Charles developed a high fever, and his CSF cultures showed *Staphylococcus aureus* ventriculitis. Before the infection was brought under control, Charles suffered frequent convulsive episodes. While receiving treatment for the infection, Charles began to experience disturbing spells of apnea, requiring constant monitoring and tactile stimulation. When his condition did not improve over several weeks of continued treatment, Charles's parents began to doubt the wisdom of the treatment program for their son. They became further discouraged after a new infection and repeated seizures developed. The Sutters decided to withdraw him from the treatment program, saying that they thought he had suffered enough pain and discomfort for his young life. They would take him home and care for him the best they could.

Dr. Kron and Ms. Paxton tried to persuade the Sutters to keep Charles in the treatment program for a while longer. They felt that all of Charles's present problems were expected and treatable. Furthermore, once Charles was withdrawn from the program, they could no longer provide treatment or follow up for him. The Sutters realized that the loss of continued treatment and follow up might be damaging to Charles, but they were adamant about their wishes. Ms. Paxton wondered if parents could make this kind of choice for their ill child. Without continued treatment, Charles's prognosis was very guarded. With continued treatment, there was a chance he would survive and receive benefit from the treatment program. Yet his parents said "no."

Case 15-2

Finding Out the Relative Benefits and Harms of Self-Care Treatment

Samantha Long is a cardiovascular clinical nurse specialist. During the past 2 years, she and her colleagues have been studying the physiological and psychologic effects of self-care activities in patients recovering from myocardial infarctions. Patients admitted to the studies have been carefully screened and selected according to the amount of myocardial damage suffered, the absence of known cardiovascular disease prior to their present illness, and the overall prognosis of the patient. To date, the results of the studies have indicated a significant positive correlation between self-care activities and psychologic status. No relationship has been found between self-care activities and physiologic effects.

Ms. Long and her colleagues would like to extend their research to include the use of self-care activities with patients having more extensive myocardial damage and those with known cardiovascular disease prior to the present hospital admission. Other studies have demonstrated that this type of patient has a higher frequency of depression and other psychologic problems as well as greater noncompliance with follow-up treatment. They are uncertain, however, whether including these patients in the study would be ethical.

Although Ms. Long has reason to believe that self-care activities will have a beneficial effect on the psychologic status of these patients, she does not know what effects self-care might have on their physiological status. She is aware that the use of self-care in the recovery of these patients poses some risks, but it is not known how serious these risks might be. Should she extend her study to include these patients?

Case 15-3
Taking Care of Baby Fae[1]

Marie Whisman, a neonatal nurse specialist, once cared for a very special baby. This baby, known to the public as Baby Fae, was born on October 14, 1984, with hypoplastic left heart syndrome, a normally fatal cardiac abnormality. The recommended treatment was a heart transplant. Because a human heart was not believed to be available for Baby Fae, her physicians considered performing a xenograft—a procedure replacing her heart with that of a baboon. The procedure was explained to her parents, their consent was obtained, and the surgery was performed on October 26, 1984. Baby Fae survived for 21 days but died from complications resulting from rejection of the xenograft.

Marie Whisman was Baby Fae's primary nurse. At the infant's funeral, Ms. Whisman read a statement about the nursing care that this special infant received. Unstated, however, were many questions about the role that nurses play in the care of patients undergoing innovative therapies that can also be described as research. Of what benefit to Baby Fae was this particular procedure? What obligation did Ms. Whisman have to Baby Fae's parents to inform them of the special risks and limited benefits of the planned procedure? Was the planned procedure of such great benefit to society that the risk to Baby Fae's life was justified? How does a nurse caring for a patient assess the risks and benefits of innovative procedures and decide whether or not he or she wants to continue to participate in care involving innovative treatment?

Ms. Whisman was the individual who touched and cared most for Baby Fae during her short life and was a participant in every procedure that was performed on the infant. What obligations does a nurse in this situation have to the infant? To the parents? To the research team?

Commentary

In all three of these cases, the first task is to determine what counts as research, what counts as therapy, and what difference it makes. The treatment of Charles Sutter, the baby born with a meningomyelocele and other problems, poses the

---

[1]Mathews, J. (1984, October 30). Baby with baboon's heart making steady progress. *Washington Post*, p. 2. Mathews, J. (1984, November 18). Head nurse shares memories of Fae. *Washington Post*, p. 14. Cummings, J. (1984, November 18). Memorial service held for Baby Fae. *New York Times*, p. L-30. Altman, L. K. (1984, November 18). Learning from Baby Fae. *New York Times*, pp. L-1, L-30.

problem well. The first ethical question raised is whether the parents made the right choice when they decided to take him home from the hospital rather than opting for the standard surgical treatment. Assuming that Dr. Kron's new treatment was not in the picture, some would argue that there is a moral, if not legal, duty on the part of the parents to have Charles treated using conventional therapeutic measures. That is not in itself a problem in research or innovative therapy but rather one of the limits on parental judgments made in the name of promoting their child's welfare. That problem is addressed in the cases in Chapter 17.

Assuming, however, that the parents have decided against the conventional therapy and that Dr. Kron is prepared to offer the innovative treatment, a new set of ethical problems arises for the parents, the physician, and the nurse, Becky Paxton. It appears that the parents and the health professionals were willing to accept the conclusion that, on balance, the risks were justified considering the potential benefits. If that is so, the treatment itself, in one sense, is not research. It is therapy—innovative therapy—but therapy nonetheless. It is justified by the judgment that the benefits to Charles outweigh the risks. Just as when the conventional therapy was rejected, this judgment is controversial. In either case, society could require that the judgment made by the individual practitioners and the individual parents be reviewed by some sort of committee. Society has not seen fit to have such review of conventional therapeutic decisions (even when the judgment is controversial). It might do so in the future, using ethics committees or some other mechanism to monitor certain kinds of problematic therapy decisions.

Society *has* seen fit to ask for such review in some decisions involving innovative therapy. Part of the reason is that some of the parties—the surgeon, for example—may have an agenda involving interests other than those of the patient. He or she may be uniquely partial to a technique he or she is developing. Or the doctor may want to accumulate several cases so he or she can publish an article on the procedure. It is now common for innovative therapies to be reviewed by institutional review boards (IRBs) especially when there is a plan to collect data and publish results.

Normally, in addition to the fact that the therapy is innovative, Dr. Kron and Becky Paxton would gather data about the procedure. They might photograph the operation, do extra tests to monitor effectiveness, or perform special follow-up studies. These steps would constitute research and would represent moving from innovative therapy to data gathering. When Ms. Paxton and Dr. Kron tried to persuade the Sutters to keep Charles in the treatment program a while longer, they may not have been motivated solely out of a commitment to Charles's welfare. They may have been afraid of losing one of the patients in their program. This is the type of special agenda that many people believe calls for additional monitoring of innovative therapies.

With that background, it is still important to determine whether the risks to Charles are justified when compared to the potential benefits. We shall see in the cases in Chapter 16 that such calls are inherently subjective. Weighing benefits and the harms depends not only on guesses about the probabilities of various outcomes but also qualitative assessments of how bad or how good the outcomes will be. The Sutters need to decide whether preserving life with fever, infections, and convulsions is good or bad on balance. They also need to decide whether the pain and the dysfunctions are justified. In principle, medical science cannot answer these questions.

On top of those problems, Dr. Kron and Becky Paxton need to decide whether they should be taking into account the potential benefits to other children if Charles continues to suffer. Some would argue that only the potential benefits to this patient can count in justifying the burdens to him.[15] Others, however, including the National Commission for the Protection of Human Subjects, permit some exceptions. They would permit research on children when the interventions for research purposes involve, at most, minimal risk or, under special conditions, "a minor increase over minimal risk."[16] The same language was incorporated into the Department of Health and Human Services regulations governing research on children.[17] In either case, the commentators seem to agree that even substantial potential benefits to society cannot justify unlimited risks to a child or other nonconsenting subject of research. At most, a minor increase above minimal risk is acceptable. That, of course, takes into account the risks taken for research, not those justified by the benefits of the proposed therapy for the patient. Dr. Kron, Becky Paxton, and the Sutters need to assess whether they will be asking more than this of Charles.

Marie Whisman, the neonatal nurse specialist caring for Baby Fae, had to face similar problems. It is possible that Baby Fae's transplant of a baboon heart could be viewed in strictly therapeutic terms. Her parents apparently made the decision—right or wrong—that the transplant was in her interest and was more plausible than any available alternative. Ms. Whisman's perspective on the risks and benefits may have differed from that of Dr. Bailey, the surgeon who performed the procedure. If it did, then she had a duty to ensure that her interpretation was presented along with the others that the parents received.

It is possible that Ms. Whisman had a very low estimate of the possible benefits and a high estimate of the potential pain and suffering in store for the baby. In that case, she might have faced the question of whether it was moral to perform innovative surgical treatment. In her judgment it could have been a case of greater than a minor increase above minimal risk, the standard called for by federal regulation. In that case, she might have had to consider withdrawing and taking actions to protect the baby's welfare.

Samantha Long's study of self-care with myocardial infarction patients poses a somewhat different problem. Some of the patients may be substantially nonautonomous—senile or mentally incapacitated. Those patients would presumably have to meet standards for risks and benefits similar to those involving children. Ms. Long and the IRB that would eventually have to approve of her study could adopt the conservative standard, permitting no risks for research and tolerating risks only when justified for the patient's own welfare. Or she could adopt the more liberal standard permitting minimal risks for proportionally greater benefits.

Many of her patients, however, are going to be adults capable of consenting to the risks of the self-care approach. Some might even find the approach so attractive that they would opt for it, taking the risks even if they were not in a study. Others could be asked to agree to take the risk of physiologic harm to make a contribution to science. Even if they thought the risks exceeded the benefits somewhat, they might be willing to assume the risks for the good of science.

That does not solve Ms. Long's problem, however. Even if she can recruit willing patients, she still needs to decide if it is moral for her to offer research that will expose the patients to risks. If she takes the stance that she has a strict duty to avoid harm, a duty based in the principle of nonmaleficence, she will not be able to proceed. If, however, she is willing to trade off benefits and harms, she might be able to proceed if the benefits exceed the harms.[18] Her critical question is whether other conditions will also have to be met. For example, if she is to avoid the ethical problem of being committed to exposing subjects to extreme harm in cases where even greater benefit is predicted, she will have to set some limits on the amount of harm she is willing to let willing volunteers accept. She may do this for paternalistic reasons, simply wanting to protect the patients from harm. She may also do it for nonpaternalistic reasons. She may reason, for instance, that she cannot in good conscience be part of placing patients, even willing ones, in jeopardy because it would not be fitting with her own character. In that case, she could say that others may want to do the study, but she cannot.

Ms. Long's task at this point is to estimate what the risks will be and then to decide whether she can, in good conscience, offer the self-care protocol to patients with more extensive myocardial damage.

Critical Thinking Question

What are the ethical questions Ms. Long needs to consider before extending her study to include patients with more extensive myocardial damage? Why?

Research Brief 15-1

Source: Higgins, P. A., & Daly, B. J. (2002). Knowledge and beliefs of nurse researchers about informed consent principles and regulations. *Nursing Ethics, 9*(6), 663–673.

Purpose: The purpose of this study was to determine the knowledge and beliefs of nurse researchers regarding informed consent principles and regulations in the United States.

Method: The study used a comparative descriptive design, stratified random sampling, and a mail survey. Potential participants ($n = 463$) were selected from four research interest groups of the Midwest Nursing Research Society. Using a random numbers list, 50 members from each research interest group were selected to receive surveys in the first quarter of 2000. The mail survey was developed using the Dillman method and included demographic items, questions regarding confidence of self-knowledge about federal regulations on informed consent, and a vignette with questions about collecting and reporting data from people who refuse to participate in a study. The study tool was pretested and revised in a series of presentations and dialogues with faculty researchers.

Findings: There were 119 surveys that were returned (59.5% return rate). The participants were largely female (97.5%); 44% had attained a master's degree, and 56% had a doctoral degree. The majority (58%) of the respondents were employed in academia; 45% reported 1–9 years of experience in research, and 19% had greater than 10 years of experience. Of the participants, 28% identified themselves as members of an IRB, and 40% reported some experience in teaching research ethics.

More than 65% of the participants were confident in their knowledge of IRB procedures, research ethics, informed consent, and the moral and legal rights to privacy protections. Only 28%, however, rated themselves as knowledgeable about federal research regulations. Those who were more confident in their knowledge of or had more practical experience with research ethics were no more likely to answer questions about current federal guidelines regulating the use of patient data from medical records correctly than those who reported less confidence or experience were.

When asked what federal regulations permit regarding the use of information from patient records for research, only 50% of the participants chose the correct answer. When asked if the nurse researcher can collect and report data on patients who subsequently refuse to participate, in order to examine and report any differences between participants and nonparticipants, 48% said that no data can be used without consent, 21% said that medical record data can be used, and 31% said that some data could be used.

Conclusions: The results of this study demonstrate that there are widely varying understandings of federal regulations and beliefs about the precise requirements of informed consent in research among nurse researchers. This indicates that further discussion of the moral right to privacy in research and requirements for informed consent for disclosure of personal information needs to take place among nurse researchers.

Implications: It is recommended that IRBs require more exact information about patient data that will be used and reported when participants refuse to participate in a research study. It is also recommended that nursing research courses devote more time to the content of the federal regulations and to the issue of access to data in medical records.

Protecting Privacy

Ensuring that the benefits of research exceed the harms and seeing that the welfare of the subject is not compromised severely for the benefit of society are not the only criteria for ethically and legally acceptable research. The federal regulations also call for "adequate provisions to protect the privacy of subjects and to maintain the confidentiality of data." In some cases, privacy violation risks can be incorporated into the calculations of benefits and harms. If a nurse discloses sensitive information from research files and that disclosure causes harm to subjects, that would count as one of the harms. However, we saw in the cases in Chapter 9 that promises to protect confidentiality of medical information may not be based solely on concern for the harm that disclosure could cause.

Sometimes this concern about *privacy protections* is expressed in terms of a "right to privacy," a right to have information about oneself kept from public scrutiny, even if that information would not necessarily cause harm. In other cases, the concern rests on an implied or explicit promise made by the one gathering the data that it will not be disclosed without the authorization of the one supplying it. This would be based in a principle of fidelity or promise keeping.

The duty to keep research data private or confidential is widely recognized, but it is also recognized that there are some limits. The following case deals with disclosures of data for research purposes when the disclosures have not been authorized.

Case 15-4
Mandatory Reporting of Drug and Alcohol Use in Pregnant Women for Research Purposes[2]

Kevin Oberman is a child health nurse in a public health agency in a large metropolitan area. Mr. Oberman is responsible for assisting new parents in their application for a certificate of live birth in their state. In addition to the usual birth information, the state asks for additional information that will be used in research studies related to newborn morbidity and mortality and parental health.

---

[2]The names in this case are fictitious, but the case is based on actual events cited in Osonoff, D. (1979, December). Registering baby: Database or private record? *The Hastings Center Report, 9*, 7–9.

One day an angry group of women stormed into his office and questioned the state's right to ask for personal information concerning pregnancy history and maternal drug and alcohol use on the state's newly revised certificate of live birth. Mr. Oberman explained the purpose for collecting the information, but he was unable to explain how the state kept this information confidential or what the information might be used for in the future.

Several months later, he learned that the women had sought legal counsel and were being supported by civil rights advocates in questioning the state's right to ask for personal information concerning pregnancy history and maternal drug and alcohol use during pregnancy on a public document. Their claims were presented in the state legislature, and legislation was passed that limited the types of questions that could be asked on public documents such as birth registration forms. Soon Mr. Oberman received directions to inform his clients about the use of the information requested on the birth registration forms, the confidentiality protection of the information, and the perceived public benefit of the data collected from the answered questions.

Other workers in his health agency strongly protested the legislation. They felt that the overall restrictions on public health research that collected data on such illnesses as fetal alcohol syndrome and fetal drug addiction were ultimately harmful to the public's health and obstructed the conduct of public health science. Mr. Oberman was sympathetic to the requirements of scientific inquiry, but he was also supportive of his clients' rights to privacy and their need to know the use of the information they provided, now and in the future. When he was asked to join in his agency's protest of the new legislation, he was not sure what he should do.

Commentary

Without knowing it, Kevin Oberman has been employed as a field worker gathering data for research that the state or other entities may eventually undertake. The problem is more complex because the nurse is not even directly involved with those who will eventually do the research using the data. Still, he must struggle with the ethical dilemma posed by patients who object to providing potentially sensitive information to a public data file.

If Mr. Oberman were to analyze the problem strictly on risk–benefit grounds, it is not clear how he would decide. The problems potentially to be addressed with such data—fetal alcohol syndrome, sudden infant death syndrome, and other conditions related to neonatal morbidity and mortality—are important. On the other hand, Mr. Oberman has clear information showing that some patients are distressed by having to provide the data. It is also clear that some of the women could be at risk of legal and psychologic problems if the information about drug and alcohol use were made public. If Mr. Oberman sees it as his duty to benefit his patient and if he considers the birth mother to be his patient, he may well consider that more harm would be done to her than good if the data were reported. Even if he considers the newborns his patients as well as the mothers, he may well reach the same conclusion. The actual infants Mr. Oberman is caring for probably will not benefit from the studies; only future infants will benefit. If, however, Mr. Oberman sees it as his responsibility to produce maximum net benefits, including benefits to others in the society, he may conclude that much more good than harm will result from the reporting of the data.

He may be faced with an argument from the women that they simply have a "right to privacy," regardless of the amount of good to others that can result from a study of the data. Then he must determine what the status of such a purported right would be. To what extent do people have a right to keep private information that could realistically be expected to help others? Some precautions could be taken with the data. The data could be reported in such a way that they were not connected with specific women. On the other hand, the state may want the data in a connectible form. For example, it might want to monitor cases where infants are thought to be at great risk in the future because of the mothers' behaviors. The state might claim a concern for the welfare of either these or future children that overrides the women's purported right of privacy.

Mr. Oberman might also determine that, even though the basis for the women's claim is not a right of privacy, confidentiality has been promised. He may find that the hospital has made such a promise or even that the state has. More critically, he may find that he, himself, has made such a promise—at least implicitly. If he subscribes to the American Nurses Association (ANA) *Code of Ethics for Nurses*, he will have promised to safeguard "the patient's right to privacy" and to "maintain confidentiality of all patient information."[19] However, after the code states that "only information pertinent to a patient's treatment and welfare is disclosed," it goes on to state that the "duties of confidentiality, however, are not absolute and may need to be modified in order to protect the patient, other innocent parties, and in circumstances of mandatory disclosure for public health reasons."[20] These two commitments seem to be directly contradictory. One cannot disclose information only for the patient's treatment and welfare and simultaneously disclose it to protect innocent parties and to conform to mandatory requirements for disclosure for public health reasons. Assuming the state has established its new certificate of live birth form with due process (by law or by administrative decision), perhaps one could argue that this is information that no one has promised will be kept confidential. In fact, it could be argued that, when the state requires disclosure by law, there is not even a right of privacy.

Mr. Oberman may find himself in an awkward position. He may be sympathetic with the women, at least to the extent of wanting to insist that the data be stored in a way that will protect their privacy, but he may also be in no position to change the state law or regulation that calls for the data. If he concludes that the law is justified, his project will be one of attempting to explain to the women why he has reached that conclusion. If, however, he thinks the law is not justified or that procedures must be established to better protect the data, then he will have to develop leverage for challenging the existing practice.

This might mean anything from requesting assurances about the storage of the data to refusing to be part of the process whereby the data are collected.

Critical Thinking Question

Do you think the privacy rights of the pregnant women in this case should be overridden for the public good? Why or why not?

Equity in Research

In addition to consideration of benefits and harms and of confidentiality, the federal regulations also require determination that the "selection of subjects is equitable." Often, there are times when it would be easier or cheaper to use special groups of subjects—prisoners, residents in a state institution, or clinic patients. If efficiency in research were the only objective, then researchers would be justified in using the most convenient subjects. However, people are increasingly concerned that the poor, the institutionalized, or the incarcerated not be singled out to make disproportional contributions to science as research subjects.[21] The path of least resistance could easily lead to persons in these groups participating overwhelmingly as subjects.

For certain studies it is impossible to use any subjects other than those who are members of these groups. A sociological study of two different ways of housing or teaching institutionalized mentally retarded persons would be an example. Experiments utilizing medical vouchers with which the poor could buy health insurance on the private market would be another. For this reason, the federal regulations ask that IRBs take into account the purpose of the research and the setting in which the research will be conducted.

Concerns of *equity* in research are driven by the principle of justice. Justice in subject selection may be in direct conflict with the requirements of the principle of beneficence. Doing the most good with limited research dollars could conflict with selecting subjects equitably. It could be that with the same budget twice as many subjects could be studied if the investigator were to limit recruitment to institutionalized populations.

The federal regulations limit concern about the implications of the principle of justice to subject selection. Other people are extending their concern to matters of actual research design.[22] They ask what should happen if the investigator designing a research project realizes that there are two different designs that could be used. One would efficiently and eloquently obtain the answer to the research question. It is an ideal design, but it places considerable burden on some very sick patients. The alternative design would place much less burden on the patients, but it sacrifices some of the efficiency in the design. If justice requires arranging things so that those who are least well-off receive the benefits, it would seem to require the second design. However, beneficence—which emphasizes maximizing net benefits—would require the first. We see, therefore, that equity is a problem not only in subject selection but in design and execution of research as well. The next two cases illustrate these problems.

Case 15-5

When the Subject Group of Choice Is Prisoners

Gail Lassiter is a doctoral student in a nursing program, and she has encountered some difficult questions about research design. Miss Lassiter is studying violent behaviors and personality variables associated with violent behaviors. She is particularly interested in this topic because she is employed in the clinic at a large city jail and has often witnessed the effects of violent behavior on unsuspecting inmates and guards at the jail. She hopes that the results of her research will ultimately help nurses, during the initial health assessment, identify inmates with a tendency toward violent behavior before they harm other inmates and guards.

Because Ms. Lassiter works in the clinic of a large city jail, it would be much easier and more efficient for her to recruit her subjects there. If she had to find a sample of persons prone to violence by going to the general population, she would either have to study very large numbers of persons picked at random or select subpopulations she believes would be likely to be violent. The latter strategy would possibly cloud the quality of the data, and the former approach would be practically impossible. Should she do this type of research using a prisoner population, and could prisoners in her own place of employment be part of the study?

Case 15-6

Inconveniencing the Dying

Martha Ward is the nurse coordinator for the clinical center of a large tertiary care unit. The unit is responsible for clinical trials involving budgets of several million dollars a year. She works directly on one project involving the monitoring of patients in a multicenter trial for carcinoma of the prostate. The patients are randomized into three cells, each receiving a chemotherapy regimen involving at least four drugs. The patients are all seriously ill. They have received conventional treatments, but their disease has progressed. Most of the men in the study are quite elderly, and many have difficulty getting around.

Ms. Ward is responsible for maintaining records for the study and also for taking routine blood samples, blood pressure readings, weight, and so on. The protocol calls for these measurements to be taken weekly, at which time the patients are expected to come to the hospital. Ms. Ward is used to such procedures. She has worked on research protocols for several years. Many of them have involved patients receiving medications on an out-patient basis and coming to the hospital regularly for data monitoring.

She is troubled by the present protocol, however. She knows how difficult it is for her patients, being seriously ill, to come to the hospital. She realizes that they have to make the trip weekly and that most of the visits are solely for the purpose of the research. She also knows that Dr. Hanson, the principal investigator for the study, has never considered any variations in the protocol that would ease the burden on these men. She wonders how much the study would be compromised if the data were gathered only when the men needed to come to the hospital for therapeutic reasons. Alternatively, she wonders whether nurses could visit the men in their homes to get the blood samples and other data.

Ms. Ward has been involved in other protocols where patients were inconvenienced for the purpose of the study, and in those cases it did not trouble her; but these men have such a difficult time getting to the hospital and are in such poor health that she wonders whether she should press for a modification in the study. Would it be ethical to compromise the quality of the data or to increase the costs of the study? Is it ethical to ask these men to come to the hospital weekly in order to get slightly better data or to save the project money?

Commentary

Cases 15-5 and 15-6 raise, in different ways, the question of whether researchers ought to be as efficient as possible in gathering data, even if it means placing disproportionate burdens on certain classes of potential subjects. The principle of justice, discussed in Chapter 5, focuses on what is fair or equitable in the distribution of burdens and benefits. We saw that some people hold that the morally correct way to distribute them is simply the way that produces the most good on balance. That would mean in these cases that Gail Lassiter would use her prisoners because they can most efficiently give her the data about persons displaying violent behavior and that Martha Ward would not raise questions about the burden to the prostate cancer victims unless she could show that the burden to these men was greater than the benefits obtained from having them come to the hospital.

The alternative position is that justice requires distributing benefits and burdens fairly. For some, that means making sure that the least well-off have their positions improved. For others, that means trying to arrange things so that people have equal opportunity for well-being. For Ms. Lassiter, it could mean that she would choose a more difficult, less efficient method for the study in order to avoid asking that prisoners carry an undue portion of the burden. To make this judgment, she would have to determine what kind of claim prisoners have. Are they among the least well-off who, therefore, have special claims not to be burdened further? Or are they people who have voluntarily engaged in antisocial behavior, surrendering any claims they would have had to be considered among the least well-off?

The elderly, critically ill men in Dr. Hanson's study, for whom mobility is difficult, would have special claims under the interpretation of justice that requires benefit to those worst off. As the protocol is designed, they are asked to make a sacrifice for the benefit of society by bearing the inconvenience of trips to the hospital beyond what is necessary for therapy. Ms. Ward is willing to make such requests of patients who are better off, as she has done in previous studies. In this study, however, the patients are probably among the least well-off of any of the people who might be affected by a change in protocol. When they are compared with those who would be hurt by changing the protocol, Ms. Ward appears to recognize that it is particularly hard to ask the persons of the community who are the least well-off to make sacrifices, even relatively small sacrifices, for the benefit of others who are better off. If Ms. Ward is guided by a principle of justice, she might be inclined to ask for changes in the protocol, either slightly reducing the quality of the data in order to make it easier on these patients or slightly increasing the budget for the project by asking that a nurse be hired to collect the data from the men at home when possible.

Critical Thinking Question

If you were a member of the IRB reviewing these research protocols, what would be your recommendations about the equity questions?

Informed Consent in Research

A final major area of ethical assessment for research involving human subjects involves *informed consent*. The federal regulations call for ensuring that informed consent be sought from each prospective subject or the subject's authorized representative and that the consent be appropriately documented. These regulations speak of the "elements" of an appropriately informed consent—that is, the kinds of information that must be included. Those elements are summarized in Table 15-1. Although the major problems concerning informed consent will be explored in Chapter 16, which deals with consent in the therapeutic setting, consent is also a major issue in research. Some problems (e.g., the consent for the use of records for research) are unique to the research context. The following cases raise these special research questions.

Case 15-7
Research Without Consent: What Do You Do with the Results?[3]

Between 1976 and 1983, Carmen Amato, a maternal–child health nurse, participated in the collection of data for a research study designed to identify major hemoglobinopathies in newborn infants. Mrs. Amato's role was to collect samples of cord blood; label them; and send them to the laboratory for testing for Rh type, Coombs, serology, bilirubin and hemoglobin type, PKU, and thyroid scan. On admission to the labor and delivery suite, pregnant women were informed that their infants' blood would undergo this examination, and consent forms were signed.

---

[3]This case is adapted from the results of a study published by Ewing, N., Powers, D., Hilburn, J., & Schroeder, W. A. (1981, June). Newborn diagnosis of abnormal hemoglobins from a large municipal hospital in Los Angeles. *American Journal of Public Health, 71*, 629–631. See also Wyatt, P. R. (1981, December). Issues surrounding genetic screening programs. *American Journal of Public Health, 71*, 1411; and Ewing, N. (1981, December). Dr. Nadia Ewing responds. *American Journal of Public Health, 71*, 1411.

Collected from more than 29,000 infants over the 7-year period, the blood samples were also examined for incidental information on genetic carrier states in the neonates. No consent was ever sought for these tests, and Mrs. Amato did not know that these data were being collected in the study. She did know that when infants were found to have a major hemoglobinopathy, the study results, along with psychologic support, education, and genetic counseling, were offered to the parents of the child. Apparently, when other genetic information was found, particularly regarding carrier states, no information was relayed to the parents. The results were simply forwarded to the referring physician and included in the infant's hospital record. Because no consent for the additional testing had been sought, the researchers assumed that the physician would be the appropriate person to assess the situation and to choose the most appropriate timing to convey the information to the parents.

Like many of her colleagues, Mrs. Amato read about the results of the research study in published reports in several professional journals. She became deeply concerned when she realized that 637 infants had been identified as having non-AA hemoglobin genotypes in the additional testing. She knew that under certain systemic disease conditions, these children were at risk of demonstrating complications of their genotype. Yet disclosure of the testing results had not been offered to parents whose children were discovered to have these genotypes. When she voiced her concern to officials in her department and to the hospital's IRB, she was told that there were no federal guidelines pertaining to the use and communication of incidentally obtained genetic carrier state information. What should she do about this information, and what could she do to avoid being involved in future research efforts that failed to disclose the results of incidental testing?

Commentary

First, what constitutes research and what constitutes therapy in this case? It is reasonable that blood would be drawn from newborns for laboratory tests even if there were no study being conducted at all. This case raises important ethical questions even if all of the work being done were undertaken solely for therapeutic purposes. For example, the fact that certain information was being withheld from the parents raises questions about withholding information of the kind addressed in Chapter 8. Some parents might have an interest in and be able to make reasonable use of the carrier status information, which adds to these moral problems.

Moreover, even if there were no research being undertaken, there appear to be questions about the adequacy of the consent for the blood samples and tests. It can be imagined that a clinician might ask for tests for hemoglobinopathy carrier state or that such information would be an inevitable by-product of the tests being performed. Even if there were no study being conducted, one might ask whether the mothers should have been asked to consent to (or refuse consent for) the generation of that information. We shall see in the cases in Chapter 16 that the answer will depend, in part, on whether one emphasizes beneficence or autonomy as the central ethical principle underlying consent requirements.

If beneficence (doing good and avoiding evil) is the key, then the clinician might argue that the patient was at absolutely no risk when this information was generated (i.e., blood was being drawn anyway). Moreover, telling the mothers about carrier status could unnecessarily result in their developing a mindset that their children were "unhealthy," creating psychologic problems for the children. On benefit–harm grounds, maybe the mothers should not have been told about the tests if they were performed for therapeutic purposes. If the blood tests were done on cord blood, who does the cord belong to—the mother or the infant? Is the mother consenting for herself or for the infant, and does this make any difference?

If autonomy is the underlying ethical concern, on the other hand, then the mothers have a right to consent (or not) to diagnostic procedures, even if there is no further risk to their infants. They may have reasons of their own for not wanting the tests performed. They may fear that they or their physicians may be influenced by the results in undesirable ways. Hemoglobinopathy studies have racial implications that some parents may object to in principle. For whatever reason, a person committed to autonomy as the basis of consent would favor disclosing information about the tests that the parents would reasonably want to know.

These samples were being analyzed, however, as part of a study specifically to gain information about the patterns of major hemoglobinopathies. As such, the parent should have been asked to consent to having the information about her child used for research purposes. In addition, if additional tests were performed, the question arises of whether the women should have been asked to agree. This question would arise even if the tests were performed on a blood sample drawn for clinical purposes. Once again, if the driving ethical principle is beneficence, then deciding whether to disclose that the data were also being used for research or that additional tests were being performed would be made on the basis of whether the disclosure does any good. However, if autonomy is the basis of consent, then these decisions would be based on whether the disclosure increases the capacity of the patient to make an autonomous choice.

In research, one of the elements of disclosure is normally the purpose of the study. Presumably this is to help subjects decide whether they wish to contribute to the objective of the investigation. Some women might, for example, not want to contribute to studies of hemoglobinopathy carrier status (perhaps because of the racial implications), even though in doing so they are not at any risk of harm. Mrs. Amato appears to be a party to both controversial therapeutic practice and the practice of research without informed consent. The question is whether either of those practices is ethically unacceptable.

If these events had occurred after April 1, 2003, they would have come under the Health Insurance Portability and Accountability Act (HIPAA) of 1996. This law covers the use and disclosure of a patient's personal health information (including information in doctors' offices and in hospitals). The patient must authorize the use and disclosure of such information. If a research use is anticipated, that use must be included in the authorization from the patient. If a clinician or researcher later decides to conduct research on stored samples, such as blood, a new authorization must be obtained.[23]

Table 15-1

Federal Regulations: Basic Elements of Consent

1. A statement that the study involves research, an explanation of the purposes of the research and the expected duration of the subject's participation, a description of the procedures to be followed, and identification of any procedures which are experimental;

2. A description of any reasonably foreseeable risks or discomforts to the subject;

3. A description of any benefits to the subject or to others, which may reasonably be expected from the research;

4. A disclosure of appropriate alternative procedures or courses of treatment, if any, that might be advantageous to the subject;

5. A statement describing the extent, if any, to which confidentiality of records identifying the subject will be maintained;

6. For research involving more than minimal risk, an explanation as to whether any compensation and an explanation as to whether any medical treatments are available if injury occurs and, if so, what they consist of, or where further information may be obtained;

7. An explanation of whom to contact for answers to pertinent questions about the research and research subjects' rights, and whom to contact in the event of a research-related injury to the subject; and

8. A statement that participation is voluntary, refusal to participate will involve no penalty or loss of benefits to which the subject is otherwise entitled, and the subject may discontinue participation at any time without penalty or loss of benefits to which the subject is otherwise entitled.

Additional elements of informed consent that should be included when appropriate:

1. A statement that the particular treatment or procedure may involve risks to the subject (or to the embryo or fetus, if the subject is or may become pregnant), which are currently unforeseeable;

2. Anticipated circumstances under which the subject's participation may be terminated by the investigator without regard to the subject's consent;

3. Any additional costs to the subject that may result from participation in the research;

4. The consequences of a subject's decision to withdraw from the research and procedures for orderly termination of participation by the subject;

5. A statement that significant new findings developed during the course of the research, which may relate to the subject's willingness to continue participation will be provided to the subject; and

6. The approximate number of subjects involved in the study.

Source: U.S. Department of Health and Human Services, National Institutes of Health, Office for the Protection of Human Subjects. (2009, January 15). Protection of human subjects. *Code of Federal Regulations, 45*(46), 116. Available at: http://www.hhs.gov/ohrp/humansubjects/guidance/45cfr46 .htm#46.116. Accessed May 10, 2010.

Research Brief 15-2

Source: Karlawish, J. H. T., Knopman, D., Clark, C. M., Morris, J. C., Marson, D., Whitehouse, P. J., et al. (2002). Informed consent for Alzheimer's disease clinical trials: A survey of clinical investigators. *IRB: Ethics & Human Research, 24*(5), 1–5.

Purpose: The purpose of this study was to identify the process of obtaining informed consent from patients with Alzheimer's disease (AD) at 39 sites participating in the Alzheimer's Disease Cooperative Study, a National Institutes of Aging (NIA)–funded network of AD clinical programs and investigators. How the sites conducted the informed consent process and the state laws, regulations, and local rules that governed the informed consent process were studied.

Method: A pilot-tested survey questionnaire was distributed via electronic mail to the principal investigators (PIs) at each of the 39 sites, with a request that it be completed by the person most familiar with the informed consent process for clinical trials. Statistical analyses were performed on the survey responses. Responses to all open-ended questions were coded independently by two individuals.

Findings: Study data indicated that either the study coordinator (22 sites) or the PI (14 sites) most often solicited informed consent from participants. Four sites (17%) reported that they use materials to assess caregiver decision-making capacity, and 12 sites (40%) reported that they use materials to assess patient decision-making capacity. The methods used to assess decision-making capacity varied from site to site. No sites used a competency assessment tool developed specifically for research involving persons with diminished capacity to make an informed decision about consent. Some sites reported that 100% of their participants were competent to consent; other sites reported that few AD participants were competent to consent. Less than 45% of the sites knew whether there were federal laws or regulations describing the kinds of persons who have the authority to provide informed consent for research on behalf of an incompetent person. Fewer than 50% of the sites knew of local laws or IRB rules describing who can provide proxy informed consent for an adult who is not competent. Seven sites either did not know or thought no laws or regulations existed that describe the kinds of persons who have the authority to provide proxy informed consent when, in fact, their states did have laws or regulations regarding proxy decision makers.

Conclusions: The findings suggest a number of areas for further study and potential improvements to the informed consent process in AD clinical trials. Further research should determine the training that study coordinators receive about informed consent; interventions to improve the informed consent process should include education of study coordinators. There is also a need to identify and test the feasibility, reliability, and validity of tools and methods for assessing the capacity of AD patients to make decisions about participating in research. Researchers also need to be informed about valid instruments that already exist for making these assessments.

Implications: There is substantial need for improvement in the process and methods of obtaining informed consent from patients with diminished capacity to make decisions about participating in research. All clinical trial sites also need education on local laws and regulations that guide informed consent, especially proxy consent on behalf of incompetent adult persons.

Case 15-8
When the Patient Does Not Remember Giving Consent

Mr. Timmons was a 48-year-old, unemployed laborer who had sustained minor injuries when he walked in front of a slowly moving car. He was intoxicated at the time and had, in fact, been known to have a long-standing alcohol addiction problem. Treated in the emergency room of a well-known medical center, he was offered the opportunity for treatment of his alcoholism if he agreed to participate in a study on alcoholic encephalopathy. Dr. Wiseman, the principal investigator (PI) of the study, and Mrs. Barnsworth, the head nurse of the alcohol research unit, explained to Mr. Timmons that the purpose of the study was to determine if a certain medication administered over a period of time would decrease encephalopathic symptoms and improve liver function in alcoholic patients. Mr. Timmons would be required to receive the medication via constant intravenous infusion 24 hours per day for 30 days. He would also be required to take multivitamins, eat three meals per day, and take other medications as required (e.g., antihypertensives for hypertension). Potential side effects of the experimental medication were explained, and the risks and benefits of the study were discussed. Mr. Timmons signed the consent form and was admitted to the research unit.

During the first 15 days of hospitalization, Mr. Timmons gradually regained his strength and began to increase his activity levels. He was cooperative with the nursing staff, was attentive to discussions about alcohol rehabilitation, and seemed content. By the 20th day, however, he began to be agitated and depressed, claiming that he was going "stir crazy." Because he felt better than when he was admitted, he especially wanted to go home. He was obviously better nourished, and laboratory testing indicated he had few signs of alcohol encephalopathy. When reminded that he had signed a consent form and had agreed to participate for a full 30 days, he claimed that he did not remember signing a consent form. He informed the nurses that he was going home whether they liked it or not.

When Mrs. Barnsworth checked the signed consent form, she noticed that it had been signed with a scribbled "X" and was almost illegible. The admission notes showed that he had been in DT's for the first 24 hours of admission but that he was not hallucinating, he knew his name, and he knew he was in the hospital. Was Mr. Timmons's consent to participate in the study valid?

Commentary

One of the characteristics of consent is that it is free. It must be a decision rendered by a substantially autonomous agent. Mr. Timmons's case raises the question of the autonomy of his actions when he expressed consent.

Mr. Timmons's consent can be questioned on the grounds that he may not have comprehended adequately what he was being told. He was intoxicated at the time. If consent is grounded in the principle of beneficence, Mrs. Barnsworth would ask the question, "Did getting the original consent do any good?" If it did not, then presumably it serves no moral purpose. She might also ask whether the process should have been delayed until Mr. Timmons could have understood the conditions to which he was consenting. Once again, she would ask whether getting the consent at that point would have done any good.

If consent is grounded in the principle of autonomy, Mrs. Barnsworth would have to ask whether getting the consent at the time it was obtained furthered Mr. Timmons's autonomy. She might also ask whether getting it at a later time would have done so.

Mr. Timmons's case raises another problem. Assuming he did at some point consent with adequate autonomy to enter the study to reduce encephalopathy, does that mean he is obligated to stay in the study until it is completed or does he have a right to cancel his consent? That problem is raised in the next case.

Critical Thinking Question

Would you consider Mr. Timmons's consent valid? Why or why not?

Case 15-9

The Research Subject with Rare Blood Cells: Is Consent Required for Cloning Them?[4]

Signe Colson was a nurse working in the leukemia research clinic of a large medical center. Mrs. Colson welcomed patients to the clinic, checked their records, recorded their vital signs, and briefly interviewed each patient for problems and/or progress since his or her last visit. Following blood work in the laboratory, other necessary tests, and an examination by his or her physician, each patient again stopped by Mrs. Colson's office to sign any necessary consent forms for the withdrawal of their blood; receive clarification on instructions for new medications, additional testing, or research protocol requirements;

---

[4]The names in this case are fictitious, but the case is based on actual events cited in the statement of John L. Moore before the Subcommittee on Investigations and Oversights, House Committee on Science & Technology hearings on the use of human patient materials in the development of commercial biomedical products (1985, October 29). See also Moore v. Regents of the University of California, 793 P.2d 479 (Cal. 1990); Annas, G. J. (1990). Outrageous fortune: Selling other people's cells. *The Hastings Center Report, 20*(6), 36–39; Trout, B. J. (1992). Patient law—A patient seeks a portion of the biotechnological patent profits in Moore v. Regents of the University of California. *Journal of Corporation Law, 17*(20), 513–538; and White, G. B., & O'Connor, K. W. (1990). Rights, duties and commercial interests: John Moore versus the Regents of the University of California. *Cancer Investigation, 8*(1), 65–70.

and obtain a return appointment. This was the time when many of the patients asked for further explanation of their physicians' recommendations and for other information important to them.

One day, Mrs. Colson found herself troubled by the questions that one of her patients was asking. Mr. Johnstone was enrolled in an ongoing study at the research center. He had previously been diagnosed as having hairy cell leukemia, a rare and potentially fatal form of leukemia. He questioned why he still needed to return to the clinic for repeated blood tests and examinations. Four years ago, Mr. Johnstone had undergone a splenectomy to slow down his leukemia and had subsequently enjoyed an extraordinary recovery from his leukemic disorder. He visited the clinic twice a year at the request of his physician, who claimed that his blood had some unique characteristics that were of interest to him and his research staff.

Mr. Johnstone was especially concerned about the consent form that Mrs. Colson had asked him to sign on this particular visit. She replied that the form was a new standard form that needed to be signed for the removal of blood from patients and that the tests were necessary for his continued health care. Mr. Johnstone, however, wanted to know more about the research activity involving his blood and whether there were any commercial products or potential financial interests involved in the research being performed on his blood. Mrs. Colson assured Mr. Johnstone that the form was only a formality made necessary by the procedural rules of the hospital, but Mr. Johnstone did not seem convinced by her explanation. She told Mr. Johnstone that she would have his physician call him to answer his specific questions. Again, she assured him that a number of the clinic's patients were involved in research studies involving their blood and that the form was a standard instrument now being used by the clinic. Later in the day, she informed Mr. Johnstone's physician of the questions he had asked and soon forgot the matter.

Two years later, Mrs. Colson was shocked to read in the newspaper that a former patient of one of the clinic's physicians was suing the medical center for use of his blood to develop commercial biomedical products without his knowledge and consent. The patient was claiming that his blood cells had been used for private commercial gain and personal financial profit on the part of the physician without his knowledge, consent, and participation. As a result of his physician's negotiations concerning his blood cells, a for-profit biogenetic firm had been granted exclusive access to the patient's blood cells and their products in exchange for payment to the physician of approximately half a million dollars and other advantages that would accrue both to the physician and his employer. The biogenetic firm had, in fact, cloned the unique genetic sequence of the patient's white blood cells responsible for producing useful substances in the treatment of leukemias. The patient was Mr. Johnstone. Had Mrs. Colson unwittingly played a role in deceiving a patient about his consent to have blood drawn for "research"?

Commentary

In contrast with Mr. Timmons in Case 15-8, Mr. Johnstone is alert, involved, and apparently autonomous. He is capable of giving and withdrawing his own consent. One question is whether, in some situations, consent is irrevocable. A second question is whether Mr. Johnstone gave an adequately informed consent.

No doubt Mr. Johnstone consented to something. He presumably consented to his blood being withdrawn and to the use of his blood for research. But presumably he had not been told that his blood would be used to develop a cell line that would have potentially significant financial implications. We shall see in the cases in Chapter 16 that it is debatable whether Mr. Johnstone was told enough for his consent to be considered informed. It could be argued that he needs to be told the information he would want to know to make an autonomous choice. In this case, would he have wanted to know that at least hundreds of thousands of dollars could be made from the use of his cells?

Even if he did give adequate consent, Mrs. Colson needs to face the question of whether he can withdraw that consent. Certain consents probably cannot be withdrawn—those on the basis of which irreversible decisions have been made, such as performing surgery, for example. The philosophic literature explores consents that contain within them the provision that the consenter cannot change his or her mind. If Mr. Johnstone's consent contained such a provision, would he still be able to withdraw it? If it did not contain this provision, should he be able to withdraw it?

If you are interested in the Mr. Johnstone case you may want to read *The Immortal Life of Henrietta Lacks*.[24] Recently released, it details the story of the woman with cervical cancer who became the source of the famous HeLa cells. Both of these cases raise serious questions about the ownership of human materials and what counts as permissible uses of these materials. Researchers are struggling to balance the autonomy and privacy rights of subjects as well to find means to notify subjects of future research that might be beneficial. Biobanking, especially commercial biobanking, raises complex issues. One biobank management model offers a means of protecting the information in biobanks, offers ways to provide follow-up information requested about the participants, protects the participant's confidentiality, and purports to adequately deal with the ethical issues at stake in biobanking.[25]

Case 15-10

Sensitive Information in the Employee's Health Record[5]

Jane Sanborn was the occupational health nurse for a federally sponsored veterans support program. Among her responsibilities was the completion of the health status section of a form that included both personal and health history gathered during periodic health examinations of the company's employees. The physician completed the medical portion of

---

[5]Adapted from Fry, S. T. (1984, November/December). Confidentiality in health care: A decrepit concept? *Nursing Economics, 2,* 413–418. See also Flaherty, M. J. (1982). Confidentiality of patients' records. In L. Curtin & M. J. Flaherty (Eds.), *Nursing ethics: Theories and pragmatics* (pp. 315–316). Bowie, MD: Robert J. Brady Company.

the health report, recorded a decision about the employee's fitness for work, and returned the report to Ms. Sanborn, who maintained a confidential file of employees' health reports and records. Employees were asked to sign a statement on the health report to the effect that information in the report relating to employee fitness for the job could be shared with the employer as necessary.

One day Ms. Sanborn received a memo directing her to send a copy of 16 employees' health records to a federal agency in Washington, DC, for participation in a study involving employee health in government-sponsored programs. The agency maintained a centralized data bank that was often used for research involving health record searches. Ms. Sanborn questioned the request and asked for more information about the particular study. No explanation was provided and the original request was repeated. Ms. Sanborn responded that she would send the health records as soon as she obtained the consent of the employees. She then discussed the matter with the physician and the administrator of the program. Ms. Sanborn was told that she should comply with the request, that it was accepted practice to send any requested employee health records because the program was federally sponsored. No consent was ever obtained from the employees. Under pressure from both the physician and the administrator, she was uncertain what she should do.

Commentary

One problem that arises in research is that of consent for the use of records. Especially for epidemiologic studies, statistical analysis of data drawn from medical records can be extremely valuable in increasing understanding of disease patterns, such as occupational health risks. Sometimes this can be done in a way that poses only limited confidentiality problems. If, for example, an occupational health nurse such as Jane Sanborn were to remove all identifying information from the files before sending them to Washington, then it would be difficult for individual patients to be identified. Of course, there are still risks of confidentiality violation. For example, if all 16 records reported a stigmatizing medical problem and those 16 employees could be identified as a group, then the removal of identifiers from individual records would mean nothing.

Aside from the confidentiality problem, are there any ethical issues raised by sending employee records for inclusion in epidemiologic research? In effect, these employees are subjects of a study without their consent. If beneficence is the basis for assessing consent, then the question would be answered by determining if getting the employees' consent would increase the net benefit. The employees in this case might be hurt by the study. They might lose their jobs if certain results are found. On the other hand, requiring the consent could harm others, if that requirement makes it significantly harder to do the study. It seems like a close call whether more good or harm would be done by requiring the consent, considering the effects on everyone (including those who may someday benefit from the research).

More importantly, some people believe that taking into account all the people affected is not the basis on which this question should be decided anyway.

They believe that the critical issue is the autonomy of the patient. The critical question for people holding this view is whether the employees (the potential subjects) would want to be asked. Some employees probably would have no objections to searches of their records without being asked provided reasonable safeguards were employed. Others, however, might object, either in principle or because they fear bad consequences.

Whether they object, Ms. Sanborn might ask whether these employees have been told what they would want to know. For example, they might have been told when they were hired that their records could be used in this way. If they had agreed then, they would have given a "blanket consent" to use the records for research. Some hospitals are now asking for such blanket consents when patients enter hospitals. If there is no blanket consent, it might be argued that reasonable employees would want to know nothing about this use of their records so that, in effect, they have been told already "all that they wanted to know." Ms. Sanborn's task is to determine how the consent requirement applies and, if it does, whether the consent is adequate for the purpose.

In the next chapter, the consent issue is presented in cases involving clinical therapy rather than research.

ENDNOTES

1. Nuremberg Code, 1947. (1995). In W. T. Reich (Ed.), *Encyclopedia of bioethics* (Rev. ed., pp. 2763–2764). New York: Simon & Schuster Macmillan.
2. U.S. Department of Health and Human Services, National Institutes of Health, Office of Protection from Research Risks. (2001, November 13). Protection of human subjects. *Code of Federal Regulations, 45*(46). See also National Commission for the Protection of Human Subjects of Biomedical and Behavioral Research. (1978). *The Belmont report: Ethical principles and guidelines for the protection of human subjects of research.* Washington, DC: U.S. Government Printing Office.
3. Federman, D. D., Hanna, K. E., & Rodriguez, L. L. (Eds.). (2002). *Responsible research: A systems approach to protecting research participants.* Washington, DC: Institute of Medicine, National Academies Press.
4. Committee on Conflict of Interest in Medical Research, Education, and Practice. (2009). *Conflict of interest in medical research, education, and practice.* Washington, DC: Institute of Medicine, National Academies Press.
5. Silva, M. (1995). *Ethical guidelines in the conduct, dissemination, and implementation of nursing research.* Washington, DC: The American Nurses Association.
6. U.S. Department of Health and Human Services, National Institutes of Health, Office of Protection from Research Risks. (2001, November 13). Protection of human subjects. *Code of Federal Regulations, 45*(46), 46.111.
7. U.S. Department of Health and Human Services, National Institutes of Health, Office of Protection from Research Risks. (2001, November 13). Protection of human subjects. *Code of Federal Regulations, 45*(46), 46.401–46.409.
8. National Bioethics Advisory Commission. (1998, December). *Research involving persons with mental disorders that may affect decisionmaking capacity* (Vol. 1). Available at: http://bioethics/georgetown.edu/nbac/capacity/TOC.htm. Accessed May 10, 2010.

9. Faden, R., Beauchamp, T. L., & King, N. N. P. (1986). *A history and theory of informed consent.* New York: Oxford University Press; President's Commission for the Study of Ethical Problems in Medicine and Biomedical and Behavioral Research. (1982). *Making health care decisions: A report on the ethical and legal implications of informed consent in the patient–practitioner* relationship (Vol. 1). Washington, DC: U.S. Government Printing Office; Veatch, R. M. (1978). Three theories of informed consent: Philosophical foundations and policy implications. In National Commission for the Protection of Human Subjects of Biomedical and Behavioral Research (Ed.), *The Belmont report: Ethical principles and guidelines for the protection of human subjects of research.* Washington, DC: U.S. Government Printing Office.

10. Levine, R. J. (1978). The boundaries between biomedical or behavioral research and the accepted and routine practice of medicine. In National Commission for the Protection of Human Subjects of Biomedical and Behavioral Research (Ed.), *The Belmont report: Ethical principles and guidelines for the protection of human subjects of research* (App. I, 1-1–1-44). Washington, DC: U.S. Government Printing Office.

11. Emanuel, E., Wendler, D., & Grady, C. (2000). What makes clinical research ethical? *Journal of the American Medical Association, 283*(20), 2701–2711.

12. Emanuel, E. J., Crouch, R. A., Grady, C., Lie, R., Miller, F. G., & Wendler, D. (Eds.). (2008). *The Oxford textbook of clinical research ethics.* New York: Oxford University Press.

13. Beecher, H. K. (1966). Ethics and clinical research. *The New England Journal of Medicine, 274*(24), 1354–1360.

14. U.S. Department of Health and Human Services, National Institutes of Health, Office of Protection from Research Risks. (2001, November 13). Protection of human subjects. *Code of Federal Regulations, 45*(46), 46.111.

15. Ramsey, P. (1970). *The patient as person* (pp. 11–58). New Haven, CT: Yale University Press.

16. National Commission for the Protection of Human Subjects of Biomedical and Behavioral Research. (1977). *Research involving children: Report and recommendations* (pp. 6–8). Washington, DC: U.S. Government Printing Office.

17. U.S. Department of Health and Human Services, National Institutes of Health, Office of Protection from Research Risks. (2001, November 13). Protection of human subjects. *Code of Federal Regulations, 45*(46), 46.406; This limit applies except in special cases in which the Secretary of Health and Human Services has given explicit approval (see section 46–407).

18. Silva, M. (1995). *Ethical guidelines in the conduct, dissemination, and implementation of nursing research* (p. 16). Washington, DC: The American Nurses Association.

19. American Nurses Association. (2001). *Code of ethics for nurses with interpretive statements* (provisions 3.1 & 3.2, p. 12). Washington, DC: Author.

20. Ibid, provision 3.2, p. 12.

21. Levine, R. J. (1981). *Ethics and regulation of clinical research* (pp. 49–67). Baltimore: Urban & Schwarzenberg; National Commission for the Protection of Human Subjects of Biomedical and Behavioral Research. (1978). *The Belmont report: Ethical principles and guidelines for the protection of human subjects of research* (pp. 8–10). Washington, DC: U.S. Government Printing Office.

22. Veatch, R. M. (1983, February). Justice and research design: The case for a semi-randomization clinical trial. *Clinical Research, 31,* 12–22.

23. U.S. Department of Health and Human Services. (2003, July 13). Standards for privacy of individually identifiable health information. *Code of Federal Regulations, 45*(Part 160, Part 164). See also Muhlbaier, L. H. (2002). *HIPAA training handbook for researchers: HIPAA and clinical trials.* Marblehead, MA: Opus Communications.
24. Skloot, R. (2010). *The immortal life of Henrietta Lacks.* New York: Crown Publishers.
25. Auray-Blais, C., & Patenaude, J. (2006). A biobank management model applicable to biomedical research. *BMC Medical Ethics, 7*(4). See also Deschênes, M., & Sallée, C. (2005). Accountability in population biobanking: Comparative approaches. *Journal of Law, Medicine, & Ethics, 33*(1), 40–53; Clayton, E. W. (2005). Informed consent and biobanks. *Journal of Law, Medicine, & Ethics, 33*(1),15–21.

Chapter 16

Consent and the Right to Refuse Treatment

Other Cases Involving Consent

Key Terms

Capacity

Comprehension

Disclosure

Incompetent patients

Informed consent

Subjective standard

Voluntariness

Objectives

1. Describe the ethical principles central to issues of informed consent or refusal for treatment.
2. Identify the four essential elements of valid decision making: disclosure, capacity, comprehension, and voluntariness.
3. Describe three standards for disclosure.
4. Describe three standards for capacity and define its essential elements.
5. Identify ethical issues involved in achieving adequate comprehension of information.
6. Describe constraints on voluntary choice.
7. Apply ethical principles to patient care situations involving surrogate consent to treatment for incompetents.

The problems of consent for research on human subjects, raised in the previous chapter, sets the stage for a more detailed examination of the ethics of consent for medical treatment and the right to refuse treatment. This is an important topic in nursing ethics because the nurse may be the patient's primary contact concerning decision making for specific treatment or procedures performed by health personnel. Although surgery, complex medical procedures, organ donation, and even routine medical tests and treatments may have been explained by other members of the healthcare team, the nurse is often in a position to clarify the explanations and make sure the consent of the patient is truly informed. In many acute care institutions, the nurse may even be a legal witness to the consent process, including the adequacy of patient consent.

In this chapter, case studies will explore the ethical dimensions of healthcare decision making. Essential elements of valid decisions, consent or refusal, include **disclosure**, **capacity**, **comprehension**, and **voluntariness**. General consensus (clinical, ethical, and legal) exists today: (1) that patients with decision-making capacity have the right to consent to or refuse all medical treatment, (2) when one loses decision-making capacity one does not lose the right to be self-determining, (3) to the extent that a patient's previously expressed preferences are known these should guide decision making, and (4) this applies to all types of medical decisions, including those about life-sustaining treatment. Unresolved issues include: (1) determinations about who should make decisions for patients who have not designated a surrogate, (2) the right of patients or their surrogates to demand medical treatment that healthcare professionals believe to be futile (which will be discussed in Chapter 17), and (3) the right of healthcare professionals to deny treatment judged to be medically futile without informing patients or their surrogates. Once the basic dimensions of **informed consent** or refusal have been explored, subsequent cases will focus on problems of comprehension during the consent process and the voluntariness of the one giving consent. Finally, the meaning of the concept of consent for **incompetent patients** will be explored.

Informed consent is a relatively new notion in healthcare ethics. It emerged in the 20th century out of two different ethical concerns.[1] First, traditional professional ethics has long been concerned about protecting the patient from harm and promoting the patient's welfare. It recognizes that the patient who is informed of potential side effects, contraindications, and so forth is often in a better position to protect his or her interests. Such a patient becomes an active partner in his or her own health care. Thus, if guided by the traditional ethical principles of beneficence and nonmaleficence, the health professional would tend to give the patient the information necessary to be reasonably informed.

There are, however, significant problems in grounding an informed consent ethic in the principles of beneficence and nonmaleficence. These principles seem to require only informing the patient, not obtaining her or his actual consent. In cases in which the physician correctly believed the treatment was in the patient's interest, merely informing on the physician's part would not offer the patient any real choice in the treatment.

A second principle, that of autonomy, has become an alternative foundation for the requirement of informed consent. It affirms the right of competent patients to control interventions involving their own bodies. Under the principle of autonomy, the patient is given the authority to evaluate treatment options based on his or her own beliefs and values. Treatments may be rejected even if they are believed by the healthcare professional to be beneficial. In fact they may be rejected even if they are deemed beneficial by the patient—if, for example, the patient would rather conserve resources for other family members. Case 16-1 involves a patient's right to refuse treatment.

In 20th-century American law, the requirement of informed consent has been grounded in the principle of autonomy, or what the courts often refer to as the "principle of self-determination." In the 1914 landmark case of Schloendorff v. Society of New York Hospital, Judge Cardozo articulated the principle that was to become the foundation of the consent doctrine:

> Every human being of adult years and sound mind has a right to determine what shall be done with his own body; and a surgeon who performs an operation without his patient's consent commits an assault for which he is liable for damages.[2]

Even with this acknowledgment that the patient is required to consent to treatment, it was still many years before it was explicitly acknowledged that in order to consent, one had to be informed. In 1960 Justice Schroeder, in the important Kansas case of Natanson v. Kline, argued that where a physician misrepresents a procedure or fails to point out its consequences, he or she may be subject to a claim of unauthorized treatment—that is, treatment without adequate consent.[3] That argument has generated a public debate over the elements of disclosure that must be transmitted for a consent to be adequately informed, one of the issues raised by the cases in the second section of this chapter.

Yet, even if we know what the elements of disclosure are—risks, benefits, alternative procedures, and other elements of information necessary for a consent to be informed—there still exists an issue of just how much of each element must be conveyed. If we agree that risks of the procedure must be explained, just how many risks must be explained for consent to be adequately informed? Certainly, not all risks must be discussed, because the list of risks for most procedures could be infinite. Some standard of reference is needed to determine which risks must be disclosed. Similarly, once we realize that alternative procedures must be disclosed, we need to identify which alternatives. Surely, not all alternatives must be disclosed because that would include untested treatments, disproved treatments, treatments based on various religious beliefs, and even illegal treatments.

Traditionally, it was assumed that professionals decided how much information was to be conveyed by appealing to the consensus of their professional colleagues. But now other standards are emerging that are based on what patients would want to know.

The movement, both in the courts and in the ethical debate, has been very much in favor of these newer standards for determining how much to disclose to patients. Determining whether they apply to the nurse as well as to the physician will be one of the critical issues in the cases in the second section of the chapter.

As discussed in Chapter 7, patients must have decision-making capacity in order to exercise self-determination by consenting to or refusing medical treatment. While the term *competence* is often used synonymously with capacity, competence is technically a legal determination. In usual healthcare decision making, nurses are concerned about whether patients have the capacity to make decisions about proposed treatment. Three standards have been proposed for determining capacity, outcome, categories, and function, with only the last standard, function, being valid.

The outcome standard is invoked when a patient's capacity is questioned because he or she is making a decision with an outcome we cannot accept (e.g., claiming a patient lacks decision-making capacity because she decides to refuse life support). Rarely do healthcare professionals challenge capacity when a patient makes a decision likely to result in the preferred outcome. It is, however, perfectly ethical and legal for patients to autonomously choose an outcome not to the healthcare team's liking.

The category standard is used to rule out whole categories of individuals such as the elderly, the homeless, those with mental health disorders, as possessing the ability to make valid decisions. Clearly, many people in these categories do possess decision-making capacity and to think otherwise is to be guilty of prejudice and bias.

The function standard states that patients possess decision-making capacity when they can do three things: (1) understand what is at stake in the decision at hand, (2) reason in accord with a relatively consistent set of values, and (3) communicate a preference. Decision-making capacity is task specific and admits of a sliding scale, with low-risk/high-benefit treatments demanding a less rigorous degree of capacity than high-risk/low-benefit treatments.

We do know that the American Nurses Association (ANA) *Code of Ethics for Nurses* includes in its first provision a forceful commitment to patient self-determination and says:

> Respect for human dignity requires the recognition of specific patient rights, particularly, the right of self-determination. Self-determination, also known as autonomy, is the philosophical basis for informed consent in health care. Patients have the moral and legal right to determine what will be done with their own person; to be given accurate, complete, and understandable information in a manner that facilitates an informed judgment; to be assisted with weighing the benefits, burdens, and available options in their treatment, including the choice of no treatment; to accept, refuse, or terminate treatment without deceit, undue influence, duress, coercion, or penalty; and to be given necessary support through the decision-making and treatment process. Such support would include the opportunity to make decisions with family and significant others and the provision of advice and support from knowledgeable nurses and other

health professionals. Patients should be involved in planning their own health care to the extent they are able and choose to participate.[4]

In the cases that follow, the problem will be to determine whether that is an acceptable summary of the nurse's role in informed consent and, if so, whether it requires the nurse to do the informing in certain cases or merely to ensure that the patient receives the information.

After we have looked at cases that pose problems about determining the elements of valid decision making and the standards for determining how much information to disclose (Cases 16-2 through 16-4), we shall examine a case (Case 16-5) in which the ethical issue is whether the patient has comprehended what has been disclosed. This will be followed by cases involving patients who, for one reason or another, may not be able to participate as voluntary, substantially autonomous decision makers. We will first look at a case (Case 16-6) involving a patient whose mental faculties can be presumed to be intact but who is in an environment where freedom to make decisions may be constrained. Our example will be from the military. Then in Case 16-7 we shall look at a patient who has a compromised capacity for rational planning and choice (i.e., a patient who has been sedated prior to the consent process).

Finally, we shall examine three cases (Cases 16-8, 16-9, and 16-10) of patients who may not be capable of substantially autonomous decision making—a clearly incompetent patient, a 7-year-old girl; a psychiatric patient; and an adolescent.

The Right to Refuse Treatment

The first issue to address is whether healthcare professionals should provide treatments that clearly seem beneficial to patients who are competent and able to comprehend what is proposed, but who voluntarily choose to refuse treatment. How would a nurse committed to benefiting the patient respond differently from one committed to respecting patient autonomy in this case?

Case 16-1
Do Patients Have a Right to Refuse Services They Do Not Want?[1]

Mr. Howard is a 63-year-old man referred to the home health nurse for evaluation and treatment of stasis ulcers on his legs. When Karla Long, the home health nurse, visited the home, she found large, oozing, sticky areas of raw tissue on Mr. Howard's legs. Ms. Long cleaned and dressed the ulcers and continued visiting the Howards several times per week.

---

[1]Adapted from Fry, S. T. (1997). Ethics in community health nursing practice. In M. Stanhope & J. Lancaster (Eds.), *Community health nursing: Promoting health of aggregates, families, and individuals* (4th ed., pp. 93–116). St. Louis, MO: C.V. Mosby Company.

As the ulcers began to heal, Ms. Long engaged the Howards in discussions about nutrition and hydration and encouraged them to start a weight reduction program (both of the Howards were grossly obese). Mr. and Mrs. Howard were not interested in weight reduction, and Ms. Long's visits were over.

Several months went by and Mr. Howard's ulcers began to deteriorate. He was hospitalized, treated, and returned home. When his condition deteriorated a second time, Mr. Howard was again hospitalized but, after a few days, he signed himself out of the hospital. Angered by Mr. Howard's decision, his physician refused to continue treating him. Ms. Long was then left without continuing physician orders to visit the home. She explained the situation to the Howards and taught Mrs. Howard to wash her husband's legs and to apply the medicine to them. Mr. Howard seemed satisfied with this. He claimed that the physicians had not really improved the condition of his legs and that he had no intention of seeking any medical help for his condition in the future. Ms. Long left her telephone number with the Howards in case they ran into any further problems.

Nearly a year passed. One summer day, Mrs. Howard called and said her husband was "awfully sick" and could not even get out of bed. The policy of the home health agency allowed Ms. Long to make a one-time-only evaluation visit, so she did. She found Mr. Howard's legs alive with the larvae of the summer flies attracted to the non–air-conditioned bedroom. She urged that Mr. Howard be hospitalized. He agreed and was transported to the local hospital by ambulance. Because of the extreme condition of his legs, a bilateral leg amputation was performed. When news of Mr. Howard's general condition got out (he had created quite a sensation in the emergency room of the local hospital), the citizens of his small town were aghast. How could a man be allowed to rot away? Where were all the home health services for the poor? Who was responsible? An investigation was done, but months later, "no fault" was found and it was announced that the community health services had sufficient mechanisms to prevent such a thing from happening again. But Ms. Long was not satisfied. Did patients not have a right to refuse services they did not want? If they refused certain services, should home health care be totally withdrawn? Should health care be provided to some individuals against their will and without their voluntary consent?

Commentary

This case raises many issues that are discussed in other chapters of this book. One issue is whether patients are entitled to complex and expensive treatment made necessary by their refusal of simpler interventions. That raises problems of justice and allocation of resources, discussed in Chapters 4 and 5. Underlying these problems is the related issue of whether the physician was ethically justified in acting in anger and refusing further therapy. The key question for Ms. Long, however, is somewhat more basic: Should Mr. Howard and patients like him be allowed to refuse the prescribed and apparently helpful treatment in the first place? And should he have been allowed to sign himself out of the hospital against the advice of his physician?

A preliminary issue, one that will be explored in more detail later in this chapter, is whether Mr. Howard was mentally competent. He made some decisions that, to many, might seem inappropriate or even irrational; however, it is generally agreed that we cannot assess whether a person is mentally competent based on the values he or she holds or the outcomes he or she prefers. Was there any evidence that Mr. Howard did not comprehend the probable outcome of refusing treatment? Was there any evidence that he was coerced into refusing treatment or that he suffered from a mental illness that led him to make the choice he made? If he were incompetent, he would not be in a position to accept or refuse proposed treatments.

Assuming Mr. Howard was mentally competent, should he have the right to refuse the treatments authorized by his physician and encouraged by Ms. Long? As we saw in the introduction to this chapter, the traditional ethic of the health professions focused on benefiting the patient and protecting the patient from harm. This raises the issues of Chapter 4 (how health professionals can judge benefits and harms) as well as those of Chapter 7 (whether patients have the right to make choices even if they are likely to turn out not to be in the patient's interest).

Assessing whether the treatments are in Mr. Howard's interest is a complex matter. Ms. Long's interventions seemed to be helping, and the ulcers deteriorated when the interventions ceased. But the burdens of the treatment also need to be assessed. Certainly, they would be inconvenient and unpleasant, both for Mr. Howard and for his wife. Likewise, Ms. Long's dietary recommendations seemed to make sense, but dieting seems to be impossibly difficult for some people. Can a case be made that, in some objective sense, Mr. Howard would be better off medically if he followed the recommended treatment? If so, would he be better off overall, taking into account his total well-being and not just his medical well-being?

Suppose Ms. Long and the physician conclude that, in spite of the complexities in determining what is in Mr. Howard's interest, they are certain he would be better off if he followed the prescribed ulcer treatment and the dietary recommendations. Should involuntary treatment then be authorized? As we saw in Chapter 4, even if the health professionals involved are convinced that a person would be better off if she or he were treated involuntarily, that does not settle the matter. It could be that the health professionals give too much emphasis to preserving life or other medical goods when they evaluate the consequences. We would probably want some more unbiased way of assessing whether Mr. Howard really would be better off. What method could be used?

Even if there were some unbiased, objective way of determining that Mr. Howard would be better off if he were treated, we still need to determine the role of the principle of autonomy in this case. As we saw in Chapter 7, the principle of autonomy holds that, insofar as a people are autonomous one is obligated to permit them to live their lives according to their own life plans—even if it could be shown that they would be worse off by doing so. Thus, those who are committed to autonomy will reach a very different conclusion from that chosen by more traditional health professionals who, paternalistically, justify efforts to benefit a person against his wishes. Should benefits or autonomy prevail here?

Critical Thinking Questions

1. Do you think Mr. Howard had a right to refuse treatment for his condition?
2. If you were Ms. Long, would you have done anything differently? Why or why not?

Research Brief 16-1

Source: Fried, T. R., Bradles, E. H., Towle, V. R., & Allore, H. (2002). Understanding the treatment preferences of seriously ill patients. *New England Journal of Medicine, 346*(14), 1061–1066.

Purpose: To identify the treatment preferences of adults with life-threatening illnesses under various conditions.

Method: This was a descriptive study. A questionnaire was administered to 226 persons who were 60 years of age or older and who had a limited life expectancy due to cancer, congestive heart failure, or chronic obstructive pulmonary disease. Study participants were asked whether they would want to receive a given treatment, first when the outcome was known with certainty and then with different likelihoods of an adverse outcome. The outcome without treatment was specified as death from the underlying disease.

Findings: The burden of treatment (i.e., length of the hospital stay, extent of testing, and invasiveness of interventions), the outcome, and the likelihood of the outcome all influenced treatment preferences. For a low-burden treatment with the restoration of current health, 98.7% of the participants said they would choose to receive the treatment (rather than not receive it and die), but 11.2% of these participants would not choose the treatment if it had a high burden. If the outcome was survival but with severe functional impairment or cognitive impairment, 74.4% and 88.8% of those participants, respectively, would not choose treatment. The number of participants who said they would choose treatment declined as the likelihood of an adverse outcome increased, with fewer participants choosing treatment when the possible outcome was functional or cognitive impairment than when it was death. Preferences did not differ according to the primary diagnosis.

Implications: Advance care planning should take into account patients' attitudes toward the burden of treatment, the possible outcomes, and the likelihood of those outcomes. The likelihood of adverse functional and cognitive outcomes of treatment requires explicit consideration.

The Elements and Standards of Disclosure

The first problem in understanding valid decision making is determining what information should be disclosed. This will depend, in part, on the ethical principle underlying consent. If the objective is to make sure that the patient's welfare is promoted, then the emphasis is likely to be on risks of side effects in response to which the patient can take action to avoid harm. If, however, the objective is to facilitate patient freedom of choice, then many other kinds of information might have to be transmitted. These might include the purpose of the intervention, the alternatives, and the side effects about which the patient can do nothing.

The federal regulations regarding research using human subjects, which were summarized in Chapter 15, include a list of "basic elements" of informed consent.[5] Those elements were presented in Table 15-1 (see page 386). Although some of those elements apply only to research consent, many are appropriate for any type of consent, including consent to routine therapy. They were built largely on an autonomy model and, therefore, contain many elements beyond those the subject would need to know to protect himself or herself from harm.

In deciding what information to disclose to the patient, some choices will have to be made. There is a very large amount of information one can communicate about any medical intervention, even a simple one. No reasonable person would want to know it all. In deciding which information is important enough to include, however, some standard is necessary. Nurses should be aware that different standards for making these choices lead to very different disclosures. Traditionally, a so-called "professional standard" was used. Under this standard, a practitioner had to disclose whatever his or her colleagues similarly situated would have disclosed.

The problem with this standard is that there are cases where a professional's colleagues would uniformly not disclose information that some patients would want to know in order to decide whether to consent to an intervention. Some physicians, for example, may tend not to disclose because they are guided by the Hippocratic principle of beneficence, whereas patients may want the information in order to exercise autonomous choice.

The nurse may face a similar problem in situations where he or she obtains consent. There may be cases where the nurse's colleagues would not disclose certain information that patients would want to know.

To get around this problem, those committed to the autonomy principle have supported a newer standard, referred to as the "reasonable person standard."[6] According to this standard, a healthcare professional must disclose whatever a reasonable person in the patient's position would need to know in order to exercise self-determined choice about an intervention.

Whereas this avoids the problem created by the professional standard whenever the consensus among professionals differs from that of reasonable patients, it still leaves another problem unresolved. Not all patients are the same. In fact, not all are reasonable. What happens when a patient would like more or less information than the hypothetical reasonable patient? A third standard, sometimes called the *subjective standard*, is emerging to deal with this problem. It requires disclosure of what a reasonable person would want to know, modified by the unique needs and desires of the patient insofar as the practitioner knows them or ought to know them. This might require, for example, asking the patient if he or she has any special concerns. It might require that the practitioner add information based on his or her particular knowledge about the patient or on what the practitioner could reasonably be expected to know about the patient.

The following cases illustrate problems the nurse confronts when attempting to ensure that all of the appropriate elements of consent are communicated to the patient and how she or he must draw upon some standard for deciding how much information to transmit.

Case 16-2

Intubating the Dead Patient: Treatment Practice Without Consent[2]

Mr. Ellsworth, who was 87 years old, was brought into the emergency room by the local rescue squad in a complete cardiac arrest. All emergency procedures were performed, including the establishment of an airway, placement of peripheral intravenous lines, urinary catheterization, and more. After resuscitation attempts were performed for 45 minutes, the patient was pronounced dead by the attending physician and family members were notified.

When the family arrived at the emergency room, Mary Pope, the evening staff nurse, found the attending physician teaching intubation techniques to five medical students. They were using Mr. Ellsworth's corpse for the practice. She quietly notified the attending physician that the family had arrived and wanted to talk to the physician. They also wanted to see their loved one's body. The attending physician, however, said he would be busy teaching the medical students for another 15–20 minutes. When she asked whether Mr. Ellsworth had given permission for his body to be used for teaching purposes, the attending physician ignored Miss Pope and asked her to tell the family that he would be busy with another patient for a few more minutes.

Case 16-3

How Much Information Did the Patient Need to Know?

Mr. Longwood was an unmarried, 64-year-old school teacher admitted to the hospital for indigestion, anorexia, and weight loss. After laboratory testing, an MRI, and a full gastro-intestinal (GI) workup, a colon mass was identified. Surgery was performed, and a large

---

[2]Case supplied by Kathleen M. Stilling, RN, MSN. Used with permission.

cancerous lesion in the colon was found and excised. When he arrived in the surgical intensive care unit (SICU), Mr. Longwood had a gastrostomy tube, a colostomy, and chest tubes. He also had an endotracheal tube in place and his respirations were maintained with a ventilator. Joellen Ullman was assigned as his primary nurse.

When Mr. Longwood regained consciousness, Ms. Ullman explained the machinery and tubing that were maintaining and monitoring his vital and bodily functions. Mr. Longwood was asked by the physician in Ms. Ullman's presence if he had any questions. He did not raise any. Dr. Jankowski did not go into any detail about the postsurgery recovery period and possible complications.

The patient, however, seemed very confused and alarmed and soon began to express anger and frustration at his altered condition. Communicating with a pad and pencil, he related how much he was appalled by the extensive and disfiguring surgery. He had signed an operative permit for abdominal surgery that listed the gastrostomy and colostomy as "possible" surgical procedures, but he had not comprehended what those procedures involved. After communicating this to his surgeon, he wrote to Ms. Ullman stating that he would not have permitted the surgery had he realized the condition that would result and had he known he had colon cancer. He wrote that he would rather have lived a shorter life without the drastic alterations to his body.

Mr. Longwood never did leave the SICU. He developed infections, abdominal wound dehiscence, and several pneumothoraxes, and he became ventilator dependent. He slipped in and out of consciousness. A cardiopulmonary arrest resulted in a tracheostomy. He also developed bradycardia, and his pulse rate dropped whenever he was suctioned. When back on the ventilator, he would revive and then beg Ms. Ullman to let him die. His surrogate decision maker (a cousin who was not close to Mr. Longwood) tended to agree with his physicians, who refused to discontinue life-prolonging measures. After weeks of difficult treatments and miserable suffering, Mr. Longwood died. Yet Ms. Ullman could not forget his pleading eyes and frequent scribbled notes asking, "Why didn't someone tell me this could happen?"

Case 16-4
Ms. Jolene Tuma and the Leukemia Patient[3]

In 1976, Ms. Jolene Tuma cared for a patient with myelogenous leukemia. The patient had been told by her physician that the condition could best be treated with chemotherapy. The physician had explained that the drugs to be used were very potent and had undesirable side effects that reduced the body's defense mechanisms and made the body susceptible to infection. Mechanisms to protect the patient from infection (reverse isolation) had been explained to the patient, and after discussing the treatment with her family, she had consented to treatment.

On the morning chemotherapy was to begin, Ms. Tuma brought the prescribed medication to the patient's room. She sat with the patient for a while discussing the patient's

---

[3]For a full discussion of this case, see Gargaro, W. J. (1982, April). Cancer nursing and the law. *Cancer Nursing*, 5, 131–132.

12-year fight against leukemia. The patient related that she attributed her past success in combating leukemia to her belief in God and to the faithful practice of her religion. The patient and Ms. Tuma then discussed the use of nontraditional treatments for leukemia, including laetrile and herbal treatments. Other alternatives, such as natural foods and massage treatments through reflexology, were also discussed. The patient indicated to Ms. Tuma that she preferred natural treatments for her disorder to the chemotherapy. She felt, however, that her family wanted her to undergo the chemotherapy treatment even though she was worried about its effectiveness and its side effects. She asked Ms. Tuma to discuss some of the alternatives for cancer treatment with her family. Ms. Tuma agreed to do so and made arrangements to meet with the patient's family that night. The chemotherapy was started with the understanding that the patient could request that it be discontinued, pending the meeting with the family.

When the family learned of the planned meeting, they immediately called the patient's physician. He did not interfere with the meeting and did not discuss the matter with the patient. He did order that the next dose of chemotherapy be withheld until after the planned meeting. Later, meeting with the family, Ms. Tuma discussed the prescribed treatment, its side effects, and alternatives provided by natural foods and herbs, as well as the fact that the patient would have difficulty obtaining treatment for her disorder, particularly blood transfusions, if she left the hospital without treatment. By the end of the meeting, the patient agreed to remain in the hospital and continue chemotherapy. The next dose of her chemotherapy had been delayed for 1.5 hours but was resumed. The patient died 2 weeks later, during which time she experienced adverse side effects from the chemotherapy and was comatose much of the time.

As a result of her actions with this patient, Ms. Tuma's license was suspended. The patient's physician had complained about her actions to the hospital, the hospital lodged a complaint with the Idaho Board of Nursing claiming interference with the patient–physician relationship, and a hearing was held. As a result of the hearing, it was determined that Ms. Tuma had engaged in "unprofessional conduct," and her license was suspended. Tuma appealed to the district court and requested a trial. The request for a trial was denied, and Ms. Tuma filed an appeal with the Supreme Court of Idaho. The court ruled in her favor, and her license was restored.

Discussions about Ms. Tuma's case appeared in the nursing literature and provoked a considerable amount of comment and interest in the role of the nurse in patient consent to treatment. What do you think Ms. Tuma's responsibilities were to the patient in this situation once she realized that the patient did not receive all the information necessary for informed consent to chemotherapy treatment?

Case 16-5
The Patient Who Waived Informed Consent

Mr. Fred Morrison, 49 years old, was admitted to the hospital for a cardiac catheterization. During the initial nursing assessment, Ms. Tricia Farraday asked Mr. Morrison why he was being admitted to the hospital. He stated that he was to have a "heart test" because his doctor thought the test was needed. When Ms. Farraday asked what kind of test his doctor wanted him to have, Mr. Morrison said he did not know but that his doctor could tell the nurse. When the assessment was finished, Ms. Farraday made a note that Mr. Morrison had a knowledge deficit about his condition and the reason for his admission. She recorded this information as part of her nursing diagnosis and conveyed the information to the nurse on the next shift.

The next morning, Ms. Farraday noticed that Mr. Morrison was being taken out of his room and sent to surgery. She inquired whether his physician or anyone else had visited him and discussed his diagnosis and the impending cardiac procedure. Checking the consent form in his chart, she noticed that it had not been signed. Ms. Farraday immediately called the resident and told him that the patient could not leave the unit until his consent form had been signed. The resident quickly came to the unit and explained the need for Mr. Morrison to sign the permit but did not explain the procedure. When the resident asked the nurse to witness the consent form, Ms. Farraday refused because the resident had not given the patient adequate information for an informed consent.

When she asked the patient what he would like to know about the procedure, Mr. Morrison claimed that he did not want to know very much. "I leave all that to my doctor," he stated. Ms. Farraday wondered whether a patient can avoid being informed and whether she ought to witness the consent form. In a situation where the patient did not want to be informed, must she still abide by the requirements for informed consent?

Commentary

These four patients all raise the question of just how much information should be disclosed for them to be adequately informed. The patient in Case 16-2, 87-year-old Mr. Ellsworth, whose body was being used as teaching material upon which medical students could practice intubation techniques, presses us to the limits of the consent requirement. If the purpose of getting consent is to protect the patient from harm, then it would seem to follow that if the patient cannot be harmed by an intervention, no consent is necessary. Mr. Ellsworth is the limiting case of a patient who cannot be harmed.

Still, the nurse, Mary Pope, may have had some concern beyond protecting Mr. Ellsworth from harm. She might have been worrying about the harm that could be done to the family waiting to visit their loved one a last time. Or she might have had in mind something beyond benefits and harms entirely. She may have been concerned about the infringement of Mr. Ellsworth's dignity or his right of self-determination.

In this particular case, the concern for self-determination or autonomy raises a problem. To what extent do the deceased have autonomy claims? To what extent could they have any claims if they are deceased? These problems are arising in ethics and law regarding the treatment of the deceased. They are philosophic questions raised when wills are read or when other wishes of the deceased are considered.

Critical Thinking Questions

1. In your opinion, to what extent do the deceased have autonomy claims?
2. To what extent could they have any claims if they are deceased and what is the basis for these claims?

At the level of law, there is a simple answer: All states have passed the Uniform Anatomical Gift Act (UAGA), which governs the use of corpses for medical purposes.[7] It is normally used in cases of transplantation of organs, but it also governs the use of the body for teaching and research as well as for other therapeutic uses beyond transplant. Among other things, it specifically requires that, before a body is used for any such purposes (including teaching) proper consent be obtained. This can come through the patient's permission in the form of a document signed while he or she is still competent or, if patient consent is not available, through the next of kin. This obviously did not happen in this case. Thus, practicing intubation techniques on Mr. Ellsworth's body can be described as use of the body without consent. The practice raises the question, however, of how much the patient or the next of kin might want to know before consenting. Obviously if Mr. Ellsworth had filled out a UAGA card some years before his death, he would have had no information at all at that time about how his body might be used. If his family had to be asked, how much and what kind of information about use of the body for teaching purposes should they be told?

A similar question arises in the case of Mr. Longwood, the 64-year-old school teacher suffering the after effects of abdominal surgery. In Mr. Longwood's case, it is clear that he, in some sense, consented to the surgery. Yet it is doubtful that he was adequately informed. His physician, Dr. Jankowski, appeared to take a position similar to that of Mr. Ellsworth's physician; that is, that information should be dispensed judiciously, only when it will do some good for the patient. It is obvious that information would have done no good for Mr. Ellsworth. It is more controversial whether it would have done Mr. Longwood any good.

Joellen Ullman, Mr. Longwood's nurse, might have disagreed with the judgment about how much should be disclosed. She might have concluded that Mr. Longwood would have been better off if he had been told about the potential surgical complications, respiratory problems, tubing, disfigurement, infections, and such.

Rather than the doctor and the nurse guessing whether Mr. Longwood would have been better off with or without the surgery, they might have reasoned that he should have enough information to exercise a choice about whether he wanted the surgery done—that is, they might have appealed to autonomy rather than beneficence. If they had done so, they would have to consider many of the same elements for consent outlined by the federal regulations that govern research. For example, they might have had to give a fair account of the potential risks as well as the benefits. They would have had to specify how much good the surgery could do as well as the reasonably foreseeable harms. And they would have had to spell out the alternatives so that the patient could make a choice among them. They would have had to ensure that he understood that he could refuse the surgery if he so desired. Review the elements of an informed consent as outlined in Table 15-1 on page 386 to see how many of them would apply to nonresearch settings, such as Mr. Longwood's surgery.

The fact that Mr. Longwood had a surrogate who approved of the physician's choice would be relevant if Mr. Longwood's own preferences were unknown, but most would consider the surrogate irrelevant if his preferences are known. Surrogates make decisions for individuals who previously had capacity using the substituted judgment standard. This standard obligates the surrogate to be a voice for the patient by making the decision the patient would most likely make—that is, one consistent with the patient's beliefs, values, decisional history, and previously expressed preferences. Nurses and other clinicians are often troubled when a surrogate appointed by patient begins to authorize decisions clearly incompatible with the known wishes of the patient. If the nurse cannot resolve these discrepancies help should be sought from an institutional ethics committee or other resource.

Even after the doctor and nurse agree on the ethical principle underlying informed consent and the elements of the consent process that need to be explained to the patient, there are still likely to be questions relating to how much detail needs be included. It is here that the controversy arises over the proper standard for disclosure in an adequately informed consent.

Under the traditional professional standard, it is possible that in both Mr. Ellsworth's and Mr. Longwood's cases there was an adequate consent. The critical question is whether these physicians' colleagues similarly situated would have disclosed anything more than they did. In Mr. Ellsworth's case, absolutely nothing was disclosed; yet the patient's attending physician might have been able to demonstrate that none of his colleagues similarly situated would have said anything either. Likewise, in Mr. Longwood's case, if the physician could demonstrate that none of his colleagues would have gone into any more detail about the potential side effects and complications of the surgery than he did, then the pro forma consent signed by Mr. Longwood might have been considered adequate. This question is really an empirical one that could be answered by asking a number of the physicians' colleagues.

The reasonable person standard for an informed consent would ask an entirely different question. It is not concerned about collegial consensus. Rather, it asks whether the patients (or the surrogate for the patient, in the case of Mr. Longwood) have adequate information to exercise a substantially autonomous choice about their care. Would reasonable patients scheduled for surgery for an abdominal mass in Mr. Longwood's condition want to know of the potential consequences and alternatives—including not doing the surgery? If they would, then the physician would have an obligation to tell Mr. Longwood about them. That question might also be answered empirically, but not by asking the physicians' colleagues. Rather it would be answered by asking a group of reasonable people whether they would want the information.

One of the problems with the reasonable person standard is raised in the cases of the patients cared for by Jolene Tuma and Tricia Farraday. Both nurses were caring for patients who seemed to have unusual information requirements. Ms. Tuma's patient seemed to want details about alternative treatments in which many reasonable people probably would not be interested. Ms. Farraday's patient, on the other hand, seemed to want virtually no information at all. In either case, it might be concluded that reasonable people would not want to know the amount and kind of information these patients wanted.

It is in situations like these that defenders of the subjective standard would be inclined to modify the reasonable person standard. Ms. Tuma's patient apparently had great interest in religious healing, unorthodox therapies, laetrile, and herbal remedies. If the professional standard were used by Ms. Tuma, there is no doubt that these alternative treatments would not be mentioned. Likewise, if Ms. Tuma were obligated to discuss only those pieces of information that the reasonable leukemia patient would want to know about, it is likely that these treatments would not be included.

But when Ms. Tuma is assessing what the reasonable patient similarly situated would want to know, does she take into account the patient's expressed interest in these nontraditional treatments? Does she have a duty to disclose what the reasonable leukemia patient with an interest in nontraditional remedies would want to know? Or do the patient's unusual interests make her an unreasonable patient?

Surely, neither Ms. Tuma nor any other healthcare professional has an obligation to try to guess whether her patients have unusual interests, such as those of her present patient. On the other hand, once those unusual interests are made known, some people would argue for the shift to the subjective standard, under which the duty of the professional is to disclose those things that a reasonable person would want to know adjusted for the unusual agenda of the present patient. Does that mean that Ms. Tuma had not only the right but also the duty to discuss with her patient the nonorthodox therapies?

The same logic might be applied to Tricia Farraday's patient, Fred Morrison. He was scheduled for cardiac catheterization, which he understood only as "heart tests." He obviously had little idea of the risks, the benefits, and the alternatives. He seemed not to have the information that the reasonable person would want to know, such as how much good the tests might do, how dangerous they are, and so forth.

Mr. Morrison is, in effect, waiving his right to be informed, expressing his confidence in his physician's judgment about the benefit–risk ratios and the wisdom of doing the tests. That may not be wise on Mr. Morrison's part. He may believe, erroneously, that deciding whether the test should be done is a medical matter to be left to an expert in cardiology. In fact, many subtle value judgments must be made. People with different risk-taking profiles might decide differently, especially in borderline cases. People with different life agendas might also decide differently. If Mr. Morrison desperately were to want to see a daughter graduate from college within the next week and is less concerned about long-term survival, he would make a different choice than if he had no crucial short-term agenda but wanted to achieve long-term survival. Those alternatives are trade-offs that are not made on the basis of cardiologic expertise. When Mr. Morrison leaves the matter up to his physician, he may simply be confused about the nature of the choice, and either his physician or someone else, such as his nurse, may have to set him straight.

On the other hand, he may understand exactly what he is doing when he waives his right to give an informed consent. When he opts instead for what could be called an uninformed consent, he may be saying that he knows his cardiologist's values well and that he knows that his cardiologist understands his own risk-taking profile and life agenda. If that is so, then perhaps it is not entirely irrational for Mr. Morrison to yield the decision making to his cardiologist.

We are still left with the question of whether it is ethical to waive receipt of the information necessary to make a real autonomous choice in such a situation. Some people might conclude that there is a moral duty to face life's critical choices and, therefore, that it is morally irresponsible to give over such choices to someone else. Maybe Ms. Farraday holds such a view.

Even if there is such a duty to make critical choices oneself, it does not follow that a nurse or a physician has the right to impose information on a patient who is consciously trying to refuse it. If the subjective standard is applied to Mr. Morrison, it may turn out that his information requirements are much less than what the reasonable person standard or the professional standard would require. In that case, holders of the subjective standard would accept Mr. Morrison's waiver.

Critical Thinking Question

If you were Ms. Farraday, would you have witnessed Mr. Morrison's consent form? Why or why not?

Comprehension and Voluntariness

Even if all of the kinds of information (the elements of disclosure) are provided and even if the proper standard for which information must be disclosed is used, still other requirements must be met. The information must be comprehended, and the one giving the consent must be capable of making substantially autonomous, voluntary choices.

Even assuming that the person is not constrained in his or her choices by a lack of freedom or by internal limitations in capacity to choose, it is still possible that information could be presented in a form or in a manner in which the individual does not comprehend. The only fail-proof guarantee that comprehension exists is to have patients repeat in their own words what they understand to be consenting to or refusing.

Decisions should be free of coercive influences. There is a continuum among persuasion, manipulation, and coercion, and nurses may find themselves discerning when best efforts to persuade a patient to choose a beneficial treatment become manipulative or coercive. It is not unusual for patients who love their families and who have gratitude to a healthcare team to feel conflicted about a desire to transition to purely palliative goals and to discontinue life-sustaining treatment, while at the same time they do not want to disappoint family members or professional caregivers who are not ready for them to "give up."

There are at least two ways in which a consent may be inadequately voluntary. Some potential decision makers may have their options constrained by external forces or pressures. This is especially relevant for those in confining institutions such as boarding schools, the military, prisons, and nursing homes. It may also apply to patients who have few choices because of a lack of resources. The first case in this section involves this situation of inadequate voluntariness. The second way in which choices can be inadequately voluntary is that there may be internal incapacities on the part of the one asked to consent. Psychiatric patients and the mentally retarded might be so constrained. So might a patient temporarily incapable of making voluntary choice because of drugs or medication affecting her or his ability to think clearly. The second case in this section presents such a problem.

Case 16-6
Immunizing Soldiers in Preparation for Warfare

Richard Nils is a first lieutenant in the Army Nurse Corps who was mobilized for Desert Storm in 1991. He helped immunize soldiers in Germany before they were sent to Saudi Arabia. At the time, he did not question what he was doing. Immunizing the troops in preparation for battle is one duty of the military nurse, and Lt. Nils was happy to be involved in such an important event. The immunizations included a botulinum toxin vaccine that had not been approved by the FDA for such use. Although this vaccine had existed for many years and had seen limited uses for medical researchers and others at unusual risk for exposure to botulinum toxin, no one had tested it in a situation like Desert Storm, where exposure could theoretically be intentional and at levels not previously envisioned. For these reasons, the FDA was not willing to certify that the botulinum toxin vaccine was known to be safe and effective for this purpose.

Now, four years later, he realizes that many soldiers involved in Desert Storm, within a year after the battle, began reporting a collection of neurological symptoms that suggested exposure to a harmful substance. The Army Medical Corps has not officially recognized the cause of these symptoms, although it is commonly referred to as Desert Storm syndrome. One suggested cause of these symptoms is the immunizations that the soldiers received before going to Saudi Arabia. It seems that at least one of the immunizing agents used in 1991 was not fully tested for use in human subjects. Neither Lt. Nils nor the soldiers knew this at the time. They assumed the military physicians knew what they were doing and that they were protecting them from potential harm while on the ground in Saudi Arabia. Lt. Nils wonders whether giving immunizations, particularly ones that had not been tested adequately, to soldiers without their consent was really ethical and whether he, as a nurse, should have done it.

Commentary

Lt. Nils needs to decide when, if ever, it is appropriate to treat patients without their consent. This case is unusual in that it occurs in the military. The military has unusual authority to suspend normal constitutional rights. For example, although we have seen that competent civilian patients have a legal right to refuse any medical treatment offered for their own welfare, the military has long claimed that this right of refusal does not always apply to its employees. Although that legal stance is open to some dispute, it is generally assumed that commanders can order troops under them to undergo medical treatments against their will. The reasoning is that providing such treatment may be necessary for the military mission.

Because the appeal is to the interests of others (the national interest in the military mission), we might view this as a special case of overruling the usual norms of consent in order to serve the interests of others. In the civilian world, if someone were to claim the right to treat against the individual's approval, that patient would have extensive legal and social protections, such as the right to challenge the decision in court or to appeal to entities such as hospital ethics committees within the healthcare system. In the military, those rights are severely limited.

Nevertheless, even though the military has theoretical authority to order its personnel to be treated without their consent, that does not mean that doing so is in all cases wise or ethical. Many available medical treatments that do not appear essential to the military mission could be offered to military personnel. Surely, employees of the military ought to be able to refuse therapies that have no impact on military objectives. For example, it is increasingly recognized that victims of war injuries who are being treated by military healthcare services and are so critically ill that they are almost certainly going to die regardless of treatment should have the right to refuse life support based on their personal beliefs and values. If the patient is going to die anyway, such refusals can hardly cause critical harm to the military. (In fact, they may actually help the mission by freeing up healthcare personnel and resources for other purposes.)

In Lt. Nils's case it might appear that immunizing troops from a potentially deadly disease really does contribute to the military mission. However, that issue is more complex than it may appear. Consider first whether a soldier who was a religious objector to routine immunizations (for measles, mumps, or tetanus) should be able to refuse. The first feature of such situations worth noting is that, contrary to common belief, the person most at risk from such refusals is actually the patient himself—the one doing the refusing. In fact, if the immunizations were completely effective, even in the case of infectious disease no one who had accepted immunization would be at risk of contagion. (Of course, not all immunizations are 100% effective, but the risk of contagion from isolated cases of refusers is minimal in a world in which almost everyone else is immunized.)

Still, in the military, a religious objector could cause serious harm to the military mission by refusing to be immunized, even if he is the only one who contracts the disease in question. He would be lost from service, at least temporarily, and healthcare personnel would have to attend to him rather than fulfilling other important tasks.

This suggests that, in the case of a clearly effective standard medical treatment, once one accepts the legitimacy of suspensions of civil rights for military personnel, one such right that could be suspended could be the right to consent or refuse consent to treatments.

Now, how should this reasoning be applied to Lt. Nils, who has to decide about the ethics of administering the botulinum toxin vaccine without consent? It is, of course, unfair to evaluate Lt. Nils's situation in light of more recent concerns that suggest to some people that the botulinum toxin vaccine may, in fact, have caused medical harm. Safety information was not known at the time. In fact, that is why the FDA had not accepted this use of the vaccine.

The problem is, how can the military appeal to the interests of others (the national interest in the military mission) as a justification for omitting consent for the administration of this vaccine while at the same time the FDA is refusing to acknowledge that the vaccine is safe and effective? It seems that the very information needed to support the claim that the administration is crucial to the national mission is not available—at least according to the national agency responsible for deciding whether drugs and biologicals are known to be adequately safe and effective. There seems to be an incongruity when one national agency claims that the administration is crucial to the national mission and another claims that it is not known whether the vaccine will work safely and effectively in this setting.

If the FDA had reassessed the situation and concluded that the vaccine was safe and effective in this setting, would it have been acceptable for a nurse, one whose professional norms seem to require respect for the autonomy of patients, to cooperate with his employer in the administration of the vaccine without adequate consent? Is it acceptable to subordinate the consent requirement for important social purposes in cases in which the proposed therapy is clearly likely to work? If so, can that same reasoning be extended to cases in which there is some reason to think the treatment will work, but it has not yet been shown to be safe and effective?

Normally, there are theoretical reasons and animal data to support the belief that experimental treatments that are ready for clinical trials may work even though they have not been fully tested. If that is the case, some would hold that it is not irrational to decide to try these treatments, especially in desperate situations in which no other known treatment is available. The more desperate the situation, the more reasonable such uses may be. In this case, there was a tradeoff between the concern about the unknown risks of the vaccine and the unknown potential benefits (to both the individual and society). Is the FDA the group that should be making the judgment that the vaccine is adequately safe and effective in this situation? Is the military command the one to make this call? Is the nurse? Or is the individual soldier?

In the cases in Chapters 4 and 5, we discovered how controversial treating patients on grounds of social benefit can be. We particularly wondered whether it should be the clinician, normally committed to the patient's welfare, who should make the decision to treat. Now it should be clear that, just as the clinician has a traditional commitment to the individual patient that could distort his or her judgment, so also military personnel, who have a traditional commitment to the social interest (even at the expense of normal civil rights), might also have distorting commitments.

Critical Thinking Questions

1. Do you think that a person automatically waives some of his or her personal rights (privacy, informed consent to treatment, etc.) merely by becoming a member of the armed services? Why or why not?

2. In what ways, if any, can the military obligation to follow orders compromise a military nurse's obligation to benefit and not harm patients? When these obligations conflict which do you think takes priority and why?

Case 16-7
Consent from a Sedated Patient

Mrs. Jorczak was a 54-year-old female diagnosed with carcinoma of the colon. Alert, oriented, and intelligent, she understood her diagnosis. Surgery was recommended, and she agreed to surgical excision of the tumor and whatever else could be done for her. Following surgery, she experienced many complications and remained in the surgical intensive care unit (SICU) for 4 weeks. She experienced cardiac failure, temporary respiratory failure, renal failure, sepsis, dehiscence, and she required multiple surgical procedures. As her complications continued, Mrs. Jorczak began to question the wisdom of the many procedures ordered for her. Her family, however, encouraged her to do whatever the physician felt was necessary.

One day, after being extubated and put on low-level vasopressors, she was asked to sign a permit for revision of her colostomy and removal of scar tissue from her previous surgical procedures. Mrs. Jorczak refused, stating that she could no longer tolerate any procedures and that she wanted to die a peaceful death. The nurse who was usually assigned to care for Mrs. Jorczak related the patient's wishes to the resident. He called the attending physician, who ordered a stat dose of valium 10 mg IM for the patient. One half hour later, the attending physician visited the patient and had her sign the permit. He then stopped by the nurses' desk and asked that the patient be prepped for surgery. The nurse asked: "Is this patient's consent valid?"

Commentary

Mrs. Jorczak appears to be the victim of an attending physician who is confused about what it means to obtain a consent from a patient. He may even use the term "consenting patient," as if getting consent means coaxing the patient to sign a sheet of paper. However, that clearly is not what consent means. It means a voluntary choice by a substantially autonomous agent. Was Mrs. Jorczak making such a choice? In recent years, there has been great effort to distinguish a legal notion of consent, which entails the event of obtaining a signature on a consent form from the ethical understanding of consent being a process involving adequate disclosure, capacity, comprehension, and voluntariness.

It is clear that patients in principle have a right to change their minds. The mere fact that the patient in this case originally refused the surgery for revision of her colostomy and removal of scar tissue does not foreclose forever her right to consent to the procedure. By the same token, had she originally consented to the surgery, she would retain the right to withdraw her consent at any time before the procedure took place.

But in Mrs. Jorczak's case, the second so-called consent—the one in which she might be said to have changed her mind—is certainly suspect. The first problem is that it was obtained while she was sedated. Generally, important decisions made while the mind is altered chemically should be viewed as suspect. If Mrs. Jorczak were permanently in a mentally compromised state (not by sedation, but by brain pathology) and that were the only communication we had from her, the case would be complicated. It could be argued that the suspect consent from the clouded mind was the best that could be done. In such a circumstance, we might argue that her approval was adequate. Alternatively, we could insist that she was incapable of substantially voluntary choice and that a guardian should be appointed for her.

In Mrs. Jorczak's case, however, we have additional information. We know what she said when her mind was clear. There is good reason to believe that her first decision was carefully thought out over a long period of time. There may even be reason to suspect that the sedation was given precisely to force the consent out of her. In that case, the nurse and the attending physician may have obtained nothing more than a piece of paper with a signature. The nurse asks if the consent is valid. She might have asked whether there was any consent at all.

What steps should be taken by an attending physician or a nurse who believes that Mrs. Jorczak needs to have the surgery even though she is unwilling to consent to it? Could they try to get Mrs. Jorczak declared incompetent? If so, on what grounds?

Consent for Patients Who Lack Decision Capacity

One strategy suggested in the two previous cases was to attempt to have the patients declared incompetent so that treatment might be rendered without their personal consent. Incompetent patients need medical treatments. They cannot themselves consent to treatment. Some provision must be made for them to be treated without their own consent.

We have already seen that if the patient who now lacks decision-making capacity was previously capable of being self-determining, the standard of substituted judgment applies. A surrogate must try to decide what the patient would have chosen based on the formerly competent patient's values. If, however, the patient lacking capacity is an infant, small child, or severely retarded adult, or if no one knows the individual, the best interests standard applies. Ethicist Loretta Kopelman analyzes the meaning of the best interests standard into several necessary and jointly sufficient conditions showing it:

1. Is an "umbrella" standard, used differently in different contexts;
2. Has objective and subjective features;
3. Is more than people's intuitions about how to rank potential benefits and risks in deciding for others but also includes evidence, established rights, duties, and thresholds of acceptable care; and
4. Can have different professional, medical, moral and legal uses, as in this dispute.[8]

Even if the function of the surrogate is to try to do what is best for the incompetent one, sometimes the judgment made by the surrogate is controversial. Sometimes he or she may sincerely try to do what is best but chooses a course with which many people would disagree. The first case in this section deals with a young girl whose parents made a controversial judgment about her best interest.

Case 16-8
The Case of the Overweight Child

Tracey Waters is a 7-year-old girl who has been overweight since she was 2 years old. She has been followed by the well baby clinic and public health nurses in her community for her weight problem, but all attempts at weight reduction and family teaching have failed. A second grader, Tracey now weighs 128 pounds. Her teacher had discussed Tracey's weight problem with Jane Seymour, the school health nurse, several weeks ago. Today, however, she reports that Tracey is beginning to fall asleep during classroom activities. When she called Mrs. Waters, she learned that Tracey is a restless sleeper at home and often wakes the family 3–4 times per night with irregular and noisy breathing.

Mrs. Seymour, finding Tracey's parents uncooperative in discussing their child's weight problems and classroom sleeping, has notified the school authorities. Upon the school's recommendation, the parents agree to a physical examination for Tracey by the health department physician. The physician recommends that Tracey be admitted to the hospital for controlled weight reduction and follow-up care. Mr. and Mrs. Waters refuse to agree to this intervention, stating that "Tracey is a lovable, chubby child, and we love her just the way she is." Mrs. Seymour is now in a dilemma. Should she assist school authorities in making a Child Protective Services referral on Tracey's behalf? Being an experienced school health nurse and having known the Waters family for many years, she wonders whether it would be morally justified to attempt to override the parents and whether overriding the family's decision in this matter is really in Tracey's long-term best interest.

Case 16-9
Refusing Treatment for a Delusional Parent

Rosa Green, a 60-year-old woman with symptoms of negativism and paranoia, is transferred from a medical unit to the psychiatric unit of a large medical center. The nursing staff members assess her to be delusional and capable of harming herself while delusional (not suicidal). Her 38-year-old son, her only living relative, is asked to consent to the use of psychotropic medications in treating his mother. Mr. Green refuses because his mother experienced multiple side effects from similar medications several years ago. Mrs. Green is discharged without treatment 12 hours later. The nurses question whether action should have been taken to initiate treatment in Mrs. Green's case without the son's consent.

Case 16-10
Involuntary Sterilization of a Problem Teenager[4]

Sheila Myers, staff nurse on a busy surgical unit, received an admission from the emergency room. The patient, 16-year-old Lisa Duncan, had an elevated body temperature (101.6°F) and significant abdominal pain. The admitting note revealed that Lisa had been sexually active since age 13, had one living child (age 2 years), and did not consistently use birth control methods. A pregnancy test performed in the ER was negative. Lisa was accompanied by her mother.

Both surgical and GYN consults recommended an exploratory laparotomy. Immediate surgery was ordered, and an operative permit was placed on her chart. The permit was for "exploratory laparoscopy, laparotomy, possible appendectomy, possible bilateral salpingo-oophorectomy, possible hysterectomy." The attending physician took the chart into the room, talked with both the mother and the daughter, the daughter signed the permit, and Mrs. Myers prepared the patient for surgery. While in the patient's room inserting a Foley catheter, Mrs. Myers asked the patient if she understood the nature of her impending surgery. The patient understood that she might have an appendectomy, but she did not seem

---

[4]Case supplied by Mary Ann Turjanica, MSN, RN. Used with permission.

to realize that she might have a hysterectomy and a bilateral salpingo-oophorectomy (S&O) and did not understand what these procedures entailed.

When the nurse explained what these procedures were, the patient became very emotional and said that she would not permit them because she wanted to have a family in the future. Mrs. Myers then discussed the matter with the patient's mother. The mother realized that an S&O and a hysterectomy were possible outcomes of the surgery and told Mrs. Myers that in view of her daughter's sexual activity, "it might not be a bad thing. I don't want her to give me any more kids to care for." She went on to relate that she was raising six other children in addition to Lisa's 2-year-old daughter and that it was very hard to cope with all these responsibilities.

Mrs. Myers called the resident and explained that the patient did not understand her surgery and that she thought the consent for surgery was probably invalid. The resident came to the unit to talk to the patient and later asked the nurse why she had gone into detail about the surgery to be performed. Mrs. Myers explained that there seemed to be some difficulty between the patient and her mother, and that Lisa did not understand that she might have a hysterectomy. After talking with the mother and realizing that the patient was 16 years of age, the resident drew up another permit with the same wording and asked the mother to sign it. When she did without question, Mrs. Myers was not sure that there was anything more that she could do. Could a mother permit involuntary sterilization of her teenage daughter under these conditions?

Commentary

Mrs. Seymour, the nurse dealing with the overweight child in Case 16-8, is asking the right questions. She recognizes that it will be difficult to determine whether seeking intervention from Child Protective Services will really be in Tracey's long-term interest. It will certainly be disruptive of family dynamics. Her parents will be treated as neglectful or abusive toward their child. Of course, it may not be that they are malevolent; it is possible for the most dedicated parents to be abusive or neglectful. It happens in many medical situations when parents have unusual views of what is in their child's interest. Nevertheless, giving the parents this label and forcing them to confront protective agency authorities will be traumatic—not only for the parents, but for Tracey.

A more complex question is whether it is morally the right thing to do. When the parents refused to give permission for their daughter's hospitalization, they were basing their judgment on some set of beliefs and values that apparently led them to the conclusion that it was not in their daughter's interest. Possibly they had ulterior motives. That might disqualify them from the decision-making role, but there does not seem to be any evidence that an ulterior motive is behind their choice. Rather, they seem simply to believe that their daughter does not need such a radical treatment and that she is just a "lovable child."

Assuming that their motives are good but that many people would disagree with their judgment, a complex ethical issue is raised for Mrs. Seymour. Is it the role of Child Protective Services to ensure that the parents really do what is best, or is it sufficient that they choose a course that is tolerable? It may be that both hospitalization and the parents' alternative are choices that some persons in the parents' position would make. It is not even clear how a social agency would go about deciding exactly which is best.

How much discretion should any family have in making these choices for its incompetent members? If the family must do literally what is best, it would have no discretion at all. If, on the other hand, it has discretion, what is the basis of that discretion?

Some are now arguing that families are important units within society and that they need considerable freedom to function well.[9] Some courts are even recognizing parental authority to refuse medical treatments for their children on these grounds.[10]

At the same time, parents cannot possibly have unlimited freedom of choice when it comes to the welfare of their children. Some decisions are simply beyond what can be tolerated. Cases in which members of the Jehovah's Witnesses refuse permission for their children to have blood transfusions are handled by the courts in this way. Treatments are ordered in those cases, even against religious objections of parents. The critical question is, at what point have the parents gone beyond what can be tolerated, beyond what can be called the "limit of reason?" That may be the question Mrs. Seymour must answer before she can determine whether to seek to have the Waterses' decision about Tracey's hospitalization overturned.

Critical Thinking Question

If you were Mrs. Seymour, the school health nurse, would you participate in making a referral to Child Protective Services on Tracey's behalf? Why or why not?

The case of Rosa Green, the 60-year-old delusional woman transferred to the psychiatric ward, presents problems similar to those of Tracey Waters. The nursing staff members, whether they realize it or not, made a critical decision when they asked Mrs. Green's son to consent (or give permission) for treatment with psychotropic medications. Normally, as an adult, Mrs. Green would have the right to consent or refuse consent for treatment. The nursing staff apparently has made the decision that she is not competent to consent or refuse consent for the proposed treatment. On what basis do physicians or nurses have authority to make this determination? Normally, if a patient is treated as incompetent, it is either because the patient falls into a category of people presumed incompetent because they fail the function standard (e.g., children, like 7-year-old Tracey Waters) or because the patient has been declared incompetent by a court. Private citizens are on shaky ground when they take it upon themselves to treat a person as incompetent. Sometimes persons are so obviously incompetent, such as when they are comatose, that no question is raised. But Mrs. Green is not that obviously incompetent. Asking her son's permission implies not only that she is obviously incompetent, but also that her son is her guardian. Both assumptions could be debated.

Once nursing staff members have decided to treat her son as her guardian, they are, in principle, committed to living with his choice, at least if he is within the limits of reason. Had he agreed to the administration of the psychotropic agents, his judgment would never have been questioned. But if he gives a controversial answer, he is in a position very much like that of Tracey Waters's parents. Once again the key question is not whether he gave the best answer, but rather whether he gave a tolerable answer. Was his answer tolerable, and what should be done if it was not?

The case of Lisa Duncan, the teenager causing problems for her mother, raises similar issues. If we could assume that her mother was her guardian and that she had the power to consent to treatments—just like the Waters family and, arguably, Mrs. Green's son—then we would need to determine only whether her mother's judgment was acceptable. Lisa Duncan, however, is 16, not 7. And she is not conspicuously delusional, like Mrs. Green. She is close to the age at which her mother would have no legal role in her medical care. Should Lisa herself be expected to give consent for her surgery? That appears to be what the staff members believed when the attending physician originally asked her to sign. It is questionable whether they can change tactics and ask her mother to sign once they discover that Lisa wants to make a choice they do not like.

But were they correct in the first place in assuming that Lisa could consent to her own surgery? Although she is almost at the age of majority, she has not reached it. She is still a minor and in normal situations would probably not be capable of giving a valid consent. There are special situations in which minors can consent to medical treatment, such as when they are emancipated—that is, legally independent of a parent's care and responsibility. They can also be determined to be "mature minors," capable of understanding the nature of the issues at stake and, therefore, treated as an adult for purposes of giving consent. Designation as a mature minor requires a judicial determination, however.

There is a third situation in which minors may approve of medical treatments without parental permission. Certain groups of treatments, including, in many jurisdictions, contraception, abortion, venereal disease treatment, and sterilization, can be authorized by the minor without parental approval. The reason for these laws is controversial. Some interpret them as saying that the minor is capable of giving a real consent—that is a substantially autonomous judgment—in these areas. It seems strange, however, that the minor could give a valid consent in these areas but not in others. The other possibility is that even though the minor cannot give a valid consent, she or he can be treated without parental involvement because the very process of getting parental involvement might discourage the adolescent from getting needed treatment. That would imply that there is not a real autonomous consent, but nevertheless there is an approval for the treatment that is legally valid even without parental permission. Recently, the role of parental notification and approval has become a major issue in state and federal litigation over abortion as well as sterilization and contraception. States have been permitted to impose requirements for parental notification and/or consent provided there is not an undue burden on the minor seeking services. Some states permit judges to review individual situations to ensure that the minor will not be victimized by a disapproving parent. In some states, it is legally acceptable for judges to grant consent in cases in which parental involvement would prove too risky for the minor.[11]

Would that same logic work in Lisa's case? In her case, the parent was actually involved and made a judgment purportedly in her best interest. It might be argued that the parent was really more concerned about her own welfare, especially the burdens of raising Lisa's children. Should that be grounds for removing the parent from the decision-making role in the sterilization? Assuming that Lisa's mother was working at least in part out of a concern for Lisa's welfare and that her judgment was within reason, what should Sheila Myers make of the fact that Lisa, herself, obviously does not approve? Should a minor always have the right to veto a medical procedure approved by the parent? If not, should 16-year-olds? Should all minors have the right to veto their parents' decisions on certain critical medical issues such as sterilizations? If so, which ones?

These questions arise in decisions made not only about overweight children, delusional adults, and sterilization procedures for adolescents, but also in even more critical decisions that are literally matters of life and death. The problems of consent and **treatment refusal** for terminal illnesses involve many of these same issues. They will be explored in the next chapter.

ENDNOTES

1. Appelbaum, P. S., Lidz, C. W., & Meisel, A. (1987). *Informed consent: Legal theory and clinical practice.* New York: Oxford University Press; Berg, J. W., Appelbaum, P. S., Lidz, C. W., & Parker, L. S. (2001). *Informed consent: Legal theory and clinical practice.* New York: Oxford University Press; Faden, R., Beauchamp, T. L., & King, N. N. P. (1986). *A history and theory of informed consent.* New York: Oxford University Press; Grisso, T., & Appelbaum, P. S. (1998). *Assessing competence to consent to treatment: A guide for physicians and other health professionals.* New York: Oxford University Press; Katz, J. (1984). *The silent world of doctor and patient.* New York: The Free Press; Lidz, C. W., Meisel, A., Zerubavel, E., Carter, M., Sestak, R. M., & Roth, L. H. (1984). *Informed consent: A study of decision making in psychiatry.* New York: The Guilford Press; President's Commission for the Study of Ethical Problems in Medicine and Biomedical and Behavioral Research. (1982). *Making health care decisions: A report on the ethical and legal implications of informed consent in the patient–practitioner relationship* (Vol. 3). Washington, DC: U.S. Government Printing Office.

2. Schloendorff v. Society of New York Hospital, 211 N.Y. 125, 105 N.E. 92, 95 (1914).

3. Natanson v. Kline, 186 Kan. 393, 350 P.2d 1093 (1960). (1972). In J. Katz, A. M. Capron, & E. S. Glass (Eds.), *Experimentation with human beings* (pp. 529–535). New York: Russell Sage Foundation.

4. American Nurses Association. (2001). *Code of ethics for nurses with interpretive statements* (provision 1.4, p. 8). Washington, DC: Author.

5. U.S. Department of Health and Human Services, National Institutes of Health, Office of Protection from Research Risks. (2001, November 13). Protection of human subjects. *Code of Federal Regulations, 45*(46), 46.116.

6. Faden, R., & Beauchamp, T. L., & King, N. N. P. (1986). *A history and theory of informed consent.* New York: Oxford University Press; President's Commission for the Study of Ethical Problems in Medicine and Biomedical and Behavioral Research. (1982). *Making health care decisions: A report on the ethical and legal implications of informed consent in the patient–practitioner relationship* (Vol. 1, pp. 102–104). Washington, DC: U.S. Government Printing Office.

7. Sadler, A. M., Sadler, B. L., & Stason, E. B. (1968, December 9). The uniform anatomical gift act. *Journal of the American Medical Association, 201*, 2501–2506.

8. Kopelman, L. M. (2007). Using the best interests standard to decide whether to test children for untreatable, late-onset genetic diseases. *Journal of Medicine and Philosophy, 32*(4), 375–394. See also Kopelman, L. M. (2007). Analyzing the best interests standard. *ASBH Exchange, 10*(3), 1, 11.

9. President's Commission for the Study of Ethical Problems in Medicine and Biomedical and Behavioral Research. (1982). *Deciding to forgo life-sustaining treatment: Ethical, medical, and legal issues in treatment decisions* (p. 215). Washington, DC: U.S. Government Printing Office.

10. In the matter of Phillip Becker, 92 Cal. App. 3d 796, 156 Cal Rptr. 48 (1979), Cert. denied sub nom. Bothman v. Warrant B., 445 U.S. 949 (1980).

11. American Medical Association, Council of Ethical and Judicial Affairs. (1993). Mandatory parental consent to abortion. *Journal of the American Medical Association, 269*(17), 82–86; Benshoof, J. (1993). Planned Parenthood v. Casey: The impact of the new undue burden standard on reproductive health care. *Journal of the American Medical Association, 269*(17), 2249–2257; Capron, A. M. (1992). Privacy: Dead and gone? *The Hastings Center Report, 22*(1), 43–45; Planned Parenthood of Southeastern Pennsylvania v. Casey. (1992, June 29). *U.S. Supreme Court Reporter, 112* , 2791–2885.

Chapter 17

Death and Dying

Other Cases Involving Death and Dying

Key Terms
Competent patient
Definition of death
Formerly competent patient
Futility
Never-competent patient
Normative futility
Palliative sedation
Physiological futility
Professional integrity
Surrogate

Objectives
1. Describe three ways to define death.
2. Describe three ethical issues that arise in end-of-life decision making for formerly competent patients.
3. Describe two types of futility judgments.
4. Identify ethical issues in end-of-life decision making by surrogates or healthcare proxies.
5. Apply ethical principles to end-of-life decision making for a never-competent patient.

Care of seriously ill and dying patients and their families presents nurses with some of the most difficult and dramatic ethical challenges they will face.[1] All of the basic principles introduced in Part II are relevant to the ethics of care for the dying patient. Many of the arguments are carried out in terms of what will benefit the patient or protect the patient from harm—that is, in terms of the principles of beneficence and nonmaleficence. On the other hand, much of the debate over the right to refuse treatment has been centered on the principle of autonomy. Patients, so it is argued, should have the right to self-determination, even regarding matters of life and death. Likewise, the general concept of respect and the related principles of truth telling and fidelity often apply in situations where patients are dying. What they should be told about a terminal diagnosis and whether family members can be consulted before they are told are issues related to these principles, discussed in Chapters 6, 7, and 8. The principle of the sanctity of human life introduces many issues that are often seen as directly relevant to the care of the terminally ill patient. The cases in Chapter 10 explored the question of whether there is an independent moral duty to avoid killing other human beings and, if so, whether that duty prohibits omitting life-prolonging treatments or only prohibits active killing, even on grounds of mercy. Those cases also examined the questions of whether withdrawal of treatment is to be thought of more as an omission or an action, whether a distinction can be made between direct and indirect killing, and whether some treatments (such as medical provision of nutrition and hydration) are so basic that they can never justifiably be omitted. All of these issues are important in end-of-life care.

The care of the terminally ill also raises some issues that are usually formulated in terms unique to these patients. The first is: What role ought the **definition of death** to play in the care of such patients? In this chapter's first case, we shall see that one of the first problems faced by the nurse may be whether to treat the patient as dead or as a still living, though terminally ill, patient. We shall see that calling a patient dead is very different legally and ethically from deciding to allow a living patient to die. There are certain procedures (e.g., organ removal for transplantation, research uses of the cadaver under the Uniform Anatomical Gift Act [UAGA], and the use of a corpse for teaching purposes) that can only be initiated after the person is pronounced dead. Some patients who are still alive, however, may appropriately be allowed to die, at least according to some systems of ethical thought.

Even if there is agreement that the nurse's patient is still alive, there is still reason to ask whether treatment should continue. These questions arise first in the case of the *competent patient* or the patient who expressed wishes while competent. Various mechanisms, sometimes called living wills or advance directives, are used by patients to express their wishes about terminal care. The nurse may face problems when he or she knows that a treatment-refusing living will has been executed, yet either the nurse or some other member of the healthcare team believes that treatment should continue. Beginning in 1976, state laws have been passed giving certain terminally ill patients the right to refuse treatments. Now almost all states have passed some such legislation, and a federal law requires that patients at the time of admission to a hospital be informed of their right to have an advance directive.[2] Furthermore, the nursing profession asserts that nurses have a major role in the implementation of this legislation.[3] Questions still arise, however, when advance directives do not completely comply with the law or when, even though they do comply, some members of the healthcare team believe that advance directives should not be followed. Cases 17-2 through 17-4 deal with competent and **formerly competent patients** who have expressed their wishes about end-of-life care.

The most complex cases involve terminally or critically ill patients who have never been competent to express their wishes (because they are infants, children, or mentally retarded) or who, though once competent, have never made their wishes known. In these cases, someone must take responsibility for deciding about their care. In some states (such as New Mexico, Arkansas, and Virginia) the law makes provisions for some other person, normally the next of kin, to become the **surrogate** decision maker or agent for the patient. In other states, the next of kin is presumed to be the appropriate surrogate and is asked whether treatment should continue.

We are learning about the limits of such surrogate decision making. The range of discretion for surrogates is not as great as that of substantially autonomous competent patients. However, it appears that surrogates should be entitled to some discretion as well. Proposals to deal with incompetent patients have included roles for the physician, the family, the courts, and special committees at the hospital level, as well as for instructions written by the patient while competent. The nurse's role in these decisions can be critical when she or he is the only one in a position to be aware that decisions are being made that may be contrary to the interests or wishes of the patient. The nurse's role as advocate for the patient comes into play here. The nurse may play other roles, as well. Increasingly, nurses are asked to serve on hospital ethics committees. The cases in the third section of this chapter (Cases 17-5 through 17-9) explore the issues of surrogate decision making.

Finally, there may be times when the limits on scarce resources do not permit the healthcare team to do all that the competent patient wants done or that the surrogate for the incompetent patient requests. Usually these issues arise when the desired treatment is very expensive or time consuming and offers little hope of benefit. Such questions are arising more and more frequently. Cases 17-10 through 17-12 explore these problems.

The Definition of Death

Medical technology has advanced to the point where it is sometimes difficult to tell whether a patient is dead or alive. The problem first arose when mechanical ventilators and other support systems permitted prolonged maintenance of patients suffering severe head trauma or prolonged periods of anoxia. Because of ventilator support, these patients could continue respiring indefinitely. With a source of oxygen, their heartbeats could often be maintained, as well. They were alive according to traditional definitions of death based on the irreversible loss of all vital functions.

This became a practical problem in the late 1960s when organ transplantation, especially heart transplantation, produced a need for organs from deceased patients whose organs were still viable. Although the need for organs was the most dramatic stimulus to the definition of death debate, many other less dramatic decisions hinged on whether the patient was alive or dead. It is not normal practice to use nursing and medical services to maintain cadavers. Deciding whether the patient is dead may determine when treatment will be stopped. Critics emphasize, however, that often it is appropriate to stop at least some medical interventions while the patient is still alive. The UAGA, which regulates the use of human tissues from newly dead individuals, authorizes use of body parts not only for transplantation, but also for research, education, and other therapeutic uses. Even if no concrete use of the newly dead body is anticipated, it is important for family members and healthcare personnel to know when the individual should be treated as dead and when as alive.

Case 17-1 illustrates the challenges of determining death.

Case 17-1

When Parents Refuse to Give Up[1]

Nine-year-old Yusef Camp began experiencing symptoms soon after eating a pickle bought from a street vendor. He felt dizzy and fell down, he could not use his legs, and he began to scream. By 10:00 P.M., he was hallucinating and was transported to the DC General Hospital by ambulance. He went into convulsions. His stomach was pumped, and they found traces of marijuana and possibly PCP. He soon stopped breathing, and by the next morning, brain scans showed no activity.

Four months later, Yusef's condition had not changed. The physicians believed his brain was not functioning and wanted to pronounce him dead based on brain criteria. Several difficulties were encountered, however. First, there was some disagreement among the medical personnel over whether his brain function had ceased completely. Second, at that time the District of Columbia had no law authorizing death pronouncement based on brain criteria. It was not clear that physicians could use death as grounds for stopping treatment. Most important, Ronald Camp, the boy's father, protested vigorously any suggestion that treatment be stopped. A devout Muslim, he said, "I could walk up and say unplug him; but for the rest of my life I would be thinking, was I too hasty? Could he have recovered if I had given it another 6 months or a year? I'm leaving it in Almighty God's hand to let it take whatever flow it will."

The nurses involved in Yusef's care faced several problems. Maggots were found growing in Yusef's lungs and nasal passages. His right foot and ankle became gangrenous. He showed no response to noises or painful stimuli. The nurses had the responsibility not only for maintaining the respiratory tract and the gangrenous limb, but also for providing the intensive nursing care needed to maintain Yusef in debilitated condition on life support systems. Had the aggressive care been serving any purpose, they would have been willing to provide it no matter how repulsive the boy's condition was and in spite of there being many other patients desperately needing their attention. However, some of the nurses caring for Yusef were convinced that they were doing no good whatsoever for the boy. They believed they were only consuming enormous amounts of time and hospital resources in what appeared to be a futile effort. In the process, other patients were not getting as much care as would certainly be of benefit to them. Could the nurses or the physicians argue that care should be stopped because he was dead? Could they overrule the parents' judgment about the usefulness of the treatment even if he were not dead? Could they legitimately take into account the welfare of the other patients and the enormous costs involved when deciding whether to limit their attention to Yusef?

---

[1]Weiser, B. (1980, September 5). Boy, 9, may not be "brain dead," new medical examiner shows. *Washington Post*, p. B1. Weiser, B. (1980, September 12). Second doctor finds life in "brain dead" DC boy. *Washington Post*, p. B10. Sager, M. (1980, September 17). Nine-year-old dies after four months in coma. *Washington Post*, p. B6.

Commentary

Many issues are raised in this complex case. First, the nurses and physicians need to understand the role of the definition of death. Apparently, some of the physicians believed that an individual should be considered dead when the brain functions are irreversibly lost—an increasingly accepted view.[4] A decision about whether to call an individual dead when his or her brain stops functioning (rather than when spontaneous heart and lung functions irreversibly cease) is not scientifically determined. No amount of scientific evidence will help one decide whether a person should be treated as dead. All states in the United States and most other countries have now passed legislation or have had court cases that have established that brain criteria should be used as the basis for death pronouncement. Moreover, the President's Commission for the Study of Ethical Problems in Medicine and Biomedical and Behavioral Research has endorsed such a position.

The first problem faced by the nurses in this case was how they should respond if physicians attempt to pronounce death based on brain function loss in a jurisdiction that has not authorized a shift in the definition of death. That, of course, is no longer a problem for nurses practicing in most states. The only exceptions are the states of New Jersey and New York. New Jersey's law considers people who have irreversibly lost brain function to be dead, but makes an exception when the patient has documented a religious objection to brain-based death pronouncement. In those cases, the traditional cardiorespiratory definition of death must be used. In the state of New York, the Department of Health advises physicians that they may take into account the views of the patient or their family when deciding whether to pronounce death based on loss of brain function. Hence, if Yusef Camp had been in New York, his parents' objection would have been sufficient for a physician to refrain from pronouncing death.

In fact, several different positions on the definition of death have emerged over the past several years.[5] Some people still hold to the notion that an individual should not be considered dead until heart and lung function cease (even if it is well established that the individual will never again regain any consciousness). They hold that they are dealing with a still-living, critically ill, comatose patient. For them, it is still possible to ask whether such a patient should be allowed to die. They might use arguments such as those discussed in Chapter 10 to conclude that the morally appropriate course is to let the still-living patient die by withdrawing support. If ventilator and other supports are withdrawn, the patient would die very soon. At issue for those concerned about organ procurement is the damage to the organs from this procedure. Defenders of this view, however, hold that organ procurement should not be the basis on which a definition of death is chosen.

A variation on this traditional view has recently received renewed interest. A 2008 report of the President's Council on Bioethics entitled *Controversies in the Determination of Death* addressed concerns about widely accepted death criteria. It noted that:

> In relatively rare cases, however, the irreversible loss of brain-dependent functions occurs while the body, with technological assistance, continues to circulate blood and to show other signs of life. In such cases, there is controversy and confusion about whether death has actually occurred. A minority of the Council endorsed the view that a person could still be alive and manifest bodily integrating capacity even though the brain was no longer functioning.[6]

Other people hold that whether a person should be treated as living should depend not so much on relatively trivial functions such as circulation and respiration, but rather on the more critical capacities to integrate bodily functions and exercise mental function. They believe that an individual can appropriately be treated the way society treats dead people whenever those functions are lost, even if the heart and lungs continue to function. It may happen that the nurse holds one of these views and the physician holds the other. In fact, it is likely that there will be differences over these nonscientific issues. Among members of the President's Council on Bioethics, the prevailing opinion is that the current neurological standard for declaring death, grounded in a careful diagnosis of total brain failure, is biologically and philosophically defensible.[7]

A third distinct position, now often called the higher-brain definition of death, has begun to emerge. It acknowledges that individuals who have lost all brain function should be treated as dead, but questions whether all individuals who retain any brain function should be treated as living. They have in mind an individual, perhaps like Yusef Camp, who still has some lower-brain functions, such as reflex arcs or even respiratory center activity. Such a patient would not be dead based on the now-legal, brain-oriented definitions of death. He or she would be vegetative. People holding this position argue that personal identity is forever lost[8] or that capacity for consciousness and social interaction is lost[9] and that, for those reasons, the individual should be treated as dead even though some nonessential brain functions remain. No jurisdiction in the world has, to date, adopted this higher-brain view.

In 2009, an Orthodox Jewish family sued the National Children's Medical Center in Washington, DC, refusing to accept that their 12-year-old son, Motl, a victim of cancer whose brain had irreversibly stopped functioning was dead. According to the family's Hasidic beliefs, death occurs when circulatory functioning ceases, which means their son would be considered alive. Cases like these reflect the lack of consensus in society today about what had previously seemed like accepted death criteria[10].

It is important for the nurses in this case to realize that even if Yusef Camp or a similarly situated patient is considered still living, it is reasonable to ask whether it is morally appropriate to stop treatment in order to let the patient die. Cases later in this chapter look at the limits of parental responsibility in making such choices.

Competent and Formerly Competent Patients

We saw in the cases in Chapter 16 that patients with decision-making capacity have the legal right to consent (or refuse to consent) to medical treatments. This is based in part on the ethical principle of autonomy. Giving patients the right to consent or refuse to consent may also tend to promote their welfare. Patients who want to refuse a treatment will tend to be harmed, at least psychologically, if the treatment is rendered. They often know whether the benefit will exceed the harm, based on their own system of values. If, however, this right to consent is based on benefits and harms—the principles of beneficence and nonmaleficence—it could be overridden in cases where there is good reason to believe that the patient would really be better off without the consent.

The right to consent is not limited in cases in which the patient is terminally ill. In fact, if the patient is inevitably dying, many would argue that the harm that could be done by the omission of treatment at the patient's request would be minimal. In any case, the right of the mentally competent patient to refuse life-prolonging treatment is now recognized widely, both as a matter of law[11] and of ethics.[12] There are certain individuals who, based on religious and philosophic objections, hold that it is morally wrong to make such decisions,[13] but they are a minority and even they tend to acknowledge the right of persons to make such choices. Many authorities in all the major Western religions accept the legitimacy of deciding to forgo certain medical treatments, even some that will prolong life.

One group of minorities that remains committed to the preservation of life (even "at all costs") is some physicians. Although it does not occur as commonly as it did in the past, nurses may find themselves facing physicians who insist that even competent patients or patients who clearly expressed their wishes while competent but are now incompetent continue to receive treatment. That is the issue in Case 17-2.

Treating Against the Wishes of the Patient

Case 17-2

The Patient Who Had a Cardiac Arrest in the Wrong Hospital[2]

Jesse Newton, a 68-year-old disabled man without living relatives, has had a 14-year history of coronary artery disease. Since the age of 54, Mr. Newton has suffered three myocardial infarctions (MIs). He now complains of angina at rest, has ventricular arrhythmias, and has been admitted to the hospital five times for treatment of congestive heart failure.

Mr. Newton was aware of his heart condition and had said that he did not wish to live as a "cardiac cripple" or to be placed on life support equipment. He discussed his concerns with his primary care physician. They both agreed that should Mr. Newton suffer another

---

[2]Case supplied by Sandra K. Reed, MSN, CCRN. Used with permission.

MI or cardiac arrest for any reason, no heroic measures would be carried out. Mr. Newton signed a living will in accordance with the legal requirements of his state and gave a copy to his cardiologist.

Several months later, while traveling in a neighboring state, Mr. Newton was involved in a single-car accident. He was transported to a local hospital for treatment of closed head injuries with temporary loss of consciousness, facial lacerations, and cardiac contusion. He was admitted to a neurosurgical nursing unit and hooked up to a portable bedside EKG monitor. During the first 8 hours of his hospitalization, his EKG demonstrated frequent PVCs, and he complained of angina unrelieved by sublingual nitroglycerin (NG) or morphine. Mrs. Sherri Brooten, the nursing supervisor responsible for the neurosurgical nursing unit, was concerned that Mr. Newton's cardiac status could not be adequately monitored on that particular unit. She began to make arrangements to transfer him to the coronary care unit (CCU).

Before the transfer could be accomplished, Mr. Newton had a cardiac arrest. He was defibrillated and his cardiac rhythm was quickly restored and maintained by medications while his respirations were maintained by hand ventilation. When he awakened after his arrest, Mrs. Brooten explained what had happened to him. Mr. Newton became agitated, saying that he did not want this to happen again and that the nurse should see his living will in his briefcase. When the advance directive was located, Mrs. Brooten showed the living will to Dr. Gross, the attending physician handling Mr. Newton's case. Dr. Gross read it and then decided that the document should be ignored. It was not valid for his state, and Mr. Newton would receive all necessary treatment while under his care. Did this decision release the nurses from all obligation to respect Mr. Newton's requests?

Commentary

Mr. Newton is one of an increasing number of patients who have thought in advance about their terminal care. He had executed a document called an advance directive, or sometimes called a living will. State-specific standard forms for advance directives are available from Last Acts Partnership (http://www.caringinfo.org/index.cfm?). This group formed as a result of a merger of several organizations furthering decision making for the terminally ill, including Choice in Dying, the group that originated the living will. Other groups, including many religious groups, have prepared documents suitable for their members.

The first question this case raises is what the physician might have meant when he stated that the document was not valid for his state. Perhaps he was aware that almost all states have passed laws specifically authorizing patients to write their wishes about terminal care in advance. These laws vary somewhat from state to state. In California's law, for example, the advance directive is legally binding only if the patient has been certified terminally ill for 14 days before the document is signed.[14] In most other states, this is not required. In some states, proxy decision makers can be designated as part of the statute. The physician might have said he believed that the statutory law in his jurisdiction did not authorize such advance directives or that such directives were not binding. In fact, a few states (such as New York and Michigan) have not passed such laws. Many other countries have no formal laws authorizing advance directives. Nevertheless, in the United States, all states, even those that have not passed specific laws, recognize the right of competent persons to refuse treatment. Directives from patients who are no longer competent are also binding, provided it is clear what the patient's wishes are and that the patient has not changed her or his mind.

Regardless of whether Mr. Newton was hospitalized in a state with an explicit law governing advance directives, other complex legal and ethical questions arise. Neither Mrs. Brooten nor the physician was in a good position to interpret all of them. For example, common law generally requires patients to consent to treatment. Patients may also refuse to consent. Would a living will written by a competent patient constitute a refusal to consent to treatment under common law, even if there is no specific statute on the matter?

Assuming that Sherri Brooten had doubts about the legitimacy of the physician's decision to treat, what ought she to have done? She was in an awkward position. If she had provided nursing care based on Dr. Gross's decision, she may have been treating against the refusal of the patient, which could have raised legal as well as ethical problems for her as well as for the physician. If she had refused to treat, however, she at least would have faced practical problems in her relation with the physician. Furthermore, if she had been wrong about her interpretation of the case, she could have been seen as abandoning a patient.

The following clinical situations were recently identified as creating the highest degree of moral distress for critical care nurses:

1. Continuing to participate in care for hopelessly ill person who is being sustained on a ventilator, when no one will make a decision to "pull the plug"
2. Following a family's wishes to continue life support even though it is not in the best interest of the patient
3. Initiating extensive life-saving actions when I think it only prolongs death
4. Following the family's wishes for the patient's care when I do not agree with them but do so because the hospital administration fears a lawsuit
5. Carrying out the physician's orders for unnecessary tests and treatments for terminally ill patients[15]

Many nurses would take some initial steps to clarify the situation. They would talk with colleagues and gather opinions on the appropriate moral and legal course. Perhaps they would speak with their supervisor. They might, if they had a good rapport with the physician, discuss their reservations about the situation with him or her directly. They might exercise their right to refuse to participate in the case on grounds of conscience. That would free them from direct involvement, but it might not absolve them of responsibility, because Mr. Newton would still be treated against his wishes.

Critical Thinking Questions

1. What additional steps might a nurse take who believes that the moral or legal rights of Mr. Newton are being violated, even if she is personally free from involvement in the case? Would it be appropriate for Mrs. Brooten to speak with nursing supervisors, with hospital administrators or attorneys, or with the chief of medicine?

2. Would it be appropriate for Mrs. Brooten to suggest to Mr. Newton that he get legal advice, that she contact a patient advocacy group, or that he transfer to another hospital where his instructions would be unambiguously valid?

3. Should Mrs. Brooten take the case to the local hospital ethics committee for further review or advise Mr. Newton to do so? Why or why not?

The Patient in Conflict with the Physician and the Family

Case 17-3
The Patient Says Yes; The Physician and the Family Say No

Frank Graham, age 58, was admitted to the emergency room unresponsive and without spontaneous respirations. He had been found on the driveway alongside his house, having fallen from a ladder while he was cleaning the rain gutters. A neighbor had started CPR, which was maintained by the rescue squad during transport to the hospital. Once in the ER, Mr. Graham was placed on a ventilator, and his blood pressure and pulse were restored. Subsequent testing ruled out a stroke or heart attack. X-rays did show a C1, C2 fracture. His initial unresponsiveness was attributed to cerebral edema. Several days later, he began to focus his eyes on his nurse, Mrs. Cauthen; he could blink and also move his eyes to commands.

A neurological consult indicated that the patient's situation was irreversible and that the family should be consulted regarding discontinuation of treatment. Mr. Graham's wife wanted to see her husband before discussing his treatment. When she visited him, he did not open his eyes and did not respond to her voice. Later that evening, she called the physician and told him that she did not want her husband's life prolonged in this manner. The physician told her that another consult was ordered for the next day. After consulting with that physician, he would then talk to her again about any decisions that would be needed.

The second consulting neurosurgeon felt that the patient was capable of understanding the situation, and he explained the nature of the injuries to Mr. Graham. He told the patient that he would not be able to survive without the support of the ventilator. He asked Mr. Graham to look in a certain direction if he wanted the ventilator continued. Mr. Graham did this several times.

The neurosurgeon and Mrs. Graham agreed that his wishes should be respected. When the attending physician read the consult report, he decided that he would not discontinue the ventilator but that he would not treat Mr. Graham's current electrolyte imbalance (hyperkalemia), arrhythmias, hypotension, or pneumonia. A do-not-resuscitate (DNR) order was written. Mrs. Graham was consulted and concurred in these decisions. Mr. Graham was not told of this last decision; he was simply told that his ventilator would not be removed unless he desired it to be removed.

Mrs. Cauthen was very uncomfortable with the kind of limited treatment being done for Mr. Graham and with the fact that he was not being consulted about his treatment. Because she was the one who spent the greatest amount of time with Mr. Graham, she felt that her nonresponse to his many developing problems was contributing to his death.

Commentary

In some ways, this case is like the previous one. Here, however, the neurosurgeon went to great lengths to involve the patient, Mr. Graham, in the ventilator decision, and the wife and attending physician agreed that his wishes about the ventilator should be respected. On what basis then, did the attending physician and Mrs. Graham take it upon themselves to decide to omit various treatments and to write a DNR order?

There is a growing volume of literature on the use of the "do-not-resuscitate" decision.[16] Some of the early guidelines written by local groups held open the possibility that a decision not to resuscitate could be made by the physician and/or family without consulting the patient, even though the patient was competent.[17] This is an example of older, paternalistic thinking, sometimes referred to as "therapeutic privilege" and rooted in the principle of beneficence. Almost all commentators now recognize, however, that if there is a presumption in favor of resuscitation, it is the patient who has the authority to confirm or cancel that presumption, as long as the patient is competent to do so. Otherwise, a patient literally could have life-sustaining therapy omitted without her or his knowledge or approval. In fact, at least one case has led to legal action for failing to resuscitate a patient without informing her in advance that she would not be resuscitated.[18]

Although no similar extended discussion of withholding treatment for other conditions such as hypotension or pneumonia has taken place, similar principles would seem to apply. In the cases in Chapter 10, treatments were deemed extraordinary if they were useless or gravely burdensome based on the patient's judgment. Were Mr. Graham to have refused these treatments, they would surely have been expendable, but given the fact that he apparently desired that the ventilator be continued, it is at least possible that he would also have desired the other treatments.

Mrs. Cauthen is thus on firm ground in feeling uncomfortable. Her judgment would be supported by the nursing profession's position that "the choices and values of the competent patient should always be given highest priority."[19] Her position is somewhat similar to that of Mrs. Brooten, the nurse in the previous case. She might explore similar options.

There is one difference that might be significant. Whereas Mrs. Brooten's patient was trying unsuccessfully to refuse treatment, Mrs. Cauthen's patient may well want the treatment that was being withheld. It was the physician and the family who decided to omit CPR and several other interventions. Yet although the patient appears to have a virtually unlimited legal right to refuse treatment, he clearly would not have the right to insist on every imaginable intervention. He would not have the right to insist on unconventional treatments or experimental treatments, for example. Before Mrs. Cauthen protests, she should explore whether a request from her patient for treatment would be of this kind.

It seems clear, however, that the treatments that Mr. Graham may really have wanted (treatments he might have requested if asked) are not of the sort that a healthcare institution could categorically refuse to provide. They are not unconventional or experimental theories. They are not comparable to laetrile or experimental therapies. They may be thought to be similar to interventions sometimes called *futile care*, but those often involve permanently unconscious and rapidly dying patients. Futile care will be discussed in cases later in this chapter. Mr. Graham, however, was neither unconscious nor inevitably dying. If that is the case, Mrs. Cauthen may well be justified in objecting. Her problem will be one of figuring what channel is most appropriate for communicating her objection. Of course, there is always the possibility that no matter how and to whom she makes her objection, the other treatments will not be done and Mrs. Cauthen will remain in moral distress.[20] Whatever Mrs. Cauthen chooses to do, she should base her decision on the commitment that the patient is the one who should make decisions about his or her care. That was a right given to Mr. Graham when it came to the ventilator. Why he was not also asked about other medical interventions is unclear.

The Problem of the Ambivalent Patient

Case 17-4

To Resuscitate or Not?

Jessica Holmes is an experienced acute care nurse specialist caring for Mr. Sweitzer, a 61-year-old man with metastatic cancer of the bone. Admitted for an above-the-knee (AK) amputation, Mr. Sweitzer developed respiratory distress immediately after his surgery. He was resuscitated successfully, but he now suffers organic brain damage and continued confusion. This once-active patient now has limited mobility and is in considerable pain from the amputation. He also seems frightened by his confusion. At times, he cries and tells Mrs. Holmes that he would rather die than live as he is living now. At other times, he cooperates with maintenance of the ventilator and acts as if he wants to live.

The mental change and ambivalence Mr. Sweitzer experiences worries his family members. They visit him often but believe that his confusion is a temporary condition and that he will soon recover and return home. They do not seem to be aware of the brain damage that he suffered after surgery.

Several days after his surgery, Mrs. Holmes observes that Mr. Sweitzer has developed an intermittent pattern of Cheyne-Stokes respirations. In discussing Mr. Sweitzer's condition with the physician, she learns that the physician wants the patient to be resuscitated if he develops cardiopulmonary arrest, despite the fact that Mr. Sweitzer has indicated otherwise. Because the family members do not really understand Mr. Sweitzer's condition, they also want everything done for their loved one. Mrs. Holmes thinks that it would be cruel to resuscitate this particular patient. What should she do?

Commentary

This case is in some ways similar to the two previous ones. It may simply be another instance of a physician refusing to follow the patient's wishes. If so, Mrs. Holmes faces a problem like those of Mrs. Brooten and Mrs. Cauthen. As in Mr. Graham's case, the family may be siding with the physician against the patient. Mrs. Holmes's problem may be more complicated, however, because it is not as clear exactly what the patient really wants. At times Mr. Sweitzer has given Mrs. Holmes a clear signal that he would rather not be treated, yet he has suffered brain damage and seems confused.

There are several possibilities. He may be competent but ambivalent. Sometimes patients are competent beyond doubt but cannot make up their minds. If that is the case, the physician and the family may be on the right track. It is not because they have the authority to decide, but because even though the patient has the authority, he is not giving a clear answer. Surely, the rule of thumb should be that when the patient is ambivalent, treatment should continue (at least until he or she makes up his or her mind).

More likely, the doubt is over whether Mr. Sweitzer really has the capacity to make a choice with adequate understanding. A treatment refusal by a clearly incompetent patient is not binding. Consider, for example, a small child who refuses surgery. We shall see in the next group of cases that for incompetent patients someone must be the presumed surrogate for the patient—whether it is the physician, the next of kin, or someone else. The problem here, however, is whether Mr. Sweitzer is competent to make these critical decisions.

Legally, no one involved—family members, Mrs. Holmes, or the physician—has the authority to declare Mr. Sweitzer incompetent. If there is doubt or if there is a dispute, some adjudication will be necessary. Mrs. Holmes's task may be to raise the question of whether a patient can be treated against his consent. It may be to question whether Mr. Sweitzer is really incompetent, as the physician and the patient's family appear to presume. She might use one of the mechanisms discussed in the previous cases or some other (such as asking for a psychiatric consult or, conceivably, if the case becomes critical, reporting the case to public authorities). In any case, if the nurse's role is to be an advocate for the patient, she will have a duty to see that Mr. Sweitzer's wishes are respected insofar as he is competent to express them and to see that his interests are served insofar as he is not competent to express his wishes. It is to the incompetent patient that we now turn.

Critical Thinking Question

If Mr. Sweitzer were your patient, which actions would you take to respect his wishes? Why?

Research Brief 17-1

Sources: Marshall, P. A. (1995). The SUPPORT study: Who's talking? *The Hastings Center Report, 25*(6), S9–S11; Hiltunen, E. F., Puopolo, A. L., Marks, G. K., Marsden, C., Kennard, M. J., Follen, M. A., et al. (1995). The nurse's role in end-of-life treatment discussions: Preliminary report from the SUPPORT project. *The Journal of Cardiovascular Nursing, 9*, 68–77; The SUPPORT Principal Investigators. (1995). A controlled trial to improve care for seriously ill hospitalized patients: The Study to Understand Prognoses and Preferences for Outcomes and Risks of Treatments (SUPPORT). *Journal of the American Medical Association, 274*, 1591–1598.

Purpose: The purposes of the Study to Understand Prognoses and Preferences for Outcomes and Risks of Treatment (SUPPORT) were to improve end-of-life decision making and to reduce the frequency of a mechanically supported, painful, and prolonged process of dying.

Method: Phase II of the study was a controlled clinical trial to test the effect of an intervention designed to improve communication about end-of-life decision making among patients, families, and physicians. The intervention was provided by a group of specially trained nurses. Patients ($n = 4804$) were enrolled in Phase II from January 1992 through January 1994 and were recruited from five large urban medical centers throughout the United States.

The Phase II intervention involved providing information to patients and families about end-of-life treatments and facilitating communication among the patient, the family, and members of the healthcare team, especially the physician. Patient/family preferences for end-of-life treatments were communicated to physicians in the usual manner—by telephone messages and nurses' notes. The nurses were specially trained to be patient advocates who helped patients to identify their values and choices, encouraged them to communicate their values and choices to their physicians, and made sure that the patients' wishes for pain management and treatment were documented in the patient care record. The nurses spent a great deal of time (an average of six discussions per patient) with patients and families to help them understand their options and to empower them with knowledge of how to navigate the healthcare system so that their wishes could be heard.

Findings: Unfortunately, the study findings indicated that the intervention was not effective in: (1) improving patient–physician agreement on CPR preferences, (2) affecting the incidence and timing of DNR orders, (3) decreasing the number of days spent by a patient in the ICU or on a ventilator, (4) improving pain management, or (5) controlling the utilization of hospital resources. One reason for the ineffectiveness of the intervention was that the nurses in their advocacy roles needed the participation and assistance of the physicians to make sure that the patient/family wishes were recognized and carried out. Physicians did not read the nurses notes and did not follow up on verbal communications provided by the nurses. This is particularly disturbing given that 41% of the patients who had not previously discussed resuscitation or prognoses with their physicians indicated a desire to do so.

Implications: The SUPPORT intervention failed to produce the intended results partly because it kept the cultural system intact—that is, it maintained the role of the nurse as the translator for patients who cannot, for whatever reasons, speak directly to their physicians. In the final analysis, the study found that there are limits to the nurse's advocacy role in the acceptance of patients' choices concerning life-sustaining treatments.

Never-Competent Patients and Those Who Have Never Expressed Their Wishes

For the competent and formerly competent terminally ill patients we have just considered, the moral conflict is over the tension between judgments about what is in the patient's interest and what serves patient autonomy. That conflict cannot arise for patients who have never been competent or who have never expressed their desires while competent. For young patients like Yusef Camp, in the opening case in this chapter, some surrogate decision maker must be found. For these patients, the moral objective is to have someone choose what will be in the patient's interest. Whereas for the formerly competent patient the surrogate decision maker will try to do what the patient would have wanted (applying the so-called substituted judgment test), for the *never-competent patient*—the small child or the severely retarded patient—the surrogate will have to try to determine what is in the patient's interest (the so-called best interest test).

Two kinds of questions arise. First, who should the surrogate be? Should it be a healthcare professional, a family member, or a court-appointed guardian?

Second, once the surrogate has been chosen, how much discretion should that person have in assessing the interests of the patient? Many of the most controversial cases have involved good-faith choices made by a designated surrogate with which many people would not concur. Do we insist that the surrogate make the best possible determination of what is in the patient's best interest or only that he or she be within reason?

Some people think that parents should not have the authority to make critical treatment choices for their infants. When an infant is severely afflicted, for example, the parents may have long-term conflicts of interest. They may have obligations to other children; they also have interests of their own. The treatment that would constitute the proper care of the infant may not be one the parents would choose. On the other hand, it is not clear that the physician is the appropriate surrogate for the incompetent patient. Clearly, physicians differ tremendously among themselves over appropriate care for infants and other incompetents. One physician might believe that the parents should be spared the agony of rearing the infant. Another physician, perhaps one who has had issues of infertility in his or her marriage or one from a religious tradition that favors sustaining the lives of such infants, might have a very different response.

Other approaches to decision making regarding never-competent patients include the use of an infant care review committee—a hospital ethics committee oriented specifically to decisions regarding critically ill infants.[21] Although some have argued that there is nothing so unique about infant care that a separate committee needs to be created, others have maintained that specialized personnel (pediatricians, specialists in handicapped infant care, special education experts, and neonatal nurse practitioners) could be included. Such committees, however, have no legal authority to make critical decisions for infants. The most they can do is provide counsel and advice. Moreover, committees appointed at local institutions might not completely neutralize the biases of individual practitioners. A particularly conservative or liberal hospital might have a committee that reflects that orientation, no matter how well-meaning the administrators were who appointed the committee, possibly leaving the incompetent patient still subject to random variations in decisions.

Another alternative to the use of parents as decision makers is to go routinely to a court or child protection agency for a publicly authorized guardian. Although that may be necessary in controversial cases, most people do not think it appropriate to resort to such bureaucratic mechanisms in all cases requiring decisions about medical care for infants or other incompetent patients.

Some people object to healthcare professionals, infant care review committees, and public agents serving as surrogates for infants because they believe that, in principle, if the patient is a minor, the choice should belong to the parents, at least if the parental choice is within reason. The parents or next of kin should have some discretion, according to this view, in deciding what counts as appropriate treatment, basing their choice on family beliefs and values. The notion of familial discretion is the issue in the next group of cases.

How Much Discretion Should Family Have?

Case 17-5

Selective Treatment of Meningomyelocele: Two Cases of Parental Choice[3]

Sherri Fincham is a pediatric nurse specialist who has worked on a pediatric neurosurgical unit for more than 10 years. She is especially well qualified to care for children born with spina bifida and meningomyelocele. She is well versed in the problems that nurses often encounter in decision making concerning these children and their deformities. Two cases represent the diverse choices that might be made by parents in the care and treatment of their children.

(1) Jimmy Adams was born with a lumbar meningomyelocele. His parents were told there was no hope, that they should "let him go." Mr. and Mrs. Adams were aware that Jimmy would have some residual handicap, but they were eager to do all they could to save his life. After 5 days, the parents took Jimmy home and sought other medical treatment. Admitted to another institution, Jimmy was leaking cerebrospinal fluid (CSF) but had good movement at his hips and toe movement on the right foot. He was alert and responsive, and he had good reflexes. Because Jimmy's back had been open for 5 days, his physicians decided not to close the wound until they had seen three consecutive negative wound cultures. Unfortunately, the wound cultures remained positive for Pseudomonas, and the infant developed ventriculitis. He was treated with bilateral external ventricular drainage (EVDs) systems and ventricular irrigations with antibiotics. The meningomyelocele was closed, and antibiotics were continued. After 10 days of negative CSF cultures, the EVDs were removed. When Jimmy later developed increased intracranial pressure, a ventriculoperitoneal (VP) shunt was inserted. His parents did not give up, and neither did Jimmy. Three months and 2 days after his birth, Jimmy was able to return home with his parents.

(2) John Brody was born with a large lumbar meningomyelocele, kyphosis, bilateral club feet, and bilateral dislocated hips. His meningomyelocele was closed, and a partial kyphectomy was performed hours after his birth. John's parents were optimistic and eager for additional information about their child's condition. As in Jimmy's case, complications soon developed. John's back began to leak CSF, and an EVD was inserted. Several days later, he developed fever and apnea spells. His CSF cultures were positive for *Staphylococcus aureus*, and ventriculitis was diagnosed. After treatment with antibiotics, he recovered, was alert and responsive, and began feeding well.

John's parents, however, had become discouraged and sought another medical opinion. They then decided against further treatment for John. When the physicians wanted to initiate further treatment, the Brodys transferred John to another hospital. They stated that they were more concerned for the quality of John's life than for whether it would be possible to keep him alive. They became very angry when Ms. Fincham and the other nurses

---

[3]Adapted from Homer, M. B. (1984). Selective treatment. *American Journal of Nursing, 84,* 309–312.

conveyed displeasure with their choices for John. The parents said they did not feel guilty about their decision but resented being made to feel guilty by the nursing staff.

Postscript: At the age of 4 years, Jimmy is walking with braces and crutches. He is moderately mentally retarded but talkative and friendly. He has not been able to develop bladder and bowel control, so he wears diapers all the time.

John was discharged from the hospital without a VP shunt at his parents' request. He died at home about 6 months later.

Commentary

The pair of cases of meningomyelocele involving nurse Sherri Fincham is typical of situations of critically ill newborns that generate great controversy today. Other cases involve infants born with Down syndrome and gastrointestinal atresias, as well as low–birth-weight infants. Common to all of these cases is the patient's obvious lack of ability to decide for himself or herself. Moreover, without treatment, the patient will almost certainly die. With treatment, the patient will live but with handicaps of varying degrees of seriousness.

In the cases of Chapter 10, we saw that the most straightforward approach to these cases begins with the assumption that the surrogate decision maker should try to serve the best interests of the patient. The President's Commission on the Study of Ethical Problems in Medicine and Biomedical Research and the Catholic Church are among the groups that have supported the notion that treatments are expendable when they are disproportionally burdensome for the patient. We also saw that two criteria are now frequently used for deciding when treatments are disproportionally burdensome. When the treatment is useless, it will offer no benefit and is surely expendable. Likewise, if there is grave burden with expectation of relatively modest benefit, the treatment is morally expendable. Mr. and Mrs. Brody made the decision that the benefits of aggressive treatment of the meningomyelocele did not justify the burdens of the treatment. It is not clear whether the Brody family was considering the burdens of the treatments themselves, the burdens of the handicapped life that would result, or the burdens resulting from the institutional care that might be necessary. All three factors have been considered by some parents. There is some controversy over which of these burdens are legitimate considerations.

The Brodys may also have taken into account burdens to other persons—themselves or other children in the family, for example. It is also not clear what role these considerations ought to play. From the case report, we have no evidence that the Brodys were malicious or that they were considering anything other than John's welfare.

The Adamses, facing an essentially similar situation, came to a very different conclusion. They thought it was in Jimmy's interest that he be treated aggressively. Ms. Fincham seems to agree more with the Adamses than with the Brodys. There is evidence that many in our contemporary society side with Ms. Fincham and the Adamses, even if substantial numbers concur with the Brodys and would make the same decision they did.

The problem for Ms. Fincham is what difference it makes that she and a purported majority of the population agree with the Adamses and disagree with the Brodys. It hardly seems the kind of issue that should be decided by majority vote. If, for example, the majority of the population believed that such infants would be better off having treatment stopped, it would hardly be a justifiable conclusion that the Adamses should be forced to stop against their will. In the case of the Brodys, Ms. Fincham has a number of avenues available to her if she wishes to intervene, including reporting the case to child abuse authorities. In fact, such a step may be required by current federal regulations governing the care of handicapped newborns.[22] They require that, in order to get federal support·for child protective services, states have mechanisms available for reporting cases of "medical neglect, including instances of withholding of medically indicated treatment from disabled infants with life-threatening conditions."[23] The only cases excluded are those in which:

1. The infant is chronically and irreversibly comatose;
2. The provision of such treatment would merely prolong dying, and would not be effective in ameliorating or correcting all of the infant's life-threatening conditions, or would otherwise be futile in terms of the survival of the infant; or
3. The provision of such treatment would be virtually futile in terms of the survival of the infant and the treatment itself under such circumstances would be inhumane.

Even in these cases, appropriate nutrition, hydration, and medication must be provided. The infants with meningomyelocele (as well as those with Down syndrome and atresias, and those with low birth weight) would appear not to fit any of these exceptions.

By contrast, the President's Commission for the Study of Ethical Problems in Medicine and Biomedical and Behavioral Research appears somewhat more open to the conclusion that parents could justifiably find some treatments unreasonably burdensome even if these conditions are not met. It speaks of situations in which benefits are ambiguous or uncertain and accepts forgoing treatment in such circumstances.[24]

If it is true that decisions about what is useless and what is a disproportional burden are inherently evaluative judgments, then it is likely that there will continue to be disagreement. The question faced by Ms. Fincham and others assessing surrogate decisions is how much discretion the parents or other surrogates should have in making the evaluations.

One approach is to insist that the guardians make the most reasonable judgments about what is in the incompetent one's best interest. That would give the incompetent patient the best chance of having his or her interest served, but it would require some routine assessment of every surrogate decision. The alternative is to give the surrogate some latitude, at least in ambiguous cases.

It is not clear why parents and other surrogates should have such latitude. Some argue that it is because the family is a fundamental unit in our society. Society expects the parents to draw on family beliefs and values in making many choices for their children, such as in choosing school systems, in socializing children in religious and other values, and so on. Some people hold that families therefore deserve some discretion beyond that given to a judge or some other decision maker who is a stranger to the patient. The President's Commission, for example, says:

> There is a presumption, strong but rebuttable, that parents are the appropriate decision makers for their infants. Traditional law concerning the family, buttressed by the emerging constitutional right of privacy, protects a substantial range of discretion for parents. . . Americans have traditionally been reluctant to intrude upon the functioning of families, both because doing so would be difficult and because it would destroy some of the value of the family, which seems to need privacy and discretion to maintain its significance.[25]

This suggests some range of discretion for parents in their decisions. The next question is just how much discretion should be allowed. Surely, parental variation cannot be unlimited. Parents must at least be within reason when they judge what is in their child's welfare. Drawing that line is a judgment call. It is slightly different, however, from the judgment call made by those who insist that the parents must choose what really is best.

What does this mean for Ms. Fincham? If she believes that the parents in these meningomyelocele cases have the duty to make what really is the best choice, then it appears that in at least one of the cases they have not done so, and she must intervene. She must ask for an ethics committee review, make a report to the child welfare agency, or seek judicial intervention. If, however, she accepts the notion of a range of parental discretion, she will have to decide not what is best in each case, but rather whether either of these pairs of parents has exceeded the reasonable limits of parental discretion.

Research Brief 17-2

Source: Wocial, L. D. (2000). Life-support decisions involving imperiled infants. *Journal of Perinatal and Neonatal Nursing, 14*(2), 73–86.

Purpose: The purpose of this study was to understand the experience of parents faced with making decisions to withhold or withdraw life-sustaining treatments from their infants in the NICU.

Method: In this phenomenological study, 20 parents (12 families) of NICU patients who died were interviewed. The majority of parents were Caucasians (97%) with some college education (67%) and with health insurance (92%).

All were living with their spouses. Relevant themes were extracted from the data until significant themes were refined and defensible based on the data. Interrater reliability was established by an audit by experienced qualitative researchers and a neonatal expert.

Findings: Parents described the context of their decision making, not the method used to make their decisions. An important aspect of the context was how their decision was carried out and how they were supported as their babies died. Holding their babies prior to death was very important to them and facilitated making their decision.

Focusing on the parents' interactions with the providers, the themes were acceptance, humility, and caring. When providers helped the parents see the reality of the situation, parents were able to accept the need to make a life-sustaining treatment decision. Providers who conveyed that they did not have all the answers were perceived by parents as more humane. Likewise, providers who showed their emotions were seen as more caring.

The themes related to the parents' information needs were need, comprehension, presentation, and trust. Parents described their massive need for information to help them make their decisions. Additionally, they needed to understand the information presented to them about their treatment options. When the information was presented in a direct manner, it was perceived as more truthful than when it was presented less directly. To believe the information presented to them, the parents had to trust the provider giving it. Parents were more likely to trust information they received directly rather than indirectly through other providers.

The major theme regarding involvement in decision making was the degree of control perceived by the parents. When parents felt they were not in control, they did not perceive that they were involved in decision making for their infants. Participation in caring for their infants increased their feelings of control and involvement.

Implications: The researchers found that parents were focused on their relationships with healthcare providers rather than the ethical nature of making decisions to withhold or withdraw treatments. Nurses were of critical importance to parents, helping them feel like parents and providing support during the difficult process of making and implementing decisions to withhold or withdraw treatments. Nurses should routinely offer parents the opportunity to hold their infants before death occurs. Nurses can help parents understand and process difficult information. Nurses should be allowed to show their emotions when caring for dying infants and their families.

Nonfamily Surrogates

Case 17-6

May a Friend Be a Surrogate?[4]

Mr. Burntree, a 67-year-old, was admitted by his internist to the medical/surgical unit with the diagnosis of probable bowel obstruction. Mr. Burntree had a history of two myocardial infarctions, chronic obstructive pulmonary disease (COPD), and arteriosclerotic heart disease (ASHD). A surgeon was consulted, and Mr. Burntree underwent surgery in the late afternoon. A cancerous growth was removed from his colon, and a permanent colostomy was performed. He returned to the unit several days later (a Friday afternoon), alert, oriented, and aware of his condition. He was receiving IV fluids at 125 ml/hr, and he had a Foley catheter in place. His urinary output for the previous 8 hours had been only 200 cc. Both the internist and surgeon were aware of this fact.

During visiting hours, Mr. Burntree was visited by Ms. Scanlon, a woman friend with whom he had made his home for the past 10 years after being divorced for about 6 years. Ms. Scanlon was very attentive toward Mr. Burntree and quite concerned about him. Later in the afternoon, Mr. Burntree's daughters called the nurses' station. They talked with Liz Holden, the evening charge nurse. The daughters were from out of town and were requesting information regarding their father's condition. Both seemed unaware of their father's postoperative diagnosis. Miss Holden advised the daughters that his condition was stable and that they could talk with their father on his room telephone.

By the end of the 3:00 to 11:00 shift, Mr. Burntree's urinary output was a total of 85 cc. Miss Holden contacted the resident on call (both the internist and the surgeon were signed out to their respective partners for the weekend) and received orders to give Mr. Burntree Lasix IV and to increase his IV fluids to 166 ml/hr.

By the next afternoon, Mr. Burntree's condition had deteriorated significantly, and his urinary output had failed to increase significantly during the night. The resident was notified during the day, and he ordered Lasix IV, oxygen per nasal cannula, and the insertion of an NG tube to low suction. Given the patient's diagnosis and condition, the day nurse requested a DNR order. The resident refused, citing his unfamiliarity with the patient, his family, and his friend. By early evening, Mr. Burntree was extremely restless and confused, at one point pulling off his oxygen cannula and trying to climb out of bed. Within an hour, the patient was diaphoretic and extremely lethargic, with Cheyne-Stokes respirations. The resident was notified, but no additional orders were given, and he did not come to visit Mr. Burntree. At this time, Mr. Burntree's daughters called again for a report on their father's condition. They were informed of his deteriorating condition. The daughters were adamant that they wanted everything done for their father and that they would arrive at the hospital within 3–4 hours.

Mr. Burntree's friend, Miss Scanlon, who had been visiting him all afternoon and evening, talked to Miss Holden and stated that she just wanted Mr. Burntree kept comfortable.

---

[4]Case supplied by Dawn G. Snyder, MSN, RN. Used with permission.

She did not want any heroic measures taken. Mr. Burntree had apparently shared his diagnosis with her, and because he had COPD, he had asked that he not be kept "hooked up to any machines" in order to live. Miss Holden assured Miss Scanlon that she would record this information and notify the physician on call.

Before she could reach the physician by phone, Mr. Burntree arrested. Whose directions, if any, should Miss Holden follow: the daughters' or the friend's?

Commentary

Mr. Burntree's case is all too typical of many terminally ill patients. He apparently had views about terminal care, but no one took the responsibility for documenting them. There are suggestions that a record of the patient's wishes be part of every routine hospital intake interview and that the patient be asked if he or she has an advance directive or would like to prepare one. The federal legislation, the Patient Self-Determination Act, requires that hospitals have in place a mechanism for asking such questions and providing counseling to patients who would like assistance.[26] Had that been done in this case, much of the confusion might have been avoided.

The first nursing intervention is a puzzling one. The day nurse apparently asked for an "order" opposing resuscitation. There is no evidence that she based the request on the patient's wishes or even those of Ms. Scanlon. Should a nurse (or a physician) contemplate nonresuscitation without some confirmation that it is the patient's or surrogate's wishes?

Liz Holden, the charge nurse, is then left in an awkward situation. If she knew of Mr. Burntree's wishes, she presumably should follow them, but the evidence of his wishes is very indirect. On the other hand, there is substantial circumstantial evidence that Mr. Burntree might have preferred to have Ms. Scanlon be his agent for transmitting his decision or making a decision on her own if his wishes could not be discerned. However, can a healthcare professional (physician or nurse) take it upon himself or herself to designate a friend, even an apparently close and devoted one, as the patient's surrogate? Can he or she do so especially when there are natural relatives standing by ready to take over the surrogate role? This case is even more complex because the legal next of kin, Mr. Burntree's daughters, did not know his condition and apparently did not have a close relationship with him. It is now common practice for clinicians to presume that the next of kin is the valid surrogate for the patient. In many states, the law specifically assigns this role to the next of kin. The obvious solution to this problem would have been for Mr. Burntree to have exercised a durable power of attorney designating Ms. Scanlon as his legal surrogate (assuming that was indeed his desire). Such designation of friends as surrogates is legally effective in all U.S. jurisdictions. It is a useful device not only for this kind of case, but also for couples living together who have never been married and for people who have two or more relatives of the closest degree of kinship.

Although in this particular case the legitimacy of Ms. Scanlon may be obvious, that is not always the case. In other cases, apparent friends may step into the decision-making role when there is no clear evidence how well they know the patient's wishes or how devoted they are to the patient. Can healthcare professionals decide by themselves which apparent friends are the appropriate agents for their patients?

Because no one took the initiative to help Mr. Burntree execute either a substantive directive or a proxy directive (durable power of attorney), Liz Holden is now in a bind. It would have been prudent for her (or anyone else sensitive to the possible chaos) to have insisted in advance that some responsible decision maker be designated, by court action if necessary. The next of kin is the presumed surrogate when none has been designated in advance by the patient. The next of kin has the responsibility first to determine what the patient would have wanted based on the patient's values (substituted judgment) and then to use his or her own judgment about what would be in the patient's best interest if the patient's own wishes cannot be surmised.

If the next of kin is the presumed guardian, the daughters would appear to have decision-making authority. Ms. Scanlon would have two possible ways of intervening. She could argue, based on the evidence she has available, that the substituted judgment based on Mr. Burntree's values should be that treatment cease. If necessary, she could initiate actions to have the daughters removed from decision-making authority if they continued to make choices contrary to Mr. Burntree's wishes. Second, Ms. Scanlon could attempt something even more radical. She could try to argue that she is, de facto, Mr. Burntree's next of kin. Whether that would be successful is debatable.

Where does that leave Liz Holden, as Mr. Burntree arrests before all of this is worked out? She has the following options:

1. She could take it upon herself to replace the daughters with Ms. Scanlon as surrogate.
2. She could accept the rule that the next of kin is the presumed surrogate until someone else is designated.
3. She could, as the day nurse may have done, simply use her own judgment and do what she thinks is best.
4. She could "err on the side of life," resuscitating Mr. Burntree this time, but then insist that the decision-making authority be clarified so that if another crisis occurs, the proper course is well worked out.

Critical Thinking Question

If you were Ms. Holden, which of the above actions would you follow? Why?

Divisions Within the Family

Closely related to the problems raised in the last case is the situation occurring when two or more family members are willing to step into the surrogate role. Whereas the friend might be eliminated as an authoritative decision maker until some official sanction is given for her or his agency, that would not be the case when the disagreeing significant others are family members. The following case is illustrative.

Case 17-7
When Parents Disagree on Death[5]

Celia Alinger, a 6-year-old girl with a closed head injury resulting from a recent automobile accident, was a very sick pediatric patient. Her respirations were maintained by a ventilator, and she received nutrition by a central hyperalimentation line. She had several bone fractures (left clavicle, several ribs) and had not regained consciousness for 5 weeks following the accident. There was a general concern that Celia had suffered permanent brain damage from the accident, but testing to date was not diagnostic. Celia also suffered from Down syndrome. Prior to the accident, Celia had attended a day school for mentally retarded persons and had been progressing well in self-care activities.

Celia's parents both worked and usually visited her separately. Mrs. Alinger was an office worker, and Mr. Alinger worked as a janitor for the city school system. They spaced their visits around the care of their two other children, ages 8 and 3, and their work schedules.

When additional testing did not rule out the possibility of permanent brain damage, Mrs. Alinger confided to Celia's nurse, Trish Kendrick, that she was very concerned about the quality of Celia's life. She said, "The children have a hard time understanding and accepting Celia now. What will it be like if Celia has permanent brain damage? Perhaps we should let her die without all this effort to keep her alive." At Ms. Kendrick's urging, she expressed her views to the attending physician.

When Mr. Alinger arrived during the late afternoon, it was apparent that he had not spoken to his wife about Celia's condition and the results of the additional testing. When the guarded prognosis was explained to Mr. Alinger, he asked the nurses if they could do more for his daughter. He wanted no treatment spared and rejected the idea that Celia might remain in a vegetative state.

At a staff–family conference several days later, it was apparent that the parents were deeply divided in their wishes regarding Celia's continued care. Mr. Alinger expressed deep feelings of guilt for driving the day of the accident and for fathering a mentally impaired child. Mrs. Alinger expressed resentment and bitterness concerning the day-to-day social interactions and psychologic burdens of having a retarded child. She did not want to

---

[5]Case supplied by Susan Ford, BSN, RN. Used with permission.

prolong Celia's life when it had such a bleak outlook. She also questioned how she could cope with the long-term management of Celia as a severely mentally and physically impaired child. The staff members were also divided in their opinions about Celia. Ms. Kendrick and the attending physician wanted to do whatever the parents wished, but because the parents could not agree, they felt caught in a double bind.

Commentary

The first critical decision made by Nurse Kendrick and the physician was will-ingness to accept whatever decision the parents reached. That separates this case from many of the others in this section where nurses were struggling with the question of whether they ought to go along with the parental decision. To say that they were willing to go along with either a protreatment or nontreat-ment decision is to say either that they are exactly at the indifference point between benefits and harms or that they have accepted the idea that parents should have a range of discretion in deciding about care for critically ill chil-dren. It is also to say that they believe that either option would be within rea-son and therefore that the nontreatment decision would be acceptable or at least tolerable, just as the protreatment one would be.

If this child were an infant, treatment probably could not have been omit-ted without violating the federal "Baby Doe" regulations summarized later in this chapter. It seems odd, but it is apparently current American law that treat-ments cannot be omitted for infants, but older children similarly situated are not given similar "protections."

Once Ms. Kendrick has accepted the idea that either decision would be acceptable, her problem (and the problem of the physician) then is to reach some resolution. It seems clear that the Alingers need help beyond what either Ms. Kendrick or the physician can provide—that is, they need some counseling to explore available community resources for the care and support of their daughter as well as other family members. If Mrs. Alinger's decision is based on her concern that she cannot cope with the long-term management of Celia, perhaps her fears can be ameliorated if she knows that social supports are avail-able. Mr. Alinger has expressed guilt feelings over his involvement in the acci-dent. He may also feel some unexpressed (and inappropriate) guilt over fathering a daughter with Down syndrome. He may well need psychologic sup-port in working through this critical decision.

This appears to be the kind of case in which the counsel of a local ethics committee would be of great help. Such a committee should have among its members or consultants not only people who can help the family work through the ethical choice, but also people who can identify resources for psychologic counseling and social support networks available in the community. Ms. Kendrick may know of other resources that could assist the parents in working through their decision, as well.

If the final decision is one that Ms. Kendrick finds morally or legally unacceptable, then she will have to consider the alternatives examined in the previous cases in this section. If the parents cannot resolve their disagreement, their own relationship may be threatened. In extreme cases, the courts have been asked to decide which of two disagreeing parents should exercise control. In the meantime, the rule of "erring on the side of life" would support continuing to treat until the controversy is resolved.

Case 17-8
The Guardianship of Terri Schiavo[6]

The following extract comes from the court record of the Florida Supreme Court in an opinion in September 2004. The names are made public in the court record and are real.

Theresa Marie Schindler was born on December 3, 1963, and lived with or near her parents in Pennsylvania until she married Michael Schiavo on November 10, 1984. Michael and Theresa moved to Florida in 1986. They were happily married and both were employed. They had no children. On February 25, 1990, their lives changed. Theresa, age 27, suffered a cardiac arrest as a result of a potassium imbalance. Michael called 911, and Theresa was rushed to the hospital. She never regained consciousness. Since 1990, Theresa has lived in nursing homes with constant care. She is fed and hydrated by tubes. The staff changes her diapers regularly. She has had numerous health problems, but none have been life threatening.

For the first 3 years after this tragedy, Michael and Theresa's parents, Robert and Mary Schindler, enjoyed an amicable relationship. However, that relationship ended in 1993 when the parents and Michael disagreed about appropriate medical treatment for Theresa. In May of 1998, 8 years after Theresa lost consciousness, Michael petitioned the guardianship court to authorize the termination of life-prolonging procedures.

Based on the information received from her physicians, Michael believed that his wife was in a persistent vegetative state, unable to recover consciousness and unable to have any awareness of her family. Based on that belief, he decided to allow his wife to die by withdrawing all "artificial life support." Terri's parents disputed this decision. They believed there were some signs that their daughter was aware of her family's presence and believed that, with new therapy, she had a possibility of recovering consciousness.

Over the many years that this case lingered, Theresa (usually called "Terri") was cared for by many nurses. What is the appropriate role of the nurse when family members disagree over medical treatment for a loved one?

---

[6]Based on Jeb Bush, Governor of Florida, et al., Appellants, v. Michael Schiavo, Guardian of Theresa Schiavo, Appellee. Supreme Court of Florida, No. SC04-925 (2004, September 23).

Commentary

Nurses usually are aware of disagreements among family caregivers over treatment decisions. In fact, nurses are often aware of each situation even before attending physicians are. What steps can and should a nurse take when such disputes arise?

In the early stages of such disputes, there is hope that the family members can reach agreement and resolve the issue. In this case, there was disagreement over issues of medical fact: whether Terri really was in a permanent vegetative state or had a realistic chance of recovery based on either presently available therapies or those that might become available in the future. If the nurse believes that the family members do not have the same understanding of the medical facts, he or she should certainly make the attending physician aware of the lack of agreement. In some cases, the physician or an ethics committee may be able to provide additional medical expertise that would clarify the correct understanding of medical facts.

It is also possible that the family members' preferred treatment decisions are based on significant moral differences that go beyond an understanding of the medical facts. The parents could conclude that Terri should continue to receive life support even if she cannot recover consciousness whereas Michael could conclude that withdrawal of support is appropriate even if she might become conscious again at some point in the future. This disagreement constitutes a moral dispute about human actions. As such, there is no reason that either the physicians' or the nurses' moral views about these matters should influence the surrogate's choice.

In some cases, even if the parties can agree on the facts and agree on whether to stop treatment, society requires that health professionals not act on such an agreement. For example, the federal Baby Doe rules require that life support continue on babies who are not terminally ill, unconscious, or otherwise suffering from a condition known to be "virtually futile and inhumane." Some well-meaning parents may decide to forgo life support when none of these conditions are met, but health professionals are obliged to treat this decision as child abuse or neglect and report the situation to the proper authorities.

In Terri Schiavo's case, however, there were no standards requiring such reporting. Nurses and physicians must accept a valid surrogate's decision to withdraw consent for life-sustaining treatments unless a court order is obtained that overrides the surrogate's decisions.

Clearly, health professionals needed to know who Terri's proper surrogate was. As a general rule, the next of kin is the presumed surrogate—in this case, Michael Schiavo, Terri's husband. He must make treatment decisions based on the patient's beliefs and values insofar as those are known and must choose what is in the best interest of the patient if her wishes cannot be determined. Others close to Terri—family or friends—may disagree with him. They may believe that he, as next of kin, is not following the patient's wishes or not pursuing her best interest. If they continue to dispute his choice after consulting with the clinical staff, the hospital ethics committee, or other trusted advisors (such as clergy), they have the right to challenge his choice in court. That is what Terri's parents did in this case.

After several court reviews, the court concluded that there was "clear and convincing evidence that Theresa Schiavo was in a persistent vegetative state and that Theresa would elect to cease life-prolonging procedures if she were competent to make her own decision." Thus, the court did not accept the parents' claims. The court's decision was repeatedly affirmed on appeal. At this point, the legislature passed an ad hoc law giving the governor of Florida the power to overrule Michael's decision. In the words of the Supreme Court:

> On October 21, 2003, the Legislature enacted chapter 2003-418, the Governor signed the Act into law, and the Governor issued executive order No. 03-201 to stay the continued withholding of nutrition and hydration from Theresa. The nutrition and hydration tube was reinserted pursuant to the Governor's executive order.[27]

On September 23, 2004, the Florida Supreme Court declared that law unconstitutional, thus reinstating the authority of the next of kin as the valid surrogate who could get the life-supporting treatment—including medically supplied nutrition and hydration—stopped on Terri's behalf. The parents continued to dispute the medical facts about whether Terri was vegetative and also continued to challenge the goodwill of her husband.[28] After the Florida courts reviewed all those claims, the U.S. Congress took the unprecedented action of passing a law giving the federal courts jurisdiction. The federal courts, however, at all levels up to the U.S. Supreme Court, refused to take any action to change the state decision. Terri Schiavo's nutrition and hydration was withdrawn, and she died March 31, 2005. Under these circumstances, health professionals had no reason not to follow the valid surrogate's understanding of his wife's wishes. In fact, had they refused to do so, they would have been treating without consent and violating both legal and ethical standards. Interestingly, the politics of the Terri Schiavo case continued to be debated.[29]

Critical Thinking Questions

1. When a nurse first perceives that family members are in disagreement about the use of life-sustaining treatment in a patient's care, who should he or she notify?

2. If the attending physician, based on one of the family member's instructions, decides to proceed with withdrawal of life support before agreement is achieved in the entire family, what should the nurse do?

3. What do you think should have happened in the Terri Schiavo case? Why?

Case 17-9

Disagreements with the Healthcare Proxy

Mr. Moore is a 42-year-old, single male with advanced hepatic cancer. He was admitted for hydration and pain management. Mr. Moore was alert and oriented at the time of his admission and was aware that he had a very poor prognosis. He had already named one of his sisters as his healthcare proxy and had clearly expressed a desire for all possible interventions including full-code status.

Within a week, Mr. Moore's condition deteriorated. His healthcare proxy was in Arizona, but two other siblings visited him daily. As his condition worsened, Mr. Moore began to express to his siblings that he was ready to die and no longer wanted a full-code status. The two siblings asked Beth Green, Mr. Moore's primary nurse, that he not be resuscitated if he should have a cardiac arrest.

By the end of 3 weeks, Mr. Moore's capacity to make decisions was an issue. He had brain metastases that were causing confusion. Mrs. Green notified the house staff and the attending physician of Mr. Moore's siblings' request to change the patient's code status. All agreed that the healthcare proxy should be called to discuss his change in condition and his request for DNR status. The healthcare proxy refused to agree to the DNR and said that she would make a decision after she saw her brother, in about 6 days. The other siblings, however, continued to pressure the healthcare team to make Mr. Moore a DNR. They could not understand why the healthcare team accepted their sister's decisions rather than the wishes of the siblings present to see Mr. Moore's changed condition. They threatened to physically block anybody who tried to resuscitate their brother.

The attending physician did not feel comfortable overriding the healthcare proxy despite a hospital policy that allowed him to do so (when it was believed that resuscitation would not benefit the patient). He was willing to go through a resuscitation effort because he believed the patient would not survive the effort (i.e., the outcome [patient death] would be the same).

Mrs. Green and the other nurses questioned what they should do if Mr. Moore coded before the healthcare proxy arrived. Mrs. Green personally believed that Mr. Moore had been competent during his discussions with his siblings and that he no longer wanted to be resuscitated. She believed that he accepted his inevitable death and did not want to undergo resuscitative efforts. The siblings who were present with him 24 hours a day believed the same, but they were unable to convince their absent sister of this fact.

Mr. Moore was decompensating at a rate that made all parties uncomfortable with the healthcare proxy's time frame. None of the nursing staff members wanted to be present if and when Mr. Moore arrested. What should Mrs. Green and the other nurses do to resolve this situation? What should they do if he arrests?

Commentary

The nurses and clinicians in this case have been introduced to the concept of proxy decision making. It appears that the patient, Mr. Moore, had made a clear and valid declaration naming his absent sister as his proxy should he ever be incapable of making decisions on his own. The critical questions in this case concern when a proxy decision maker assumes responsibility and what standard the proxy should use. A proxy expressed in a durable power of attorney for health care is the person the patient wants to make decisions for him or her if he or she is ever incapable of doing so. This means that as long as Mr. Moore is mentally competent to express his own views, then he has the authority to do so. During the time he is competent, his own decision is decisive, not those of any of his family, whether the sisters at his bedside or the out-of-town proxy.

As Mr. Moore deteriorates, he at some point is no longer capable of making his own decisions in a substantially autonomous manner. There seems to be no doubt that at this point someone else should take over. Normally, that would be the proxy. The standard used by the proxy varies depending on the circumstances. If the proxy knows nothing of the patient's own views, she would apply the best interest standard—that is, attempting to do what is best for the patient. (This standard is discussed further in the cases later in this chapter.) However, the best interest standard applies only when the proxy has no basis for knowing the patient's own wishes, as expressed while he was competent. In this case, the proxy is under the assumption that her brother wanted all possible interventions, including full-code status. This was Mr. Moore's choice when he entered the hospital and named his sister as proxy. In deciding not to agree to a DNR order, the sister is making a substituted judgment for her brother based on his wishes as she knows them.

Mr. Moore changed his mind, however, telling his other sisters that he was ready to die and no longer wanted a full-code status. Unfortunately, he did not express this change of mind to his proxy. The sisters and Mrs. Green could argue that the absent sister is failing to fulfill her duties as proxy by not making a substituted judgment based on Mr. Moore's changed views. Although a proxy is usually given some discretion in deciding what the patient would have wanted, it seems it would be hard for the proxy in this case to sustain her position that Mr. Moore really wanted to be resuscitated in the event of an arrest.

This leaves us wondering what Mrs. Green and the sisters should do if they are convinced that the proxy is failing in her duty to make a substituted judgment. The local institution apparently has a policy that would permit the physician unilaterally to override the proxy in cases like this one, but he refuses to do so. That policy is controversial, however. In most jurisdictions, the authority of the proxy is established by law. The moral basis of the proxy's authority is the autonomy of the patient to pick an agent while he or she is competent. Mr. Moore could have picked the physician, Mrs. Green, or one of the other sisters, but he did not. We must assume he freely chose the sister that he did. This suggests that any hospital policy that appears to authorize physicians to unilaterally override a proxy is in violation of the law. Likewise, if the sisters at the bedside were to try to override the proxy decision and the physician acted on the sisters' judgment, he would probably be acting illegally.

Could Mrs. Green solve this problem simply by refusing to respond to the code? Probably not. First, even if she refused to respond, others probably would. If she is convinced that it is wrong to resuscitate Mr. Moore because she thought it was not in her patient's interest, the result would still be that his wishes (as expressed by his proxy) were not respected. Refusing to treat when a valid surrogate has refused to authorize an instruction not to resuscitate could be considered abandonment. On the other hand, if she refused to resuscitate because she understood that to be Mr. Moore's instructions, given while he was still competent, she would be on more solid ground. Nevertheless, it would be a controversial and irreversible action, one that could be challenged by the physician or by Mr. Moore's absent sister.

Unless it can be established that Mr. Moore refused treatment while he was still competent, there seems to be no one on the scene capable of overriding the decision of a valid surrogate. It would be best for all parties if Mrs. Green and the sisters could convince the proxy of Mr. Moore's more recent wishes. If that fails, action may have to be taken to disqualify her as a proxy. If a designated proxy is clearly failing to make a correct substituted judgment, then the proxy can and should be removed. This could take judicial intervention, because no one on the scene appears to have that power.

Futile Care

Recent acceptance of the right of competent patients and valid surrogates to refuse life-prolonging treatment has led to a newer kind of ethical problem in the care of terminally and critically ill patients. Many patients are concluding that some treatment proposals offer more potential burden than benefit; clinicians are also realizing that in some cases, aggressive life-support efforts are so unlikely to succeed that they can be deemed futile. At the same time, a minority of patients and families retains the more traditional commitment to attempting to preserve life even in cases where the chances of success are minimal. Increasingly, clinicians are insisting that some of these efforts are inconsistent with their understanding of what counts as good healthcare practices. Nurses and physicians are finding themselves in situations where patients or families demand efforts that appear heroic but clinicians are convinced there is no chance of restoring the patient to what the clinician takes to be minimally acceptable health. In some cases, it is a foregone conclusion that the patient's life can be preserved only for a very brief time. Nurses and other healthcare professionals are claiming a right to determine that some demands for care are so unreasonable that they can be unilaterally rejected, even when the patient or surrogate is insisting that every effort be made to prolong life.[30]

These demands of healthcare professionals have led to considerable controversy over the very meaning of the term *futility*.[31] A distinction is now made between two different types of judgments regarding futility. Decisions by clinicians that interventions requested by patients or surrogates are not capable of producing the effect sought constitute one type of futility judgment. A demand from a desperate family that CPR be given 60 minutes after a cardiac arrest when such an intervention could not restart circulation is an example of this kind of futility judgment. These are now referred to as *physiological futility*.

In many other cases, however, families are demanding interventions that will have the physiological effect of changing the time and the way the patient dies. On their part, clinicians may believe that the change is of no value. For example, an 87-year-old woman named Helga Wanglie was left in a persistent vegetative state after a cardiac arrest following a series of respiratory tract infections. Her clinicians were convinced that there was no possibility of her ever recovering consciousness. Nevertheless, her husband insisted on a ventilator for life support. He did so on the grounds that not only he, but also his wife, were strongly pro-life and that she had long insisted that she would want her life prolonged even if she were in an unconscious condition. Her husband was not arguing about her prognosis; he conceded that the clinicians were correct in claiming that further life support could not restore consciousness. Still, he rejected the value judgment of the clinicians that unconscious life is not worth preserving.[32] Here the disagreement is not over the medical facts and prognosis; it is over the value of preserving unconscious life. This is now being called a judgment of *normative futility*.

Much of the dispute today is over whether health professionals have the right to refuse to participate in life-supporting interventions that will prolong life, at least for a while, in a way that the clinician believes is useless or disproportionately burdensome, perhaps even cruel and inhumane. Critics are claiming that even if clinicians should have a right to refuse to deliver physiologically futile care, the decision about normative futility is fundamentally not a medical one.[33] It is a value judgment raising much more complex questions.

Part of the complexity is over the reason that clinicians might want to refuse to provide such life support. One reason could be that substantial resources would be consumed for what they believe is a useless pursuit. If no benefit comes to the patient from this expenditure of resources and other patients could benefit from them, then morality seems to require refusing to provide wasteful and futile care. (This concern for the welfare of other patients will be taken up in the following section of this chapter.)

The resource allocation concern, however, is not the only reason that clinicians are demanding the right not to be party to aggressive life-supporting efforts for permanently unconscious and dying patients, even if such support will postpone somewhat the time of death. They are also concerned about what is now being called *professional integrity*. They claim that health professionals have an understanding of the purpose of health care and that they should have the right to refuse to deliver services—even services that will effectively change the timing of a patient's death—when the interventions are not consistent with their understanding of the purpose of health care. The following two cases deal with interventions nurses deem futile even though providing them would have some effect on the way the patients die. In these cases, resources are not the primary issue. That problem will be reserved for the following section. Here the issue is whether the care being demanded is consistent with the nurses' understanding of the nursing role.

Case 17-10

Life-Support for the Anencephalic Infant[7]

Baby Sharon was born at Southside Hospital in October 1992 with anencephaly, a congenital malformation in which a major portion of the brain, skull, and scalp is missing. Baby Sharon lacks a cerebrum, and she is permanently unconscious. Thus, she has no cognitive abilities or awareness. She cannot see, hear, or otherwise interact with her environment. She does, however, have brain stem functions such as respiration and brain stem reflexes.

When Baby Sharon had difficulty breathing on her own at birth, the hospital physicians placed her on a mechanical ventilator. This respiratory support allowed the doctors to confirm the diagnosis. They gave Sharon's mother, Ms. Tucker, the diagnosis and prognosis of Sharon's condition. The physicians explained to Ms. Tucker that most anencephalic infants die within a few days of birth due to breathing difficulties and other complications. Because aggressive treatment would serve no therapeutic or palliative purpose, they recommended that Sharon be provided only with supportive care in the form of nutrition, hydration, and warmth. Physicians at the hospital also discussed with Ms. Tucker the possibility of a DNR order that would provide for the withholding of life-saving measures in the future.

The treatment physicians and Ms. Tucker failed to reach an agreement as to the appropriate level of care for Sharon. Ms. Tucker insisted that Sharon be provided with mechanical breathing assistance whenever the infant developed difficulty breathing on her own, whereas the physicians maintained that such care was inappropriate. Ms. Tucker appealed to her firm Christian faith that all life should be protected. She said she believed that God would work a miracle if that was his will. Otherwise, she believed God, not other humans, should decide the moment of her daughter's death.

As a result of this impasse, Southside Hospital sought to transfer Sharon to another hospital. This attempt failed when all the hospitals in the area with pediatric intensive care units declined to accept the infant.

All parties agreed that cost of care was not the issue. Ms. Tucker was a member of an HMO that agreed to pay for all treatment. Ms. Tucker was not married to the baby's father. Since Sharon's birth, the father had been only distantly involved in matters relating to the infant. Neither Southside Hospital nor Ms. Tucker ever sought the father's opinion or consent regarding Sharon's medical treatment.

Because of Ms. Tucker's continued insistence that Sharon receive ventilator treatment, the baby's physicians requested assistance from Southside Hospital's ethics committee in overriding the mother's wishes. A three-person ethics committee subcommittee consisting of a family practitioner, a psychiatrist, and a minister met with Sharon's healthcare providers. The subcommittee concluded that Sharon's ventilator treatment should end because "such care is futile." It recommended waiting a reasonable time for the family to adjust to

---

[7]This case is based on In the Matter of Baby K, 1993 WL 343557 (E.D. Va.); In the Matter of Baby "K" 1994 WL 38674 (4th Cir Va.). Details and names have been changed.

the idea of terminating aggressive therapy. If Ms. Tucker refused to follow this advice, the subcommittee recommended that the hospital attempt to resolve the matter through the legal system. In the meantime, Sharon was stable most of the time, needing ventilator assistance only occasionally. She was transferred to a local nursing home with the understanding that she would be returned to Southside Hospital's emergency room in the event of respiratory crisis.

Martha Houston was a per diem nurse who worked from time to time in the emergency room of Southside Hospital. From her conversations with other nurses, she knew that the ER might have to provide emergency ventilatory support for Sharon when needed. She had a distinct sense that providing this kind of treatment in cases like Sharon's was not the real purpose of nursing, although she understood that even the physicians who objected to the treatment as futile had agreed to the emergency ventilation while the case was being settled in the courts. That did not completely settle the matter for Mrs. Houston, however. Because the hospital had adequate staffing, other patients would not be at risk by providing the emergency ventilation. Nevertheless, she had a lingering discomfort when she realized that if she accepted future assignments at Southside Hospital, she could well be forced to participate in interventions she considered useless and outside her understanding of the purpose of emergency room nursing. She wondered if it would be ethical to object to participating in this intervention.

Case 17-11
Family Demands and Professional Integrity

Suzanne Grimes, RN, was assigned to care for Mr. Desmond, a 67-year-old man with chronic obstructive lung disease and cor pulmonale who had developed tracheal necrosis and paratracheal abscesses from prolonged mechanical ventilation. Several days ago, his physicians had decided that his trachea could not be repaired. Now they discovered that he was also suffering from sepsis. After discussing Mr. Desmond's prognosis with his physician, his family had agreed to discontinue treatment. Mr. Desmond was now semicomatose and incapable of participating in this critical decision. The plan was to make Mr. Desmond as comfortable as possible until his inevitable death from sepsis and respiratory failure.

During the morning, Mr. Desmond was visited by his oldest daughter who lived thousands of miles away and had not seen her father for several years. She was visibly alarmed by Mr. Desmond's condition and by the fact that no treatment was being carried out for his declining physical condition. After conferring with the rest of the family, she announced that the family would like to try an alternative treatment for Mr. Desmond. They called the physician and requested that massive doses of vitamins be given to him. The physician agreed to their request. He then called Miss Grimes and asked her to begin instituting massive intravenous vitamin therapy.

Miss Grimes protested the use of this form of therapy in the care of an inevitably dying patient. She consulted her supervisor. The supervisor agreed with the physician and the family. "I don't understand why you are protesting about vitamins," the supervisor said. "It won't take much of your time to administer them, it won't cost the family a lot of money; and it might help them cope with their father's imminent death," she told Miss Grimes. "Besides, vitamins won't hurt Mr. Desmond. He won't notice them because he is dying anyway. So why the fuss?"

Miss Grimes still disagreed with the plan. She argued, "We are giving the family false hopes and we are setting a precedent for family requests for any treatment on dying patients." According to Miss Grimes, it was not so much the cost of the requested therapy as the fact that a family could make requests of nursing staff that were of no proven benefit to the dying patient. Was it fair that families could make such requests? Miss Grimes did not think so.

Commentary

These two cases both raise the problem of whether nurses and other healthcare professionals can appeal to their understanding of the purpose of their profession in refusing to participate in interventions sought by surrogates for patients who are critically or terminally ill.

Sharon, the anencephalic infant whose mother insisted that, based on her religious belief, all life should be preserved, clearly could have had the exact timing of her death changed by emergency ventilation in moments of respiratory crisis. In fact, the infant upon which this case is based lived for two-and-a-half years following a court decision that support should be provided. There is no doubt that without the ventilatory intervention she would have died much sooner. Thus, the claim of the hospital providers was not that the ventilation would have no physiological effect on Sharon.

Their real concern and that of Mrs. Houston, the per diem nurse working in the emergency room, was whether ventilation intervention is consistent with the practice of good health care. Apparently, Mrs. Houston had doubts that the purpose of emergency room nursing was to prolong life in what was believed to be only a temporary delay in the moment of death of the child.

Some might dispute Mrs. Houston's understanding the purpose of ER nursing. Some health professionals hold the traditional view that preservation of life is a fundamental goal for all health practice, but increasingly members of the health professions are recognizing that sometimes mere preservation of life, especially unconscious life, serves no real purpose. Holders of this newer view stress other goals such as cure of disease, relief of suffering, and promotion of health.

In Sharon's case, the disease (anencephaly) could not be cured. Moreover, because she was permanently unconscious, she was beyond suffering. Likewise, promotion of her health did not seem to be an option. Temporary ventilation, from Mrs. Houston's point of view, seemed to offer no benefit at all. In fact, it seemed like an indignity to continue to maintain life in such a patient.

Assuming that was the nurse's view, how should she interact with Ms. Tucker, the mother whose religious values led her to see an important reason to preserve even unconscious life? One of the fundamental issues raised by so-called "futile care cases" is whether it is up to the various health professions to determine the scope of their practices. Traditionally, professions have defined their purposes or objectives. This tradition, however, is increasingly being called into question. Professions have "public roles" and are created not by members of the professions themselves, but by society. At least insofar as licensure creates monopoly control over the practice of nursing or doctoring, these professions are increasingly acknowledging that the purposes of their roles will be subject to negotiation and mutual agreement. There may be times when the public's understanding of the professional role and the profession's own understanding of it are not identical. Differences have arisen recently, for instance, over such issues as participation in medical execution and warning the public about dangerous patients. The issue is whether the public or the profession should define the professional's role in such controversial areas.

In the case of care deemed futile by many members of the health professions, we face a problem of differing moral understandings of the objectives of the use of professional skills. We know that a minority of the population, including some nurses, believes strongly that even permanently unconscious life is worth preserving. If we could arrange nursing practice so that nurses who have such values were the ones on call to provide such care, then no individual consciences would be violated. Some would claim that even though a number of nurses hold that there is value in preserving unconscious life, they are mistaken—the real purpose of nursing does not include efforts to preserve such lives. But is it possible to sustain the claim that there is one and only one correct understanding of the purpose of nursing and that practitioners can have certain knowledge of what that one purpose is?

This seems to be a fundamental clash between a professional's right to practice her profession as she sees fit and a mother's right to have her baby kept alive under conditions the healthcare team has the skill and resources to provide. When these cases have been adjudicated in the courts, with rare exceptions the courts have found that patients or their surrogates have a right to pursue treatments that will predictably extend life, at least in cases in which insurers are willing to pay the bills and other patients' interests are not seriously jeopardized. The health professionals already providing ongoing care have been found to have a duty to continue those interventions.

A similar issue arises in the second case, that of Suzanne Grimes, the nurse responsible for the care of Mr. Desmond. She perceives that the family has opted for a totally useless therapy. She might object purely out of concern for the patient. Or because the vitamin therapy is not going to burden the patient, she might well be indifferent to the proposed treatment.

But Miss Grimes clearly feels uncomfortable with the proposed vitamin therapy. Partly, she seems concerned that family members can ask for utterly useless interventions and obtain them. One reason for her to object could be that providing intravenous megavitamin therapy involves some costs and requires nursing time. Other patients' interests could be compromised by the time devoted to the useless intervention. But, as Miss Grimes's supervisor has pointed out, very few resources will be expended on this particular intervention.

The real underlying issue, once again, may be that the professional nurse feels that her professional integrity is jeopardized if she is made to deliver a treatment that seems incompatible with her understanding of the purpose of her profession. If the treatment is utterly useless, why should a nurse have to devote her energy to the procedure just because a family member believes it might help?

It seems reasonable to concede that it is very unlikely that the vitamins will help. But earlier in this chapter we discussed the emerging theory that family members should be given some discretion in their choices for incompetent loved ones, provided those choices are within reason.

This leaves Miss Grimes with three possible objections to the family's decision. First, she could argue that the oldest daughter has exercised undue influence and that, therefore, the decision should not be honored. She might hold that the wife, as next of kin, should be the real decision maker, assuming that Mr. Desmond could not participate. If the wife had, in fact, accepted the treatment proposal after being persuaded by her daughter, however, Miss Grimes has little grounds for claiming that the valid surrogate disagreed with the vitamin therapy.

Second, she could argue that the family decision about what would serve Mr. Desmond's interests is so grossly in error that it should be overturned. Just as hospital attorneys go to court to override parents who make unreasonable treatment refusal decisions for their children, so they could seek to overturn a familial decision that was so implausible that it would constitute abuse of the patient. That creates problems as well, however. It would require a court action to have the family removed from the decision-making process. Furthermore, it is highly debatable whether the family's decision is so contrary to Mr. Desmond's interests that a court should intervene. After all, he is not likely to be hurt from the treatment.

That leaves one other possibility: that even though the family decision is tolerable in terms of Mr. Desmond's interest, requiring Miss Grimes to participate in the family's choice of treatment violates her rights to practice nursing as she understands its purposes. Could Miss Grimes sustain such an argument here?

Critical Thinking Question

If you were Miss Grimes, how would you resolve the conflicts in Case 17-11? Why?

Limits Based on the Interests of Other Parties

Thus far, the cases in this chapter have focused on the principle of autonomy and its conflict with the patient's welfare (beneficence). This problem arose first with competent and formerly competent patients and then with patients who have never expressed their wishes about terminal care while competent. Even then we saw that some degree of familial autonomy is being advocated by many participating in the current debate. At the same time, the principle of beneficence seems to place some limits on the range of familial and other surrogate choices. Sometimes the welfare of these incompetent patients seems to require overruling parents and other surrogates.

There are other cases in which the welfare of other parties may be in conflict with the decision rendered by the patient or surrogate. This may arise when the patient is permanently comatose and, by many people's judgment, has no further possibility of benefit from treatment. It may also arise when the patient might benefit but the benefits are extremely small compared with the potential social or economic costs to others. These problems are related to the ethics of allocation of scarce resources. The principle of beneficence (now interpreted broadly to include the welfare of all affected parties) is in potential conflict with the principles of autonomy and justice. Increasingly, as a society we are having to ask whether patients or their surrogates should ever be prohibited from having the care they desire because of burdens to other parties. In the 1950s, Pope Pius XII, in clarifying the concept of extraordinary means, stated that means may be expendable if they involve grave burden to oneself or another.[34] In the future, nurses will be facing these social conflicts—arising particularly in the care of the terminally ill—more and more.

Case 17-12
The Economic Side of Prolonging Life

Leon Davies, age 16, has Duchenne muscular dystrophy. Despite his relatively young age, his disease is at an advanced stage. He has already lost the functional use of all extremities, is dependent for all activities of daily living, and suffers frequent sleeplessness and headaches because of breathing difficulties. Leon's father died when Leon was an infant. His mother is disabled and lives on a fixed income in a small rural community in another state. Because of his mother's inability to care for him, Leon has been in the custody of the Department of Social Services for the past 7 years. He has been placed in a private institution for children with physical disabilities, where he is supported by a combination of federal and state funds. He sees his mother about twice a year and considers the staff of the institution his "real family." As his physical condition has deteriorated, staff members have noted that Leon is becoming uncooperative and distant from them and from peers. They are often unsure about what to do to relieve his headaches and sleeplessness.

Recently, Leon's physician has talked with him about the possibility of being placed on a respirator to prolong his life. It has been made clear that such a decision would probably improve his sleeping and decrease his headaches but that Leon should not expect improvement in any of his other functions.

Simone Gauthier, a nurse and the director of the institution where Leon lives, has discussed Leon's care with his physician and has concluded that it is unlikely that Leon would be able to stay at her facility if he were placed on a respirator. The institution does not maintain 24-hour nursing care, and staff members would be unable to provide the level of care that he would need if he were on a respirator. She also wonders whether the state could afford the approximately $200,000 extra a year required to provide respirator care for Leon. Mrs. Gauthier has tried to talk with Leon about his own wishes with respect to being on a respirator, but Leon has been vague. He finally said that he did not know what decision to make. Neither Mrs. Gauthier's institution nor the physicians have discussed what they plan to do for Leon when his inevitable respiratory failure occurs.

Commentary

The first issue raised by this case is whether Ms. Gauthier is motivated out of concern for burdens to others or out of what is best for Leon Davies. She seems to have shifted her focus from the welfare of the individual patient to a more social perspective, observing, for example, that the extra $200,000 per year for respirator care is a great deal of money. At some point, a limit must be reached.

The question must be raised of whether this kind of issue is appropriate to the clinical nurse's agenda. If a decision is made that Leon Davies's treatment should be limited in order to protect the welfare of others, should the nurse be the one raising the issue, or should someone else—an administrator, the board of trustees, or health insurance planners—be setting these limits? Because Mrs. Gauthier is the administrator of Leon Davies's institution, perhaps her nursing background provides her with a unique perspective in raising the issue.

Whoever makes these choices will face the alternatives for allocating scarce resources discussed in the cases in Chapters 4 and 5. It is not obvious that just because resources are scarce, the patient who is expected to receive the least benefit has the least claim on them. The administrators of the system might give the resources to those who are most willing to pay for them, they might use them where they will do the most good, or they might distribute them to those in greatest need. Should nurses make these choices themselves, or should they turn to someone else for the decisions?

Case 17-13

Request for Assistance in Dying when Removing a Life-Sustaining Treatment Is Not an Option

Trevor Miles is an educated, articulate, wealthy, and until recently, healthy 78-year-old, single male. He has lived a rich and full life and sees nothing but diminishment in his future with a life increasingly constricted to his condominium. A recent fall resulted in a fracture of his pelvis and leg. He bitterly resents not being able to walk his dog, Whistles. Looking ahead to the future he sees nothing but further diminishment. His fall was the result of a TIA, and he suspects that Parkinson's disease is in his future. When he told someone that he wished he could just fall asleep and never wake up, his friend told him that he should just stop eating and drinking. His friend works for a hospice and suggested he call the local hospice to see if they would care for him during his time of debilitation since it was clear that Trevor could not remain in his condominium alone while he died.

Trevor's few close friends think that what he wants to do is terrible and none are willing to care for him while he dies of dehydration. Bert Roser is the intake nurse at the hospice who first hears his request. He immediately calls the Medical Director to see if this would be an appropriate admission since he is not aware of the in-patient hospice unit ever serving in this capacity. Bert is moved by Trevor's request but he is not sure that it would be good for the hospice to get the reputation of helping folks who want to cause their own deaths.

Margaret Sybilla is a 69-year-old woman who has battled cancer for 32 years—with five major recurrences. Her husband died early, and she raised three daughters, who are now all married with children. She buried her mother and a brother. She is a retired high school teacher and recently has worked tirelessly for her local SPCA. Now she is tired, tired, tired. For years she fought the cancer wanting to raise her daughters, get them through college, and see a grandchild. But at present she is finding life too threatening and she wants to "go to God." She has researched her options on the Internet and comes to the hospice wanting *palliative sedation*. Her family supports her. The hospice has a policy which states that palliative sedation needs to be used for the imminently dying and that it should not be used to treat existential suffering or angst. Margaret does not meet these criteria. When she is told that palliative sedation is used for intractable pain, delirium, agitation, dyspnea, and then asked to evaluate her pain on a scale of 1 (no pain) to 10 (worst pain) she says her pain is about a 1 or 2. She says that she will not commit suicide because she does not want her family to have to live with this legacy. She also says that she does not want to stop eating and drinking because this will "drag" on for days. Staff report that she uses lots of "code language" and winking, seeming to suggest that she knows they cannot give her a lethal prescription because assisted suicide is illegal in their state but that they should be able to accomplish the same thing via palliative sedation.

Some of the staff are angry that she wants them to do what she will not do for herself. Others believe that the hospice policy is wrong and that palliative sedation should be allowed for existential suffering since it most certainly is a "distressing symptom." Greta Stihls is the nurse manager of the hospice and is conflicted about how the hospice should respond to Mrs. Sybilla's request. She contacts the Medical Director and ethics committee. What recommendations should come from the hospice ethics committee about meeting Mrs. Sybilla's needs?

Commentary

Dr. Timothy Quill and others described six "Last Resort" Palliative Interventions that can be valuable options to patients who have witnessed a bad death and fear a similar experience:

1. Standard pain management,
2. Forgoing life-sustaining therapy,
3. Voluntarily stopping eating and drinking,
4. Terminal sedation (heavy sedation to escape pain, shortness of breath, or other severe symptoms)
5. Assisted suicide, or
6. Voluntary active euthanasia,

Acknowledging that the list is written from least contentious ethically and legally to most, he writes:

> Knowledge of the range of possibilities can also help clinicians better respond to the relatively rare patients who pain and suffering become intolerable, without violating their own values and without abandoning their patients. Clinicians who care for severely ill patients must become aware of these options and decide which ones they are willing to provide as a last resort. The challenge is to find the least harmful alternative given the patient's circumstances and the values of the patient, family and clinicians involved.[35]

Clearly the nurses and other healthcare professionals in both of these cases are struggling to determine if it is ethical for them to be complicit in the autonomous choices of Mr. Miles and Mrs. Sybilla as they respectively choose to end their lives by voluntarily stopping eating and drinking or terminal sedation. Society at large and the healthcare community specifically lack consensus about these "last resort" palliative interventions and about the appropriateness of the healthcare institutions being complicit in their use.

Greta Stihls, Mrs. Sybilla's nurse, is particularly troubled by her request. The hospice has a policy stating that palliative sedation should only be used for patients who are imminently dying and not for relief of existential angst. The medical director shared with her a recent article contrasting proportionate palliative sedation and palliative sedation to unconsciousness and seems to want to honor Mrs. Sybilla's request, even if this means changing hospice policy or making an exception. The article states:

> Despite receiving state-of-the-art palliative care, some patients still experience severe suffering toward the end of life. Palliative sedation is a potential way to respond to such suffering, but access is uneven and unpredictable, in part because of confusion about different kinds of sedation. Proportionate palliative sedation (PPS) uses the

minimum amount of sedation necessary to relieve refractory physical symptoms at the very end of life. To relieve suffering may require progressive increases in sedation, sometimes to the point of unconsciousness, but consciousness is maintained if possible. Palliative sedation with the intended end point of unconsciousness (PSU) is a more controversial practice that may be considered for much fewer refractory cases.[36]

What are the responsibilities of nurses caring for patients like Mr. Miles and Mrs. Stihl's concerning decisions for individual patients, institutional policy, and establishing "best practices" for end of life care?

Critical Thinking Questions

1. If you were Bert Roser how would you respond to Mr. Miles? How would patient advocacy be described in this situation? Is cooperating with a patient's voluntary stopping of eating and drinking compatible with the ethics of the nursing profession? How should the hospice resolve its reservations about admitting Mr. Miles?

2. If you were Greta Stihls how would you respond to the request made by Mrs. Sybilla? How would patient advocacy be described in this situation? Is assisting in palliative sedation to the point of unconsciousness compatible with the ethics of the nursing profession? How should the hospice resolve its reservation about acceding to Mrs. Sybilla's request?

ENDNOTES

1. As we go to publication, the ANA is reviewing a new position statement on *Registered Nurses' Roles and Responsibilities in Providing Expert Care and Counseling at the End of Life*. Check their website to see the final version: www.nursingworld.org.
2. United States, Omnibus Budget Reconciliation Act of 1990, sec. 4206: Medicare provider agreements assuring the implementation of a patient's right to participate in and direct health care decisions affecting the patient. [and] sec. 4751: Requirements for advance directives under state plans for medical assistance. Statutes at Large. 1990 November 5 (date of enactment). 104. 1388/115–117, 1388/204–206.
3. American Nurses Association. (1991). *Nursing and the Patient Self-Determination Act* (Position statement). Washington, DC: Author.
4. President's Commission for the Study of Ethical Problems in Medicine and Biomedical and Behavioral Research. (1981). *Defining death: Medical, legal, and ethical issues in the definition of death*. Washington, DC: U.S. Government Printing Office.
5. For recent developments in the definition of death debate, see Youngner, S. J., Arnold, R. M., & Schapiro, R. (Eds.). (1999). *The definition of death: Contemporary controversies*. Baltimore: Johns Hopkins University Press.

6. President's Council on Bioethics. (2008, December). *Controversies in the determination of death*. Washington, DC: U.S. Government Printing Office.

7. Ibid, p. 89. They do, however, reject the somatically integrated whole philosophical argument and propose in its stead a fundamental openness to the surrounding environment argument (p. 90).

8. Green, M. B., & Wikler, D. (1980). Brain death and personal identity. *Philosophy and Public Affairs, 9*(2), 105–133.

9. Veatch, R. M. (1976). *Death, dying, and the biological revolution*. New Haven, CT: Yale University Press.

10. This story is available at: http://www.msnbc.msn.com/id/27611868/. Accessed February 7, 2010.

11. In re Quinlan. 70 N.J. 10, 355 A.2d 647 (1976).

12. President's Commission for the Study of Ethical Problems in Medicine and Biomedical and Behavioral Research. (1983). *Deciding to forego life-sustaining treatment: Ethical, medical, and legal issues in treatment decisions*. Washington, DC: U.S. Government Printing Office.

13. Bleich, J. D. (1979). The obligation to heal in the Judaic tradition: A comparative analysis. In F. Rosner & J. D. Bleich (Eds.), *Jewish bioethics* (pp. 1–44). New York: Sanhedrin Press.

14. California "Natural Death" Act. Cal. Stat., Chapter 1439, Code, Health, and Safety, sections 7185–7195 (1976).

15. Elpern, E. H., Covert, B., & Kleinpell, R. (2005, November). Moral distress of staff nurses in a medical intensive care unit. *American Journal of Critical Care, 14*(6), 523–530.

16. Miles, S. H., Cranford, R., & Schultz, A. L. (1982, May). The do-not-resuscitate order in a teaching hospital. *Annals of Internal Medicine, 96*, 660–664; Minnesota Medical Association. (1981, January 24). *Do not resuscitate (DNR) guidelines*. Minneapolis, MN: Author; Youngner, S. J., Lewandowski, W., McClish, D. K., Juknialis, B. W., Coulton, C., & Bartlett, E. T. (1985). "Do not resuscitate" orders. *Journal of the American Medical Association, 285*, 54–57.

17. Beth Israel Hospital, Guidelines: Orders not to resuscitate. (1983). In President's Commission for the Study of Ethical Problems in Medicine and Biomedical and Behavioral Research, *Deciding to forego life-sustaining treatment: Ethical, medical, and legal issues in treatment decisions* (p. 503). Washington, DC: U.S. Government Printing Office.

18. Frances Okun v. The Society of New York Hospital. Supreme Court of the State of New York. County of New York. Summons. Index number 13167/84 (1984, June 1).

19. American Nurses Association. (1992). *Position statement: Nursing care and do-not-resuscitate decisions*. Washington, DC: Author. See also American Nurses Association. (2001). *Code of ethics for nurses with interpretive statements* (pp. 8–9). Washington, DC: Author.

20. Jameton, A. (1984). *Nursing practice: The ethical issues*. Englewood, NJ: Prentice Hall; Yeo, M., & Moorhouse, A. (1996). *Concepts and cases in nursing ethics* (2nd ed., pp. 277–280). Ontario, Canada: Broadview Press; Rodney, P. (1988). Moral distress in critical care nursing. *Canadian Critical Care Nursing Journal, 5*(2), 9–11.

21. U.S. Department of Health and Human Services. (1985, April 15). Infant care review committees—Model services and treatment for disabled infants; Model guidelines for health care providers to establish infant care review committees. *Federal Register: Notices, 50*(72), 14893–14901.

22. U.S. Department of Health and Human Services. (1985, April 15). Child abuse and neglect prevention and treatment program. Final Rule: 45 CFR 1340. *Federal Register: Rules and Regulations, 50*(72), 14878–14892.

23. Ibid.

24. President's Commission for the Study of Ethical Problems in Medicine and Biomedical and Behavioral Research. (1983). *Deciding to forego life-sustaining treatment: Ethical, medical, and legal issues in treatment decisions* (p. 218). Washington, DC: U.S. Government Printing Office.

25. Ibid., pp. 212, 215.

26. McCloskey, E. L. (1991, June). The Patient Self-Determination Act. *Kennedy Institute of Ethics Journal, 1*, 163–169.

27. Jeb Bush, Governor of Florida, et al., Appellants, v. Michael Schiavo, Guardian of Theresa Schiavo, Appellee. Supreme Court of Florida, No. SC04-925 (2004, September 23).

28. Chachere, V. (2005, February 25). Abuse allegations add new twist to Schiavo drama. *Herald Tribune*, p. B7.

29. Gilgoff, D. (2005, April 4). Life and death politics. *U.S. News & World Report*, pp. 15–21.

30. Cranford, R. E. (1994). Medical futility: Transforming a clinical concept into legal and social policies. *Journal of the American Geriatrics Society, 42*(8), 894–898; Jecker, N. S., & Pearlman, R. A. (1992, June). Medical futility: Who decides? *Archives of Internal Medicine, 152*, 1140–1144; Jecker, N. S., & Schneiderman, L. J. (1993). Medical futility: The duty not to treat. *Cambridge Quarterly of Healthcare Ethics, 2*, 151–159; Murphy, D. J. (1994). Can we set futile care policies? Institutional and systemic challenges. *Journal of the American Geriatrics Society, 42*(8), 890–893; Taylor, C. (1995). Medical futility and nursing. *IMAGE: Journal of Nursing Scholarship, 27*(3), 301–306; Tomlinson, T., & Brody, H. (1990). Futility and the ethics of resuscitation. *Journal of the American Medical Association, 264*, 1277.

31. Cranford, R., & Gostin, L. (1992, Winter). Futility: A concept in search of a definition. *Law, Medicine & Health Care, 20*, 307–309; Youngner, S. J. (1988). Who defines futility? *Journal of the American Medical Association, 260*, 2094–2095.

32. Angell, M. (1991). The case of Helga Wanglie: A new kind of "right to die" case. *New England Journal of Medicine, 325*, 511–512; In re the Conservatorship of Helga Wanglie, State of Minnesota, District Court; Probate Court Division, County of Hennepin, Fourth Judicial District (1991, June 28); Miles, S. H. (1991). Informed demand for non-beneficial medical treatment. *New England Journal of Medicine, 325*, 512–515.

33. Lantos, J. D. (1994). Futility assessments and the doctor–patient relationship. *Journal of the American Geriatrics Society, 42*(8), 868–870; Veatch, R. M. (1994). Why physicians cannot determine if care is futile. *Journal of the American Geriatrics Society, 42*(8), 871–874; Veatch, R. M., & Spicer, C. M. (1992). Medically futile care: The role of the physician in setting limits. *American Journal of Law & Medicine, 18*(1 & 2), 15–36.

34. Pope Pius XII. (1958). The prolongation of life: An address of Pope Pius XII to an international congress of anesthesiologists. *The Pope Speaks, 4,* 393–398.
35. Quill, T. E., Lee, B. C., & Nunn, S. (2000). Palliative treatments of last resort: Choosing the least harmful alternative. *Annals of Internal Medicine, 132*(6), 488–493.
36. Quill, T. E., Lo, B., Brock, D. W., & Miesel, A. (2009). Last-resort options for palliative sedation. *Annals of Internal Medicine, 151*(6), 421–424.

Appendix

Ethics Resources on the Web
Bioethics Research Library
at Georgetown University

Bioethics, General

Site: American Society for Bioethics and Humanities (ASBH)
Organization: American Society for Bioethics and Humanities (ASBH)
Location: Glenview, IL, United States
http://www.asbh.org
As the professional society for bioethics, the ASBH site provides information about the organization and links to their reports, books, and newsletter. ASBH members have formed a number of affinity groups, including one for nursing (see http://www.asbh.org/membership/affinity.html).

Site: Association for Practical and Professional Ethics (APPE)
Organization: Indiana University
Location: Bloomington, IN, United States
http://www.indiana.edu/~appe/
As a membership organization devoted to the interdisciplinary study and teaching of practical and professional ethics, the APPE site focuses on posting descriptions of its programs (such as Ethics Bowl and the Pre-College Ethics Interest Group), job announcements, and grant opportunities.

Site: Bioethics and Today's News
Organization: The Johns Hopkins University, Bioethics Institute
Location: Baltimore, MD, United States
http://www.bioethicsinstitute.org/
The Bioethics Institute home page features links to recent news stories and blog postings on bioethical issues.

Site: Bioethics.net
Organization: *The American Journal of Bioethics*
Location: Kansas City, MO, United States
http://www.bioethics.net
In addition to featuring its publication *The American Journal of Bioethics*, this site
links to resources on bioethical issues, online news stories and blog postings as well
as its own blog at http://blog.bioethics.net/.

Site: Bioethics Research Library at Georgetown University
Organization: Kennedy Institute of Ethics, Georgetown University
Location: Washington, DC, United States
http://bioethics.georgetown.edu/
The bioethics library site provides access to and instructions for searching the
following databases:

> ETHXWeb - a bibliographic database of bioethics and professional ethics
> literature;
> GenETHX - a bibliographic database of literature on genetics and ethics;
> Syllabus Exchange database - a database of bioethics syllabi for courses
> from high school through graduate education, with links to the full text of
> each syllabus available online;
> International Bioethics Organizations database - a database of bioethics
> organizations from around the world; and
> Bioethics Thesaurus database - a database of the terms in the Bioethics
> Thesaurus.

These databases can be searched for nursing ethics resources by using library's
classification scheme designation for nursing ethics: 4.1.3
This site also provides searchers with the opportunity to request customized reference service.

Site: Bioethics Resources on the Web
Organization: The National Institutes of Health (NIH), Inter-Institute Bioethics
Interest Group (BIG), Office of Extramural Research (OER)
Location: Bethesda, MD, United States
http://bioethics.od.nih.gov/
The NIH bioethics portal organizes its resources into the following categories: Bioethics
and the NIH, General Resources, Organizations of Interest, Other Federal Resources,
and Specific Topics (Research Ethics, Genetics, and Medicine and Health Care).

Site: Center for Bioethics Resources & Links
Organization: University of Minnesota, Center for Bioethics
Location: Minneapolis, MN, United States
http://www.ahc.umn.edu/bioethics/resource/home.html

Along with an Ask an Ethics Question feature, the Center for Bioethics Web site provides summaries and overviews of bioethical issues, links to full-text bioethics documents (such as the Minnesota Health Care Directives form), and hosts the EthicShare database and Web site (https://www.ethicshare.org/).

Site: Ethics Matters
Organization: University of San Diego, Values Institute
Location: San Diego, CA, United States
http://ethics.sandiego.edu/
Focusing on resources for ethics instruction, this site contains links to videos, full-text articles, and links to other Web sites for both ethical theory and applied ethics topics. Discussion questions are included for each section.

Site: Eubios Ethics Institute
Organization: Eubios Ethics Institute
Location: Bangkok, Thailand
http://www.eubios.info/
This site links to e-books on Asian bioethics, teaching guides, and historic documents relating to the Eubios Ethics Institute.

Site: Global Ethics Observatory (GEObs)
Organization: United Nations Educational, Scientific and Cultural Organization (UNESCO), Social & Human Sciences, Ethics of Science and Technology
Location: Paris, France
http://www.unesco.org/shs/ethics/geobs/
UNESCO's Global Ethics Observatory (GEObs) consists of six databases available in UNESCO's six official languages (Arabic, Chinese, English, French, Russian, and Spanish): Who's Who in Ethics, Ethics Institutions, Ethics Teaching Programs, Legislation and Guidelines, Codes of Conduct, and Resources in Ethics. An interactive geographic search feature is provided to retrieve all information by region or country. Searches in several of these databases can be limited to nursing/nursing ethics. In the Who's Who in Ethics database, the Professional Background value can be limited to Nursing and the Area of Interest in Applied Ethics value can be limited to Nursing Ethics. In the Ethics Teaching Programs database, the Topics value can be limited to Nursing Ethics. In the Codes of Conduct database, the Field of Activity value can be limited to Nursing. In the Resources in Ethics database, the Area of Ethics value can be limited to Nursing Ethics.

Site: Library of Bioethics and Medical Humanities Texts and Documents
Organization: University of Buffalo, Center for Clinical Ethics and Humanities in Health Care
Location: Buffalo, NY, United States
http://wings.buffalo.edu/faculty/research/bioethics/texts.html

This electronic library features classic bioethics texts such as *The Belmont Report: Ethical Principles and Guidelines for the Protection of Human Subjects in Research*, encyclicals of the Roman Catholic Church on bioethical issues, and the *Advisory Committee on Human Radiation Experiments: Final Report*. The site also links to bioethics reports from state and federal agencies.

Site: National Bioethics Advisory Commission
Organization: National Bioethics Advisory Commission (NBAC) (defunct)
Location: Rockville, MD, United States
http://bioethics.georgetown.edu/nbac/
NBAC was established by a presidential executive order in 1995; its charter expired on October 3, 2001. The NBAC reports and meeting transcripts are archived and available full text on the site of the National Reference Center for Bioethics Literature.

Site: Nuffield Council on Bioethics
Organization: Nuffield Council on Bioethics
Location: London, Great Britain
http://www.nuffieldbioethics.org/
The full text of the council's reports and discussion papers are provided on their site along with drafts of works-in-progress.

Site: Online Ethics Center at the National Academy of Engineering (OEC)
Organization: National Academy of Engineering
Location: Washington, DC, United States
http://www.onlineethics.org/
Focusing on science and technology, OEC's site contains essays, case studies, articles, guidelines, and teaching materials on ethical issues with environmentalism, professionalism, research, technology, and business.

Site: OTA Legacy
Organization: Princeton University
Location: Princeton, NJ, United States
http://www.princeton.edu/~ota/
This electronic archive of the publications of the Congressional Office of Technology Assessment (OTA) (which closed on September 29, 1995) also contains a history of the OTA and full-text articles on its importance.

Genetics and Ethics

Site: Dolan DNA Learning Center
Organization: Cold Spring Harbor Laboratory
Location: Cold Spring Harbor, NY, United States
http://www.dnalc.org/

In addition to animated educational materials on molecular biology, this site contains an image archive of the American eugenics movement as well as simulated gene sequencing exercises.

Site: Genome.gov
Organization: National Human Genome Research Institute (NHGRI),
National Institutes of Health
Location: Bethesda, MD, United States
http://www.genome.gov/
As the site for the completed Human Genome Project, the site features links to the continuing international genome sequencing programs, clinical research centers, and Ethical, Legal and Social Implications Program (ELSI) projects and publications. One ELSI project is the Policy and Legislation Database containing the full-text of federal and state regulations on such issues as genetic testing, patenting, informed consent, and confidentiality.

Site: Human Genome Project Education Resources
Organization: Human Genome Project, Department of Energy
Location: Oak Ridge, TN, United States
http://www.ornl.gov/sci/techresources/Human_Genome/education/education.shtml
As part of the US Department of Energy's genome gateway, DOEGenomes.org, this site contains full-text documents such as *Genomics and Its Impact on Science and Society: The Human Genome Project and Beyond* and *Your Genes, Your Choices*, as well as the *Genome Education Modules* produced as part of the Biological Sciences Curriculum Study (BSCS). Also included are video and audio files (PBS) that can be downloaded for educational purposes, and the archives of their *Human Genome News* newsletter.

Site: National Information Resource on Ethics and Human Genetics
Organization: National Reference Center for Bioethics Literature, Kennedy Institute of Ethics, Georgetown University
Location: Washington, DC, United States
http://bioethics.georgetown.edu/
This site contains a DNA patent database, annotated bibliographies on genetic topics, full-text government reports and historic documents on ethics and genetics, and a searchable database on ethics and genetics.

Site: Trust It or Trash It?
Organization: Genetic Alliance
Location: Washington, DC, United States
http://www.trustortrash.org/
This online reference tool was designed by the Genetic Alliance, a consumer advocacy group, to enable the public to evaluate the quality of online genetic information.

Nursing Ethics

Site: Center for Ethics and Human Rights
Organization: American Nurses Association (ANA)
Location: Washington, DC, United States
http://nursingworld.org/MainMenuCategories/EthicsStandards.aspx
This site provides links to ANA statements on such topics as stem cell research, assisted suicide, and foregoing nutrition and hydration. A page is devoted to the ANA *Code of Ethics for Nurses*, and includes background materials as well as the code itself (http://nursingworld.org/MainMenuCategories/EthicsStandards/ CodeofEthicsforNurses. Aspx).

Site: ICN Code of Ethics
Organization: International Council of Nurses (ICN)
Location: Geneva, Switzerland
http://icn.ch/ethics.htm
The ICN's Code of Ethics is freely available in 12 languages.

Site: International Centre for Nursing Ethics (ICNE)
Organization: University of Surrey
Location: Surrey, Guildford, United Kingdom
http://www.nursing-ethics.org/
ICNE's site contains commentary on current events as well as the Table of Contents and editorials published in their journal, *Nursing Ethics*.

Site: Nursing Ethics Network (NEN)
Organization: Emmanuel College of Nursing
Location: Boston, MA, United States
http://jmrileyrn.tripod.com/nen/nen.html
The special feature of the NEN site is the ability to e-mail another nurse about a specific ethical issue in clinical practice. This site also provides abstracts of research on nursing ethics topics and links to other ethics resources.

Glossary

advance directive: A legal document in which a competent adult indicates his or her end-of-life wishes, reflecting values of the individual—especially the life-sustaining treatments he or she wants (or does not want) under various circumstances.

advocacy: Active support of an important cause; speaking on behalf of another person.

aggregate good: The good or human welfare of a group or population.

allocation of health resources: The decision-making process by which goods and services are distributed to people. Macro allocation decisions occur at the level of policymaking and establish how costs should be distributed, which goods and services will be distributed, and the process of distribution. Micro allocation decisions occur at the individual level and concern who will receive the goods or services to be distributed.

assisted suicide: Ending one's own life with the help of another person.

autonomy: The ethical principle that obliges one to allow individuals to self-determine their plans and actions. It entails respecting the personal liberty of individuals and the choices they make, based on their personal values and beliefs.

beneficence: The ethical principle that obliges one to provide good (promote someone's welfare, for example); cf. nonmaleficence, which obliges one to avoid doing harm (prevent putting someone at risk for harm, for example).

bioethics: Applied ethics inquiry in the biomedical sciences that attempts to provide moral responses to difficult questions arising in health care, technology use, and related public policy.

caring: A trait of human character that expresses concern about how another person is experiencing his or her world, often expressed by behavior that protects and preserves the health, welfare, and human dignity of another; a virtue of individuals found in certain relationships to another (mother/child; nurse/patient; etc.).

code of ethics: A formal statement by an individual or group that establishes and prescribes moral and nonmoral standards and behaviors.

competency: The legal term for the capacity or ability to perform some task; for example, making healthcare decisions or deciding whether to participate in a research study.

confidentiality: The ethical obligation to keep someone's personal and private information secret or private.

conscientious objection: An objection based on moral or religious grounds.

cultural values: Moral and nonmoral beliefs, attitudes, and standards that derive from a particular cultural group.

decision-making capacity: (a) the ability to comprehend information relevant to the decision at hand, (b) the ability to deliberate in accordance with his or her own values and goals, and (c) the ability to communicate with caregivers.

disclosure: What must be told to a patient or surrogate as a condition of obtaining valid consent or refusal (e.g., risks, benefits, alternative procedures, the option of nontreatment).

doctrine of double effect: Derived from Catholic moral theology, a doctrine that makes a distinction between killings that are directly intended and those that are unintended. The doctrine holds that evil consequences, even deaths, are morally permissible provided that four conditions are met: (1) the action is good or indifferent in itself; (2) the intention of the agent is upright; that is, the evil effect is not intended; (3) the evil effect must be equally immediate causally with the good effect; that is, it is not a means to the good effect; (4) there must be a proportionally grave reason for allowing the evil to occur.

durable power of attorney: A legal document that empowers someone other than the patient (that is, a surrogate) to make decisions when the patient loses decision-making capacity. It is limited in that the surrogate decision maker may not fully understand the patient's healthcare preferences.

egalitarianism: A belief in human equality, especially in regard to social, political, and economic rights and privileges. As a social philosophy, it may advocate the removal of inequalities among people.

emotivism: An ethical theory maintaining that ethical judgments are expressions of one's feelings and desires.

ethical behavior: Conduct characterized by actions in response to moral standards or norms.

ethical conflict: An opposition between two or more moral positions (principles, virtues, or values) or between moral and nonmoral positions.

ethics environment: Features of an environment with the potential to promote or compromise moral integrity and moral agency.

ethical practice: A general pattern of moral conduct within a domain or sphere of life. In nursing, the domain of nurses' moral behavior, actions, decisions, and ethical decision making in response to moral conflicts.

ethical principle: A general right-making characteristic of actions; a guide to moral decision making and moral action (e.g., autonomy, beneficence, and justice).

ethical sensitivity: The ability to recognize values and value conflicts.

ethical theory: An integrated body of principles, rules, and virtues governing moral choices. Consequential theories claim that certain acts are right and others are wrong because of their consequences (e.g., utilitarianism). Nonconsequential theories claim that certain acts are right and others are wrong because of the features of the acts (right-making or wrong-making characteristics) or their conformity (or nonconformity) to duty or obligations (e.g., formalism).

ethics: An integrated system or theory pertaining to the moral practices, beliefs, and standards of individuals and/or groups. Also, a particular form of inquiry about morality, (i.e., normative ethics and non-normative ethics).

etiquette: Prescribed requirements for polite social behavior, actions, decisions, and ethical decision making in response to conflicts of morals or customs.

euthanasia: An act or omission that intentionally results in the death of a person for reasons of mercy. Active euthanasia is an action that results in killing someone or ending someone's life by any method such as lethal injection or a lethal dose of medication. Passive euthanasia is the withholding or withdrawing of a life-sustaining measure to allow a person to die.

existential advocacy: Assisting others to authentically exercise their freedom of self-determination. By authentic is meant a way of reaching decisions which are truly one's own—decisions that express all that one believes important about oneself and the world, the entire complexity of one's values.

fidelity: The ethical principle that obliges one to remain faithful to one's commitments; relates especially to the keeping of promises and the protection of confidentiality.

futility: The state of serving no useful purpose or of being ineffective.

hedonism: A theory of ethics maintaining that pleasure or happiness is the highest good.

human dignity: Excellence of the human condition; deeply valued inner sense of well-being and personal worth.

individual good: The good or human welfare of the individual person.

informed consent: An individual's autonomous authorization of a medical intervention or of participation in research. A consent is valid if and only if the individual is competent to make the consent, material information is adequately disclosed to the individual, the individual understands the information, and the consent is voluntarily given.

integrity: Firm adherence to moral values or norms.

intuitionism: An ethical theory maintaining that our basic ethical principles and value judgments are intuitive or self-evident. Ethical judgments are true or false, but are not factual and cannot be justified by empirical observation, argument, or reasoning. They are only known through intuition.

justice: The ethical principle that obliges one to treat those who are equal, in relevant respects, in the same manner. When individuals are unequal, in relevant respects, one is obliged to treat them in a fair manner. This often means that those who have greater need may justly receive more of a particular resource than those with lesser need.

libertarianism: A belief in absolute and unrestricted freedom of thought and action.

living will: A document containing a person's preferences, usually addressing mechanical or artificial life-sustaining treatments in the event of a terminal illness or condition. It becomes effective when the person is unable to participate in decisions about his or her care. Living wills are limited in that laws in some states may limit how they are used, and they may be written so that they take effect only under very narrow circumstances.

metaethics: The analysis of the language, concepts, and methods of reasoning in ethics; also, the analysis of the logic of moral justification.

moral agency: The capacity for a person to act morally/ethically on his or her own (moral) authority.

moral character: The perseverance, strength of conviction, and courage that enables a person to carry out a plan of moral action that he or she deems imperative.

moral development: A series of stages through which one develops moral reasoning, abilities, and skills.

moral dilemma: A situation in which there are two equally justifiable courses of action or judgments and the individual is uncertain which one to pursue or choose.

moral distress: A situation in which the individual knows the right course of action to follow and can morally justify that action but is unable to carry it out because of one or more constraints. The constraints may include legal rules, institutional policies, lack of decision-making authority, and lack of recognition of the individual's moral agency.

moral ideal: A conception of moral perfection or excellence that specifies conduct or character traits beyond the call of duty.

moral integrity: That condition of soundness or wholeness that exists when there is a good fit between who a person is (human being, spouse, parent, nurse) and what is reasonable to expect of the person given his or her identities. Moral integrity entails a good fit between who one is and a particular vision of the good life.

moral motivation: A genuine desire and interest to achieve the right moral outcomes. It involves one's sense of moral responsibility and integrity, and a commitment to achieving moral ends.

moral reasoning: The cognitive process by which one chooses among principles, virtues, and values to come to some decision about one's moral behavior. This process takes place after recognition of moral conflicts (ethical sensitivity or moral sensitivity) and usually results in judgment about an action or rule (moral behavior).

moral residue: What a person experiences after compromising or allowing others to ethically compromise oneself.

moral uncertainty: A situation in which the individual recognizes that ethical norms are in conflict but is uncertain which norms they are, feels uncomfortable about the situation, or does not have full information about the situation.

moral values: Values ascribed to human actions, behaviors, institutions, or character traits when evaluated by some ultimate or universal standard. Cf. nonmoral values.

mores: A set of culturally defined goals and the rules governing how one attains those goals. The goals to be attained include certain dispositions, character traits, or virtues.

naturalism: An ethical theory maintaining that ethical judgments are based on natural phenomena or natural inclinations and desires given by nature or by God.

nonmaleficence: The ethical principle that obliges one to avoid doing harm.

nonmoral values: Values related to personal preferences, beliefs, or matters of taste.

non-normative ethics: A type of ethics inquiry that describes the phenomena of moral beliefs and behavior (descriptive ethics) or analyzes the moral language and concepts used in ethics inquiry and the logic of moral justification (metaethics).

normative ethics: A type of ethics inquiry that examines standards (norms) or criteria for right or wrong conduct and character. Using ethical theories such as utilitarianism, formalism, and pragmatism, it defends a system of moral principles and rules for determining which actions are right and which are wrong.

nursing ethics: The philosophical analysis of: (1) the moral phenomena found in nursing practice, (2) the moral language and ethical foundations of nursing practice, and (3) the ethical judgments made by and about nurses. It can also address the normative aims and content of nursing practice.

palliative sedation: The use of sedative drugs for the purpose of lowering levels of awareness of pain and other distressing symptoms.

paternalism: The overriding of autonomous individual choice or actions in order to provide benefit to an individual or to prevent harm from occurring to the individual. Some ethical theories hold that paternalistic actions are morally justified when the benefits realized are great and the harms avoided are significant. Other ethical theories impose additional requirements to justify paternalism.

personal values: Moral and nonmoral evaluative beliefs, attitudes, and standards considered important to the individual and that are among the factors forming the basis for his or her behavior and choices.

primum non nocere: A principle often encountered in physician ethics: "first of all do no harm;" sometimes erroneously believed to be included in the Hippocratic oath.

privacy: State of being private, of not having personal information or observation disclosed to others; nondisclosure of the self.

professional values: Moral and nonmoral evaluative beliefs, attitudes, and standards that are derived from one's professional group or from expressed views about a professional group.

rationing: Restriction of certain provisions (such as food, treatments, or medications) or resources (such as healthcare services, nursing care, organs, or technologies) by some method of distribution.

respect for persons: The ethical principle that obliges one to respect the inherent dignity and fundamental rights of persons (i.e., rights to autonomy, privacy, freedom).

responsibility: The obligation to carry out duties associated with a particular role assumed by the individual.

right: A just claim or title; that which is due someone. Legal rights are valid claims recognized by the legal system. Moral rights are valid claims derived from ethical theory. Cultural rights are customs, traditions, or ideals that may be upheld or protected by the law or other culturally created forces.

right to health: A morally just claim or entitlement to bodily well-being or freedom from illness, debilitating disease, or risk of illness or disease. A negative right to health is a moral right not to have one's health endangered by the actions of others. A positive right to health is a moral right to obtain resources or services to guarantee bodily well-being or a state free of illness or debilitating disease. A right to health care is a positive moral right to goods and services aimed at maintaining and improving whatever state of health one already has.

sanctity of human life: The ethical principle that obliges one to view human life as sacred; not to take human life even for noble reasons.

stoicism: A theory of ethics maintaining indifference to pleasure, the repression of emotion, and submission of the will without complaint.

surrogate: An individual who makes decisions on behalf of someone who does not have decision-making capacity. When the surrogate has been legally designated, for example in an advance directive, the surrogate is referred to as a healthcare proxy.

unethical behavior: Individual behavior that violates (usually knowingly and willingly) fundamental norms of ethical conduct toward others.

value(s): A rational conception of the desirable; a standard or quality that is esteemed, desired, and considered important. Values are expressed by behaviors or standards that a person endorses or tries to maintain. Values are typically organized into a hierarchic system of importance to the individual.

value conflict: An opposition or clash among one or more values considered important by an individual or a group.

veracity: The ethical principle that obliges one to tell the truth and not to lie to or deceive others.

viability: The capacity to survive outside the mother's womb without artificial support.

virtue: A persistent disposition (such as honesty or kindness) or trait of character (such as conscientiousness) that is considered praiseworthy and is acquired, in part, through teaching and practice, and perhaps by grace. A disposition or habit to undertake certain types of actions in certain types of situations in accordance with moral obligation or moral ideals is often called moral virtue.

well-being: The state of being happy or having one's welfare protected.

Index